POWER IN THE BLOOD
A Handbook on AIDS, Politics, and Communication

POWER IN THE BLOOD
A Handbook on AIDS, Politics, and Communication

Edited by

William N. Elwood
Behavioral Research Group
University of Texas

LEA **LAWRENCE ERLBAUM ASSOCIATES, PUBLISHERS**
1999   Mahwah, New Jersey   **London**

Lawrence Erlbaum Associates, Inc., Publishers
10 Industrial Avenue
Mahwah, NJ 07430

Cover design by Michael A. Nelson

Library of Congress Cataloging-in-Publication Data

Power in the blood : a handbook on AIDS, politics, and communication / edited
by William N. Elwood.
     p. cm. — (Communication series: applied communications)
Includes bibliographical references and indexes.
ISBN 0-8058-2906-7 (alk. paper)
1. AIDS (Disease)—Social aspects—United States. I. Elwood, William N.
II. Series.
RA644.A25P69 1999
362.1'969792'00973—dc21   98-7516
                                                                      CIP

Books published by Lawrence Erlbaum Associates are printed on acid-free paper,
and their bindings are chosen for strength and durability.

Printed in the United States of America
10 9 8 7 6 5 4 3 2 1

To God, wondrous, witty, and wise;
To Michael, with love and respect;
To this book's contributors, tenacious and insightful;
To individuals infected and affected by HIV and AIDS,
particularly our research participants; and,
To David, who, I am happy and proud to say,
will not go gently.

Contents

Part VII
The Synthesis: Conclusions and Projections

About the Editor

William N. Elwood, Ph.D., is adjunct assistant professor of behavioral sciences in the Center for Health Promotion Research and Development in the University of Texas School of Public Health, and senior research scientist with the Behavioral Research Group of NOVA Research Company. His articles appear in *AIDS Care, Communication Studies, Connections*, the *Journal of Psychoactive Drugs*, the *Journal of Psychology and Human Sexuality*, and *Metaphor and Symbolic Activity*, among other publications. He is the author of *Rhetoric in the War on Drugs: The Triumphs and Tragedies of Public Relations* (1994), and editor/contributor of *Public Relations Inquiry as Rhetorical Criticism: Case Studies of Corporate Discourse and Social Influence*, which received the National Communication Association's award for best public relations book of 1996. Dr. Elwood's research has been funded by the World Health Organization, the National Institute on Drug Abuse (NIDA), and the Texas Commission on Alcohol and Drug Abuse. The associate American editor for *AIDS Care*, Dr. Elwood also serves on the Texas Drug Epidemiology Workgroup and NIDA's Border Epidemiology Workgroup. He has served as a member of the State of California's University-wide AIDS Research Program grant application review board and the City of Houston HIV/AIDS Prevention Community Planning Group, the mandated organization that sets priorities for the distribution of CDC funds for HIV prevention program efforts. His biography appears in *Who's Who in America, Who's Who in the South and Southwest*, and *Who's Who in Medicine and Medical Research*. Dr. Elwood lives in Houston, Texas.

Acknowledgments

A book always consists of more than its editor and contributors. *Power in the Blood* owes its initial inspiration to my colleague Bob Denton, who, in response to my idea for a book proposal said, "You know, that's a good idea, but what we really need is a book on the politics of AIDS." His initial comment inspired the process that led to *Power in the Blood*.

Mike Nelson has inspired and supported me in ways personal and professional. I am grateful for the balance he brings to my life and for his artwork, which I consider to be the best cover in the Lawrence Erlbaum Associates book catalogue. Edsel J., Baba K., and Fala Gioia Marie, constant companions and cooperative coworkers, listened, guarded, played, barked, meowed, walked on keyboards, basked under the glow of the desk lamp, and provided mirth, divergence, and balance.

Mark Williams has been a thoughtful mentor and scrupulous coauthor and reviewer, although he likely never thought he'd be scanning manuscripts for this book when he bought his elaborate computer—or when we met almost 15 years ago. I am grateful for his friendship and for introducing me to the field of HIV/AIDS research.

Michael Hamm has been my mentor and friend for even longer. I know no finer example of a friend. From encouraging a reluctant undergraduate through graduate and doctoral student, to currently sending magazine and newspaper clippings or the AIDS organization newsletter from my hometown, he has influenced my personal and professional progress. Thank you, Michael, and thank you, God.

The late Wesley Perrin, whom I never met, but whose ghost figuratively dwells with me at times, raised two children and countless animals—two of whom I am proud to call my own. God rest you, Wesley.

Linda Bathgate and Dorothy Gribbin at Lawrence Erlbaum Associates managed individuals and issues with grace and professionalism. Their efforts, and those of their LEA colleagues, rendered *Power in the Blood* as you see it. Thank you, Dorothy and Linda, for making this a memorable process.

The research participants I have interviewed not only have provided rich data for the projects on which I have worked, but also have influenced me profoundly. Although most of them have been members of disadvantaged populations, and are frequently stereotyped as ignorant and inarticulate, I frequently found them to be intelligent and eloquent individuals whose responses have shaped how I think about theory and praxis, love and sex, and how researchers and "real people" talk about all of it. In turn, I hope that you, too, are influenced by the experience of this work.

—*William N. Elwood*

Introduction

This is a book about you. An overstatement? Perhaps. At the very least, however, this is a book that interests you. That's not surprising; just about everyone in the United States, indeed, in every country, is affected by HIV/AIDS: They know someone, are related to someone, or *are* someone living with the virus or with AIDS. Sadly, they mourn someone who died from HIV disease before the advent of the "cocktail" prescription pharmaceuticals that have extended the lives of many HIV-infected people. Regrettably, this person could be one of the individuals for whom these celebrated prescriptions are not effective—or who cannot receive such treatment for lack of finances or health insurance. If none of these categories suits you, here is one that does: Every year, some of your tax dollars are allocated for HIV prevention materials and to provide services to people living with HIV and AIDS. The early feminist movement was driven by the idea that the personal is political. In the 1990s, there may be nothing more personal or political than HIV/AIDS.

WHAT'S THIS BOOK ABOUT?

If you opened this book because you are interested in another exposé on the HIV/AIDS crisis, you will be surprised for two reasons. First, *politics* is not simply about elections, the policy process, or how someone instantly gains the upper hand. It is about how individuals in a society influence one another regarding what ideas and behaviors are appropriate. In short, everyday life is fraught with politics. Second, our everyday political experiences are much more important and exciting than a single "conspiracy" to analyze, because these experiences shape our perceptions on which election-oriented campaigns and policy discussions are based. To illustrate how these initial perceptions come into being is to explain the basis for what conveniently comes to mind when we think about "the politics of AIDS."

Communication is the unique human ability to convince other people that certain ideas deserve attention, and that particular perspectives on those ideas are better than other perspectives that may exist or emerge (see also Elwood, 1995b, p. 7). When other people follow the perspective you advocate, they also will believe that only certain ideas, behaviors, and policies are important—whether it is that drug injectors should not share their equipment, that casual sex partners always should use protection, that the federal government should fund HIV/AIDS research, that people with HIV deserve civil rights protection, or that these same people can receive hugs and handshakes without infecting another person.

WHAT'S IN THIS BOOK?

This book explains the governmental, intrapersonal, interpersonal, public, and programmatic areas in which AIDS, politics, and communication intersect. You will find orientation and synthesis sections as well. So although some chapters explore policy issues, others explain other important topics related to how we understand HIV and AIDS. For example, you may live in a city that closed its public pool after an HIV-infected person swam in it, or you remember the public outcry when Greg Louganis revealed his HIV infection years after his celebrated head injury and dive at the Olympics. One chapter in the first section illuminates how we can behave irrationally in such cases because the primary archetype of blood overrides our scientific understanding of how people are infected with HIV. Among the other issues explored in this opening section are the influence of language use and change in the research process and the unexpected results of HIV/AIDS fundraising through the selling of products. You also will read about additional ways to think about power, politics, HIV prevention, and people living with HIV and AIDS.

Among the intrapersonal chapters, you will find an explanation of how words become political when men seek settings that impede any kind of talk so they can have unprotected sex without the option of negotiating condom use with their partners. If you have ever wondered how people can rationalize risky behaviors when they also can cite accurate HIV prevention information by chapter and verse, you will find multiple chapters that address just this issue. And if you have ever been confounded by the many constraints that face women's abilities to protect themselves from HIV infection, there is a chapter that outlines them. In fact, you will find at least six chapters that address women's issues regarding power relations and personal HIV prevention, stigmas that preclude them from seeking HIV treatment, and breastfeeding.

If you are concerned about media influences, you will find chapters that explain how early news coverage shaped the way we continue to talk about HIV/AIDS, how news and program content influence our perceptions and behaviors, and how we must consider demographics more carefully as we craft prevention messages in the future. The chapters in the program section range from the information dissemination process at the National Institutes of Health (NIH), to analyses of outreach education, needle-exchange policy process, HIV treatment, and prevention in Kenya and Southeast Asia.

WHO SHOULD READ THIS BOOK?

You. You picked it up, didn't you? This book explains how we think and talk about AIDS and how those thoughts and words influence our individual behaviors and our behavior with others. You obviously have an inquisitive mind. You have chosen the right book. You can apply this information in your life, in your research, in your class discussions, in your program design and in your grant application. These days, even community-based organizations have to base their proposals in research findings. Many of these chapters provide models to follow and provide additional literature to read and cite. If you are reading this book for a course that addresses communication, HIV/AIDS, or politics, it likely will provide a strong point of departure. It is organized and written to be a multidisciplinary endeavor.

The people who wrote these chapters are well-regarded experts and have conducted solid research. They represent a wide range of fields including communication, psychology, public health, anthropology, political science, and law. They know what they are talking about and how to talk about it to you. So if you are expecting a lot of $5 words, you will be disappointed. You may have to reach for the dictionary once or twice, but even the *Reader's Digest* makes you do that!

WHAT IS THIS BOOK'S OVERALL PURPOSE?

This is a book about the importance of talk. Talk may be the most important component to HIV prevention and treatment. When people do not talk to their partners about the behaviors that can transmit HIV and other diseases, let alone their known or unknown HIV statuses, they will not talk about HIV prevention methods. When researchers do not talk to laypeople about their findings, we cannot put those findings into practice. When people from various disciplines who conduct HIV/AIDS research do not share their findings with one another, they potentially prevent the joint use of effective strategies that can help others.

A few years ago, I left a meeting of NIH grantees and told one of the scientists that I was headed for a national communication conference. This woman, a psychology professor, expressed her surprise that there were a sufficient number of people conducting communication research to have a conference about it. I informed her that the association had thousands of members, and that there were communication professors at countless colleges and universities. This story is not a recruitment message; it demonstrates that communication researchers must continue to disseminate their findings on HIV/AIDS to other AIDS researchers from other disciplines.

Because that is what it is all about. If human beings cannot talk about the sexual and drug use behaviors that risk the transmission about HIV, we cannot stop the spread of the virus. If patients will not explain exactly how they consume the medicines their physicians prescribe, we will never know how to treat HIV and its related diseases properly. And if the people in different fields, on different levels, do not talk to each other, we will not learn the innovations any of us make. We are all in this together. *Power in the Blood* is a book that assembles many of us and speaks to many others.

POWER IN THE BLOOD
A Handbook on AIDS, Politics, and Communication

I

THE POLITICAL:
INTRODUCTORY PERSPECTIVES

1

Burden of Sin: Transmitting Messages and Viruses in a Stigmatized Plague

William N. Elwood
Behavioral Research Group
University of Texas—Houston School of Public Health

Social and behavioral scientists have spent countless hours and dollars conducting research to design influential teaching methods so people do not get it. Pharmaceutical companies race their respective research protocols to get new drugs to treat people who have it—and to satisfy desperate activists and eager stakeholders. The U.S. Public Health Service offers special deadlines for proposals to research it (U.S. Department of Health and Human Services, 1995). Elizabeth Taylor became a tireless spokesperson and fundraiser for it—and made such occasions prestigious social and newsworthy events ("AIDS Victims Remembered," 1996). Durex (1996, 1998) met sufficient criteria to be the official condom manufacturer at the XI and XII international conference dedicated to it. Dresses from the collection of Diana, Princess of Wales, were auctioned so that $2.88 million of the proceeds could benefit people who have it (Bumiller, 1997; Efimades, Green, & McNeil, 1997).

"It," of course, is HIV/AIDS, the virus and syndrome, respectively, with which few wish to be infected and seemingly everyone wants to be associated. The chapters in this book, however, have little to do with benevolent female celebrities at the end of this millennium; instead, they analyze many of the choices that celebrated and everyday people make in regard to HIV and AIDS.

At first blush, one might think that a handbook on AIDS, politics, and communication would examine solely policy issues and their discussion. For example, if a president chooses to say little or nothing about HIV or AIDS in the public arena, citizens with no direct experience with the illness may think it merits scarce attention and resources (Nelson, chap. 5 of this volume; Perez & Dionisopoulos, 1995) and that people who endure with HIV/AIDS deserve persecution (Goldberg, 1989). If a president chooses to make a speech about HIV/AIDS and says, "The gay people who have AIDS are still our sons, our brothers, our cousins, our citizens. They're Americans, too. They're obeying the law and working hard. They're entitled to be treated like everybody else" (Clinton, 1995, p. 1196), he defines such individuals as deserving of civil rights protection and health services (see McKinney & Pepper, chap. 7 of this volume) and as unworthy of persecution or scapegoating. Similarly, if a youthful, photogenic princess chooses to hug AIDS patients during photo opportunities when much of the world's population thinks such individuals should be quarantined like tuberculosis patients of old, she defines such people as safe for casual contact and deserving of compassion (Alderson, Hastings, & Ridley, 1997; Anthony, 1997).

These familiar examples demonstrate famous people using their great influence as regards HIV and AIDS. Still, a reader may think that these examples are not expressly political—just words, mere rhetoric—because they are not linked to specific policy actions. According to Adrienne Rich, any human discourse "is in some way political" (p. 83). She argued against the idea that communication is political only when it proposes policy actions: "There are words that uphold the status quo either by what they don't say or by what they do say, what they affirm. And any status quo is political" (in Trinidad, 1991, p. 83). Longtime AIDS activist Larry Kramer (1989) ventured as far as to posit that anything involving HIV/AIDS also involves politics.

Whereas politics once was conceived as "the art of preventing people from taking part in affairs which properly concern them" (Valéry, 1995), the advent of HIV/AIDS has provided previously marginalized groups with a forum to define themselves and their needs beyond those related to HIV prevention. For example, government-funded needs assessment projects seek out gender-transposed (transsexual, transgendered) people to determine how to allocate resources for prevention efforts in the following year. Yet such a project also allows what seemingly are men in dresses to voice their needs to be regarded as female in countless situations (see Yep & Pietri, chap. 15 of this volume). While I was writing this chapter, I spoke with a 14-year-old street youth who explained to me how she convinced HIV-infected male adolescents to have unprotected intercourse with her so she, too, could be infected. You may wonder why anyone would endeavor consciously to acquire HIV; however, after homeless adolescents eke out a basic existence using only their minds and bodies, they begin to perceive of HIV/AIDS as the means to an all-expenses-paid vacation. To many individuals, an HIV diagnosis is a death sentence; to a homeless youth, it is the entree to a regular monthly income, a housing allowance, guaranteed health care, and respectful asexual attention from the adults who provide those services. The many examples discussed thus far demonstrate the wide variety of politics involved with HIV/AIDS. This book examines many of the communicative decisions that influence people to think individually about HIV/AIDS, to act regarding people with HIV and AIDS, and to discuss with others the means to prevent its transmission.

Just as in previous epidemics, the decisions people make have profound implications. In the Middle Ages, a frightened European populace was decimated by a plague because the people knew neither prevention nor panacea for what they then called "the Pestilence or Great Mortality" (Tuchman, 1978, p. 101). Indeed, "ignorance of the cause" for what later was identified as the Bubonic Plague "augmented the sense of horror," leading to a popular decision that "there could be but one explanation—the wrath of God" (Tuchman, 1978, p. 103). When ashes, sackcloth, prayers, and rituals failed as prophylaxis, the populace did the next best thing: They decided Jewish people were responsible for the epidemic's creation and spread in order to rid the world of Christianity. The distraught Christians began to persecute the Jews through quarantine, mass execution, and other methods (Tuchman, 1978).

The themes of scapegoating, quarantines, and divine invocations resonate in the great mortality of this century, and demonstrate the continued underlying intersection of epidemics and Christianity in the Western world. Sontag (1966) opined, "Ours is an age which con-sciously pursues health, and yet only believes in the reality of sickness" (p. 49). Echoing past epidemics and reactions to them, Sontag (1990) maintained, "Illnesses always have been used as metaphors to enliven charges that a society was corrupt or unjust. . . . Disease imagery is used to express concern for social order" (p. 72). Van der Vliet's (1996) analysis of international concerns in the HIV/AIDS epidemic finds that persistent and less tolerated prejudices were granted new life by couching them in terms of HIV prevention:

In the United States, fears of changing sexual mores allowed homophobia to re-emerge as a fear of AIDS. In France and elsewhere in Europe, threats of job losses to waves of new immigration revived old xenophobic attitudes, this time in the guise of fears about foreigners bringing AIDS into the country. In South Africa, fears of a new social order reactivated racism masquerading as concerns about AIDS in desegregated swimming pools and lavatories. AIDS was seen as divine retribution, punishment for immorality, an answer to overpopulation. (pp. 3–4)

According to Sontag (1990), to have a disease is to have "punishment that fits the objective moral character" (p. 46), whereas recovery is viewed as an individual's "test of moral character" (p. 43). To recover, then, is to be redeemed; to die, to be held reproachable for the sins of society. Consider also that we have declared "war" on illnesses since "the identification of bacteria as agents of disease. . . . Not only is the clinical course of the disease and its medical treatment thus described, but the disease itself is conceived of as the enemy on which society wages war" (Sontag, 1990, pp. 55–56). Given this fusion of military and moral perspectives on disease, it can become culturally acceptable to wage war not only against a virus, but also against people who suffer from it—endowing the entire effort with "the religious significance of a secular crisis" (Ivie, 1992; see also, e.g., Elwood, 1994, 1995a). This union of disease, religion, and war is encapsulated best in the lyrics to my favorite Protestant Christian hymn:

Would you be free from the burden of sin? . . .
Would you o'er evil a victory win? . . .
There's wonderful power in the blood. (Jones, 1982)

HIV, the human immunodeficiency virus generally acknowledged to debilitate people's immune system to the extent that they become vulnerable to a variety of opportunistic infections that constitute acquired immune deficiency syndrome (AIDS), is transmitted through activities traditionally associated with sin: sexual intercourse and psychoactive substance use. Specifically, the virus is transmitted through semen, blood, vaginal secretions, and, perhaps, other body fluids (for a thorough and practical description of HIV risk behaviors and the course of HIV disease to AIDS, see Smith, 1996, pp. 1–25).

In the context of HIV and AIDS, blood has tremendous power to transmit disease and to stigmatize infected individuals. In the United States, a mysterious constellation of diseases, only known later as HIV and AIDS, began to afflict predominantly gay men and injection drug users—two of the bigger "sinner" groups in our society of Puritan heritage. Echoing the cries of the 14th century and consistent with Sontag's observations regarding human perceptions of illness, certain members of the populace suggested that HIV and AIDS served as just punishment from a God angered by these individuals' behaviors; this suggestion grew more generalized as members of the "general population" became infected with HIV and died from complications related to AIDS (Burkett, 1995; Rotello, 1997; Shilts, 1988; Smith, 1996). The serological test for HIV antibodies provides the opportunity to educate infected individuals about treatment options and practices to avoid transmitting the virus to others. Nevertheless, receiving one's seropositive test results can have the affect not only of a death sentence, but also induction into a league of loathed and fearsome persons.

The chapters that follow address these issues and as issues related to the behavioral choices people make. These chapters examine *politics* in its broadest sense—as the complex constellation of social relations among individuals, not solely an examination of the policy process. Perhaps the most important human behaviors regarding HIV and AIDS are symbolic ones. *Communication* is the symbolic means humans use to describe self, feelings, situations, issues, and behaviors to induce responses to such descriptions, usually recognition or suasion, from others (see also Elwood, 1995b, p. 7). It is the means of politics, "the strategy that underlies social behavior and alignments" (van der Vliet, 1996, p. 4; see also Edelman, 1967, 1971, 1977, 1988). Consequently, how one delineates an issue has profound implications because the description that becomes used most frequently influences how other people think about an issue, the people associated with it, and how one should take action (see Elwood, 1995b; Vibbert, 1987). Human discourse organizes and governs societal practices; it dictates what constitutes "truth," what constitutes appropriate behavior, and how one may constitute "self" in regard to these dictates (see Foucault, 1961, 1970, 1972, 1978, 1980, 1989, 1990)— particularly as regards membership in an HIV "risk group" (van der Vliet, 1996) and as a person living with, or even without, HIV (see, e.g., Odets, 1995; Sawyer, 1996).

In short, people achieve *power,* or pervasive terminological influence, through commu-nication. On a public level, once a particular description becomes commonplace, certain behaviors and policies become acceptable, whereas others simply seem unfit relative to the hegemonic descriptions. For example, proposals to quarantine people with HIV could not gain broad support in the United States because opponents could argue that a proposal to segregate people with an infectious, not contagious,[1] disease conflicts with the American value of civil rights. In a private context, a serodiscordant couple, partners of differing HIV status, may decide to avoid intercourse and engage in other sexual acts because they perceive condoms as a barrier to intimacy and still wish to reduce the risk of infecting the one partner. Whether communication occurs between two people or millions, human discourse influences how people think about HIV, people infected with the virus, and what to do as regards transmission, treatment, and tolerance. As the means human beings use to influence others in their social order, all communication—or the lack thereof—has powerful political implications, whether the context is a legislator railing against an increase in funding for Ryan White Act programs or a man attempting to penetrate a new sexual partner without wearing a condom, mentioning his positive HIV status, or discussing protective measures with that partner. Indeed, there are power imbalances in sex, disease, and communication; contributors to this book examined these relationships and present some surprising results.

The late Princess of Wales was eulogized for her nonverbal symbolic action to influence perceptions of people with AIDS; her mother-in-law spoke wise words that apply to this field. Speaking generally to citizens of the Commonwealth of Nations, the countries of the former British empire, the Queen easily could have addressed a conference on communication, politics, and HIV/AIDS: "We have the means of sending and receiving messages, we can travel to meetings in distant parts of the world, we can exchange experts; but we still have difficulty in finding the right messages to send, we can still ignore the messages we don't like to hear, and we can still talk in riddles and listen without trying to comprehend" (HM The Queen, 1991, p. 121). At present, people in many disciplines are reconsidering the theories and praxes we have used to prevent the transmission of HIV and to encourage treatment compliance among HIV-infected people (Booth & Watters, 1994; Fishbein, 1997; National Institutes of Health Consensus Panel, 1997; Patton, 1996; Zimmerman & Vernberg, 1994). In other words, we still are trying to find the right messages to send. This book is part of an extended dialogue between message senders, their intended recipients, and the people who

---

[1]Contagious diseases, including colds, influenza, and tuberculosis, are transmitted "casually," through such means as the air and physical surfaces like doorknobs and countertops. HIV is considered an "infectious" disease because one must engage in specific behaviors to be exposed only to certain body fluids of a person infected with the virus (see, e.g., Smith, 1996, p. 9).

design and study them—to provide descriptions and analyses of people involved with HIV who are distant to us, so that the issues involved with HIV's power in the blood can be transferred to powerful communication strategies for prevention, treatment, and social relations.

REFERENCES

AIDS victims remembered. (1996, October 13). *Houston Chronicle,* p. 2A.

Alderson, A., Hastings, C., & Ridley, Y. (1997, September 7). A friend for life to the sick and hurting. *The Sunday Times* (London), Section 1, p. 19.

Anthony, T. (1997, September 1). World mourns Princess Diana: Americans made her their own. *Houston Chronicle,* pp. 1A, 26A.

Booth, R. E., & Watters, J. K. (1994). How effective are risk-reduction interventions targeting injecting drug users? *AIDS, 8,* 1515–1524.

Bumiller, E. (1997, June 26). That was some closet: Auction of Princess Diana's frocks pulls in $3.25 million for cancer and AIDS charities. *Houston Chronicle,* p. 18A.

Burkett, E. (1995). *The gravest show on earth: America in the age of AIDS.* Boston: Houghton Mifflin.

Clinton, W. J. (1995, July 6). Remarks at Georgetown University. *Weekly Compilation of Presidential Documents,* pp. 1190–1200.

Durex. (1996). Sheik Sensi-Creme Condom, Official Condom of the XI International Conference on AIDS [Product box]. (Distributed by London International U.S. Holdings, Inc., Sarasota, FL).

Durex. (1998). Durex Lubricated Latex Condoms, Official Condom of the XII World AIDS Conference, Geneva 1998 [Product box]. (Distributed by the LI Group, London, England).

Edelman, M. (1967). *The symbolic uses of politics.* Urbana: University of Illinois Press.

Edelman, M. (1971). *Politics as symbolic action: Mass arousal and quiescence.* New York: Academic Press.

Edelman, M. (1977). *Political language: Words that succeed and policies that fail.* New York: Academic Press.

Edelman, M. (1988). *Constructing the political spectacle.* Chicago: University of Chicago Press.

Efimades, M., Green, M., & McNeil, E. (1997, July 7). Going, going, gown! In a high-spirited—and higher-priced—contest at Christie's, bidders plunk down $3.26 million for Princess Diana's posh hand-me-downs. *People Weekly,* pp. 46–48.

Elwood, W. N. (1994). *Rhetoric in the war on drugs: The triumphs and tragedies of public relations.* Westport, CT: Praeger.

Elwood, W. N. (1995a). Declaring war on the home front: Metaphor, presidents, and the war on drugs. *Metaphor and Symbolic Activity, 10,* 93–114.

Elwood, W. N. (1995b). Public relations is a rhetorical experience: The integral principal in case study analysis. In W. N. Elwood (Ed.), *Public relations inquiry as rhetorical criticism: Case studies of corporate discourse and social influence* (pp. 3–12). Westport, CT: Praeger Publishers.

Fishbein, M. (1997, February 11–13). *Theoretical models of HIV prevention.* Paper presented at the NIH Consensus Development Conference, Natcher Conference Center, National Institutes of Health, Bethesda, MD.

Foucault, M. (1961). *Madness and civilization: An archaeology of medical perception* (A. M. Sheridan Smith, Trans.). New York: Pantheon.

Foucault, M. (1970). *The order of things: An archaeology of the human sciences* (A. M. Sheridan Smith, Trans.). New York: Pantheon.

Foucault, M. (1972). *The archaeology of knowledge* (A. M. Sheridan Smith, Trans.). New York: Pantheon.

Foucault, M. (1978). *The history of sexuality: Vol. I. An introduction* (R. Hurley, Trans.). New York: Pantheon.

Foucault, M. (1980). *Power/knowledge: Selected interviews and other writings, 1972-1977* (C. Gordon, Ed., C. Gordon, L. Marshall, J. Mepham, & K. Soper, Trans.). New York: Pantheon.

Foucault, M. (1989). Sexual choice, sexual act. In *Foucault live: Interviews, 1966-1984* (S. Lotringer, Ed., J. Johnston, Trans.). (pp. 211-231). New York: Semiotext(e).

Foucault, M. (1990). *Michel Foucault: Politics, philosophy, culture: Interviews and other writings, 1977–1984* (L. D. Krizman, Ed.). New York: Routledge.

Goldberg, W. (1989). *Fontaine: Why am I straight?* [video]. Los Angeles: Tall Pony Productions/Whoop, Inc.

HM The Queen. (1991). The Queen's Christmas message, 1983. In P. Lichfield (Ed.), *Elizabeth R: A photographic celebration of 40 years* (p. 121). New York: Doubleday.

Ivie, R. L. (1992, April 14). *The rhetorical transaction of significance.* The annual Grazier memorial lecture presented at the Department of Communication, University of South Florida, Tampa.

Jones, L. E. (1982). There is power in the blood. In J. W. Peterson & N. Johnson (Compilers), N. Johnson (Ed.), *Praise! Our songs and hymns* (p. 283). Grand Rapids, MI: Singspiration Music/Zondervan Corporation.

Kramer, L. (1989). *Reports from the holocaust: The making of an AIDS activist*. New York: St. Martin's Press.

National Institutes of Health Consensus Panel. (1997, February 11–13). *Interventions to prevent HIV risk behaviors: National Institutes of Health consensus development statement*. Bethesda, MD: National Institutes of Health.

Odets, W. (1995). *In the shadow of the epidemic: Being HIV-negative in the age of AIDS*. Durham, NC: Duke University Press.

Patton, C. (1996). *Fatal advice: How safe sex education went wrong*. Durham, NC: Duke University Press.

Perez, T. L., & Dionisopoulos, G. D. (1995). Presidential silence, C. Everett Koop, and the *Surgeon General's Report on AIDS. Communication Studies, 46*, 18–33.

Rotello, G. (1997). *Sexual ecology: AIDS and the destiny of gay men*. New York: Dutton.

Sawyer, E. (1996, July 7). *Remarks at the opening ceremony, Vancouver*. Speech presented at the opening ceremony at the XI International Conference on AIDS, Vancouver, BC, Canada.

Shilts, R. (1988). *And the band played on: Politics, people, and the AIDS epidemic*. New York: Penguin.

Smith, J. M. (1996). *AIDS and society*. Upper Saddle River, NJ: Prentice-Hall.

Sontag, S. (1966). *Against interpretation, and other essays*. New York: Farrar, Straus & Giroux.

Sontag, S. (1990). *Illness as metaphor and AIDS and its metaphors*. New York: Anchor.

Trinidad, D. (1991, December 31). Adrienne Rich charts a difficult world: The acclaimed poet talks of art, anger, and activism [interview]. *The Advocate, 593*, 82–84.

Tuchman, B. W. (1978). *A distant mirror: The calamitous 14th century*. New York: Ballantine.

U.S. Department of Health and Human Services. (1995, May). *Application for a Public Health Service grant, PHS 398*. Bethesda, MD: National Institutes of Health.

Valéry, P. (1995). Definition of politics from *Tel quel*. In *Infopedia: The ultimate multimedia reference tool* [CD-ROM, Future Vision Multimedia, Inc.; 0000-0055-08].

van der Vliet, V. (1996). *The politics of AIDS*. London: Bowderdean Publishing Company.

Vibbert, S. L. (1987, May). *Corporate communication and the management of issues*. Paper presented at the International Communication Association convention, Montreal.

Zimmerman, R. S., & Vernberg, D. (1994). Models of preventive health behavior: Comparison, critique, and meta-analysis. In G. L. Albrecht (Ed.), *Advances in medical sociology: A reconsideration of health behavior change models* (Vol. 4, pp. 45–67). Greenwich, CT: JAI.

2

Pink Water: The Archetype of Blood and the Pool of Infinite Contagion

Kevin A. Clark
University of Texas, Austin

> The red saccharinity of blood flows over the prescientific religious imagination as an unsettling, real presence. Nothing possessed greater concretion than the metaphorical, nothing more bodiliness than the symbolic.
>
> —Camperosi (1988/1995, p. 71)

> Infectious diseases to which sexual fault is attached always inspire fears of easy contagion and bizarre fantasies of transmission by nonvenereal means in public places.
>
> —Sontag (1989, p. 27)

With its unpredicted emergence and unpredictable course, the pandemic of AIDS has thoroughly insinuated itself into the anxious imagination of the American public. The fascination with AIDS in the medical establishment has focused on the human body as an object of curiosity, examination, and hypothesis. As the object of rhetorical criticism, the body has been scrutinized as a nexus of power between larger systems of societal domination and more intimate patterns of corporeal control, including its treatment in medical discourse (e.g., Patton, 1985, 1990; Treichler, 1988). Whether entrenched in medical or rhetorical realms, the fantasy of AIDS contagion is attached to the stigma of marginalized groups thought prone to spreading sexual filth and disease. As long as undesirable others, with their undesirable practices and afflictions, are kept at a safe distance from the "purity" of the "general population," fears of contagion may be considerably reduced (M. Douglas, 1966).

The stigma of AIDS found itself irretractably attached to the stigma of homosexuality in the earliest years of the pandemic, as the syndrome was first termed the *gay plague* and *GRID*, or "gay-related immune deficiency." Although HIV, the virus thought to cause AIDS, may be transmitted in heterosexual intercourse, heterosexuals may view themselves as inherently different from gay people and so create a psychological boundary that keeps them "protected" from the disease (Land, 1992, p. 1).

However, a "second" AIDS epidemic of fear has emerged that has blood, rather than sex and the sexual body, as its point of departure. In this chapter, I examine the archetype of blood as it escapes the comfortable boundaries of stigmatized others and creates new and less easily assuaged fears of contagion at large. Although the bygone culture of blood pollution has seemingly lapsed into superstition, the potent symbolism of blood continues to work its (black) magic today in new fears of HIV transmission. Disembodied and nonsexual, and so

9

its degree of contamination uncertain, "tainted" blood may be present in anonymous donations, in randomly invasive medical instruments, or in a combination of the two—in unmarked medical wastes that routinely yet unpredictably wash ashore. Discourse is rife with new, frenzied levels of fear and anxiety as corporeal and noncorporeal notions of contagion coalesce in the accidental, public spilling of blood during athletic competition.

HISTORY OF CONTAGION I: BLOOD AND MAGIC

Blood as an archetype is particularly useful for understanding the rhetorical dimensions of contagion, as archetypes are "neither in the physiology of the brain, the structure of language, the organization of society, nor the analysis of behavior, but in the process of imagination," according to psychoanalyst Hillman (1975, p. xi). Archetypes underlie abstractions (Burke, 1969), are the "lexicon" of transcendent myth (Rushing, 1985, p. 192), and are the "inherited response-pattern of the race" (Wimsatt & Brooks, 1957, p. 709). Blood, in contrast to sexual habit, makes a potent archetype because boundaries of purity and pollution are at first more difficult to establish. Whereas boundaries of sexuality partition out entire groups, blood boundaries exist in everyone at skin level; thus, superstitious images of blood first arose with individual sightings of blood issuing from animal and human wounds. Hunters past and present have believed that life is contained in blood and that such power is transferable to their own bodies; for example, the Masai tribesmen today drink the blood of lions, and the warriors of ancient Scythia drank the blood of their first opponents killed in battle (Page, 1981).

The mundane power of life in human blood evolved into a higher power of creation, absolution, and eternal life in Western religious belief and practice. Humankind was born of a blood clot (Koran 96:1–2), and the blood of Christ could "annihilate the stench of sin, the fetor of the excremental human being, the acrid fusty stench of the polluted community, [and] the miasmas of malignity" (Camperosi, 1988/1995, p. 72). The Eucharist, which became the central ritual of the Church, requires that each parishioner consume wine that, once consecrated, becomes the blood of Christ. Whether this conversion, or transubstantiation, was literal or merely symbolic became the focus of considerable debate in the ninth century (Langmuir, 1990), and even today, holy relics, including samples of blood, have lasting symbolic significance for churches (e.g., see Hundley, 1996).

Medical science, in contrast, was more productive in anchoring the archetype of blood to material bodies as objects of inquiry. The common medical practice of bloodletting conveyed a sense of the power of blood across the centuries, from ancient Egypt to 19th-century Europe, because it was not merely surgery to remove diseased tissues, but was also a means to let evil humors out of the body. In the Middle Ages, medical and religious practice merged in great celebrations of therapeutic bloodletting, where the ailments and sins of whole crowds were purged *en masse,* as during the Parisian festival of St. Bartholomew on August 24 (Camperosi, 1988/1995). Like transubstantiation, bloodletting became more symbolic and less attached to "true" medical practice, as "sympathetic" chicken eggs were filled with human blood, waved over ill patients, and then buried to "contain" bodily and spiritual impurities (Page, 1981, p. 21).

The individual body could find cure or salvation through the power of blood; its particular malady or sin could be absolved by focusing attention on the entrance or exit of blood. However, real rhetorical power lay in the ability of the priest-barber-surgeon to determine and articulate not only the nature of the problem, but its cause as well. And in whatever direction cause is found to lie, one will also find—or cast—a shadow of blame. In this way, symbolic borders are constructed between groups that divide the pure from the impure, the good from the evil, the majority from the outcast. With borders established, a group believing its power in jeopardy could accuse another group—usually a defenseless one—of draining "good" blood and so potency from its ranks, or of tainting the general pool of blood with an "evil" batch. Articulation of the interplay of good and evil thus shifts from the balance of humors within the individual body to the polarized good and evil communities within society. Where once the medico-religious practitioner used blood to fortify the body or bloodletting to relieve the body of ill humors, the political practitioner now blamed those who would relieve the body politic—the greater community—of its power or who would pollute the blood of the common good.

Bloodlettings were a matter of public record, but the stealing and tainting of blood was performed "covertly" and so made for easy accusations against undesirable groups. For example, second-century Christians were charged with secretly killing Romans to use their blood in private ceremonies (Langmuir, 1990), though Christians themselves maintained that the Church would grow with the spilling of their *own* blood: "We become more numerous each time we are mown down; the blood of Christians is seed" (Tertullien, 1961, p. 108; my translation). Christian soldier became soldier of democracy in the American Revolution, as the "tree of liberty must be refreshed from time to time with the blood of patriots" (Jefferson, 1944, p. 436). Here, the good blood of a group is spilled to increase its own potency, without regard to the taking or the spoiling of the blood of any surrounding groups.

As Christians and democrats grew in number and prominence through public blood baths, minority groups dispersed into dark enclaves, where practices were private and so suspect. Through "blood libel," Christians accused Jews in the Middle Ages for a variety of societal "ills," including poor economies, disease, and even the attempted overthrow of Christian society (Langmuir, 1990). Some Christians believed that Jews gained their power through the abduction and murder of a Christian child, whose blood was allegedly "[d]rawn from the veins . . . collected in cups, dried into powder, and sprinkled on Seder wine and matzo" during Passover (Hsia, 1992, pp. 88–89; see also Leikin, 1993).

Jews not only took Christian blood, it was said, but tainted it, too. By poisoning wells with human blood, they supposedly spread the Black Death of 1347–1350 (Langmuir, 1990; Strack, 1909) and were consequently massacred in large numbers (Hsia, 1992). A blood libel trial in 1913 raised worldwide concern about magical conspiracies: "Who would have supposed that in the 20th Century . . . we would see a court solemnly discussing Black Magic . . . and whether Jews drink Christian blood?" (*London Times* report, cited in Leikin, 1993, p. 221). The question was premature, as a Nazi propaganda pamphlet in 1935 quoted from Martin Luther's *The Jews and Their Lies*: "We do not kidnap their children and pierce them through; we do not poison their wells; we do not thirst for their blood" (Langmuir, 1990, p. 309). The consequences of this indictment may be found in the genocide of the Holocaust.

HISTORY OF CONTAGION II: SEX AND SCIENCE

Blood libel sounds archaic in the light of modern technological progress, yet fierce accusations, the partitioning of groups, and extraordinary blame emerge anew in the era of AIDS. This time, rhetoric attempts to remove itself from the hysterical superstition of unseen powers and veers instead toward calm, scientific justification. As sex emerges as the primary marker of identification, boundaries of clear-minded, "rational" purity prevail in an efficient *cordon sanitaire,* whereby the culture of the ingroup is defensively constructed against suspicious outgroups and internally strengthened by a consensus about fundamental principles (Ross, 1989).

The first "border of sanitation" is, again, the boundary of the body itself, with its natural integrity of skin and its rhetorical integrity of an obsession with cleanliness, as Americans attempt to seal themselves off from the surrounding pollution of modern life. Although some "internal" microbes (such as *e. coli* bacteria) are vital and many "external" areas are not very harmful to a healthy body, we have adopted, since the 1950s, an "us versus them" cultural anxiety toward germs, where our bodies are germ-free and the outside world is contaminated (Patton, 1985). Advertisements push products for destroying unidentified germs in households and in public places by "showing" us where they are—or, more important—where they *might* be (kitchen countertops and automatic teller machine keys). The fear of contamination, of pollution crossing the thresholds of our skin, is thus heightened by a lack of information about exactly what and where the germs are. In light of this fear, Americans are particularly anxious to know how to avoid what they perceive to be the most serious germ of all—HIV—in everyday life.

The simplest of medical guidelines for the prevention of HIV focus on maintaining corporeal boundaries, or, in former Surgeon General C. Everett Koop's (1990) words, having "respect for our bodies" (p. 28). Body-focused rhetoric is not so disruptive as it tends to be vague in providing detail about which "bodily fluids" contain and convey HIV across corporeal lines. Specifically identifying fluids as sexual fluids, which in turn implicates the ways in which they are transported, would, in the mind of the reader, impute groups of individuals, separate from the main of society, involved in secret—and therefore abhorrent—practices. Despite Dear Abby's assurances that "explaining is not condoning" (Van Buren, 1990, pp. 68–69), explaining the means of transmission has rhetorical implications for either condoning or condemning certain practices (such as gay sex) and, so, certain people (such as gays).

Jews and gays have concomitant histories as minorities, their oppression based on successive waves of prejudice and segregation. "Inferior" minority groups often separate themselves into corners, form their own belief systems and identities, and so are increasingly less understood because of their seeming absence. Distant corners soon become dark corners that fuel rumors of mysterious and evil deeds. However, pogroms against Jews were based on emotional, hearsay tales of blood theft and contagion, whereas the initial stigmatization of gay men *presupposed* emotionally disengaged scientific rhetoric about AIDS—a disengagement that becomes engaged in a moral and magical contagion of its own. Scientific talk in the modern age also has much greater dissemination than did blood libels through totalizing organizations of "medical surveillance" and "media coverage" (Patton, 1985, p, 20).

The prescientific medicine of bodily humors focused on the balance of good and evil blood within the individual; modern medicine, in contrast, has developed a great taxonomy of grouping individuals with similar practices or conditions in the science of epidemiology. Such is the case with AIDS: Because its first patients in the West were gay, medical authorities and the media termed the disease the gay plague and GRID. At least one medical expert even chastised the medical establishment for *avoiding* such terminology in favor of "long, cumbersome circumlocutions" (Grmek, 1989/1990, p. 10)—terms such as *AIDS,* presumably. With the twin stigmas of deadly illness and sexual minority, AIDS found its most potent "semantic epidemic" (Treichler, 1988, p. 37) in the rhetorical boundaries between gay men and the "population at large" (Klaidman, 1991, p. 146), the "general population" (Margaret Heckler, in Adams, 1989, p. 133), or the "general public" ("As AIDS Scare Hits," 1983, p. 71). Although it was assumed that AIDS was an autochthonous disease, or a disease originating *and* appearing in the enclaves of young, gay, urban professionals, the stigma of youth (e.g., see Zaslow, 1990) and big-city dwelling (e.g., see Flynn, 1990) failed to take hold.

Gay men are often identified by their sexual behavior, but sexual disease became "scientized" before the issue of AIDS arose at all. Venereal diseases, involving the simple contact of genitalia, were in the Victorian age regarded as "venial," or forgivable, sins of passion (both words are derived from *Venus,* the goddess of love); today, the expanded notion of sexually transmitted diseases (or STDs) categorizes diseases more scientifically, based on identification of the microbes or parasites themselves. Seemingly neutral in the use of the term sex, STDs presuppose a wide range of sexual activity, including emotionally charged thoughts of anal sex and diseases spread by contaminated feces (Patton, 1985)—thoughts not mentioned by the Victorians, and thoughts that soon tied dirty, unnamable (sometimes deviant) sex acts to the cool detachment of scientific rhetoric.

In the mid-1980s, it was hoped that AIDS would stay within its "natural limits" (Grover, 1988, p. 28) of gay men; the best hope of the 1986 International AIDS Conference was not cure or even mass prevention (which would have been the focus of a body-barrier campaign), but "containment" within those gay boundaries (Treichler, 1988, pp. 5–6). Of course, gay men were not the only group afflicted with AIDS in the United States, but they were the "cultural medium" in flourishing, culturally bordered-off gay enclaves that allowed the more virulent strains of HIV to come about (Grmek, 1989/1990, p. 168) in "super vectors" of rampant transmission (Adams, 1989, p. 125). More than just a Petri dish for disease, gay men as deviants also were to blame for their plague (P. H. Douglas & Pinsky, 1992; Land, 1992; Patton, 1985; Ryan, 1976; Sontag, 1989). From there, the even more suspect bisexual man provided a "bisexual bridge" from the "demi-monde" of hidden homosexuality to the heterosexual world of girlfriends and wives (Gagnon, 1989, pp. 55–60). Even if gay men were not responsible for the pollution within their own community, they could still be cordoned off into boundaries of disease rather than "lifestyle" as a means to prevent contagion, as much as to care for them, just as lepers had been relegated to leprosaria and tuberculosis patients to sanitariums in years past (Land, 1992).

Heterosexuals, in contrast, believed themselves safe from the pandemic by virtue of their self-identification as straight and, more particularly, as nongay. Because gays are indistinguishable in appearance from straights, and it was difficult determining just who occupied the "underworld," it became important to set up psychological and rhetorical boundaries between the normal/pure "me" and the abnormal/impure other (Ryan, 1976, pp. 13–14), through a "bizarre dance in which the search for difference, the desire to discover the mark of the beast divides one from the other, renders us dubious of ourselves and distrustful of those we meet" (Davies, Hickson, Weatherburn, & Hunt, 1993, p. 44). Alas, this "difference" became a matter not for the worrisome, "dubious" eyes of the individual heterosexual, but for the rhetoric of the straight community as it codified its behavior as normal and the behavior of gay men as abnormal (M. Douglas & Calvez, 1990).

The conflation of "high-risk groups" with "high-risk behaviors" (Powell, 1990, p. 50) rhetorically maintains boundaries between gay and straight communities and so the cultural perception that straights are not at risk for HIV transmission (Erni, 1994), *regardless of their behavior,* as long as they stay within the culturally straight community. For example, one surgeon told us with authority that high-risk sex is synonymous with a high-risk group, which in turn is depraved in any account: "Medically speaking, the homosexual lifestyle is a harmful lifestyle fueled by a sexual addiction that has no limits" (Day, 1991, p. 126). Another surgeon informed us that it is a medical point and not a "moralistic" one to tell gay men not to have sex, although he imputed gay men as a whole as blameworthy rather than directing attention on the particular modes of transmission, which may indeed be, in some instances, heterosexual (in Adams, 1989, p. 8).

The power of scientific rhetoric in the straight community is so strong that some experts recommend avoiding terminology connected to the "individual pathology" of the person and instead focus on AIDS-related stigma such as "AIDS phobia" and "AIDS hysteria" as socially constructed (Herek & Glunt, 1988). In other words, the hegemonic process of blaming the victim derives from "systematically motivated, but unintended, distortions of reality" (Ryan, 1976, p. 11) created by society: "[P]eople select certain risks for attention to defend their preferred lifestyles and as a forensic resource to place blame on other groups. . . . That is, what societies choose to call risky is largely determined by social and cultural factors, not by nature" (Royal Society, cited in Bloor, 1995, p. 96).

Unfortunately, heterosexuals will not adopt safer sexual practices if they do not perceive themselves to be vulnerable to AIDS (Siegel & Gibson, 1988)—a situation unlikely in a pure/impure, innocent/guilty, straight/gay, scientific, and "collective fantasy of dualism" (Erni, 1994, p. 29).

THE BLOOD CONTAGION OF AIDS

Though the sexual contagion of HIV/AIDS continues to grow within communities both gay and straight, the reiteration and production of cultural boundaries and norms through scientific rhetoric at first assures the "population at large" that they are safe from the scourge. However, this rhetoric seems less able to contain the panic of a second, blood-borne pandemic. The calm, medical reassurances that offered "protection" against a gay sexual disease are useless against the fear of anonymous, amorphous blood; in other cases, "reassuring" rhetoric exacerbates the same fear it was meant to assuage. Alas, the Black Death has become here a Red Death of sorts, as the gay community is thought to be polluting not the common water wells of medieval times, but today's common blood supplies.

Anxieties abound in the second AIDS epidemic when semantic paradoxes rupture the comfort zones of rhetorically safe, heterosexual culture. Undesirable groups and activities become bracingly synonymous categories when a term such as high-risk group is used to refer to gay men as a whole; in contrast, heterosexuals are, by default, soothingly synonymous with "nonrisk behavior." Medical authorities affirm neat conflations in noting that the lowered rate of HIV transmission among gay men is due to a "saturation" of "highly sexually active" men having sex behind distant, nonthreatening borders (Bloor, 1995); less or nonsexually active gay men do not enter into the equation (or simply do not exist at all in this formulation). In contrast, an epidemic *of* heterosexuals is unlikely to be "self-sustaining" (Bloor, 1995), because, we are told, their "activities" do not pose much risk of transmission. An epidemic *among* heterosexuals is, however, possible through various "bridges" to homosexuals and *their* activities. In general, the straight community can feel free from risk because bisexual relations and intravenous drug use—the primary bridges—are "chosen" activities outside their cultural boundaries. However, a paradox of uncertainty emerges as the possibility that a homosexual, blameworthy disease may infect heterosexuals through *nonsexual, involuntary* means—through blood.

Beacause AIDS found an early association with gay men, those who did not self-identify as gay did not concern themselves with sexual contagion. Fear became evident, though, as rumors concerning the second, blood-borne epidemic began to surface, fueled by a lack of knowledge about what agent within blood made it so dangerous. As thoughts of blood contagion first arose, new boundaries of containment began to form at the lowest level, with the integrity of the individual body. In particular, people took charge of their safety at body level—the only level in which they felt they had control—by refusing to be involved in blood donation programs. In contrast to earlier beliefs that bloodletting was a way to purge oneself of bad humors, misplaced fear led some to believe that *giving* blood was one way to contract AIDS. In 1983, for example, blood donations dropped by one fourth in New York City, largely, it is estimated, because of the fear of contracting AIDS ("As AIDS Scare Hits," 1983, p. 71). As late as 1987, more than two fifths of Americans continued to believe that donating blood was risky (Adams, 1989), though public health activists alerted the public time and again that it was safe. In some instances, as when Jonas Salk proved that polio vaccinations were safe by inoculating himself, activists announced their own *personal* lack of fear in giving blood (Capps, 1990) or even made a public show of it ("As AIDS Scare Hits," 1983, p. 71).

There was less control in the other direction, however, because most blood recipients require blood in the sudden trauma of an emergency or operating room, especially in life-or-death situations. Beyond the bounds of the body, then, people began to fear for the widened boundaries of the circles of family and friends who might require blood from the large, anonymous donor pool; this is the first level at which people began to resist the recommendations of the medical establishment. Indeed, what was once perceived as a medical "act of mercy" was now a "mortal menace" (Grmek, 1989/1990, p. 38). In particular, most health facilities did not allow the "private pooling" of blood because, as one blood program director noted, "we'd see little pockets of donors" for these family groups alone, and "eventually the blood banks would be destroyed" for those without such close connections ("As AIDS Scare Hits," 1983, p. 72). With a veritable "social explosion" of fear (Grmek, 1989/1990) of possible infection from large donor pools, some heterosexual communities formed their own "blood clubs" of family and friends, and even one blood bank in San Francisco, finding itself in danger of contamination with gay blood, allowed directed donation programs, bending to "public [heterosexual] pressure" (Eckert, 1985). Some experts also disagreed, saying that an "unnecessarily large," volunteer donor pool would lead to inadequate screening for "risk factors" related to contaminated blood (Baroody, 1985). Here, of course, risk factors refers to high-risk groups; eventually gay men (regardless of behavior) were asked not to make donations.

The rhetoric of stigmatization and blame was directed at bloodthirsty medieval Jews for the supposed abduction and ritual cannibalization of children; similarly, the rhetoric of blood contamination in the 1980s focused on the gay contamination and subsequent killing of "innocent" children through donated blood (Patton, 1985). Even a supposed bastion of unbiased information, the Centers for Disease Control in Atlanta, published a rhetorically charged chart of demographic groupings of AIDS cases through 1984. Some of the groups listed include "homosexuals" and "recipients of blood transfusions," with subdivisions that divide these groups into "adults/adolescents" and "children." Ostensibly a simple, scientific chart, with the usual entries such as "homosexual adults" (with the largest number of cases) and "child recipients" (with some cases), there is the glaring positioning at the top of "child homosexuals" with the expected case load of "0" (Wallace, 1985, p. 112). Of course, this entry indicates the conflation of high-risk group and high-risk behavior, as surely some children are homosexual. But the positioning of such a simple "statistic" highlights the blameworthiness of gay men, who have now not only infected themselves (noted by the neat containment of the single, well-bounded category of homosexuals), but have also infected children, who cannot engage in homosexual activity, as there are no child homosexuals.

Just as Jews had been accused of anonymously, intentionally, and vengefully poisoning well water to exacerbate the spread of the bubonic plague, gays were implicated with the anonymous, intentional, and vengeful contamination of the "general" pool of the blood supply. This indicated a shift from "transactions between friends and family who cared about one another" to "transactions between strangers," who had little incentive for "honesty and caution" (Eckert, 1985, p. 68). Unintentional pollution becomes intentional pollution as gay men begin to be accused not just of ignoring public health guidelines not to donate blood, but of maliciously attempting to contaminate the blood supply. Asymptomatic—and so invisible—"revenge infectors" have long been feared and blamed for epidemics, though in the AIDS epidemic, at least, some authorities have suggested that those who know they are infected are more likely to *reduce* risk behavior (Bloor, 1995).

Nonetheless, there are many urban myths of the seemingly "normal" yet vengeful, sexually infectious Typhoid Mary, who has sex with unsuspecting partners, only to reveal his or her "condition" in foreboding, morning-after messages, such as the hand-scrawled, "Welcome to the AIDS Club." Although some of these stories have been shown to be hoaxes (e.g., see Stein, 1993), in one trial, an HIV-seropositive man was charged with "intent to inflict bodily harm," as he allegedly revealed that he would use the virus to "take as many people down" with him as he could (Westfall, 1991, p. B1). Randy Shilts (1987) followed the more "scientific" phenomenon of Gaeten Dugas, the French-Canadian flight attendant who was traced as "Patient Zero" in the beginning of the AIDS epidemic. Not just an initial vector of disease, Dugas enjoyed his own morning-after messages in the darkness of the bathhouses, where he would reveal to his partners after a round of sex that he had "gay cancer," and was heard to say, "I'm going to die and so are you" (Shilts, 1987, p. 165). Naming the individual revenge infector allows for fascinating storytelling, but the indistinguishable gay man somewhere within the general public becomes a far more frightening prospect for the heterosexual, as he may be anyone anywhere. For example, the assumed safe-blood boundaries of the family provide a false sense of security that, once made known, serves to increase suspicion and fear beyond what was necessary in the sexual plague. In one instance, a physician noted her own reluctance at accepting anything but the "purest" (and assuredly heterosexual) blood for her hypothetical children: "If my children had been unfortunate enough to have been in an accident, I know that I would have wanted them to have my mother's, my aunt's or even my best friend's blood rather than blood that came from the Castro" (Day, 1991, pp. 102–103). Although she stated that "some of [her] closest friends are homosexual" (Day, 1991, p. 4), she must assume her "best friend" is not; otherwise, latent fears of gay-driven infection would be realized. Suspicion of possible bridges of infection to her mother or aunt would push her fear to stratospheric levels, as everyone then becomes suspect.

Individual, personal vendettas such as these, whether directed at a particular demographic group or at random, "foolish" partners, have their own myth-making power. The accusations, as with the blood libel against Jews, become powerfully convincing as the revenge infectors in question are only vaguely individuated in the imagination, existing as shadowy groups just out of the sight of close scrutiny. For example, as far back as the early 18th century, Daniel Defoe's (1722/1968) account of plague-ridden London critically appraises the impressive stories of revenge infection by dark and mysterious refugees. The idea of a vengeful gay community—as opposed to individual gays—first emerged when it was suggested that gay men should be excluded from blood donation drives. In 1984, just as the U.S. Department of Health and Human Services had considered screening out all "male homosexuals," regardless of behavioral factors, from blood donations, some medical experts warned that full exclusion might "alienate" some gay people to donate "out of spite" (Eckert, 1985, p. 64). Higher, and so more plausible, motives were offered by one physician, as she believed that gay men will donate (supposedly contaminated) blood as an act of national terrorism, unless "certain medical and political demands are being met" (Day, 1991, p. 98). Presumably, these demands included pushing the slow-acting Reagan administration to focus its attention more squarely on the plague at hand (M. Douglas & Calvez, 1990).

The case of AIDS in hemophiliacs enhances the pointed finger of blame against homosexual blood killers of children, who have gained the most sympathetic notoriety for their condition. The stigmatization of gay men operates in an inexorable logic of binary pairs, as young hemophiliacs are depicted as "innocent" victims, in marked contrast to the generally unspoken but syllogistic assumption that gay men are responsible for their own infection and reprehensible for their spread of their disease to other groups—in this case, through contaminating the blood pools from which blood-clotting factors are extracted for treatment of hemophilia. Youth is vital in the contrast with gay men (there would seem to be no gay boys) such that one patient is emphatically described as not simply young, but as a "young eighteen-year-old . . . youth" (Grmek, 1989/1990, p. 37). Vital, too, is heterosexuality, as young patients are described solely by their inhibited dreams of wedding bells: "Planned marriages which seemed before the [epidemic] to have been made in heaven have not occurred" (Adams, 1989, p. 102). In the most famous case, Ryan White, "with his almost saintly grace" (Bremner, 1990, p. 5D), "taught us that AIDS was claiming the lives of thousands, including the young and innocent" (Futterman, 1990, p. 3F). For gay men, the image of infector and infected are one, and the carry-over of this stigma is challenged in White's case: One mourner at his funeral hoped that "the people in his hometown remember that (contracting the disease) was not Ryan's fault. He [also] wasn't going to hurt anybody" (Cook, 1990).

Infection with HIV from medical syringes or invasive instruments has the potential for a more focused blame because particular individuals, rather than group-diluted pools of blood, are implicated. The most notable case of a health care worker infecting a patient occurred when a young woman, Kimberly Bergalis, was diagnosed with AIDS in 1991. Bergalis was not a member of any high-risk group, so tracing the time and place of infection became a matter of well-directed blame toward David Acer, a gay dentist who apparently knew he was infected and was thought to have contaminated his own dental instruments. Here, a gay man allegedly infected through nonsexual means a straight female *virgin,* who thus suffered not a sexual rape of her body but instead the destruction of the rest of her childhood through the "devastating rape of her personhood and her future" (Wells, 1991, p. 26A). Here stood two polarized images of stigma and blame. On the one hand, the media depicted Acer as a Jekyll-and-Hyde chimera of deception, seemingly a "gentle man" but also a "vengeful serial killer who deliberately injected his blood into [his patients'] bodies because he believed America would continue to ignore AIDS until 'it starts affecting grandmothers and young people'" (Lawson, 1996, p. D1). On the other hand, Bergalis was described as a "beautiful young lady" who died of AIDS "through no fault of her own" (Chipponeri, 1991, p. 3D). She stood before Congress to say, "I didn't do anything wrong, yet I'm being made to suffer" (in Painter, 1991, 1D). Though more recent studies question the role of her dentist in infecting her and even her virginity (see, e.g., Burkett, 1995), the shadow of blame had been irrevocably cast in the American mindset.

A third, strange scenario of the blood contagion of AIDS comes about as medical syringes wash up on popular East Coast beaches. Here, containers of unmarked and possibly tainted pools of blood become doubly randomized in their potential to cause anxiety, as the containers themselves are usually anonymous and appear on shore in random, unpredictable intervals. Because blame is far more difficult to trace, fear intensifies, though it is more diffuse and undirected. Television broadcasts magnified this hysterical fear even further, as they played over and over again the "sightings" of stray needles along stretches of sand (Lyall, 1991, pp. B1–B2), giving the appearance that medical wastes are more common than they actually are. Beachgoers themselves apparently became so hysterical that they did not just see infected blood where empty syringes lay, but saw the whole gamut of infected medical supplies: "Soon, plastic Popsicle packages were being identified as syringes. Cigar holders became blood vials, household gloves became surgical gloves and pieces of animal carcasses turned into human organs" (Lyall, 1991, p. B2). Hyperbole becomes satire as one humorist reflected on the beach medical waste scare with the succinct synopsis that people were practically envisioning "entire operating rooms washing up on the beaches of New Jersey" (Seligmann, 1989, p. 93). The least likely outcome of an outing at the beach is also one that becomes the most cogent and the most succinct—a straight line from point A, visiting, to point B, dying of AIDS: "[P]eople immediately thought they were going to come to the beach, step on a syringe, receive a puncture wound and contract the AIDS virus within six months" (J. S. Lescinski, cited in Lyall, 1991, p. B1).

Some backtracking of blame is accomplished, as some of the wastes are found to be from individual users via local sewers rather than from hospitals ("Back to the Beach," 1989; "High Tide," 1989). However, fear emerges anew, as sewers suggest dirty back alleys and so the dirty, illicit behavior of intravenous-drug users. Attempts to locate a particular revenge infector fail, though the myth of the "mad midnight dumper" takes hold ("State Officials," 1988). Anxiety is most pronounced, once again, in the supposition that children will be at the most risk of infection, because medical wastes may wash ashore next to an elementary school (Perino, 1996) or neighborhood children may become too curious (Fried, 1992; Nitkin, 1994).

"Hypervigilance" toward the gay community *and* the medical community comes onto the scene as a final rhetorical outlet for the (heterosexual) public (Herek & Glunt, 1988). Here, the public finds that it is suspicious not only of the gay community for "ignoring" medical guidelines to close down bathhouses and to cease donating blood, but of the medical community as well for what it perceives to be a lack of honesty in pursuing safety measures in a time frame that matches the public's frenzied need to know and need to act. As much as dark and shadowy gays must be mistrusted to do the right things, the medical community has likewise become the suspicious "AIDS establishment" (Adams, 1989), entrenched in deceitful "AIDSpeak" (Shilts, 1987).

Rather than allaying fears, layered medical reassurances, whether quantitative or qualitative, serve to increase panic. Quantitative risks expressed as statistics are particularly frightening: Risk percentages, no matter how small, are still noticeably—and measurably—distant and distinct from no risk. Unfortunately, science must operate logically on the notion of the null hypothesis, which states that never-can-happen scenarios cannot be proved; only the opposite, it-might-happen scenario can be proved by the single example. In the unusual fear, say of contagion via toothbrushes, scientists are unable to assert with absolute certainty that it will never happen; they can only attempt to calculate odds. For example, as of mid-1983, it was estimated in statements to the public that the odds were 10 million to 1 against someone contracting AIDS through a blood transfusion. This might-be vision remains in play indefinitely for the public's attention and can be disrupted only by a single case of actual transmission. Here, what might be possible at last becomes what is proven possible.

Sometimes qualitative terms must be used instead of statistical ones, as rates of HIV transmission are often difficult to quantify (Bloor, 1995). For example, transmission of HIV via blood products is "extremely small" (Bloor, 1995, p. 7), and that of health care workers to patients is "extremely unlikely" (P. H. Douglas & Pinsky, 1992, p. 22) and "essentially nil" (Elvin, 1991, p. A6). Similarly, the chances of stepping on a syringe that has washed ashore is "virtually nil" ("Back to the Beach," 1989). Relative risks are also posed; for example, HIV is noted to be more fragile than the viruses that cause colds or flus (P. H. Douglas & Pinsky, 1992). Unfortunately, though, as colds and flus are thought to be easily contracted, an image of easy contagion persists, without regard to the differences in risk. In other risk comparisons, the types of illness juxtaposed are so different that no clear image of risk can be imagined at all, and so little fear is quelled. For example, a blood bank director noted that "more people die of bee stings than of transfusion-related AIDS" (Eckert, 1985, p. 65).

Rather than curbing fears, however, long odds produce an "emotional gestalt of 100 percent" (Holly Atkinson, cited in Klaidman, 1991, p. 16), as any chance of infection brings to mind a visceral response of great catastrophe, as in a nuclear war. Thus, medical advice entreating one to "pay attention to the technical details, even those that seem mundane" is counterproductive in reducing fears of contagion (Klaidman, 1991, p. 234). Likewise, emotional absolutism in the lay press that insists on *perfectly* effective safety guidelines might, in fact, interfere with incremental steps geared toward calm, rational responses to epidemics (Cates & Hinman, 1992).

THE POOL OF INFINITE CONTAGION

[T]he epidemic has spilled over, from the original U.S. male homosexual population, to flood other sectors to a previously unimagined extent. (Grmek, 1989/1990, p. 90)

Corporeal symbols of sex and noncorporeal symbols of blood foment fear and anxiety at new levels, as diver Greg Louganis injures himself during an important dive at the 1988 Olympics. The singular and very public incident of the spilling of blood during athletic competition juxtaposes a previous image of athletic, heterosexual masculinity with the stigma of the gay male body, and the image of a "red badge of courage" gained in pursuit of national pride is exchanged for uncertain risks for other divers—and the public as a whole—in the dilution of blood into a pool of seemingly infinite contagion.

As diver Greg Louganis attempted a difficult dive—dubbed the "Dive of Death" (Wulf, 1995, p. 87)—at the 1988 Summer Olympics in Seoul, he hit his head on the springboard and landed in the water, his head bleeding from a small gash. He was subsequently praised for bearing the pain, completing his remaining dives, and winning several gold medals. However, in early 1995, Louganis announced that he knew he was HIV-seropositive at the time of the dive. In this simple setup are the beginnings of great anxiety, as paradoxical images clash in the oft-rerun loop of his dive, involving both his body and the blood in the pool. Coverage of AIDS issues in the media usually involves the selection of just one theme (such as sexuality or drug use), as each subissue has its own trajectory of reportable meanings, and these monovocal fragments produce an illusion of control of the whole issue of AIDS (Treichler, 1989). Similarly, audiences prefer the control afforded them when issues—and choices—are dispensed to them within an adequate time frame, as when these monovocal fragments are presented over months or years (Herek & Glunt, 1988). In the case of Louganis, though, several themes play out at the same time, creating overtones of a multiplicity of meanings, which, when combined, create feelings of immense anxiety in the receptive audience. For example, people tend to distort reality or construct experiences that help them avoid a fundamental anxiety about death, but the public specter of possible HIV transmission makes them confront their own death (Herek & Glunt, 1988; Siegel & Gibson, 1988). Thus, the ambiguity and uncertainty that create anxiety must be linguistically managed to reduce panic (Treichler, 1988).

The 1995 re-viewing of the 1988 dive first creates apprehension about Louganis' body. Once described as an "Adonis-like" athlete before the simultaneous announcement of his homosexuality and his HIV-seropositive status, the image of Louganis must be modified in the imagination of his viewers to suit his double-stigma status as gay and infected (Erni, 1994). Because the media tell us that the AIDS sufferer looks a "lot like you, . . . a lot like me" (in Crimp, 1992, p. 119), it is important for us to reorganize that image, using a representative heuristic (Siegel & Gibson, 1988) to ignore the traits that are similar to ours and to emphasize the traits that can best match the stereotypes we already have in mind. Stereotypes are useful in that we can access them quickly and efficiently (Turow, 1984), hence reducing the anxiety by some degree. Indeed, we must know who is queer to relieve apprehension (Patton, 1990).

Once we know that Louganis is gay, we backtrack our earlier perception of him as masculine and athletically fit. His "carved, deep-chested body" (Skow, 1988, p. 59) and "handsome" face (Wulf, 1995, p. 87) are characteristics that will slowly vanish as payment for both his gay disease and his gay vanity (Adams, 1989), as was said of Gaetan Dugas before him (Grmek, 1989/1990). Indeed, in gazing at him, "we seek to find 'the other,' the sallow cheek, the shadow beneath the eye, the glint of fear" (Davies et al., 1993, p. 44). We are uncomfortable in remembering that we were not able to tell that he was infected, as was conceivably the case with the evil contagion of Jews in the Middle Ages (M. Douglas, 1992), but we are happy to make the connection now that he is both gay and infected, so at least that component of his image is stable. The years that have passed before we were able to make that connection are not important, as even some physicians today believe that the 16th-century thinker Erasmus was gay—and died of AIDS (Grmek, 1989/1990, p. 111).

The viewer can also now see the look of shame (or *aidos* in Greek, merely one letter away from *AIDS*) on his face, as he becomes embarrassed not just for his faulty dive, but for knowing that he may have infected others (M. Douglas, 1966; Visser, 1984). Certainly, Louganis received considerable criticism for his poor judgment in not informing the officials there of his status in case of emergency situations. Although current medical discourse suggests that he may have risked infecting his physician, Dr. James Puffer, who was not wearing gloves at the time, much of the discourse concerning risk and contagion has been centered on the drops of blood in the pool, outside the bodies of both Louganis and Puffer.

Released from the body, these drops of blood *qua* blood become blood *qua* sign as they are "freed from their . . . points of reference" and "embark upon an endless process of self-reproduction" (Baudrillard, 1993, p. 6). In other words, the infected blood as a signifier replaces the image of gay sexuality (Treichler, 1988), not unlike the disembodied belief in the power of blood in the Middle Ages and rather like the disembodied fears of blood contagion evident in discourse about the blood supply, medical instruments, and spare syringes. Some medical descriptions model this view of a "conscious" virus, as "virions," or virus particles, "swim cell-free in the blood looking for more cells to infect" (Adams, 1989, p. 82).

Just as the archetype of blood shows its qualifiable, not quantifiable, state of power, so, too, does the dispersion of the few drops of blood in the pool, as the pool itself is then imagined as polluted and infectious throughout. In a scientific synecdoche of sorts, where the part is seen as the whole, and the whole for the part, blood and water are one. The singular drops of blood pollute the entire pool of water, because a little evil taints all of its surrounding good, as has been seen in discussions of miscegenation. In American conceptions of race, the "one-drop rule" establishes the standard: A single drop of "Black blood" makes a person Black and effectively taints the gene pool from that point forward. Anthropologists term this the "hypo-descent rule," as racially mixed persons are assigned the status of the subordinate group (Davis, 1991, p. 5) The evil is clear: In popular, historical connotations, such mixing leads to "blood poisoning and other physical deterioration, to mental inferiority, and to immorality and cultural degeneracy" (Davis, 1991, p. 25). So, too, does the inferior, tainted blood of Louganis contaminate the pool for those who are "superior" in their heterosexual, uninfected status.

Discourse of risk is very strong in the frenzied fear of visibly contaminated pool water. Louganis (1996) himself worried, in retrospect, about what exactly happened: "Did I get any blood in the pool? Is the filtration system working? Did they allow ample time before the next diver dove? Did any blood spill on the pool deck?" (p. 6). Assurances of safety begin at lower levels of credibility and move ever higher from there, beginning with coach Ron

O'Brien, who parroted general guidelines in noting that "the risk of his spreading the virus through an open cut was infinitesimal" (in Wulf, 1995, p. 88). Health officials once again promise the public that there is "almost no risk" of infection from trace levels of blood in the pool (Rochell, 1995). At last, Dr. Anthony Fauci, a prominent expert on AIDS, responded with a series of cumulatively lesser risk factors—a series that still does not serve to mollify fears of contagion: "[T]here would have been an extraordinary low risk of infecting anyone . . . First, there's the profound dilutional effect—at most, there may have been a minuscule amount of blood in a pool filled with tens of thousands of gallons of water. Second, the chlorine in the pool would have killed the virus" (cited in Louganis, 1996, p. 7).

Perhaps the best explanation for the anxiety caused by repeated viewing of Louganis' dive can be found in a theory of magical contagion—a theory that ties together old notions of blood and magic into the modern world. In this law of contagion, actual, logical, risks of pollution, infection, and so forth, are not so much considered as is the emotional gestalt mentioned earlier, where something is contagious, regardless of the risk comparison or percentage, or it is not. For example, in one experiment, participants refused to try on a sweater they were told was worn by Hitler, though it had been freshly laundered and so had no "real" properties of infection. Similarly, participants refused to wear a sweater they were told was worn by an AIDS patient (Nemeroff & Rozin, 1994). Thus, mere belief in contagion is enough to cause anxiety, if not outright behavioral changes, even without physical proximity to the threat (M. Douglas & Calvez, 1990).

The ultimate relief for the anxiety caused by the replaying of Louganis' dive is death itself, justly delivered, to protect society as a whole: "Pollution, once it appeared, threatened every citizen . . . and anyone could take it upon himself to expel it by killing the offender. Here the motive was not honor or shame or vengeance but a kind of impersonal civic responsibility" (Visser, 1984, p. 199).

Louganis did receive death threats after his announcement (Perry, 1995), and one may wonder if the killer would feel a sense of "impersonal civic responsibility" in slitting his throat and watching his "faggot blood run in the street" (Henry, 1994, p. 57). The evil purged, in this view, would be for the common good.

CONCLUSION

Arising from the seeming safety of sexual and sexuality difference, a second AIDS epidemic of fear has emerged that has blood, rather than sex and the sexual body, as its point of departure. The archetype of blood plays into the imagination of the American people by crossing the preformed, anxiety-free boundaries of stigmatized others and by creating new and less easily assuaged fears of contagion. The ancient culture of blood pollution has not lapsed into superstition, as the power of blood continues to work its spell even today in new fears of HIV transmission. Disembodied and nonsexual, and so its degree of contamination uncertain, tainted blood may be present in a variety of situations and its characteristics are perhaps most pronounced in the rhetoric surrounding Greg Louganis' ill-fated Olympic dive. The power of blood continues to confound, mystify, and frighten the public even today, as the pool of infinite contagion has grown far beyond the bounds of the Olympic pool. The endless ocean itself was feared to be contagious when, following the crash of TWA Flight 800 in July, 1996, packages of HIV-contaminated blood were dispersed, presumably risking the lives of rescue divers (Baker, 1996; "United Way," 1996). Of course, we are told that "even if the package had broken at sea, contamination would have been virtually impossible"

(Baker, 1996, p. A17). Logic tells me this is true; emotion, and the fear of magical blood contagion, tell me otherwise.

REFERENCES

Adams, J. (1989). *AIDS: The HIV myth.* New York: St. Martin's Press.

As AIDS scare hits nation's blood supply. (1983, July 25). *U.S. News & World Report,* pp. 71–72.

Back to the beach; medical waste. (1989, July). *The University of California, Berkeley Wellness Letter, 5* [On-line], 2. Available: Lexis-Nexis Library: News File: Allnws

Baker, A. (1996, August 13). Pieces of a shattered puzzle. *Newsday* [On-line serial], p. A17. Available: Lexis-Nexis Library: News File: Allnws

Baroody, W. J., Jr. (1985). Foreword. In R. D. Eckert & E. L. Wallace (Eds.), *Securing a safer blood supply: Two views.* Washington, DC: American Enterprise Institute for Public Policy Research.

Baudrillard, J. (1993). *The transparency of evil: Essays on extreme phenomenon* (J. Benedict, Trans.). New York: Verso.

Bloor, M. (1995). *The sociology of HIV transmission.* London: Sage.

Bremner, C. (1990, April 13). AIDS victim's death moves a nation. *The Times,* p. 5D.

Burke, K. (1969). *A rhetoric of motives.* Berkeley: University of California Press.

Burkett, E. (1995). *The gravest show on earth: America in the age of AIDS.* Boston: Houghton Mifflin.

Camperosi, P. (1995). *Juice of life: The symbolic and magic significance of blood* (R. R. Barr, Trans.). New York: Continuum Publishing Company. (Original work published 1988)

Capps, K. (1990). Volunteer your time. In S. Alyson (Ed.), *You can do something about AIDS* (pp. 42–44). Boston: The Stop AIDS Project, Inc.

Cates, W., & Hinman, A. R. (1992). AIDS and absolutism: The demand for perfection in prevention. *New England Journal of Medicine, 327,* 492–493.

Chipponeri, J. (1991, December 22). Re: AIDS used to justify military ban on gays, Dec. 10 [Letter to the editor]. *St. Petersburg Times* [On-line], p. 3D. Available: Lexis-Nexis Library: News File: Allnws

Cook, B. (1990, April 9). Vigil honors White [Regional News]. *United Press International* [On-line]. Available: Lexis-Nexis Library: News File: Allnws

Crimp, D. (1992). Portraits of people with AIDS. In L. Grossberg, C. Nelson, & P. Treichler (Eds.), *Cultural studies* (pp. 117–133). New York: Routledge.

Davies, P. M., Hickson, F. C. I., Weatherburn, P., & Hunt, A. J. (1993). *Sex, gay men and AIDS.* London: Falmer Press.

Davis, F. J. (1991). *Who is Black?: One nation's definition.* University Park: University of Pennsylvania Press.

Day, L. (1991). *AIDS: What the government isn't telling you.* Palm Desert, CA: Rockford Press.

Defoe, D. (1968). *A journal of the plague year.* Bloomfield, CT: Sign of the Stone Book. (Original work published 1722)

Douglas, M. (1966). *Purity and danger: An analysis of concepts of pollution and taboo.* New York: Praeger.

Douglas, M. (1992). *Risk and blame: Essays in cultural theory.* New York: Routledge.

Douglas, M., & Calvez, M. (1990). The self as risk taker: A cultural theory of contagion in relation to AIDS. *The Sociological Review, 38,* 445–464.

Douglas, P. H., & Pinsky, L. (1992). *The essential AIDS fact book.* New York: Pocket Books.

Eckert, R. D. (1985). Blood, money, and monopoly. In R. D. Eckert & E. L. Wallace (Eds.), *Securing a safer blood supply: Two views* (pp. 1–84). Washington, DC: American Enterprise Institute for Public Policy Research.

Elvin, J. (1991, September 30). Down on Koop. *The Washington Times* [On-line], p. A6. Available: Lexis-Nexis Library: News File: Allnws

Erni, J. N. (1994). *Unstable frontiers: Technomedicine and the cultural politics of "curing" AIDS.* Minneapolis: University of Minnesota Press.

Flynn, R. L. (1990). What a caring city can do about AIDS. In S. Alyson (Ed.), *You can do something about AIDS* (pp. 141–144). Boston: The Stop AIDS Project, Inc.

Fried, J. P. (1992, January 19). Closed beach tied to man on barge. *The New York Times,* p. A31.

Futterman, E. (1990, April 13). Two who helped us face our prejudice. *St. Louis Post-Dispatch* [On-line], p. 3F. Available: Lexis-Nexis Library: News File: Allnws

Gagnon, J. H. (1989, Summer). Disease and desire. *Daedalus: Journal of the American Academy of Arts and Sciences,* pp. 47–77.

Grmek, M. D. (1990). *History of AIDS: Emergence and origin of a modern pandemic* (R. C. Maulitz & J. Duffin, Trans.). Princeton, NJ: Princeton University Press. (Original work published 1989)

Grover, J. Z. (1988). AIDS: Keywords. In D. Crimp (Ed.), *AIDS: Cultural analysis, cultural criticism* (pp. 17–30). Cambridge, MA: MIT Press.

Henry, W. A., III (1994, June 27). Pride and prejudice. *Time*, pp. 54–59.

Herek, G. M., & Glunt, E. K. (1988). An epidemic of stigma. *American Psychologist, 43*, 886–891.

High tide for ocean legislation. (1989, June 15). *The Record* [On-line], p. A15. Available: Lexis-Nexis Library: News File: Allnws

Hillman, J. (1975). *Re-visioning psychology* (1st ed.). New York: Harper & Row.

Hsia, R. P.-C. (1992). *Trent 1475: Stories of a ritual murder trial.* New Haven, CT: Yale University Press.

Hundley, A. R. (Ed.). (1996). *Let's go: Europe 1996.* New York: St. Martin's Press.

Jefferson, T. (1944). Letters. In A. Koch & W. Peden (Eds.), *The life and selected writings of Thomas Jefferson* (pp. 349–730). New York: Random House.

Klaidman, S. (1991). *Health in the headlines: The stories behind the stories.* New York: Oxford University Press.

Koop, C. E. (1990). Looking to the future. In S. Alyson (Ed.), *You can do something about AIDS* (pp. 28–30). Boston: The Stop AIDS Project, Inc.

Land, H. (1992). Introduction: Meeting the AIDS challenge: An overview. In H. Land (Ed.), *AIDS: A complete guide to psychosocial intervention* (pp. 1–10). Milwaukee: Family Service America, Inc.

Langmuir, G. I. (1990). *Toward a definition of antisemitism.* Berkeley: University of California Press.

Lawson, K. (1996, November 15). "Patient A" dissects famous AIDS case. *The Arizona Republic/The Phoenix Gazette* [On-line], p. D1. Available: Lexis-Nexis Library: News File: Allnws

Leiken, E. (1993). *The Beilis transcripts: The anti-semitic trial that shook the world.* Northvale, NJ: Aronson.

Louganis, G. (1996). *Breaking the surface.* New York: Penguin.

Lyall, S. (1991, September 11). Beach medical waste: Debris but no panic. *The New York Times*, pp. B1–B2.

Nemeroff, C., & Rozin, P. (1994). The contagion concept in adult thinking in the United States: Transmission of germs and interpersonal influence. *Ethos, 22*, 158–186.

Nitkin, D. (1994, October 18). Beach cleanup needles officials; woman collected syringes from sand. *Sun-Sentinel* [On-line], p. 1B. Available: Lexis-Nexis Library: News File: Allnws

Page, J. (1981). *Blood: The river of life.* Washington, DC: U.S. News Books.

Painter, K. (1991, December 18). Guilt, innocence and AIDS. *USA Today* [On-line], p. 1D. Available: Lexis-Nexis Library: News File: Allnws

Patton, C. (1985). *Sex and germs: The politics of AIDS.* Boston: South End Press.

Patton, C. (1990). *Inventing AIDS.* New York: Routledge.

Perino, G. (1996, January 17). Bad site for hospice [Letter to the editor]. *The Record* [On-line], p. 17. Available: Lexis-Nexis Library: News File: Allnws

Perry, T. (1995, March 20). [Perspectives section]. *Newsweek*, p. 19.

Powell, J. (1990). Working with the media. In S. Alyson (Ed.), *You can do something about AIDS* (pp. 49–52). Boston: The Stop AIDS Project, Inc.

Rochell, A. (1995, March 29). Dispelling myths about how virus is transmitted. *Atlanta Constitution* [On-line], p. 3B. Available: Lexis-Nexis Library: News File: Allnws

Ross, A. (1989). *No respect: Intellectuals and popular culture.* New York: Routledge.

Rushing, J. H. (1985). *E.T.* as rhetorical transcendence. *Quarterly Journal of Speech, 71*, 188–203.

Ryan, W. (1976). *Blaming the victim.* New York: Vintage Books.

Seligmann, J. (1989, November 27). The '90s: Back to the future. *Newsweek*, p. 93.

Shilts, R. (1987). *And the band played on: Politics, people, and the AIDS epidemic.* New York: St. Martin's Press.

Siegel, K., & Gibson, W. C. (1988). Barriers to the modification of sexual behavior among heterosexuals at risk for acquired immunodeficiency syndrome. *New York State Journal of Medicine, 88*, 66–70.

Skow, J. (1988, October 3). Splashes of class and acts of heroism. *Time*, pp. 58–59.

Sontag, S. (1989). *AIDS and its metaphors.* New York: Farrar, Straus & Giroux.

State officials want Bush to stem ocean pollution [Regional News]. (1988, December 12). *United Press International* [On-line]. Available: Lexis-Nexis Library: News File: Allnws

Stein, G. (1993). *Encyclopedia of hoaxes.* Detroit: Gale Research, Inc.

Strack, H. L. (1909). *The Jew and human sacrifice: Human blood and Jewish ritual* (H. Blanchamp, Trans.). London: Cope & Fenwick.

Tertullien [Tertullian]. (1961). *Apologétique* [Apology] (2nd ed) (J.-P. Waltzing, Trans.). Paris: Société d'Édition <<Les Belles Lettres>>.

Treichler, P. (1988). AIDS, homophobia, and biomedical discourse: An epidemic of signification. In D. Crimp (Ed.), *AIDS: Cultural analysis, cultural criticism* (pp. 31–70). Cambridge, MA: MIT Press.

Treichler, P. (1989, October). Seduced and terrorized: AIDS and network television. *ArtForum*, pp. 147–151.

Turow, J. (1984). *Media industries: The production of news and entertainment.* New York: Longman.

United Way president establishes fund to help victims' families (1996, July 19). *USA Today* [On-line], p. 6A. Available: Lexis-Nexis Library: News File: Allnws

Van Buren, A. (1990). An open letter to parents. In S. Alyson (Ed.), *You can do something about AIDS* (pp. 67–69). Boston: The Stop AIDS Project, Inc.

Visser, M. (1984). Vengeance and pollution: Orestes' trail of blood. *Journal of the History of Ideas, 45,* 193–206.

Wallace, E. L. (1985). The case for national blood policy. In R. D. Eckert & E. L. Wallace (Eds.), *Securing a safer blood supply: Two views* (pp. 85–153). Washington, DC: American Enterprise Institute for Public Policy Research.

Wells, R. J., Jr. (1991, December 20). The consequences [Letter to the editor]. *Star Tribune* [On-line], p. 26A. Available: Lexis-Nexis Library: News File: Allnws

Westfall, B. (1991, September 26). Ferguson denies keeping AIDS secret. *The Columbian* [On-line], p. B1. Available: Lexis-Nexis Library: News File: Allnws

Wimsatt, W. K., Jr., & Brooks, C. (1957). *Literary criticism: A short history.* Chicago: University of Chicago Press.

Wulf, S. (1995, March 6). Heart of the diver: His Olympic triumph marred by the terrors of AIDS, Greg Louganis talks about growing up gay. *Time,* pp. 87–88.

Zaslow, J. (1990). Education doesn't happen only in schools. In S. Alyson (Ed.), *You can do something about AIDS* (pp. 34–36). Boston: The Stop AIDS Project, Inc.

3

Initiating or Avoiding Activism: Red Ribbons, Pink Triangles, and Public Argument About AIDS

Matthew J. Sobnosky
College of William and Mary

Eric Hauser
Wayne State University

A November 1995 issue of *The Advocate,* a national gay and lesbian news magazine, poses an intriguing question about the acquired immune deficiency syndrome (AIDS)[1] epidemic in contemporary America: "It's the only disease to have its own gift shop. Have we gone too far in commercializing the epidemic?" (Foster, 1995, p. 3). In the accompanying article, Dave Mulryan, a New York advertising executive who advises companies seeking access to gay markets, explained, "Politics ignored this disease, so we did a very American thing: We commercialized it. If we can't talk about AIDS in the political arena, well, we can talk about it in the commercial arena" (in Foster, 1995, p. 38). Muiryan referred to the increasing number of consumer products that feature a red ribbon or some other emblem of AIDS activism. Nor is *The Advocate* being facetious about the existence of an "AIDS gift shop." The same article describes Under One Roof, a San Francisco shop that carries only merchandise from Northern California AIDS organizations. According to Martin Spector, the executive director, the shop carries "pins, earrings, candles, bumper stickers, stamp pads, stickers, T-shirts, coffee mugs, calendars, bracelets, coloring books, Keith Haring tote bags, ties, note cards, watches, books, dominoes, and yo-yos" that feature a red ribbon or some other emblem associated with AIDS, and donates all profits to the fight against AIDS (in Foster, 1995, p. 36).

Mulryan, Spector, and others who promote the sale of AIDS-related merchandise and memorabilia see the commercial use of symbols such as the red ribbon as a way of introducing a discourse about AIDS into American public consciousness. More important, however, the "commercialization" Mulryan described creates a space in public discourse for activists to propose a language for understanding the AIDS epidemic that challenges prevalent social understandings of AIDS and people with AIDS. Such a language is necessary, activists argue, because the ways in which society has defined AIDS have led to policies that have, at best,

---

[1]Many of the terms surrounding the AIDS controversy are problematic. For consistency, we use the term AIDS to refer both to acquired immune deficiency syndrome and to the controversy that surrounds it. We use the term HIV to refer specifically to the human immunodeficiency virus. Unless otherwise stated in the text, we use the phrase, "people with AIDS" to refer both to people with a clinical diagnosis of AIDS and those who are HIV-seropositive. For a more thorough discussion of the problems associated with the terms AIDS and HIV, see Crystal and Jackson (1991).

ignored and, at worst, exacerbated the consequences of the spread of HIV. Thus, activists have employed alternate forums in their attempt to redefine the AIDS issue in contemporary society.

In this chapter, we focus on the use of visual symbols as a way of initiating public discourse about AIDS. Specifically, we argue that AIDS activists use visual symbols as a way of introducing public discussion of AIDS into places from which it has been previously excluded, as a way of generating an activist-informed mainstream discourse about AIDS. Such a strategy is necessary because current public discussion of AIDS is shaped by the early identification of HIV and AIDS with marginal groups and aberrant behavior, most notably male homosexual sex and injection drug use. Because people with AIDS are defined as marginal, the issue of HIV/AIDS also becomes marginal, and is thus is delineated outside the public sphere of discourse. AIDS, therefore, becomes an issue of concern primarily to specific segments of society: doctors and researchers who investigate treatment for AIDS, people with AIDS and their caregivers, who deal with the ravages of AIDS on individuals, and "risk groups," who must negotiate the terrain of AIDS transmission and prevention among themselves. Little space is left for discussion of the public responsibility for AIDS research, or for the need for compassionate public policies to ease the financial and psychological costs of treating individual people with AIDS.

This chapter is important for three reasons. First, it contributes to an understanding of publicity as a dimension of rhetoric. Several recent studies have drawn attention to the decline of public argument in contemporary society (Fisher, 1989; Goodnight, 1982; Olson, 1991; Olson & Goodnight, 1994). Social and political forces, they argue, increasingly assign controversial issues to either the private sphere, where they are resolved by individuals, or the technical sphere, where decisions are made by technical experts (Goodnight, 1982). An important (but often overlooked) implication of this tendency to attenuate the public dimension of controversial issues is that it also mitigates the need for a public response to crises such as HIV/AIDS. Goodnight offered the environmental movement as an example of a controversy where public concern has been supplanted by technical expertise. The environmental movement, he argued, had its roots in wilderness preservation, a concern of a variety of different public interest groups. In the 1970s, however, as environmental concerns began to conflict with the demands of the economy, people deferred increasingly to ecologists to balance the competing interests, thus replacing public concern with technical expertise.

AIDS activists, however, have challenged very directly attempts to exclude AIDS from the public sphere. Previous studies have documented the effectiveness of AIDS activists in challenging prevailing definitions of the epidemic. Brashers and Jackson (1991) argued that the activist group AIDS Coalition to Unleash Power (ACT UP) influenced the direction of AIDS research by educating activists about research and using their newly acquired expertise to lobby for changes in the research process. Fabj and Sobnosky (1995) identified argumentative strategies by which activists assert their right to speak to issues surrounding AIDS research. Both these studies, however, focus on activist attempts to challenge the definition of AIDS by technical experts. This study, like Christiansen and Hanson's (1996), focuses on activists' attempts to influence the way HIV/AIDS is popularly understood. Additionally, we examine the use of visual symbols as a specific strategy for introducing discourse about AIDS into popular consciousness.

Second, this study expands our understanding of the ways in which marginalized groups seek access to power in contemporary society. Clearly, the people most affected by AIDS—gay men, injection drug users, the urban poor—were marginal in society even before the onset of the AIDS epidemic. Further, the association of a fatal, infectious disease with these groups frequently has been used as "proof" that they deserve their marginal status. At the same time, AIDS activists use the tragic suffering of people with AIDS to generate support for their cause. Gilder (1989) wrote, "One way for the gay community to achieve collective power again lies in their rejection of the labels of 'objects' or 'victims,' and work for a self-interpretive construction of AIDS and its definition" (p. 36). We argue that AIDS activists constitute what Fraser (1993) called a "subaltern counterpublic" (p. 123) who develop an alternate understanding of an issue among themselves before challenging a mainstream definition of an issue. Thus, this study shows how a counterpublic can influence the larger public in its understanding of a controversial issue.

Third, this study expands our understanding of the rhetoric surrounding the HIV/AIDS epidemic. Clearly, AIDS is one of the most important and controversial issues facing contemporary society. Discourse about AIDS intersects with numerous other discourses, including those about reform of our medical system, civil rights protections for lesbians and gays, and the right of the government to regulate private behavior in the public interest. The fundamental issue at the heart of the AIDS crisis—the extent of public responsibility for the plight of individuals or groups—will continue to generate controversy in a variety of arenas, including welfare reform, crime, public education and housing, and health care. A deeper understanding of AIDS activism and the rhetoric of exclusion to which it responds helps to inform our understanding of these other controversies as well.

In this chapter, we first identify some of the rhetorical dimensions of the concept of "public space" as a site of social participation and activism. Second, we examine the rhetoric of exclusion by which people with AIDS are denied access to public space. Third, we examine the strategies by which activists assert their right to occupy public space.

PUBLIC SPACE IN CONTEMPORARY SOCIETY

The idea of public space stands at the center of modern notions of democratic participation in social decision making. Goodnight (1982) suggested that arguments in contemporary society develop in three different spheres: the personal, the technical, and the public. Each sphere has different requirements for arguments and different practices for resolving conflicts. More important to the study of HIV/AIDS, however, is that arguments that develop in different spheres require different responses from the community. If an issue is argued primarily within the private sphere, it will be resolved privately, among the parties involved, with little concern for the community as a whole. Technical issues, on the other hand, are resolved by experts who possess the specialized knowledge and skills required by technical problems. Public interest can enter the technical decision-making process, as when Congress appropriates money to be given to researchers whose work has military application, but decisions are usually made on technical grounds. AIDS activists have also attempted to influence the nature and direction of scientific research, with some success (Brashers & Jackson, 1991). Public arguments, however, stress common involvement in a controversy. Goodnight noted, "The interests of the public realm . . . extend the stakes of argument beyond private needs and the needs of special communities to the interests of the entire community" (pp. 219–220). When issues cannot be resolved on personal or technical grounds, they spill over into public space, demanding the attention of the whole community.

The importance of public space, then, becomes obvious: Issues receive attention and resources from the community to the extent that they are recognized as public. For this reason, a vital public sphere is necessary to democratic decision making. Without access to public space, groups and individuals cannot place their concerns before the community for discussion and resolution. Therefore, research on the public sphere explores the practices by which issues are included in or excluded from public discussion.

Fraser (1993) added an important dimension to the discussion of the public sphere. She argued that there exist multiple publics, rather than a single, monolithic public. Her notion of subaltern counterpublics is particularly useful here. Subaltern counterpublics are, according to Fraser, "parallel discursive arenas where members of subordinated social groups invent and circulate counterdiscourses to formulate oppositional interpretations of their identities, interests, and needs" (p. 123). She explained that a group can foster concern about an issue among its members, and then place it on the public agenda. Feminism, she argued, provides a clear example of a subaltern counterpublic, with its journals, conferences, bookstores, and other forums, in which issues of concern to women can be developed before they are placed before the "public at large."

The idea of multiple publics affords a perspective from which to view the rhetoric of AIDS activists. In official public spheres, which enjoy official sanction from state institutions and the mainstream media, AIDS emerges as a private issue, which deserves minimal attention from the public at large. Because media outlets and public figures are unwilling to talk frankly about gay male sexuality and injection drug use, public discussion of AIDS is restricted mainly to warnings about condom use and statements of support and compassion for some people with AIDS. In an analysis of public service announcements (PSAs) about AIDS, Myrick (1996) noted that the ads themselves contain little information about AIDS, but ask viewers to call a toll-free phone number for more information. He explained, "While the audience [of the PSAs] seems to be given more direct access to information about the subject, this direct information remains twice removed from the viewer; the implication is that knowledge about AIDS must be kept secret, hidden—most important private" (p. 72).

In contrast, activists constitute a subaltern counterpublic, in which AIDS concerns the whole community. Responding to "official" ambivalence about AIDS, activist rhetoric has both fostered a sense of identity community among those most directly affected by AIDS (Christiansen & Hanson, 1996; Dow, 1994; Gilder 1989; Myrick, 1996) and offered direction for an appropriate response to the epidemic (Fabj & Sobnosky, 1993, 1995; Gamson, 1989). Activist rhetoric asserts that "All people with AIDS are innocent" (Crimp & Rolston, 1990, p. 54). The lack of public concern for AIDS has exacerbated the medical epidemic, creating a political and social crisis as well. At the root, however, are public inaction and inattention. As activists put it, "We Die. They do nothing" (Crimp & Rolston, 1990, p. 82). Activists argue that only when the public at large appreciates the impact of AIDS on all of society will we begin seriously to address the AIDS crisis. Thus, one major goal of activist rhetoric is to foster discussion of AIDS in public forums.

OFFICIAL SILENCE AND THE EXCLUSION
OF AIDS FROM PUBLIC LIFE

At first glance, the argument that HIV/AIDS is defined as a private issue seems incredible. After all, the idea that AIDS is a political as well as medical crisis has been a commonplace among commentators and critics from the earliest days of the epidemic. Presidents Ronald Reagan, George Bush, and Bill Clinton have all appointed presidential advisory councils on AIDS, and President Clinton has appointed three "AIDS czars" to head the Office of National AIDS Policy, charged with coordinating the federal response. Further, governmental agencies, most notably the Centers for Disease Control and the National Institutes of Health, spearhead the HIV/AIDS research effort, and a plethora of federal, state, and local programs help to provide services to people with AIDS.

On closer inspection, however, a paradox becomes evident. For although there is a great deal of talk about AIDS in public forums, much of it is aimed at avoiding any real discussion of the disease. Of course, in the early years of the epidemic, politicians and media outlets tried as much as possible to ignore the existence of the AIDS epidemic (see, e.g., Kinsella, 1989; Shilts, 1987). Emblematic of this official "silence" about AIDS was the fact that President Reagan did not mention the term AIDS in public until 1985, and did not give an address on the subject until 1987, by which time over 20,000 people in America had died from the disease (see Shilts, 1987). Even President Clinton, who unarguably has done more about HIV and AIDS then either of his predecessors, restricts his public statements about the disease and its consequences to vague statements of support for research and calls for a compassionate response to people suffering with AIDS.

This official silence about AIDS leads to a fragmented understanding of the disease. Events such as the AIDS epidemic assume their social meaning as they are discussed and debated in public spheres. Procter (1990) explained how public arguments take form: "While a constant flow of arguments may surround us, some coalescing event is necessary to crystallize the arguments for a brief moment" (p. 118). When such events occur, "society must talk about [them] to develop a contextual placement that defines their cultural meaning" (Klumpp & Hollihan, 1979, p. 3). As people look to make sense of events, "prominent rhetors from various ideologies compete in a struggle to identify the public with their view of the meaning of events," until eventually, "one of the many explanations succeeds in encapsulating the rhetorical, sociological, political, and ideological resources of the events and emerges as the drama with which the culture identifies" (Klumpp & Hollihan, 1979, p. 3). Once an event has been defined, we can respond to it.

Such an event has not occurred in the AIDS epidemic. Many point to the 1985 disclosure that actor Rock Hudson had AIDS and his subsequent death from the disease as such a moment (e.g. Shilts, 1987). Certainly, the revelation that a famous movie star had contracted a disease associated primarily with marginal groups of the population brought increased press attention to the AIDS epidemic (Kinsella, 1989). Further, as Dow (1994) argued, "The Hudson revelations forced the public, the media, and the federal government to see AIDS in a new way," and began "a shift in orientation toward AIDS among the general public" (p. 225). Despite some movement in cultural understanding of AIDS, however, Hudson's "outing" as a person with AIDS and his death failed to generate discussion that led to a resolution of the cultural meaning of AIDS. As Gilder (1989) argued, "The social (and even the medical) meaning of AIDS is still a matter of dispute. Many different social actors are warring with each other over the proper constitution and construction of a powerful symbol" (p. 28). As a result, public discussion of AIDS is fragmented.

We begin our analysis by examining media coverage in the wake of Hudson's death for the characterization of AIDS it provides. We look at more recent coverage as a point of comparison. We focus primarily on national news magazine stories that address AIDS because national news magazines have a truly national focus. Further, news magazines provide a more interpretive approach to the news than do other media outlets, and attempt to place events into a context (Elwood, 1994; Kinsella, 1989). The national focus and the contextualizing function of news magazines offer an effective way to follow the emerging dramatization of AIDS.

The notion of AIDS as a problem to be addressed personally and privately is a central element in talking about the disease. Accounts of AIDS stress abandonment and rejection as part of the disease. This idea of rejection is so central to social understanding of AIDS that *Newsweek* chose to insert a box titled, "A Family Gives Refuge to a Son Who Has AIDS," in its 1985 "Special Report" on AIDS (Seligman, 1985a), implying a family who chose to care for one of its members is deserving of special note. The same "Special Report" features another insert, titled "Only Months to Live and No Place to Die," which tells the story of Robert Doyle, a Baltimore construction worker with AIDS (Seligman, 1985b). Doyle's story typifies the theme of abandonment. Doyle was treated for pneumonia at Johns Hopkins Hospital, until doctors decided they could do no more for him and discharged him. According to the story, "His parents are dead and he was estranged from his two brothers. Even his 65 year-old lover, fearing for his own health, rejected Doyle, insisting that he leave their apartment" (p. 24). The story continues to detail how Doyle grew sicker and sicker, until he was taken in by a "Good Samaritan," only to be rejected again when he "bloodied his sheets," and "she decided that Doyle's condition might threaten the lives of her two children" (p. 24). Eventually, he ended up with a couple who promised to care for him until he "chose to leave or died" (p. 24).

Several features of Doyle's story deserve note, as they typify how exclusion of people with AIDS is dramatized. First, the story begins with rejection by family, in this case a gay partner. Second, the story points out that rejection is not always automatic, nor always motivated by fear or hate. In Doyle's case, two families promised to care for him, only to reject him when the reality of living with AIDS set in. The message is clear: The idea of caring for someone with AIDS may be noble, but when it presents a risk to home and family, pragmatic self-interest must intervene. Finally, the story ends before Doyle's death. In this instance, the report ends with Doyle "drifting in and out of consciousness, and too weak to utter more than a few words" (Seligman, 1985b, p. 24). He has instructed his caregivers, we are told, "not to take any 'heroic' measures to prolong his life" (p. 24). Thus, the story ends where it began: a person with AIDS, dying in a strange environment, without support from family and friends.

Lack of a clear cultural understanding of AIDS and the ambiguity of official statements on AIDS also leads people to err on the side of caution when responding to HIV and AIDS. As Gilder (1989) argued, "The tentative nature of public health statements about AIDS has resulted in an increase of public alarm about the disease, and has opened the mind of the public to more 'irrational' appeals" (p. 35). This is most clear in discussions of AIDS and children. A 1985 *Time* story, titled, "The New Untouchables" (Thomas, 1985) quotes Fred Schmidt, a New York State Assemblyman, summarizing the feelings of many parents at a meeting to discuss admitting a child with AIDS into the New York City schools: "There is no medical authority who can say with authority that AIDS cannot be transmitted in school. What about somebody sneezing in the classroom? What about the water fountain? What about kids who get in a fight with a bloody nose? They don't know" (p. 24). Darlynn Spizzeri, a New York City woman who kept her daughter from attending school because there might be a child with AIDS at the school, reasoned thus: "[W]e are afraid our children will catch the disease even if those so-called, quote-unquote experts say it is impossible" (in Adler, 1985, p. 18).

This uncertainty, however small, has led to numerous attempts to keep children with AIDS out of schools. When officials do not act, parents take matters into their own hands. Ryan White, a teenager from Kokomo, Indiana, became something of a national celebrity as a result of his fight to attend school and otherwise live as a teenager. Before his death from AIDS in 1990, he had twice appeared on the cover of *People* magazine, and a memoir of his struggle with AIDS was published in 1991 (White & Cunningham, 1991). Despite his celebrity, White has had his home shot at by someone who wanted to keep him out of school (Findlay, 1991). Nor is White's case unique. The Ray family in Arcadia, Florida, for example, had their home burned down when they attempted to send their children who had AIDS to school. All of these instances represent the triumph of fear over medical knowledge, because we know that AIDS cannot be spread through casual social contact.

Nor are schoolchildren the only victims of ignorance about AIDS. "The New Untouchables" (Thomas, 1985) cites numerous examples of people's response to AIDS. In some instances, the precautions people take seem reasonable. The story reports, for example, that "some dentists have taken to wearing gloves and surgical masks with all patients" (p. 26), a practice that has since become almost universal and routine. In other instances, however, extreme precautions seem less warranted. The town of Williamson, West Virginia, closed the town swimming pool after Michael Sisco, who had AIDS, swam in it. He said, "It's reopened now but nobody uses it, even though they have drained the water and repainted it. Maybe they feel that if there's any small chance they could get AIDS, they don't want to go in" ("Speaking of the Plague," 1991, p. 25). More recently, American Airlines was criticized in 1993 for removing from a flight a person with AIDS because he might represent a health threat to other passengers (Gallagher, 1993).

Further, because AIDS is frequently associated with gay men, people attempt to isolate themselves from AIDS by avoiding contact with gay men. The story reports that "in New York City, some diners avoid restaurants that have gay waiters" (Thomas, 1985, p. 26), a dubious proposition at best. A story in *Newsweek* documents the extremes to which some go in isolating themselves from potential sources of AIDS transmission: "The smell of fear is abroad; it is the smell of the insecticide with which a north-side Atlanta man was dousing his backyard one recent afternoon, defending against mosquitoes who might have just taken a nip out of one of the guests of his gay neighbor's barbecue" (Adler, 1985, p. 18). Nor is the fear of mosquitoes as AIDS carriers restricted to Atlanta. Thomas (1985), in "The New Untouchables," reported that the New Orleans AIDS task force received calls asking if mosquitoes could spread the disease. Dr. Louise McFarland, the director of the agency, pointed out the absurdity of the question: "If that were true, the whole city of New Orleans would have AIDS" (p. 24). More recently, in 1993, American Airlines found itself criticized by AIDS activists after a flight crew requested that the blankets and pillows from an airliner that flew people to Washington, DC, for a gay rights march be removed and that the plane be disinfected. In a highly publicized incident in 1995, Secret Service agents wore rubber gloves during a visit by a group of gay and lesbian elected officials to the White House (Billard, 1995). The Clinton Administration quickly apologized for the incident, but the message it sent about AIDS was clear: The only way to avoid AIDS is to avoid contact with those who might have it.

Perhaps most tragic is the extent to which people with AIDS internalize the ostracism forced on them by the public at large. Contrary to the myth of the person with AIDS as an irresponsible predator seeking to spread the disease to as many other victims as possible, many people with AIDS isolate themselves out of shame and fear of spreading the disease to others. Andrew Hiatt, the subject of a *Newsweek* story about a family caring for a member with AIDS, told a typical story. He said using sterilized dishes and special towels made him feel "like a piece of crawling crud that no one could touch" (Seligman, 1985b, p. 26). Beatrice von Guggenberg, another person with AIDS, said, "My roommate heard me crying, and reached out to me. I said, 'Don't touch me.' I had internalized society's stigma" ("Speaking of the Plague," 1991, p. 24). This, of course, is the ultimate goal of any social exclusion policy: If people isolate themselves, then the rest of us will be not have to worry about isolating them.

Clearly, public understanding of AIDS focuses on the disease as a source of marginality in contemporary society. Gamson (1989) argued, "The construction and reconstruction of boundaries has been, then, an essential aspect of the story of AIDS. The innocent victim is bounded off from the guilty one, pure blood from contaminated, the general population from the AIDS populations, risk groups from those not at risk" (pp. 359–360).

Through the construction of such boundaries between "people with AIDS and risk groups" and "the general population," AIDS becomes a private issue, of concern only to those who have already contracted the virus or whose group membership places them at risk for the disease. The solution to the AIDS epidemic also becomes personal, through sexual monogamy or safer sex. Any need for a public policy is mooted. In this context, public signs of AIDS activism and AIDS awareness assume an important role in initiating public discussion of AIDS.

CREATING A SPACE FOR AIDS

As political statements, the two most common symbols of AIDS activism, the "Silence = Death" logo and the red lapel ribbon, could not be further apart. "Silence = Death," which first appeared on posters in New York City in 1987, contains an explicit call to action, and implies that those who are not actively fighting AIDS are contributing to the epidemic. Further, the words, *Silence = Death,* appear beneath a pink triangle, associating the fight against AIDS with the fight for gay rights. AIDS activists Crimp and Rolston (1990) explained the significance of the logo:

> Our emblem's significance depends on foreknowledge of the use of the pink triangle as the marker of gay men in Nazi concentration camps, its appropriation by the gay movement to remember a suppressed history of our oppression, and now, an inversion of its positioning (men in death camps wore triangles that pointed down; SILENCE = DEATH's points up). SILENCE = DEATH declares that silence about the oppression and annihilation of gay people, *then and now,* must be broken as a matter of our survival. (p. 14)

Not surprisingly, the Silence = Death logo was appropriated by ACT UP, and has come to represent a confrontational approach to AIDS activism.

The red lapel ribbon, in contrast, gently reminds us of the continued existence of the AIDS crisis, and asks us to be sensitive to the suffering of people with AIDS. Red ribbons are often associated with celebrity involvement in the fight against AIDS because the red ribbon as a symbol of AIDS awareness has received wide exposure at entertainment industry awards ceremonies since it made its first appearance at the 1991 Tony Awards, where award presenters and recipients wore red ribbons to call attention to the continuing AIDS crisis. Red ribbons are also often associated with personal involvement in the AIDS crisis because they are frequently distributed at memorial services for people who have died from complications associated with AIDS. Further, because they are not specifically associated with gay men or other so-called risk groups, red ribbons remind us that we cannot hide from the AIDS crisis, however hard we might try.

Both the Silence = Death logo and the red ribbon, however, serve the same broad purpose: drawing public attention to the continuing AIDS crisis. When they appear on clothing, buttons, posters, bumper stickers, and other personal and public property, red ribbons, pink triangles, and other visual symbols associated with AIDS activism serve as constant, portable reminders of the need for personal and social response to the presence of AIDS in society. AIDS activists have mixed feelings about the proliferation of AIDS-related merchandise and other AIDS memorabilia. On one hand, red ribbons and other emblems bring public attention to the continued existence of the AIDS crisis. As Michaels and Simons of the West Coast Ribbon Project wrote in a *Los Angeles Times* guest editorial in 1993, there is a definite value to celebrities who wear red ribbons: "If a certain celebrity does nothing else but spread [AIDS awareness], then he or she will have done something good and important with the power that comes with being famous" (in Weir, 1993, p. 36). Perhaps even more important, AIDS merchandise represents an important source of funding for AIDS service and research organizations. The American Foundation for AIDS Research (AmFAR), for example, reported generating $100,000 from the sale of red ribbon T-shirts, $50,000 from the sale of sterling silver ribbon pins, $30,000 from an "Art Against AIDS" calendar, and $500,000 from product tie-ins with Clairol Professional Color (Foster, 1995, p. 37). In a time of increased competition for research dollars, activists and researchers cannot ignore such a large potential source of income.

At the same time, others fear that red ribbons and other emblems of AIDS awareness have become empty displays, which allow people to feel good about themselves while ignoring the continued existence of the AIDS crisis. Susan Linn, of A Different Light bookstore in West Hollywood, which also sells AIDS-related merchandise, expressed this concern: "There are many who would rather hold a red ribbon coffee mug than hold a guy with Kaposi's sarcoma. These products are 'feel good' things and bring people together, but they don't always solve much" (in Foster, 1995, p. 38). AIDS activist icon Larry Kramer put it even more bluntly: "If every famous person who wore a red ribbon made a phone call to Bush or Clinton instead, this plague would be over" (in Weir, 1993, pp. 35–36).

Clearly, visual displays such as red ribbons have a great deal of potential as a way of publicizing the AIDS crisis. At the same time, visual displays also offer an easy way out of the AIDS crisis, as people adopt red ribbons as fashion accessories, largely devoid of any connection to the AIDS crisis. In this section, we argue that visual displays allow AIDS activists and others concerned with the AIDS epidemic to respond to the exclusion of AIDS from the public sphere. Specifically, we argue that visual displays of AIDS awareness and activism enable activists to open a space for public discussion of AIDS. At the same time, the ambiguity of these symbols can obscure their meaning, allowing them to deflect attention from the reality of AIDS.

Visual emblems help to create a space for public discussion of AIDS by going places from which AIDS is normally excluded. The red ribbon developed its association with celebrity concern about AIDS, for example, at the Tony Awards in 1991. Ironically, the ribbon, which is usually associated with a nonconfrontational approach to AIDS awareness, had been developed by the AIDS activist art collective, Visual AIDS, in response to the proliferation of yellow ribbons showing support for the American military effort in the Persian Gulf (Weir, 1993). Part of the power of the ribbon as a symbol was that it contrasted the amount of money spent on the Gulf War effort with the money spent on HIV/AIDS research. Presenters and award recipients wore ribbons to draw attention to the fact that AIDS has hit the entertainment industry especially hard. The ubiquity of the red ribbon at entertainment industry awards programs mirrors symbolically the ubiquity of HIV and AIDS in the entertainment industry.

Obviously, celebrities with political agendas do not need a red ribbon, or any other visual symbol, to speak to political issues from the stage. Awards programs have long been a platform for people to express their concern for political issues. The ribbon, however, allows people to express that opinion silently if they choose—clearly, not all those who wear ribbons make speeches. Nor does wearing a ribbon preclude more direct statements about AIDS, and in fact may help audiences accept political statements at ceremonial occasions. At the 1993 Academy Awards, for example, Susan Sarandon and Tim Robbins emphasized the need for public response to AIDS, and criticized the Congress and President Clinton for their unwillingness to allow immigrants with HIV into the United States. Public statements on AIDS, however, seem more appropriate in a forum where AIDS awareness is already an accepted part of the proceedings. Sarandon and Robbins received less criticism for "politicizing" an awards program than have others who have promoted other issues from the platform.

The use of visual displays to initiate public discussion of AIDS is not limited to awards programs. John Weir (1993), a columnist for *The Advocate,* explained the use of the red ribbon among theater audiences in New York:

> During the past two years, the ribbon has emerged as an integral part of most New York theatergoing experiences. At the end of one of the final performances of [Larry] Kramer's . . . *The Destiny of Me,* lead actor Jonathan Hadary . . . interrupted the curtain call to urge the audience to make a contribution on the way out to the AIDS charity and ribbon merchandiser Broadway Cares/Equity Fights AIDS. "And take a red ribbon to wear," he said. The moment was remarkable not just for its intimacy but because of the audience's acceptance of a brief AIDS interlude as just as common to New York theater as the bad orange soda that used to be sold in lobbies during intermission. (p. 37)

Once again, the visual display of a red ribbon has helped to transform a public event into a forum for discussion of AIDS.

Perhaps even more important, red ribbons have come to represent AIDS awareness among those with little or no direct experience with AIDS. Martin Spector, executive director of Under One Roof, a San Francisco shop specializing in merchandise from Northern California AIDS organizations, explained that people from small towns see his shop as providing a necessary service: "They thank us for giving them an outlet to fight AIDS. . . . Buying a product gives them a type of emotional support they're not getting from society at large" (in Foster, 1995, p. 36). Daniel Wolfe, a spokesperson for the Gay Men's Health Crisis, a New York City AIDS service agency, echoed the importance of red ribbons for people outside of large cities with visible gay communities: "A red ribbon coffee mug doesn't necessarily translate the same to a woman in Oklahoma City as to a man in Chelsea [a New York City neighborhood with a large gay male population]" (in Foster, 1995, p. 36).

The usefulness of visual emblems in promoting discussion of AIDS is not limited to the red ribbon, however. The Silence = Death logo accomplishes the same goal. The emblem originally was designed to promote AIDS awareness, and precedes by several months the formation of the direct action group, ACT UP, with which it has come to be associated. Clearly, the logo, with its reference to Nazi persecution of gay men, is more confrontational than the ribbon, which is more commonly thought of as a fashion accessory. It serves the same function, however. As Crimp and Rolston (1990) explained,

> It is not merely what SILENCE = DEATH says, but how it looks, that gives it its particular force. The power of this equation under a triangle is the compression of its connotation into a logo so striking you ultimately *have* to ask, if you don't already know, "What does it mean?" And it is the answers we are constantly called upon to give to others—small, everyday direct actions—that make SILENCE = DEATH signify beyond a community of lesbian and gay cognoscenti. (p. 14)

Very clearly, the purpose of the logo is not only to call attention to AIDS, but to initiate discussion of the AIDS crisis.

In an issue of *The Advocate,* Matt Fuller (1994), who volunteers for the People With AIDS Coalition in New York City, described his personal use of the pink triangle: "Just before the beginning of summer, I had the words HIV POSITIVE along with a pink triangle tattooed prominently on my right arm. I felt the time had come to be visible. Most people would rather not think about AIDS. I would rather not either, but I no longer have that luxury. Like my tattoo, AIDS is not going away, not for a long time. So this is my reminder to everyone that we are still here, that the fight against AIDS is not over" (p. 6). Shortly after receiving the tattoo, Fuller vacationed in the Cayman Islands, which have a reputation of being conservative. Contrary to his expectations, Fuller's tattoo generated surprisingly little controversy: "Of course there were murmurs and double takes, but of the few direct questions and comments we heard, most were positive—mainly wishes of good luck" (p. 6). He continued, "I am not naive enough to think that noticing my tattoo while standing next to me by the pool or in a gift shop radically changed anyone's perception about what it's like to live with HIV, and I suspect there were many negative comments we did not hear, but even a negative reaction can be a good thing if it means that someone has been forced to confront the reality of AIDS" (p. 6). As with the red ribbon, Fuller and others who tattoo themselves with symbols of AIDS activism introduce AIDS into areas from which it might otherwise be excluded.

The convenience of visual displays is not without potential costs, however. Although visual symbols may be easier to display, they are also often more ambiguous than other forms of public argument. As Crimp and Rolston (1990) noted, for example, one cannot fully understand the Silence = Death logo without knowledge of the use of pink triangles in Nazi concentration camps. Similarly, the red ribbon can only stimulate public discussion about AIDS to the extent that those who see it recognize it as a sign of AIDS awareness. Writer Paul Rudnick explained the potential costs of ambiguity:

> I was at the first preview of the show [failed Broadway musical *Nick and Nora*] and there was an usher handing out ribbons at the door. Well, some woman in front of me who hadn't ever seen a red ribbon before was surprised when the usher explained to her what it was for. "I thought it was just a memento of the performance," she said. And so now, every time I see somebody wearing one on the street, I want to rush up to them and say, "*Nick and Nora*, first preview, you were there!" (in Weir, 1993, p. 36)

Though characteristically exaggerated, Rudnick's comment highlights the possibility of mis-interpretation inherent in a symbol like a ribbon. The proliferation of ribbons as symbols of awareness complicates this possibility even further, as groups drawing attention to a variety of issues adopt the ribbon as a symbol of awareness (see Weir, 1993).

Even more serious is the argument that adopting a visual display replaces, rather than stimulates, public discussion of the disease. Many have charged that the wearing of red ribbons in particular has become an empty gesture, which signifies a desire to be seen as socially conscious, rather than a concern for the suffering of people with AIDS. Actor Rob Lowe put it bluntly: "I guess it's getting to the point where it's bad if you're not wearing one of these things" (in Weir, 1993, p. 36). The power of the symbol is diminished if it is seen as an obligation, rather than a choice.

Weir (1993) explained, "The ribbons have become a cultural icon, prone to cynical abuse by presidents' wives, merchandising strategies, and political manipulation" (p. 38). Weir referred to Barbara Bush, who wore a ribbon on her lapel during the final night of the 1992 Republican National Convention, but removed it before she joined her husband at the podium for the closing ceremonies. Many interpret her actions as an attempt to curry favor with gay and lesbian voters, without alienating the socially conservative wing of the Republican party. Further, the association of red ribbons with celebrities appeals to some. Screenwriter Michael Zam argued that people wear ribbons as a sign of solidarity with celebrities, rather than with people with AIDS. Wearing a red ribbon, he says, allows people to believe "that they're not going to work, they're going to the Grammy's" (in Weir, 1993, p. 36).

CONCLUSION

The greatest challenge facing people with AIDS and AIDS activists continues to be the need for more effective treatments for people with HIV and AIDS. Recent results with new drug treatments show great promise, but new AIDS treatments remain beyond the reach of many people with AIDS and many people with HIV and AIDS do not respond to new therapies. Equally challenging, however, has been the need to focus public attention on AIDS and on the need for research and treatment about AIDS. As the first section of this chapter shows, public discourse about AIDS focuses not on the need for public response to the crisis, but rather on ways to deflect public responsibility for slowing the spread of AIDS and for fighting the disease. The use of red ribbons, pink triangles, and other visual displays has met with some success as a way of creating a space in public discourse for a genuine discussion of AIDS and its impact on society. Clearly, activists cannot ignore the potential of such displays as a way of stimulating public discussion of AIDS. The question becomes, How can activists most effectively exploit the argumentative potential of such displays, without falling into the trap of trivializing such an important issue?

We offer two suggestions. First, activists should try to heighten the association between AIDS activism and AIDS emblems. Although celebrities wearing ribbons at awards ceremonies is an important effort, it becomes more powerful when some of those celebrities address more explicitly their concerns about AIDS awareness. For this reason, many activists prefer the symbolism of Silence = Death to that of the ribbon. As Crimp and Rolston (1990) explained, Silence = Death demands further explanation from those unfamiliar with its meaning. Even the original Silence = Death posters included an accompanying message: "Why is Reagan silent about AIDS? What is really going on at the Centers for Disease Control, the Federal Drug Administration [sic], and the Vatican? Gays and lesbians are not expendable . . . Use your power . . . Boycott . . . Defend yourselves . . . Turn anger, fear, grief, into action" (in Crimp & Rolston, p. 30). Even though subsequent uses of the logo have omitted the accompanying text, the close association of the logo with the group ACT UP has helped to preserve the political message of the symbol.

Red ribbons, on the other hand, have no ready source of clarification. Ironically, the merchandising efforts criticized by activists may help to more clearly identify the message of awareness and concern behind the red ribbon. As groups more aggressively promote red ribbon merchandise, they also further the identification of red ribbons with the AIDS crisis. Activist rhetoric that incorporates red ribbons may also further this identification.

Second, activists must monitor carefully the contexts in which red ribbons appear. Because symbols are effective as ways of opening space for discourse about AIDS, they are most effective when used in contexts where such discourse is possible. When people wear red ribbons or use products that feature red ribbons, they can explain the ribbon's symbolism and use the opportunity for "small acts of activism" like those referred to by Crimp and Rolston (1990). When used to promote merchandise among gay men, on the other hand, ribbons are potentially more exploitative. Even though profits from tie-ins are frequently donated to research, uses of the ribbon and other displays that may potentially "decontextualize" AIDS symbols should be very carefully considered.

This chapter has examined two competing views of AIDS in contemporary society: a popular view, which leads to the exclusion of AIDS from the public sphere, and an activist rhetoric, which attempts to place AIDS on the public agenda. Thus far, activist rhetoric has made only small inroads into the social construction of AIDS. One success, however, is the decreasing use of the terms *AIDS patient* and *AIDS victim,* which have been replaced in many media with the activist term *person with AIDS.* Similarly, media coverage of the epidemic makes less frequent reference to "innocent victims" of AIDS, who acquired the disease through blood transfusions, implying that people who contract AIDS through sexual encounters, mostly gay men, and injection drug users are somehow guilty. Activist rhetoric has, however, gained currency within a smaller public, comprised largely of gay men, lesbians, and people with AIDS and their caregivers, for whom AIDS is a very immediate issue. In much the same way that domestic violence was originally viewed as an issue deserving social concern primarily among feminists (Fraser, 1993), AIDS is currently being reinterpreted and redefined within a smaller public. Such a step, according to Fraser, makes it easier to influence the broader community.

The move from a small group to the larger community can be long and difficult. Feminists, who Fraser (1993) cited as "the most striking example" (p. 123) of a subaltern counterpublic that has succeeded in influencing the larger community, have engaged in a sustained effort that began three decades ago and is only now producing results. AIDS advocates face even greater challenges to engage the community in the fight against AIDS. They face the powerful stigmas of homosexuality and drug use associated with AIDS. In addition, activist ranks are continually thinned by the death of people with AIDS, which saps morale. Activist Peter Staley explained, "There used to be so much optimism. Now it's like, 'Yeah, we created the Office of AIDS Research.' And then you go off to your next funeral that week" (in Horowitz, 1995, p. 37). In such a context, the risk of trivializing AIDS through empty displays of activism seems outweighed by the need to keep the issues surrounding AIDS in public discourse.

ACKNOWLEDGMENTS

Earlier versions of portions of this chapter were presented to the Speech Communication Association Convention in New Orleans, Louisiana, November 1994, and the Speech Communication Association Convention in San Antonio, Texas, November 1995.

REFERENCES

Adler, J. (1985, September 23). The AIDS conflict. *Newsweek,* pp. 18–24.

The Advocate. (1995, November 28). [Contents], p. 3.

AIDS: What is to be done? [Forum]. (1985, October). *Harper's Magazine, 271,* 39–52.

Billard, B. (1995, July 25). Shooting straight. *The Advocate,* pp. 26–27.

Brashers, D. E., & Jackson, S. (1991). "Politically-savvy sick people": Public penetration of the technical sphere. In D. W. Parson (Ed.), *Argument in controversy* (pp. 284–288). Annandale, VA: Speech Communication Association.

Christiansen, A. E., & Hanson, J. J. (1996). Comedy as cure for tragedy: ACT UP and the rhetoric of AIDS. *Quarterly Journal of Speech, 82,* 157–170.

Crimp, D., & Rolston, A. (1990). *AIDS demo graphics* [sic]. Seattle: Bay Press.

Crystal, S., & Jackson, M. (1991). Health care and the social construction of AIDS: The impact of disease definitions. In J. Huber & B. E. Schneider (Eds.), *The social context of AIDS* (pp. 163–180). Newbury Park, CA: Sage.

Dow, B. J. (1994). AIDS, perspective by incongruity, and gay identity in Larry Kramer's "1,112 and Counting." *Communication Studies, 45,* 225–240.

Elwood, W. N. (1994). *Rhetoric in the war on drugs: The triumphs and tragedies of public relations.* Westport, CT: Praeger.

Fabj, V., & Sobnosky, M. J. (1993). Responses from the street: ACT UP and community organizing against AIDS. In S. C. Ratzan (Ed.), *AIDS: Effective health communication for the 90s* (pp. 91–109). Washington, DC: Taylor & Francis.

Fabj, V., & Sobnosky, M. J. (1995). AIDS activism and the rejuvenation of the public sphere. *Argumentation and Advocacy, 31,* 163–184.

Findlay, S. (1991, June 17). AIDS: The second decade. *U.S. News & World Report,* pp. 20–22.

Fisher, W. R. (1989). *Human communication as narration: Toward a philosophy of reason, value, and action.* Columbia: University of South Carolina Press.

Foster, R. D. (1995, November 28). Shopping for life: For some, AIDS is no longer a disease—It's a T-shirt. *The Advocate,* pp. 35–39.

Fraser, N. (1993). Rethinking the public sphere: A contribution to the critique of actually existing democracy. In C. Calhoun (Ed.), *Habermas and the public sphere* (pp. 109–142). Cambridge, MA: MIT Press.

Fuller, M. (1994, November 29). Marked man. *The Advocate,* p. 6.

Gallagher, J. (1993, December 28). Flight risk. *The Advocate,* pp. 31–32.

Gamson, J. (1989). Silence, death, and the invisible enemy: AIDS activism and social movement "newness." *Social Problems, 36,* 351–367.

Gilder, E. (1989). The process of political *praxis:* Efforts of the gay community to transform the social signification of AIDS. *Communication Quarterly, 37,* 27–38.

Goodnight, G. T. (1982). The personal, technical, and public spheres of argument: A speculative inquiry into the art of public deliberation. *Journal of the American Forensic Association, 18,* 214–227.

Horowitz, C. (1995, February 20). Has AIDS won? *New York,* pp. 30–37.

Kinsella, J. (1989). *Covering the plague: AIDS and the American media.* New Brunswick, NJ: Rutgers University Press.

Klumpp, J. F., & Hollihan, T. A. (1979). Debunking the resignation of Earl Butz: Sacrificing an official racist. *Quarterly Journal of Speech, 65,* 1–11.

Myrick, R. (1996). *AIDS, communication, and empowerment: Gay male identity and the politics of public health messages.* Binghamton, NY: Haworth.

Olson, K. M. (1991). Constraining open deliberation in times of war: Presidential war justifications for Grenada and the Persian Gulf. *Argumentation and Advocacy, 28,* 64–79.

Olson, K. M., & Goodnight, G. T. (1994). Entanglements of consumption, cruelty, privacy, and fashion: The social controversy over fur. *Quarterly Journal of Speech, 80,* 249–276.

Procter, D. E. (1990). The dynamic spectacle: Transforming experience into social forms of community. *Quarterly Journal of Speech, 76,* 117–133.

Seligman, J. (1985a, August 12). A family gives refuge to a son who has AIDS. *Newsweek,* p. 24.

Seligman, J. (1985b, August 12). Only months to live and no place to die. *Newsweek,* p. 26.

Shilts, R. (1987). *And the band played on: Politics, people, and the AIDS epidemic.* New York: St. Martin's Press.

Speaking of the plague. (1991, June 12). *Time,* pp. 23–26.

Thomas, E. (1985, September 23). The new untouchables. *Time,* pp. 24–26.

Weir, J. (1993, May 4). The red plague: Do red ribbons really help in the fight against AIDS? *The Advocate,* pp. 34–38.

White, R., & Cunningham, A. M. (1991). *Ryan White: My own story.* New York: Dial.

4

The Medicalization of Discourse Within an AIDS Research Setting

Clyde B. McCoy
Christine Miles
Lisa R. Metsch
University of Miami School of Medicine

The University of Miami's Community AIDS Research and Evaluation Studies (Miami CARES) in conjunction with the Comprehensive Drug Research Center/Health Services Research Center maintains a central assessment center that is conveniently located near many hospitals and clinics. Many research studies are carried out simultaneously in the assessment center, but the communication process begins before clients ever enter the door. Staff outreach workers make contact with potential clients in parks, housing projects, and other public locations. It takes time to build a relationship of trust to the point that an individual will be willing to come to the assessment center and take part in a detailed and time-consuming interview. However, because the University of Miami has been conducting research in the community for many years, it has a favorable "street reputation." Clients generally are referred through friendship networks and many people who have been eligible for one study are eager to take part in other studies whenever possible. Staff outreach workers become known and trusted in the community and are sometimes approached by people who have heard about studies and would like to take part in them.

When a potential client comes to the assessment center (transportation by van is frequently provided), they see a large imposing building with "University of Miami Assessment Center" clearly visible on it. The building blends into the setting of hospitals and clinics in the neighborhood. For security reasons, it is necessary to be buzzed in, and there is a security guard on the premises. Once inside, clients find a waiting room with a receptionist behind a glass partition. Further inside there are examining rooms and a phlebotomist (known by clients as "the blood lady"). Faculty and staff wear ID badges with names followed by impressive strings of initials such as MD and PhD. Some wear white coats and carry clipboards. Everyone is very polite and professional. When a client has been determined to be eligible to take part in a particular research study, it is necessary for the client to sign various permission forms. Once again, the process is similar to paperwork procedures that clients may be familiar with in a doctor's office, for example, the assignment of insurance benefits. Within this setting it is not surprising that a medical model of communication should develop.

The assessment center is frequently referred to as a "clinic" by clients and it is also known on the street as the "AIDS building" and "the place where they take the blood." Because of

39

the building's association with blood tests for HIV, clients will sometimes assume that other medical services can be provided there. Clients will often ask interviewers if they are doctors or medical students. They expect the staff to be highly knowledgeable about medical issues and they expect to be treated for medical problems on site. Some expect to find a drug treatment center on site. Because of these expectations, staff must be aware of service providers so that clients can be referred to the appropriate agency.

The fact that the physical setting alone communicates that the assessment center is a medical facility is demonstrated by the fact that recently an elderly Hispanic man had to be escorted off the premises by a Spanish-speaking security guard because he refused to accept the explanation that the medical tests he needed could not be performed at this location.

It is evident that the clients perceive the assessment center as some type of medical facility, an impression that is fostered by study procedures and terminology. Appointments for follow-up visits are scheduled as they would be in a doctor's office. Blood tests and urinalyses are performed and test results are communicated. Study participants are referred to as "clients." The questionnaires that are administered generally include limited medical histories (particularly concerning reproductive health, histories of sexually transmitted diseases, pregnancies, abortions, and number of children). Sometimes clients are asked about their use of various types of health care facilities and whether or not they have ongoing health problems. They may be asked to rate their general health on a Likert scale. Some studies conducted at the assessment center include medical procedures such as acupuncture or may include screening for blood cholesterol levels, syphilis, and tuberculosis. Toxicological screens are run to validate clients' self-reports of drug use.

Once admitted into a study, typically the first step is the administration of a detailed questionnaire. Study questionnaires are carefully designed in an attempt to obtain information that is precise, accurate, and consistent, and interviewers are carefully trained in questionnaire administration. However, despite the care that is taken to minimize communication problems, there are many hurdles to be overcome. Much of the research conducted involves determination of HIV risk behaviors, so clients must be asked about various drug habits and sex behaviors as well as being educated regarding HIV transmission.

Because in the English-speaking world, the strongest taboos are associated with sex, death, and bodily functions, it is obviously impossible to discuss HIV transmission methods and risk behaviors without discussing taboo topics. In language, taboo is manifested by topics that cannot be discussed "in polite company" or by words and expressions that cannot be used at all. Historically, the strongest taboos have been associated with words referring to sex and, in the past, legal sanctions such as fines or even imprisonment have been imposed on those who use such words in print or in public forums. Of course, use of taboo words is common in some segments of society, but use of taboo words in inappropriate settings can provoke strong reactions such as shock, disgust, or moral indignation. To quote an old bumper sticker, "sex is a four-letter word." It is important to note that the taboo is not necessarily against the underlying concept (e.g., sexual intercourse) but may be against specific words (e.g., what is euphemistically referred to as "the *F* word"). It should be pointed out that there is nothing intrinsically good or bad about any particular string of sounds. The acceptability of any particular word is a reflection of community standards. Such community standards are subject to change and may vary within subcultures.

Evasion is one common response to taboo and clients' use of vague terms such as "be with," "do," or "had" to describe sexual activity are examples of evasive language behavior. Clients will often admit that these topics are difficult to discuss and will sometimes try to evade uncomfortable topics by using conversational tactics such as redirection, for example, not answering directly, but saying something like, "Moving right along. . . ."

One way to handle the discomfort inherent in discussing taboo topics is to be as clinical as possible. Within the research setting, the use of medical terminology is distancing and lessens the emotional impact of the topic under discussion. However, the gain in comfort level may be compensated for by a loss of comprehension if clients are not familiar with the terms being presented. For these reasons, it is important to train the interviewers to overcome their own discomfort and to use other terms when appropriate. This may include using "street language" to help explain a concept. Some questionnaires have been designed to include prompts for the interviewer to use if the standard terminology is not understood. Sometimes clients will suggest alternate expressions if they are unsure of a term. For example, one client asked if anal sex meant "poking in the butt." Although interviewers need to be relatively "shock-proof" regarding clients' choice of vocabulary, it is not always appropriate for interviewers to use street language themselves even when it is mutually understandable because it can be perceived as disrespectful or demeaning to the client. Thus, it is necessary for the interviewer to walk a very fine line, deciding which terms are necessary for mutual understanding without offending the client.

A recent focus group for assessment center staff highlighted communication issues and several areas of potential difficulty were discussed. It was stressed that many clients are not aware of clinical/medical terms for body parts and sexual activities. The situational appropriateness of vocabulary choice was brought out by the fact that staff members who routinely and comfortably suggest alternate terms to clients were uncomfortable explaining which terms they used within the context of the focus group. For example, one staff member said that the clinical-sounding term *penis* can be replaced by ". . . [uncomfortable silence] . . . You know, it starts with a *d*. I can't say this, you know, his dick."

Many clients are unfamiliar with the terms *oral*, *anal*, and *vaginal sex*. Clients generally refer to vaginal sex as "regular sex." One client assumed that vaginal sex meant having sex with a virgin. Fortunately, he asked for clarification. Staff members assume that not everyone will ask for clarification. Some clients will be too embarrassed to admit that they do not know the meaning of a specific term and will answer "yes" or "no" depending on whether they think the underlying concept is good or bad (which they will determine by the interviewer's nonverbal communication such as tone of voice). The interviewers are sensitive to this possibility and compensate for it by asking for the same information in different ways.

Many women are unfamiliar with the term *pelvic exam* (even if they have had several children); however, most are familiar with the term *Pap smear*. Many clients are unfamiliar with the names of specific sexually transmitted diseases (STDs), although they are generally familiar with the symptoms of venereal disease and use other terms, such as *clap*. One of the least familiar STDs is chlamydia.

A very important clinical term that is subject to misinterpretation is a *positive HIV test result*. Many people assume that positive is good, so if they are told that their test results were positive, they may believe that they do not have HIV. The staff responsible for posttest counseling must very carefully explain that *positive* means that traces of HIV antibodies have been found and further explanation may be required.

Other terms that are important to the research process include terms such as *risk*, *risk behavior*, and *risk group*. It is important to remember that ordinary people do not reason the way the experts do and do not assign risk the same way. It is then reasonable to question whether researchers and respondents share a common conceptual system. For the HIV researcher, reduction in risk behavior is basically understood to mean using sterile needles, disinfecting drug works with bleach, using condoms, reducing the number of sex partners, and so on. If a client is not performing these particular actions, it is assumed that he or she is not making efforts to reduce risk. This assumption would overlook the fact that many clients are engaging in a variety of behaviors they feel will lower their risk of contracting HIV. These behaviors can be learned in the course of conversation and over time as trust builds up. Client-initiated risk reduction methods that have been reported at the assessment center include urinating after sex, using bleach to clean sex organs, bathing in bleach, using the medicine of someone who has HIV (in hope that it will prevent infection), and the use of aloe, herbal teas, and antibiotics.

Many clients believe that it is possible to determine whether someone has HIV by looking at them carefully. Some people say, "Well, I haven't got it yet," and they may then assume that they are immune to HIV or at least are very unlikely to get it (because everyone in this society has some medical concept of immunity). Other clients have a fatalistic worldview and do not see any point in risk reduction methods as explained to them. They feel that they will contract HIV if it is their fate to do so and there is no point in trying to change things. In Miami, there are some groups of people who do not accept a germ theory of disease. These individuals may feel that HIV is transmitted through curses, negative mind-sets, or some other process. It is important to be aware of the existence of these belief systems so that they can be addressed by appropriate education.

It is also important to realize that clients typically do not see themselves as members of risk groups; although, if asked, they may accurately assign someone else who performs the same behaviors into a recognized risk group. Clients have a psychological need to see themselves as individuals and may respond, "I'm just me."

From a research perspective, there is an understanding that a risk is an action taken to achieve a positive effect when the outcome is uncertain and there is significant probability of a negative outcome. According to George Lakoff (1991), a professor in the Department of Cognitive Science, University of California, Berkeley:

> It becomes natural to see a risky action metaphorically as a financial risk of a certain type, namely, a gamble. At this point mathematics enters the picture, since there is a mathematics of gambling, namely, probability theory, decision theory and game theory. . . . As a result, it is not uncommon for behavioral scientists to think that the mathematics of gambling theory literally applies to all forms of risky action, and that it can provide a general basis for the scientific study of risky action, so that risk can be minimized.

Within the populations typically studied by behavioral scientists, the positive effects of risky action would include sexual pleasure, drug-induced euphoria, money, and not being sick, among others. The negative effects would include STDs, HIV, financial costs to the state, and so forth. The "equation" is lopsided because the positive outcomes are limited to the individual, but the negative outcomes have a negative impact on society as a whole (e.g., financial costs of medical treatment, loss of productive man-hours, jail time).

For research purposes, it may be helpful to classify a client's sexual practices by number and type of sex contacts. In some cases, terminology has been so badly misconstrued that the questions have been eliminated. One example had to do with a question that asked on how many occasions the client had engaged in sexual activity. So many clients assumed that they were being asked about sexual encounters on special occasions such as birthdays or weddings that the question was eliminated, but the problem would not have been noticed if the interviewers had not been perceptive. Similar problems occurred with an attempt to classify homosexual behavior as either *active* or *receptive*. The terms active and receptive are helpful to researchers but are not commonly used or understood on the street. The terms *homosexual*, *heterosexual*, and *bisexual* are not used because of confusion over the terms and the fact that cultural definitions differ. Typically, among men in Hispanic cultures, only receptive partners are considered to be homosexual. The use of categorizations of oneself as heterosexual or homosexual may also hide the fact that people may engage in nontypical behaviors within specific contexts (such as jail), although their essential self-concept of sexual orientation remains unchanged. For these reasons, it has been found to be more helpful to ask questions regarding very specific sex acts such as, "Did you put your penis in his mouth?"

In some cases sexual behavior is not consensual and discussing the behavior may bring up deep feelings, including anger and shame. Rape, incest, and domestic violence in general are very sensitive topics and interviewers must be very empathetic to the strong emotions that clients sometimes experience during the course of an interview. As one staff member said, "We go through a lot of tissues here." It should be pointed out that sometimes a question that does not in any way specifically relate to traumatic issues may spark a memory in a client's mind and she or he will react strongly and, apparently, inappropriately. Also, discussing sexual behavior may in itself be perceived as erotic, as one staff member reported having to stop an interview because the client became sexually aroused when questioned about his sexual activities. It is therefore necessary for the staff to be responsive to the problems that the client is dealing with. This may mean taking a break in the interview, breathing deeply, getting something to drink, or otherwise allowing clients to compose themselves before continuing.

In an attempt to classify human relationships as though they were botanical specimens that could be categorized by genus and species, there have been frequent attempts to classify sex partners by using terms such as *casual partner*, *main partner*, *new partner*, and *regular partner*. These terms are useful but also can be somewhat difficult to classify. Does a casual partner mean that black tie is optional, or are blue jeans de rigeur? Occasional misunderstanding has also been reported with the term regular partner because it can be confused with a prostitute's "regulars." This confusion results in further confusion between commercial and noncommercial sexual behavior. The term *commercial sex* is not used by clients but is used by researchers to classify riskier behavior. Clients generally use the terms *johns*, *dates*, or *tricks* to indicate a commercial transaction. Briefly stated, the complexities of many clients' lives are difficult to classify. For example, if a client has ongoing personal relationships with people with whom she does drugs and who sometimes give her money and/or drugs and with whom she has sex occasionally, what type of relationship is that? There are elements of commercial transactions because drugs and/or money may be exchanged, but there is also friendship. Occasionally interviewers resort to novel ways to try to get at the underlying commercial or noncommercial aspect of a given sex act. Examples of interviewer-generated terminology include asking clients about "unjob sex" or "other-than-money sex." It is very difficult to expect a client to break down complex relationships to fit a particular taxonomy that may be convenient for the researcher. One study has attempted to clarify the term casual partner by defining it as "someone that the client does not love, does care about, and has had sex with more than once"; however, staff members report that there is still confusion regarding this definition. Anyone who has agonized over whether or not they really loved someone can sympathize with this dilemma.

During the focus group, it was pointed out that condom use is generally equated with "safer sex." Clients assume that safer sex means using a condom every time, and it is generally up to the interviewers to expand the concept by discussing other options such as abstinence, monogamous relationships, or, at least, reduction in the number of sex partners. The term *sex partner* is problematic itself because it may imply an equality similar to that in a business partnership. When interviewers tell people that they must insist their sex partners begin to use condoms, the underlying assumption behind the word *partner* belies the reality that, for many women in particular, sex is not an equal partnership. Introducing condom use into an established relationship can inject an element of distrust or upset a power structure and the response may be domestic violence.

It is difficult enough to insist on condom use in commercial sex transactions. Sometimes johns offer to pay more for unprotected sex. Other times, a sex worker may not have condoms but will conduct transactions anyway due to the pressure to obtain money and/or drugs. Clients often refer to this type of behavior as "survival," just doing what they have to do to get through the day. Also judgment is impaired when one or more of the individuals involved is under the influence of drugs. However, in general, clients feel personally empowered to insist on condom use during commercial transactions when condoms are available. Slogans such as "no glove, no love" provide a helpful way to make the point.

It is much more difficult to insist on condom use in a committed loving relationship where trust is a major factor in intimacy. A request to use barrier protection forces the individuals involved to consider that at least one of the sex partners may be involved in risky sex or drug behaviors. Denial of that risk may be psychologically necessary in order for the relationship to continue. A related issue is the problem that language that is appropriate for studying HIV risk and educating people regarding HIV risk behaviors does not translate well into intimate encounters. For example, "Darling, you remind me of moonlight, roses, and condoms; by the way, you need to complete this questionnaire regarding your personal history of HIV risk behaviors," is not likely to set the stage for a romantic encounter. It is evident that even catchy slogans cannot erase the difficulties inherent in communicating the need for barrier protection within an intimate relationship.

Because injection drug users are at high risk for contracting HIV, additional terms that are important to researchers include needle risk terms such as *share* and *clean*. However, these terms may be subject to different interpretations. To different clients, a clean needle may be one that has never been used, one that has been soaked in bleach, or one with no visible residue. Field workers have noted that a clean needle may be used with "dirty" water, cookers, or cottons. It is equally problematic to ask clients about sharing needles. Clients who are married or long-term running buddies typically will not consider the needle that both of them use to be shared. Is it sharing, for the purposes of a research study, if a client uses a sterile needle and then gives it to someone else, even though his or her personal risk of HIV transmission is not increased by this behavior? Some injection drug users exchange syringes and/or solution even though they do not technically share needles. These risky behaviors have been observed in the field by outreach workers but it appears that clients do not have specific terms for them. Researchers sometimes use the terms *front loading* and *back loading* to describe different methods of exchanging syringes and solution, but most injection drug users do not use these terms and they are subject to misinterpretation. However, it is important to note that field work has alerted researchers to risky behavior that might otherwise have been overlooked and a careful interview that asks clients specifically how they shoot up and how they transfer their drug works will elicit these behaviors, even without an agreed-upon terminology.

Clients occasionally will use medical terms to describe the effects of various drugs or combinations of drugs. Typically they can classify drugs as *depressants* or *stimulants*, although, of course, other common terms such as *uppers* and *downers* are also used. Sometimes the effects of street drugs are compared to the effects of prescription drugs and a general impression might be that clients make very little distinction between the use of prescribed and nonprescribed drugs. If true, this would lend some credence to the theory that at least some drug users are attempting to self-medicate for some underlying medical condition. In general clients do not use the term *addiction* or refer to themselves as *addicts* (with the exception of injection drug users who do use the term self-referentially). Instead, they make reference to *drug problems, drug habits,* and *drug use.* Noninjection drug users refer to injection drug users as *junkies* and look down on them; however, injection drug users may look down on users of crack cocaine.

We have discussed verbal communication, including the use of medical terms, within a behavioral science research context, but various aspects of nonverbal communication also deserve mention. First, clients have different educational levels and different learning styles. In order to be sure that the basics of HIV transmission and condom use are communicated, various nonverbal methods are used. Some of the adjuncts to spoken communication may include the use of comic books, diagrams, and anatomically correct models, which are of particular use in allowing clients to practice using condoms correctly.

A second, important nonverbal aspect of interviewing drug users is the difficulty faced when obtaining information from a respondent who is under the influence of a drug at the time of the interview. It is very rare for an interview to be terminated, but sometimes interviewers must suggest that a nervous, fidgety client walk around the room to work off some energy or suggest that a client who is nodding off take some deep breaths and have a hot drink.

Other aspects of nonverbal communication are probably influenced by the medical setting. In a recent assessment center focus group, staff stressed that clients are respectful of both staff and the physical plant. It should be noted that before the University of Miami converted the facility that currently houses the assessment center, this building was often targeted for broken windows and graffiti; however, since the first day the building was reopened as the assessment outreach center, no graffiti or broken panes have occurred.

It seems likely that the medical setting reinforces the social dynamics of power and prestige associated with the medical profession. These dynamics are compensated for by staff making efforts to put clients at ease and to make them feel comfortable. It also has been noticed that more accurate information can be obtained when clients feel more comfortable and accepted. One example is the common use of aliases within the drug-using community. Sometimes, on follow-up visits when a comfortable, trusting relationship has been established, clients will say that they want the interviewers to know their real names. Clients also may admit to more socially stigmatized behaviors when they are comfortable and sure that they will not be subjected to judgmental attitudes. Because the point of social research activities is to obtain accurate information, it is obviously of critical importance to foster such feelings of comfort and acceptance.

Although the preceding discussion has considered important aspects of discourse analysis, including some aspects of nonverbal communication within a behavioral research context, it may also be helpful to consider some assumptions and frameworks underlying the research process and that may not be immediately apparent. Our examination of a behavioral science research process within a medical context raises questions about the operative conceptual frameworks inherent in the process and why they are important.

First, it is arguable that much of social reasoning relies on a system of metaphorical thought. We understand and explain the world by expanding concepts from the concrete to the abstract. This metaphorical reasoning is so much a part of ordinary reasoning that we are unaware of the process and accept inherently metaphorical structure as literal truth. In this use of the term *metaphor*, we are not concerned with the literary use of the term. When a poet declares that his love is like a red, red rose, we do not expect her to be tall and thin with red hair. We understand that the poet is comparing aspects or qualities of his love to qualities of the rose, for example, the quality of beauty. This literary form of metaphorical reasoning does not create a problem for everyday communication because it is not taken literally. However, if a student says, "I spent two hours studying last night," this is also an example of metaphorical reasoning, but it *is* understood quite literally. We do not stop to think that *money* can be spent literally but *time* cannot be spent literally. However, because in Western culture there is an understanding that time is money, the concept of spending time makes sense.

Any metaphor/concept/model highlights certain aspects of a situation and hides others. For this reason, it is important to consider as many models or metaphors as possible. Contrary to what may be taught in English class, "mixing metaphors" is very valuable because the more different views we have of a subject, the greater the probability of understanding what a thing is really like. Each perception of reality will highlight some aspects that are not apparent in any other particular view. An explanation of this concept is the familiar story of the three blind men who encountered an elephant for the first time. The first man touched the elephant's trunk and declared that "an elephant is like a snake." The second man touched the side of the elephant and proclaimed "An elephant is like a sturdy wall." The third man grabbed the elephant's tail and stated that the first two men were both wrong because it was very clear that an elephant is like a rope. The three men argued and came to blows, each determined that his view and his alone was correct, when their understanding of "elephantness" would have been greatly enhanced by incorporating all three views.

It is especially incumbent upon society at this time to consider the metaphors, concepts, and frameworks underlying our understanding of HIV risk behaviors and the people who take part in these behaviors. It is crucial to understand that metaphor has the power to create a reality rather than simply providing a means of conceptualizing a preexisting reality. As people act in terms of a new metaphorical understanding, cultural change results. An example of this process is the "Westernization" of other cultures, which is in large part a result of introducing the Western metaphor time is money. This metaphor is one of several that underlie the Western perception of work as an exchange of time for money. Other cultures, however, may perceive work primarily as a sacred duty, a family obligation, a means of creative self-expression, or some other underlying metaphor.

Because metaphorical frameworks have logical presuppositions and implications, they provide a coherent way to organize aspects of experiences and social realities. Thus metaphorical reasoning guides future actions and affects social policy. Needless to say, those in power get to impose their metaphors. As an example of this process, a government may declare a "war on AIDS." The classic view of war demands a villain, an innocent victim, and a hero. The resulting conceptual need for an innocent victim probably underlies the use of hemophiliacs and babies as "poster children" to promote funding for the war on AIDS. Arguably, homosexuals and injection drug users are perceived as the villains and medical researchers poised to offer a cure for AIDS will be proclaimed the heroes. Logical extensions of this model include a threat to national security, and imposition of sanctions that are constructs underlying the calls for quarantine and punitive measures.

In the studies of medicine and human behavior, we have developed several conceptual frameworks to aid our understanding; however, each one of these models, paradigms, or constructs has perceptual and conceptual limitations. We consider several frameworks that can be used to examine social problems such as HIV transmission and seek to answer the questions (a) Who is to blame for the problem? and (b) Who is responsible for solving it? First, we examine four models, the *moral model*, the *enlightenment model*, the *medical model*, and the *compensatory model*, as we move toward a proposed *holistic/contextual model* (Brickman, 1982; Rosenstock, 1990).

Moral Model.   Within the moral model, people are held responsible for both their problems and their solutions. It can be explained as a societal attitude of "You got yourself into this mess, now get yourself out."

Enlightenment Model. Within this model, people are enlightened to the fact that they are to blame for their own problems. Improvement is possible, however, if they submit to the discipline of outside authoritative agents. Alcoholics Anonymous is an example of this model.

Medical Model. People are not blamed for the origins of their problems, nor are they held responsible for solutions to their problems. A typical example would be a bacterial infection. The doctor prescribes antibiotics and the patient is expected to follow the advice of the service provider.

Compensatory Model. People are not blamed for causing their problems, but are responsible for compensating for their handicap by acquiring the power or skills to overcome their problems.

Moral Model: You are to blame for the problem. You are responsible for the solution.	Medical Model: You are not to blame for the problem. You are not responsible for the solution.
Enlightenment Model: You are to blame for the problem. You are not responsible for the solution.	Compensatory Model: You are not to blame for the problem. You are responsible for the solution.

There are clear elements of the moral model in society's response to the HIV epidemic. People who have contracted HIV because of sexual practices or injection drug use are definitely considered to be at fault for their problem. However, it is outside of the control of the ordinary person on the street to provide a solution to the problem (e.g., a cure for AIDS). This leaves society with a dilemma that can be explained as follows. Morality is perceived as a kind of accounting system: A wrongdoer incurs a debt and he must be made to pay. For example, we commonly say of a criminal who has served jail time that he or she has paid his or her debt to society. Justice involves balancing the moral books, which can be accomplished by a return to the situation prior to the wrongdoing, by recompense, or by punishment. When applied to the situation of the transmission of HIV, a return to the situation prior to infection is not possible, nor is recompense possible in any meaningful way. This leaves society with a punitive attitude toward those who are perceived as spreading HIV. An example of this attitude is the degree of public outrage when an HIV-seropositive prostitute continues to ply his or her trade, even though the people who use the services of the prostitute do not fit the stereotype of the innocent victim. Under this model, the person with HIV clearly can be perceived as a villain and no one is a hero.

Although no one individual can be held responsible for developing a cure for AIDS, the moral model certainly holds individuals responsible for making positive changes to the extent that is possible. These positive changes not only could include obtaining appropriate health care and medications, but also will be perceived to include behavioral changes such as using condoms.

A situation that conforms to the enlightenment model could include an individual who is blamed for contracting HIV through behavioral means but who has been led to believe that improvement or a solution may be possible if he or she will submit to exacting regimes of one kind or another. Unfortunately, there are always people who will seek to profit by promising "cures" for HIV or AIDS if the patient will follow specific (and usually expensive) practices, no matter how bizarre or unproven they may be. Even legitimate programs that position themselves as authority figures fall into this category.

Within the context of HIV/AIDS, the medical model is most consistent with looking at the epidemic from the perspective that assigning blame for method of transmission is irrelevant. The cause of the problem is the virus and the solution will also be medical (not behavioral) such as a vaccine, or a medication that cures AIDS. There has been a conscious effort among many to propagate the medical model as an alternative to the moral model relative to drug users at risk for HIV. Previously, this population was often brought to our attention by the criminal justice system and had already been labeled *deviant*, *delinquent*, or *criminal*, a population to be protected against rather than perceived as being in need of medical care or treatment. However, accomplishing transition to this model also has its own consequences, especially in discourse as described throughout this chapter.

Within the context of the present HIV/AIDS epidemic, the compensatory model is probably most often seen in regard to people who have not acquired HIV through negatively sanctioned behavior. Individuals who fall into this category would include medical professionals who acquired HIV through needle stick injuries. Society does not assign blame in these cases, but they are expected to make positive changes to the best of their abilities.

Although these four models adequately cover the issues of blame and responsibility, we still need further clarification regarding the issue of positive and/or negative behavior change. Some other models may need to be incorporated into our understanding, and one place to look is at common conceptual frameworks that are essentially metaphorical in nature. Four that are discussed here are the *reciprocal model*, the *rational model*, the *cost–benefit analysis model*, and the *puzzle model*.

Reciprocal Model. The reciprocal model says that if I do something good for you, you owe me something positive. It may be appropriate to do a little self-examination at this point and consider whether or not research studies have an underlying attitude of reciprocity. It is possible for researchers to feel that they are providing valuable services to clients. We pay people to come in and talk to us; we provide medical tests, counseling, and education. Do we then feel that on some level the client owes us something, and if so what? Clients may feel that they owe us something and respond by telling us what they think we want to hear. We may feel that clients owe us positive behavior change and this assumption may underlie some of the frustration commonly experienced by staff when clients fail to change.

On the other side of the coin, if I do something bad for you, you owe me something negative. It is this underlying concept that explains why some people, on finding that they are HIV-seropositive, respond along the lines of, "Someone gave it to me and I'm going to give it to someone else."

Rational Model. Rationality is commonly seen as the maximization of self-interest. A rational person is perceived as someone who acts in his or her own best interests, that is, to maximize well-being. This model has clear expectations that people will make positive behavior changes as soon as behavioral risks and benefits have been explained to them. It is only rational to stop using drugs or to start using condoms. Therefore, those who do not make these changes are perceived as irrational. Drugs are perceived as powerful, harmful, and responsible for the actions of people who are under their influence and, therefore, "irrational." Drug use therefore explains the irrationality and treatment programs for drug abuse can be perceived as the cure-all. Other sources of explanation for what is perceived as irrational behavior will be sought for individuals who do not use drugs. It is possible that this underlying concept is behind the trend to call almost everyone an addict of some sort: food addicts, sex addicts, chocoholics, and so on. Almost everyone's behavior can be perceived as irrational on some level, and then the inherent irrationality explains the behavior in a neat, although circular, argument.

Cost–Benefit Analysis Model.   Under this metaphor, politics (or social welfare) is perceived as a business. A well-run business should keep track of costs and benefits. This is the kind of reasoning that lets us decide if a given objective is "worth" the "cost" (which may or may not be financial). This metaphor has the effect of turning qualitative effects on humans into quantifiable costs and gains.

Puzzle Model.   Research in general is most often conceptualized as solving a puzzle and this can be a very useful framework. It highlights the cerebral activity involved and the fact that the search for the "missing pieces" can be cooperative in nature. Less obvious expectations based on this metaphorical understanding include a strong desire for elements to fit together neatly and not to overlap. This can result in frustration when the "pieces" of social behavior under study do not fit neatly into preconceived categories. There may also be an underlying assumption that there is only one correct solution to the puzzle.

No doubt other conceptual frameworks can be thought of that will be equally helpful to an overall understanding of human behavior, including that of behavioral scientists, as it relates to HIV transmission. These frameworks can then be incorporated as we strive to develop a "holistic" model. It would appear to be somewhat presumptuous, however, to think that we can devise one model that would be appropriate in every context. It is important to remember that individuals and groups do not necessarily share conceptual frameworks. Therefore, it is important to be open to the metaphors that are most meaningful within specific groups and to develop and focus on language that will fit their needs. Possibly the area in need of most attention currently is the development of culturally sensitive conceptual frameworks that will facilitate the discussion of issues such as HIV risk and protective behaviors (such as condom use) within an intimate context. Each of us should be aware of the limitations of the metaphorical frameworks that direct our discourse and decision making, because our outcomes may be limited by the metaphors that led to our conclusions.

ACKNOWLEDGMENTS

This chapter is dedicated to the loyal, hardworking, insightful, and sensitive professionals who have led us over the last decade to a richer and fuller appreciation and understanding of our clients, our task, and ourselves.

Chapter Dedicated to the Miami CARES Outreach/Assessment Center Staff
1987–1997

Gibson Aristide
Renae Arlt
Lori Barbera
Siouxniqua Bowens
Samual Comerford
Yolanda Davis

Elaine Dyer
Marta Galvez
James Griffin
Paola Gutierrez
Beverly Holmes
Yves Jeanty
Monica Jones
Virginia Locascio
Lawrence Magilner
Elizabeth Matos
Carolyn McKay
Lulus McQueen
David Mobley
Rose Marie Pierre
Cheryl Riles
Gilliane St. Amand
Rose Salas
Lazara Seoane
Bilal Shabazz
Dennis Taylor
Elaine Walden

REFERENCES

Brickman, P. (1982). Models of helping and coping. *American Psychologist, 37,* 368–384.
Lakoff, G. (1991). *Metaphor in politics* [online essay]. Available on Internet: http://metaphor.uoregon.edu/lakoff-1.
Rosenstock, I. M. (1990). The past, present, and future of health education. In K. Glanz, F. M. Lewis, & B. K. Rimer (Eds.), *Health behavior and health education* (pp. 409–411). San Francisco: Jossey-Bass.

II

THE CIVIC: CAMPAIGNS AND POLICY

5

The Reagan Administration's Response to AIDS: Conservative Argument and Conflict

Victoria Stephan Nelson
North Park University

In January 1981, Ronald Reagan was inaugurated as the 40th president of the United States. In June of that year, the Centers for Disease Control (CDC) noted what would become known as the nation's first AIDS cases. Thus from its inception, the Reagan administration was linked to the unprecedented crisis. Dr. June Osborne, Dean of the University of Michigan's School of Public Health, observed, "It would be hard to imagine that the Greek gods could have given us a more cruel irony than this epidemic, during this administration, at this time, in this culture" (in Westmoreland, 1987, p. 48).

The government's response to AIDS during the Reagan years could best be characterized by its production of reports. This chapter examines the controversies that erupted over the *Surgeon General's Report*, as well as two other federally mandated publications: "Understanding AIDS," an informational brochure mailed to each American household, and the *Report of the President's Commission on AIDS*, initiated in 1987. The sections that follow examine conservative argument and assess its impact upon the government's actions in response to the epidemic.

As of April 1984, more than 4,000 cases of AIDS had been reported to the CDC. Approximately 1,800 persons had died (Shilts, 1987). Fear began to spread as the "gay plague" appeared in other populations: hemophiliacs, blood-transfusion recipients, and children (Keerdoja, 1983, p. 10). In late April, Health and Human Services Secretary Margaret Heckler announced the successful isolation of the virus (then called HTLV III) believed responsible for AIDS. Heckler also assured the public that a vaccine would be available for testing within 2 years. She stressed the Reagan administration's commitment to finding a quick solution to the growing epidemic. That commitment was questioned when the Office of Management and Budget called for an 11% reduction in AIDS research spending in 1985, even as the numbers of new cases continued to climb (Shilts, 1987).

By 1986, the hope for rapid development of a testable vaccine had all but disappeared, whereas the death toll grew: 17,000 were infected and 8,000 had died. Public health officials felt pressured to try to determine the scope of the epidemic. Testing blood for the presence of the antibody is the only method of determining whether a person has been infected with the virus. President Reagan (1987) advocated increased testing in his single public speech on the epidemic. Tension grew between factions supporting the rights of individuals to privacy and protection from discrimination, and those calling for a more vigilant approach to the protection of public health. Because the primary means of transmission were known (sharing injection drug needles, sex with an infected partner, and birth to an infected mother), it became clear that behavioral changes were necessary to reduce the spread of infection. Advocates of AIDS education maintained that if one knew the facts about transmission, then one would presumably avoid high-risk behaviors. There were not many other options. Drugs that might alleviate the symptoms of HIV infection were scarcely available, and the process for evaluating new drugs was mired in controversies of its own.

With vaccine research stalled, and with proposed spending cuts of up to 22% pending, public education seemed to be the most appropriate answer. "There continues to be a great deal of confusion in the public's mind about AIDS," said a spokesperson for the Public Health Service. "People are frightened" (Weinraub, 1986, p. 7). Part of this confusion stemmed from the retraction of earlier assurances pronounced by public health officials and researchers. At last, President Reagan responded by requesting that the surgeon general, Dr. C. Everett Koop, prepare a major report on AIDS. The appointment of Dr. Koop, a pediatrician, had been endorsed by conservatives who favored his strong antiabortion sentiments.

THE RISE OF THE NEW RIGHT

Discourse must, in this epidemic, intervene in the absence of medical solutions. The dissemination of appropriate information appeared to be a practical and necessary start toward mitigating the dilemma. Yet these reports sparked considerable controversy. Many of the objections to public education came from newly empowered conservative critics, whose support of Mr. Reagan had been a crucial factor in the elections of 1980 and 1984. Barbara Ehrenreich (1990) described the genealogy of this political movement as the ideological offspring of Barry Goldwater and George Wallace: "Goldwater contributed to the traditional conservative themes: militarism, anticommunism, and the need to shrink the role of government to make way for truly 'free' enterprise" (p. 162). So-called "country club" Republicans had long felt comfortable with these issues; however, according to Ehrenreich, "If the right was to move beyond its blue-blood constituency and tuxedoed image, it would have to follow the trail Wallace blazed into America's smokestack cities and blue-collar suburbs. It would need new issues, and if it was to successfully mobilize Middle America, it would need an enemy" (p. 162).

These were abundant in post-1960s America. The rise of the "New Right," a group often associated with conservative Christians, was due in part to the ability of fundamentalists to "muster doomsday fears and to draw upon a sense of America's having 'gone wrong,' having strayed from the paths of righteousness, by pointing to such signs of national degeneracy as the Supreme Court's 1973 decision on abortion, the accessibility of pornography, gay activists' demands for civil rights, and the widely perceived decline of America's military prestige in relation to Soviet power" (MacKinnon, 1992, p. 123).

The New Christian Right was able to capitalize on these fears through the medium of the "electronic church," wherein televangelists preached a conflated message of spiritual, political, and social concerns (MacKinnon, 1992, p. 123). Adherents were drawn from the ranks of disaffected Democrats, many of whom occupied the lower-middle-class socioeconomic stratum.

By the 1980s organizations such as the Moral Majority, led by the Reverend Jerry Falwell, had begun to make use of their political influence. Falwell was at the forefront of the conservative fundamentalist crusade against homosexuals. In a 1987 editorial, Falwell proclaimed, "AIDS is a lethal judgment of God on the sin of homosexuality and it is also the judgment of God on America for endorsing this vulgar, perverted lifestyle" (p. 2). Charging that "homosexuals and the pro-homosexual politicians have joined together with the liberal, gay-influenced media to cover-up the facts concerning AIDS," Falwell began yet another fundraising drive to expose the "real" facts (p. 2). "If we don't take immediate action," he warned apocalyptically, "AIDS will prove to be the final epidemic—with millions dying each year—even your loved ones" (in Doan, 1987, p. 12). Homosexuals and AIDS became the twin demons of some of the president's most vocal supporters. The debate over AIDS was dominated by these voices; therefore, conservative presumptions in argument are worthy of attention.

LIBERAL AND CONSERVATIVE PRESUMPTIONS IN ARGUMENT

The controversies surrounding the development and distribution of the AIDS reports are representative of an ongoing public argument. Goodnight (1980) proposed that "a private disagreement becomes a public argument when the consequences of choice go beyond the interlocutors (and perhaps even the immediate audience) to involve the interests of the community" (p. 308). The choice, in this example, is primarily whether to employ explicit language in widely disseminated reports aimed at public education, or whether the interests of the community are better served by testing and identifying carriers of the virus. Argument revolved around the necessity of public education when the use of graphic language might promote, rather than discourage, sexual activity. The best answers to these questions could not be ascertained by the disputants who voiced the concerns of their representative constituencies. Those fearing identification and retribution were naturally opposed to widespread testing, whereas those fearing further contamination and personal harm tended to favor it. The use of sexually explicit language in AIDS education was seen as necessary by public health officials, and as reprehensible by conservatives who had been Koop's staunchest supporters.

Public argument, according to Goodnight (1980), is grounded in the perception of individual risk. In this case, the loss of privacy and protection for those afflicted was weighed against the risk of an ever-widening spiral of disease and death. The task of public education conveyed through government reports was contrasted with the risk of seeming to encourage behaviors objectionable to conservatives. These issues can be examined in light of Goodnight's observations regarding the liberal and conservative presumptions in argument.

Goodnight (1980) suggested that that the liberal welcomes changes directed at individual improvement. People are believed to be basically good; aberrant behavior is more likely the consequence of flawed social conditions or policies, than an inevitable element of human nature. Reason is venerated above superstition and prejudice. The liberal is "outer-directed" and demonstrates concern about social well-being (p. 319). Government is seen as a powerful implement that should be used to "bring relief to the poor and suffering" (p. 319). The conservative is suspicious of political, social, or institutional change, preferring instead to defend the status quo. The conservative is "inner-directed" and seeks personal, not social, improvement (p. 322). Individuals are "not naturally good or selfless" (p. 322), and laws or regulations are necessary only to restrain reckless behavior. Otherwise, the intrusion of government into one's private life should be minimized: "Social order is construed to be the natural relation among people who . . . try to work out personal problems, and if collective action is necessary, convince their family, community, then region to take action. . . . It is the duty of conservatives to oppose unnecessary programs and to decrease superfluous ones that exist" (p. 322). Thus government intervention, particularly in the realm of private matters, should be sought only as a last resort. Self-reliance and self-control ought to preclude bureaucratic meddling.

How then should government best address the present exigence? To put it another way, how should an administration, led by a conservative-minded president who vowed to reduce the federal role in order to get government "off our backs," respond to a situation that calls for governmental intrusion into person's private behaviors, indeed, into their bloodstreams? In 1987 the question was crucial, because the wrong decision could result in the most dire consequences.

The importance of self-control and the notion of personal, as opposed to social, reform are reflected in the debate about the responsibility of the individual in maintaining health. Our cultural dialectic of responsibility and rights is evident in the discourse, as are the liberal and conservative presumptions described in Goodnight's (1980) article. John Knowles (1990), former director of Massachusetts General Hospital and past president of the Rockefeller Foundation, provided a spirited argument, representative of the conservative view, in an article entitled "The Responsibility of the Individual":

> Prevention of disease means forsaking the bad habits which many people enjoy—overeating, too much drinking, taking pills, staying up at night, engaging in promiscuous sex, driving too fast, and smoking cigarettes. . . . On the one hand, Social Darwinism maintains its hold on the American mind despite the best intentions of the neoliberals. Those who aren't supine before the Federal Leviathan proclaim the survival of the fittest. On the other, the idea of individual responsibility has been submerged to individual rights—rights, or demands, to be guaranteed by government and delivered by public and private institutions. The cost of sloth, gluttony, alcoholic intemperance, reckless driving, sexual frenzy and smoking is now a national, and not an individual responsibility. This is justified as individual freedom—but one man's freedom in health is another man's shackle in taxes and insurance premiums. (p. 377)

Knowles (1990) rather succinctly touched upon the major tenets of conservative ideology in the preceding passage. In contrast, Robert Crawford (1990) condemned Knowles' argument as merely a strategy of blaming the victim so as to shift the cost of health care to the individual: "In the new system the pariahs of the medical world and larger numbers of people in general could be diagnosed as lifestyle problems, referred to a health counselor, and sent home. At the very least, the victim-blaming ideology will help justify shifting the burden of costs back to users. A person who is responsible for his or her illness should be responsible for the bill as well" (p. 390). Absent from Knowles' argument is any consideration of the social conditions that might encourage such behaviors as a way of either seeking pleasure or escaping from pain. No doubt individuals are, to a degree, responsible for their actions. But people do not live out their lives in a vacuum. We are all affected by others perhaps less conscientious, by organizations, or by situations over which we may have little control: the unreasonable superior, the sick child, the abusive spouse, the crime-infested neighborhood, the nuclear power plant, the contaminated water supply, the filthy air, and so on. These, too, have a considerable effect upon the health of the individual.

Advertising and other media also promote the very excesses decried by Knowles (1990). As Garvey (1987) put it, "Television, radio, and other forms of noise are absolutely pervasive, and have become whatever culture we have. They stress individualism, selfishness, greed, envy, and narcissism. They create a restlessness and need for distraction which are more than annoying; these things are killing us. Perhaps some of what can seem like mindless reaction is in fact an expression of despair" (p. 694).

Knowles' (1990) position as delineated in the excerpt is both a model of, and precursor to, similar arguments made by conservatives in response to government actions prompted by the growing AIDS epidemic. The moral message implicit in Knowles' statement equates illness with sinful excess. Conversely, self-restraint, control, and temperance will lead to good health. Thus it is the obligation of the individual to act accordingly. If a person chooses to indulge, then he or she should not have the right to look to the rest of society for relief from a self-inflicted condition. And people, given their natures, will not always act as they should.

A 1987 Gallup poll indicated that the conservative emphasis on individual responsibility had some resonance with the public. Asked whether they agreed with the statement: "In general, it's people's own fault if they get AIDS," 51% of respondents responded in the affirmative. Forty-three percent agreed with the statement, "I sometimes think AIDS is a punishment for the decline in moral standards" (Elder, 1991, p. 13).

The fear that immoral, irresponsible, if not socially deviant, individuals could spread the virus into broad segments of the population prompted calls for the testing and identification of the infected. In his 1987 address to the American Foundation for AIDS Research (AmFAR), President Reagan expressed concern that "innocent people" were being exposed to the virus: "If a person has reason to believe that he or she may be a carrier, that person has a moral duty to be tested for AIDS; human decency requires it. And the reason is very simple: Innocent people are being infected by this virus, and some of them are going to acquire AIDS and die" (p. 586). This statement left the unfortunate impression that those who had died heretofore were not innocent or, at least, were responsible for their illness.

Reagan (1987) also announced plans to institute testing programs in veterans' hospitals and federal prisons, as well as a plan to exclude immigrants based on their HIV status. He encouraged states to initiate mandatory blood testing as part of the marriage application process. The speech was greeted with boos and shouts of "No! No!" according to the transcript (p. 586). Those opposed to mandatory testing feared that the identification, exposure, and contact tracing of HIV-positive persons would discourage those truly at risk from being tested. Voluntary, confidential testing and counseling were less likely to result in discrimination toward those with HIV. Charging the administration with abject neglect of the epidemic's first 6 years, a critic of testing alleged that it was merely a politically expedient ploy in a campaign year: "Republicans, particularly conservative Republicans, are on the hustings with this solution. This answer appears simple and straightforward, and when it is combined with conservative, religious, and moralistic concerns, it appeals to Americans ignorant of the real social, political, health, and constitutional issues" (Wood, 1987, p. 43). Conservatives did seem to have control over the debate. The responses of the Reagan administration can thus be considered in the context of an era dominated by the political influence of conservative thought.

THE SURGEON GENERAL'S REPORT

The *Surgeon General's Report on Acquired Immune Deficiency Syndrome* was released on October 22, 1986. The 36-page booklet was written by Dr. Koop, and was the result of meetings conducted with dozens of groups, from gay-rights activists to Catholic bishops. The report provides detailed explanations of the virus, the ways in which it is transmitted, and what can be done to avoid infection. There are several illustrations, including a picture of a condom, a rectum, and a cross-section of rectal tissue. The language is explicit and clinical: "AIDS is *not* spread by common everyday contact, but by sexual contact (penis-vagina, penis-rectum, mouth-rectum, mouth-vagina, mouth-penis). . . . If you test positive or if you engage in high-risk activity and choose not to have a test, you must protect your partner by always using a rubber (condom) during (start to finish) sexual intercourse (vaginal or rectal)"

(U.S. Department of Health and Human Services, 1986, pp. 5, 17). In addition to endorsing the use of condoms, Dr. Koop stated, "Education concerning AIDS must start at the lowest grade possible . . . There is now no doubt that we need sex education in schools and that it must include information on heterosexual and homosexual relationships" (p. 31).

In contrast to the proposed policy of widespread testing advanced by the president, the surgeon general discredited the necessity of testing: "Compulsory blood testing of individuals is not necessary. The procedure could be unmanageable and cost-prohibitive. It can be expected that many who test negatively might actually be positive due to recent exposure to the AIDS virus and give a false sense of security to the individual and his/her sexual partners" (U.S. Department of Health and Human Services, 1986, p. 31).

Whereas Dr. Koop was praised for his clarity by liberal-minded politicians including Democratic Representative Henry Waxman of California, and by organizations such as Planned Parenthood and the National Gay and Lesbian Task Force, the reception on the right was less than supportive. Gary Bauer, the president's chief adviser on domestic policy, criticized the report: "I don't see why a third grader needs to know anything about condoms or sexual practices—and I'm not going to give the go-ahead to the local schools to talk to my nine-year-old daughter about sodomy" (in Whitman, 1987, p. 27).

In a letter to Republican politicians who had planned a dinner honoring Koop, conservative organizers Phyllis Schlafly and Paul Weyrich (1987) hinted darkly of complicity with the ideological enemy: "Many believe that his statements about AIDS are a cover for the homosexual community. His report on AIDS . . . reads as though it were edited by the National Gay Task Force" (p. 16–17). They urged sponsors to withdraw their support: "This dinner will clearly play right into the hands of those promoting the gay-rights agenda, which is to teach children how to use condoms for premarital promiscuity with either sex while opposing measures that are desperately needed to protect the uninfected from the infected" (Schlafly & Weyrich, 1987, pp. 16–17). In response to these objections, 11 sponsors, including then-presidential hopefuls Robert Dole, Jack Kemp, and Pierre du Pont, withdrew their support (Schlafly & Weyrich, 1987).

Schlafly, Weyrich, and Bauer were not alone in condemning the surgeon general. Writing in the *National Review,* Wayne Lutton (1987) lamented, "Conservatives who have applauded Dr. Koop's previous public stands . . . are likely to experience a deep sense of dismay—indeed of betrayal—once they become familiar with his work on AIDS" (p. 55). Lutton accused Koop of deliberately and falsely minimizing the threat, thus rendering AIDS "the first politically protected disease in history" (p. 55). He went on to speculate about Koop's criminal liability: "By advising people that sex is safe where AIDS is present—if only they use condoms—Dr. Koop may be guilty of inducing people to engage in dangerous—perhaps lethal—behavior. Whether or not Koop's utterances constitute criminal negligence, or even implicate him as an accessory to murder, is an intriguing legal question" (p. 56).

To all of this and more, Koop replied, "I am the surgeon general of the heterosexuals and the homosexuals, of the young and the old, of the moral and the immoral. I don't have the luxury of deciding which side to be on" (in Whitman, 1987, p. 28). Although attempting to cast the issue as medical, rather than moral, Dr. Koop and his report nevertheless became part of the debate. The reaction aroused by the *Surgeon General's Report* exemplifies Johnstone's (1965) observation that "the tension between conserving old knowledge and changing to new knowledge is the very impulse of argument" (pp. 4–5).

Such synthesis of old and new knowledge had not yet been achieved. The histrionic tone of the responses polarized the discourse and precluded the possibility of achieving consensus. The irrationality of the arguments reflected a deliberate misreading of the report and a certain recklessness with the available evidence. It is rather silly to suggest that the surgeon general of the United States is unaware of the failure rate of condoms, and that therefore he might be subject to prosecution for murder. In lieu of national sexual abstinence, condoms offered the sole, admittedly imperfect, option.

To suggest that Koop adhered to an agenda whose aim was to "teach children how to use condoms for premarital promiscuity with either sex" was equally unproductive. Koop's response was dismissive of the criticism: "Sodomy in the third grade! There's no way that even an imbecile could have interpreted what I said as that. . . . It's crude to say it, but she doesn't have any idea of the configuration of an eight-year-old penis to a condom" (in Fettner, 1987, p. 36).

Reflecting on this debate, a writer in the *New Republic* suggested, "It is dishonesty that underlies the entire moralistic scheme to exaggerate the heterosexual AIDS problem. Frustrated with the failure of the message 'sex will cost your soul,' the moralistic have cynically replaced it with 'sex will cost your life.' Moral suasion is replaced with mortal terror" (Fumento, 1988, p. 21).

Appeals to fear of disease have long been used as a deterrent to excessive sexual indulgence. A similar case was advanced in 1910 by one Dr. Howard Kelly, who became alarmed at the sudden influx of immigrants whose "lower ideals" he held responsible for an increase in venereal disease. The fear of contagion was advanced as a "deterrent to licentiousness": "If we could in an instant eradicate the diseases, we would also forget at once the moral side of the question, and would then, in one short generation, fall wholly under the domination of the animal passions, becoming grossly and universally immoral" (in Eisenberg, 1986, p. 21).

Surely this presents a rather dismal view of human nature. It also suggests that appeals to restraint alone are bound to fail. Conservatives seemed reluctant to remove the element of fear without which the moral argument presumably held no sway. In his discussion of appeals to fear, Aristotle (1987) observed, "When it is advisable that the audience should be frightened, the orator must make them feel that they really are in danger of something, pointing out that it has happened to others who were stronger than they are, and is happening, or has happened, to people like themselves, at the hands of unexpected people, in an unexpected form, and at an unexpected time" (p. 629).

The decision to employ fear appeals as a device for advancing what is, in essence, an argument for morality may have been an unfortunate strategy. In order to sustain the argument's force, the threat must become real. When, in fact, the epidemic did not cause substantial devastation in the broader, middle-class, heterosexual population, the appeals for an acceptable standard of behavior evaporated with the imminent fear of HIV and AIDS. Thus, conservatives lost an opportunity to seize a moment of public awareness and uncertainty and advance a moral standard consistent with their ideology. As with the other reports, attempts to stifle public discussion also hampered efforts to provide information to the public.

"AMERICA RESPONDS TO AIDS"

October 1987 was designated as "AIDS Awareness Month," in order to inaugurate the government's education campaign. The centerpiece of the educational effort was an eight-page brochure with the theme: "America Responds to AIDS." Produced by the public relations firm of Ogilvy and Mather at a cost of $4.5 million (or $562,500 per page), the brochure was intended to fulfill a congressional appropriation of $20 million to be used for an educational or informative mailing that would be sent to every household in America. The balance of the funds would cover the printing and mailing costs.

But "alas," lamented a writer in *Science* magazine, "America will not get a chance to respond because the brochure has become hopelessly bogged down by bureaucratic intransigence and political meddling" (Booth, 1987b, p. 1410). The pamphlet was to have been approved by the newly created Presidential Commission on the Human Immunodeficiency Virus, in September 1987, but the members "just felt like we weren't ready to tackle the mailing yet," according to then-chairman W. Eugene Mayberry of the Mayo Foundation (Booth, 1987b, p. 1410). It is not surprising that conflict over the content of the brochure delayed the mailing for nearly 9 months. The original version had to pass the scrutiny of the Centers for Disease Control, the Public Health Service, the Office of Management and Budget, the Secretary of Health and Human Services, the President's Commission on HIV, the National Institutes of Health and, finally, the President's Domestic Policy Council.

The composition of the commission itself was a source of controversy, as is noted later. After passing through so many levels of federal bureaucracy, the brochure nevertheless remained controversial. The language it employed was considered to be chosen so carefully that the intent of the message was lost. The word *condom* appeared only 3 times; *family* or *families* was used 12 times, but the word *homosexual* was never used once in the eight-page brochure, despite the fact that in 1987 the overwhelming majority of persons with AIDS were homosexuals (Raymond, 1988, p. 2513). The brochure then went back to the drawing board.

The final version was ultimately mailed to 108 million households in May 1988. Some of the earlier omissions had been corrected: *homosexual* appeared twice, *condoms,* a surprising 15 times. Overall the brochure emphasized "safe" behavior. Under that heading, three suggestions were offered: not having sex; having sex with one mutually faithful, uninfected partner; and not injecting illicit drugs. Unlike the clinical, rather neutral tone of the *Surgeon General's Report,* the message emphasized here was one of avoidance through individual control of behavior:

> Who you are has nothing to do with whether you are in danger of becoming infected with the AIDS virus. What matters is what you do . . .
>
> Dating doesn't mean the same thing as having sex. Sexual intercourse as a part of dating can be risky. One of the risks is AIDS . . .
>
> The most effective way to prevent AIDS is by avoiding exposure to the virus, which you can control by your own behavior . . .
>
> Children must be taught values and responsibility. . . . These skills can be reinforced by religious and community groups. However, final responsibility rests with the parents. (U.S. Department of Health and Human Services, 1988, pp. 2–7)

The brochure was intended to "prompt feelings of pride, patriotism, and reflect the American mosaic," according to a memorandum issued by the Centers for Disease Control (Booth, 1987b, p. 1410). Indeed, the brochure concludes with a perky encouragement to all Americans to "keep an upbeat attitude" in dealing with AIDS (U.S. Department of Health and Human Services, 1988, p. 7).

However, some critics within the government felt that the brochure was completely unnecessary. An unnamed White House official "exploded" when told of remarks made by a Public Health Service physician who praised the brochure. According to the *Chicago Tribune,* the official blasted the mailing as "a total waste of money, because the only people catching the infection now are people who don't read the mail or even have an address—they're junkies" (Crewdson, 1988, p. A3). Domestic policy chief Bauer also doubted the efficacy of the brochure: "I question whether a 60-year-old couple in Topeka, Kansas, needs to be informed to avoid sharing dirty needles or engaging in anal intercourse" (in Booth, 1987b, p. 1410).

Although critical of the brochure, these remarks again point to the debate surrounding the degree to which the general population was at risk, and thereby in need of information and education. They also indicate the dually employed, yet contradictory arguments advanced by conservatives.

During the past few years, the trend in new cases of HIV infection has shifted from homosexuals to minorities, drug addicts, women, and children, but the much-feared "break-out" into the general population has not occurred. The National Research Council's report supports this finding. It has determined that the epidemic will not spread into the broader population, but is instead tragically "concentrating in pools of persons who are caught in the 'synergism of plagues': poverty, poor health, and lack of health care, inadequate education, joblessness, hopelessness, and social disintegration" (Jonsen & Stryker, 1993, p. 7). In contrast, "many geographical areas and strata of the population are virtually untouched by the epidemic and probably never will be" (Jonsen & Stryker, 1993, p. 7).

Despite these trends, some conservatives inflated the risk of falling victim to HIV in order to promote their values, hence the appeals to fear and the apocalyptic warnings of those such as Jerry Falwell. But others sought to dismiss the risk, believing that those who could had already heeded the message: "What exactly is it that people don't know? Is there a breathing American who doesn't know that you can get AIDS from sex or a dirty needle? If there is, he probably is not the kind of person who reads his mail," declared Gary Bauer (in Booth, 1987b, p. 1410).

A report undertaken by the General Accounting Office (GAO) found that efforts to educate the public, as well as the president's repeated insistence on testing, had produced unintended complications: "Education campaigns will only increase the strain on the testing and counseling centers as more and more low-risk individuals come in to be assured that they have not been exposed to the virus" (in Booth, 1987a, p. 21). Medical centers were already reporting delays of up to 10 weeks for those seeking to be tested. The GAO recommended an increase of $180 million to meet the costs of testing those with known risk factors, as well as those who did not engage in risky behaviors but were nevertheless sufficiently persuaded, or frightened, to be tested for the antibody (Booth, 1987a, p. 21).

Contradiction arose within the controversy. Conservative critics could not have it both ways. Public health officials were obliged to either inform the citizenry about AIDS (explicit language notwithstanding) in order to protect the nation's health, or they had to begin a campaign to test everyone. This ambivalence and the subsequent inability to develop an acceptable policy suggested a crack in the ideological foundation that had held together through the mid-1980s. Government now seemed to be "promoting unnecessary programs" and needlessly upsetting people with information about the risks of behaviors that some of them may not have even imagined. Furthermore, the identification of increasing numbers of infected persons led to demands for a proliferation of services, prompting this complaint from the head of the Conservative Caucus Foundation: "It's wrong to force monogamous taxpayers to fund homosexual activity" (McLaughlin, 1987, p. 24).

A fatal viral infection that threatened homosexuals and drug addicts could well seem a distant concern to "married people who are uninfected, faithful, and don't shoot drugs," identified in the brochure as "not at risk" (U.S. Department of Health and Human Services, 1988, p. 4). On the other hand, the threat to the general population must be made vivid enough to encourage mutually monogamous relationships among heterosexuals, if not abstinence. The tension inherent in the discourse undermined the conservative emphasis on safe behavior: "Jack Kemp pointed out in an address that there's no need, moral concerns aside, for condom education for third graders. But there's also no need, moral concerns aside, for impressing upon third graders the importance of chastity, at least in order to prevent AIDS" (Fumento, 1988, p. 21).

Thus, government officials beholden to conservative supporters were caught between several evils. The choices were either to inform the public at all levels about AIDS even if that led (inexplicably) to an increase in sexual curiosity seeking and more new cases; or, to inform them in such a way that young people in particular would be terrified into chastity and drug-free living, even if the threat would not endure over time. Third, one could restrict, even eliminate the brochures, reports, and other educational materials, thereby downplaying the risk, even if that jeopardized the uninfected, and provoked cries of a cover-up. "In condemning and ostracizing the 'sinners' among us, we will likely also endanger the 'saints' " (Wood, 1987, p. 38).

In essence, an examination of this debate reveals that there are multiple discourses of AIDS, each arising from different definitions of the situation (see also Plummer, 1988). The value-neutral, medical conceptualization of the illness is evident in the *Surgeon General's Report*. AIDS is viewed primarily as a medical problem, originating in a virus. Avoidance of infection is possible, but such measures require frank discussion of body parts and practices, nothing new to most physicians. Medical intervention, with an emphasis on ridding the body of disease, is the appropriate response.

A counter-rhetoric seeks to wrestle the definition away from the medical domain and ground it instead in morality. This is discernible in the discourse of Falwell, Schlafly, and to a degree, Reagan. AIDS is conceptualized as retribution; its origin is sin. Those who are HIV-seropositive can be categorized as innocent or guilty. Control of the virus is possible only through changes in behavior. Identification and, if possible, isolation of carriers are seen as proper interventions.

A third discourse is evident in Bauer's argument, with credit to Knowles. AIDS is regarded a social problem, but one that involves marginalized, if not expendable, populations. Ronald Bayer (1987), who has written extensively on the social implication of the epidemic, referred to a public official's remark that "there are two kinds of AIDS patients, dead ones and dying ones; therefore, the expenditure of large sums of money on the health care of such individuals is ill-considered" (p. 35). This view locates the origins of AIDS in self-induced behaviors (gay sex, illicit drug use, promiscuity) and, as a matter of personal choice, it does not warrant external intervention. It certainly does not justify government's intervention. Individuals, free to undertake risky behaviors, are likewise equally free to endure the consequences.

The discourse of medicine runs counter to that of morality. The discourse of morality prompts the counter-rhetoric of gay activists seeking to destigmatize and demoralize the epidemic, keeping the issue on political grounds even as they warily evaluate the medical argument. The dismissive quality of the third discourse provokes calls for compassion. Although these simplified descriptions are separated into discrete units on the page, they become somewhat tangled in the public mind, leading to the sort of comment offered by a White House official: "You can't let yourself be accused of not caring about dying people, especially if you're a moralistic conservative" (in Barnes, 1987, pp. 10–11). True, countered Tim Westmoreland (1987), himself a government bureaucrat, but, "An administration that would cut funds for childhood polio immunization, that allows infant mortality to rise around the country, and that discharges elderly people from the hospital while they are still sick will not turn to gay people as the first group to whom they will suddenly show compassion" (p. 51).

The confusion that results from AIDS' complexity and contrariness seems to have resulted in a kind of rhetorical paralysis during the Reagan administration. The adoption of one of the aforementioned strands of argument would have meant forsaking all others, something the president's advisors were unwilling or unable to do. Though issues may be self-contradictory, governments are expected to discover a consistent position and to stick with it. For this administration, the consistent approach meant ordering up yet another report.

THE PRESIDENTIAL COMMISSION

One week after the release of the surgeon general's 1986 report, the National Academy of Sciences issued a 390-page report that criticized the Reagan administration's efforts to combat AIDS. A private organization, the academy is chartered by Congress to advise the federal government on scientific matters. Though some of its findings were similar to those of Dr. Koop, the academy's report described the efforts at public education as "woefully inadequate," and urged an increase in expenditures of up to $2 billion to combat the epidemic. It also called for sweeping changes in the government's response to AIDS. One of the most urgent recommendations was for the creation of a national commission to study the epidemic and to coordinate efforts to halt its spread (Boffey, 1986).

It was not until July 1987 that the Presidential Commission on the Human Immunodeficiency Virus finally took shape, and there was controversy from the outset regarding the selection of its members. The 13-member panel included such diametrically opposed persons as John Cardinal O'Connor of New York, and Dr. Frank Lilly, a gay geneticist. The cardinal offered to participate in the "first few meetings," but hinted that he would resign from the panel shortly thereafter, "because his other duties, including caring for AIDS patients in New York City, demanded so much of his time" (Maclean, 1987, p. A5). The appointment of a gay commission member drew criticism from conservatives who had "waged a rear-guard struggle" to bar homosexuals from the panel. The members also drew criticism for their lack of experience with AIDS (Witkin, 1987, p. 8). Confusion arose over the role of the commission, and how much it could be expected to accomplish.

In an effort to clarify its mission, the panel appeared before a congressional subcommittee on September 30, 1987. Several suggestions were offered. Senator John Danforth of Missouri proposed the idea of a television show, in which the president would ask questions of medical experts. "Why not," mused the senator, "have the president play the role of an uninformed John Q. Public and ask the experts, for example, if he could get AIDS by standing in an elevator with someone harboring the virus." Senator Lowell Weicker was not amused: "To date, your commission has yet to prove that it is not merely an extension of the far right moralizing this administration has employed as its first line of offense in the AIDS battle" (in Booth, 1987c, p. 149).

Within a week of this meeting, both the chairman and cochairman of the panel abruptly resigned. The executive director had been fired the previous month. The departure of the commission's preeminent physicians left the panel even less competent to deal with the complexities of a public health crisis.

In an effort to end the strife, President Reagan appointed Retired Admiral James Watkins to head the panel, and the commission began on its uncertain course. Meanwhile, a coalition of community health and civil rights groups, working with the American Civil Liberties Union, filed suit against the commission, charging that its members did not represent the interests of those whom it must serve (Maclean, 1987).

Yet, despite the controversies, the commission managed to release its 200-page report by June 1988. Compared to the critical reception of the *Surgeon General's Report,* the Presidential Commission's study generated virtually no political response in a busy election year. The report is consistently critical of the way the Reagan administration dealt with AIDS—an evaluation that earned praise from some gay-rights groups ("Prescriptions," 1988). The panel's 579 recommendations appeared likely to go unmet in the waning months of a lame-duck administration.

The report did endorse the president's call for greater testing, but on a voluntary, confidential basis. Although endorsing early childhood education, the commissioners noted the importance of a comprehensive approach to all aspects of good health. The question of HIV/AIDS education was seen as linked to the issues of drug education, sex education, and the problem of teenage pregnancy (Presidential Commission, 1988). The epidemic could not be addressed without consideration of these additionally sensitive issues.

Reaction to this report was markedly subdued: "President Reagan responded last week with a hem and a haw to the recommendations of his own advisory commission. Reagan called for several studies, a couple of conferences, and one expeditious review," opined the journal *Science* (Booth, 1988, p. 778). *The New York Times* reported that Reagan met the panel with "praise for its work but without commenting on its call for an executive order or new federal laws" (Boffey, 1988, p. A1). The story goes on to note that senior White House officials expressed "unease" about the sections of the report that criticized the Reagan administration's response to the first 8 years of the epidemic, preferring to " 'downplay the report' by handling it without fanfare" (Boffey, 1988, p. A1).

Perhaps most telling is the photo that accompanies the story. Rather than the standard White House "photo op" taken in one of the receiving rooms wherein guests are often shown with the president, seated in armchairs before the fireplace, Admiral Watkins is pictured speaking to reporters on the White House driveway. The press conference was held well outside the building, as if the commissioner himself were contaminated.

CONCLUSION

The reports examined herein proved to be time-consuming and inefficient responses to an epidemic whose new cases grew exponentially in the mid-1980s. None of the reports had the reception that its authors no doubt hoped for. When a report itself becomes the subject of controversy, constructive discussion of the central issue is foreclosed. Commissioner Watkins urged that the debate over AIDS policy not become sidetracked on issues such as condoms or needle exchange programs: "We waste a lot of rhetoric and excessive time on a couple of little issues while behind us the forest is burning" (in Boffey, 1988, p. A1).

A brochure that tries hard not to offend anyone may employ such vapid language that its persuasive potential is lost. Likewise, when a group is characterized by so much internal strife and bureaucratic mismanagement, it may find that its report, though substantive, was simply generated too late in the political life cycle of public issues. Precious time was lost as the nation waited for the initiatives of the incoming Bush administration. Any meaningful discussion of AIDS must include accurate information about transmission and prevention. But a universal document, such as a government report, will probably not address all audiences appropriately.

Appeals to fear have failed to stem the explosion in sexual activity. A 1993 study conducted by the Alan Guttmacher Institute found that one in five Americans, or 56 million people, are currently infected with a sexually transmitted disease (Barringer, 1993). The Census Bureau has released figures that indicate that nearly one fourth of the nation's unmarried women, ages 18 to 44, have had children (deParle, 1993).

The issue of testing, like the collectively inconsistent arguments about risk, turned conservative argument inside-out, creating confusion among the public and schisms among the ranks. Liberals such as Senator Ted Kennedy expressed concern about the obtrusive role of government in testing and tracking persons with HIV: "We'll never defeat the disease unless we protect those who harbor the virus from painful and irrational consequences" (in Harbrecht, 1987, p. 53). Meanwhile, conservatives argued on behalf of coercive federal and state measures: "Ironically, conservatives [lost] because they've failed to act like conservatives. The AIDS crisis called for what used to be thought of as conservative virtues: caution before all the evidence is in and dispassion when weighing public policy. Instead, conservatives have reacted as hysterically as their radical adversaries" (Fumento, 1988, p. 23). These conflicts persisted into the Bush administration, and continue still, leaving controversy again unresolved.

REFERENCES

Aristotle. (1987). *Rhetoric* (R. Roberts, Trans.). In R. M. Hutchins (Ed.), *The works of Aristotle* (Vol. 2). Chicago: Encyclopedia Britannica, Inc.

Barnes, F. (1987, April 27). Presidential AIDS. *New Republic, 196*, 10–11.

Barringer, F. (1993, April 1). Report finds 1 in 5 infected by viruses spread sexually. *The New York Times*, p. A1.

Bayer, R. (1987). Five dimensions to the politics of AIDS. In J. Griggs (Ed.), *AIDS: Public policy dimensions* (pp. 35–39). New York: United Hospital Fund of New York.

Boffey, P. M. (1986, October 30). Federal efforts on AIDS criticized as gravely weak. *The New York Times*, p. A1.

Boffey, P. M. (1988, February 25). Panel on AIDS urges growth in health care. *The New York Times*, pp. A1–A2.

Booth, W. (1987a, August 21). Experts fault leadership on AIDS. *Science, 237*, 838.

Booth, W. (1987b, September 18). The odyssey of a brochure on AIDS. *Science, 237*, 1410.

Booth, W. (1987c, October 9). President's AIDS panel in disarray. *Science, 238*, 149.

Booth, W. (1988, August 12). AIDS report draws tepid response. *Science, 291*, 778.

Crawford, R. (1990). Individual responsibility and health politics. In P. Conrad & R. Kern (Eds.), *The sociology of health and illness: Critical perspectives* (pp. 381–389). New York: St. Martin's Press.

Crewdson, J. (1988, January 27). White House blasts AIDS mailing campaign. *Chicago Tribune*, p. A3.

deParle, J. (1993, July 14). Census reports a sharp increase among never married mothers. *The New York Times*, p. A1.

Doan, M. (1987, May 4). Jerry Falwell's anti-AIDS dollar drive. *U.S. News and World Report*, pp. 12–13.

Ehrenreich, B. (1990). *Fear of falling: The inner life of the middle class*. New York: Harper Perennial.

Eisenberg, L. (1986). The genesis of fear: AIDS and the public's response to science. *Law, Medicine and Health Care, 14*, 244–252.

Elder, J. (1991, May 19). Many favor wider testing for AIDS virus, poll finds. *The New York Times*, p. A13.

Falwell, J. (1987, April). AIDS: The judgment of God. *Liberty Report, 2*, 3.

Fettner, A. G. (1987, May 12). Citizen Koop. *Village Voice*, pp. 35–36.

Fumento, M. J. (1988, August 8). The political uses of an epidemic. *New Republic*, pp. 19–23.

Garvey, J. (1987, December 4). A fact of life: AIDS & explicit education. *Commonweal, 114*, 694–695.

Goodnight, G. T. (1980). The liberal and conservative presumptions: On political philosophy and the foundation of public argument. In J. Rhodes & S. Newell (Eds.), *Proceedings of the first summer conference on argumentation* (pp. 304–332). Annandale, VA: Speech Communication Association.

Harbrecht, D. A. (1987, October 12). Congress heads for an ugly battle over AIDS. *Business Week*, p. 53.

Johnstone, H. W., Jr. (1965). Some reflections on argumentation. In H. W. Johnstone & M. Natanson (Eds.), *Philosophy, rhetoric and argument* (pp. 1–9). University Park: Pennsylvania State University Press.

Jonsen, A. R., & Stryker, J. (Eds.). (1993). *The social impact of AIDS in the United States*. Washington, DC: National Academy Press.

Keerdoja, E. (1983, May 30). Homosexual plague strikes new victims. *Newsweek*, p. 10.

Knowles, J. H. (1990). The responsibility of the individual. In P. Conrad & R. Kern (Eds.), *The sociology of health and illness: Critical perspectives* (pp. 370–380). New York: St. Martin's Press.

Lutton, W. (1987, January 30). Hazardous to your health. *National Review*, pp. 54–56.

MacKinnon, K. (1992). *The politics of popular representation: Reagan, Thatcher, AIDS, and the movies.* London: Associated University Press.

Maclean, J. N. (1987, October 16). New AIDS panel boss tells his agenda. *Chicago Tribune,* p. A5.

McLaughlin, J. (1987, May 8). AIDS in '88. *National Review,* p. 24.

Plummer, K. (1988). Organizing AIDS. In P. Aggleton & H. Homans (Eds.), *Social aspects of AIDS* (pp. 23–24). Philadelphia: Falmer Press.

Prescriptions aplenty to defeat AIDS. (1988, May 16). *U.S. News and World Report,* pp. 7–8.

Presidential Commission on the Human Immunodeficiency Virus. (1988). *Report of the presidential commission on the human immunodeficiency virus.* Washington, DC: U.S. Government Printing Office.

Raymond, C. A. (1988). Nation will receive AIDS brochure in "largest government mailing ever." *Journal of the American Medical Association, 259,* 2513–2514.

Reagan, R. (1987). *Public papers of the presidents of the United States.* Washington, DC: Office of the Federal Register, National Archives and Record Service.

Schlafly, P., & Weyrich, P. (1987, August). Disowning the surgeon general. *Harper's Magazine,* pp. 16–17.

Shilts, R. (1987). *And the band played on: Politics, people and the AIDS epidemic.* New York: St. Martin's Press.

U.S. Department of Health and Human Services. (1986). *Surgeon general's report on acquired immune deficiency syndrome.* Washington, DC: Author.

U.S. Department of Health and Human Services. (1988). *Understanding AIDS.* Washington, DC: Public Health Service, Centers for Disease Control.

Weinraub, B. (1986, February 6). Reagan orders AIDS reports, giving high priority to work for cure. *The New York Times,* p. B7.

Westmoreland, T. (1987). AIDS and the political process: A federal perspective. In J. Griggs (Ed.), *AIDS: Public policy dimensions* (pp. 47–53). New York: United Hospital Fund of New York.

Whitman, D. (1987, May 25). A fall from grace on the right. *U.S. News and World Report,* pp. 27–28.

Witkin, G. (1987, August 3). Ronald Reagan's AIDS panel: More gray than gay. *U.S. News and World Report,* p. 8.

Wood, G. J. (1987). The politics of AIDS testing. *AIDS and Public Policy Journal, 2,* 43–45.

6

Politically Privileged Voices: Glaser and Fisher Address the 1992 Presidential Nominating Conventions

Kathleen M. German
Miami University, Ohio

Jeffrey L. Courtright
University of North Dakota

Since the first public awareness, AIDS has been a delicate political issue because of its early and continuing association with stigmatized individuals. According to CNN Medical News Correspondent Andrew Holtz, "[E]ver since the beginning of the epidemic, politics and morality have been intertwined with the health debate on AIDS" (Randall, 1992). As a result, few political leaders have risked taking action regarding the disease (Johnson, 1988). Ironically, it is the lack of government leadership that was largely to blame for the rampant spread of the disease in the early 1980s (Simons, 1996).

Despite more recent recognition of the role of government leadership in the epidemic, AIDS has remained a precarious political issue because of public attitudes. Dennis Altman (1987) summarized the nature of public opinion about AIDS: "Since the media began discussing the illness in late 1981, the public at large has fluctuated between short-lived panic about its spreading . . . and regarding it as a curse of 'the other,' something that strikes only those groups already singled out for misfortune" (p. 12). Continuing stigmatization of people with AIDS, especially gay men, led former Surgeon General C. Everett Koop to explain the reason for public disapproval: "People get AIDS by doing things that most people do not do, and do not approve of other people doing" (Juhasz, 1990, p. 35). Such social disapproval acts to "prevent AIDS from becoming a public issue in any real sense" (Fabj & Sobnosky, 1995, p. 169).

In 1992, AIDS emerged for the first time as an issue in a presidential campaign. At the time, Holtz pointed out: "Polls indicate many citizens, particularly younger ones, feel threatened by AIDS and want strong federal action against the disease. But it's not clear that concern will have a direct effect on how voters decide who they want in the White House leading the fight" (Randall, 1992). Although some political strategists thought AIDS could be the wedge issue of the campaign, just as the Willie Horton question encouraged voter response in 1988, most acknowledged that the issue was risky for Republicans, who might appear to be repressive, as well as for Democrats, who could not afford to be perceived as promoting it (Schmalz, 1992a).

This chapter focuses on how the AIDS issue was framed by Democrats and Republicans in the 1992 presidential campaign, particularly through the speeches of Elizabeth Glaser and

Mary Fisher during the nominating conventions. Both political parties minimized the potentially risky decision to feature HIV-seropositive speakers by highlighting the voices of wealthy, White, heterosexual mothers.

THE DEMOCRATIC NATIONAL CONVENTION

The 1992 campaign was dominated by a single issue—the economy. Voters attributed slow growth rates and astronomical deficits to 12 years of Republican leadership. Incumbent President George Bush failed to inspire fiscal confidence; voters did not find his economic plans credible. In short, Bush was trapped by the lackluster performance of the economy (Fineman & McDaniel, 1992). With the fading Soviet threat, there was no outside threat to divert public attention from domestic stagnation. Democrats linked the sluggish economy with feelings of alienation and disenfranchisement, voicing those feelings symbolically as outsiders (Dunham & Garland, 1992).

The Democratic convention was held in Madison Square Garden, and planners scheduled convention events to attract television viewers. Cautious optimism prevailed, in spite of former California Governor Edmund G. (Jerry) Brown, Jr., who continued to withhold endorsement of Bill Clinton into the first day of the convention. There was also the nagging memory of Michael Dukakis' 17-point lead at the end of the 1988 convention that turned into an 8-point deficit by election day.

Throughout the primaries, Clinton trailed George Bush and Ross Perot in popularity, but prior to the convention Clinton managed to recast his party's platform and image to reflect a moderate approach, captured in the "new covenant." Early in the convention, Clinton avoided divisive splits in the party. His choice of Al Gore for vice president, for example, was unorthodox but very popular with delegates. Independent candidate Ross Perot's unexpected withdrawal from the race on July 16 gave fresh impetus to Clinton's campaign. During his acceptance speech, Clinton made an immediate and obvious bid for Perot voters. By the conclusion of the convention, Clinton had taken the lead in every national opinion poll (Apple, 1992; Holmes, 1992; Ifill, 1992; Toner, 1992).

Among the top three problems cited by voters in a Gallup poll as worsening during the Bush administration were crime (59%), health care (59%), and AIDS (58%) (Klein & McDaniel, 1992). The Democratic Party addressed all three concerns during the convention. And, although AIDS had long been an issue for gay activists, it had never been treated as a political issue during a national convention (Schmalz, 1992b).

Several factors influenced the discussion of AIDS as a political issue. First, the number of voters likely to be influenced by the discussion of AIDS favored the Democrats, who were most apt to gain minority constituencies by introducing it. Whereas approximately 38% to 40% of gay and lesbian voters described themselves as Republican, most others were aligned with the Democratic Party (Duignan-Cabrera, 1992). However, married people with children were 57% of the electorate. They were more conservative, especially on values issues like gay rights and pornography (*McLaughlin Group*, 1992). As a result, placing AIDS on the political agenda was a risk calculated to court minority constituencies favoring more attention to the disease, but at the same time potentially offending the conservative or independent voter.

In addition, the antigay rhetoric of the primary season, particularly from Republican candidate Pat Buchanan, probably constrained the endorsement of gay issues. Buchanan's strong rhetoric certainly influenced the Republican primaries and undoubtedly carried over into the general campaign after the conventions. During the primaries, for instance, Buchanan indicted Bush's morality via the issue of gay pornography. One Buchanan ad showed a film clip of gay African-American men dancing together. In spite of protests from "good people," the narrator concluded, Bush funded such pornographic art (Fineman, 1992). The political dilemma, faced immediately by GOP candidates in the primaries and eventually by Clinton in the general election, was that the campaign must become more conservative to answer Buchanan's challenge but avoid alienating voters, especially women, in the process.

Finally, within the Democratic Party, gay advocates were divided over the priority of issues. Some factions accused gay leaders of neglecting AIDS in favor of a broader political agenda, including equal job opportunities, the rights of homosexual couples to marry or adopt children, and tolerance of gays in the military (Rogers, 1994). And, increasingly vocal protests came from opponents who claimed diseases like cancer, heart disease, and diabetes were neglected because of increased allocations for AIDS research (Cowley & Hager, 1993; Krauthammer, 1990).

In response to these concerns, the Democratic Convention was orchestrated to appeal primarily to a collage of groups—women, the middle class, African Americans, and others who felt disenfranchised. Overall, the Democrats depicted themselves as the party of change and "painted their nominee as a son of the poor with middle-class values and a world-class vision" (Shribman & Noah, 1992, p. A16). Columnist Gwen Ifill (1992) summarized the thrust of Clinton's image making during the Democratic convention: "He sought to portray himself as a man who completely identifies with the concerns of people who have felt neglected and burdened" (p. A10).

The results of the Democratic convention were immediate and impressive. Clinton had established a strong lead in the polls, scoring a 51% approval rating, compared to 36% for Bush (Clymer, 1992). Although Bush threatened Clinton's lead in the polls with immediate gains from the GOP convention, those gains evaporated within days. Bush stalled at approximately 17 points down in the polls. The economy remained the top concern for voters, followed closely by health care and crime. AIDS crystallized questions about access and affordability in the health care debate.

Elizabeth Glaser's Speech

Elizabeth Glaser and Bob Hattoy were the first openly HIV-infected speakers to address a national political convention. The issue of whether Glaser or Hattoy represented AIDS accurately was raised even before they took the rostrum. Hattoy, an environmentalist, was dismissed almost immediately by Republicans and the press because he was a member of the Clinton campaign staff. New York gay rights leader Thomas B. Stoddard commented, "She's a celebrity, and he's a campaign worker. It's a false image of AIDS. . . . These people are well-to-do with access to the best health care. The true nature of HIV is the lack of basic health care that tens of thousands of individuals must confront by nature of poverty and other conditions" (Schmalz, 1992b, p. A10).

Glaser's message was more effective than Hattoy's for the general public, partially because she was a political outsider. She was invited to speak only after confronting Mickey Kantor, Clinton's campaign chairman, convincing him that she had something to say. In addition, Glaser was less stigmatized: "That she was the wife of a TV star and got AIDS 'innocently'— through a blood transfusion—made her presence palatable to politicians and others who had shunned other AIDS activists" (Levy, 1994, p. 4D).

Glaser's (1992) message featured children, a theme that everyone could endorse. Her role as cofounder of the Pediatric AIDS Foundation in memory of her daughter Ariel strengthened her acceptance. Glaser's account framed the speech—she began with the story of how she contracted the disease through a blood transfusion during childbirth and then gave it to her two children. Glaser ended with the description of her daughter's death.[1]

This personal narrative functioned in two ways. First, it heightened emotions by personalizing the issue. Glaser embodied the effects of the illness. She was living testimony of the urgency of the issue because she was in a "race with the clock." Access to the finest health care did not save Ariel and probably would not save either Glaser or her son. Even Orrin Hatch, conservative Republican senator from Utah, said, "I never really centered on the fact there were a significant number of children who suffered. She brought that home to me" (Levy, 1994, p. 4D). The impact of AIDS on the Glaser family embraced mainstream Americans.

Glaser's personal story also served as a way for her to describe her emotions and suggested, by implication from the example set by her daughter, the response required of her listeners: "My daughter lived seven years, and in her last year, when she couldn't walk or talk, her wisdom shone through. She taught me to love when all I wanted to do was hate. She taught me to help others, when all I wanted to do was help myself. She taught me to be brave, when all I felt was fear." Wisdom, love, help, and bravery were the qualities Glaser endorsed through her narrative. Because these virtues are accepted as fundamentally Christian, Glaser would not offend her most conservative listeners. The narrative also identified her subtly with traditional values through motherhood and reinforced her role as an "innocent" victim of the disease.

If the Glaser family had been devastated by AIDS, the implicit message was that anyone could get it. Their story made HIV and AIDS everyone's problem. In this way, narratives are fundamental in framing the experience of those discriminated against because they give voice to those who have been silenced (Eckart, 1993).

Although Glaser included everyone in the threat, she excluded the Republican administration as the answer. Through the story of her naive attempts to get answers on Capitol Hill, she illustrated the lack of response from Republicans. In spite of two commission reports, Bush had failed to take action, leading Glaser to conclude, ". . . words and ideas are not enough." Thus, Glaser's story became political. As an outsider, she blamed the spread of the disease on inaction in the Bush administration.

In particular, Glaser echoed the Democratic agenda as she focused on the economic aspects of her disease. She transformed her personal story into an economic issue with the question: "Do you know how much my AIDS care costs? Over $40,000 a year. Someone without insurance can't afford this." Ultimately, Glaser asked for the restoration of faith in an America where everyone counts and everyone has access to health care. Her argument rested on the concept of individual opportunity fundamental to the American dream. Her case was a foil for another political objective—namely the election of Democratic candidates; she asked for a partnership of President and Congress to end gridlock on health care for AIDS patients. They offered honesty and accountability, which she contrasted sharply with the current administration: "When anyone tells President Bush that the battle against AIDS is seriously underfunded, he juggles the numbers to mislead the public into thinking we're spending twice as much as we really are." She concluded by mocking Bush's "thousand points of light," which had failed to illuminate her house.

The Response to Glaser's Speech. For the most part, the Democratic national convention was "dull and tedious, devoid of high drama and excitement; 96 hours of speeches hardly anyone listened to" (Queenan, 1992, p. 16). Even so, there were occasional moments of

---

[1]All references to the speech are transcribed by the first author from the televised broadcast of the convention, cited as Glaser (1992).

inspiration and excitement. Elizabeth Glaser's speech was rated among the highlights of the convention (Elving, 1992). Kennedy (1994) wrote, "Thousands of delegates, dignitaries and guests stood frozen in place at the Democratic national convention in New York City as she told of the death of her 7-year-old daughter, Ariel, in 1988 from AIDS" (p. B11). Others, including Clinton, were visibly overcome by Glaser's story (Gallen, 1994).

Although there was some disagreement over the priority of the AIDS issue, Glaser "spoke to a converted audience, many of whom wore the red ribbons that symbolize sympathy with sufferers of AIDS" ("Teaching Mercy," 1992, p. A20). Differences on the AIDS issue were subsumed by a general atmosphere of sympathy. In addition, delegates to the Democratic convention were united by the common goal of ending 12 years of Republican leadership.

THE REPUBLICAN CONVENTION

In the wake of the Democratic convention bounce, Republicans were hard pressed to produce a suitable response at their August convention in Houston. Under pressure to acknowledge AIDS, the GOP turned to Mary Fisher, Elizabeth Glaser's perfect clone.

The speaking situation Fisher encountered in Houston was far from ideal (Kaminski, 1992). Not only had the Republican Party sidestepped the AIDS issue over the years (Kosterlitz, 1992), but three major factors compounded the rhetorical problems she faced. First, a conservative, "Christian" faction of the party helped to shape the party platform. Unlike 1988, individuals representing gay rights issues were not allowed to address the Republican platform committee (Schmalz, 1992a). Although the 1992 platform called for "a national response to AIDS 'shaped by compassion,' " opposed to " 'any discrimination against Americans who are its victims' " (Doherty, 1992), it rejected "some of the basic recommendations of many public health experts" (Kosterlitz, 1992, p. 1935). Conservatives prevailed in disputes over platform planks on gay rights and abortion questions (Schmalz, 1992a), and religious conservatives insisted that (a) specific language in the platform make it clear that syringe and condom distribution would not cure AIDS; (b) AIDS should be described as similar to "any other sexually transmitted disease," rather than a disease like cancer or heart disease (Doherty, 1992); and (c) AIDS education should stress "marital fidelity, abstinence, and a drug-free lifestyle" (Kosterlitz, 1992, p. 1935). In short, the platform reached out to the far right, making AIDS a moral issue, not a health care crisis.

Second, Fisher addressed a largely unsympathetic audience. One commentary described the audience as "delegates from the religious right who were likely to view AIDS in terms of sin and to Republican operatives who were prepared to exploit anti-gay and anti-AIDS hysteria for political gain" ("Teaching Mercy," 1992, p. A20). Whereas Elizabeth Glaser addressed a sea of red-ribboned delegates, sympathetic to AIDS, the only AIDS ribbon Fisher would see was worn by Betty Ford, wife of the former president ("Teaching Mercy," 1992).

Third, the scheduling of speakers stood in stark contrast to Fisher's desire to reach out to all Americans. The convention began with a prime-time invective from primary candidate Patrick Buchanan. Fisher was preceded by First Lady Barbara Bush, who emphasized the importance of family, but would be followed by a highly partisan, profamily, anti-Democrat speech by Marilyn Quayle, wife of the vice president (Grady, 1992). Because of the convention's mixed messages, several media commentators would term the entire week "ironic" (Richmond, 1992).

In spite of their invitation for Fisher to speak, delegates to the Republican convention were in no mood to hear her message. The Republican Party platform, a largely unsympathetic audience, and the clashing messages of other speakers isolated Fisher.

Mary Fisher's Speech

As a result of these obstacles, Fisher attempted a delicate balance as she sought to share her message about AIDS while supporting the Republican candidate, George Bush. Like Glaser, Fisher (1992) relied on her compelling personal story to frame her appeal (Doherty, 1992). The first half of Fisher's message asserted the common struggle of all AIDS victims. Through no fault of her own, Fisher "contracted this disease in marriage"[2] after her husband purportedly became infected with the virus by sharing drug injection needles (Randall, 1992; Thomas, 1992). She alluded to her marriage and omitted the circumstances of her husband's infection, identifying families—men, women, parents, and children—as victims.

In the last part of her address, Fisher sounded the clarion call in the fight against AIDS. Knowing that she probably would die of the disease, she implicitly invited her audience to think about when "our children will be grown." Assuming an almost prophetic voice, she related, "I want my children to know that their mother was not a victim. She was a messenger." In this way, her focus moved from present to future. By naming herself a messenger, she also assumed a prophetic tone that allowed her to envision the future as in this admonition: "Learn with me the lessons of history and of grace, so my children will not be afraid to say the word AIDS when I am gone. Then their children, and yours, may not need to whisper it at all." As she moved from present to future, Fisher transcended her unique position as a White mother with AIDS to include all her listeners as real or potential victims. Fisher's focus on children and family also blended with the Republican convention theme.

Fisher's desire to tailor the AIDS issue to the requirements of her party created her greatest rhetorical difficulties. She needed to back the conservative agenda, minimize partisanship, and support Bush in the process. She attempted to overcome the resistance to her message and juggle these challenges through three strategies.

First, she asserted her similarity to other victims, suggesting that all human beings are targets for the disease. In this way she established that the disease does not discriminate: "[The AIDS virus] does not ask whether you are Black or White, male or female, gay or straight, young or old." In this strategy she shifted the focus of blame to the virus: "The AIDS virus is not a political creature. It does not care whether you are Democrat or Republican." With this refocusing, Fisher concluded that because AIDS could affect anyone, AIDS therefore was a public responsibility. This strategy effectively made AIDS the menace and removed any onus from the Republican Party. Because the threat was now external, the Republican Party could unite against it. With this strategy, Fisher transcended internal party squabbles and focused her listeners on a common enemy.

Finally, Fisher challenged her listeners to respond to the disease with humanity by asking them "to lift the shroud of silence which has been draped over the issue of HIV/AIDS." Fisher cited George and Barbara Bush's compassion and affection for her and her parents, and asked her audience to feel the same charity toward all AIDS victims. Fisher ended the argument with an overarching challenge: "We may take refuge in our stereotypes, but we cannot hide there long. Because HIV asks only one thing of those it attacks: Are you human?" With this personification of the AIDS virus as the external enemy, Fisher reasserted the connection of all her listeners as part of the human family.

In her only direct partisan appeal, predictably, Fisher avoided criticism of the Bush administration and comparisons between Bush and Clinton (Randall, 1992; Schmalz, 1992c). In the middle of her address, Fisher joined politics and family implicitly by making Bush the

---

[2]This and all subsequent references to the speech are taken from the televised broadcast of the convention, cited as Fisher (1992).

symbolic patriarch. She praised his quiet leadership in which "much good has been done; much of the good has gone unheralded." In addition, Fisher deflected criticism and united the audience against the threat of the external enemy when she said: "We do the President's cause no good if we praise the American family but ignore a virus that destroys it." With this statement, the argument came full circle. The values of family were tied directly to the cause Fisher endorsed. A listener could not reject the AIDS victim without also rejecting the family.

Fisher's appeals to children and family reached out to all Americans and asked them to take action: "We must be consistent if we are to be believed. We cannot love justice and ignore prejudice, love our children and fear to teach them." By setting up AIDS as the enemy of the family and challenging her audience to fight this threat, Fisher appealed not only to AIDS victims but to all humanity. For her Republican audience, however, her challenge to stereotypes likely posed the greatest threat (Schellenberg, Keil, & Bem, 1995). As a Republican mother with AIDS, she advised them not to look at people with HIV as outcasts or victims but as human beings "worthy of compassion."

Response to Fisher's Speech. As a representative of all AIDS victims, how effective Fisher would be as a convention speaker remained an open question. The tensions Mary Fisher balanced among the Republican right, AIDS activists, and Bush backers revealed the irony media commentators found throughout the convention. Although many listeners were moved by the ideals expressed in her speech, the seemingly subdued efforts to maintain her identity as a Republican worked to undermine them. The very access her party provided to her served to contradict Fisher's attempts to align herself with "typical" people living with HIV and AIDS: "With her shoulder-length blond hair styled just so and wearing a dark-blue pantsuit with white blouse and pearl earrings, Ms. Fisher is right out of Republican central casting: the Muffy-Buffy-Jody look writ expensive" (Schmalz, 1992c, p. A10). Even references to her family implicitly reminded insiders that she was as much a representative of the Republican Party as of AIDS activists. Her father, Max Fisher, reputedly worth hundreds of millions of dollars, was a major fundraiser for the Republican Party since the days of Richard Nixon. Fisher herself served in the Ford administration. In short, Fisher was "caught between the worlds of Republican politics and AIDS activism, both of them at times uneasy about her" (Schmalz, 1992c, p. A10).

Reactions to Fisher's speech were fairly positive (e.g., "Teaching Mercy," 1992). June Osborn, chairperson of the National Commission on AIDS, contended, "Atypical patients can break through the walls of racism and bigotry that keeps 'others' from being heard by middle America" (Trafford, 1992, p. Z6). Some AIDS activists, in contrast, saw Fisher being "used as the AIDS poster girl by a party that they believe has done little to fight the disease or provide moral leadership" (Schmalz, 1992c, p. A10). Confronting complex circumstances, Fisher would negotiate her identity as an AIDS victim as she had done in previous situations—with a fundamental paradox. But, as a *Washington Post* editorial asserted, "Regardless of politics, Fisher's message hits home" (Trafford, 1992, p. Z6). She spoke on behalf of AIDS victims while pointing out that she was not "the typical face of AIDS" (Schmalz, 1992c, p. A10).

COMPARISON OF THE TWO SPEAKERS

It can be argued that AIDS became an issue in the 1992 presidential campaign during the primaries when GOP candidate Pat Buchanan forced the Republican Party to acknowledge the extreme right. He defined issues such as AIDS in moral terms to frame his political position. Bush and other primary candidates responded by moving to the right. Because of this, Clinton could raise the AIDS issue during the Democratic convention to illustrate the narrowed boundaries of the Republican Party.

Phillip Wander (1996) posited that "politics begins with rhetoric, what is being said, who is saying it, and for whom" (p. 15). So it was with the AIDS issue. The Democratic Party chose Elizabeth Glaser, an HIV-infected mother, to illustrate, both literally and symbolically, the exclusion of AIDS victims during a Republican administration. The Republicans, in turn, were forced to respond or to look even more uncaring than they were portrayed. The result was an invitation to Mary Fisher to address the Republican convention.

Both speakers sidestepped the traditional association of AIDS with sexual morality, thereby minimizing the stigma accompanying the disease for mainstream Americans and limiting the appearance of an endorsement on the part of their party. Glaser tied the question of AIDS to the Democratic attacks on the economy by raising the problem of access to health care for all AIDS patients, not just the wealthy and well insured. Because of Republican hostility, Fisher developed a more abstract dichotomy, pitting her listeners against the disease, which she personified as an external enemy.

Additional comparisons between the speakers can be made in both content of the speeches and the style of development. First, both speakers asserted that they did not represent political parties, but rather, universal human interests. They claimed to include everyone by endorsing fundamental human values. Although both speakers claimed to be apolitical, they were ultimately both partisan.

Glaser was obvious in her indictment of the Republicans for their lack of leadership. She blamed the Republicans, in particular the Bush administration, for failing to stem the AIDS epidemic. Fisher was more oblique, focusing on the President Bush's support for her and her family, rather on the actions of her party. She transcended the immediate political environment to link the AIDS issue to the need for solutions. Both speakers solicited change: Glaser sought to replace Republican leaders with Democrats; Fisher requested changes in attitudes that would dissolve barriers and stereotypes (Seabrook, 1992).

Both speakers functioned as sources of maternal strength and knowledge, albeit in different ways. Glaser related that her daughter Ariel taught her how to confront death; Fisher acted as the source of knowledge, relaying the hope that her sons (and, potentially others) would learn from her. These differences in the maternal voice set up the individual style of each speech. Glaser's speech was highly narrative; she related what she had learned through the events of her life. Fisher advanced her argument in a propositional format, associating the details of her experience with the lessons to be learned.

AFTERMATH

During the final days of the campaign, Magic Johnson, named by President Bush to a post on the National Commission on AIDS, sent a stinging letter of resignation and voiced his public support for Governor Clinton. Fisher replaced Johnson on the Commission, continuing to represent AIDS victims on a political level. Elizabeth Glaser died of complications from AIDS on December 4, 1994. She was memorialized along with Ron Brown and others at the 1996 Democratic convention. To date, Mary Fisher remains active in various causes.

During the years following the 1992 presidential campaign, the AIDS issue has become normalized. The role of the AIDS victim has evolved into a cameo alongside representatives of other causes—Sarah and Jim Brady for gun control, Christopher Reeve for spinal cord injuries, and Carolyn Mosley-Braun for African-American women. During the 1996 Democratic and Republican conventions, each cause was showcased through representative speakers. Fisher again spoke on behalf of AIDS.

In the years following the 1992 election, the visibility and number of AIDS activists in Washington have increased (Rogers, 1994). The federal government has addressed the issue primarily through funding and recognition of AIDS related problems such as employment discrimination and military service of HIV-infected personnel.

The response of the Clinton administration has varied. On the one hand, there has been strong support for budgetary increases in AIDS research spending even in a period of fiscal restraint. On the other hand, however, many would argue that recognition of the human cost of AIDS has often been neglected. Clinton has been confronted on numerous related issues such as protection of Medicaid benefits for people with full-blown AIDS, needle-exchange programs, and a greater leadership role in the fight against the epidemic. He has been criticized on occasion for the lack of progress on AIDS. The frustration that has built in recent years has led critics to label presidential actions "political theatre" (Dunlap, 1995, p. A14).

Although there has been increased dialogue about AIDS, mainstream Americans continue to confront it as the story of personal lives—acceptable on a case-by-case basis as we encounter individuals struggling with the disease. The framework set by the personal narratives of Glaser and Fisher in 1992 persists as we confront individual tragedies rather than a public epidemic. The limitations of dealing with AIDS on such a basis was addressed by Fabj and Sobnosky (1995), who claimed: "AIDS is often addressed as a personal issue. . . . AIDS activists, however, seek to make AIDS policy a topic for public deliberation" (p. 165). They seek to extend the debate into the public sphere, making it a policy issue rather than a private, moral problem. However, public commitment may be illusive, because that would require recognition of everyone's responsibility for stemming a disease that has, so far, been blamed on its victims. The point was best summarized by Susan Sontag (1988): "Every feared epidemic disease, but especially those associated with sexual license, generates a preoccupying distinction between the disease's putative carriers . . . and those defined—health professionals and other bureaucrats do the defining—as the general population" (p. 27).

In the aftermath of the 1992 presidential campaign, AIDS has become "normalized." That is, it no longer inspires frantic activity or reaction. Writing about AIDS, journalist Jeffrey Schmalz (1993) concluded, "It is at once everywhere and nowhere, the leading cause of death among young men nationwide, but little threat to the core of American political power, the white heterosexual suburbanite" (p. 58). To the extent that the dialogue about AIDS has moved from limited communities into the mainstream, spokespersons like Glaser and Fisher have helped to normalize the disease. However, the very fact that they are wealthy, White, heterosexual mothers encourages us to ignore those who have been stigmatized and those who still bear the brunt of the epidemic.

REFERENCES

Altman, D. (1987). *AIDS in the mind of America*. Garden City, NY: Anchor.

Apple, R. W. (1992, July 17). A candidate, and a race, transformed. *The New York Times*, p. A1.

Clymer, A. (1992, August 26). Bush's gains from convention nearly evaporate in latest poll. *The New York Times*, pp. A1, A13.

Cowley, G., & Hager, M. (1993, August 9). The politics of the plague. *Newsweek*, p. 62.

Doherty, R. (1992, August 19). Like Democrats, Republicans put AIDS in prime time. *The Reuter Library Report* [On-line]. Available: Nexis

Duignan-Cabrera, A. (1992, August 24). Gay GOPs: The enemy within. *Newsweek*, p. 43.

Dunham, R. S., & Garland, S. B. (1992, October 26). The year of the woman—Really. *Business Week*, pp. 106–107.

Dunlap, D. W. (1995, December 7). A plea to Clinton to lead US efforts against AIDS. *The New York Times*, p. A14.

Eckart, D. R. (1993). Discrimination, feminist narratives, and policy arguments. *Women & Politics, 13*, 19–37.

Elving, R. D. (1992, July 25). Political conventions: Time for them to go? *Congressional Quarterly Weekly Report, 50*, 2238.

Fabj, V., & Sobnosky, M. J. (1995). AIDS activism and the rejuvenation of the public sphere. *Argumentation and Advocacy, 31*, 163–184.

Fineman, H. (1992, March 9). Nasty as they wanna be. *Newsweek*, pp. 32–34.

Fineman, H., & McDaniel, A. (1992, August 31). Bush: What bounce? *Newsweek*, pp. 26–31.

Fisher, M. (1992, August 19). *Convention address on AIDS*. West Lafayette, IN: Purdue University Public Affairs Video Archives.

Gallen, D. (1994). *Bill Clinton: Those who know him*. New York: Richard Gallen.

Glaser, E. (1992, July 14). *National AIDS policy address*. West Lafayette, IN: Purdue University Public Affairs Video Archives.

Grady, S. (1992, August 24). Ladies' night saved Bush's convention [Editorial]. *The Record*, p. A11.

Holmes, S. A. (1992, July 17). Perot says Democratic surge reduced prospect of victory. *The New York Times*, p. A1.

Ifill, G. (1992, July 17). Democratic team opens by appealing to middle class. *The New York Times*, pp. A1, A10.

Johnson, J. (1988, December 2). Bush is urged to be a leader in the fight on AIDS. *The New York Times*, p. A9.

Juhasz, A. (1990). The contained threat: Women in mainstream AIDS documentary. *Journal of Sex Research, 27*, 25–46.

Kaminski, M. (1992, August 21). AIDS forces party to confront its contradictions: Republican Party convention in Houston. *The Financial Times*, p. 5.

Kennedy, R. (1994, December 5). Elizabeth Glaser dies at 47: Crusader for pediatric AIDS. *The New York Times*, p. B11.

Klein, J., & McDaniel, A. (1992, August 24). What went wrong. *Newsweek*, pp. 22–25.

Kosterlitz, J. (1992, August 22). The GOP's wake-up call on AIDS. *The National Journal*, p. 1935.

Krauthammer, C. (1990, June 25). AIDS: Getting more than its share? *Time*, p. 80.

Levy, D. (1994, December 5). AIDS activist Glaser was a voice for children. *USA Today*, p. 4D.

McLaughlin Group on Campaign '92. (1992). New York: Cistems.

Queenan, J. (1992, July 20). Stalking the wild Democrats. *Barron's*, pp. 16–18.

Randall, G. (Anchor). (1992, August 13). How crucial is political support in the AIDS fight? In *Inside politics* [On-line]. Newport Beach, VA: Cable News Network. Available: Nexis

Richmond, R. (1992, August 20). Family-values theme "ironic" to several TV commentators. *The Orange County Register*, p. A6.

Rogers, P. (1994, September 19). Surviving the second wave. *Newsweek*, pp. 50–51.

Schellenberg, G. E., Keil, J. M., & Bem, S. L. (1995). Innocent victims of AIDS: Identifying the subtext. *Journal of Applied Social Psychology, 25*, 1790–1800.

Schmalz, J. (1992a, August 16). AIDS test. *The New York Times*, pp. A1, A9.

Schmalz, J. (1992b, August 20). A delicate balance: The gay vote; gay rights and AIDS emerging as divisive issues in campaign. *The New York Times*, pp. A1, A10.

Schmalz, J. (1992c, July 14). Two speak as one: Those with AIDS reach for constituency. *The New York Times*, p. A10.

Schmalz, J. (1993, November 28). Whatever happened to AIDS? *The New York Times Magazine*, pp. 56–61, 81, 85.

Seabrook, C. (1992, August 19). Conventions paint a distorted picture of AIDS patients: Stories of poor, black, Hispanic victims go untold. *The Atlanta Journal and Constitution*, p. A8.

Shribman, D., & Noah, T. (1992, July 14). New challenges hit Democrats at convention. *The Wall Street Journal*, p. A16.

Simons, M. (1996, June 7). HIV virus still spreading rapidly, UN says. *The New York Times*, p. A3.

Sontag, S. (1988). *AIDS and its metaphors*. New York: Farrar, Strauss & Giroux.

Teaching mercy to Republicans. (1992, August 22). [Editorial]. *The New York Times*, p. A20.

Thomas, C. (1992, August 28). What Mary Fisher didn't say about AIDS [Editorial]. *St. Louis Post-Dispatch*, p. 3C.

Toner, R. (1992, July 17). Withdrawal by independent follows campaign turmoil. *The New York Times*, p. A1.

Trafford, A. (1992, August 25). Messengers on AIDS. *The Washington Post*, p. Z6.

Wander, P. (1996). Marxism, post-colonialism, and rhetorical contextualization. *Quarterly Journal of Speech, 82*, 402–435.

From Hope to Heartbreak:
Bill Clinton and the Rhetoric of AIDS

Mitchell S. McKinney
Bryan G. Pepper
University of Oklahoma

In December of 1992, as part of the World AIDS Day observance, thousands of citizens in Los Angeles signed a giant card that was sent to the recently elected U.S. president, Bill Clinton. One message for the new president, from Robert, pleaded, "We have lost too many lives, too many years to AIDS while the White House has sat and done nothing. You are our hope" (Boxall, 1992, p. B3). One year later, in December of 1993, President Clinton addressed an audience of health care providers on World AIDS Day at Georgetown University Medical School. During his speech, the president received yet another message from a concerned citizen. As the president spoke, a "finger-pointing protester" (Friedman, 1993, p. A1) shouted, "Look at your record, Bill—one year, no results. The Manhattan Project on AIDS that you promised during the campaign—where is it? Thirty recommendations of George Bush's Commission on AIDS you promised to get implemented during your campaign. Where are they? One year. Slick Willie. The Republicans were right. We should have never trusted you!"

These messages, from hope to heartbreak, characterize the range of responses to Bill Clinton's presidential leadership on AIDS. Indeed, as candidate Clinton in 1992 openly sought their support, gay men and lesbians for the first time in the history of presidential elections became "major players" in the national political process. Jeffrey Schmalz (1992), describing the emergent status of gay politics, concluded that the gay community had been "scared into action by AIDS, drawing on lessons of AIDS organizing and fund raising . . . they have learned how to play the [political] game" (p. 29). Whereas candidates in presidential contests have competed for such titles as the "environmental president," or the ever-popular "education president," not until the candidacy of Bill Clinton in 1992 had one sought to be recognized as our "AIDS president."

Bill Clinton campaigned for such recognition by assuring voters that one of the very reasons he wanted to become president was to do something about AIDS. During the first presidential debate of the 1992 campaign, Governor Clinton declared to his national audience, "I'm proud of the leadership I'm going to bring to this country in dealing with the AIDS crisis" ("Transcript of First TV Debate," 1992, p. A14). Candidate Clinton's commitment to AIDS was even more determined when speaking to gay and lesbian audiences. At a Los Angeles rally, for example, Clinton stated, "If I could wave my arm and make HIV-positive go away and all of you that have it, I would, so help me God I would, and I'd give up my race for the White House for that" (in Maraniss, 1992, p. A1). Clinton's response to Bob

Rafsky, a member of the AIDS activism group ACT-UP, is representative of the expectations created during Clinton's initial campaign for the presidency. During Governor Clinton's address to a predominantly gay audience at a New York nightclub, Mr. Rafsky vigorously asserted, "Bill, we're not dying of AIDS as much as we are from 11 years of government neglect." The empathetic Clinton replied: "And that's why I'm running for President, to do something about it. I'll tell you what I'll do, I'll tell you what I'd do. First of all I would not just talk about it in campaign speeches; it would become a part of my *obsession* as President . . . I feel your pain, I feel your pain" ("Heckler Stirs Clinton Anger," 1992, p. A9).

Whereas Clinton actively sought the mantle of our first AIDS president, when measured by past presidents, such a standard would not be very difficult to achieve. This fact would provide President Clinton with an easy reply to those who questioned his commitment to addressing AIDS. Although some would charge that he was not doing nearly enough, Clinton would frequently argue that he was doing much more than any of his predecessors had ever attempted. Indeed, as Perez and Dionisopoulos (1995) explained, Ronald Reagan served almost two full terms before he ever publicly acknowledged that AIDS even existed. Much like his former boss, George Bush, too, had difficulty dealing with AIDS. In his bid for reelection, during the first 1992 presidential debate, President Bush had to explain the "wide-spread feeling that [his] administration [was] not doing enough about AIDS," and to explain why members of his own AIDS Commission, such as professional basketball star Magic Johnson, had quit due to the Bush administration's failure to act on Commission recommendations ("Transcript of First TV Debate," 1992, p. A13). George Bush's tepid commitment to AIDS was further illustrated at the 1992 Republican National Convention where former presidential candidate Patrick Buchanan was allowed to deliver a keynote address in which he demonized, among others, the "militant" and "amoral" homosexuals (McKinney, 1996, p. 146); and at the same gathering, Barbara Bush discreetly removed her red AIDS ribbon before joining President Bush on the podium (Schmalz, 1992). With such deathly silence characterizing the approach of the current and former presidents, those most directly affected desired a president willing to publicly acknowledge AIDS, and someone willing to provide strong leadership in directing our government's response. Bill Clinton offered himself as that man.

The purpose of this chapter is to analyze the performance of Bill Clinton as AIDS president. Specifically, this analysis utilizes a rhetorical model of presidential leadership and provides an exegesis of Clinton's rhetorical response to AIDS. Beyond providing a description of the frequency of presidential AIDS talk, this analysis examines the primary strategies Clinton used to construct AIDS as a political issue, as well as those strategies through which he attempted to distance himself from AIDS. In understanding Clinton's rhetorical construction of AIDS, we analyze his discourse by examining his interpretive logic, Clinton's notion of a "New Covenant" for the American people, and discuss the extent to which this covenant includes those with AIDS. Clearly, one can conclude that AIDS was not part of Ronald Reagan's or George Bush's American story, but what of our current president? Our primary goal in this chapter is to provide a better understanding of how AIDS, in Bill Clinton's America, is woven into our national dialogue.

ANALYZING PRESIDENTIAL AIDS TALK

The present analysis is chiefly concerned with how AIDS becomes part of our national dialogue through the communicative activity of President Bill Clinton. Such a focus of study implies two fundamental assumptions: first, that talk about AIDS matters; and that presidential talk, in particular, is important and worthy of analysis. Certainly, if one starts with an understanding that language shapes reality, we can conclude that our discourse about AIDS does influence our understanding of AIDS. Here, the work of Grover (1992) is instructive, in which she has analyzed the key terms that have been utilized in public discourse to describe AIDS. As she explained, "I saw more clearly the dimensions of the problems language created about AIDS. Media, medical, and government formulations about AIDS made life more complicated or stressful to my friends who were ill, to my students and my fellow activists" (p. 230). Our analysis of presidential AIDS talk is not to suggest that "the virus is just a discursive construction" (Grover, 1992, p. 238), but the ways in which we symbolically construct AIDS greatly influence how we understand and deal with the disease. Bateson and Goldsby (1988) wrote eloquently about the potential power of AIDS talk:

> If we were able, as a society, to talk openly about matters related to sex and to feel compassion equally for all our neighbors, the AIDS epidemic would probably be under control by now. Instead, we are in a situation where help has been withheld because of unstated ideas about who is and is not deserving, where essential information is not imparted to those who need it, and where many lack the trust and self-esteem needed to use the information available to them. The perennial problems of our society and of the world, which we have not had the resolution or imagination to address, are the principal sources of our vulnerability. (p. 122)

If talk about AIDS matters, then why might presidential discourse represent a significant source of AIDS talk? In addition to the direct influence that presidential persuasion can have on governmental actions in dealing with AIDS, the president is granted a privileged voice in our public or civic conversation. Several studies (e.g., Arno & Feiden, 1986; Joseph, 1992) have shown that AIDS and the people affected by the disease are most often marginalized in public discourse. The president, as "interpreter-in-chief" (Stuckey, 1991), can utilize the power of presidential talk to help people interpret the social and political realities of AIDS.

Once in office, Bill Clinton began to understand the power of his role as interpreter-in-chief, and specifically, the importance of including AIDS as part of his presidential narrative. In his 1993 World AIDS Day speech at Georgetown University Hospital, Clinton (1993d) confessed that his own efforts to give voice to the AIDS crisis had been largely inadequate and he pledged to do more:

> The theme of World AIDS Day is "Time To Act." The argument that Jeffrey Schmalz made in his article was that we also ought to talk more. And for those of us in positions of leadership, talking is acting; I have to tell you that one of the things that I underestimated when I became President was the actual power of the words coming from the bully pulpit of the White House to move the country. . . . But I do think sometimes all of us underestimate the power of our words to change the attitudes and the range of behavior of other people, not just me, but you, too. (p. 2488)

Ironically, this would be one of only two AIDS-specific addresses given by the president during his first 4 years in office.

METHODOLOGY

This study seeks to understand the AIDS talk of Bill Clinton during his first term as president. The primary data for analysis included the recorded public utterances of the president (as compiled in the *Weekly Compilation of Presidential Documents*) from January 20, 1993, through January 20, 1997, the period spanning the president's first and second inaugural addresses. In addition to the primary data, Clinton's 1992 campaign speeches were retrieved from the SUNSITE Internet archive; and finally, *The New York Times* transcripts and excerpts of selected addresses were used to supplement speeches and remarks found in the *Weekly Compilation.*

The fundamental unit of analysis in this study is the AIDS speech act, or instances in which Clinton spoke about AIDS.[1] These speech acts were classified as either primary or secondary. A primary AIDS speech act was an entire presidential address or announcement devoted exclusively to the discussion of AIDS. Secondary speech acts were those instances in which the topic of AIDS would be discussed by the president in a secondary manner, usually as a passing reference or when used as an example in an address, press conference, or announcement that dealt mostly with a topic other than AIDS. In identifying each speech act, researchers analyzed how AIDS was discussed, the audience to whom the address was made, and whether or not the president voluntarily initiated the discussion, or if his mention of AIDS was in response to a question asked by a citizen or journalist. Such classification and quantification of presidential AIDS talk is similar to Hart's (1987) method of analyzing speech acts (see also Smith, 1983, 1996). The following section reports our findings, followed by an interpretation of the president's rhetorical construction of AIDS based on his own interpretative logic.

FINDINGS

Candidate Clinton pledged in his 1992 campaign that he would "discuss the AIDS crisis with the American people early and often" ("Magic Johnson Talks," 1993, p. A6) and, as already noted, AIDS "would become part of [his] obsession as President" ("Heckler Stirs Clinton Anger," 1992, p. A9). How successful was the president in keeping such pledges? In total, Bill Clinton spoke publicly about AIDS on 99 occasions during his first 4 years in office. To interpret this figure, several factors must be taken into account. First, in nearly 25% of the instances in which Clinton addressed AIDS, it was not of his own initiation, but rather in response to a question posed by a citizen or reporter. Also, and perhaps most revealing, only 6 of these 99 instances of AIDS talk were substantive, or speech events devoted exclusively to discussion of AIDS. The remaining instances were very brief or passing references in which discussion of AIDS would be included in discourse dealing primarily with other topics.

Of his six substantive AIDS speech acts, only on *two* occasions during his first 4 years did the president deliver a full address devoted exclusively to the discussion of AIDS. First, in December of 1993 Clinton delivered an address on World AIDS Day at Georgetown University Medical Center (Clinton, 1993d); and then in December of 1995, the president spoke to an audience of AIDS activists and health care providers at the first-ever White House Conference on HIV and AIDS (Clinton, 1995d). His remaining four AIDS speech events were actually administrative functions that required the president to make specific AIDS remarks. These instances of AIDS talk include his remarks on June 25, 1993, when announcing the appointment of Kristine Gebbie as the first AIDS policy coordinator (Clinton, 1993e); remarks made the following year when announcing Gebbie's replacement, Patsy Fleming, as the second AIDS policy director (Clinton, 1994b); his brief comments in July of 1995 preceding the first meeting of the Presidential Advisory Council on HIV/AIDS (Clinton,

---

[1]Use of the term *speech act* in the present analysis—similar to the approach taken by Hart (1987) and Smith (1983, 1996)—refers to a presidential speech event, and is used to highlight the "performative" function of presidential discourse. Adapted from Austin's (1962) and Searle's (1969) notion of speech acts, Hart explained such a focus on the act of presidential speaking: "Broadening Austin's conception a bit, we can view all speeches as having performative aspects, especially if they are the speeches of the most powerful person in the land. When a president speaks, doing is almost always being done. By giving an inaugural address, a president makes himself president" (p. 45).

1995c); and finally, public comments in May of 1996 at a signing ceremony for the reauthorization of the Ryan White Care Act (Clinton, 1996b).

Of his six substantive discussions on AIDS, five took place within the confines of the White House (the World AIDS Day speech was also delivered in Washington, DC); and all six of these speech acts were with audiences consisting primarily of AIDS activists and health care providers. None of the six events received extensive media coverage. The president's Rose Garden announcement of Kristine Gebbie as our nation's first AIDS policy coordinator was broadcast live in midmorning by CNN, and the 1993 World AIDS Day address received most of its media coverage in "sound-bite" form due to a "protester" who interrupted the speech (Devroy, 1993). Here, it is important to note the extent to which the president seemingly ignored wider audiences when speaking in a substantive manner about AIDS.

During his campaign, in fact, Clinton was encouraged by gay activists to speak about AIDS with "non-traditional groups," defined as an audience not primarily gay or of activists directly involved with AIDS (Maraniss, 1992, p. A1). Also, as Clinton was entering office in 1992, the National Commission on AIDS, formed by the Bush administration, urged the president to take the lead in educating the public and to be willing to "discuss the AIDS crisis with the American people . . . Americans have heard almost no discussion of AIDS by our President during the first 12 years of the AIDS epidemic" ("Magic Johnson Talks," 1993, p. A6). Interestingly, even the president, when speaking to the "safe" groups most directly involved with AIDS, admonished, "Our task is to lift the visibility of this issue. . . . AIDS affects all Americans. . . . It really is a part of our common ground. I think we can attack this disease without attacking each other" (Clinton, 1995b, p. 1320). Although understanding that all Americans needed to know more about AIDS, apparently Bill Clinton was not willing to be that messenger. As our analysis discusses in greater detail, Clinton actually employed different rhetorical strategies when addressing the general public than when speaking to those most directly involved with or affected by AIDS.

SILENCE AND SURROGATES

Yet another way of analyzing Clinton's discourse that provides additional information about his speech acts is to examine the frequency of his AIDS talk throughout his first 4 years in office. Table 7.1 indicates the number of instances the president spoke publicly about AIDS during each year of his first term.

In analyzing these data, it is clear that Clinton, to the extent to which he did publicly address AIDS, was rather consistent across the 4 years, *except for the year 1995*. In 1995, we see that presidential talk about AIDS decreased 50%, when the other 3 years are averaged. What brought about this decrease in the frequency of AIDS talk? The notion of silence as political strategy (Brummett, 1980; Perez & Dionisopoulos, 1995) suggests that candidates

TABLE 7.1
Number of Times the President Spoke Publicly
About AIDS During Each Year of His First Term

Year	Number of AIDS Speech Acts
1993	30
1994	26
1995	14
1996	29

employ a strategy of calculated silence usually during a perceived crisis and for a specified time period. In President Clinton's case of AIDS silence in 1995, the perceived crisis most likely was the Republican takeover of the Congress in the fall of 1994.

Less than 1 month after the "Republican Revolution" in Congress, Clinton began implementing his strategic silence on AIDS. Unlike the major address on World AIDS Day he delivered in 1993, the president decided to mark the 1994 observance with a "secret" meeting at the White House with a small group of young people living with AIDS (Broder & Jackson, 1994). In fact, Clinton's only public words on World AIDS Day, 1994, were given in a Rose Garden ceremony involving the Joint Chiefs of Staff in which the president announced he would ask Congress for an additional $25 billion in military spending. Commenting on the president's actions, AIDS Action Council Director Christine Lubinski feared "that Clinton's response to the November elections would be fiscal infatuation with the military and diminished commitment to dealing with the AIDS epidemic" (Broder & Jackson, 1994, p. A9).

The next step in silencing AIDS talk in the Clinton administration came just a week following the president publicly ignoring World AIDS Day. This time, Surgeon General Elders, one of the president's chief AIDS surrogates, was too frank in her public discussion of AIDS prevention; due to her "inappropriate" views, Elders was asked to resign. On December 8, 1994, Elders addressed the United Nations World AIDS Day conference. Following her speech, she responded to a question regarding AIDS prevention and sex education: "As per your specific question in regard to masturbation, I think that is something that is part of human sexuality, and it's a part of something that perhaps should be taught" (Panetta, 1994, p. 2). In announcing Elders' resignation, White House Chief of Staff Leon Penetta stated the following day, "The President feels that's wrong, feels that it's not what schools are for, and it is not what the Surgeon General should say." Members of the press suggested that Elders' firing may have been influenced by the Republicans gaining control of the Congress, as one of the first questions asked following Panetta's statement was, "Would she have been fired before the election?" (Panetta, 1994, p. 3).

In assessing the appropriateness of Elders' views and the extent to which they deviated from the president's, it is interesting to note that in February of 1994, Clinton visited a junior high school and was asked by a teenager what the president could do about AIDS prevention. President Clinton (1994a) responded,

> Now, the only thing we know that works with regard to AIDS is not to get it. And we know that AIDS is spread primarily in two ways: because of drug users using unsafe needles and because of unsafe sex, primarily homosexual sex but not exclusively. Now, so what we're trying to do is to be honest, brutally honest about that, talk to young people, tell them that your life is on the line and the only safe way, the only way to avoid dying from AIDS that we know right now is not to get it. And that's the truth. (p. 201)

In considering the president's attempt at sex education, we see that he, like Elders suggested, found it necessary to discuss sex with schoolchildren while addressing AIDS prevention. Although the president claimed that these discussions needed "to be honest, brutally honest," apparently Elders' honesty was too much for the president and the new Republican-controlled Congress.

The president's discussion with the children at Kramer Junior High is instructive in yet another way. This response drew charges from activist groups that disagreed with Clinton's version of the "truth" about AIDS, arguing that the president was wrong to single out homosexual sex as a primary cause of AIDS. In her White House press briefing the day following this comment, Press Secretary Dee Dee Myers was asked to react to charges that the president "was spreading homophobia." Myers (1994) dismissed this notion by comment-ing: "I mean, clearly the President has been a strong supporter of doing more to fight AIDS and to fight the misperceptions about AIDS and to fight the fear about AIDS. And he'll continue to do that. That's why he appointed an AIDS Czar in Kristine Gebbie . . . He'll continue to fight the disease and work with the AIDS groups to do so" (p. 3).

Myers' comment illustrates yet another component of strategic silence, the use of surro-gates. Perez and Dionisopoulos (1995) explained that a prime tactic that allows a political leader to be strategically silent on a controversial issue is to depend on surrogates to do one's speaking. This tactic of strategic surrogate discourse was utilized in the Reagan presidency, in which the Secretary of Health and Human Services Margaret Heckler declared AIDS as "the No. 1 priority" of the administration, whereas President Reagan was unwilling to speak publicly about AIDS (Perez & Dionisopoulos, 1995, p. 20). Clinton, too, would often abdicate the power of his bully pulpit by deferring public discussion of AIDS to surrogates. The primary source of surrogate discourse in the Clinton administration came with the creation of the position of AIDS Policy Coordinator, the so-called "AIDS Czar."

In the 1992 campaign, one of the specific promises that candidate Clinton made was the creation of a new cabinet-level position to coordinate the federal government's efforts to combat AIDS (Foreman, 1993). Kristine M. Gebbie, a state public health administrator, was named the first White House AIDS Coordinator on June 25, 1993. Once Gebbie was named the first AIDS policy coordinator, the president would regularly use the existence of this position as an argument in defense of his commitment to fighting AIDS. For example, in Billings, Montana, at one of his frequent "town meetings," the president was faced with a citizen questioner who charged that he was not doing enough to fight AIDS. Clinton (1995a), following his usual line of defense, responded: "First of all, it's not true that I have made no major speeches about AIDS. I appointed the first AIDS czar the country ever had. . . . This administration has done far more on research and care and raising the visibility of the issue than anyone ever has" (p. 955).

The creation of an AIDS czar, as Krauthammer (1992) noted, provides the political leader with a handy administrative response for those problems that have no easy solutions. In short, czardom in the political process is a rhetorical strategy to suggest action: "When met with a problem that we have no idea how to solve, we endow someone with a title that implies absolute power and order him [sic] to start giving orders" (Krauthammer, 1992, p. A27). The notion of a powerful AIDS czar created great expectations during the campaign. Candidate Clinton, when making the pledge to appoint a czar, also called for a "Manhattan Project" on AIDS (Hilts, 1993b, p. A2). Invoking the intense project to develop the atomic bomb in World War II, our new AIDS czar would supposedly lead an urgent and focused government effort to find a cure for AIDS. Disillusionment with the AIDS czar and abandonment of the so-called Manhattan Project once taking office were primary criticisms of those who had high hopes that Bill Clinton would be their true AIDS president.

During this period of strategic presidential AIDS silence, the administration did employ several "political gestures" (Edelman, 1988, p. 24) as symbolic attempts to improve relations with the now-alienated homosexual and AIDS constituencies. For many reasons, this once supportive group of supporters was no longer solidly behind the president who had previously "felt their pain." Beginning with the administration's handling of the gays in the military issue (Bostdorff, 1996), alienation continued to build with disillusionment regarding the role of the AIDS czar, the seeming abandonment of the grand AIDS Manhattan Project, the firing of Jocelyn Elders, and the administration's refusal to oppose a Colorado constitutional amendment that sought to ban civil rights protections for homosexuals (Dunlap, 1995b). The Clinton administration realized the need to repair relations with the disaffected gay and lesbian community, and its first move was to develop yet another presidential surrogate. In June of 1995, the first-ever White House Liaison for Gay and Lesbian Issues was created. Upon accepting her new position at a White House meeting with gay and lesbian activists—a meeting the president did not attend—Marsha Scott alluded to Clinton's noticeable silence: "I know some of you think many of us in the Administration have lost our voice . . . but the voice is coming back" (Dunlap, 1995b, p. B7).

The very same week in which the new liaison was announced, the White House was going all out with its political gestures to show that the Clinton administration had not forgotten AIDS or gay and lesbian concerns. The day following the announcement of the new liaison, a White House briefing with elected gay officials was held; the very next day, the administration announced the creation of a Presidential Advisory Council on HIV/AIDS. At each of these events, due to Clinton's conspicuous absence, it was left to his surrogates to defend the administration's commitment to fighting AIDS. Ironically, at the briefing for gay elected officials, attendees were greeted by White House Secret Service guards wearing protective rubber gloves fearing "the risk of infection from HIV" (Dunlap, 1995a, p. A22).

As Brummett's (1980) notion of strategic silence suggests, the silence usually lasts for a specified period. Bill Clinton did in 1996, at long last, regain his voice and willingness to publicly address AIDS. In reviewing his total 1996 AIDS talk, it is clear that the breaking of Clinton's silence was necessitated by his reelection campaign. Indeed, 22 of the 29 AIDS speech acts during this year occurred in campaign-related addresses in which the president attempted to persuade his audience that he deserved another 4 years to continue fighting AIDS. Here, his message was constructed in two primary ways. First, his commitment to AIDS should be measured largely, he argued, by his efforts to increase funding for research; and, second, this increase in funding facilitated the development of new drugs that would prolong the life of those living with HIV/AIDS. Such a construction of AIDS allowed the president to directly link his actions to the recent advancements in the treatment of AIDS, while also speaking of the virus in a hopeful manner. In his acceptance speech at the Democratic National Convention, Clinton delivered what represents his standard AIDS "speech module" (Trent & Friedenberg, 1995, p. 156) used throughout the campaign: "We have increased our investments in research and technology . . . more rapid development of drugs to deal with HIV and AIDS and moving them to the market quicker have [sic] almost doubled life expectancy in only four years. And we are looking at no limit in sight to that. We'll keep going until normal life is returned to people who deal with this" (Clinton, 1996a, p. 1578).

CLINTON'S CONSTRUCTION OF AIDS

Whereas Bill Clinton's AIDS talk during his reelection campaign focused on increased funding for the development for new AIDS treatments, what other ways did he discuss or construct AIDS? Perhaps the most significant approach to analyzing Clinton's AIDS talk is to examine the various ways in which he included AIDS in his national narrative. This section offers a general description of the rhetorical strategies Bill Clinton used to construct AIDS as a political issue. The final section of this chapter then explains how his primary construction of AIDS fits within his interpretive logic, the notion of a New Covenant for the American people, and discuss the extent to which this covenant includes those citizens with AIDS.

In analyzing each of Bill Clinton's AIDS speech acts, several distinct categories emerged. Of the 99 AIDS speech acts that Clinton made as president, 22 of these occasions, as already

TABLE 7.2
Bill Clinton's Rhetorical Construction of AIDS During First Term

Rhetorical Strategy	Frequency of Strategy
AIDS as health care	50%
(AIDS as cause of rising health care costs 42%)	
(Health care reform as benefit to those with AIDS 8%)	
Increased funding for AIDS / Ryan White Act	20%
AIDS as world plague	8%
AIDS and Medicaid	6%
AIDS surrogates (references to Gebbie, Fleming, Elders, etc.)	5%
Sex education and AIDS prevention	4%
Compassion / inclusion for those with AIDS	4%
Public's irrational fears of AIDS	2%
AIDS related to drug abuse	1%

noted, were campaign-related events in 1996. Discounting his construction of AIDS as campaign rhetoric, Table 7.2 represents the various ways in which Clinton constructed AIDS throughout his first 4 years as president.

By far, throughout his first term, AIDS for Bill Clinton was tied to one of the cornerstones of his 1992 campaign, health care reform. Of the total 56 AIDS speech acts during 1993 and 1994, 41 of these discussions related AIDS to health care reform. Thus, AIDS as health care reform constituted the primary approach to AIDS during the first 2 years, silence prevailed during his third year, following the Republican takeover of Congress, and then AIDS as campaign rhetoric reappeared in the final year.

In constructing AIDS as an issue of health care reform, two very different strategies were used, depending on the audience being addressed. First, in numerous speeches to general, or non-gay/activist audiences, Clinton would invoke AIDS as one of several "problems" contributing to our nation's high cost of health care. These problems were most often described as being caused by irresponsible individuals who made it difficult for "hardworking" Americans to afford health care. In announcing his "Health Security for All Americans Act" before a joint session of Congress and a nationally televised audience, Clinton (1993a) admonished: "In short, responsibility should apply to anybody who abuses this system and drives up the cost for honest, hard-working citizens . . . the outrageous costs of violence in this country . . . we also have higher rates of AIDS, of smoking and excessive drinking, of teen pregnancy, of low birth weight babies. We have to change our ways if we ever want to have an affordable health care system" (p. 1843).

As previously noted, Bill Clinton did not always construct AIDS as weakening our health care system. In the few instances in which the president would address a primarily gay audience, or would respond to a question from someone with AIDS, the disease would not be constructed as contributing to the costs of health care; rather, a reformed health care system would be described as a *benefit* to those living with AIDS. In these instances, the president abandoned his strategy of blame and sought to identify with his audience by pointing out how he was trying to help those with the AIDS virus. To a citizen with AIDS in Kansas City, Clinton (1994c) offered the reassurance that "for someone like you who has very expensive medical bills for medicine, you would benefit enormously because of the very reasonable copay and deductible and annual limit" (p. 730).

Beyond constructing AIDS in relation to health care, a secondary rhetorical strategy for AIDS talk that Clinton employed throughout his first term was to prove his commitment to AIDS based on increased federal funding, especially during a period of budgetary crisis. This rhetorical strategy was used primarily when speaking to activist groups. In reporting to his Advisory Council on HIV/AIDS, Clinton (1995c) spoke of his commitment by noting "As you know, I have been strongly committed to an increasing Federal response to the AIDS crisis. In spite of the fact that we have cut and eliminated hundreds and hundreds of programs since I have been President, we increased overall AIDS funding by 40 percent and funding for the Ryan White Care Act by over 80 percent since I've been President" (p. 1320).

In addition to discussion of AIDS in relation to health care and the need for increased federal funding of AIDS, several additional categories emerged from the analysis of Clinton's AIDS talk. Among the categories previously discussed in this chapter include the mention of AIDS in relation to presidential surrogates, and also discussion of sex education and AIDS prevention. In a few instances, and usually when addressing an international audience, Clinton would discuss AIDS as a threatening world plague. Describing world threats to democracy in an address to the United Nations, Clinton (1994e) proclaimed, "The dangers we face are less stark and more diffuse than those of the cold war, but they are still formidable . . . diseases like AIDS that threaten to decimate nations" (p. 1863). Also, during his struggle with Congress over funding for Medicaid, Clinton (1995d) did point out on several occasions that "Medicaid [is] the program that provides health care funding to half of all Americans with AIDS as well as the poor and elderly in nursing homes" (p. 2134). Finally, in one instance Clinton (1994c) directly linked drug use and AIDS when he noted, "The craving for drugs is an enormous factor in the spread of AIDS" (p. 245).

The two remaining categories are interesting to examine as one considers the degree to which these constructions are largely missing in Clinton's overall AIDS message for America. First, we see that discussion of the need to show compassion for and include in our social community those with AIDS, along with addressing the public's irrational fears of AIDS, represent a very small portion of Clinton's AIDS talk. Going further with this analysis, it is also apparent that the very audiences who need these messages are most often ignored. Almost always, when speaking of AIDS in a way that affirms the dignity of those living with the disease and includes them as valuable members of our society, the president would be addressing a mostly gay/activist audience. In his remarks on signing the Ryan White Care Act in 1996, Clinton (1996b) described AIDS as our common concern: "People with AIDS deserve not only the best medical care, but also our compassion and our love. . . . [AIDS] has shaken the faith of many, but it has inspired a remarkable community spirit . . . we know that AIDS affects all Americans. Every person with HIV or AIDS is someone's son or daughter, brother or sister, parent or grandparent. We cannot allow discrimination of any kind to blind us to what we must do" (p. 898).

On a few occasions while speaking to non-gay or activist audiences, Bill Clinton would discuss the need for compassion and inclusion for those with AIDS. In analyzing this discourse, it seems that a certain type of compassion and inclusion is advocated. In these instances, the president would ground his argument for compassion in the narrative form, usually recounting a personal acquaintance with AIDS. The president's (1992a) most often used AIDS anecdote is a story he developed in campaign '92 and one he would use several times throughout his first term:

> When I was in Des Moines, Iowa in the campaign, I saw a white lady holding an African-American baby that had AIDS. She was from Iowa. The kid was from Miami. She had been abandoned by her husband. She had two children of her own. She was living in an apartment house, working at a meager job. She thought it was God's will that she take a child who had AIDS and was abandoned. And she did it. If she could do it, a lot of the rest of us should as well. Someone has got to care for these children. (p. 7)

Such calls for compassion and inclusion, pleas usually made by Clinton when addressing nongay audiences, illustrate what has been described as the "innocent victim." Here, Bill

Clinton is able to associate himself with AIDS and express genuine concern without identifying with the "guilty" AIDS victims. As McAllister (1992) pointed out: "Scholars have noted the creation of a 'victim continuum' for people with AIDS, which distinguishes the 'innocent victims' from the 'guilty victims.' On one end of the continuum are those 'innocent' people, those portrayed as guiltless bystanders who, through no fault of their own (in fact, maybe even through the fault of others), have contracted AIDS. On the opposite end are guilty victims, those whose conscious behavior has led to the disease" (p. 213).

The only instance during Clinton's first 4 years in which he pleads the cause of so-called "guilty victims" with a nongay audience was his address at Georgetown University in July of 1995. In this speech on the obligations of citizenship, Clinton argued that we should not exclude those with AIDS, even the homosexual, from our national community. As the president (Clinton, 1995b) asserted, "The gay people who have AIDS are still our sons, our brothers, our cousins, our citizens. They're Americans, too. They're obeying the law and working hard. They're entitled to be treated like everybody else" (p. 1196).

CLINTON'S NEW COVENANT

In understanding President Clinton's AIDS talk, it is useful to situate this discourse within his broader interpretive schema. As Smith (1994, 1996) has described in some detail, Bill Clinton campaigned for office on the rhetorical vision of a new covenant, a message crafted in the form of the political jeremiad. Jeremiadic design, rooted in the traditional Puritan message, constructs a special or chosen people who covenant with God so that they might fulfill their divine mission. The problems that they face serve as a test to strengthen the people, or as punishment for following false prophets. Translating this religious message into a civic doctrine, the logic of the political jeremiad suggests that citizens are experiencing trials in the form of social ills, and that this social tribulation has occurred due to the people's willingness to follow a misguided or false political leader; thus, a new leader is needed to guide the people back to the promised land of peace and prosperity. Smith (1996) cogently described Clinton's use of jeremiadic logic in his 1992 campaign message:

> Candidate Clinton explained that a chosen people ("the forgotten middle class") was incurring tribulations in the forms of recession, crime, drug abuse, AIDS, riots, rising health care costs, and inadequate education because they had followed false prophets (Reagan, Bush, Quayle et al.) who had led them away from the "first principles" that had always made America great. Jeremiadic logic reasons that followers must heed their leader's call to fundamental principles and obligations so that the afflictions will be lifted by divine intervention. (p. 226)

To better understand Bill Clinton's new covenant and the way in which AIDS is part of this narrative, it is important to consider the development of Clinton's campaign message. As a founding member of the Democratic Leadership Council, an organization made up of the party's more conservative leaders, candidate Clinton labeled himself a "new Democrat" and realized that his margin of victory would come largely from the former Reagan Democrats; in campaign '92, this constituency would become Clinton's "forgotten middle class." The "new" in his new Democrat title could also be interpreted as Clinton's desire to become the first Democratic nominee since Jimmy Carter to succeed in ascending to the White House. For Clinton, this would be done by not repeating the errors of former nominees Mondale and Dukakis, their mistake of embracing the party's traditional liberal views; Clinton, instead, would craft his message to appeal to those who found comfort in Ronald Reagan's "righting" of America. Indeed, in both form and content, Clinton's appropriation of the political jeremiad, developed in campaign '92 as his new covenant, is a variation on the new right's economic message of bootstrap materialism and narrow moralism.

Patton (1985), in her early analysis of the politics of AIDS, described Ronald Reagan's "Calvinist" message in which economic advantage would come to those deserving of opportunity and willing to work hard. In this supply-side ethic, the predestined wealthy among us would allow enough riches to "trickle down" on those willing to work their way up the ladder of economic success. Describing this so-called "Reaganomics," Patton noted, "The wealthy who engage in capitalism (not charity) are altruistic because they engender opportunities for the whole economy . . . This parable of wealth and poverty, faith and doubt gives hope to the lower classes in the most crass Horatio Algeresque sense" (p. 91). Examining the social element of Reagan's Calvinist message, Patton pointed out that this dialogue was driven largely by the fundamentalist-Christian agenda: "Implicit in their rhetoric, and explicit in their policies, is a notion of racial purity and absolute community consensus that decries pluralism and abhors 'mixing' . . . New right Calvinism accedes to a program of 'Christ against culture' by allowing leaders to prove their election in symbolic or real battle with the evil forces of homosexuality, abortion, miscegenation, etc." (p. 84).

In Ronald Reagan's America, the directive was to work yourself into prosperity and to act "right." Certainly, it was not right to be homosexual, and AIDS was seen as a just punishment for such deviance. This view is articulated by North Carolina Senator Jesse Helms' argument that the government should not "waste" money on research for a disease caused by "deliberate, disgusting, revolting conduct . . . a disease transmitted by people deliberately engaging in unnatural acts" (Seelye, 1995, p. A12).

Clinton's new covenant, like Ronald Reagan's narrative, suggests that America's greatest challenge is lack of economic prosperity. Indeed, as Clinton's campaign slogan stated, "It's the economy, stupid . . . and health care, too!" Unlike Reagan, however, Clinton's economic message was directed not toward those at the top, but rather the forgotten middle class who had been tricked into believing that if they would just work hard enough, they too would be materially blessed. In revealing the hoax, Clinton (1991) explained to voters:

> For 12 years of this Reagan–Bush era, the Republicans have let S&L crooks and self-serving CEOs try to build an economy out of paper and perks instead of people and products. It's the Republican way: every man for himself and get it while you can. They stacked the odds in favor of their friends at the top, and told everybody else to wait for whatever trickled down. And every step of the way, the Republicans forgot about the very people they had promised to help—the very people who elected them in the first place—the forgotten middle-class Americans who still live by American values and whose hopes, hearts, and hands still carry the American Dream. (p. 9)

Clinton's covenant extended to the forgotten middle class a pledge that if they were willing to be responsible, which meant "work hard and play by the rules," their government, in turn, would invest in their future through improved educational opportunities, the creation of "high-skill, high wage" jobs, and improved health care. In accepting his party's nomination, Clinton (1992b) pledged, "And so, in the name of all the people who do the work, pay the taxes, raise the kids and play by the rules, in the name of the hard-working Americans who make up our forgotten middle class, I accept your nomination for President of the United States. . . . For too long, those who play by the rules and keep the faith have gotten the shaft, and those who cut corners and cut deals have been rewarded" (p. 1).

As described, Clinton shares with Reagan and Bush a political construction of AIDS that is largely negative. For Reagan and Bush, AIDS is seen as suffering due to moral deviance; as part of Clinton's new covenant, AIDS is constructed as a cause of his vaunted middle class' economic suffering. In his inaugural address, Clinton (1993b) continued the jeremiadic positioning of AIDS as a threat, in which he alluded to the disease as a "plague" upon the country, "Today, a generation raised in the shadows of the cold war assumes new responsibilities in a world warmed by the sunshine of freedom but threatened still by ancient hatreds and new plagues" (p. 75). Here, his words suggest that the baby boomers, having survived the cold war, would now have to face the haunting specter of AIDS dimming their prospects for a bright future. As the previous section of this chapter discussed, the president's primary rhetorical approach would continue to construct AIDS as a threat to the middle class' ability to prosper economically. AIDS, along with the many other social blights including teen pregnancy, drug use, violence, low-birthweight babies, are caused by those not acting "responsible" and whose actions contribute to increased health care costs for his forgotten middle class. Such blame is illustrated when Clinton (1993a) attempted to describe why our health care system was in such a mess:

> We have a higher percentage of poor people, a higher percentage of people with AIDS, a higher percentage of teenage births and low birth weight babies, and a much higher percentage of violence than any of our competitors. And that's all a health care issue. You pay for it when those folks show up every weekend all shot up and cut, and they don't have any health insurance. They pass it on to you. So, you pay for that. That's another big cost that makes our system more expensive. (p. 2034)

CONCLUSION

The preceding analysis reveals much about Bill Clinton's presidential leadership on AIDS. This chapter began by noting Clinton's campaign assurances that "AIDS would become part of [his] obsession as President" ("Heckler Stirs Clinton Anger," 1992, p. A9), and that he would "discuss the AIDS crisis with the American people early and often" ("Magic Johnson Talks," 1993, p. A9). Once in office, President Clinton found little time—and perhaps political courage—to honor such pledges. Certainly, achieving an increase in federal funding for AIDS-related causes can be used as one measure of Clinton's commitment to fighting AIDS. Fulfilling one's fiscal responsibility, however, largely ignores the president's obligations as interpreter-in-chief. Here, we must conclude, Bill Clinton's rhetorical leadership on AIDS is woefully lacking.

First, as discussed throughout this chapter, Clinton's substantive instances of AIDS talk occurred primarily with gay and activist audiences. These rhetorical acts served much like "preaching to the choir." Although devoting most of his AIDS discourse to convincing those directly involved with AIDS that he cared, the president unfortunately was not willing to use his privileged position and rhetorical power to educate the American people about the disease. Another interesting finding from this analysis reveals Clinton's tendency to construct AIDS differently when addressing gay versus nongay audiences. Finally, the present analysis also illustrates that Bill Clinton, when forced to be politically cautious in dealing with such "liberal" issues as AIDS, shunned personal involvement and instead employed the strategies of silence, surrogates, and political gestures to demonstrate his commitment.

Perhaps the most disappointing finding of this analysis was the primary way in which Bill Clinton constructed AIDS. Whereas this nation endured more than a decade of a political construction of AIDS as plague, or as punishment for deviant behavior, we are told in Bill Clinton's America that AIDS is now largely an economic curse or punishment on the middle class—a punishment brought about by those who are irresponsible and who undoubtedly do not play by the rules. Clinton's new covenant notion of helping those who are responsible and who play by the rules deserves a more critical examination as it relates to AIDS. Although a thorough analysis of this matter is beyond the scope of the current chapter, one can easily see the inherent contradiction in this notion of playing by the rules, especially when these rules are often designed to deny one's ability to engage in "life, liberty, and the pursuit of happiness." Whether a rule denying those who are infected with HIV from immigrating to the United States (Hilts, 1993a), a rule forcing military discharge of those who test HIV-seropositive (Hilts, 1992), or in much broader terms, a rule such as the so-called "defense of marriage" law (Moss, 1996), it is impossible for those with AIDS to play by *the rules* and thus enjoy the benefits of Bill Clinton's new covenant.

In searching for glimmers of hope in Clinton's AIDS talk, we do find some evidence, however limited, that Bill Clinton's vision for America just might include those with AIDS. As previously noted, in his Georgetown University speech in July of 1995 the president indicated that those with AIDS deserve to be part of our community: "The gay people who have AIDS are still our sons, our brothers, our cousins, our citizens. They're Americans, too. They're obeying the law and working hard. They're entitled to be treated like everybody else" (Clinton, 1995a, p. 1196). Indeed, AIDS seen not as economic plague but rather as opportunity to build a community that includes all citizens should become the president's dominant AIDS message. As Arthur Schafer (1991) has so eloquently stated, "The plague 'within each of us' is not the submicroscopic virus as much as it is an extreme alienation from our fellow human beings . . . the AIDS epidemic is as much a threat to our cultural values as it is to our lives, our health-care system, and our economy . . . There is still time to counteract, decisively, the plague mentality. The survival of our common humanity is at stake" (p. 10).

Shall we dare hope, once again, that there is still time for President Clinton to realize that the power of AIDS can be found in its ability to transform the way we treat one another, in its challenge to our capacity for creating community.

REFERENCES

Arno, P., & Feiden, K. (1986). Ignoring the epidemic: How the Reagan administration failed on AIDS. *Health PAC Bulletin: Health Policy Advisory Center, 17*, 78–11.

Austin, J. L. (1962). *How to do things with words.* Oxford, England: Oxford University Press.

Bateson, M. C., & Goldsby, R. (1988). *Thinking AIDS.* Reading, MA: Addison-Wesley.

Bostdorff, D. M. (1996). Clinton's characteristic issue management style: Caution, conciliation, and conflict avoidance in the case of gays in the military. In R. E. Denton & R. L. Holloway (Eds.), *The Clinton presidency: Images, issues, and communication strategies* (pp. 189–223). Westport, CT: Praeger.

Boxall, B. (1992, December 2). AIDS activists prepare plea to Clinton for help. *Los Angeles Times*, p. B3.

Broder, J. M., & Jackson, R. L. (1994, December 2). Clinton observes world AIDS day with low-key private meeting. *Los Angeles Times*, p. A9.

Brummett, B. (1980). Towards a theory of silence as a political strategy. *Quarterly Journal of Speech, 66*, 289–303.

Clinton, W. J. (1991, November 20). *A new covenant for economic change.* Internet: Sunsite.

Clinton, W. J. (1992a, September 11). *Remarks by Governor Bill Clinton at University of Notre Dame.* Internet: Sunsite.

Clinton, W. J. (1992b, July 16). *A vision for America: A new covenant.* Internet: Sunsite.

Clinton, W. J. (1993a, September 22). Address to a joint session of the congress on health care reform. *Weekly Compilation of Presidential Documents,* pp. 1836–1846.

Clinton, W. J. (1993b, January 20). Inaugural address. *Weekly Compilation of Presidential Documents,* pp. 75–77.

Clinton, W. J. (1993c, October 8). Remarks at a Democratic National Committee breakfast. *Weekly Compilation of Presidential Documents,* pp. 2026–2035.

Clinton, W. J. (1993d, December 1). Remarks at World AIDS day at Georgetown University Medical Center. *Weekly Compilation of Presidential Documents,* pp. 2486–2490.

Clinton, W. J. (1993e, June 25). Remarks on the appointment of Kristine M. Gebbie as AIDS policy coordinator and an exchange with reporters. *Weekly Compilation of Presidential Documents*, pp. 1168–1170.

Clinton, W. J. (1994a, February 3). Remarks and a question and answer session at Kramer Junior High School. *Weekly Compilation of Presidential Documents*, pp. 195–205.

Clinton, W. J. (1994b, November 10). Remarks announcing Patsy Fleming as National AIDS Policy Director and an exchange with reporters. *Weekly Compilation of Presidential Documents*, pp. 2356–2358.

Clinton, W. J. (1994c, February 9). Remarks at Prince George's county correctional center, MD. *Weekly Compilation of Presidential Documents*, pp. 244–248.

Clinton, W. J. (1994d, April 7). Remarks in a town hall meeting in Kansas City, MO. *Weekly Compilation of Presidential Documents*, pp. 718–736.

Clinton, W. J. (1994e, September 26). Remarks to the 49th session of the United Nations general assembly in NYC. *Weekly Compilation of Presidential Documents*, pp. 1862–1867.

Clinton, W. J. (1995a, June 1). Remarks at a town meeting in Billings, MT. *Weekly Compilation of Presidential Documents*, pp. 950–962.

Clinton, W. J. (1995b, July 6). Remarks at Georgetown University. *Weekly Compilation of Presidential Documents*, pp. 1190–1200.

Clinton, W. J. (1995c, July 28). Remarks to the presidential advisory council on HIV/AIDS and an exchange with reporters. *Weekly Compilation of Presidential Documents*, pp. 1320–1321.

Clinton, W. J. (1995d, December 6). Remarks to the White House conference on HIV/AIDS. *Weekly Compilation of Presidential Documents*, pp. 2133–2138.

Clinton, W. J. (1996a, August 29). Remarks accepting the presidential nomination at the Democratic National Convention in Chicago. *Weekly Compilation of Presidential Documents*, pp. 1577–1586.

Clinton, W. J. (1996b, May 20). Remarks on signing the Ryan White Care Act amendments of 1996. *Weekly Compilation of Presidential Documents*, pp. 898–900.

Devroy, A. (1993, December 2). AIDS patient, protester ask Clinton to do more. *The Washington Post*, p. A31.

Dunlap, D. (1995a, June 16). Clinton creates group to improve campaign against AIDS. *The New York Times*, p. A22.

Dunlap, D. W. (1995b, June 14). Clinton names first liaison to gay and lesbian groups. *The New York Times*, p. B7.

Edelman, M. (1988). *Constructing the political spectacle*. Chicago: University of Chicago Press.

Foreman, C. H. (1993, Summer). AIDS and the limits of czardom. *The Brookings Review*, pp. 18–21.

Friedman, T. L. (1993, December 2). President defends his efforts in combating AIDS. *The New York Times*, p. A1.

Grover, J. Z. (1992). AIDS, keywords, and cultural work. In L. Grossberg, C. Nelson, & P. Treichler (Eds.), *Cultural studies* (pp. 227–239). London: Routledge.

Hart, R. P. (1987). *The sound of leadership: Presidential communication in the modern age*. Chicago: University of Chicago Press.

Heckler stirs Clinton anger: Excerpts from the exchange. (1992, March 28). *The New York Times*, p. A9.

Hilts, P. J. (1992, December 10). Clinton team is urged to reorganize nation's effort to fight AIDS. *The New York Times*, p. D19.

Hilts, P. J. (1993a, February 9). Clinton to lift ban on HIV-infected visitors. *The New York Times*, p. A20.

Hilts, P. J. (1993b, June 27). Into the maelstrom. *The New York Times*, p. A2.

Joseph, S. C. (1992). *Dragon within the gates: The once and future AIDS epidemic*. New York: Carroll & Graf.

Krauthammer, C. (1992, November 13). The quest for magic wands. *The Washington Post*, p. A27.

Magic Johnson talks; risky sex falls. (1993, January 29). *The New York Times*, p. A6.

Maraniss, D. (1992, May 20). Democrat takes stand at gay fund-raiser. *The Washington Post*, p. A1.

McAllister, M. P. (1992). AIDS, medicalization, and the news media. In T. Edgar, M. A. Fitzpatrick, & V. S. Freimuth (Eds.), *AIDS: A communication perspective* (pp. 195–221). Hillsdale, NJ: Lawrence Erlbaum Associates.

McKinney, M. S. (1996). *Building community through communication: Expressions of voter anger and alienation in the political process*. Unpublished doctoral dissertation, University of Kansas, Lawrence.

Moss, J. J. (1996, June 25). Bill Clinton. *The Advocate*, pp. 44–52.

Myers, D. D. (1994, February 4). *Press briefing by press secretary Dee Dee Myers, Washington, DC*. Internet: Texas A&M White House Archive.

Panetta, L. (1994, December 9). *Press briefing by chief of staff Leon Panetta, Washington, DC*. Internet: Texas A&M White House Archive.

Patton, C. (1985). *Sex and germs: The politics of AIDS*. Boston: South End Press.

Perez, T. L., & Dionisopoulos, G. N. (1995). Presidential silence, C. Everett Koop, and the surgeon general's report on AIDS. *Communication Studies, 46*, 18–33.

Schafer, A. (1991). AIDS: The social dimension. In C. Overall & W. P. Zion (Eds.), *Perspectives on AIDS: Ethical and social issues* (pp. 1–12). Oxford, England: Oxford University Press.

Schmalz, J. (1992, October 11). Gay politics goes mainstream. *The New York Times Magazine,* pp. 1–3, 29, 41–42, 50–51.

Searle, J. R. (1969). *Speech acts.* Cambridge, England: Cambridge University Press.

Seelye, K. A. (1995, July 5). Helms puts the brakes to a bill financing AIDS treatment. *The New York Times,* p. A12.

Smith, C. A. (1983). The audience of the rhetorical presidency: An analysis of president constituent interaction, 1963–1981. *Presidential Studies Quarterly, Fall,* 613–622.

Smith, C. A. (1994). The jeremiadic logic of Bill Clinton's policy speeches. In S. A. Smith (Ed.), *Bill Clinton on stump, state, and stage* (pp. 73–100). Fayetteville: University of Arkansas Press.

Smith, C. A. (1996). "Rough stretches and honest disagreements": Is Bill Clinton redefining the rhetorical presidency? In R. E. Denton & R. L. Holloway (Eds.), *The Clinton presidency: Images, issues, and communication strategies* (pp. 225–247). Westport, CT: Praeger.

Stuckey, M. E. (1991). *The president as interpreter-in-chief.* Chatham, NJ: Chatham House Publishers.

Transcript of first TV debate between Bush, Clinton, and Perot. (1992, October 12). *The New York Times,* pp. A11–A14.

Trent, J. S., & Friedenberg, R. V. (1995). *Political campaign communication.* Westport, CT: Praeger.

Scapegoating and Political Discourse: Representative Robert Dornan's Legislation of Morality Through HIV/AIDS

R. Anthony Slagle
St. Cloud State University

> As with all kinds of sex, attempts at prevention aren't going to stop them. They only increase the quotient of guilt and self-loathing—results exceptionally costly, both in economic terms and those of mental health. . . . The one facet of the AIDS epidemic that I think almost everyone prefers to overlook is this: *Something infectious is going around.*
>
> —Kramer (1990, pp. 235, 266)

Since the early 1980s, the AIDS epidemic has attracted varying degrees of attention in the realm of politics. For the first several years of the epidemic, then-President Ronald Reagan did not mention the disease once in political discourse (Shilts, 1987). Other politicians have been cautious about bringing up HIV and AIDS as a political issue because it is an issue that many people believe is not a serious problem; it is perceived as a disease that affects only a small minority of the population. Furthermore, many politicians are likely reluctant to fight for money for HIV/AIDS research because they are concerned that to do so might be political suicide. The voting public still perceives HIV/AIDS as a problem that a few specific disenfranchised groups have brought upon themselves (Brandt, 1988). In more direct terms, it is not a popular issue for politicians to embrace because HIV/AIDS is perceived to be a disease of homosexual men and illicit drug users. Other politicians have been very vocal about the disease, but have characterized it as a deserved punishment for people who cannot control their immoral behavior. In all fairness, a handful of politicians have embraced the issue and have sponsored legislation to help stop, or at least slow, the epidemic. Unfortunately, these politicians are a small minority even as we find ourselves well into the second decade of the epidemic.

From the earliest days of the AIDS epidemic, a common perception has been that it is a gay disease. This characterization is common because HIV has profoundly affected the gay community from the very beginning of the epidemic. However, we now know that this characterization is simply untrue. This initial perception, despite the efforts of many people, has been difficult to overcome. Unfortunately, many conservative politicians, particularly those who identify as members of the "religious right," have perpetuated the myth that HIV/AIDS is a gay disease.

I have three main goals for this chapter. First, I demonstrate how Burke's notion of the *scapegoat* is useful in understanding how we talk about social problems. In general, I emphasize how the radical religious right has responded to the HIV/AIDS epidemic. In particular, I discuss the discourse of former Representative Robert Dornan (R–California). Dornan was a vocal member of Congress when it came to the issue of HIV/AIDS, and probably addressed the issue on the floor of the House more than any other member of Congress. Dornan, in fact, was quick to point out that he gave well over 200 speeches on the issue (Cong. Rec., 6/27/96). Dornan has not been the only conservative member of Congress to address the issue, nor has he been the only politician to use gay men as a scapegoat in his rhetoric, but he has been fairly representative of the apocalyptic discourse that is prevalent among members of the religious right. Extremist discourse, like Dornan's, raises grave concerns about the legislation of health policy in the United States, because the politicians who engage in this type of discourse appear to be more concerned with solving what they perceive to be social and spiritual decline in the United States, rather than focusing on how to deal with serious health concerns.[1] Dornan is an important rhetorical figure, then, because he has been a leader of this movement in Congress. To understand how such discourse works is to illuminate the power of the rhetor. By understanding why such discourse is effective, and by understanding the flaws in such reasoning, Congress and the general public can move past placing blame to dealing with a serious public health issue.

Second, I illuminate why much discourse about HIV/AIDS has stepped outside the bounds of epidemiology and scientific rationality, and focused, instead, on issues of morality. In particular, Dornan focused on the fact that HIV/AIDS is the result of spiritual and moral decline in the United States.

Third, and finally, I suggest that the rhetorical strategies of the radical religious right are not only a hateful attack on a marginalized group, but by using such divisive rhetoric—and suggesting that gay sex is the root of the AIDS epidemic—all people are put at greater risk for infection with HIV.

A great deal of discourse about HIV/AIDS has focused on the perceived moral ills of a few marginalized groups that have been labeled as "high risk": gay men and injection drug users. In this chapter, I focus specifically on the scapegoating of gay men, because this is the group that is the target of most of Dornan's rhetoric. The perception that HIV/AIDS is a "gay disease" has been a problem since the earliest documented cases in 1981 (Brandt, 1988; Shilts, 1987; Treichler, 1988). Much of the discourse about the epidemic, at least from the conservative right, points to unacceptable and uncontrolled behavior as the cause of AIDS rather than a virus (Fee, 1988). Instead, much of the conservative rhetoric places blame, instills guilt, and perpetuates the view that the disease is a deserved punishment for deviant behavior.

BURKE'S CONCEPTION OF THE RHETORICAL SCAPEGOAT

According to Burke (1966), the notion of the rhetorical scapegoat stems directly from the principle of perfection that is found in his definition of the human being as the "symbol-using, symbol-making, and symbol-misusing animal" (p. 16). In Burke's view, we must come to realize "just how overwhelmingly much of what we mean by 'reality' has been built up for us through nothing but our symbol systems" (p. 5). Burke claimed that, unlike other animals, human beings rely on symbols to understand our history, to communicate in the present, and

---

[1]I agree with Paul Monette's (1994) description of this kind of moralizing: "I think what's happened to our freedom of religion is that we're free to be nutcake fundamentalist Christians and hate everybody else. Meanwhile, no one seems capable of drawing the line between freedom of religion and the naked politics of hate" (p. 120).

to envision the future. Other animals, in Burke's view, do not have this ability; they simply exist in the present (in other words, they exist in the realm of motion, not action).[2]

Symbols, obviously, are ambiguous because they represent things that they are not (Burke, 1966). Because of the ambiguous nature of symbols, human beings are "rotten with perfection" (Burke, 1966, p. 18). Basically, Burke argued that because of our ability to symbolically envision a reality different from the one in which we find ourselves, humans are always striving to reach a more perfect state of being. In other words, no matter what our state of affairs, we can always imagine something better. The notion of the scapegoat is necessary for human beings to strive for this perfection.

According to Burke (1973), the scapegoat is used to place blame on a rhetorical or actual "other," in order to make the world easier to accept. Burke explained that the process of scapegoating "delegates the personal burden to an external bearer, yet the receiver of this burden possesses consubstantiality with the giver, a pontification that is contrived . . . by objectively attributing one's own vices or temptations to the delegated vessel" (p. 45).

To put it another way, the "giver" divorces him or herself from any personal responsibility in a situation by placing the full responsibility for the situation on the scapegoat. The primary reason that human beings do this, as Bertelsen (1993) pointed out, is that:

> This cathartic purging . . . satisfies our need to make our version of events socially palatable. We rely on catharsis to mediate our relationships. In an attempt to resolve human divisiveness, we often engender symbolic enactments designed to induce others to see events the same way we do. Ironically, we often rely on division for cathartic satisfaction. In an attempt to transcend the inherent divisiveness of the human condition, we resort to victimage and scapegoating. Such strategies attempt to purify, cleanse, or make more acceptable a version of reality capable of uniting competing versions, groups, or nations. (p. 242)

We all engage in scapegoating at times to make unpleasant situations more acceptable to us. We do this by divorcing ourselves from accepting any level of responsibility that we personally have, or any responsibility that we have as a community, and we point the finger at a rhetorical or actual other. The goal of scapegoating is to make the rhetor closer to perfect by rhetorically separating him or herself from the perceived problem.

SCAPEGOATING AND THE HIV/AIDS EPIDEMIC

Scapegoating is common in terms of how all human beings talk about social problems. This technique is strongly apparent in the history of disease in general, and in terms of HIV/AIDS in particular. Fee (1988) confirmed that when we are "dealing with major disease problems, we often try to find some social group to blame for the infection" (p. 123). Indeed, because the epidemic affected the gay male community so significantly in the early years of the epidemic, gay men became an easy scapegoat for the disease. As Treichler (1988) noted, "Many were [and are] reluctant to move away from the view of AIDS as a 'gay disease.' For some the name GRID[3] would always shape their perceptions" (p. 202).

Furthermore, AIDS has been used as a justification to criticize people for their immoral behavior. As Brandt (1988) pointed out, "[t]he AIDS epidemic thus offered new opportunities

---

[2]Obviously, Burke's view of symbols is controversial. In particular, many have argued that it is arrogant to assume that human beings are the only animals that use symbols. I am sensitive to these concerns, yet this issue is not where I would like to focus my attention in this chapter.

[3]One of the first names for AIDS was *gay-related immunodeficiency* (GRID). Another common name for the disease was *gay cancer*, because of the high incidence of Kaposi's sarcoma in gay patients with the disease.

for expressions of moral opprobrium. Patrick Buchanan, conservative columnist and former Reagan speechwriter, explained, 'The poor homosexuals—they have declared war upon Nature, and now Nature is exacting an awful retribution' " (p. 155).[4] Finally, as Rosenberg (1988) pointed out, the general perception has been that although certain people are innocent victims of the disease, other groups are more deserving of infection: "Of course, it was to have been expected that patients who contracted AIDS through blood transfusions or *in utero* are casually referred to in news reports as innocent or accidental victims of a nemesis both morally and epidemiologically appropriate to a rather different group" (p. 29).

The use of scapegoating is prevalent in discourse about HIV and AIDS. In fact, the use of the strategy is apparent not only in the discourse of the conservative right. Indeed, the gay community—perhaps feeling the pressure from being labeled as the source of the problem by the conservative right—has used this technique as well (Shilts, 1987; Treichler, 1988). For example, the gay community was quick to point the finger at a sexually promiscuous flight attendant for the early spread of the virus. Specifically, the now infamous "cluster study" carried out by the Centers for Disease Control offered compelling evidence that a French Canadian flight attendant, Gaeten Dugas, had been sexually intimate with a significant number of the men who were diagnosed early in the epidemic. Gaeten Dugas became known as "Patient Zero," and to this day he is depicted as the "Typhoid Mary" of the AIDS epidemic. Treichler noted that the focus on Dugas was largely the result of Randy Shilts' account of the early years of the AIDS epidemic, *And the Band Played On*. She noted, "Yet Shilts himself, whose own account of AIDS begins with the mysterious illness in central Africa of a Danish lesbian physician, nevertheless focuses more intensely on a sexually appetitive Canadian airline attendant, a gay man who came to be identified by the CDC as 'Patient Zero.' Of course, as soon as the advance publicity on Shilts's book went out, the *New York Post*'s headline blared: 'THE MAN WHO GAVE US AIDS!' " (p. 217).

The gay community was quick to blame Dugas, and to separate themselves from him by contending that not all gay men are promiscuous.

REPRESENTATIVE DORNAN AND THE LEGISLATION OF MORALITY

In a rather lengthy address on the floor of the House, Dornan rose to speak on a matter of personal privilege (Cong. Rec., 6/27/96). Under personal privilege, members of the House are entitled to address the legislative body when they believe that their reputation has been impugned. In this particular instance, Dornan rose to defend himself against criticism from Representative Steve Gunderson (R–Wisconsin), one of three openly gay members of the House of Representatives.[5]

---

[4]Brandt (1988) also noted:

> Some have seen the AIDS epidemic in a purely "moral" light: AIDS is a disease that occurs among those who violate the moral order. As one journalist concluded: "Suddenly a lot of people fear that they and their families might suddenly catch some mysterious, fatal illness which until now has been confined to society's outcasts." AIDS, like other sexually transmitted diseases has been viewed as a fateful link between social deviance and the morally correct. Such fears have been exacerbated by an expectant media. "No one is safe from AIDS," announced *Life* magazine in bold red letters on its cover. Implicit was the notion that 'no one is safe' from gays and intravenous drug users. The diseases had come to be equated with those who are at highest risk of suffering its terrible consequences. (p. 155)

[5]Representatives Barney Frank (D–Massachusetts) and Gerry Studds (D–Massachusetts) are the only other openly gay members of Congress. Steve Gunderson was, until his retirement, the only openly gay Republican member of Congress at that time.

Gunderson had criticized Dornan for his prejudiced views about the gay community in general. In particular, Gunderson's remarks came in defense of a gay circuit party and AIDS fundraiser (Cherry Jubilee) held in a federal building that Dornan had been critical of on a separate occasion. Gunderson argued:

> The gentleman from California [Dornan] has every right to dislike me if he so chooses. But he has no right to misrepresent the facts, nor the motives of others in this, his latest, attempt to smear the gay community. . . . This is a much bigger issue than a personal or ideological dispute. This is a question of whether individuals in American society should be able to intentionally misrepresent the facts, question others' motives, and intentionally falsify information in an attempt to discredit other elements in society. If there is to remain any element of mutual respect in a diverse society, we must reject intentional efforts to personally destroy those with whom we might disagree. (Cong. Rec., 5/14/96, p. H4923)

Although Dornan's criticism of this event was based partly on the issue of groups using federal buildings, his attacks on the gay community and AIDS activists are striking. Despite Dornan's attempts to shadow his heterosexist views by focusing on an administrative issue, it is impossible to miss the crux of his position. For example, Dornan contended, "Our toleration of low standards here in Congress over the years that I have observed is at the core of my challenge today, Mr. Speaker. Our Federal buildings, and I have been told today they are going to do it again next April for the third time, our Federal buildings must never, never be used to facilitate, if not glorify, immorality" (Cong. Rec., 6/27/96, p. H7053).

For Dornan, then, the issue is not about the use of public buildings by private groups; he is opposed to the fact that the building was used by a group of gay men—a group that he finds morally objectionable. He further argued, "We in Congress are culpable for any immorality taking place on public citizen-owned property in Washington. And if we fail as custodians of these beautiful citizen-owned buildings, you bet, culpable [*sic*]. And what dangerous policy are we following if we dismiss the consequences of glorifying homosexuality right here in our Capitol?" (Cong. Rec., 6/27/96, p. H7053). In all likelihood, Dornan would not have objected to the use of the building by a group that he did not find morally objectionable. Dornan's remarks on this occasion are a fair representation of his record in terms of his attacks on the gay community.

Much of Dornan's speech on the afternoon of June 27, 1996, is spent defending his record on HIV/AIDS. Specifically, Dornan rejected Gunderson's view that he is not concerned about the epidemic. In fact, Dornan contended that he had given the epidemic more attention than any other member of Congress. He said:

> [I]t is interesting to know over the last ten years, Mr. Gunderson has spoken on this floor about AIDS about eight times. Unbelievable for a self-proclaimed person who is involved. . . . I, on the other hand, addressed this Chamber on the subject of AIDS, I repeat, about 200 times. That is Mr. Gunderson's rate times twenty-four. This speech tonight alone contains more references to AIDS both in quantity and quality than Mr. Gunderson's eight short speeches over sixteen years all run together. (Cong. Rec., 6/27/96, p. H7055)

One of the assumptions that Dornan made is that *quantity* and *quality* are somehow equivalent. Put another way, Dornan implied that because he spent so much energy addressing the issue, he must be compassionate. This is a huge leap in logic for the congressman.

The majority of Dornan's remarks to the House have pointed the finger at the gay community for the spread of the epidemic. Dornan, for example, refused to accept that not all gay men are promiscuous. In fact, he argued, "I said on this floor that in the early years of the AIDS crisis, the pollution of our blood supply was being incubated by promiscuity. Some people on this floor said incubated by sodomy. Well, sodomy by its nature involves promiscuity" (Cong. Rec., 2/4/93, p. H543). This is significant because by equating homosexuality with promiscuity, and promiscuity with HIV, homosexuality is the cause of AIDS in Dornan's view.

Dornan insisted that homosexuality leads to disease, or at the least, to emotional problems. Dornan maintained that homosexuality "is grounded in a sex act, and variations on that eros theme, in conduct that is defined in that dictionary behind me as 'sodomy,' and sodomy can never be anything but a selfish, hedonistic, and impotent ritual that bears only the lifeless fruits of disease and emotional distress" (Cong. Rec., 6/27/96, p. H7066).

On another occasion, Dornan claimed that "homosexual activists refuse to apologize for or give up the wild, promiscuous lifestyle that is the main driving, evil engine of this public health catastrophe of 360,000 dead people" (Cong. Rec., 6/6/96, p. H5993).[6] Arguably, there are some gay men who are promiscuous, just as there are heterosexuals who are promiscuous. The most disturbing aspect of Dornan's rhetoric is that he relied heavily on generalizations about the sexual behavior of gay men. The result of this scapegoating has been that Dornan has been at the center of attempts to legislate morality in terms of sexuality.

Dornan's rhetoric is deeply rooted in his religious beliefs, and he made no attempt to deny this fact. Indeed, his opening remarks on the question of personal privilege make strong reference to biblical scripture. He explained that "I mentioned Moses, I mentioned that in God we trust, I mentioned Abraham, I mentioned a few lines from the end of Cecil B. DeMille's classic *Ten Commandments* [sic] 'and they did give themselves up to vile afflictions' " (Cong. Rec., 6/27/96, p. H7051). References like this are common in Dornan's speeches. He contended that homosexuality is unacceptable, and Americans should not be asked to accept gays and lesbians because they are deviant. He explained:

> I would further add that there are many other reasons to oppose the norming of the abnormal. Reasons such as respect for the desires of the God of both the Old and New Testaments, or for the course of nature itself, or what Jefferson's Declaration calls "nature's God," or for the survival of the traditional family of one man and one woman bound together in mutual respect and love, sacrificing their selfish interests to procreate, nurture, and maintain what our founders called "posterity," i.e., all of our innocent children yet unborn. This is a legacy that has been time-tested, for millennia, and by its very success it is undeniably the proven path. [sic] (Cong. Rec., 6/27/96, p. H7066)

Dornan's argument that homosexuality will lead to a decline in the traditional family is unfounded. Aside from Dornan's biblical interpretation of homosexuality, Dornan provided no support for how homosexuality will destroy the family. Furthermore, Dornan ignored Gunderson's argument that the event in question is an excellent example of family values. Gunderson argued, "Cherry Jubilee represented the best of the American family. If family means 'unconditional love' then no group has rallied to care for its own more than the American gay community. When others cast the AIDS victims out of their houses, out of their communities, and out of their churches, the gay community raised unparalleled funds to meet the needs of its victims" (Cong. Rec., 5/14/96, p. H4925).

Furthermore, Dornan maintained that homosexuality is incompatible with a Christian life. He contended:

---

[6]Dornan's discourse is characterized by generalizations. In addition to characterizing all gay men as promiscuous, he tended to characterize all gay men as activists.

What possible claims can homosexual activists make toward Christian loyalty. A true Christian must be able to say with believability, "I try to walk in the footsteps of my Savior Jesus Christ." For someone to claim, without shame, that the disgusting display of hedonism at the majestic, publicly-owned Andrew W. Mellon Auditorium [the Cherry Jubilee] had anything to do with Jesus Christ or his followers is to exercise raw evil egotism. Dr. Billy Graham had it exactly right. We are "a nation on the brink of self-destruction." (Cong. Rec., 6/27/96, p. H7066)

Dornan's implication is that homosexuality is leading the country into moral destruction. Although he was responding to Gunderson's argument that the event epitomized Christian ideals, he did not respond to Gunderson's rationale. In particular, Gunderson contended, "Cherry Jubilee represented the best of America's Judao-Christian [sic] ethic. They saw the least of these among us who needed food, and clothing, and shelter. And through such events as this, they tried to provide it. They became the love of God personified, as they become their brothers' keepers" (Cong. Rec., 5/14/96, p. H4925). Dornan dismissed Gunderson's arguments by not responding to them directly.

Religious references, like these, are common in Dornan's speeches on HIV/AIDS, as well as in his speeches more generally aimed at gay men, lesbians, and bisexuals. The religious views of all citizens should be respected; however, Dornan's remarks are inappropriate in this forum because of the separation between Church and State that is fundamental to legislative activity in the United States. Most of the criticism that is leveled at Dornan, and the religious right in general, stems from the fact that it is inappropriate for Congress to legislate religious dogma. Indeed, such attempts stand in direct opposition of the purpose behind the "freedom of religion" clause in the First Amendment that guarantees that all religious beliefs will be respected. Dornan, though, insisted that he was justified in pushing his agenda because that is why he was elected. He explained, "Let me turn around another Gunderson insult: [sic] He accused me of trying, quote, 'to personally destroy those with whom (I) might disagree' [sic] . . . we, who truly believe we are our brother's keeper, . . . are not trying to destroy your risk-takers, we're trying to save your immortal souls, and your mortal lives in the measure" (Cong. Rec., 6/27/96, p. H7064). Dornan ignored the fact that the religious beliefs of other citizens are not harmonious with his own. In Dornan's case, I refer to the legislation of morality based on the Bible, but this concern could extend beyond Christianity. Citizens should become concerned when any elected official attempts to legislate any brand of religious dogma. On the other hand, because Christianity is the dominant religious affiliation in the United States, it is unlikely that we would see much legislation based on other doctrine.

Dornan's use of religious dogma serves another significant rhetorical function beyond providing him with the evidence for his argument. Specifically, the fact that Dornan used his religious beliefs extensively to support his claims gave him the opportunity to evade criticism. When Dornan has been criticized by other members of Congress, or members of the press, he has responded that to attack him is to attack his religion. Specifically, in replying to Representative Steve Gunderson, he explained:

When Mr. Gunderson attacks my belief system on what constitutes serious sin and what constitutes serious corruption of youngsters through bad example, he also attacks my religion. The Catholic Church and Pope John Paul II are unrelentingly slandered by the top and the middle management of the homosexual food chain. However, thanks to God's unrelenting love, when death is near, it's back to the arms of Holy Mother Church. *Dominus vobiscum.* (Cong. Rec., 6/27/96, p. H7062)

Although Dornan was accurate that his religious beliefs are under attack, what he failed to realize is that if he did not attempt to legislate his own religious beliefs, such attacks would be unnecessary. Dornan tried to dodge criticism by hiding behind the freedom of religion clause in the First Amendment, and yet he incited the criticism by bringing religious dogma into legislative debate. This defense is ironic, given that Dornan evidently lacked tolerance for the beliefs of others. In the interest of legislative debate, religious references probably should not be tolerated at all. However, to the extent that religious dogma is given a voice on the floor of Congress, alternative perspectives not only are justified, but also are necessary in terms of pointing to the fact that not all people share the same views; alternative perspectives are necessary to strike a balance. Put another way, the critical-thinking process that we expect to be at the center of legislative decision making, demands that we—and our legislators—seek out as many perspectives as possible.

The most striking feature of Dornan's discourse is that he consistently blamed gay men for spreading the virus. In fact, Dornan not only blamed the gay community for the spread of HIV/AIDS, but he also tended to point the finger at gays, lesbians, and bisexuals as being the root problem in what he saw as a decline in traditional family values in the United States.

Dornan contended that except for a relatively small number of people, gay men are the largest population infected with the HIV. Indeed, Dornan was correct in making this argument. The disturbing thing about Dornan's claim is that he portrayed the people that infected others as callous and uncaring. He argued, "Except for those 4,000 defenseless children and the innocent victim recipients of infected tissue or infected blood products, such as hemophiliacs, it's conduct driven. And except for, sadly, the innocent victims of lying philanderers, who callously infected their unknowing partners in the name of love. It's conduct driven" (Cong. Rec., 6/27/96, p. H7060).

Dornan's perspective is disturbing for a number of reasons. First, although he pointed out that there are a handful of people who can and should be viewed as "innocent victims," Dornan implied that people who were infected through sexual activity deserve the virus. In other words, because HIV is conduct driven, people who engage in (homo)sexual conduct deserve the consequences of their actions. Dornan was correct in arguing that to a large extent, HIV infection is conduct driven. However, he ignored the fact that politicians have hampered both educational and research efforts. In other words, for Dornan, the issue is not about teaching people to practice safer sex. Instead, Dornan placed the blame solely on what he saw as immoral sexual behavior.

In terms of creating a scapegoat, this is a significant rhetorical turn. Burke (1966, 1973) noted that in order to create a scapegoat the rhetor must, in some way, make the scapegoat "worthy" of sacrifice. In this case, sexually active individuals are worthy because they took an action and they deserve the consequences of their behavior.

A second striking feature of Dornan's statement is the way that he demonized those who infected others through sexual activity. In particular, Dornan was referring to gay men. Although this particular statement is not making a direct reference to gay men, the focus of Dornan's speech is on gay sexual behavior and promiscuity (which he assumed, necessarily, go hand-in-hand)[7]; it is reasonable to infer that it is gay men that Dornan had in mind here. In fact, Dornan was emphatic that heterosexual transmission of HIV is exaggerated. On one occasion he cited conservative commentator Wes Pruden on these exaggerated figures, who pointed out that, *The Wall Street Journal* reported this week that the Centers for Disease Control (CDC) has routinely and deliberately exaggerated the risks to heterosexuals because government officials who lobby Congress for federal research money think it's easier to get money for 'straights' " (Cong. Rec., 5/10/96, p. E773). Not surprisingly, Pruden's conclusions

---

[7]Dornan, unquestionably, was critical of any person who is sexually active outside the institution of marriage. However, Dornan spent very little energy on the issue of heterosexual promiscuity, and focused his attack on gay men.

are similar to Dornan's: that it is male-to-male sex that is the root of the problem. This is a dangerous conclusion to reach, obviously, because it implies that heterosexual sex is not a significant risk. The reality, of course, is that unsafe heterosexual sex practices are equally as risky as unsafe homosexual sex practices. Regardless of the actual demographics[8] of people with HIV, the grim reality is that anyone who engages in unsafe behavior is at risk. This should go without saying, and yet Dornan made it seem that only gay men are at risk for infection.

GAY MEN, AIDS, AND MORALISTIC RHETORIC

The view that homosexuality is at the heart of the AIDS epidemic is a common view among a substantial number of people, particularly in the United States where HIV and AIDS have decimated the gay community from the very first identified cases in the early 1980s. As Fee (1988) pointed out, "AIDS is popularly seen as caused by gay promiscuity and, even more broadly, as a punishment for unconventional or unapproved sexual behavior, rather than simply as the result of infection by a microorganism" (p. 41). The implication of Dornan's rhetoric, which is not uncommon among members of the religious right, is that if gay men would stop having sex, the virus could be controlled. Furthermore, because Dornan assumed that homosexuality is the cause of HIV/AIDS, he implied that gay men place heterosexuals at risk for the infection.[9] Indeed, as Brandt (1988) explained, there are historical parallels between HIV and other diseases: "Underlying the fears of transmission were deeper concerns about homosexuality. Just as 'innocent syphilis' in the first decades of the twentieth century was thought to bring the 'respectable middle class' in contact with a deviant ethnic, working-class 'sexual underworld,' now AIDS threatened heterosexuals with homosexual contamination. In this context, homosexuality—not a virus—causes AIDS" (p. 155). For Dornan, like many others, it was necessary to rhetorically construct a world that places the blame on a group that he found to be morally bankrupt. This divisive strategy helped Dornan create a reality in which he (and all other heterosexuals) are inherently superior.

Dornan claimed that his approach to HIV/AIDS in one of "love the sinner, and hate the sin." Dornan, in fact, admitted that he is also guilty of sin: "I am a sinner. Most of us around here commit at least little, small sins on a pretty regular basis, . . . Everyone of us, every day with every suffering person can and should say, there but for the grace of God go I" (Cong. Rec., 6/27/96, p. H7055). The difference between Dornan and the groups that he attacked is that Dornan perceived his own sins to be relatively minor in comparison. He had difficulty, however, separating the sinner and the sin. Put another way, Dornan had a tendency to hate gay men because he defined this group of human beings solely by their sexual behavior.[10] The conclusion that Dornan, and many others, reach is that gay men, almost exclusively, are to blame for the spread of HIV. In an attempt to defend himself from attacks by Representative Gunderson and others, he piously remarked, "How can I, a God-fearing American, a very lucky husband of 41 years, a father of 5 stalwart children, God-loving adult children, a grandfather of 10—number 11 is in the hanger [*sic*]—and a very hardworking double House

---

[8]Statistics about HIV/AIDS are suspect for many reasons, and they should be taken with a grain of salt. Anonymous test results, for example, are not reported to the CDC. Furthermore, because many still perceive AIDS as a gay disease, few heterosexuals are tested for the virus. On the other hand, education has varied widely among different segments of the population, which may account for skewed statistics.

[9]Indeed, this is consistent with Dornan's objections to gays in the military. He assumed that gay men will spread HIV among the troops, either through sexual contact or infected blood transfusions (Cong. Rec., 2/4/93, 11/2/95).

[10]Dornan explained that "[i]n law, homosexuality is no more nor less than a sex act" (Cong. Rec., 6/27/96, p. H7055).

chairman who is trying his best to slow the AIDS death toll, how could I possibly smear homosexual activists, as Mr. Gunderson accuses, given what they've done and continue to do to themselves?" (Cong. Rec., 6/27/96, p. H7060). Dornan seemed to forget that in the same speech he equated homosexuality with pedophilia and ephebephilia,[11] he stereotyped gay men as sexually compulsive, and he characterized gays as people that "live on the edge" (Cong. Rec., 6/27/96, p. H7060). In another speech, Dornan characterized bisexual men and women as "fence straddlers" (Cong. Rec., 9/8/95, p. H8719) who want to raise their "Benetton kids in swinging orgy households" (Cong. Rec., 9/8/95, p. H8719). Finally, Dornan referred to same-sex partnerships as an assault on traditional families[12] (Cong. Rec., 7/13/94). Dornan vehemently argued that his "motives are based on compassion and on love for my fellow man and a pure desire to defend innocent youth and children" (Cong. Rec., 6/27/96, p. H7055). For a man who claimed that he was not "out to smear homosexual activists," his characterizations of this community certainly leave a lot to be desired in terms of creating a compassionate tone.

CONCLUSION

The discourse of the radical religious right provides a strong example of how scapegoating is used as a rhetorical strategy in order to make sense of a social problem. Although this analysis is critical of this conservative group, it is important to realize that we all use scapegoats at various times in order to make our world more acceptable. That is to say that we all create scapegoats, we point the finger at other groups or individuals, in order to put a clear line of division between ourselves and situations that we find unpleasant.

The conservative, religious right discourse about HIV and AIDS, exemplified by Representative Robert Dornan, is dangerous, I believe, for several reasons. First, this discourse tends to view the spread of HIV as spread solely through male-to-male sex, and thus sends a dangerous message to heterosexuals. That is, this approach makes it seem as if there is little risk of infection if one does not engage in gay sexual activity. If people accept that they are "more likely to be struck by a personal lightning bolt from God" than to be infected with HIV, the perception is created that heterosexuals are safe from infection.

Second, the dogmatic rhetoric of this conservative politician stereotypes all gay men as sexually compulsive. Dornan, for example, did not see any problem with this approach. In fact, he argued, "Mr. Gunderson whines that straight Members [sic], such as I, unfairly use, quote, 'stereotypes,' unquote, when analyzing homosexual conduct. Well, Mr. Speaker, just what would be considered typical versus stereotypical conduct?" (Cong. Rec., 6/27/96, p. H7059). In all fairness to Dornan, there is probably very little difference between the two words in this particular instance. To argue that a particular sexual behavior is typical of gay men is to create a stereotype. By playing a semantic game, Dornan attempted to avoid the actual issue that Gunderson raised: that not all gay men are sexually compulsive, that not all gay men are drug users, that not all gay men are pedophiles, and so on.

Third, religious references in such discourse can be, and indeed are, used to protect politicians from criticism. When Dornan, for example, was criticized, he attempted to shield himself from criticism by invoking the First Amendment. In other words, he contended that

---

[11]Dornan explained that "[e]phebephilia, like pedophilia, is a mortal sin of seduction, a transgression against teenage youths 18 and 19 years old" (Cong. Rec., 6/27/96, p. H7060).

[12]Dornan argued, "Our society, especially as it is steeped in illegitimacy and divorce, need [sic] to unashamedly promote traditional marriage. Traditional marriage is better than same-sex partnerships and our institutions should say so. Anything less is an attack on the family" (Cong. Rec., 7/13/94, p. H5608).

to criticize him is to criticize his religion. This kind of devious rhetorical positioning is pretty convenient for politicians like Bob Dornan, but it runs the risk of stifling serious debate. As I have argued previously, critical thinking and decision making demand that alternative perspectives are given a voice. I would hope that the legislative bodies in this country are skeptical of approaches like the one that Dornan used in his discourse.[13]

Fourth, and finally, we must realize that although scapegoating techniques are fairly common, we should be careful to identify when these strategies are being used by the rhetor. Scapegoating techniques not only tend to construct a society in which differences are devalued, but they in fact reinforce the disenfranchisement that marginalized groups already face every day. In the case of disease in general, and HIV/AIDS in particular, prejudice and intolerance find justification through scapegoating. As Risse (1988) explained:

> In the face of epidemic disease, mankind has never reacted kindly. Collective fears, anxiety, and panic prompted a number of measures designed to protect the still healthy by cleaning up an environment deemed to be harmful, . . . we should also remember that the response to disease is a powerful tool to buttress social divisions and prejudices. . . . Flight and denial come first, followed by scapegoating of those who are judged to be different by virtue of religious beliefs, cultural practices, or economic status. (p. 57)

My own hope is that we, as a society, can begin to move beyond the harmful stereotypes that have been common in discourse about HIV and AIDS. It is critical if we are to move forward in the fight against the epidemic that we stop blaming certain groups and individuals, that we recognize that HIV is an infectious virus and not a punishment for certain behaviors, and that we begin working together to slow the spread of the virus and develop treatments for those who are suffering.

ACKNOWLEDGMENTS

The author thanks Mary Garrett and William Elwood for their helpful advice on this chapter.

REFERENCES

Bertelsen, D. A. (1993). Kenneth Burke's conception of reality: The process of transformation and its implications for rhetorical criticism. In J. W. Chesebro (Ed.), *Extensions of the Burkeian system* (pp. 230–247). Tuscaloosa: University of Alabama Press.

Brandt, A. M. (1988). AIDS: From social history to social policy. In E. Fee & D. M. Fox (Eds.), *AIDS: The burdens of history* (pp. 147–171). Berkeley: University of California Press.

Burke, K. (1966). *Language as symbolic action*. Berkeley: University of California Press.

Burke, K. (1973). *The philosophy of literary form*. Berkeley: University of California Press.

139 Cong. Rec. H543–H550. (Daily Ed. February 4, 1993). Statement of Representative Dornan.

139 Cong. Rec. H8358. (Daily Ed. October 21, 1993). Statement of Representative Dornan.

140 Cong. Rec. H4922–4925. (Daily Ed. May 14, 1996). Statement of Representative Gunderson.

---

[13]This chapter would be deficient without noting an important postscript to Dornan's tenure in the U.S. House of Representatives. In a very close election, Dornan was defeated in his reelection attempt in November 1996. Dornan had been critical of the Clinton administration during the entire first term of Clinton's presidency. For example, Dornan argued, "President Clinton's administration is in a meltdown and they are contaminating the rest of us. It is going to be three long, painful years to November 5, 1996, when we get rid of this moral sickness" (Cong. Rec., 10/21/93, p. H8358).

In an ironic twist, Clinton was reelected to a second term and Dornan was defeated. This was not the first time that Dornan lost a reelection bid; he was defeated in 1982. In all likelihood, Dornan will attempt to regain his seat in 1998.

140 Cong. Rec. H5608–5609. (Daily Ed. July 13, 1994). Statement of Representative Dornan.

141 Cong. Rec. H8714–8720. (Daily Ed. September 8, 1995). Statement of Representative Dornan.

141 Cong. Rec. H11758–11765. (Daily Ed. November 2, 1995). Statement of Representative Dornan.

142 Cong. Rec. E773. (Daily Ed. May 10, 1996). Statement of Representative Dornan.

142 Cong. Rec. H5990–5996. (Daily Ed. June 6, 1996). Statement of Representative Dornan.

142 Cong. Rec. H7051–7066. (Daily Ed. June 27, 1996). Statement of Representative Dornan.

Fee, E. (1988). Sin versus science: Venereal disease in twentieth-century Baltimore. In E. Fee & D. M. Fox (Eds.), *AIDS: The burdens of history* (pp. 121–146). Berkeley: University of California Press.

Kramer, L. (1990). *Reports from the holocaust: The making of an AIDS activist.* London: Penguin.

Monette, P. (1994). *Last watch of the night: Essays too personal and otherwise.* San Diego: Harcourt Brace.

Risse, G. B. (1988). Epidemics and history: Ecological perspectives and social responses. In E. Fee & D. M. Fox (Eds.), *AIDS: The burdens of history* (pp. 33–66). Berkeley: University of California Press.

Rosenberg, C. E. (1988). Disease and social order in America: Perceptions and expectations. In E. Fee & D. M. Fox (Eds.), *AIDS: The burdens of history* (pp. 12–32). Berkeley: University of California Press.

Shilts, R. (1987*). And the band played on: Politics, people and the AIDS epidemic.* New York: St. Martin's Press.

Treichler, P. A. (1988). AIDS, gender, and biomedical discourse: Current contests for meaning. In E. Fee & D. M. Fox (Eds.), *AIDS: The burdens of history* (pp. 190–266). Berkeley: University of California Press.

III

THE INTRAPERSONAL:
INDIVIDUALS AND BEHAVIOR

Reducing HIV Risk Behaviors of Drug-Involved Women: Social, Economic, Medical, and Legal Constraints

Sally J. Stevens
Southwest Institute for Research on Women

John G. Bogart
Attorney-at-Law

Women constitute the fastest growing group of people with HIV/AIDS in the United States (Centers for Disease Control [CDC], 1996). The proportion of AIDS cases in female adolescents and adults in the United States has increased steadily from 7% to 18% in 1994 (CDC, 1995). By mid-1996, over 78,000 cumulative AIDS cases were reported in female adolescents and adults (CDC, 1996).

Minority women have been most affected by the AIDS epidemic. Whereas African-American and Hispanic women account for only 21% of all U.S. women, they make up 74% of the cumulative AIDS cases (CDC, 1995). The median age for women with AIDS is 35 years. However, recent data indicate that young women are becoming infected at a higher rate. The number of AIDS cases diagnosed among teenage women 13 to 19 years of age increased more than 11 times between June 1989 and December 1995, and for women 20 to 24 years the number has increased more than 7 times (CDC, 1996). Injection drug use accounts for 16% of AIDS diagnosis in 13- to 19-year-olds and 31% in women who are 20 to 24 years old. Heterosexual contact accounts for 54% and 51%, respectively (CDC, 1996). Based on reported AIDS cases, 70% to 80% of persons infected through heterosexual transmission are women; most are young, minority, indigent women using crack cocaine and exchanging sex for money or drugs (Holmberg, 1996).

Unfortunately, the number of women to become infected with HIV is likely to increase due to a number of reasons. Theoretical models used to develop HIV prevention programs have generally not taken into account the gendered nature of sexual behavior and risk reduction (Amaro, 1995), and gender-specific medical, social, economic, and legal issues that affect women's ability to engage in risk reduction or protective behavior have not been adequately addressed. Most HIV prevention programs provide brief interventions for individuals or for at-risk social networks, and are limited to fewer than four sessions. Many of the medical, social, economic, and legal issues that surround women's HIV risk-taking and protective behaviors are gender specific and encompass broader issues that are not likely to be adequately addressed in a two- or three-session intervention. Fortunately, however, research has begun to illuminate those issues that may be particularly important in developing gender-specific HIV prevention strategies and interventions for women at risk for becoming infected with HIV.

MEDICAL, SOCIAL, ECONOMIC, AND LEGAL ISSUES
IN WOMEN'S HIV RISK AND PROTECTIVE BEHAVIORS

Medical Issues

Medical issues that place women at increased risk of becoming infected with HIV include issues such as: the relative efficiency of male-to-female sexual transmission, genital health and the presence of a sexually transmitted disease (STD), poor nutrition, lack of medical and preventative care, lack of acceptable female-controlled protective barriers, and reproductive issues. With regard to efficiency of HIV transmission, women are more likely to become infected by a man than a man is by a woman (Haverkos & Quinn, 1995; Padian, Shiboski, & Jewell, 1990; Sack & Streeter, 1992). A woman's reproductive organs are designed to hold semen, allowing more time for HIV to be absorbed into her body. Adolescent girls' risk of becoming infected may be even greater than that of mature women because the squamocolumnar junction of the cervix is large and more exposed. A large squamocolumnar junction is related to increased incidence of genitourinary tract infections and ecotopy in sexually active adolescent girls. In turn, this increases the likelihood of being infected with HIV or other STDs (Bowler, Sheon, D'Angelo, & Vermund, 1992).

Efficiency of vaginal HIV transmission is increased if there is a cut, lesion, abrasion, or ulcer in the vaginal lining or on the cervix, as these conditions allow HIV easier access into the bloodstream. Consequently, women who accidentally cut the vaginal tissue with a tampon or fingernail, or engage in rough vaginal sex such as frequent and multiple partners, vaginal fisting, or who use sex toys that cause genital tears, are at greater risk for becoming infected with HIV. Additionally, the presence of an STD also increases the possibility of becoming infected with HIV. Although both women and men with STDs are at increased risk, the presence of an STD may not be detected in the vaginal cavity or on the cervix, making HIV transmission unknowingly easier for women (Aral & Holmes, 1991; Rolfs, Goldberg, & Sharrar, 1990; Siegal et al., 1992). Additionally, women who use drugs are more likely to have experienced an STD sometime during their lifetime. In a national sample ($N = 1,108$) of injection drug– and crack cocaine–using women, 79% reported ever having an STD (Stevens, Estrada, & Estrada, 1998).

Nutritional differences between men and women exist in urban areas of the United States, with women's nutritional intake being worse than her male counterpart (Patton, 1994). Poor nutrition results in lower overall health status and worsens anemia, a condition that is particularly common among women of childbearing age. Drug-using women often report poor nutritional standards, whether due to the drug's impact on appetite, women's priority to spend money on drugs, or women's poverty status. In our National Institute on Drug Abuse (NIDA) AMOR[1] residential treatment for mothers and children study, as well as our Center for Substance Abuse Treatment (CSAT) Desert Willow residential treatment for pregnant and newly postpartum women's services study, women reported poor nutritional intake. Drug use itself was most often blamed for poor nutritional standards. Lack of money, however, is also an issue. In a separate NIDA-funded study, COPASA,[2] 34% of the 159

---

[1]AMOR is an abbreviation for Addicted Mothers and Offspring in Recovery.
[2]COPASA is an abbreviation for Community Outreach Project on AIDS in Southern Arizona.

women who were sex partners of male drug users, reported that they did not have enough food for 3 days.

Medical benefits and health prevention (including HIV) programs for low-income women are lacking. Many indigent women do not have health coverage or access to health care, significant barriers in obtaining primary and prevention health services. Women employed in nontraditional settings or small companies that do not offer health coverage as a benefit often cannot obtain state-funded health care because their annual income surpasses the allowable limit. Moreover, women who depend on a man to support them (and their children) may not be covered under his employer's policy if spousal benefits are not provided, or, if she is not married to the man. Only 64.8% of the 159 women who were sex partners of injection drug– and crack cocaine–using men in our NIDA COPASA female sexual partners substudy reported that they had medical coverage for themselves. This percentage is higher than that reported by some studies, given that Arizona has a relatively efficient and inclusive indigent health care program. Supporting the idea that women put others' health care needs ahead of their own, 78.7% of the female sexual partners who had children ($N = 108$), reported having health care coverage for their children. Again, given Arizona's inclusive indigent health care program, this percentage could be much higher if the enrollment process were easier and having health care was more of a priority for these women.

Historically, the majority of HIV prevention programs focused on reaching the most-at-risk populations, which included men who have sex with men, injection drug users (IDUs), and women who traded sex for money or drugs. As heterosexual contact further emerged as a major mode of HIV transmission, prevention efforts began to target men and women who use crack cocaine, due to its effect on sexual risk-taking behavior. With recent data indicating that women are the fastest growing population becoming infected with HIV, new initiatives emphasize reaching women (Coyle, 1998). However, reaching, engaging, and intervening with women at risk for HIV may need to employ different strategies than that previously used for a more male-focused prevention plan.

Prevention programs that emphasize condom use need to be redesigned to meet the challenges faced by women. Prevention programs for men attempt to convince men to use condoms. Prevention programs for women must assist women to successfully influence the behavior of their partners. Women often lack the power within relationships to insist that a condom be used and lack the resources to leave relationships that put them at risk (Elwood, Williams, Bell, & Richard, 1997; Weissman & National AIDS Research Consortium, 1991). Data from the NIDA COPASA project indicate that even among high-risk injection drug– and crack cocaine–using women, the percentage of condom use is relatively low. At baseline women ($N = 252$ matched pairs) reported having unprotected sex 68.7% of the time. Six months following an HIV prevention intervention this percentage decreased by only 16.6% to 52.1%. Compared to men enrolled in the study, these women reported not only higher percentages of unprotected sex at both baseline and follow-up, their overall decrease in unprotected sex from baseline to follow-up was also smaller. Difficulty in helping women to get their male sex partners to use condoms is also supported by data from the NIDA COPASA female sex partner of male drug users substudy. After participating in a five-session HIV risk reduction intervention, these women ($N = 75$ matched pairs) did not significantly reduce their percentage of unprotected sex. Other risks, however, were significantly reduced, including the number of sex partners ($p < .000$) and the number of sex acts ($p < .000$). Anecdotal data indicate that these women found it easier to say "no" to sex than to negotiate condom use.

The female condom has been touted as giving women more control in protecting themselves against HIV and other STDs. However, significant increases in their use have not been noted, perhaps because many women are still unfamiliar with it and/or because of its relatively high cost. Only 41% of the women enrolled in the Desert Willow project knew that a female condom should not be reused and only 18% knew that the female condom could be inserted up to 8 hours in advance of having sex. Research on the use of the female condom does, however, indicate that many drug-using women are willing to experiment with the female condom (Ashery, Carlson, Falck, Siegal, & Wang, 1995). In a study conducted by Eldridge, Lawrence, Little, Shelby, and Brasfield (1995), 23% of the low-income African-American women rated the female condom as their first-choice barrier method of five possible alternatives. In our NIDA-funded COPASA female condom substudy on the perceived benefits and acceptance of the female condom, only 10% of the low-income minority women surveyed preferred the female condom over the male condom. However, 26% said that they would use the female condom if it were readily available, 63% said they would recommend it to a friend, and 53% reported that using the female condom gave them more control. Given this, information and a demonstration of the female condom using a vaginal replica should be included in HIV prevention interventions for women.

Other desperately needed protective strategies to combat sexual transmission of HIV are underway. Although results of studies on Nonoxynol-9 (a biodetergent compound) have been mixed, the development of acceptable and effective microbicides is slowly emerging as a research focus. In part, companies have lacked interest in the development of microbicides due to fear of liability claims and the perceived lack of potential gross profit (Center for Women Policy Studies, 1994; Elias & Heise, 1993). Unlike the male and female condom, the use of microbicides as a prevention method can be employed without the man's permission or knowledge. Also, unlike the male and female condom, the development and use of microbicides could possibly allow for pregnancy to occur while simultaneously protecting against HIV and other STDs.

The decision to reproduce is a major decision in a woman's life. Women who use condoms for pregnancy prevention or prevention of STDs and HIV may forego condom use to promote pregnancy. For women whose sexual partner engages in injection drug use or risky sexual behavior with others, becoming pregnant means placing oneself and the unborn "baby" at risk for HIV through semen that may carry the virus. Women who have sex with women are also at risk from male donor sperm used for reproductive purposes (Stevens, 1997). Once pregnant, drug-using women may not seek out preventive health or medical care for fear of losing custody of her unborn "baby" at delivery. This is also true for drug-using women with children.

Social Issues

Female-centered HIV prevention efforts, particularly those that target poor and addicted women, must take into account the broader social context of women's lives. Many social issues should be addressed, including women's role within the family; power differentials in relationships; violence and the threat of violence; and social and family support. With regard to women's role within the family, women's gender-role socialization teaches women that their own health needs are secondary to her family (Center for Women Policy Studies, 1996). As reported earlier, data from the COPASA female sexual partner substudy show that indigent women are more likely to enroll their children in Arizona's health care program (78.7%) than they are likely to enroll themselves (64.8%).

Hierarchy, and related concepts such as "power," have been presented as alternatives to "sex" for explanations of attitudinal and behavioral differences between men and women (Griscom, 1992). Although power and sex may not be mutually exclusive categories (Smuts, 1991), power differentials between men and women impact women's abilities to incorporate drug and sexual risk reduction behaviors in their lives. Women who depend on men to supply them with drugs and injection drug equipment often inject *after* the man in a drug injection episode (Su et al., 1996). Social network analysis has also demonstrated power differentials within the group. Those with less power, or who are considered lower on the "hierarchy," inject after those with more power. Additionally, crack cocaine–using women are often at the mercy of a man who supplies the drug, exchanging unprotected sex for crack (De Groff & Stevens, 1992).

Women, once engaged in a sexual situation, tend to have less power than men to control the encounter or to terminate a partnership over the issue of unsafe sex (Shervington, 1992). Part of the reason that many women lack the power to insist upon condom use is that they are not financially independent. Seventy-two percent of the 152 women surveyed at the Desert Willow project reported that they received money from their family, friends, or mates during the 30 days prior to treatment entry. Data from the COPASA female sexual partner substudy indicated that only 23% of the women were employed. Moreover, women are often fearful of accusations of infidelity or abandonment if they were to suggest using a condom. Of the 151 women enrolled in the COPASA female sexual partner substudy, 40% indicated that they felt better about themselves if a man was living in the house, and 43% said that it was important to them to have a man living in the house in spite of the fact that the men were current injection drug and/or crack cocaine users. Additionally, physical violence and even its threat often prevents women from asking their male partners to use a condom.

The pervasiveness of male violence against women, including forced sex within marriages, is a reality that HIV prevention programs must address. Domestic violence is thought to exist in up to 33% of all families (Harvey, 1994), with an even higher percentage for families (partners) who use alcohol or drugs. Data from the Desert Willow project substantiate that a higher percentage of substance abusers report violence between partners. Approximately two thirds (66.7%) of the Desert Willow women reported having been violently pushed or shoved by their partner and 61.1% reported having been physically thrown around by their partner. Although data from some studies indicate that both women and men can be abusive, women more frequently report engaging in violence out of self-defense and report sustaining more serious injuries (Murphy, Stevens, McGrath, Wexler, & Reardon, 1998; White & Kowalski, 1994). Data from the Desert Willow project also support these findings. Over one fourth of the women (27.8%) reported needing medical help because of the severity of the beating sustained from their male partner, whereas only 5.6% of the women reported that they injured their partner severely enough for him to seek medical help.

Violence, substance abuse, and HIV risk behavior are clearly intertwined. When substance use occurs, violence and HIV risk behavior increases. When the women at the Desert Willow project were asked about the most recent time they had sex, 87% of the women reported using drugs before or during sex, and 82% reported not using a condom. When asked about lifetime experience of sex with partner, 33% reported having been physically forced to have sex by their partner and 66.7% reported that their partner demanded sex when they did not want it. Not surprisingly, 61.1% reported having been afraid of their partner. Violence and the fear of violence is a significant factor in inhibiting women from getting treatment, getting HIV testing, sharing HIV test results with partners, and protecting themselves from (re)infection (Brown, 1995). Women who are beaten or sexually abused by their mate are simply not in a position to ask the man to wear a condom. Additionally, women who have a history of physical or sexual abuse during childhood have reported engaging in riskier HIV behavior than those not abused as children (He, McCoy, Stevens, & Stark, 1998; Paone & Friedman, 1995).

The level of social and family support has been associated with HIV status. Brook and Brook (1995) conducted a study of female IDUs in which half of the sample were HIV-seropositive. Results indicated that peer and family risk factors were more marked in seropositive subjects. These factors included parent–child conflict, lack of mutual parent–child affection, low sibling support, low significant other support, and peer deviance/drug use. Other studies indicate that social isolation impacts HIV risk behaviors and consequent health outcomes, including HIV status. McCoy, Metsch, Smith, and Weatherby (1995) found that social support was associated with serostatus in a group of socially isolated female migrant workers. Although some of the women reported support from female relatives, specifically mothers and sisters, very few named boyfriends or spouses.

Data obtained from women enrolled in the Desert Willow project ($N = 106$) indicate that the women had fewer than two friends that they could count on for social support prior to treatment entry. In the focus group discussions that followed the administration of the questionnaire, many of the women indicated that their sexual partners did not encourage (or allow) them to have male or female friends. They said they had little choice in friendships and that their degree of socialization was dependent on their male partner's permission. To verify this, a second questionnaire was later administered. Women were asked whether their male partners wanted them to have (a) male friends, and (b) female friends; and whether their partners (a) demanded obedience, and (b) became angry if she disagreed. Results indicated that 89.9% of the women said that their male partners did not want them to have male friends and 72.2% said that their male partners did not want them to have female friends. Furthermore, 77.8% reported their partner had demanded obedience and 83.3% reported that their partner had become angry when they disagreed.

Economic Issues

Economic issues are at the root of many HIV risk behaviors. In general, issues such as poverty and employment, trading sex for money or drugs, assistance with economic hardships, and provision of appropriate and affordable women-centered drug treatment are issues that impact HIV risk–taking behavior of drug-involved women. Poverty results in personal deprivation for women, including deprivation of primary and prevention health care. As a result, the increasing rates of poverty among women have serious immediate and long-term consequences for the overall health status of women (Thomas, 1994). Many drug-involved women live at or below the line of poverty. Of the 387 injection drug– and crack cocaine–using women enrolled in the COPASA project, 93% reported an income of under $1,000 and 78% reported an income of under $500 during the 30 days prior to the baseline interview. Of the 152 women enrolled in the Desert Willow project, only 15% reported having been employed during the 30 days prior to treatment entry. Those who were employed had an average monthly income of only $531.

Studies on the relationship between employment and health indicate that employed women evidence better health status (Bullers, 1994), whereas being unemployed is correlated with high-risk sexual activity (McCoy & Inciardi, 1993). With the August 22, 1996, passage of the Personal Responsibilities and Work Opportunities Act, 50% of Aid to Dependent Families (AFDC) recipients (of which 88% are women) are expected to be employed by 2002. Although being employed may improve women's health, many women, particularly drug-using women, lack the skills or education necessary to secure employment (Karuntzos, Caddell, & Dennis, 1994). Other women may not be able to be employed due to language barriers or other family responsibilities such as taking care of aging parents. It is estimated that two thirds of the chronically poor never graduated from high school and one third of the current welfare caseload will be unable to cope in the real job market (Hunger Awareness Resource Center, 1996). Consequently for some women, the passage of this bill may increase their (a) level of poverty,

(b) dependency on men, (c) inability to end violent or HIV-risky relationships, and (d) need to trade sex for money, drugs, and/or subsistence. For women who live in poverty, AIDS is only one of many life problems, and is often rated as being less serious than unemployment, lack of child care, and crime victimization (Kalichman, Hunter, & Kelly, 1992).

Women who are dependent on trading sex to support themselves are at increased risk of becoming infected with HIV (Campbell, 1991; Worth, 1989). "Trading" behavior is a result of being in a desperate and powerless circumstance, including being homeless and living in poverty (Elwood et al., 1997). Research indicates a sizable overlap between drug use and the trade of sex for money and drugs. Des Jarlais and colleagues (1987) reported that approximately 50% of female prostitutes acknowledged injection drug use. Booth and Koester (1995) found that 30% to 50% of female IDUs relied on prostitution for economic support. Forbes (1993) reported that trading sex became the standard means for obtaining drugs for about 40% to 60% of female crack cocaine users (CCUs) interviewed. This high rate of commercial sex associated with chronic drug use and the consequent spread of HIV poses a threat for the female drug user, for her sex and needle-sharing partners, and for her unborn baby if she were to become pregnant. Again, for these women the perceived risk of becoming infected with HIV may be considerably less than the risk of being arrested, beat up, assaulted, raped, robbed, overdosing, and so on (Connors, 1992).

Help for the addicted woman is difficult to find. As of January 1, 1997, disability benefits under the Social Security and Supplemental Security Income (SSI) to individuals whose disability is based on alcohol and/or drug addiction is prohibited ("Questions and Answers," 1996). Insurance benefits and managed care often limit the type of treatment (outpatient vs. residential), as well as the number of sessions. For the disenfranchised addicted woman who lives in poverty, has experienced abuse as both a child and as an adult, lives in a violent household, *and* has children, barriers to entering and staying in drug treatment and/or HIV prevention programs are numerous. Two of the more noted barriers are lack of transportation and inability to access trustworthy child care (Wechsberg, 1995). Other barriers include desire to continue using drugs, family (particularly sexual partners) pressure to not enter treatment, lack of choice of treatment modality, and the need to financially support self and others.

Legal Issues

There are numerous legal barriers that prevent people, especially women, from engaging in HIV risk protective behavior. Although not all-inclusive, the most significant are laws that prevent the advertisement of contraceptive devices, especially condoms; laws that make possession of drug paraphernalia criminal, especially syringes; laws prohibiting or inhibiting sex education in public schools; the lack of laws requiring the testing of donor sperm for artificial insemination; inadequate delivery systems for legal services to women and children at risk; increased legal scrutiny, regulation, and supervision of women's bodies, to include the custody and control of their children; revisions in federal entitlement programs and the implementation of federal block grants to the states for services; and revisions in the U.S. immigration laws. Although these all constitute legal barriers, they are also inextricably intertwined with society's social, moral, and economic interests. Most significantly, they all seem to involve, or revolve about, empowerment between the sexes, and the subjugation of women by the male element.

One of the more acknowledged legal barriers is the passage of laws that restrict syringe sales and exchanges, and regulate the possession of drug paraphernalia, which includes "hypodermic syringes, needles and other objects used, intended for use or designed for use in parenterally injecting drugs into the human body" (Arizona Revised Statutes, § 13-3415). Several states require a prescription to purchase syringes, and the majority of the U.S. states have laws that regulate the possession of syringes. As a result, syringe availability in many states is scarce, pressing drug injectors to share whatever syringes are available (Booth, Koester, Reichardt, & Brewster, 1993; Singer, Irizzary, & Schensul, 1991). Nevertheless, the scarcity of syringes does not seem to prevent users from sharing and borrowing needles among themselves, prompting HIV researchers to advocate for reassessment of such laws (Koester, 1994), and for needle-exchange programs, which have been shown to reduce the risk of HIV transmission ("Legal, Policy Barriers," 1997).

Research on female drug injectors indicates that they often inject after the male in a drug injection episode (Su et al., 1996), placing them at more risk for becoming infected. The most pervasive barriers for clean needle use among minority female injectors include: first, not having clean needles; second, being high and not interested in needle cleaning; and third, not having disinfectant available (Nyamathi, Lewis, Leake, Flaskerud, & Bennett, 1995). These results suggest that needle-exchange programs may be particularly beneficial for women injectors. Preliminary data from Estrada and Estrada (1997) indicate that women are receptive to needle-exchange programs. Of the 135 people who used the needle-exchange program in South Tucson between December 1996 and March 1997, 50% of the women (compared to 12% of the men) who participated in the needle-exchange program used the program more than once.

Legal constraints with regard to sex and HIV prevention include laws that prohibit contraceptive (condom) advertising, laws that inhibit sex education in public schools, and the lack of regulation requiring testing of donor sperm for use in artificial insemination. These laws involve oversight on the part of our public officials or, most significantly, incorporate the social and moral values of our legislators. HIV/AIDS education in curriculum within schools is left to the discretion of each state. As a result, some states limit the instruction of sex education, which inherently involves HIV/AIDS prevention. Some states, such as North Carolina, choose to teach students that the only way to practice safe sex is to not have sex ("AIDS Policy & Law," 1997). Moreover, laws that prohibit condom advertising (on television, radio, and other advertising media) also leave young adults uninformed about how they can protect themselves against infection. With the number of diagnosed AIDS cases among teenage women ages 13 to 19 years having increased by more than 11 times between June of 1989 and December of 1995, more appropriate and factual HIV/AIDS curriculum is called for, as well as relevant and effective media campaigns. Education and media advertising may help women overcome their reported discomfort in addressing condom use with their partner, a major barrier to condom use reported by women (Nyamathi et al., 1995). As women become more confident in negotiating condom use, frequency of condom use has been shown to increase (Sacco, Levine, Reed, & Thompson, 1991).

More than 80,000 women are artificially inseminated each year with sperm from unknown donors, yet only 20 states have laws mandating HIV testing of semen donors or their donated sperm. Notwithstanding, CDC guidelines call for two tests, one on the donor at the time of donation and a second test on the semen 6 months later when antibodies to the virus should be detectable ("AIDS Policy & Law," 1997). Without implementation of the recommended testing guidelines, women who want to become pregnant through artificial insemination may be putting themselves, their sex partners, and their unborn children at risk for HIV infection.

The need for a delivery system for legal services for the poor is an important one. Recent statistics indicate that less than 20% of poor Americans' legal needs are being met (Arizona Bar Foundation, 1997). Klein, Dubler, DiStabile, and Solomon (1995) studied the legal needs of poor, minority women infected with HIV. Legal needs included: help with housing (41%), government entitlements (35%), living will or health care proxy (32%), loans or unpaid bills (26%), child care (16%), child support (15%), and welfare (14%). Some reasons women with

HIV/AIDS are not served are: lack of education about the legal system and what it can provide, dislike of the legal system, child-care and transportation needs, the fear of loss of financial and family support, and failure of service providers to ask women what their needs are or provide for those needs in a timely manner. These same factors may be true for women who are at risk for HIV (Pilar, 1995). Fear and underuse of the legal system may be even more pronounced for women who use drugs, who are involved with a partner who uses drugs, and/or trades sex for money or drugs. Data from drug-using women in the Desert Willow and AMOR projects indicate that 75% of the 166 women reported having been raped sometime during their life. Of the 49 women who were asked whether they pursued prosecution, only 30.6% ($n = 15$) said they had attempted. This fear and underuse of the legal system by drug-using women is further elevated when women are pregnant and/or have children of whom they want to retain custody. Education and guidance regarding legal services that are available, and how to obtain these legal services, would help to alleviate this problem.

As the pendulum of societal interest and concern for its citizenry swings, so does the legal scrutiny, regulation, and supervision of women's bodies. For the most part, the legal constraints upon women's bodies involve women's direct involvement with their children, to include unborn children. As science and technology have advanced, "viewing" of the fetus has become possible through video and sonograms. Advances in the area of neonatology have led to the legal construction of "fetus as patient," an entity requiring a separate physician, and often a separate legal advocate (Hartouni, 1991; Kolata, 1989). As a result, state courts, and especially juvenile courts, have subsequently begun to assume jurisdiction over the content of pregnant women's wombs. Drug-using women have been charged with manslaughter ("Woman Charged With Manslaughter," 1995), "transportation of drugs" (through the umbilical cord; Dinnerstein, 1995), and potentially for "delivery of a controlled substance" (through the umbilical cord). Pregnant women who smoke, drink, have sex, take legal/illegal drugs, fail to obtain prenatal care, and so on, are increasingly subject to legal scrutiny or possible criminal prosecution. Many women report that they do not seek prenatal care or substance abuse treatment because they are afraid of being arrested, having their children removed from their custody, or having an unborn "baby" taken away at birth (R. McGrath, personal communication, December 10, 1995).

Recently, the federal government has passed legislation vastly changing federal entitlement programs and immigration policy, the full impact of which has yet to be determined. The Welfare Reform Act of 1996 (PL 104-193) reduced federal entitlement programs, and implemented block grants to the individual states for funding distribution on a state-by-state basis, as each state believes appropriate. Although restrictions of disbursement will vary from state to state, some restrictions already evident are that recipients of food stamps, supplemental social security, and the like, may be ineligible for assistance after 2 years. Likewise, some states are requiring aid recipients to work in order to obtain assistance, which then inherently involves difficulties with transportation, child care, physical and mental capabilities, job skills, and the like. At this time, the state-by-state details have not been worked out, and the full impact of the Welfare Reform Act of 1996 cannot be determined. However, there is no question that the poor, untrained, uneducated, and needy ultimately will be left without a safety net, which then places poor and needy women, especially women with children, under the power and authority of whomever may be willing to support them or provide them shelter, food, and clothing.

Likewise, the Illegal Immigration Reform and Immigrant Responsibility Act of 1996 will impact upon women at risk. Women illegally in the United States may be "removed" from the United States, whereas their children, some of them U.S. citizens, are left in limbo. Because the Act, for all intents and purposes, denies judicial review, no court has jurisdiction to review the discretionary decisions or actions of the Attorney General and the Immigration Service. Again, this places women, and especially women with children, at the mercy of those who would "assist" them, either with financial assistance or under threat of being reported to the authorities and removed from the United States.

The net impact perceived with the revisions in federal entitlement programs and U.S. immigration laws is increased social control over women, their bodies, and their children. Not only is there an increase in social control, but the lack of societal assistance to women at risk concurrently increases the power of the man over the woman. Women, especially unskilled/uneducated women with children, inherently become more dependent on men who are at times abusive, domineering, drug abusing, and high risk taking. With dependency comes "lack of voice," which leads to HIV risk taking on the part of women in order to keep themselves and their children with a roof over their head, clothes to wear, and food to eat. This male dominance can only increase and compound as society's social, moral, and economic interests remove the safety net of programs designed to provide drug treatment for women and their children, and to assist women who do not have the education, training, job skills, citizenship, and/or financial resources necessary to support themselves and their children.

THE NEED FOR WOMEN-CENTERED HIV RISK REDUCTION INTERVENTIONS

HIV risk reduction interventions for drug-involved men and women, in general, have not been gender specific. Many of the theoretical models used to guide HIV interventions have been developed by men, for men, and tested on a predominantly male population. Although certain elements of these models are applicable to women, none captures the unique medical issues, social context, economic hardships, and legal struggles and concerns that affect women's HIV risk–taking behaviors. More appropriate theoretical models might include those based on learned helplessness (Abramson, Seligman, & Teasdale, 1978; Uomoto, 1986), Maslow's theory of self-actualization (McConnell, 1980), or theories that consider the role of oppression (Freire, 1970). Additionally, comprehensive theories, such as feminist theory, that take into account these wider issues, the diversity of women, their subjectivity, and the ever-changing context of women's lives (Agger, 1993; Doyal, Naidoo, & Wilton, 1994; Hermann & Stewart, 1994; Thomas, 1994) may be more useful in developing women's-centered HIV risk reduction interventions.

A women's-centered intervention must first reach women at risk for HIV infection. Women, particularly disenfranchised drug-using women, are a difficult, hidden population to reach. HIV prevention programs need to be willing to go to the women, in their communities, their homes, the day-care centers of their children, neighborhood centers, hotels used for prostitution, housing projects, back alleys, and streets. Posters, pamphlets, first aid kits, bleach kits, hygiene packets, food boxes, kitchen towels, and so on can provide a means for advertising the prevention project. Because men often control the day-to-day activities of the women, advertising of the program should be done discreetly, perhaps only noting a "health care" project that offers many health-related services and that does not alienate men or women from entering the project. Additionally, providing additional services helps to recruit women for services. Pregnancy testing, well baby checks and immunizations, food boxes, hygiene and bleach packets, condoms, child friendly lounging areas, STD testing, and acceptance of personal mail will draw women to the center where HIV prevention messages and interventions can occur. Moreover, HIV prevention must include transportation and child care.

Once recruited to participate, a women's-centered intervention should begin by recognizing the very basic biological differences between men and women. Communication and education about their own bodies must be facilitated, identifying factors that make it easier for HIV to enter their bloodstream when having vaginal sex. Because women often do not have control over condom use, perhaps the most important information we can give women is to educate them on how to keep their genital area healthy. Women should know that any trauma to their genital area makes it easier for HIV to enter their bloodstream. Trauma can be inflicted through rough sex, tampon insertion, STDs, multiple and frequent partners, use of spermicide, vaginal douching, and so on, causing cuts or lesions and/or loss of healthy bacteria. Second, women should be given STD screenings on a regular basis, as well as education about identification and treatments for STDs. Third, women should be educated about the female condom. If a woman is interested in using the female condom for protection, training on correct insertion and removal is necessary. Although the female condom may not be an option for many women, it should be included as an alternative in HIV prevention programs that target women.

A women's-centered intervention should provide hands-on instruction and rehearsal about how to clean a needle, even if the woman is not an IDU but rather a sex partner of an IDU. Consequently, with this knowledge she has an option to clean her partner's needles or teach her partner how to clean his needles effectively. Women should be reminded that use of the male condom is still her best protection against HIV and other STDs. If she has a male partner who is willing to use a condom, she should insist upon its use. Women also should be taught how to put on and take off a male condom. She should be informed that her partner should use condoms made of latex, that condoms should be kept out of the heat, that they should not be used after the expiration date, and so on. Furthermore, women need to be taught negotiation skills so that they can promote the cleaning of needles, or negotiate the use of condoms. Women should also be encouraged to examine their past experiences and how gender-role expectations and past experience reinforce current behavior, including how past violent sex experiences often set women up to choose abusive partners. Such information will hopefully assist women in avoiding future violence-oriented relationships and sex experiences. Women then can choose better, and more respectful, sex partners.

Women's-centered interventions should also include activities that promote empowerment such as identification of positive social support and support systems, discussion of alternatives to male domination, provisions for job training, and encouragement to engage in drug treatment and/or support groups. Moreover, women need to become knowledgeable about the legal impact of their behavior. They need to be encouraged and empowered to stand up for their legal rights and utilize the legal system for their own safety and protection as well as the safety and protection of their children.

Finally, women must be taught, and assisted, in communication skills. With communication comes strength, both for the individual woman, and for women as an identifiable, specific, at-risk group. Women must learn how to communicate with their sex and/or drug-using partners, with their families, and with their support groups. Communication provides the vehicle to reduce HIV exposure, and is the catalyst for female empowerment, both individually and as a group. Communication can provide the information and skills to reduce HIV exposure, and enables the at-risk woman to overcome the social, moral, cultural, and economic barriers that have traditionally supported male domination and placed the woman at greater risk of HIV infection. Moreover, communication is absolutely necessary to organize groups, who can then communicate with legislative and public health officials to alter the system that denies women empowerment within our society. With communication also comes power, and with power comes change, change that can reduce HIV risk behavior of drug-involved women.

REFERENCES

Abramson, L. Y., Seligman, M. E. P., & Teasdale, J. D. (1978). Learned helplsessness in humans: Critique and reformation. *Journal of Abnormal Psychology, 87,* 49–74.

Agger, B. (1993). *Gender, culture and power: Toward a feminist postmodern critical theory.* Westport, CT: Praeger.

AIDS Policy & Law. (1997). *HIV/AIDS and the states: Looking back at 1996.* Horsham, PA: LRP Publications.

Amaro, H. (1995). Love, sex, and power: Considering women's realities in HIV prevention. *American Psychologist, 50,* 437–447.

Aral, S. O., & Holmes, K. K. (1991). Sexually transmitted diseases in the AIDS era. *Scientific American, 264,* 62–69.

Arizona Bar Foundation. (1997). *Justice for all.* Pheonix: State Bar of Arizona.

Ashery, R. S., Carlson, R. G., Falck, R. S., Siegal, H. A., & Wang, J. (1995). Female condom use among injection drug- and crack cocaine-using women. *American Journal of Public Health, 85,* 736–737.

Booth, R., & Koester, S. K. (1995). Gender differences in sex-risk behaviors, economic livelihood, and self-concept among drug injectors and crack smokers. *American Journal of Addictions, 4,* 313–322.

Booth, R., Koester, S., Reichardt, C. S., & Brewster, J. T. (1993). Quantitative and qualitative methods to assess behavioral change among injection drug users. *Drugs and Society, 7,* 161–183.

Bowler, S., Sheon, A. R., D'Angelo, L. J., & Vermund, S. H. (1992). HIV and AIDS among adolescents in the United States: Increasing risks in the 1990s. *Journal of Adolescence, 15,* 345–371.

Brook, D. W., & Brook, J. S. (1995, June). *Women at risk: Psychosocial factors in HIV transmission.* Paper presented at NIDA's 1995 conference on AIDS and Drug Abuse, Scottsdale, AZ.

Brown, V. B. (1995, February). *HIV infection in women: Models of intervention for violence against women.* Paper presented at the HIV Infection in Women Conference: Setting a New Agenda, Washington, DC.

Bullers, S. (1994). Women's roles and health: The mediating effect of perceived control. *Women and Health, 22,* 11–30.

Campbell, C. A. (1991). Prostitution, AIDS, and preventive health behavior. *Social Science & Medicine, 32,* 1367–1378.

Center for Women Policy Studies. (1994). *Women-controlled microbicides for HIV prevention of HIV/STDs.* Washington, DC: Author.

Center for Women Policy Studies. (1996, April). *Building a national policy agenda: Ten principles for women-focused HIV/AIDS prevention.* Washington, DC: Author.

Centers for Disease Control and Prevention. (1995). *HIV/AIDS Prevention.* Atlanta: Centers for Disease Control and Prevention.

Centers for Disease Control and Prevention. (1996). *HIV/AIDS Surveillance Report, 8,* 1.

Connors, M. M. (1992). Risk perception, risk taking and risk management among intravenous drug users: Implication for AIDS prevention. *Social Science Medicine, 34,* 591–601.

Coyle, S. L. (1998). Women's drug use and HIV risk: Findings from NIDA's Cooperative Agreement for Community-Based Outreach/Intervention Research Program. *Women & Health, 27,* 1–18.

De Groff, A., & Stevens, S. J. (1992). *HIV and crack cocaine use: Issues in prevention strategies: Final report* (Submitted to the Arizona Department of Health Services). Tucson, AZ: Tucson AIDS Project.

Des Jarlais, D. C., Wish, E., Friedman, S. R., Stonebruner, R., Yancovitz, S. R., Mildvan, D., El-Sadr, W., Brady, E, & Cuadrado, M. (1987). Intravenous drug use and the heterosexual transmission of the human immunodeficiency virus: Current trends in New York City. *New York State Journal of Medicine, 30,* 283–286.

Dinnerstein, M. (1995, November). *The cultural body.* Paper presented at the Joint Seminar: El Colegio de la Frontera Norte, El Colegio de Sonora, University of Arizona, Tucson.

Doyal, L., Naidoo, J., & Wilton, T. (1994). *AIDS: Setting a feminist agenda.* Bristol, PA: Taylor & Francis.

Eldridge, G. D., Lawrence, J. S., Little, C., Shelby, M. C., & Brasfield, T. L. (1995). Barriers to condom use and barrier method preference among low-income African American women. *Women and Health, 23,* 73–90.

Elias, C. J., & Heise, L. (1993). *The development of microbicides: A new method of HIV prevention for women.* New York: The Population Council.

Elwood, W. N., Williams, M. L., Bell, D. C., & Richard, A. J. (1997). Strawberry fields: Powerlessness and HIV prevention among people who trade sex for drugs. *AIDS Care, 9,* 273–284.

Estrada, A. L., & Estrada, B. D. (1997). *South Tucson needle exchange preliminary report.* Unpublished report, University of Arizona, Tucson.

Forbes, A. (1993). Crack cocaine and HIV: How national drug addiction treatment deficits fan the pandemic flames. *AIDS and Public Policy, 8,* 44–52.

Freire, P. (1970). *Pedagogy of the oppressed.* New York: Seabury Press.

Griscom, J. (1992). Women and power: Definition, dualism, and difference. *Psychology of Women Quarterly, 16,* 389–414.

Hartouni, V. (1991). Containing women: Reproductive discourse in the 1980s. In C. Penley & A. Ross (Eds), *Technoculture*. Minneapolis: University of Minnesota Press.

Harvey, D. (1994). *Domestic violence monitoring program: Program summary*. Unpublished manuscript.

Haverkos, H. W., & Quinn, T. C. (1995). The third wave: HIV infection among heterosexuals in the United States and Europe. *International Journal of STD and AIDS, 6,* 1–6.

He, H., McCoy, H. V., Stevens, S. J., & Stark, M. J. (1998). Violence and HIV sexual risk behaviors among female sex partners of male drug users. *Women and Health, 27,* 161–174.

Herrmann, A. C., & Stewart, A. J. (1994). *Theorizing feminism: Parallel trends in the humanities and social sciences.* Boulder, CO: Westview.

Holmberg, S. (1996). The estimated prevalence and incidence of HIV in 96 large US metropolitan areas. *American Journal of Public Health, 86,* 642–654.

Hunger Awareness Resource Center. (1996). *Welfare reform to impact food banks.* Tucson, AZ: Hunger Awareness Resource Center.

Kalichman, S. C., Hunter, T. C., & Kelly, J. A. (1992). Perceptions of AIDS susceptibility among minority and non-minority women at risk for HIV infection. *Journal of Consulting and Clinical Psychology, 60,* 725–732.

Karuntzos, G. T., Caddell, J. M., & Dennis, M. L. (1994). Gender differences in vocational needs and outcomes for methadone treatment clients. *Journal of Psychoactive Drugs, 26,* 173–180.

Klein, R. S., Dubler, N., DiStabile, P., & Solomon, L. (1995, February). *Self-reported legal needs of women at risk for HIV infection.* Paper presented at the HIV Infection in Women Conference: Setting a New Agenda, Washington, DC.

Koester, S. K. (1994). Copping, running, and paraphernalia laws: Contextual variables and needle risk behavior among injection drug users in Denver. *Human Organization, 53,* 287–295.

Kolata, G. (1989, May 14). Operating on the unborn. *The New York Times Magazine,* p. 35.

Legal, policy barriers inhibit effective prevention of HIV/AIDS transmission. (1997, February). *AIDS/STD News Report,* p. 3.

McConnell, J. V. (1980). *Understanding human behavior.* New York: Holt, Rinehart & Winston.

McCoy, H. V., & Inciardi, J. A. (1993). Women and AIDS: Social determinants of sex-related activities. *Women and Health, 20,* 69–86.

McCoy, H. V., Metsch, L., Smith, S., & Weatherby, N. L. (1995, February). *Social isolation and HIV-related health outcomes: Women migrant workers.* Paper presented at the HIV Infection in Women Conference: Setting a New Agenda, Washington, DC.

Murphy, B., Stevens, S. J., McGrath, R., Wexler, H. K., & Reardon, D. (1998). Women and violence: A different look. *Drugs and Society, 13,* 148–164.

Nyamathi, A. M., Lewis, C. Leake, B., Flaskerud, J., & Bennett, C. (1995). Barriers to condom use and needle cleaning among impoverished minority female injection drug users and partners of injection drug users. *Public Health Reports, 17,* 166–172.

Padian, N. S., Shiboski, S. S., & Jewell, N. (1990, June). *The relative efficiency of female-to-male HIV sexual transmission.* Paper presented at the Sixth International Conference on AIDS, San Francisco.

Paone, D., & Friedmann, P. (1995, February). *Sexual abuse as a risk factor for HIV infection.* Paper presented at HIV Infection in Women Conference: Setting a New Agenda, Washington, DC.

Patton, L. (1994). *Last served? Gendering the HIV pandemic.* Bristol, PA: Taylor & Francis.

Pilar, J. P. (1995, February). *Overcoming legal service barriers for women with HIV.* Paper presented at the HIV Infection in Women Conference: Setting a New Agenda, Washington, DC.

Questions and answers. (1996). *Social Security Administration News Briefs, 6,* 3.

Rolfs, R. T., Goldberg, M., & Sharrar, R. G. (1990). Risk factors for syphilis: Cocaine use and prostitution. *American Journal of Public Health, 80,* 853–857.

Sacco, W. P., Levine, B., Reed, D. L., & Thompson, K. (1991). Attitudes about condom use as an AIDS-relevant behavior: Their factor structure and relation to condom use. *Psychological Assessment: A Journal of Consulting and Clinical Psychology, 3,* 265–272.

Sack, F., & Streeter, A. (1992). *Romance to die for.* Deerfield Beach, FL: Health Communications Inc.

Shervington, D. (1992, December). *Personal testimony.* Hearings before the Obstetrics and Devices Panel of the Center for Devices and Radiological Health, U.S. Food and Drug Administration, 49th meeting, Washington, DC.

Siegal, H. A., Carlson, R. G., Falck, R., Forney, M. A., Wang, J., & Li, L. (1992). High-risk behaviors for transmission of syphilis and human immunodeficiency virus among crack cocaine–using women. *Sexually Transmitted Diseases, 19,* 266–271.

Singer, M., Irizzary, R., & Schensul, J. J. (1991). Needle access as an AIDS prevention strategy for IV drug users: A research perspective. *Human Organization, 50,* 142–153.

Smuts, B. (1991). Male aggression against women: An evolutionary perspective. *Human Nature, 3,* 1–44.

Stevens, S. J. (1997, October 14). *AIDS and drug abuse.* Paper presented at the Implementing Consortium Project: Aspirations, Challenges, and Connections, Tijuana, Mexico.

Stevens, S. J., Estrada, A. L., & Estrada, B. D. (1998). HIV sex and drug risk behavior and behavior change in a national sample of injection drug and crack cocaine using women. *Women and Health, 27,* 25–48.

Su, S. S., Pach, A., Hoffman, A., Pierce, T. G., Ingles, J. S., Unfred, C., & Gray, F. (1996). *Drug injector risk networks and HIV transmission: A prospective study.* Unpublished report to the National Institute on Drug Abuse.

Thomas, V. G. (1994). Using feminist and social structural analysis to focus on the health of poor women. *Women and Health, 22*(1), 1–15.

Uomoto, J. (1986). Examination of psychological distress in ethnic minorities from a learned helplessness framework. *Professional Psychology, Research and Practice, 17,* 448–453.

Wechsberg, W. (1995). Strategies for working with women substance abusers. In B. S. Brown (Ed.), *Substance abuse treatment in the era of AIDS* (pp. 119–152). Rockville, MD: Center for Substance Abuse Treatment.

Weissman, G., & National AIDS Research Consortium. (1991). AIDS prevention for women at risk: Experience from a National Research Demonstration Program. *Journal of Primary Prevention, 12,* 49–63.

White, J. W., & Kowalski, R. M. (1994). Deconstructing the myth of the nonaggressive woman: A feminist analysis. *Psychology of Women Quarterly, 18,* 487–508.

Woman charged with manslaughter for crack use before stillbirth. (1995, October 18). *Substance Abuse Funding News,* p. 10.

Worth, D. (1989). Sexual decision-making and AIDS: Why condom promotion among vulnerable women is likely to fail. *Studies in Family Planning, 20,* 297–307.

The Politics of Silence: Communicative Rules and HIV Prevention Issues in Gay Male Bathhouses

William N. Elwood
Mark L. Williams
Behavioral Research Group
University of Texas—Houston School of Public Health

Politics frequently is understood as a linguistic process (Edelman, 1971, 1977, 1988). Using this operational definition, people attempt to persuade others to accept their definition of issues because specific definitions influence people to accept specific policy outcomes, or to consider certain issues, rather than others, as important (Brummett, 1979; Elwood, 1995, chap. 1, this volume; Vibbert, 1987). Thus, politics involves symbol usage by symbol-using, symbol-misusing animals (see Burke, 1966), a symbolic process of acquiring power, or pervasive terminological influence, over other people (Edelman, 1971; Elwood, chap. 1, this volume). Such power can influence events, policies, and actions of other individuals (Hale, 1983; Mumby, 1988). Indeed, scholars of discourse from ancient Greece to the present day concur that human discourse is political because linguistic choices portray a particular version of reality that benefits some and dispossesses others (Aristotle, 1984, 1991; Hart, 1982; Trinidad, 1991). Foucault ventured as far as to assert that discourse and power are inextricably intertwined (1961, 1970, 1972, 1978); his later idea of the *power/knowledge regime* posits that discourses organize and govern societal practices, dictate what constitutes "truth," what constitutes appropriate behavior, and how one may constitute "self" in regard to these dictates—particularly as regards (homo)sexuality (1980, 1989, 1990). In other words, individuals with power have pervasive terminological control to define appropriate behaviors and policies.

What happens, then, when language itself becomes that which is regulated? And when the dearth of language leads to policy outcomes of pandemic proportions? The purpose of this chapter is to answer these two questions. For although gay bathhouses in the United States have been the object of policy discussions since their inception (e.g., Bérubé, 1996), the discursive practices within them—or, rather the lack thereof—have been ignored. Yet these practices reinforce a power dynamic that facilitates the transmission of HIV and other STDs. To illustrate this idea, we first discuss the nexus of politics and bathhouses. Second, we present the political uses of silence adapted to bathhouses. Third, we describe the study and method for analysis. Fourth, we present data to support our thesis. Fifth, and finally, we discuss our findings and the implications for transmission and intervention.

BATHHOUSES, POLITICS, AND POLICY

Although some people might dispute Kramer's (1989) claim that any issue involved with HIV and AIDS is inherently political, anyone likely would agree that bathhouses have been a political issue since the advent of the HIV/AIDS epidemic. In fact, Bérubé (1996) traced the history of bathhouses as sites of male sexuality and finds that American urban bathhouses have been associated with legislation and law enforcement since the beginning of the 20th century. Early in the HIV/AIDS pandemic, identification of bathhouses as sites of unprotected sex with multiple partners, and popular outrage at their existence, led to bathhouse closings in many cities. Health officials, policymakers, and political activists in New York, San Francisco, and other cities argued over the premise that "bathhouses guaranteed the rapid spread of AIDS among gay men" (Shilts, 1987, p. 306). Since that time, bathhouses or their variants have reopened in American cities, and unprotected sexual behaviors and illegal drug use, thought to exacerbate sexual risk behaviors, among men who have sex with men (MSMs) in bathhouses and other venues have been reported (Battjes, 1994; Elwood, 1996; Elwood & Williams, 1998; Elwood, Williams, & Bowen, 1996; Heitz, 1997; Leigh, 1990; McCoy & Inciardi, 1995; Meyer & Dean, 1995; Odets, 1994; Ostrow, 1994; Peterson et al., 1992; Sadownick, 1996; Strathdee et al., 1996).

Perhaps the most recent—and ironic—situation in which bathhouses, politics, and HIV/AIDS converge is that of a member of the Presidential AIDS Advisory Committee, who died in a Palm Springs, California, bathhouse cubicle surrounded by seven bottles of a nitrite compound (Britton, 1996; "Conversations," 1996; for a discussion of gay irony, see Pronger, 1993). Nevertheless, the debate over the public health threat of bathhouses has reemerged in many American cities as sexually oriented establishments open for business (e.g., Clark, 1996; Heitz, 1997; Johnson, 1997; "Licensed sex clubs," 1996). Opponents argue that bathhouses are settings that encourage risky sexual behaviors, and that without bathhouse venues, the men who ordinarily frequent them would be unable to find other settings in which to engage in unprotected sex with numerous male partners (see Orta, 1996; Webber, 1996). Proponents posit that bathhouses provide men with the opportunity to socialize, to express their gay identity, and, of course, to have sex observed by others in a protected setting. Without bathhouses, proponents argue, many of these men would frequent public sex environments, thus disturbing the peace and increasing their chances of disease transmission because such settings leave them without access to condoms (Mohr, 1996; Quinn, 1996; Zappas, 1996). The lack of previous research to cite has resulted in a policy argument on both sides that is based almost entirely on anecdotal information.

Nevertheless, researchers recently have begun to explore the idea that some MSMs may seek out sexual environments including bathhouses as situations in which they fulfill a desire to escape cognitive awareness of very rigorous HIV prevention norms and standards. Fatigue, fatalism, or other negative affect over HIV may lead people to "cognitively disengage" within sexual situations, and not to follow their norms for HIV risk reduction or intentions toward safety. Thus, substance use in bathhouses and other sexual settings facilitates this cognitive disengagement, wherein people enact "automatic" sexual scripts and/or become more responsive to external pressures toward risk (McKirnan, Ostrow, & Hope, 1996; Ostrow & McKirnan, 1997; M. L. Williams, Elwood, & Bowen, 1997). Concurrent with such reasons to attend bathhouses is the predominant communication rule for silence in bathhouse public areas to ensure the expediency of men's sexual encounters (Elwood & M. L. Williams, 1997; see also Henriksson & Mansson, 1995; Weinberg & C. J. Williams, 1975). Not only does silence make sex between men expedient, but also it can facilitate the transmission of HIV and other STDs during sex. For example, Prestage and Drielsma (1996) found a relationship between silence and sexual risk behaviors among bisexual men who frequented public sex environments.

POLITICS, SILENCE, AND BATHHOUSES

As stated earlier, Foucault posited that power operates through the apparatus of human discourse; however, Bruneau (1973) argued that "much political power" is "derived and . . . maintained by the manner in which silence is used" (p. 59). Similarly, Kane (1984) stated that silence is "a moment in language" that "has specific meaning and purpose" (p. 17). Part of that meaning and purpose has been to escape from the heterocentric world (e.g., Bérubé, 1996; Rich, 1983). In bathhouses, silence allows MSMs to fulfill a common human desire, "to turn away from the real world which presents problems that sometimes seem overwhelming, and to turn instead to a fantasy world of our own making" (Kaplan, 1994, p. 46). Specifically, bathhouses allow MSMs to escape compulsory heterosexuality, to foster a gay identity (Bérubé, 1996); silence allows them to preserve their outside world identities and to pursue fantasy sex with other male bathhouse patrons (e.g., Elwood & Williams, 1998; McKirnan et al., 1996).

Although silence can facilitate patron anonymity and sexual escapism in bathhouses, it also can provide the means by which men can consciously pursue unprotected anal sex with other men. Previous research demonstrates that condom use and other sexual risk reduction practices require negotiation between partners (e.g., Bartos & Middleton, 1996; Browne & Minichello, 1994; Kellar-Guenther, chap. 16 of this volume; Sheer, 1995; Wingood, Hunter-Gamble, & DiClemente, 1993). When silence is the communication norm within bathhouses (Elwood & M. L. Williams, 1997; Weinberg & C. J. Williams, 1975), condom negotiation becomes improbable, if not impossible. Thus, silence facilitates a policy, or practice, of unprotected anal sex between men—some of whom can exploit the practice to achieve their goal of unprotected anal sex with others.

SILENCE AS POLITICAL PRACTICE

Writing about the presidency, Brummett (1980) "propose[d] a theory of . . . *strategic silence* in politics" (p. 289). He argued, "Silence becomes strategic only when talk is expected. Silence is strategic when someone has pressing reason to speak, but does not" (p. 289). Although presented originally in a public policy context, Brummett's ideas are cogent in the context of HIV prevention in bathhouses. The norm of silence in bathhouse public areas has been documented. Although this norm may conflict with condom negotiation, it also is possible that just as presidents have used silence strategically to achieve their own policy ends (Bostdorff, 1994; Brummett, 1980; Perez & Dionisopoulos, 1995), some men may use silence strategically to achieve their goals of unprotected anal sex.

Indeed, Bruneau (1973) posited that silence is about "exerting control." In "interactive silences[,] the burden of speech is often the burden of the subordinate. This burden often presses toward respectful silence, depending on the strength of authority management of silence" (pp. 30–31). Similarly, Hart (1982) stated, "Politics is personhood writ large, an arena in which a leader attempts to make his mark" (p. 368). In the arena of bathhouses, active/insertive partners make their mark by enforcing silence and using the opportunity *not* to negotiate safer sex practices, although this opportunity may be interrupted by a condom request from a passive partner. Silence, however, creates "unchecked inference about one's motives and actions" (Bruneau, 1973, pp. 29–30). The passive partner may attribute altruistic or healthy motives to the insertive partner's nonuse of condoms (i.e., HIV-seronegative status), while he maintains the respective silence of a subordinate.

The process for presenting our data analysis for the strategic use of silence, in this case, bathhouses, follows Brummett's (1980) directive: "The critic should note to whom the silence is directed and should examine the relationship between the silent persona and the target and how the silence affects the relationship. . . . So the critic should ask what the meaning of the silence is for the target audience and for the indirect audience, if any" (p. 295). The purpose of this chapter is to illuminate the relationship between the silent persona and the target individual and how such silence influences the possibilities for HIV and other STD transmission.

METHOD AND DATA

These data are part of a larger study examining the attitudes toward condom use of individuals who use illicit drugs and whose sexual behaviors place them at risk of HIV infection. Between December 1995 and February 1996, we conducted interviews with men who reported recently having had sex with a man in a bathhouse. Candidates for the study were recruited through advertisements in local newspapers and by referral from men already participating in the study (cf. Patton, 1990). Candidates were asked to call one of the investigators to determine study eligibility. During the initial phone conversation, candidates were screened to match the following criteria: 18 years of age, reported sex in a bathhouse within the 6 months prior to the phone conversation, and verbal consent to be interviewed. To conclude the phone interview, participants who met study eligibility criteria and who were willing to be participate in the study made an appointment to be interviewed at a later date. Interviews were conducted in a small, private office. At the time of the office interview, we again informed participants of the study's purpose and what we expected during the interview process, and we asked them to give informed consent to be interviewed. Once informed consent was given, the interview process commenced. As part of the interviewing process, men were asked to describe the bathhouses they had visited and the general behaviors and behavioral norms that they believed occur in bathhouses. Those men who could not accurately describe a typical bathhouse or seemed unfamiliar with the behaviors and norms that occur in a bathhouse setting were interviewed, but data resulting from their interviews were excluded from analysis. A gratuity was paid to men for their time involvement.

Data were collected using a semistructured interview guide, which included questions concerning sociodemographic characteristics and life history. Although the semistructured guide served as a prompt and guide for the interviewer, participants were encouraged to elaborate on topics that appeared to contain information relevant to the study. Interviews were audio recorded and transcribed verbatim into text files. Text files were content coded using a subjective/objective analytical strategy (Maxwell, 1996). The coding scheme itself was derived from Murdock et al.'s (1985) *Outline of Cultural Materials* (*OCM*), "a manual which presents a comprehensive subject classification system pertaining to all aspects of human behavior and related phenomena" (p. xi). Although originally created by and for anthropologists, the *OCM* was revised in its fifth edition for research in "psychology, sociology, political science, economics, geography, and general science" (p. xi) and can be adapted for use on individual studies. For example, the *OCM* includes only one code, 343, for "bathhouses," used in its more traditional sense of "washing and bathing facilities" (p. 82). We expanded this one code through additional letters and numbers for such phenomena as "perceived effects of being in a bathhouse" (343A), and "communication rules specific to a bathhouse" (343A1).

Objective analytical criteria codes were derived from the theory of reasoned action (Ajzen & Fishbein, 1973, 1980) and the idea of silence as a communication rule in bathhouses. Interviews were coded using the theory of reasoned action for the pros and cons of condom use, barriers and facilitators of condom use, intentions to use condoms during future sexual encounters, and perceived norms regarding condom use. Data were then reanalyzed to add codes derived regarding silence. Other predetermined codes included HIV/AIDS knowledge, HIV/AIDS inaccuracies, and historical and current drug use. Subjective analytical coding criteria were developed based on the principles of grounded theory (Glaser & Strauss, 1967). Coded data were assessed for patterns of thought and behavior that became apparent as data were analyzed. Data that best illustrate analytical patterns were excerpted for presentation in the text that follows. In presentation of the data, the four-digit codes following data represent unique participant identifiers.

Forty-one men agreed to participate in the study and provided data that form the basis of this analysis. Twenty-eight of the men in the study were White, 8 were Hispanic, 3 were African-American, and 2 men categorized themselves as "other." Thirty of the men reported that they were single at the time of the interview; 8 reported being married to other men, and 3 reported being married to women. Thirty-four men self-identified as gay, 5 as bisexual, and 2 as heterosexual. Nine participants reported having one or more female sex partners in the last 6 months. Four participants reported using injection drugs and 13 reported having smoked crack cocaine.

Silence in Bathhouses

As stated previously, an existing communication rule in bathhouses precludes men talking in public areas where sex occurs (Elwood & M. L. Williams, 1997; Weinberg & C. J. Williams, 1975). For example, a 33-year-old, gay-identified Hispanic man said,

R: When I first started to go there, I would see somebody and say something like, "Hi Bill! What's goin' on?" And, you know, people would kind of look at you like, "Shh, just don't talk in here."
I: Why? Why are you not supposed to talk?
R: I don't know. I never figured that part out. (1029)

Whereas the previous respondent could not cite a rationale for this rule, most participants, when asked, provided reasons related to their desires for taciturn efficiency in their sexual encounters within the setting. Said a 35-year-old, gay-identified White man, "I think people usually go to bathhouses because they just want sex. You can do it and you can leave, with no questions asked. You don't have to make up an excuse. You don't have to wake up in bed with them the next morning and say you have to be somewhere" (1019).

This latter theme of not having to make excuses or not feeling compelled to establish and perpetuate an illusion of intimacy appears in the comments of a married, African-American, 28-year-old bisexual man, who said that he appreciated the lack of conversation in bathhouses because he was reluctant to disclose any details about himself: "It takes the whole lying factor out, and, in turn, you can be as anonymous as you want to be. You don't have to say where you came from. You don't have to say anything. I think that makes it pretty safe for some people to go there because they can be anonymous" (1017). Ironically, the previous respondent considers "safe" sex to be "anonymous" sex. Although such silence may preserve men's identities, it also provides an opportunity for its strategic use to facilitate unprotected anal intercourse.

Top Men Rule: Condom Use and Communication

Succinctly put, according to one participant, "If you're on top, you're in charge" of both condom use and oral communication (1015):

S: To be honest, when I see it [unprotected anal sex] go on at a bathhouse, if I see two guys having it, I automatically assume that they're infected and they just don't care. If a guy is willing to be the bottom when having anal intercourse and not insist on a condom, then I assume he's infected, which makes me even more leery to use them. That's totally assumption. I have nothing to base that on.

I: What else? What else do you think?

S: Um, the awkwardness of it. Having to tell somebody to put it on if you're going to be the bottom is sometimes hard to do. It's easier to put it on if you're the top. You just do it. If you're the bottom, you have to say, "Excuse me." It's not easy to do, especially when the code of the bathhouse is silence, where you don't speak. Especially if you're in a public area, people that speak are kind of shunned—not shunned, but you just don't talk. So, if you're having sex, you can't stop and tell someone to put a condom on, unless you do it yourself. (1015)

Consistent with the idea that the man "on top" is in charge of oral discourse and condom usage, one 26-year-old, gay White man reiterated throughout his interview that his large penis and the silence at bathhouses allow him to satisfy his desire for unprotected insertive anal sex. Shortly before the following block description of condom use, he said, "When I was younger I thought sex meant a little bit more. But now it doesn't. My view towards sex is, like I said, just the anonymity":

Life's too short to feel guilty about what I should've, could've. But, hey, their eyes are on the prize and I guess they're just not going to think about asking me to wear a condom. I'll wear one if they ask, but I'm not going to offer. I hate 'em. (1035)

When we asked this participant to reflect on why he thought his bathhouse sex partners did not request that he wear a condom, he replied,

S: I don't know. I guess I've never thought about it. Maybe because they look at me and they don't want to bother with that part of it. They just want to get right to it.

I: They have their eyes on the prize, too.

S: Right. Maybe I look clean. I don't know. I have no idea. Maybe they look at the size of me and say "Well, [pause]." I have no idea. I have no idea. I think maybe it's the eyes on the prize and they don't want to bother with it. (1035)

Unlike the previous participant, another gay White man, 26, perfunctorily reported a preference for condom use during anal sex; however, the conditions he listed under which he would use condoms in bathhouses made it unlikely that such prevention behavior would occur with any frequency:

But, it's a give or take at the baths. If they're there and convenient and, if I have them, then I'll probably use them. That means I'll plan to use it when I go there. If I don't have it, it's not used probably unless they request it. Of course, I've never been penetrated there, you know. (1010)

According to these participants, there is a clear, unsolicited theme of condom use *only* when receptive partners request them. Although these men frequently reported that silence was the rule in bathhouse public areas, and that they were willing to wear condoms if asked, no participants who reported receptive anal sex in bathhouses reported perceiving that condom use, or initiating the negotiation of condom use, was their responsibility. For example, a 25-year-old Hispanic man recounted this episode that occurred in the maze, a dark room subdivided similar to a boxwood garden maze or the circuitous puzzle one would find in the newspaper:

> There was this big Black man. He was gorgeous, you know? A real man. Tall, really broad shoulders and a big chest, big muscles everywhere, and a really big cock. I just had to have him, you know? I thought about using condoms, I did, but I didn't want to talk because it might break the moment, or he might go away. I just had to have him, so I backed onto him and he really filled me up. It felt so good. I even thought that we should have used a condom while he was fucking me; I knew what the risks were, but I didn't care. (1012)

This participant's story demonstrates his internalization of silence rules—that subordinate individuals have the daunting responsibility to initiate discourse; nevertheless, the preeminent way for a subordinate to demonstrate respect for the "top man" is to remain silent. This story clearly demonstrates the participant's internalization of this standard (Bruneau, 1973). Under this rubric, top men can pursue their desire for unprotected sex successfully.

Just as an earlier participant attributed positive HIV serostatus to men he observed having unprotected anal sex in a bathhouse, the following man attributed possible HIV infection and definite psychological problems to men who allow him penetrate them without protection:

> My main thought is, "Okay, I'm sticking my dick in your ass. And you're here in the bathhouse, and I've seen you here before, and you let me and half dozen other people in there tonight, and, you're just sick. You're just out to get a disease, baby. You're depressed, you're fucked up, and you're really sad. And if you're gonna let me stick my dick in there, all right, I'll stick my dick in there. I'm gonna get my rocks off and, I'll try not to come in you, but, you know, fuck it, I'm sorry. That's just life." You know, I think people are responsible for their own HIV status. And if a bottom is out there getting fucked without a condom—and I assume that that's one of the main routes of transmission—they're just stupid. I'm sorry, I mean, this disease has been around for, you know, 15 years. I hear about AIDS, and condom usage has been, I think I came out when safe sex, this thing started. I came out in like '86, you know? And condoms were being talked about back then. It wasn't real popular, but it was like an idea that was starting to catch on. And here we are 10 years later and you're doing it—you know, where've you been? How many friends have you lost? Are you on some kind of death wish? And if they're positive and letting somebody do it, it's like, you know, you don't care about yourself. (1011)

This example also has an ironic quality, in that the respondent attributed poor mental and physical health to his receptive anal partners, never acknowledging his complicity in the process, let alone his own risk for infection (and potential transmission) of HIV and other STDs.

Changing the Rules: Using Condoms in Bathhouses

Some men recognize the silence norm in bathhouse public areas, and thus only have anal sex in private rooms where oral communication is acceptable (Elwood & M. L. Williams, 1997). The following 38-year-old White participant delineated this strategy as well as his less-than-100% compliance rate:

> Condoms are free as you walk in the door. And I'll reach in and have a handful as I walk in the door. Most of the time, I don't have [anal] sex. We have oral sex, you know, in open places. But if we're gonna have sex, I usually go back to a room or a cubicle. If you have

rented it, and they always have condoms. And I'm not gonna sit here and tell you I use condoms 99.9 percent of the time, but I try to use them 75 percent of the time. (1020)

This same participant explained, "Even if they don't suggest it first, if they don't offer to put it on, if you ask them to put a condom on, most will" (1020). He continued, "I've had maybe one who refused to wear it, and he wouldn't have sex." The following participant succinctly described the feelings of "most other gay men" regarding condoms: "I think they wish they didn't have to use it. They would prefer not to. But it's necessary to stay alive" (1016). This 42-year-old top man not only reported using condoms regularly at bathhouses, but also described his ritual to eroticize condom use:

S: The man I had sex with put it on me . . . in his room. I was asked to come in. The first thing I asked him was, "Do you have a condom?" He said, "yes," so I didn't hesitate then.
I: Did you like him putting a condom on you better than doing it yourself?
S: I think it, there was more of a comfort level there for both of us.
I: Why?
S: I don't know. I liked the idea of him putting it on. (1016)

Although some men—top or bottom—may engage in HIV risk reduction behaviors in bathhouses, at least one participant's story suggests that the politics of silence has lethal implications. The following participant stated that he suspected he "was HIV for years," and finally got tested "after taking so many of my friends to the clinic." Even after this 37-year-old, gay White man had proof he was infected with HIV, he continued to have unprotected insertive and receptive anal sex in bathhouses:

No, I was hot and heavy crazy about it and I knew I was HIV, but it never really put the hammers to my head until the doctor said, "I don't want you to work any more," because, uh, neuropathy is a nerve disorder. . . . Until [I went on disability], I was a lot less inhibited. I really didn't care. I was doing a lot of crystal, coke, whichever I could afford, always alcohol. And I was a lot freer with my selections. I really didn't care as long as I got off in the way I wanted to get off. That's basically what it boiled down to. Me, with my kind of guilty conscience, now I'm worried, scared to death, that I got a person real sick or something. (1021)

DISCUSSION

The purpose of this study was to explain how men use silence in bathhouses to achieve their desire for unprotected anal sex. In examining the data, we chose to look at men's descriptions of bathhouses and their attitudes toward condoms and toward the sexual behaviors that occur in bathhouses. Through this examination, we found the theme that the customary practice of silence that protects men's identities and facilitates expedient sex also facilitates a practice of unprotected anal sex. In general, subordinate individuals are obligated to initiate speech, but also are "pressed for respectful silence" (Bruneau, 1973, p. 31). In the case of bathhouses, receptive partners serve as subordinate individuals. Provided the dual responsibility to initiate discussion and to demonstrate respect by remaining silent, receptive partners thus are torn between negotiating condom use and "breaking the moment" by violating the silent respect to their insertive partners. All too frequently, they opt for silent respect and unsafe sex.

The examples cited here demonstrate participants' knowledge of these practices. Insertive partners state that they will wear a condom if their partners request it, and that few actually utter such requests. Receptive partners' comments reflect a concerns for condom use and that such requests would result in a termination of such coupling.

Nevertheless, these findings demonstrate men still perceive the setting of the bathhouse in much the same way as Weinberg and C. J. Williams (1975) described it over 20 years ago—as uniquely sexual settings where they are almost assured of satisfaction. Bathhouses, indeed, remain sexual settings in which anonymous sex among men can take place without fear of arrest or civic disclosure. They also remain essentially silent places to ensure the confidentiality of men's identities and to expedite sexual encounters themselves. The advent of HIV has changed the impact of silence in bathhouses, however.

The practice of silence in bathhouses has acquired a political dimension, as men rely on this long-standing practice to obtain unprotected anal sex, despite warnings that this sexual practice places them at acute risk for infection with HIV and other STDs. The practice of silence is particularly advantageous for insertive partners, as long-standing etiquette places subordinates in the double bind of initiating discourse and demonstrating respect for another through silence. The stories participants told demonstrate their knowledge of this etiquette— and how to maneuver the etiquette to avoid safer sex practices. These men dislike wearing condoms but will use them only if asked by their receptive partner; they consciously use silence to achieve their desires for unprotected sex.

The opportunity for sex with multiple partners in bathhouses, and the propensity of some men to practice unprotected anal sex in bathhouse environs, suggests multiple opportunities for HIV and other STD transmission. This pilot study did not offer blood tests, nor required men to reveal their serostatus; many, in fact, did not know their HIV status. Thus, a detailed discussion of transmission opportunities is beyond the scope of this study. The qualitative data do suggest, however, that MSMs who desire unprotected anal sex may attend bathhouses because the number of men and the practical policy of silence allow them to escape the realities of HIV prevention and thus satisfy desires that risk disease transmission.

IMPLICATIONS

Data from this study suggest the importance of studying silence among individuals and how such silence influences their relationships. It also reiterates not only the importance of studying silence as a political strategy, but also that such strategies have profound implications for people other than presidents. In the context of HIV prevention, scholars may wish to study the functions of silence and their political, or power, implications in more private heterosexual and homosexual encounters.

Results from this study also indicate the need for additional research on why men attend bathhouses. We need data that describe not simply the kinds of sex MSMs have in bathhouses, but also the psychological characteristics of insertive and receptive men. For example, detailed descriptions of the types of men who, respectively, silently acquiesce to unprotected receptive anal sex, and those who request condom use out loud, can lead to targeted safer sex interventions. More specific suggestions regarding intervention content are beyond the scope of this study.

A definite recommendation of this study is to change the rule for silence in bathhouses. Although this recommendation does not extend to compromising the identities of patrons, it wholeheartedly proposes normalizing the negotiation of sexual practices and risk reduction activities. Additional research can lead to the content of such interventions.

Nevertheless, HIV and AIDS has taught gay men to be more altruistic to others. Many men practice their altruism by monetary gifts to AIDS charities, by purchasing products knowing some of the proceeds will benefit AIDS charities, and by caring for friends and strangers debilitated by AIDS (e.g., Sobnosky & Hauser, chap. 3 of this volume; Harney, chap. 13 of this volume). They have not expressed their altruism, however, in their sexual practices with one another. When faced with a malleable opportunity to have unprotected anal sex, many men will take it—even when they know that such sex may infect another man with HIV. What men should practice was expressed even before we knew the links between HIV and AIDS: "If you love the person you are with—*even for one night*—you will not want to make them sick" (Berkowitz & Callen, 1982, p. 167). Clearly, the politics of silence in bathhouses demonstrates the need to teach men that human discourse and condom use are preeminent ways to be their brothers' keepers.

ACKNOWLEDGMENTS

This research was supported by grants from the National Institute on Drug Abuse Community Research Branch. The interpretations and conclusions expressed in this chapter are solely those of the authors.

REFERENCES

Ajzen, I., & Fishbein, M. (1973). Attitudinal and normative variables as predictors of specific behaviors. *Journal of Personality and Social Psychology, 27,* 41–57.
Ajzen, I., & Fishbein, M. (1980). *Understanding attitudes and predicting social behavior.* Englewood Cliffs, NJ: Prentice-Hall.
Aristotle. (1984). *The rhetoric and poetics of Aristotle* (W. R. Roberts & I. Bywater, Trans.). New York: Modern Library.
Aristotle. (1991). *On rhetoric: A theory of civic discourse* (G. A. Kennedy, Trans.). New York: Oxford University Press.
Bartos, M. R., & Middleton, H. (1996, July). *Gay men in regular relationships and HIV risk.* Poster presented at the XI International Conference on AIDS, Vancouver, BC, Canada.
Battjes, R. J. (1994). Drug use and HIV risk among gay and bisexual men: An overview. In R. J. Battjes, Z. Sloboda, & W. C. Grace (Eds.), *The context of HIV risk among drug users and their sexual partners, NIDA research monograph 143* (pp. 82–130). Washington, DC: U.S. Department of Health and Human Services.
Berkowitz, R., & Callen, M. (1982, March 15–28). Sex in an epidemic. *Native,* pp. 164–167.
Bérubé, A. (1996). The history of gay bathhouses. In Dangerous Bedfellows [E. G. Colter, W. Hoffman, E. Pendleton, A. Redick, & D. Serlin] (Eds.), *Policing public sex: Queer politics and the future of AIDS activism* (pp. 187–220). Boston: South End Press.
Bostdorff, D. M. (1994). *The presidency and the rhetoric of foreign crisis.* Columbia: University of South Carolina Press.
Britton, J. (1996, November 20). Clinton appointee found dead in bathhouse. (San Diego) *Update,* p. A1.
Browne, J., & Minichello, V. (1994). The condom: Why more people don't put it on. *Sociology of Health and Illness, 16,* 229–251.
Brummett, B. (1979). A pentadic analysis of ideologies in two gay rights controversies. *Central States Speech Journal, 30,* 250–261.
Brummett, B. (1980). Towards a theory of silence as a political strategy. *Quarterly Journal of Speech, 66,* 289–303.
Bruneau, T. J. (1973). Communicative silences: Forms and functions. *Journal of Communication, 23,* 17–46.
Burke, K. (1966). Definition of man. In K. Burke (Ed.), *Language as symbolic action: Essays on life, literature, and method* (pp. 3–20). Berkeley: University of California Press.
Clark, K. (1996, September 12). Return of bathhouses sparks renewed debate over sex, AIDS. *The Texas Triangle,* pp. 3, 8.
Conversations with Nicole [Column]. (1996, November 21). (San Diego) *Gay and Lesbian Times,* p. 5D.
Edelman, M. (1971). *Politics as symbolic action: Mass arousal and quiescence.* New York: Academic Press.
Edelman, M. (1977). *Political language: Words that succeed and policies that fail.* New York: Academic Press.

Edelman, M. (1988). *Constructing the political spectacle.* Chicago: University of Chicago Press.

Elwood, W. N. (1995). Public relations is a rhetorical experience: The integral principal in case study analysis. In W. N. Elwood (Ed.), *Public relations inquiry as rhetorical criticism: Case studies of corporate discourse and social influence* (pp. 3–12). Westport, CT: Praeger.

Elwood, W. N. (1996). *Trends among abusers in Houston: A report from special studies and the streets.* Austin: Texas Commission on Alcohol and Drug Abuse.

Elwood, W. N., & Williams, M. L. (1997). *Gentlemen don't speak: Communication rules and HIV risk behaviors in male bathhouses.* Manuscript submitted for publication.

Elwood, W. N., & Williams, M. L. (1998). Sex, drugs, and situation: Attitudes, drug use, and sexual risk behaviors among men who frequent bathhouses. *Journal of Psychology and Human Sexuality, 10,* 23–44.

Elwood, W. N., Williams, M. L., & Bowen, A. M. (1996, July). *Psychosocial determinants of HIV risk reduction behaviors among men who frequent bathhouses.* Poster presented at the XI International Conference on AIDS, Vancouver, BC, Canada.

Foucault, M. (1961). *Madness and civilization: An archaeology of medical perception* (A. M. Sheridan Smith, Trans.). New York: Pantheon.

Foucault, M. (1970). *The order of things: An archaeology of the human sciences* (A. M. Sheridan Smith, Trans.). New York: Pantheon.

Foucault, M. (1972). *The archaeology of knowledge* (A. M. Sheridan Smith, Trans.). New York: Pantheon.

Foucault, M. (1978). *The history of sexuality: Vol. 1. An introduction* (R. Hurley, Trans.). New York: Pantheon.

Foucault, M. (1980). *Power/knowledge: Selected interviews and other writings, 1972–1977* (C. Gordon, Ed., C. Gordon et al., Trans.). New York: Pantheon.

Foucault, M. (1989). Sexual choice, sexual act. In S. Lotringer (Ed.), *Foucault live: Interviews, 1966–1984* (J. Johnston, Trans., pp. 211–231). New York: Semiotext(e).

Foucault, M. (1990). *Michel Foucault: Politics, philosophy, culture; Interviews and other writings, 1977–1984* (L. D. Krizman, Ed.). New York: Routledge.

Glaser, B. G., & Strauss, A. L. (1967). *The discovery of grounded theory: Strategies for qualitative research.* Chicago: Aldine.

Hale, M. Q. (1983). Presidential power: Presidential influence, authority, and power and economic policy. In D. H. Nelson & R. L. Sklar (Eds.), *Toward a humanistic science of politics: Essays in honor of Francis Dunham Wormuth* (pp. 399–437). Lanham, MD: University Press of America.

Hart, R. P. (1982). A commentary on popular assumptions about political communication. *Human Communication Research, 8,* 366–389.

Heitz, D. (1997, July 8). Men behaving badly: The recklessness of the 1970s and early '80s has reappeared on the party circuit, where gay men are indulging in illicit drugs and wild sex with increasing abandon. *The Advocate,* pp. 26–29.

Henriksson, B., & Mansson, S-A. (1995). Sexual negotiations: An ethnographical study of men who have sex with men. In B. Henriksson (Ed.), *Risk factor love: Homosexuality, sexual interaction, and HIV prevention* (pp. 147–174). Göteburg, Sweden: University of Göteburg Institute for Social Research.

Johnson, S. (1997, March 20). Strip clubs win round in court: County can't enforce two new regulations on topless dancers. *Houston Chronicle,* pp. 33A, 37A.

Kane, L. (1984). *The language of silence: On the unspoken and unspeakable in modern drama.* Rutherford, NJ: Fairleigh Dickinson University Press.

Kaplan, A. (1994). The life of dialogue. In R. Anderson, K. N. Cissna, & R. C. Arnett (Eds.), *The reach of dialogue: Confirmation, voice, and community* (pp. 34–46). Cresskill, NJ: Hampton Press.

Kramer, L. (1989). *Reports from the holocaust: The making of an AIDS activist.* New York: St. Martin's Press.

Leigh, B. C. (1990). The relationship of substance use during sex to high-risk sexual behavior. *Journal of Sex Research, 27,* 199–213.

Licensed sex clubs near reality in San Francisco. (1996, October 20). *Houston Chronicle,* p. 21A.

Maxwell, J. A. (1996). *Qualitative research design: An interactive approach.* Thousand Oaks, CA: Sage.

McCoy, C. B., & Inciardi, J. A. (1995). *Sex, drugs, and the continuing spread of AIDS.* Los Angeles: Roxbury Publishing Company.

McKirnan, D, J., Ostrow, D. G., & Hope, B. (1996). Sex, drugs, and escape: A psychological model of HIV-risk sexual behaviours. *AIDS Care, 8,* 655–669.

Meyer, I. H., & Dean, L. (1995). Patterns of sexual behavior among young New York City gay men. *AIDS Education and Prevention, 7*(Suppl.), 13–23.

Mohr, R. D. (1996). The bathhouse controversy roars on. *The Guide, 16*(6), 18–22.

Mumby, D. K. (1988). *Communication and power in organizations: Discourse, ideology, and domination.* Norwood, NJ: Ablex.

Murdock, G. P., Ford, C. S., Hudson, A. E., Kennedy, R., Simmons, L. W., & Whiting, J. W. M. (1985). *Outline of cultural materials* (5th edition). New Haven, CT: Human Relations Area Files, Inc.

Odets, W. (1994). AIDS education and harm reduction for gay men: Psychological approaches for the 21st century. *AIDS and Public Policy Journal, 9,* 3–15.

Orta, J. (1996, September 5). Community must act to keep bathhouse from becoming "HIV incubation factory" [Letter to the editor]. *The Texas Triangle,* p. 3.

Ostrow, D. G. (1994). Substance use and HIV-transmitting behaviors among gay and bisexual men. In R. J. Battjes, Z. Sloboda, & W. C. Grace (Eds.), *The context of HIV risk among drug users and their sexual partners, NIDA research monograph 143* (pp. 88–113). Rockville, MD: National Institute on Drug Abuse.

Ostrow, D. G., & McKirnan, D. (1997). Prevention of substance-related high-risk sexual behavior among gay men: Critical review of the literature and proposed harm reduction. *Journal of Gay and Lesbian Medical Association, 1,* 97–110.

Patton, M. Q. (1990). *Qualitative evaluation and research methods.* Newbury Park, CA: Sage.

Perez, T. L., & Dionisopoulos, G. D. (1995). Presidential silence, C. Everett Koop, and the *Surgeon General's Report on AIDS. Communication Studies, 46,* 18–33.

Peterson, J. L., Coates, T. J., Catania, J. A., Middleton, L., Hilliard, B., & Hearst, N. (1992). High-risk sexual behavior and condom use among gay and bisexual African-American men. *American Journal of Public Health, 82,* 1490–1494.

Prestage G., & Drielsma, P. (1996). Indicators of male bisexual activity in semimetropolitan New South Wales: Implications for HIV prevention strategies. *Australian and New Zealand Journal of Public Health, 20,* 386–392.

Pronger, B. (1993). Gay irony. In A. Minas (Ed.), *Gender basics: Feminist perspectives on women and men* (pp. 79–83). Belmont, CA: Wadsworth.

Quinn, D. (1996, September 12). Texas bathhouses part of national trend. *The Texas Triangle,* pp. 3, 9.

Rich, A. (1983). Compulsory heterosexuality and lesbian existence. In A. Snitow, C. Stansell, & S. Thompson (Eds.), *The powers of desire: The politics of sexuality* (pp. 177–205). New York: Monthly Review Press/New Feminist Library.

Sadownick, D. (1996). *Sex between men: An intimate history of the sex lives of gay men postwar to present.* New York: HarperSan Francisco.

Sheer, V. C. (1995). Sensation seeking predispositions and susceptibility to a sexual partner's appeals for condom use. *Journal of Applied Communication Research, 23,* 212–229.

Shilts, R. (1987). *And the band played on: Politics, people, and the AIDS epidemic.* New York: Penguin.

Strathdee, S. A., Hogg, R. S., Martindale, S. L., Cornelisse, P. G. A., Craib, K. J. P., Schilder, A., Montaner, J. S. G., O'Shaughnessy, M. V., & Schechter, M. T. (1996, July). *Sexual abuse is an independent predictor of sexual risk-taking among young HIV-negative homosexual men: Results from a prospective study at baseline.* Paper presented at the XI International Conference on AIDS, Vancouver, BC, Canada.

Trinidad, D. (1991, December 31). Adrienne Rich charts a difficult world: The acclaimed poet talks of art, anger, and activism [Interview]. *The Advocate,* pp. 82–84.

Vibbert, S. L. (1987, May). *Corporate communication and the management of issues.* Paper presented at the International Communication Association convention, Montreal.

Webber, G. (1996, June 28). Gay today: Before and after [Opinion column]. *Houston Voice,* p. 10.

Weinberg, M. S., & Williams, C. J. (1975). Gay baths and the social organization of impersonal sex. *Social Problems, 23,* 124–136.

Williams, M. L., Elwood, W. N., & Bowen, A. M. (1997). *Escape from risk: Attitudes and beliefs of men who have sex with men in bathhouses.* Manuscript submitted for publication.

Wingood, G. M., Hunter-Gamble, D., & DiClemente, R. J. (1993). A pilot study of sexual communication and negotiation among young African American women: Implications for HIV prevention. *Journal of Black Psychology, 19,* 190–203.

Zappas, M. (1996, September 19). Behavior, not bathhouses, contribute to AIDS epidemic [Letter to the editor]. *The Texas Triangle,* p. 3.

11

Redefining Categories of Risk and Identity: The Appropriation of AIDS Prevention Information and Constructions of Risk

Antonio Estrada
Gilbert A. Quintero
Mexican American Studies and Research Center
University of Arizona

One of the most politically volatile diseases in modern history, HIV/AIDS has induced a number of broad social transformations in communities throughout the world. In the United States, the character and extent of the HIV epidemic challenges American society to contend in a more open manner with stigmatized and morally loaded sets of behaviors revolving around sexuality, drug use, and contagion. The societal reaction to the AIDS pandemic has been shaped not only by the natural history and organic pathology of the retro-virus, but also by a variety of social arrangements, cultural structures, and political institutions.

Within local arenas of interpersonal communication, HIV/AIDS has served to shape the regulation of various social relationships in a number of different ways. In the broadest terms, HIV/AIDS has highlighted the structural inequities underpinning the political ecology of disease, because traditionally peripheral groups, including ethnic minorities, the poor, drug users, prostitutes, and homosexuals, have borne a disproportional brunt of the epidemic. The sometimes dramatic impact of AIDS in diverse communities has provided the impetus for collective organization and political action. A climate of contention has developed as affected groups actively organize themselves and demand entitlement in order to more effectively vie for and gain access to important resources to fight the epidemic. As a consequence of these developments, the pandemic has brought attention to particular segments of society that are economically, socially, and politically marginalized and heretofore largely ignored.

The epidemic called AIDS has influenced the establishment of social groups in other ways as well. Information about HIV, generated within the context of applied health research, including public health, epidemiology, biomedicine, and the social and behavioral sciences, has played a significant role in channeling perceptions of what type of people are more likely to carry HIV and what practices are most conducive to its transmission. These categories of risk, practice, and identity help situate the disease within the boundaries of certain social and cultural groups. But this information, often encapsulated in various prevention messages and concepts, is activated within a social frame of local attitudes, perceptions, and beliefs. Because of this, coordinated responses to the disease, often circulated through the mass media, have shaped the social processes and semantics underlying lay categories and conceptions of risk, vulnerability, drug use, and sexuality. Ultimately, these processes have a direct bearing on the regulation of relationships within specific social groups.

In this chapter we explore some of these developments by examining how certain ideas about HIV and AIDS are actualized in local contexts. More specifically, we describe how one particular high-risk group, injection drug users (IDUs) in Tucson, Arizona, appropriate and internalize HIV prevention concepts, messages, and procedures in order to navigate through their interpersonal relationships and the demands of their social life worlds. Despite exposure to special prevention messages and a high level of awareness, many IDUs still engage in behaviors conducive to the transmission of HIV/AIDS. In a world infused with potential harm, IDUs manage their perceived vulnerability by appropriating prevention concepts and categories to relativize and constitute their own personal risks. This is accomplished through a number of different strategies including reinventing categories of identity associated with risk groups that allow for the discrimination between "low-risk" (i.e., "clean") and "high-risk" (i.e., "careless") people, utilizing HIV test results for social purposes, and relabeling "unsafe" behaviors (e.g., condomless sex) as "safe." By focusing on the local semantics of categories like "high-risk groups" and "safer sex," this chapter underscores the role certain prevention messages and concepts play in negotiating risk behaviors within the surround of interpersonal social relationships.

BACKGROUND

Salient characteristics of the human immunodeficiency virus (HIV), including its modes of transmission and its resistance to vaccines and other medical regimens, indicate that AIDS is noncurable but, theoretically, almost always preventable. Despite promising recent advances in drug therapies there are no pharmacological means of curing or preventing AIDS. As a result, a vast array of prevention programs, drawing together the skills and perspectives of health educators, epidemiologists, community activists, and social scientists, focus on the development of interventions to stem the transmission of HIV. The general strategy of these efforts centers on the identification of practices conducive to the transfer of HIV, the communication of the potential danger posed by these activities to those who engage in them, and the assumption that, given adequate information, individuals will modify behaviors that place them at risk for contracting HIV. Communication, in the form of pamphlets, public service announcements, and other prevention messages, is at the foundation of this prevention process and has met with arguable degrees of success (Becker & Joseph, 1988; Catania, Kegeles, & Coates, 1990; Elwood & Ataabadi, 1996, 1997).

Throughout the course of the HIV/AIDS epidemic in the United States, certain conceptual frames have gained dominance in the prevention process. From the beginning a lexicon of risk and identity evolved that continues to maintain a special currency in the development and implementation of HIV prevention programs. Indeed, the demarcation and development of key categories and concepts, including certain target risk groups (e.g., IDUs, homosexual men) and high-risk practices (e.g., syringe transfers, condomless anal sex), has proven integral to the composition and maturation of prevention messages and interventions (Bayer, 1989; Oppenheimer, 1988; Shilts, 1987).

The overarching, ubiquitous category organizing the HIV prevention agenda, as well as the discourse on HIV/AIDS, is "risk." By identifying certain practices (e.g., needle sharing) as conducive to the spread of HIV and associating specific target groups (e.g., IDUs) with these and other risky behaviors, prevention efforts are designed to prompt individuals into recognizing the heightened probability of HIV infection linked to these and other activities and populations. Ideally, those engaging in HIV-related risk behaviors should, after exposure and integration of prevention information, label specific practices as risky and in need of change. Motivated to avoid infection, these individuals modify their behaviors accordingly and, as a result, HIV transmission diminishes. Thus, IDUs are exhorted to clean their syringes with bleach and not to share their "works" just as those engaging in sexual intercourse are encouraged to practice safer sex or no sex at all. One result of these education campaigns has been a reported decrease in factors facilitating HIV infection (see Becker & Joseph, 1988; Fisher & Fisher, 1992). But whereas many studies point to the apparent success of various prevention efforts, others indicate that behavioral change is often ephemeral. An extensive and growing literature makes clear that the communication and comprehension of prevention messages often does not lead to desired behavioral changes over time (Connors, 1992; DiClemente, Forrest, & Susan, 1990; Lear, 1995; McKeganey, Barnard, & Watson, 1989; Page & Wingerd, 1993; Sibthorpe, Fleming, Tesselaar, & Gould, 1991; Stall, McKusick, & Wiley, 1986).

A number of critiques have been offered to explain this discrepancy between cognitive knowledge and social practice. Many researchers underscore the importance of understanding the various social and structural parameters governing the construction and internalization of risk in specific interactional settings. Often, prevention efforts seem motivated by the underlying assumption of a single rationality influencing decision making, a simple cost–benefit analysis engaged in by a "rational man," rather than programs that account for the multiplicity of risk construction. The traditional anthropological concern with documenting local constructions of meaning has prompted efforts at situating risk and decision-making processes within particular social arenas. This approach to understanding risk as a collective construct based on politics generated and evaluated within specific social groups (Douglas, 1992) has added a needed depth to representations of perceptions of vulnerability and how they are created, actualized, and maintained.

Attention to the social underpinnings of risk construction has provided a productive locus for the study of behaviors relevant to the transmission of HIV. Rhodes (1995), for instance, argued for the utility of situating risk assessment by identifying the social realities that shape not only the relative perceptions of risk but also the structure of HIV risk behaviors and individual evaluations of those behaviors. Although IDUs recognize a host of potential hazards related to HIV transmission, IDUs also must consider these hazards alongside other, often more immediate, concerns to form a "hierarchy of risk priorities." In a social world fraught with a multitude of threats to bodily and psychic integrity, IDUs learn to accept some risks through a process of routinization.

A similar tack is taken by Ramos, Shain, and Johnson (1995), who proposed the application of a socially situated "ethno-theory" to uncover the dynamics, experiences, and rationales underlying the construction of risk. These researchers focus on how people at risk for HIV infection (IDUs, prostitutes) utilize background "commonsense knowledge" as a baseline to evaluate specific circumstances, relations, and social interactions in calculating their own risk and vulnerability. The use of such knowledge, in conjunction with the distancing formula that produces the feeling that AIDS happens to someone else, prevents individuals from perceiving themselves as at risk for HIV—especially within the context of conjugal relationships with well-known intimates and companions. The authors' example is one of many (e.g., Clatts, 1995; Kane, 1991; Lear, 1995; Parker, 1995; Sibthorpe et al., 1991) that provide convincing documentation of the multiple strategies employed by individuals to lessen and manage perceived risk.

These studies point to the relevance of local factors in the construction of personal felt risk and in the conduct of risk behaviors. Common to all is recognition that the information produced and promulgated through prevention programs and other venues is situated within a social and cultural matrix where individuals, guided by the exigencies of their own local worlds, integrate, act upon, and ultimately derive their own meanings for prevention messages and other educational efforts. The implications of these studies for HIV prevention should be apparent. Increased attention to the social details channeling the construction of risk not only offers a deeper understanding of rationales underlying the conduct of risk behaviors but also might potentially provide information needed to identify the situational factors and processes mediating against effective behavior change. Ultimately, such an understanding may provide for the development of more situationally appropriate intervention programs.

Other critics of constructs of risk and identity stress similar limitations of the prevention project. The apparent discrepancy between knowledge of risk factors and actual behavior modification is attributed to the conceptual underpinnings of prevention efforts. The weaknesses of prevention lie in the persuasive organizational frames underlying HIV/AIDS intervention efforts. From this point of view, the demonstrated inability of prevention programs to effect significant change in risk behaviors is a direct upshot of the current approach to HIV intervention that privileges the construction of risk behaviors and risk groups. This regnant emphasis in prevention efforts tends to reify already stigmatized members of society (e.g., IDUs, homosexuals) and in so doing provides a conceptual buffer that allows others (heterosexuals, non-IDUs) to distance themselves from feeling vulnerable to HIV infection. After all, if an individual is not a member of a high-risk group, or does not identify with such a category, why should she or he feel at risk for contracting HIV? As a result of such attitudes, the populace, by and large, does not see the relevance of AIDS in their lives (Kane, 1991, 1993; Schiller, Crystal, & Lewellen, 1994). Thus, public health efforts, as they are currently organized and promulgated, inadvertently might lend a sense of exemption to those individuals whose behaviors in fact may be conducive to HIV transmission, but who do not identify with risk groups.

From an anthropological point of view, one of the more compelling critiques of this order is offered by Schiller (1992), whose perceptive analysis focuses on the overall impact of the conceptual categories organizing the response to HIV. The age-old social penchant for locating pathology in the "cultural other" is manifested in the contemporary epidemiological category of the risk group. "Culture" has proven to be an indispensable conceptual means to distance and subordinate marginalized social groups. At the same time, the concept of culture allows for the construction of culturally homogenous groups of people from sets of individuals who are, in fact, socially diverse. In this analysis, the continued currency commanded by risk group categories lies not so much in any efficacy such classifications may provide to fight the spread of HIV, but more in the benefit these taxonomies afford to the dominant classes of society. The construction and promulgation of concepts like risk groups allows certain institutions, including biomedicine, to reassert legitimacy, authority, and hegemonic control in the face of threatening social and demographic change.

The results of these circumstances are by no means simply academic; they carry far-reaching implications for disease prevention and control, and call attention to important aspects of power relations within American society. Schiller (1992) summarized:

> Among the serious consequences of the construction of AIDS risk groups seen as culturally distinct from the rest of the population have been: (1) misunderstanding who is at risk and who is not; (2) poor targeting of health education efforts; (3) the resultant spread of disease because people do not understand who is really at risk; (4) the stigmatizing, distancing, and silencing of the population with AIDS; and (5) a concentration on HIV disease itself without placing it in the context of conditions that have a direct impact on AIDS education and HIV disease, diagnosis, and treatment. (p. 246)

In general, then, it is possible to discern two broad concerns in anthropologically oriented studies of risk and HIV. There are those studies emphasizing the construction and perceptions of risk in local social contexts, and those studies taking a broader focus, which includes attention to the power differentials made apparent in the construction of risk group boundaries. Although warranted attention has been focused on local constructions of risk, the reification of risk groups, and the influence risk group construction has on the distancing of risk, particularly by those who are not part of advertised risk groups, less concern has been directed at how people in high-risk groups appropriate prevention concepts and procedures to construct local definitions of risk categories. We now turn our attention to these aspects of politics, communication, and AIDS.

METHOD

The data presented here were collected as part of a larger ongoing effort, the One to One Project, which focuses on the development, implementation, and evaluation of a culturally innovative, community-based HIV prevention program for Mexican-American IDUs and their sexual partners in Tucson, Arizona. The initial formative phase of the One to One Project involved an ethnographic research component that focused on understanding the patterns of HIV risk management and potential points of intervention in this population. The information derived from this research informed our efforts in preparing a culturally innovative intervention program specifically targeting Mexican-American drug injectors ("tecatos") and their sexual partners. Data collection focused on the development of a better understanding regarding the culturally specific attitudes, values, and beliefs related to drug use, sexuality, and HIV/AIDS. Although the ostensive focus of the investigation was Mexican-American IDUs, Anglo and Native-American drug injectors and their sexual partners also were interviewed. All interviewees were either IDUs or sexual partners of IDUs.

Two interview instruments were utilized in the course of the data collection procedure. An open-ended interview format investigated several pertinent cultural domains including: interpersonal relationships and communication, gender roles, decision-making and power relations, sexuality, drug use, condom use, knowledge of HIV/AIDS, and experience with behavior change. In addition, a structured interview instrument focusing on demographics, employment, condom use, drug use, and sexual activity was utilized.

Using an opportunistic sampling plan participants were recruited over a 4-month period in the spring of 1996. Respondents were enlisted into the study in several ways. First, one member of the research team who had been employed as an outreach worker for a NIDA cooperative research project was utilized as a gatekeeper into the IDU community. His professional and personal familiarity with the drug-using community facilitated contact and recruitment of 14 participants (Mexican-Americans and Pascua Yaquis) residing in four barrios in Tucson. Second, nine interviewees were recruited through project announcement flyers posted at a local methadone maintenance clinic. Third, a snowballing technique was utilized where respondents brought in their sexual partners or friends to participate in the research project. This procedure provided 17 respondents. Other participants were recruited from an ongoing cooperative research project ($n = 19$) and by word of mouth on the street ($n = 10$). Criteria for participation in the research included active injection drug use within the last 30 days and/or sexual relations with an active IDU. Respondents had to be at least 18 years of age, agree to the audiotaping of an hour-and-a-half-long ethnographic interview, and complete a 30-item demographic questionnaire. Respondents received $15 compensation for their interview time. A total of 69 interviews were conducted.

Data from the structured questionnaire were entered into a database and analyzed with the SPSS software program. Tape recordings of the open-ended interviews were transcribed and coded using Tally, a software package for the analysis of qualitative data. All interview transcriptions were coded according to content. Codes themselves were multilevel and indexed important cultural domains, specific risk behaviors, and attitudes relevant to intervention. The ethnographers (two), graduate research assistant, and research coordinator each coded individual interviews in turn so that all preceding codes were subsequently checked by others. Coding questions, including inconsistencies, were noted and discussed at weekly meetings. Tally was used to collate all information coded for risk behaviors and perceptions. Through this process all interview data relevant to risk were identified and evaluated. These data form the basis for the following presentation.

DESCRIPTION OF SAMPLE

As noted in Table 11.1, 38% (26) of the interviewees identified themselves as Hispanic, 35% (24) indicated they were Anglo, and 26% of this group identified as Native-American. Respondent ages ranged from 19 to 66 years of age (mean = 36.68; median = 36). Fifty-five percent were men and 45% were women. Thirty-eight percent of the sample had less than a high school education. Twenty-two percent had completed high school and 23% had completed some college, but had not obtained a degree. A high unemployment rate (51%) characterized this group of individuals. Sixty-one percent received less than $500 a month.

A high rate of drug use characterized this sample and multiple drug use was common. The vast majority of the sample (93%) had experienced injection drug use. Among the drugs most widely used in the last 30 days were heroin (79.7%), cocaine (43.5%), marijuana (42%), and speedball, or heroin and cocaine mixed (26.1%). Drug use data are outlined in Table 11.2.

As indicated in Table 11.3, interviewees exhibited a wide range of sexual experiences, including current sexual relationships, sexual preferences, number and frequency of sexual relationships, and condom use. All women and 84% of men reported having a current or past sexual partner who used drugs. Women (94%) were more likely than men (71%) to have had a sexual partner who also injected drugs. The number of lifetime sexual partners in this group ranged from 1 to 1,000 (mean = 49; median = 16). Three respondents (two men and one woman) reported that they were unsure about how many partners they had, but were certain that the number exceeded 1,000. All three were either currently working as prostitutes or had done so in the past. Ninety percent identified as heterosexual, 4% as gay (men only), and 6% as bisexual. Sixty-nine percent reported only one sexual partner during the last 6 months. Thirty-three percent had never been married, 23% were married or living with someone, and 26% were divorced. At the time of the interview, 16% of the sample indicated that they were not in a relationship. Of these 11 individuals, 7 reported abstinence for a 6-month period. Seventy-eight percent said that they had been in a monogamous relationship during the last 30 days. Six percent reported more than one sexual partner during this same time period.

THE APPROPRIATION OF CATEGORIES
OF RISK AND IDENTITY

Interviews with IDUs revealed consciousness of a world full of risks. In this environment interviewees constructed their own categories and assessments of danger by appropriating an existing lexicon of risk groups and behaviors and applying it to their own particular situations. Heroin addicts and their sexual partners rely upon AIDS prevention categories as taxonomic keystones utilized to organize perceived risks for HIV/AIDS. These individuals manage their

TABLE 11.1
General Characteristics

Gender	n	%
Male	38	55.1
Female	31	44.9
Race/Ethnicity		
Anglo (non-Hispanic)	24	34.8
Black (non-Hispanic)	1	1.4
Native-American	18	26.1
Hispanic	26	37.7
Age (years)		
≤30	17	24.6
31–40	29	42.0
41–50	18	26.1
≥50	5	7.2
Education		
No formal schooling	1	1.4
<8th grade	7	10.1
<High school	18	26.1
High school	15	21.7
GED	9	13.0
Trade/technical school	2	2.9
Some college	16	23.2
College graduation	1	1.4
Employment Last 30 Days		
Unemployed	35	50.7
Employed full-time	10	14.5
Employed part-time	6	8.7
Full-time homemaker	1	1.4
Retired	1	1.4
Disabled	14	20.3
Other	2	2.9
Income in Last 30 Days		
<$500	42	60.9
$500–$999	19	27.5
$1,000–$1,999	4	5.8
$2,000–$3,999	4	5.8

Note. $N = 69$.

vulnerability by appropriating prevention concepts and categories to negotiate intimate relationships and situate personal risks. This appropriation is accomplished in a number of different ways, including reinventing categories of identity associated with risk groups to discriminate between low-risk and high-risk people, and relabeling unsafe behaviors as safe.

The Construction of High- and Low-Risk Groups. Lay appropriation of categories of risk and identity, including the construction of high-risk and low-risk groups, is central to conceptions and values surrounding HIV risk behaviors among IDUs. In a social world full of

TABLE 11.2
Drug Use

Multiple Drugs Used in Last 30 Days	n	%
No	2	2.9
Yes	67	97.1
Drugs Used in Last 30 Days		
Marijuana	29	42.0
Crack	11	15.9
Cocaine	30	43.5
Heroin	55	79.7
Speedball (heroin and cocaine)	18	26.1
Amphetamine/Methamphetamine	2	2.9
Other	12	17.4
Injection Drug Use Status		
Injector	64	92.8
Noninjector	5	7.2

Note. N = 69.

risks, IDUs assess and categorize individuals who are potentially carriers of HIV into high- and low-risk groups. These appraisals help frame behaviors and interactions with other social actors, figure into the calculus of what are acceptable and unacceptable risks, and ultimately, carry implications for the effectiveness of intervention messages and the transmission of HIV.

Although IDUs recognize that their sexual and drug use behaviors may increase their likelihood for contracting HIV, they often manage these perceptions of risk by emphasizing the danger posed by high-risk groups that they do not identify with. For many IDUs these high-risk groups are made up of unthinking, often reckless people—especially uncontrolled addicts, prostitutes, homosexuals, and sexually promiscuous individuals. The common denominator that underlies and unifies the high-risk category is carelessness, whether in sexual activity or drug use, a carelessness that demonstrates an indiscriminate attitude and a perceived likelihood of infection. Because many IDUs employ a number of different strategies to "be careful," some of which are discussed further later, they often do not feel that they are at a great risk themselves, even if they do occasionally share needles or have sex without a condom.

Interviewees expressed that they could lessen the chances of HIV transmission to an acceptable level if they avoided potentially dangerous interactions with people in high-risk categories. A number of strategies are employed to assess individuals and the risk they pose. In the arena of sexual activity "getting to know someone," observing an individual's personal habits and hygiene, and learning who a person "runs around with," were the most common artifices utilized to determine which risk category someone fell into. Many interviewees expressed an ability to discriminate between careless and careful people and thereby distinguish between potentially safe and unsafe sexual or running partners. Once enough information is known about a person's behavior and background an informed judgment can be made regarding what mutual activities might be risky. But IDUs also rely on other devices in calculating risks.

The Role of HIV Testing in Constructions of Risk.   HIV antibody testing, an important facet of HIV intervention programs, provides another key means of constructing risk. Negative test results are put to use in several different ways that not only help achieve a number of social ends, but also carry important implications for the prevention of AIDS. Test results

TABLE 11.3
Sexual Relationships

Sexual Relations With Drug-Injecting Partner	n	%
No	13	18.8
Yes	56	81.2
Sexual Preference		
Heterosexual	62	89.9
Gay (men only)	3	4.3
Lesbian (women only)	0	0.0
Bisexual	4	5.8
Sexual Partners in Lifetime		
≤8	21	30.4
9–17	13	18.8
18–27	12	17.4
28–35	5	7.2
50–74	6	8.7
≥75	9	13.0
Not Sure	3	4.3
Sexual Partners in the Last 30 Days		
0	11	15.9
1	54	78.3
10	2	2.9
20	2	2.9
Marital Status		
Single (never married)	23	33.3
Living with sexual partner	5	7.2
Married/common law married	16	23.2
Separated	4	5.8
Divorced	18	26.1
Widowed	3	4.3
HIV Status		
No HIV+ status disclosed	63	91.3
Disclosed HIV+ status	6	8.7

Note. $N = 69$.

can assist in the assessment of risk posed by others and help verify that a person is really safe. In general, negative results allow intimates to feel more at ease with each other. For some IDUs, testing is a mutual procedure they undergo with new partners and is becoming a routinized script in the early development of relationships; that is, testing is part of getting to know each other. Negative test results are also used to negotiate the termination of condom use in some relationships or to avoid condom use altogether, as indicated by the following exchange between the researcher and a 28-year-old Mexican-American woman (3003) who is the sex partner of an IDU:

[How would you determine whether or not it was necessary to use condoms?]

Well, I should be using them 'cause he's an IV drug user, just for my safety, that's very necessary to have.

[You said you should be using them?]

I should be using them but I don't.

[Why?]

I mean, we both got tested, we go get tested so, so far so good. But I know that's a big risk to be taking, and we have a couple times talked about it. "Yeah, we should be using condoms." But we just never do. I really don't know why. I don't know if we're just lazy about it or what. We shouldn't be, I mean, that's our life we're playing with.

Several interviewees noted that negative test results are not only routinely shared with actual and potential sexual partners, but also with other IDUs in needle-sharing situations. Thus, HIV test results are used not only for the resolution of the risk classification of others, but also to project a safe image of self.

IDUs use negative test results as empirical encouragement that the strategies they have used to lessen and manage risk have, in fact, succeeded. Whereas some IDUs reported a change in risk behaviors after getting tested, others assumed a negative result substantiated their abilities to avoid infection. Testing also provides a means to lessen anxiety after slips, such as sharing needles or having unprotected sex with a person whose risk status is questionable. HIV testing is just one part of a larger set of strategies, including getting to know someone and seeing who people run around with, that taken together form the basis for the lay appropriation of yet another prevention concept: safer sex.

Making Sex Safer and Condom Use.   The practice of safer sex, as an index of condom use, was explored in ethnographic interviews. Discussions centered on this category revealed that many informants were aware that safer sex required important and sometimes comprehensive changes in their behavior. As one interviewee noted, "You gotta change your lifestyle in order to have safer sex." But these changes in lifestyles and patterns of behavior are themselves variable and reflect, in part, not only the diverse strategies, rationales, and assessments underlying the construction of risk among IDUs, but also the character of a spectrum of social and sexual relationships.

Although many of those interviewed noted that safer sex was linked to condom use, other meanings were mentioned as well. Safer sex was equated with monogamy, long-term relationships, and marriage, as well as "fluidless sex." Masturbation, "clean works," "protecting yourself," "being clean," abstinence, heterosexual intercourse, and "respect" were also mentioned as safer sex by our interviewees.

Other notions regarding safer sex are more disturbing in light of transmission risks and intervention goals. One informant, a 31-year-old Mexican-American male IDU noted, "Safe sex means that you're 100 percent sure that if you have sex without a condom that you're gonna be okay afterwards" (3012). Such sentiments were not uncommon. Consider the following statement, offered by a 34-year-old Anglo female IDU (3101): "[Safe sex is] being able to have sex with somebody and not have to worry or think about it afterwards if you got a disease or something or if you're HIV positive. Just being assured that everything's okay."

Sex is made safer by utilizing any one or combination of the strategies and procedures discussed previously. The ability to properly utilize these artifices to discriminate between high-risk and low-risk people underlies notions of perceived risk and vulnerability and often constitutes the definition of safer sex. Safe sex is "knowing who you're having sex with," and in this context condom use and nonuse can become not just a prophylactic measure against HIV infection but a tangible signifier of levels of intimacy, trust, and the developmental stage of a relationship. Similar sentiments were noted by a 42-year-old Anglo female IDU in a discussion regarding the need to use condoms with a partner: "I say it would be a matter of bein' with a person six months to a year, being positive that he had been with nobody else but you and having those tests done, like I said, when you first get together, a six-month window and then in another six-month window I think could be completely positive" (3102).

For others, past life experiences and current circumstances make feelings of vulnerability and risk more immediate. The danger posed by HIV in sexual relationships brings a certain level of awareness and a host of worries regarding not only one's own personal past, but the sexual past of current or potential partners. This is illustrated in the following exchange with a 41-year-old Anglo former prostitute and IDU.

[You mentioned earlier that you don't use condoms with your regular partners, did you say?]

With my man no.

[No?]

I do not like condoms. I've used a million of 'em and I don't like 'em. I could have AIDS right now just from being with Andy. I have no idea. I haven't been checked since I've been with him. It worries me but Andy's pretty much like I am about sex and I know, you know, and now that I've been with him this long, your past kinda comes up, slaps you on the face, especially as much as we're on the street. And he's just a real loner and he hasn't been, from what I can see, but with two women in the two years he's been here. One of 'em worries me a lot, but the other one doesn't. But he's an extremely clean, conscientious, hygienic man, you know. I've got my fingers crossed [laughs]. (3107)

Within the context of a relationship, condom use is seen by many as a barometer of distance and intimacy and indicates what type of relationship a person is in. The shift from use to nonuse of condoms in a relationship, or vice versa, points to changes in the course and development of personal bonds. At times this developmental shift in a relationship may be facilitated by undergoing and/or sharing HIV test results. In any event, condom use in the initial stages of relationships often gives way to nonuse as partners get to know each other better and establish certain levels of commitment, intimacy, and familiarity.

Such sentiments were well summarized by the following interviewee, a 32-year-old Anglo male IDU, in his discussion regarding condom use as a measure of intimacy and trust in a relationship:

I guess that there's a trust issue or something. One of the things that you want to express to a sexual partner is that somehow you trust them, that you, you know, if your sexual partner is into a developed relationship and not like anonymous sex or something like that but, that you really trust them. And an extension of that is you trust that they are aware of their own sexual histories, and would not put you at risk. Somehow insisting that a partner use a condom, if they don't want to use one, it's kind of an expression of a lack of trust. That's the only thing that I can think of that is a problem in condom use. (4600)

A number of rationales, strategies, and feelings underlie condom use and enter into the calculation of risk, which makes consistent use problematic. One interviewee, a 19-year-old Anglo man and a sex partner of an IDU, summed up some of these difficulties in using condoms:

When you're with a primary partner you know you're gonna be with that person for at least from six months to a year, minimum, and, when you know yourself that, they haven't ever been involved with drugs and, you know, you find each other, find out each other's backgrounds, I think it makes it a lot easier not to use condoms. I mean, there's always that chance that you could contract AIDS somehow, somewhere, but it's not, it's not quite as high risk when you're with one person only, than it is with three or four. (4101)

Note once again how observation, history, and the underlying notion that certain procedures can be used to avoid high-risk groups and situations are reiterated here.

The determination of risk categories, the use of various strategies to get to know someone, including the utilization of HIV test results, and the decision to begin, continue, or terminate condom use—in short, "being careful"—are of critical importance within the context of intimate relationships in the age of AIDS. For the addict with no active sexual relationships, or those within mutually monogamous partnerships, these strategies have less relevance. But for those in other sexual relationships, the confidence they place in their abilities to discern between a high-risk and low-risk person may have far-reaching consequences.

To various degrees, these strategies and categorizations are reflected in reported condom use in this group. The data in Table 11.4 present a mixed picture of condom use among IDUs and their primary sexual partners. Although a number of respondents were consistent in either their use or nonuse of condoms, others were more sporadic. Those who never used condoms tended to be in more exclusive relationships of longer duration, whereas those that always used condoms with their primary partner revealed that they were HIV-seropositive. A variety of explanations for the use patterns of those falling between these two extremes emerged over the course of our ethnographic interviews. Often, these sporadic patterns reflected changes in a relationship as it developed from a more open, potentially transitory association to a more permanent, and exclusive, arrangement. Thus, these changing use patterns are one indicator of a process whereby people became more comfortable with each other, either through observation, history taking, HIV testing or status disclosure, or some combination of these and other strategies, and make risk assessments and judgments based on this information. Other variations in condom use within this group were attributed to changing birth control needs, health concerns associated with a urinary tract infection, and partner infidelity.

As outlined in Table 11.5, patterns of condom use with nonprimary sexual partners reveal similar variations. The most consistent users were individuals who were either HIV-seropositive or prostitutes. The former were motivated to use condoms in consideration of their sexual partners' health, whereas the latter used condoms to protect themselves in situations where they felt at risk. Although some prostitutes were consistent in their use, others did not use condoms with regular clients whom they felt they knew well or with whom they had established a long-term relationship. The underlying motivations and rationales underlying sporadic users included assessments of risk, closeness, and trust. In these cases, once again, underlying categories of risk and identity shape the practice of behavior conducive to HIV transmission.

TABLE 11.4
Condom Use

Condom Use With Main Partner	n	%
No main sex partner ever	1	7.2
Never	49	71.0
Almost never	4	5.8
Sometimes	6	8.7
Almost always	6	8.7
Always	3	4.3

Note. N = 69.

TABLE 11.5
Condom Use

Condom Use With "Casual" Partner	n	%
No "casual" sex partner ever	5	7.2
Never	42	60.9
Almost never	3	4.3
Sometimes	2	2.9
Almost always	6	8.7
Always	11	15.9

Note. $N = 69$.

Seventy-five percent of individuals engaging in injection drug use ($n = 64$) reported that they did not use condoms with their main sexual partner at the time they were interviewed. Of the 69 respondents, 71% reported that they had never used condoms with their main sexual partners. Of 64 respondents who said that they had been involved in a sexual relationship they did not consider to be a main partnership, 66% reported that condoms were never used. Such relationships ranged in duration from a "one-night stand" to 5 years in length.

DISCUSSION

A number of researchers argue that the professional construction of risk, through reification of social groups and particular sets of behaviors, fosters a climate wherein certain segments of society may uncritically assume that they are not in any urgent danger of contracting HIV. Prevention concepts and media messages overwhelmingly locate the high risk of HIV transmission within the parameters of certain stigmatized segments of society, especially IDUs, prostitutes, and gay men. For those who, for whatever reason, find themselves outside the boundaries of these social categorizations, the perceived immediacy of felt HIV risks is cognitively and socially distanced.

What the current study suggests is that this process of categorization and distancing is not the exclusive prerogative of the "general public," but even includes those who fall within the social boundaries of certain widely circulated high-risk groups. IDUs appropriate the lexicon, concepts, and procedures of intervention messages and utilize them to manage the vulnerabilities centering around the felt risks of HIV infection and, in so doing, fulfill personal psychosocial ends.

The information presented here adds an interesting dimension to those theoretical arguments suggesting that the construction of the social other is an integral part of a process whereby certain privileged segments of society systematically pathologize and exclude those who are culturally and socially distant from political power (Gilman, 1985; Gusfield, 1996; Schiller, 1992). Although our aim here is not to contest the legitimacy of these claims, it seems clear that the demarcation of social boundaries, pathology, and exclusion is not confined to the dominant classes of society, nor solely a simple tool of hegemonic domination. The contagious cultural other is constructed not only by those powerful groups who wish to separate specific populations from political power, but also by insiders within those very groups that are systematically marginalized.

This insight points out the need for a fuller understanding of the intricacies and social parameters utilized by actors to classify and construct others within specific social groups. What modes of status and power do these local constructions reveal? Our data suggest that a dimension of acceptable patterns of drug use and sexual activity underlies these classifications. These patterns point to important levels of responsibility, carelessness, and control. These conceptualizations help navigate potentially dangerous situations by keeping certain people and risks at length on a socially apparent, if not always biologically real, level. But these same strategies and rationales provide a means to develop closer, more intimate, relationships. The IDUs we interviewed readily adopt conventions to both distance and bring them closer to others.

In addition, the reified categories of risk and identity promulgated by many AIDS researchers belie a social reality characterized by variation and plurality. The social construction of IDUs and other groups (e.g., Hispanics, gay men) as more or less monolithic cultural groups ignores important aspects of variability within these groups. This variability is indexed when IDUs note sets of identifiable patterns of behavior, including drug use patterns and sexual behaviors, that help constitute categories of risk and identity within their own group.

This study also adds dimension to the impact HIV/AIDS has had on how people evaluate others in social situations, especially in the context of intimate social and sexual relationships. In a changing landscape of relationships and the transformation of intimacy and sexuality wrought by drastic changes in the modern social order (Giddens, 1992), HIV continues to have an enduring influence in situating relationships. Sexuality is not only an arena where assessments and categorizations pertinent to HIV risks become actualized, but also the realm where drug use patterns, condom use, and the social use of HIV test results intersect. Although needle behaviors of IDUs have been targeted for intervention for some time, sexual activities are also important in understanding and stemming the transmission of HIV. HIV/AIDS has helped to create boundaries between individuals and social groups at the same time it has demonstrated, in growing seroprevalence rates, the imaginary nature of those boundaries.

In order to better understand the character of such boundaries, it is necessary to examine just how such boundaries are constructed. This requires us to look beyond risk at the importance of local constructions of risk and the tools and resources people use to make these constructions. What social purposes do they put these constructions to?

How are local risk constructions linked to professional concepts and discourses of risk? How does risk figure into levels of intimacy in relationships, the determination of acceptable risk, and the limits of vulnerability? Clearly, categories of risk and identity continue to shape the course of interactions and intimate relationships in important ways that we are only beginning to understand.

To conclude, this study illuminates how a set of social categorizations, concepts, and procedures that are a valuable part of HIV prevention efforts are reportedly enacted by IDUs within certain social contexts. The categories and concepts circulated by AIDS prevention programs have a direct, if not always apparent, influence on the regulation of relations within IDU social networks. Ideas regarding risk groups, safer sex, and HIV test results are actualized in specific interactions and often serve to structure the patterns of relationships IDUs share with people around them. Ultimately, this study points to some of the parameters governing the regulation of relationships among people by illustrating how macrocommunications are enacted in microcontexts.

REFERENCES

Bayer, R. (1989). *Private acts, social consequences: AIDS and the politics of public health.* New York: The Free Press.
Becker, M. H., & Joseph, J. G. (1988). AIDS and behavioral change to reduce risk: A review. *American Journal of Public Health, 78,* 394–410.

Catania, J. A., Kegeles, S. M., & Coates, T. J. (1990). Towards an understanding of risk behavior: An AIDS risk reduction model (ARRM). *Health Education Quarterly, 17,* 53–72.

Clatts, M. C. (1995). Disembodied acts: On the perverse use of sexual categories in the study of high-risk behavior. In H. ten Brummelhuis & G. Herdt (Eds.), *Culture and sexual risk: Anthropological perspectives on AIDS* (pp. 241–255). New York: Gordon & Breach.

Connors, M. M. (1992). Risk perception, risk taking and risk management among intravenous drug users: Implications for AIDS prevention. *Social Science and Medicine, 34,* 591–601.

DiClemente, R. J., Forrest, K. A., & Susan, M. (1990). College students' knowledge and attitudes about AIDS and changes in HIV-preventive behaviors. *AIDS Education and Prevention, 2,* 201–212.

Douglas, M. (1992). *Risk and blame: Essays in cultural theory.* New York: Routledge.

Elwood, W. N., & Ataabadi, A. N. (1996). Tuned in and turned off: Out-of-treatment injection drug and crack users' response to media intervention campaigns. *Communication Reports, 9,* 49–59.

Elwood, W. N., & Ataabadi, A. N. (1997). Influence of interpersonal and mass-mediated interventions on injection drug and crack users: Diffusion of innovations and HIV risk behaviors. *Substance Use and Misuse, 32,* 635–651.

Fisher, J. D., & Fisher, W. A. (1992). Changing AIDS-risk behavior. *Psychological Bulletin, 111,* 455–474.

Giddens, A. (1992). *The transformation of intimacy: Sexuality, love, and eroticism in modern societies.* Stanford, CA: Stanford University Press.

Gilman, S. (1985). *Difference and pathology: Stereotypes of sexuality, race and madness.* Ithaca, NY: Cornell University Press.

Gusfield, J. R. (1996). *Contested meanings: The construction of social problems.* Madison: University of Wisconsin Press.

Kane, S. (1991). HIV, heroin, and heterosexual relations. *Social Science and Medicine, 32,* 1037–1050.

Kane, S. (1993). National discourse and the dynamics of risk: Ethnography and AIDS intervention. *Human Organization, 52,* 224–228.

Lear, D. (1995). Sexual communication in the age of AIDS: The construction of risk and trust among young adults. *Social Science and Medicine, 41,* 1311–1323.

McKeganey, N., Barnard, M., & Watson, H. (1989). HIV-related risk behavior among a non-clinic sample of injecting drug users. *British Journal of Addiction, 84,* 1481–1490.

Oppenheimer, G. M. (1988). In the eye of the storm: The epidemiological construction of AIDS. In E. Fee & D. M. Fox (Eds.), *AIDS: The burdens of history* (pp. 267–300). Berkeley: University of California Press.

Page, J. B., & Wingerd, J. L. (1993, March). *"I'm protected somehow": Discrepancies between knowledge and action in HIV prevention.* Paper presented at the meeting of the Society for Applied Anthropology, San Antonio, TX.

Parker, R. G. (1995). The social and cultural construction of sexual risk, or how to have (sex) research in an epidemic. In H. ten Brummelhuis & G. Herdt (Eds.), *Culture and sexual risk: Anthropological perspectives on AIDS* (pp. 257–269). New York: Gordon & Breach.

Ramos, R., Shain, R. N., & Johnson, L. (1995). "Men I mess with don't have nothing to do with AIDS": Using ethno-theory to understand sexual risk perception. *Sociological Quarterly, 36,* 483–504.

Rhodes, T. (1995). Theorizing and researching "risk": Notes on the social relations of risk in heroin users' lifestyles. In P. Aggleton, P. Davis, & G. Hart (Eds.), *AIDS: Safety, sexuality, and risk* (pp. 125–143). Washington, DC: Taylor & Francis.

Schiller, N. G. (1992). What's wrong with this picture? The hegemonic construction of culture in AIDS research in the United States. *Medical Anthropology Quarterly, 6,* 237–254.

Schiller, N. G., Crystal, S., & Lewellen, D. (1994). Risky business: The cultural construction of AIDS risk groups. *Social Science and Medicine, 38,* 1337–1346.

Shilts, R. (1987). *And the band played on: Politics, people, and the AIDS epidemic.* New York: St. Martin's Press.

Sibthorpe, B., Fleming, D., Tesselaar, H., & Gould, J. (1991). Needle use and sexual practices: Differences in perception of personal risk of HIV among intravenous drug users. *Journal of Drug Issues, 21,* 699–712.

Stall, R., McKusick, J., & Wiley, J. (1986). Alcohol and drug use during sexual activity and compliance with safe sex guidelines for AIDS: The AIDS behavioral research project. *Health Education Quarterly, 13,* 359–371.

12

Perceptions of Condoms and Barriers to Condom Use Along the Trans-Africa Highway in Kenya

Kenzie A. Cameron
University of Georgia

Kim Witte
Michigan State University

Solomon Nzyuko
African Medical and Research Foundation, Nairobi, Kenya

If we are not yet infected, then we are still at risk.
—Commercial Sex Worker along the Trans-Africa Highway in Kenya (Summer 1995)

Many individuals are susceptible to and at risk for contraction of human immunodeficiency virus (HIV), the virus that causes Acquired Immune Deficiency Syndrome (AIDS). HIV/AIDS is a disease that is not contained by a country's borders; it is a global disease that continues to spread at staggering rates.

Current estimates reported by the World Health Organization (WHO) in its publication, *The Weekly Epidemiological Report,* documented a 19% increase in reported AIDS cases of adults and children worldwide since July 1, 1995 (WHO, 1996). Based on a country-by-country analysis, WHO estimated that, since the pandemic had its start in the late 1970s and early 1980s, approximately 25.5 million adults and more than 2.4 million children worldwide have been infected with HIV (WHO, 1996). WHO estimated that 21 million adults and 800,000 children are *currently* living with HIV/AIDS (WHO, 1996). These estimates show an increase of 24% from those estimates listed as of December 15, 1995 (WHO, 1995, 1996).

The majority of AIDS cases in the world are currently found in Sub-Saharan Africa, where HIV seroprevalence rates have been suggested to range from less than 1% up to 20% of the adult population ("East and Central Africa," 1993). Recent epidemiological reports rank Kenya as the fourth highest country in terms of estimated numbers of HIV infections (WHO, 1995). The number of reported cases continues to rise in Kenya, with transmission of HIV often occurring along the trucking routes that connect major cities in Kenya, where there is a norm of multiple sex partners, both for the male truck drivers and their assistants, as well as for the women living at or near the truck stops (Nzyuko, 1991; Orobuloye, Caldwell, & Caldwell, 1993). There are three major groups along the highway that appear to be contracting HIV at faster rates than those individuals living in other areas of Kenya: commercial sex workers, truck drivers and their assistants, and young men who live and work at the truck stops (Conover, 1993; Kigondu et al., 1993; Nzyuko, Nyamwaya, Lurie, Hearst, & Mandel, 1995; Omari et al., 1993). Past research indicates that commercial sex workers have been reported to have HIV seroprevalence rates ranging from 27% to 88% (Anarfi, 1994; Conover, 1993; WHO, 1992a). In addition, Kenyan truck drivers have been reported to have HIV seroprevalence rates reaching 19% (Conover, 1993).

AIDS was made a "notifiable disease" by the Kenyan government under the Public Health Act in 1987, at which time 1,497 cases had been reported from all of the Kenyan provinces (Agata, Muita, Muthami, Gachihi, & Pelle, 1993; Rachier, 1993). Current estimates are in excess of 1 million cases of HIV infection within the provinces of Kenya. Such an increase is staggering and underscores the need for research and projects designed in attempts to further individuals' knowledge of HIV/AIDS and to determine appropriate prevention campaigns and intervention strategies.

A STUDY OF PERCEPTIONS OF CONDOM USE IN KENYA

This chapter relates results from a formative evaluation, conducted in the summer of 1995, of perceptions and beliefs about HIV transmission. The larger project, from which information for this chapter has been drawn, was undertaken in order to evaluate HIV/AIDS prevention campaign materials targeted toward individuals who live and work along the Trans-Africa Highway in Kenya (Cameron, Witte, Lapinski, & Nzyuko, 1996; Witte, Cameron, Lapinski, & Nzyuko, 1997). Nine focus groups were conducted at three sites along the Trans-Africa Highway. The populations sampled for this study were commercial sex workers, truck drivers and their assistants, and young men who lived and worked at the selected truck stops. These three populations were selected based on past research identifying these populations as contracting HIV at increased rates, as noted earlier. Three focus groups were conducted among each of the three populations.

Sites

The three sites at which the focus groups were conducted were chosen to represent a broad geographical range and to allow the inclusion of a cross-section of Kenyan citizens. Following is a brief description of each site (Simba, Mashinari, and Malaba) at which focus groups were conducted.

Simba. Simba, Kenya, began as a small village in the colonial days and, until recently, served primarily as a shopping site for the Masai and Kamba communities. Since 1990, it has expanded rapidly as a truck stop. It is 135 kilometers southeast of Nairobi along the Trans-Africa Highway (Nairobi-Mombasa section), is located on the rail, and has a railway station. No formal population estimates exist but public health estimates suggest a population of approximately 1,000. There are more than 50 commercial buildings in the Simba area. The rural flavor of the truck stop, as well as the large influence of the Masai nomads who shop and use the health clinics in the town, make it a unique community.

Mashinari. Mashinari, Kenya, is a truck stop 208 kilometers southeast of Nairobi along the Trans-Africa Highway (Nairobi-Mombasa section). It began in 1967 as a campsite for the Mashinari Construction Company, which was then constructing the Trans-Africa Highway. It has grown rapidly in the past 10 years and now holds more than 80 commercial buildings. No formal population records exist but public health workers estimate that Mashinari consists of approximately 2,000 permanent residents. The infrastructure of Mashinari is still developing; currently Mashinari boasts a water supply, a post office, and telephone access, and plans for the introduction of electricity are underway. The truck stop includes several private health clinics as well as a nursing home.

Malaba. Malaba, Kenya, is a town with a population exceeding 5,000. Currently, there are over 200 commercial establishments, as well as 13 bars and restaurants, in this truck stop located 520 kilometers west of Nairobi. The town also houses a police station, several private health clinics, a railway station, a cereals and produce port depot, as well as customs and immigration offices, as Malaba lies on the Kenya/Uganda border. Malaba is one of a number of border towns to Uganda. Due to its status as a border town, truck traffic is dense. Many truck drivers stay for an extended period of time in Malaba, in order to clear their cargo for border inspection. Malaba is administered by town council of five elected councilors, headed by a chairman.

Participants

Obtained from these three sites, a total of 64 individuals participated in the study. The study participants ranged in age from 17 to 57 ($M = 24.52$). Each of the participants was asked to take part in a discussion concerning health problems in the area. Commercial sex workers accounted for 24 of our participants, ranging in age from 17 to 32 ($M = 22.42$). Nineteen participants were truck drivers and their assistants, with ages ranging from 24 to 57 ($M = 31.05$). The young men provided us with 21 of our participants, aged 18 to 23 ($M = 20.30$). These 64 participants provided us with the perceptions, beliefs, and fears that we describe later.

Procedure

Subjects participating in the study were recruited using a snowball sample and word of mouth. Often, the researchers acquired the assistance of an ingroup member (e.g., a member of the community, a public health official) to facilitate the gathering of participants. The subjects were informed that they would be compensated for their time and participation.

The focus group moderator was a Kenyan native, known to some of the subjects, who spoke Swahili, English, and Kamba fluently. Participants were provided the opportunity to choose the language in which they would like to conduct the discussion. All participants chose Swahili.

The focus groups lasted between $1\frac{1}{2}$ and 2 hours and were audiotaped. Informed consent was solicited and received verbally. An extensive focus group protocol was then followed, during which participants were asked to reflect upon and discuss their perceptions of the causes of HIV/AIDS, recommended responses to avert contraction of HIV, perceived threat of contraction of HIV, efficacy of recommended responses to avert HIV, barriers to protecting oneself from contraction of HIV, current HIV/AIDS prevention campaign materials, and to offer ideas and suggestions for future HIV/AIDS prevention campaigns.

The protocol was developed to correspond to the underlying theoretical framework of the Extended Parallel Process Model (EPPM; Witte, 1992), which focuses on threat (susceptibility and severity) and efficacy (self- and response efficacy). A myriad of issues, including political, cultural, and relational issues surrounding HIV/AIDS, were brought to the forefront during these discussions. The results reported in this chapter include only those results pertaining to perceptions of condoms and barriers to condom use.[1]

BARRIERS TO CONDOM USE AS A PREVENTIVE MEASURE AGAINST CONTRACTION OF HIV

A portion of the focus group protocol centered on learning how the participants viewed condom use. This chapter focuses on the many obstacles, or barriers, that were suggested by the participants regarding condom use. The results provide descriptive examples of the breadth of issues affecting, and possibly interfering with, the promotion efforts of various governmental and nongovernmental agencies working to decrease the spread of HIV in Kenya. The categories of themes of barriers to condom use were determined through content analysis of the transcripts of the focus group sessions. Following transcription of the audiotapes, and translation of the transcripts into English from Swahili, two coders analyzed the results question by question. No significant response differences appeared to exist across sites, therefore the responses were pooled across sites. Following is a qualitative presentation of the thematic categories that emerged when the participants' responses were content analyzed. The focus of the qualitative analysis is initially upon general perceptions of condom use, followed by a description of the emergent themes regarding barriers to condom use.

Perceptions of HIV/AIDS and Condom Use

In general, participants suggested that condoms hypothetically could work as a preventive measure against contraction of HIV. Yet, based on their personal experiences they did not believe that condoms were an *effective* preventive measure. The most commonly cited reason for the belief in the lack of efficacy of condoms was condom breakage, which is addressed later.

During the discussions, the participants suggested a number of potential barriers to condom use. These barriers emerged from the stories that the participants shared about their personal experiences or the experiences of individuals known to them. These obstacles to condom use provide a depiction of the multitude of competing demands, resources, interests, and beliefs that the participants face on a daily basis.

Although the majority of the individuals who participated in the focus groups knew that condoms were a preventive measure against contraction of HIV, most participants reported that their condom use was infrequent ($M = 2.83$, $SD = .70$, where 5 represented "Never," and 1 represented "All of the time").[2] Based on their sexual activity of the past year, individuals reported that, on average, they had sexual intercourse two to four times a week ($M = 4.71$, $SD = 1.62$, where 1 represented "less than once a month," 2 represented "once a month," 3 represented "once a week," 4 represented "twice a week," 5 represented "3–4 times a week," and 6 represented "once a day").

The reported number of partners in the past month ranged from 0 to 30 ($M = 5.12$, $SD = 6.30$) and in the past year from 0 to 60 ($M = 19.23$, $SD = 16.84$). Participants voiced many

---

[1]For further information on the recruitment of participants, mechanics of the focus group discussions, and discussion of other results, please see Cameron et al. (1996), Witte, Cameron, and Nzyuko (1996), and Witte et al. (1997).

[2]Following the focus group discussions, each participant met individually with the moderator for a face-to-face interview. The results presented in this section are drawn from data obtained during these individual interviews. See Cameron et al. (1996) and Witte et al. (1997) for further discussion.

reasons for their lack of condom use. Upon analysis, these reasons appear to fit in thematic categories of power and negotiation issues, economical and structural issues, relational issues, and cultural issues. We turn now to a description and analysis of these themes.

Power and Negotiation Issues

Condom use, whether it be the suggestion by one partner to use condoms, the mutual decision of both partners to use condoms, or the process in which the partners engage while negotiating condom use, has always been filled with a variety of power issues. These issues may manifest in one's beliefs of what one can and cannot say in a certain situation, one's access to a desired resource (e.g., the female condom), or one's perception of one's ability and right to discuss topics such as condom use.

The Verbalization of One's Desire to Use Condoms. Metts and Fitzpatrick (1992) noted that the suggestion of condom use itself is inherently face threatening because such a suggestion could appear to challenge the identity that an individual desires to project in a given encounter. To suggest condom use is to relate one's fear of contraction of HIV and other STDs (Metts & Fitzpatrick, 1992), which may be seen by the other partner as threatening, and may serve to imply distrust between the partners. The suggestion that one wants to use condoms can be seen as an affront by the individual to whom condom use is suggested. The receiver may question if the suggestion is fueled by one's caring about the partner, by one's distrust as to whether or not the partner is infected, or by one's past sexual encounters, potentially raising questions of promiscuity or the HIV status of the individual suggesting condom use (Metts & Fitzpatrick, 1992). A request for condom usage may thus provoke issues of power in a relationship.

The participants voiced numerous examples of power issues. In addition, as many of the participants engaged in sex with commercial sex workers, or were commercial sex workers themselves, the power issues took on yet another dimension. The participants noted extreme fears of being seen as infected, if they were to suggest condom use to their partners. In addition, they perceived powerlessness in their ability to suggest condom use to their partners—especially the commercial sex workers, as they were well aware that they were providing a service for which they were being paid. One commercial sex worker noted, "Here it is not easy for a woman to face a man and tell him to use a condom. Women tend to be on the receiving end, they wait for the man to suggest condom use."[3] Another commercial sex worker echoed a similar thought, "We are women, we are weak and shy, we cannot ask them to use condoms."

The Female Condom. In an attempt to gain more power in a sexual situation, many women asked if it would be possible for them to obtain the female condom. When questioned, these women stated that they were not all that familiar with the female condom and its proper use. They did not know (nor were they highly concerned) about the success rates of the female condom. Their desire to obtain female condoms was driven by the belief that, were they to have the female condom made available to them, it could provide them increased power in the condom negotiation process. The women felt that access to a female condom would give them the option of telling the men, "If you don't know how to use yours, use mine." Some women noted that if they were the ones to use the condoms, the men may not perceive the condoms to be as inconvenient as a male condom, and may therefore be more receptive to condom use.

---

[3]The unattributed quotes noted in this chapter were voiced by participants during the focus group discussions.

Empowerment. Even though some of the women hoped to have access to the female condom in the near future, it was noted that, in the end, the man was paying for the sexual acts. If the man insisted on no condom use (whether it be a male or female condom), then one must acquiesce to the wishes of the man, as he controlled the income of the women in that particular setting. "A given evening at a truck stop provided only so many potential clients; if a woman were to displease them by insisting on condoms—well, plenty of other girls were willing" (Conover, 1993, p. 66).

One commercial sex worker, in summing up the situation of condom use and power noted: "[Some men] claim that if it is just death, everybody must one day die . . . at such moments the woman is powerless and just succumbs to the wishes of the man." As suggested by this statement, many of the power issues appeared to center around the women's feeling of a lack of power, as the man's power was increased due to the fact that he was the paying client. The conflict of economic necessity and condom usage was readily apparent in such interactions.

The need to promote empowerment of women regarding sex and condom use has been documented. Ngugi (1993) and Anarfi (1994) suggested that education and counseling of women regarding condom use, as well as attempts to increase the social status of women, are vitally needed in order to decrease the rate of spread of HIV. The female participants were eager to learn how they could effect condom use in their relationships. However, power and negotiation issues are not the only obstacles to condom use faced by individuals in the truck stop communities.

Economic and Structural Issues

In addition to power issues that are seen in personal relationships, there are broader power issues affecting decisions such as condom use. The economics of commercial sex work, as noted previously as influencing factors such as a woman's empowerment, exist in conjunction with broader, more diverse economical and structural issues. The economy of the country, as well as available resources, play a large role in condom-related issues. The focus group participants noted that the supply of condoms was often inadequate, the quality of some of the more available condoms was often perceived to be low, and improper storage procedures led to the deterioration and subsequent bursting of condoms when used during sexual intercourse. Breakage problems then caused individuals to further doubt the efficacy of condoms in protecting themselves against contraction of HIV.

Condom Supply. Individuals at each of the three truck stops visited during this project commented on the lack of condoms available in their small communities. Some individuals focused more on the lack of variety of condoms and the expense. For example, the participants noted that they preferred some of the more expensive condoms, which were often manufactured abroad, but they could not afford to buy them. The cost of the preferred condoms may well equal the amount of money that the commercial sex workers would receive for engaging in sexual intercourse. One commercial sex worker bluntly stated, "I cannot buy condoms, food for me and my children, and pay my rent because I have not enough money."

Participants also noted an extreme need for more condoms, of any variety, to be brought to the truck stops for retail. As part of their participation in the focus group, individuals were provided with condoms, as well as instructions as to how to use condoms properly. Supply-and-demand issues were readily apparent in such exchanges: The participants consistently asked if we had more condoms to give to them. Unfortunately, the number of condoms available for distribution through this project was limited. Alternate sources were attempted, which provided us a firsthand experience of the inadequate supply of condoms at the various truck stops as we vainly searched for more condoms and found that kiosks and stores were sold out of their supply of condoms.

Upon reaching Malaba, a town on the Ugandan border, sources noted that there had not been a new shipment of condoms to Malaba for over 6 months. Malaba is a border town where many truck drivers remain for multiple nights, as they wait for their cargo to clear customs. These truck drivers seek out the local commercial sex workers in order to pass their time in an enjoyable manner as they wait for their cargo to be inspected. According to public health workers and peer educators, although there had been repeated requests for more condoms, apparently the shipments never reached Malaba. One shipment consigned for Malaba was left in Buzia, a town approximately 30 kilometers from Malaba. Reactions to the lack of condom shipments ranged from speculations that the shipments were never sent in the first place, to suggestions that the shipments may have been depleted in transit, as most truck stops were in the similar position of not having sufficient amounts of condoms to meet consumer demand.

Another issue related to condom availability was the hours of operation of local kiosks. When available, condoms would be sold at kiosks at the truck stops. However, kiosks close at night. Thus, in addition to an overall insufficiency in the condom supply, it was noted that, at times when there may be condoms hypothetically available for purchase at the truck stops, it may still seem impossible to obtain the condoms if the kiosks are closed.

Condom Storage and Quality. In addition to the difficulties in obtaining condoms, at least two more economical and structural obstacles affect condom use in Kenya, even when the condoms reach the truck stops. Storage facilities are often unsatisfactory: Sources noted that boxes of condoms were left in places where they may be rained upon, and left in places where the condoms were exposed to the damaging rays of the sun. In addition, due to shipment difficulties, it was possible that the only condoms available at a particular truck stop were expired. Although individuals knew that expired or damaged condoms should not be used, and some even feared that expired condoms carry HIV (see later discussion), these condoms may be used during sexual intercourse. As a result of using expired condoms, individuals would experience repeated problems with condom breakage, which served to reduce even further individuals' perceptions of the efficacy of the condoms as a preventive measure against contraction of HIV. Such negative experiences with condoms and condom breakage, reported by most of the participants, did not encourage the individuals to continue their use of condoms.

Relational Issues

Obstacles to condom use included relational concerns in venues other than power, for example, when participants discussed the use or lack of use of condoms during sexual intercourse. During the focus groups, varied relational barriers to condom use were suggested, including issues surrounding multiple acts of sexual intercourse when faced with a limited supply of condoms, issues pertaining to relationship development, physical pleasure, competing relational goals, and issues of trust.

Multiple Acts of Sexual Intercourse. Initial responses to what can be viewed as relational barriers to condom use focused on some practical issues raised by the participants. Having already noted the frequent inadequate supply of condoms in many of the communities, participants commented on a different facet of the unavailability of condoms as a factor in the low usage rates of condoms. Many of the condoms were sold either singly, or in packages of three. Individuals who chose to have multiple acts of sexual intercourse during the night, not an uncommon choice, especially for the commercial sex workers, faced the possibility of running out of condoms. Even if their initial sexual encounters of the evening included using condoms, their limited supply of condoms (possibly a package of three condoms) may be used up before one's desire is satiated. One young man said, "[It] is not easy [to use condoms consistently] because one may get a partner and have only two pieces of condom. After using the two condoms, one may still be having a strong desire to continue and hence one is compelled to go at it skin to skin." Another young man offered a suggestion of what to do when faced with an insufficient condom supply: Use and reuse the condoms, for example, "for three rounds." This young man knew that condoms were not intended to be reused and that condoms do not provide adequate protection if they have already been used, yet he questioned which was the lesser of two evils: to reuse a condom, which may allow for some protection, or to abandon condom use and continue having sexual intercourse without protection. The option of not having sexual intercourse, of abstaining, was repeatedly dismissed by the majority of the sample as being "impossible."

Some commercial sex workers indicated that they had limited success in requesting and attaining condom usage from their partners—at least initially. However, either due to shortage of condoms, or increasing desire, the commercial sex workers said that, as the night continued, condom usage often declined: "[Some men who use condoms] . . . may persevere during the early hours of the night, but by midnight they insist on skin to skin."

Relationship Development.   Another facet of multiple acts of sexual intercourse that emerged was the relationship development between the partners. Such a relationship could serve to decrease one's desire for or belief in the necessity of condom use, as suggested by one young man: "Once you get a caring partner, the desire to have skin to skin is high and possibly when you attempt condom use if only for the first round, and then get into skin to skin due to both the drive and the personal conviction that you are now familiar to one another and generally view the partner as too good to have the virus."

It was found that, along the trucking routes, sex work appears to be more relational than anonymous (although there are cases where the commercial sex workers did not know their clients). That is, the majority of the commercial sex workers reported that they had several "regular" partners or repeat clients with whom they had long-standing relationships. These clients would seek out their particular "friend" whenever they stopped at that particular truck stop.

Physical Pleasure and the "Reality" of Sexual Intercourse.   When speaking of relational issues regarding sexual intercourse and condom use, our participants spoke of the aspect of physical pleasure. They suggested that, when one views oneself to be in some sort of relationship, one wants the sexual experience to be "real." Reality in the sexual experience to them meant no condom use. One commercial sex worker noted, "There are some men who say they don't experience the expected pleasure, hence, skin to skin or steel to steel is the only enjoyable way of having sex."

Related to physical pleasure was the perception of commercial sex workers that they were not having sex if the man did not ejaculate into them directly. The use of condoms was seen, from such a view, as a barrier to true or real sex, for it would take away such an experience. Both women and men cited the *need* for the sexual activity to be skin to skin and for the woman to be able to feel the man's "full length" inside of her in order for the experience to be real and pleasurable. Indeed, many participants accused their partners of "pinching" (intentionally breaking) the condom so that, during sexual intercourse, the condom would *not* act as a barrier. It was implied that the reason for pinching of condoms was to reach the reality of sexual intercourse, to attain skin-to-skin contact.

Competing Relational Goals. Another relational issue suggested by the participants was the aspect of the competing goals they perceived in their relationships. Both women and men indicated that sexual pleasure was a goal of intimate relationships, and the men often said that "the need for sex" was a reason to seek the company of commercial sex workers. Some men suggested the necessity of developing a libido-suppressing drug, for they claimed that there were times when they perceived it to be completely beyond their control to suppress their libido, for example, when a particularly attractive partner was in close proximity. The men also strongly endorsed the belief that a man has sexual drives that *need* to be satisfied and cannot be ignored. As one young man stated, "Condom use is best because usually man's nature is that they are never satisfied and in their many movements they may come across girls who they feel they must have sex with. Due to such eventualities, condom will be most appropriate." Further, many said that they had even been told by medical personnel that back problems they experienced were caused by infrequent sex. Thus, for men, sex was seen as crucial to both sustain physical health and to meet their needs.

In contrast, the women noted that commercial sex work was their means of income. Although both the men and the women talked of the pleasure obtained from the sexual experiences, for the men it was often a release of sexual desire, or a need, a hunger that they felt they could not control until they returned to their wives. The women, although many enjoyed the experiences, looked to their sex work as an income. For some it was the only source of income; for others it was supplemented by other jobs that they hold in the community. The commercial sex workers themselves often had children and some had husbands. The husbands often knew of the women's sex work, and encouraged it, for it brought income to the family. Thus, the competing demands of sexual desires and economical needs were continually at play in many of these encounters.

Relational Trust. A final relational issue focused upon levels of trust within the relationships. Some participants indicated that they were not sure that they could completely trust their partners. Thus, they *advocated* the use of condoms in sexual relationships. For example, one commercial sex worker said, "Having one partner helps. However, this one partner may not be faithful. Hence, you are still exposed." Other individuals suggested that trust was not always apparent in many of the transient relationships that could be found along the highway, and agreed that condom use would be advisable. Although the participants recognized the potential benefits of condom use, they were often reminded in some way of the difficulty of obtaining and consistently using condoms during sexual intercourse.

Cultural Issues

A final theme that emerged during discussions of obstacles to condom use was one of cultural issues. A number of culturally relevant barriers were suggested, including: difficulties in communicating about condom use; perceptions of individual risk; questions pertaining to foreign involvement in HIV/AIDS campaigns, and in the manufacturing and distribution of condoms; as well as various issues resulting from cultural beliefs and practices.

Communication About Condom Use. Although the participants were candid in their discussion of sex and condom use, there appeared to be a lack of knowledge about how to communicate condom use within sexual relationships. In addition to relational problems, experienced when two partners prepare to discuss condom use, these individuals faced the difficulty of communicating about an economically driven sexual act. Sexual intercourse is a form of income for the women, and many of the women felt powerless to insist on or even suggest the use of condoms to their paying clients. Many women recognized that, were they to refuse to participate in sexual intercourse without condoms, their client could and would easily turn to other women in the community who would agree to his suggestion of skin-to-skin contact. Thus, the bind became an economical one within the culture of the truck stop itself. One could choose to earn wages that evening, or to see one's wages go to another woman who agreed to the client's request.

The Risk Factor.   Cross-culturally, research indicates the attitude that HIV/AIDS is a disease that affects "the other." Individuals often perceive themselves as not being at risk for contraction of the disease based on stereotypes of who is at risk for HIV contraction, as well as self-images that exclude the possibility of being infected with HIV (Manning, Balson, Barenberg, & Moore, 1989). Although many of the participants perceived that it was likely that they were infected with HIV, they also suggested that they viewed other individuals as being more susceptible to contraction of the virus.

Beliefs as to who was responsible for spreading the virus were also focused on some other person or group. For example, truck drivers blamed women for the spread of HIV, saying, "Women should be immunized so as to cut down the spread of HIV." Another truck driver suggested, "These women also need to be kept away because there are some who get lifts from truck drivers to very far countries such as Tanzania, Rwanda, etc., where they get infected and then bring the virus back to the unsuspecting population." These same truck drivers who suggested that the women are acting as vectors to the virus through the women's travels to other countries are also traveling to the same countries on their truck route and participating in sexual experiences with the women at the truck stops in other countries.

Foreign Involvement.   During the focus group discussions, it became evident that there were many reservations, as well as feelings of distrust, toward foreign involvement in all aspects of the AIDS crisis. HIV/AIDS campaigns and the manufacturing processes of condoms were questioned, and perceptions of potential hidden agendas of the distribution of free condoms were shared.

A few individuals quite candidly suggested that AIDS is an invented disease, invented by those individuals who wanted to take away some of the pleasures of life. Some participants shared their version of the AIDS acronym: the American Invention to Discourage Sex. Although this phrase was presented in a jovial manner, the number of times that it was repeated by different individuals suggests that some believe that AIDS is not necessarily a deadly disease, but may be an invention. A young man remarked that by using such a description, individuals could downplay the threat of AIDS in their minds and "dismiss the reality of AIDS."

Another concern that emerged was in regard to the appropriateness and effectiveness of foreign condom use in Kenya. During an individual conversation, one man stated that he believed the erection power of the African man to be much greater than that of the American man. Consequently, he believed that American-manufactured condoms were tested on American men, who are not "as strong," and therefore the condom manufacturers, seeing the condoms pass American standards, failed to take into consideration the sexual superiority of the African man. Thus, these American-manufactured condoms would burst for the African man during intercourse. This man suggested that the reasons for the sexual superiority of the African men were the higher temperatures (heat) that the African man must endure, as well as effects from continual exposure to the sun. Although this man did appear to be slightly concerned with the continual breakage of condoms that he experienced, he repeatedly attributed the source of the breakage not to a defect in the condom that could be corrected, but to his prowess and erection power. His narrative suggested that when he found himself in sexual situations when a condom burst during intercourse, the fact that the condom was no longer serving as a protective barrier did not appear to be a matter worthy of concern. Rather, he took pride in the bursting of the condom, for he believed such a bursting to be an irrefutable demonstration of his sexual prowess and power.

In addition to questions about the manufacturing of condoms by foreign companies for distribution in Kenya, questions of the trustworthiness of foreign condoms were raised. Although participants often asked if we had foreign condoms for distribution, they also raised doubts about condoms imported from abroad. Some individuals believe that the lubricant found on some foreign condoms may be the HIV itself. The participants provided reasons as to why such perceptions exist. They told us that there are suspicions that AIDS is an invented disease, either a disease invented to discourage sex, as noted previously, or a disease invented in order to suppress certain cultures or races. Some participants suggested that the spread of HIV may be the attempt of a foreign country to dominate and suppress countries such as Kenya. One commercial sex worker stated, "There are people speculating that some of the condoms distributed have HIV and there are consignments which have been destroyed in some countries. Possibly, the lubricant on the condoms is the HIV, *and more so given that these condoms come from abroad* [emphasis added]." Truck drivers and their assistants, as well as the young men, corroborated this statement, remarking that there were many rumors circulating that condoms, specifically those distributed free of charge, are contaminated with the virus itself.

One factor leading to such perceptions was the "dumping" of shipments of condoms. Apparently, from time to time, a shipment of condoms, usually from abroad, will be destroyed and not distributed. Reasons given for such destruction may be that the condoms were expired, or were defective in some way. When situations such as these arise, questions surface as to the "true" reason for the destruction of these condoms. An explanation suggested was the rumor that the condoms were indeed destroyed due to a defect: This defect was that the condoms were contaminated with HIV. Other reports have noted the belief that expired condoms actually *carry* HIV (Conover, 1993). One woman was surprised to learn that condom use is promoted in the Western world; she believed that condom use was solely a Kenyan or African practice. There continues to be much misinformation regarding condoms and condom usage, misinformation that gains increased momentum and force with each repetition.

Cultural Beliefs and Practices. A variety of research has indicated the need to address culture and cultural beliefs when viewing health issues (e.g., Cameron, 1996; Clark, 1983; Fabrega, 1977; Michal-Johnson & Bowen, 1992; Quesada & Heller, 1977; Ruiz, 1985; Witte & Morrison, 1995). During the focus group discussions, the participants noted a number of cultural beliefs and practices relevant to the use or the lack of use of condoms during sexual intercourse. Fatalistic outlooks, the practice of polygamy, wife inheritance, the need to procreate, the recreational aspect of sexual intercourse, and available testing procedures were couched in terms of being related to the culture and atmosphere of the truck stops, as reported by the participants.

Belief in fatalism, or believing that all events are inevitable, is a cultural belief that is commonly noted. An individual who had traveled for a period of time with truck drivers along the Trans-Africa Highway once wrote an article examining sexual behaviors and AIDS, in which he commented, "I wondered if what had been called Africa's fatalism was just a reasonable response to the fact that there was only so much you could do" (Conover, 1993,

p. 75). A few seemingly fatalistic remarks were made during the focus group sessions, as noted earlier when one woman stated, "[Some men] claim that if it is just death, everybody must one day die."

The culture and atmosphere of the truck stops themselves appeared to contribute to the perceptions of sexual intercourse and HIV/AIDS. Many of the commercial sex workers were married or involved in significant relationships. Their sex work was condoned by their significant others because it was a source of income. Polygamy is still practiced in the culture; in one focus group two wives of the same man were participants. There are also beliefs surrounding death that have sexual implications for those who remain. A commercial sex worker stated, "When a man dies in a homestead, there are some cultural practices which demand that if there is a woman having her period [she] should cleanse herself through extramarital sex before the deceased is buried." In addition, participants spoke of wife inheritance: When a man dies, his kin inherit his wife and take her as their wife (in addition to any other wives that family member may already have).

Another issue that arose was the intense desire to multiply. Participants shared that producing a male heir was very important, for it meant that the man's line would continue. Due to this strong desire to multiply, condom use was seen by some as a vile, negative practice. One young man claimed, "Use of condoms is not appropriate because it is like throwing one's children away, it is just like murder so it is very bad." Another young man even linked the need to propagate to the specter of AIDS itself: "This disease has no cure and also since as young men, many of us don't have wives, and we are afraid that once we are infected we die without any heirs."

According to the participants, sexual intercourse itself is viewed in a number of ways in the Kenyan culture. In addition to being the process through which one may create an heir, the pleasure derived from sexual intercourse is a high priority. At some truck stops, the impression given was that sexual intercourse was one of the few recreational activities readily available to the inhabitants and those travelers (truck drivers and their assistants) who may be at the truck stop. With regard to how individuals at the truck stop may perceive and even attempt to rationalize the threat of AIDS, Anarfi (1994) noted: "The long incubation period makes people think of AIDS as a problem of tomorrow, not today. For many people the only means of escape from a harsh existence are alcohol, drugs, and sex" (p. 9).

A final cultural issue related to HIV/AIDS that could fuel continuing beliefs in fatalism or decrease further one's attempts to practice safer sex is the lack of sufficient HIV testing available to individuals. Much of the confusion regarding the separation of HIV and AIDS resulted from the fact that most individuals do not know that they are infected with HIV until they begin to develop signs of AIDS. Many individuals were cognizant of the thought that they may well have been exposed (and possibly repeatedly exposed) to individuals who are infected with HIV. The reasons for lack of testing do not stem from issues of fear of finding out one's HIV status, but, rather, from the lack of available HIV-testing opportunities, which suggests that this issue may be a structural one as well.

When questioned as to what could be a way of protecting oneself against HIV transmission, one young man responded, "Be screened periodically to ascertain the safety." Yet, individual interviews with the participants revealed that *none* of the participants had ever been tested to determine their HIV status. Another study, which offered HIV testing as part of the study, found that 94% of the participants, who were commercial sex workers, were *willing* to be tested for the virus (Njoki et al., 1993).

Cultural issues as a whole appear to play a large role in sexual practices, whether they be evidenced through condom usage, beliefs held, customs adhered to, or opportunities available to the individuals within that culture. Culture, therefore, can be seen as an influential variable in many of the decisions made by individuals. Cultural issues, in addition to power and negotiation issues, economical and structural issues, and relational issues, act as factors influencing individuals' sexual behaviors as well as their condom use behavior.

CONCLUSION

Studies such as the one from which this information was drawn can add to a base of information from which future studies can extend. By obtaining information regarding perceptions of condoms and barriers to condom use, future health promotion campaigns focused on HIV/AIDS prevention can address better the concerns of the target audience. Although there are limitations to this work, the most prevalent being the limited generalizability that this study may offer, the information gathered in this study enables us to present specific comments and reactions regarding obstacles that HIV/AIDS prevention campaigns may encounter. In addition to the obstacles listed here, one also finds other barriers, for example, challenges with the dissemination of campaign materials.

The topic of barriers to condom use is an inherently political one. Particularly when studied in the realm of commercial sex work, as was the setting for this study, one can see how power and negotiation issues, economical and structural issues, relational issues, and cultural beliefs and practices coalesce and create an environment in which it can be quite difficult, for a plethora of reasons, to promote a health protective behavior such as condom use. As this chapter has delineated, numerous barriers to condom use, ranging from feelings of powerlessness to the need for the income derived from commercial sex work, and from inadequacies of condom supply to cultural beliefs promoting procreation, face individuals to whom seemingly simple messages such as "AIDS Kills: Use a Condom" are promoted. As this chapter describes, barriers to condom use are prevalent and diverse, and in order to attain change and to attain greater use of condoms during sexual intercourse, various issues must be addressed. Many of these issues need to be addressed in a political forum: The need to promote and achieve wider distribution of condoms, particularly to the rural truck stops, the often-voiced need of the necessity of the condom supply to meet the demand, and the underlying structural issues, which may include training in proper condom storage, as well as proper condom usage, are only a few of the myriad of issues that are raised by those individuals who live and work in the truck stop communities.

A study such as this one highlights the need for international *collaboration* when developing health promotion campaigns. In 1992, WHO published a series of booklets on AIDS and on efforts to combat the spread of the disease. As suggested by WHO (1992b), the need exists to "mobilize and unify national and international efforts" regarding action against the spread of AIDS (p. 18). Almost all of the continents are affected by this virus; it is truly a worldwide pandemic. WHO (1992b) noted that, by 1992, the majority of countries had begun to implement AIDS programs at the national level, and that funding was obtained from a variety of assistance agencies, some of them governmental, some nongovernmental. WHO (1992b) urged that global actions be taken so that the response to AIDS may be a unified response. WHO (1992b) stressed that AIDS programs will not be effective if they do not have the support of the highest level political organizations. Some countries have suffered a complacency about the possibility of the incredible destructiveness of the virus, preferring to believe that their country is not affected by HIV/AIDS. WHO (1992b) suggested that epidemiological and sociobehavioral work are two potentially effective ways of attempting to overcome such complacency, particularly complacency by governments.

HIV/AIDS is a political issue, and at the same time is a danger to the world. It is a disease that crosses cultural, social, and economic boundaries; a disease that ignores political affiliations; and a disease that conquers those who are afflicted. The politics of AIDS are, in a way, simple: HIV/AIDS is a pandemic, one that must be addressed, and one that will not go away by being ignored. Those individuals who are not yet infected with HIV may indeed face the risk of infection. The obstacles on the path to combating AIDS are many, and research and action are needed to break down such barriers. International collaboration, heightened awareness, and an acceptance of the need for such research are all steps on the path of HIV/AIDS research. Such steps on journeys such as this one, which may well be long, are often best taken in the company of others. "For the sake of our common survival, we must act with courage and urgency. With every passing day, HIV claims thousands of lives. The only possible answer to the new AIDS challenge lies in global solidarity" (WHO, 1992b, p. 23).

ACKNOWLEDGMENTS

This research was supported by an All-University Grant awarded by Michigan State University. We are grateful for the support of many individuals who assisted us with the project. Particularly, we would like to thank Dr. David Nyamwaya, Peter Omondi, AMREF, the numerous public health officials who assisted us, the many individuals who helped to recruit participants, and all of our participants who spoke freely and candidly with us. In addition, we acknowledge the coding assistance of Maria Knight Lapinski, of Michigan State University.

REFERENCES

Agata, N., Muita, M., Muthami, L. N., Gachihi, G. S., & Pelle, H. (1993). Epidemiology of HIV/AIDS in Kenya. *1st Kenya HIV/AIDS/STD Conference: Program and Abstracts,* p. 18.

Anarfi, J. K. (1994). HIV/AIDS in Sub-Saharan Africa: Its demographic and socio-economic implications. *African Population Paper, 3.* Nairobi, Kenya: African Population and Environmental Institute.

Cameron, K. A. (1996, August). *Individual and relational barriers to condom use: A cross-cultural study.* Paper presented at the biannual meeting of the International Society on Social and Personal Relationships, Banff, Alberta.

Cameron, K. A., Witte, K., Lapinski, M. K., & Nzyuko, S. (1996, November). *Preventing HIV transmission along the Trans-Africa Highway in Kenya: Using persuasive message theory to conduct a formative evaluation.* Paper presented at the annual meeting of the Speech Communication Association, San Diego.

Clark, M. M. (1983). Cultural context of medical practice. *The Western Journal of Medicine, 139,* 2–6.

Conover, T. (1993, August 16). A reporter at large: Trucking through the AIDS belt. *The New Yorker, 69,* 56–75.

East and central Africa worst hit. (1993, May/June). *AIDS Analysis Africa,* p. 5.

Fabrega, H., Jr. (1977). Group differences in the structure of illness. *Culture, Medicine and Psychiatry, 1,* 379–394.

Kigondu, C. S., Nyunya, B. O., Ogutu, J. O., Nyonyintono, R. M., Sanghvi, H. C. G., Bwayo, J. J., & Omari, M. A. (1993). *1st Kenya HIV/AIDS/STD Conference: Programs and Abstracts,* p. 31.

Manning, D., Balson, P. M., Barenberg, N., & Moore, T. M. (1989). Susceptibility to AIDS: What college students do and don't believe. *Journal of College Health, 38,* 67–73.

Metts, S., & Fitzpatrick, M. A. (1992). Thinking about safer sex: The risky business of "Know your partner" advice. In T. Edgar, M. A. Fitzpatrick, & V. S. Freimuth (Eds.), *AIDS: A communication perspective* (pp. 1–19). Hillsdale, NJ: Lawrence Erlbaum Associates.

Michal-Johnson, P., & Bowen, S. P. (1992). The place of culture in HIV education. In T. Edgar, M. A. Fitzpatrick, & V. S. Freimuth (Eds.), *AIDS: A communication perspective* (pp. 147–172). Hillsdale, NJ: Lawrence Erlbaum Associates.

Ngugi, E. N. (1993). What is the epidemiology of HIV/AIDS of women and how is it changing? *1st Kenya HIV/AIDS/STD Conference: Programs and Abstracts,* p. 25.

Njoki, A. K., Bwayo, J. J., Omari, M. A., Karuga, P., Plummer, F. A., & Moses, S. (1993). A study on female commercial sex workers associated with long distance truck drivers. *1st Kenya HIV/AIDS/STD Conference: Programs and Abstracts*, p. 40.

Nzyuko, S. (1991, July/August). Teenagers along the Trans-Africa Highway. *AIDS and Society*, p. 10.

Nzyuko, S., Nyamwaya, D., Lurie, P., Hearst, N., & Mandel, J. (1995, October). *Adolescent high risk sexual behavior along the Trans-Africa Highway*. Paper presented at the AMREF/AIDS Scientific Conference, Tanzania.

Omari, M. A., Bwayo, J., Mutere, A. N., Plummer, F. A., Moses, S., Ndinya-Achola, J. A., & Kreiss, J. K. (1993). Correlates of HIV infection in long distance truck drivers in Kenya. *1st Kenya HIV/AIDS/STD Conference: Programs and Abstracts*, p. 35.

Orubuloye, I. O., Caldwell, P., & Caldwell, J. C. (1993). The role of high-risk occupations in the spread of AIDS: Truck drivers and itinerant market women in Nigeria. *International Family Planning Perspectives, 19*, 43–48.

Quesada, G. M., & Heller, P. L. (1977). Sociocultural barriers to medical care among Mexican-Americans in Texas: A summary report of research conducted by the Southwest Medical Sociology Ad Hoc Committee. *Medical Care, 15*(Suppl.), 93–101.

Rachier, A. D. O. (1993). HIV/AIDS and the law. *1st Kenya HIV/AIDS/STD Conference: Programs and Abstracts*, p. 55.

Ruiz, P. (1985). Cultural barriers to effective medical care among Hispanic-American patients. *Annual Review of Medicine, 36*, 63–71.

Witte, K. (1992). Putting the fear back into fear appeals: The extended parallel process model. *Communication Monographs, 59*, 330–349.

Witte, K., Cameron, K. A., Lapinski, M. K., & Nzyuko, S. (1997, May). *A theoretically based evaluation of HIV/AIDS prevention campaigns along the Trans-Africa Highway in Kenya*. Paper presented at the annual meeting of the International Communication Association, Montreal, Quebec.

Witte, K., Cameron, K. A., & Nzyuko, S. (1996). *HIV/AIDS along the Trans-Africa Highway in Kenya: Examining risk perceptions, recommended responses, and campaign materials*. Final report of project funded by Michigan State University AURIG grant.

Witte, K., & Morrison, K. (1995). Intercultural and cross-cultural health communication: Understanding people and motivating healthy behaviors. *Intercultural and International Communication Annual, 14*, 216–246.

World Health Organization. (1992a). *AIDS in Africa: A manual for physicians*. Geneva, Switzerland: Author.

World Health Organization. (1992b). The global AIDS strategy. *WHO AIDS series, 11*. Geneva, Switzerland: Author.

World Health Organization. (1995, December 15). *Weekly Epidemiological Record, 70*, 353–360.

World Health Organization. (1996, July 5). *Weekly Epidemiological Record, 71*, 205–212.

IV

THE INTERPERSONAL: RELATIONS AMONG INDIVIDUALS

Lesbians on the Frontline: Battling AIDS, Gays, and the Myth of Community

Diane M. Harney
Pacific Lutheran University

Humans seek the positive in any disaster. Some, seeking an upside to the AIDS epidemic, claim the epidemic has engendered a positive change in gay and lesbian culture. High on the list of "epidemic positives" identified in popular media is the creation of a unified gay/lesbian[1] community working side by side, fighting AIDS. According to Andrew Kopkind (1993), "Devastated by a plague that threatens the very existence of their community . . . AIDS has given a new sense of solidarity to lesbians and gay men who for years have often pursued separate agendas" (pp. 590, 600). In August 1992, a *Time* magazine cover story claimed that "the wildfire of the AIDS epidemic has made gays a community even as it has consumed their lives" (Henry, 1992, p. 35). Such claims attempt to make sense of the epidemic. But, these claims are incomplete, idealistic, and fail to understand the complexity of lesbian responses to AIDS and their relations with gays.

Popular theory holds that "AIDS has healed the great divide between lesbians and gay men, caused lesbian-feminists to finally value their friendships with men and promoted the creation of a truly co-sexual community" (Rofes, 1996, p. 258). This myth holds that, as the result of AIDS activism, relations between lesbians and gays are now marked by respect and equality. Initially, the AIDS crisis did redirect, redefine, and refocus the rhetorical and political trajectory of the gay movement and the lesbian movements toward unification of the two communities. However, over time, this unification has evolved into a range of organizations and activities with supporters carefully choosing where to expend their energies based on self-interests. Some would view this division as a failure of community and potentially devastating for AIDS activism.

A more accurate picture of AIDS activism can be drawn from texts commonly circulated within gay and lesbian communities,[2] which highlight the continued separation between the two groups. Examination of these texts, targeting gay and lesbian audiences, explains the

---

[1] In this chapter, gay refers to homosexual men; gay/lesbian refers to a unified or singular group; gay and lesbian refers to separate groups.

[2] Community texts include publications such as *The Advocate, off-our-backs, Gay Community News*, and the writings by authors such as Susan Schulman, Cindy Patton, Eric Marcus, Darrell Yates Rist, and others.

difficulty in finding common ground, and illustrates the myth of community. This chapter concludes that AIDS activism, although having a positive impact on participants, has failed to build a unified community at this time. Instead, this separation is predictable and AIDS activism provided a reasonable step necessary to a possible unification movement.

This study examines, from a lesbian perspective, the complex nature of gay and lesbian relationships as they converged around AIDS activism. To that end, this chapter discusses the post–World War II relationship between gays and lesbians, the nature of collective action, and lesbian involvement in AIDS activism and the tensions that emerged. Finally, these issues are discussed from the perspective of the complexities of coalitions and communities.

THE EMERGENT MOVEMENT

Migration to large metropolitan areas and the conservative sociopolitical environment of the post–World War II era marked the beginning of the modern gay and lesbian movements. Key to the establishment of the gay and/or lesbian movements was awareness of their identity as a minority group. Identity politics—the identification of oneself as a member of a specific group with shared experiences and concerns—defined the movement. The reason identity politics became the dominant model was that fighting against a cultural construction of one's identity as inferior requires people come to see themselves as different than those cultural images. It requires group members see themselves and the group of which they are a part as valuable, based on a revised definition of what is desirable or acceptable.

The first ongoing organization of the "Homophile Rights" movement, the Mattachine Society, a discussion group, was founded in December 1950, in Los Angeles. Similar groups, consisting primarily of men, sprang up in metropolitan areas such as Chicago, New York, and San Francisco. In 1955, the Daughters of Bilitis (DOB) was formed in San Francisco to provide social, educational, and consciousness-raising opportunities for lesbians. The primary focus of both groups was to help individual members develop a positive self-image and to provide a safe social environment. Although seen as radical at the time, these groups adopted a conservative, accommodationist philosophy in which homosexuals were to be treated like anyone else.

A changing environment in the 1960s led activists to bolder and more public action. The Council on Religion and the Homosexual was founded in 1963. In the spring of 1967, lesbian and gay students at Columbia University organized the Student Homophile League, which spread to Cornell, New York University, and Stanford (Faderman, 1991). Some organizations gained recognition and legitimacy in the larger arena. When DOB held its 1966 convention, the *San Francisco Chronicle* ran a four column article headlined "San Francisco Greets Daughters." The New York Civil Service Commission, which had rejected applicants suspected of being homosexual, began approving homosexual hires. After years of harassment, the San Francisco police made efforts to cooperate with homosexual groups by providing security at events.[3]

The "Stonewall Rebellion," which began June 27, 1969, in response to a police raid on a Greenwich Village gay bar, the Stonewall Inn, marked the beginning of "gay liberation," a period of consolidation of gay and lesbian communities in urban areas, the development of subcultures, and the formation of well-defined settings and institutions. Holding that

---

[3]See L. Ebreo (1965, December); "A Homosexual Ghetto?," *The Ladder, 10*(3), 8; "U.S. Homophile Movement Gains National Strength" (1996, April), *The Ladder, 10*(7), 4–5; B. Grier (1968, October/November); "A Suggested Policy: Confrontation and Implementation [Editorial]" (1969, February), *Homophile Action League Newsletter (1),* 4.

invisibility perpetuated oppression by allowing myths to remain unchallenged, identity shifted from mentally ill or deviant—an identity defined by those outside the communities—to societally oppressed, an identity claimed within the communities. More gays and lesbians began to affirm their identity based on their identification with this large community that shared the goal of societal legitimization. Coming out, publicly announcing one's homosexuality to the world, increased visibility and provided a foundation for building a mass movement.

In the post-Stonewall era, identity-based gay and lesbian movements have been successful in creating safe places where life can be lived openly. Bars, coffeehouses, bookstores, and community centers have thrived. For gay men, asserting their gay identity was less important than ending bar raids and having access to gay sex and social life. Rather than challenging the social and political systems, gay politics sought to end harassment and promote privacy rights within the existing systems. For lesbians, identity focused on the elimination of patriarchal oppression and the building of women-identified communities. Lesbian communities have been more focused on issues of identity and relationship. A crucial feature of the lesbian movement was the integration of lesbian-feminism, which intensified differences with gays and made it difficult to articulate shared goals.

The tradition of gay and lesbian identities, prior to the onset of AIDS, effectively created barriers to building effective coalitions or alliances. In the then-radical *No Turning Back: Lesbian and Gay Liberation for the '80s* (Goodman, Lakey, Lashof, & Thorne, 1983), the authors strongly advocated the development of separate gay and lesbian communities. In their opinion, separation allows individuals to recognize how they have been hurt without blaming it on individual members of the oppressor class. The development of separate spaces encourages the development of culture, style, and spirituality, which may be repressed by the dominant culture.

Furthering the tradition of separation has been the lack of a central organization to direct a gay and lesbian movement. Rather, movement activists and intellectuals worked through a variety of organizations, such as the National Gay Task Force (NGTF), the Lambda Legal Defense and Education Fund, and the Human Rights Campaign Fund (HRCF). These organizations have worked within existing legal and political structures to ensure protection against housing and employment discrimination, and privacy rights. Communication with gay and lesbian audiences was facilitated through a variety of national and local publications. Beyond these organizations, which are seen as elitist by some gays and lesbians (Minkowitz, 1991), individual communities, defined by geography, affection, or interests, sprang up across the country, but, until the HIV/AIDS epidemic, these communities failed to emerge as a unified activist force.

THE NATURE OF COLLECTIVE ACTION

Group theory is based on the assumption that groups will act when necessary to further common or group goals. Group actions in support of group interests are supposed to follow logically from the widely accepted premise of rational, self-interested behavior. In other words, if members of a group have a common interest, it should logically follow that that the members would act together to achieve that interest. Group existence to further the interests of group members is hardly novel. Aristotle held that we journey together with a view to a particular advantage, and similarly political association seems to have come together originally, and to continue in existence, for the same the advantages it brings (Cooper, 1932). Kenneth Burke, in *A Rhetoric of Motives* (1950/1969), described identification between individuals as emotional or ideological commonalities. He noted that these commonalities operate in a dialectic, that there is an ever-present tension to the identifications we create and break.

At issue here are the connections and interests served by AIDS activism for lesbians. Specifically, assuming a degree of rational behavior, what benefits might be derived from participation in AIDS activism by lesbians? For lesbians working with gays as AIDS activists, there were two distinct interests: fighting stigma and gaining legitimacy for lesbian issues.

Working Together: Painted With the Same Brush

Early in the crisis the nature of the disease was unclear. Both conservative and mainstream political and cultural commentators were quick to highlight the fact that most of the people who first were diagnosed with the disease in the United States shared the common trait of homosexuality. The earliest name for AIDS was GRID—gay-related immune deficiency. Much of the dominant culture did not distinguish between lesbians and gays and used labeling and stigmatizing to separate what was acceptable behavior from unacceptable behavior. AIDS provided a new weapon for those who categorize homosexuality as deviant or immoral.

According to Maxine Wolfe, a professor at the City University Graduate Center, "The majority of people don't make distinctions between lesbians or gays. In their minds, we're queer" (in Schulman, 1994, p. 120). Sandy Feinbloom, of the Gay Men's Health Crisis, echoed this perspective, "There are certain people who, when they hear *homosexual* don't distinguish between gay men and lesbians" (in Schulman, 1994, p. 121). According to Brouwer (1995), "In the early stages of the AIDS epidemic, while gay men comprised the overwhelming number of AIDS diagnoses, lesbians saw in the public and government's responses to AIDS, and to those who had AIDS, a means of identifying with the syndrome. Specifically, the homophobia that AIDS dredged up against gay men implicated lesbians as 'sexual deviants' " (p. 6). Because of the syndrome's adverse impact on gays, it can be argued that gays had no choice but to engage in a range of community-building activities, but lesbians were equally victimized by AIDS phobia. As a result, fighting AIDS requires addressing the disease *and* the stigmatization.

Simply stated, lesbians found themselves painted with the same brush as gay men—at-risk, transmitters of a fatal disease—a community of people doomed by their own behavior. It was through their perceived identification with the gay rights movement that lesbians were drawn into the vortex that was AIDS.

Healing: I Like You, You Like Me

The second interest served by AIDS activism was less clearly apparent. Many lesbians saw activism as a means of gaining support and legitimacy from the gay community. The two communities had long functioned as separate entities. Divisions among lesbians and gays included not only education, income, and social status, but also attitudinal and behavioral differences that created obstacles to the building of a gay/lesbian community. Lesbians knew how few men had offered support for women's shelters or rape crisis centers. They had seen gay men develop their own, segregated communities, which not only excluded but often denigrated lesbians.

Many felt that identity politics had damaged both communities and had prevented a united battle against homophobia. According to author Terry Wolverton (1992), "I no longer believe in those separate, isolated worlds, in which lesbians' interests are inimical to those of gay men. Misunderstanding persists, as does inequality. Many gay men remain indifferent to lesbian oppression, and many lesbians still prefer to keep separated from the gay community. Still, a movement is afoot; a gradual process of reunification has begun" (p. 230).

THE NATURE OF LESBIAN ACTIVISM

AIDS activism provided an opportunity to serve both interests: the need to fight homophobia and the desire to gain the respect and support of gays for broader "community" issues. Response to the AIDS crisis had an enormous impact on lesbians: "Many of us involved in the women's movement turned our attention to the lesbian/gay movement. There were many reasons for this shift. AIDS is a clear, delineated crisis, and there is an urgent need to help people in our community" (Winnow, 1992, p. 70).

What compelled lesbians to become AIDS activists? There is no single explanation. Numerous lesbian authors and activists have provided insight into possible lesbian motivations—altruism, the feminist experience, identification, and survival. AIDS and lesbian activist, Cindy Patton, described her personal impulse to become involved in AIDS activism: "At a time when so many people's lives are being ruined not just by getting AIDS but by the cultural backlash of the epidemic, to refuse to participate in a cultural event which is so politically charged, to decide it doesn't apply to you, is very strange and wrong" (in O'Sullivan, 1990, p. 124). Reflecting the lesbian-feminism perspective, Eve Kosofsky Sedgwick (1991) explained the drive toward activism:

> The contributions of lesbians to current gay and AIDS activism are weighty, not despite, but because of the intervening lessons of feminism. Feminist perspectives on medicine and health-care issues, on civil disobedience, and on the politics of class and race as well as of sexuality, have been centrally enabling for the recent waves of AIDS activism. What this activism returns to the lesbians involved in it may include a more richly pluralized range of imaginings of lines of gender and sexual identification. (pp. 38–39)

Amber Hollibaugh (1997) suggested, "For some of us it was the shared gay identity we felt with gay men which brought us forward early in the epidemic; for some of us it was the dramatic increase in the already devastating daily occurrences of homophobia and gay bashing which occurred because of the government's misrepresentations of AIDS as a gay disease" (p. 670).

Suddenly gays and lesbians shared concerns. Gays had come to the issues that lesbians had long been addressing. Because of society's homophobic response to AIDS and government indifference, lesbians seemed compelled to respond to the AIDS epidemic:

> A male-dominated movement that had rarely ventured beyond 'safety' gay issues, like police harassment of gay men in parks and rest stops and bars, was suddenly addressing topics that lesbians and feminists had worked on for more than a decade—the bias of mainstream health care deliverers, the expansion of a self-help model of care, Medicaid reform, welfare benefits reform, sex education, the use of reproduction technologies to prevent transmission of disease, racial prejudice and federal government inaction. When AIDS broadened the gay-male movement, lesbians became invaluable in ways we had not been before. (Vaid, 1995, p. 294)

The urgency of the epidemic—its ability to ravage so many, so quickly; its appropriation as a justification for homophobic policies—demanded a unified response by lesbians and gays.

Early in the epidemic, lesbians were able to use their political histories as organizers and health, feminist, and civil rights activists to inform the responses to AIDS.

Shifting the Focus

As it became clear there would be no quick cure, lesbians involved in AIDS activism found themselves asking how the health community was dealing with women with AIDS. It did not take long for lesbian activists to reach the conclusion that, "HIV exposes all the inequalities of women's positions in society: poorer; less access to health care for themselves; little support in their roles as carers" (Scharf & Toole, 1992, p. 64). As evidence of the discrimination, in a 1988 *Village Voice* piece, Susan Schulman (1994) cited statistics showing women with AIDS live an average of 298 days after diagnosis; men live 400 days. Many lesbians saw a conflict between AIDS activism and other lesbian issues. In addition, some began to ask, "If a cure for AIDS happened tomorrow, wouldn't all those gay men go home and not care about access issues [and,] would gay men have done the same thing for lesbians if the situation had been reversed?" (Wolfe, 1997, p. 641).

Susan Chu, epidemiologist with the Centers for Disease Control, noted that women constituted the fastest growing group of people with AIDS: "By 1991 HIV can be expected to become one of the five leading causes of death in women of reproductive age" (in Crane, 1990, p. 42). Yet women seemed invisible in both AIDS research and treatment. Ten years into the epidemic, Scharf and Toole (1992) articulated the concerns of HIV positive women. They asked, "What are the causes of death in women who are infected by HIV; do these fit into the current definition of AIDS; what is the picture, the 'natural history,' of HIV in women; what are women-specific HIV-related illnesses and conditions? Do women have access to drug trials; and, are drugs safe for women, if tested only on men?" (p. 66).

Lesbians, many of whom were grounded in the feminist tradition, found themselves conflicted by the AIDS activist movement. At low risk for infection and having given of their energies, there was the strong sense that the medical establishment was ignoring the impact of AIDS on women and that their deeds were undervalued by gays. Lesbian activists turned their attention to the plight of women with AIDS.

The Battle for Inclusion

AIDS has been defined by markers. By 1990, there was a wealth of evidence that suggested that HIV progressed differently in female bodies than in male. HIV manifests itself in gynecologic disorders such as chronic vaginitis, which is the same as thrush and which the CDC recognized as HIV related when found in the mouth, but not when it is in the vagina. Because of definitional exclusion, women found it difficult to gain access to services, drug therapies, and medical care.

A second concern raised by lesbian activists was that the male symptom–dominated definition had impact that extended beyond medical benefits. An AIDS diagnosis allowed for presumptive disability, with immediate Social Security benefits. The result was:

> An HIV-positive gay man who felt healthy, who had no pain, no loss of energy or weight, but suffered from a yeast infection in his throat had AIDS, according to the CDC—and thus was eligible for presumptive disability, according to Social Security. An HIV-positive woman who had lost weight, was in chronic pain from pelvic inflammatory disease, could barely get around and suffered from the same yeast infection, in her vagina instead of her throat, did

not have AIDS, according to the CDC—and thus was ineligible for presumptive disability, according to Social Security. (Burkett, 1995, p. 194)

Over time, men with AIDS became less stigmatized but women with AIDS, who manifested different symptoms, continued to be marginalized.

Not only did women find themselves ineligible for services provided men diagnosed with AIDS, but also women were widely excluded from drug trials. The result of this exclusion were delays in making life-extending drugs such as DDC, AZT, and protease inhibitors available to women. Researchers justified women's exclusion from drug trials on the grounds that women might conceive during the trial. As a result of this paternalism, in 1990 women represented only 6% of the participants in the AIDS Clinical Trial Group at the National Institute of Allergy and Infectious Diseases (NIAID). According to Marion Banzhaf, coordinator of the Women and AIDS Network in New Jersey: "It's no different than how women have been treated forever by the medical profession. They look at us only as receptacles for breeding. NIAID's division on AIDS has a maternal and pediatric committee, but it has no women's committee in spite of emerging statistics on women as the second wave of the epidemic" (Crane, 1990, p. 43).

DuPont pharmaceutical spokesman Roger Morris claimed that the reason women were excluded from DuPont-funded trials was their concern about reproductive damage, which can result in lawsuits (Schulman, 1994). Dr. Michael Grieco of Saint Luke's Ampligen Program cited other reasons for women's exclusion. "The best patients," he said, "have been male homosexuals. Women have less compliance. There's less education, motivation, and understanding. It is different taking someone who is productive in the arts than someone living as a minority person. They're not going to have the same grasp" (Schulman, 1994, p. 177).

According to noted AIDS researcher, Dr. Mathilde Krim, "Women have been excluded [from clinical trials for AIDS] because of the assumption by doctors that they are IV drug users and therefore undesirable patients" (Schulman, 1994, p. 176). Within the stigmatization of an AIDS diagnosis, women were further stigmatized by assumptions by both the government and the medical community.

Reasonable Reaction or AIDS Envy

Although many lesbians continued to work with service and activist groups, many began to question their involvement. As the AIDS crisis continued, two issues arose for lesbians: What impact did AIDS activism have on other women's health issues; and, Had lesbians received a quid pro quo from gays for their efforts?

"Angry that almost a decade of lesbian leadership and care giving in the AIDS arena has seen little substantive response from gay men on women's issues, some lesbians [have] confronted gay men on unkept promises and continued self-centered agendas" (Rofes, 1997, p. 653). The result was a growing division among activists that was detrimental to the development of a gay/lesbian community. As AIDS activist Jackie Winnow (1992) put it, "Groups facing health crises are often pitted against each other, and it is important for us to understand the reasons for those divisions. Many people with cancer are upset about the attention paid to AIDS. This inequity is not the fault of the people with AIDS, but rather of the systems that create the divisions. People start fighting over the same piece of the pie. That is not an accident" (p. 73). All other issues of importance to the lesbian community became what Winnow described as second stage and were seen as less deserving of attention.

Women's health activist groups, such as Women's Health Action Mobilization (WHAM!) found it difficult to project the single-minded urgency characteristic of AIDS. According to WHAM! founder Dolly Meieran, "The biggest obstacle to portraying women's health care as facing a crisis is the scope of the issue. A virus is very concrete, all of the systemic sorts of things [affecting women's health] are much harder to see" (in Brownworth, 1990, p. 45).

When it became clear that most lesbians did not have to worry about AIDS, some lesbian journalists began writing about breast cancer as their own epidemic and demanded funding for "lesbian-specific breast cancer" as well as chronic fatigue immune deficiency syndrome (CFIDS) and other women-centered health concerns. According to a lesbian cancer survivor, "Our community doesn't seem to see any disease but AIDS, anyone who's ill but gay men." She asked, "Doesn't anyone see that lesbians are sick and dying everywhere? Do we have to drop dead on the AIDS quilt for it to make a difference?" (in Brownworth, 1990, p. 44).

Some thought the lesbian response was pathetic or laughable. Others felt by "pushing a lesbian agenda where it had no place, they have managed to undercut their own effectiveness in promoting a wider women's agenda that is urgent" (Burkett, 1995, p. 213). Gay author Stephen Miller (1993) wrote, "There are lesbian-feminists who argue AIDS has received too much attention compared to breast cancer. They seem to be experiencing a bad case of 'death envy,' unable to accept that lesbians might not be the most victimized of victims" (p. 37). Writing in 1989, Darrell Yates Rist proclaimed that "even lesbians . . . have taken to keening that the whole community is dying—so compulsive is the human need to partake in the drama of catastrophe" (p. 196). Accusing lesbians of hysteria and envy dismissed lesbians' work in AIDS activism, denied the legitimacy of their concerns, and served to further destabilize the possibility of identification among gays and lesbians.

Lesbians also felt betrayed by the service organizations that they had helped to build. On February 25, 1991, 20 women and 2 men gathered outside the office of the Gay Men's Health Crisis to opine that the "world's oldest and largest AIDS service organization had betrayed a community that was instrumental in building it" (Gessen, 1991, p. 55). Chanting "GMHC, you forgot about me! Lesbians die from AIDS" (Gessen, 1991, p. 55), the protesters, members of Dyke Action Machine! (DAM), a Queer Nation spin-off, contended that GMHC had failed to implement services designed specifically for the lesbian community. In addition, charges were leveled that GMHC discriminated against lesbians in its hiring practices.

Lesbian anger is an understandable reaction to the drama that has been AIDS. The crisis has given gays visibility and garnered sympathy from a variety of sources. Pride rallies have become AIDS rallies. Gay/lesbian publications, although adopting more inclusive language, run pages of information on health and disease problems with little relevance to lesbians. Lesbian rights activist Jane Shore articulated the frustration of many lesbians: "It would be nice if for once gay men would acknowledge lesbians' [contribution to the health care movement]. Have you ever seen anyone anywhere—especially in the gay male press—give credit to lesbians for the AIDS health-care movement? I know that Larry Kramer et al. think they started it, but the reality is that feminists—primarily lesbians—started the self-help health-care movement 20 years ago. . . . The boys look at our model, decide it works, and move on" (in Brownworth, 1990, p. 44).

DISCUSSION

The journey of lesbian AIDS activists provides a unique opportunity to understand the power of rhetorical division and reciprocity within groups and the nature of the community-building process. To understand this journey, one must examine the necessary conditions for rhetorical success and community building.

The success of group action, which can lead to political success and the development of community, depends on rhetorically amplifying certain concerns and ideological imperatives while diminishing other concerns and markers of difference. The ability of group members to negotiate between competing concerns and imperatives is dependent on the group creating and fostering a stable, unifying group identity. For example, differences in race or class might be diminished among female group members wishing to present coherent, public discourse about gender inequities. According to ACT UP (1990), "Changing governmental and social policies requires joint work among AIDS activists. Building coalitions and working together isn't easy. Often, everyone has to suspend some issues to be able to work together and build a basis of respect" (p. 82). The success of amplification and diminution mandates the suspension of personal issues. Suspension as a strategy is essential for generating identification among AIDS activists.

Although many activists suspended their personal issues or other markers of difference, divisions arose from lesbian perceptions of inequitable suspensions between gays and lesbians in AIDS activism. Whereas AIDS galvanized many gay and lesbian activists, others focused on the lack of concern for issues such as fair employment and housing legislation, the rise in antigay legislation, services for gay and lesbian youth, and other heath issues (Rist, 1989) that historically have been part of lesbian activism.

Failed Reciprocity

Accusing lesbians of "AIDS envy" and denigrating lesbian-identified issues, gay writers, such as Miller and Rist, destabilized identification among men and women not only in AIDS activism but also in gay/lesbian community building. Besides being dismissive of lesbians' hard work in AIDS activism, this rhetoric of division denies the authenticity and integrity of lesbians' suspension of gender and personal interest. Ultimately, it furthers skepticism about the ability to create plausible identifications.

The rhetoric of division by gay men is not surprising. Both gays and lesbians acknowledge the tendency of gay men to be highly self-involved in their political vision. Gay scholar Thomas Yingling (1991) described the inequities in suspension and identification:

> In its unyielding equation of value with white male-embodied masculinity, American culture imprints a double-bind on those on its margins: gay people of color and lesbians, for instance, may well find themselves alienated from white gay male culture but they may also recognize that their own political future and visibility are bound in complex and equivocal ways to the struggle of gay white men. . . . The dialectic of that recognition does not often work the other way: gay white men are less likely to see their own political fortunes at stake in what happens for people of color or women. (p. 294)

Preexisting tensions and divisions between the two communities manifested themselves in perceived inequities in identification between gays and lesbians.

The refusal of gay men to acknowledge lesbian/feminist issues such as equal work-equal pay, nationalized day care, or breast cancer research, is a refusal to engage in identification across gender that is reciprocal to the cross-gender identification that lesbian AIDS activists make. Lou Ann Matossian (1993) wrote, in the lesbian journal *off our backs*, "To tell the truth, I have always been more than a little suspicious of the gay[lesbian]-rights movement. . . . Many lesbians, myself included, have offered and received genuine support from individual men. . . . Yet such alliances come at a price. . . . To be gay-identified (or 'queer-identified,' to use the trendy term), is to identify our political interests with those of men, in a movement that still refuses to acknowledge feminist issues as its own" (p. 6). Patton (1990) captured the conflict when she asked, "What is AIDS doing for (lesbian and gays') ability to construct categories? What's the effect of the AIDS crisis on our ability to construct our identity?" (p. 130). Failure to acknowledge and discuss status inequalities limits the ability to challenge them, and, in order to guarantee a true public sphere with participatory parity, it is essential that inequities be addressed. This failure destabilizes the cohesiveness of any lesbian/gay rights community.

Working Toward Community

The term *community* has been widely misused to describe gays and lesbians. Most definitions of community stem from scholarly examinations that stress either shared geography or value systems and experiences to which individuals have been socialized. Rosenthal (1996) suggested that the essential component for the political development of communities "is the elaboration of interpersonal networks that may or may not be locality based" (p. 46). Consequently, the development of gay and lesbian communities would depend more on the connection between individuals to social networks and groups of varying degrees of formality than on locality.

Lehr (1993) claimed the failure to create a gay/lesbian community is the result of identity politics which "encompasses a celebration of [each] group's uniqueness as well as an analysis of its particular oppression" (p. 248) rather than creating a broader, unified community. Instead of rushing to label gays and lesbians as a single community, it is more appropriate to understand their relationship as a *coalition*—a necessary precursor to the formation of community. A coalition refers to groups or individuals that have come together around a particular issue or to achieve a particular goal. The primary features of a coalition are the existence of enduring differences in their values, preferences, beliefs, and perceptions of reality; an imbalance in the distribution of power; and conflict (Spicer, 1997). Coalitions are a recurring group phenomenon in which power is unevenly distributed. Goals and decisions emerge from bargaining, negotiation, and jockeying for position among coalition members. The decision to align with and against others is far from trivial—it determines the survival of existing power structures and introduces patterns of positive and negative sentiment that affect morale and the possibility of cooperation and accommodation (Buchli & Pearce, 1975).

Alliances, which further developing relationships, grow out of coalitions: "Out of our vision of alliance we see allies as people who struggle together on a number of progressive fronts, not just a single issue" (Albrecht & Brewer, 1990, p. 4). To form alliances, there must be acknowledgment of the other groups' histories and concerns and an understanding of the connection between forms of oppression. Addressing the potential of a gay and lesbian alliance, Schulman (1994) stated, "If gay men prioritized women's lives with the same commitment that women have made to them, then women's issues would be organic and homogenous to our organizing and not the special responsibility of the women in the movement" (p. 218). Such action, by gays, represents an essential step to move existing coalitions toward the building of alliances, and, ultimately, to the building of a unified community.

CONCLUSION

If tensions increase and the anxiety of division overwhelms, then perhaps the separation and isolation of lesbians and gay men is inevitable. Such a solution would be a political tragedy. To claim the existence of a gay/lesbian community based solely on affectional orientation oversimplifies the nature of community and fails to acknowledge the broad diversity of gays and lesbians. It is clear that many lesbians and gays are no longer willing to sustain the fiction of universal identification imposed by outside groups.

Unified, to some degree, gays and lesbians have been able to work together on specific issues. Advocacy organizations such as the National Gay and Lesbian Task Force, the Lambda Legal Defense and Education Fund, and the Human Rights Campaign Fund have had success creating a legitimate political identity for gays and lesbians. Out of AIDS activism, numerous groups have evolved to address other issues of importance to both gays and lesbians such as homophobia or violence. Although groups such as ACT UP and Queer Nation offend some by the nature of their in-your-face activism, they have provided a place in which gays and lesbians have redirected the energy of AIDS activism into gay/lesbian activism. According to Wolfe (1997), "One of the most important roles that ACT UP plays is that it is a place where many younger gay men and lesbians have come to understand that what we want is the right to exist—not the right to privacy; the right to a life, not a life-style; and a life that is as important as anyone else's but not any more important than anyone else's" (p. 641). In the new activist organizations, "There is not ideology, not statement of purpose. It is a place to bring ideas for action and find other people to work with you" (Podolsky, 1990, p. 52).

The question now is how to avoid the fragmentation of a potential gay/lesbian movement into smaller and smaller interest groups. How can gays and lesbians negotiate the dialectic between division and identification in order to retain and foster the political and rhetorical energy of AIDS activism into a gay/lesbian movement? Brouwer (1995) offered a series of prescriptions:

First, gays and lesbians must move beyond identity politics. Former executive director of the National Gay and Lesbian Task Force Urvashi Vaid (1995) warned lesbians and gays that "our investment in identity-based organizing . . . actually holds us back: we are unable to coalesce across identities" (p. 285). Although identity politics has helped lesbians and gays know and find each other, it is not sufficiently encompassing to serve as a unifying theory or identity as a means for organizing lesbians and gays together politically.

Second, gays and lesbians must recognize and respect the fluidity of individual identifications. Kenneth Burke (1950/1969) offered a notion of multiple voices within the individual that is especially helpful to understanding activism and the personal conflict that may occur:

> These voices may be treated . . . as a concerto of principles mutually modifying one another, they may likewise be seen, from the standpoint of rhetoric, as a parliamentary wrangle which the individual has put together somewhat as he [or she] puts together his [or her] fears and hopes, friendships and enmities, health and disease, or those tiny rebirths whereby, in being born to some new condition, he [she] may be dying to a past condition, his [her] development being dialectical, a series of terms in perpetual transformation. (p. 38)

Gay men have been less likely to recognize the consubstantiality of lesbian and gay interests. However, the growth of Queer Nation, ACT UP, and other activist groups has broken new ground in gay and lesbian relations.

The 1970s gave birth to three distinct movements—the gay community, the lesbian community, and the gay and lesbian movement. The latter was pieced together for political expediency. In the wake of AIDS a new vision is emerging, the possibility of creating a shared gay/lesbian community. Through hard work and political commitments in the AIDS struggle, new friendships have grown and flourished. AIDS activism has helped many in the gay community to move from an isolated position to understanding issues long the focus of lesbians (Osborn, 1991). This relationship is fragile and must be nurtured. It must not be rushed by the application of inappropriate labels and the use of divisive rhetoric. A new respect for each other is the first of many steps necessary in order to build a gay/lesbian community.

REFERENCES

ACT UP/New York. (1990). *Women and AIDS*. New York: AIDS Book Group.

Albrecht, L., & Brewer, R. M. (1990). *Bridges of power*. Philadelphia: New Society Publishers.

Brouwer, D. (1995, November). *Lesbians and gays fighting AIDS (and each other): The negotiation of identification and division in AIDS activism*. Paper presented at the annual meeting of the Speech Communication Association, San Antonio, Texas.

Brownworth, V. (1990, October 23). Lesbians press for more attention their health concerns. *The Advocate*, pp. 44–45.

Buchli, R. D., & Pearce, W. B. (1975). Coalition and communication. *Human Communication Research, 1*, 213–221.

Burke, K. (1969). *A rhetoric of motives*. Berkeley: University of California Press. (Original work published 1950)

Burkett, E. (1995). *The gravest show on earth: America in the age of AIDS*. New York: Picador USA.

Cooper, L. (1932). *The rhetoric of Aristotle*. New York: Appleton–Century–Crofts.

Crane, T. (1990, November 6). The battle against AIDS intensifies for women. *The Advocate*, pp. 42–44.

Faderman, L. (1991). *Odd girls and twilight lovers: A history of lesbian life in twentieth-century America*. New York: Penguin.

Gessen, M. (1991, April 9). New York lesbians demand AIDS care from GMHC. *The Advocate*, p. 55.

Goodman, G., Lakey, G., Lashof, J., & Thorne, E. (1983). *No turning back: Lesbian and gay liberation for the '80s*. Philadelphia: New Society Publishers.

Henry, W. A. (1992, August 3). An identity forged in flames. *Time*, pp. 35–37.

Hollibaugh, A. (1997). Lesbian leadership and lesbian denial in the AIDS epidemic: Bravery and fear in the construction of a lesbian geography of risk. In M. Blasius & S. Phelan (Eds.), *We are everywhere: a historical sourcebook of gay and lesbian politics* (pp. 669–677). New York: Routledge.

Kopkind, A. (1993, May 3). The gay movement. *The Nation*, pp. 577, 590, 592, 594–596, 598, 600–602.

Lehr, V. (1993). The difficulty of leaving "Home": Gay and lesbian organizing to confront AIDS. In R. Fisher & J. Kling (Eds.), *Mobilizing the community: Local politics in the era of the global city* (pp. 246–269). Newbury Park, CA: Sage.

Matossian, L. A. (1993, July). A lesbian-feminist goes to the march on Washington. *off-our-backs, 23*, 6.

Miller, S. (1993, November). Diversity or duplicity? *Christopher Street, 207*, 36–37.

Minkowitz, D. (1991, November 5). The conference made me feel like a working-class spy. *The Advocate*, p. 37.

O'Sullivan, S. (1990). Mapping: Lesbians, AIDS, and sexuality [Interview with Cindy Patton]. *Feminist review, 34*, 120–135.

Osborn, T. (1991, January 29). Is a unified queer nation possible? *The Advocate*, p. 90.

Patton, C. (1990). *Inventing AIDS*. New York: Routledge.

Podolsky, R. (1990, October 9). Birth of a Queer Nation: New activists say there's more to do than just act up. *The Advocate*, pp. 52–53.

Rist, D. Y. (1989, February 13). AIDS as apocalypse: The deadly cost of an obsession. *The Nation*, pp. 181, 196, 290–297.

Rofes, E. E. (1996). *Reviving the tribe: Regenerating gay men's sexuality and culture in the ongoing epidemic*. Binghamton, NY: Harrington Park Press.

Rofes, E. E. (1997). Gay lib vs. AIDS: Averting civil war in the 1990s [From *Out/Look*, 1990]. In M. Blasius & S. Phelan (Eds.), *We are everywhere: A historical sourcebook of gay and lesbian politics* (pp. 652–659). New York: Routledge.

Rosenthal, D. B. (1996). Gay and lesbian political mobilization and regime responsiveness in four New York cities. *Urban Affairs Review, 32*(1), 45–70.

Scharf, E., & Toole, S. (1992). HIV and the invisibility of women: Is there a need to redefine AIDS? *Feminist Review, 41*, 64–67.

Schulman, S. (1994). *My American history: Lesbian and gay life during the Reagan/Bush years* [Collection of previously published essays]. New York: Routledge.

Sedgwick, E. K. (1991). *Epistemology of the closet*. Berkeley: University of California Press.

Spicer, C. (1997). *Organizational public relations: A political perspective*. Mahwah, NJ: Lawrence Erlbaum Associates.

Vaid, U. (1995). *Virtual equality: The mainstreaming of gay and lesbian liberation*. New York: Anchor.

Winnow, J. (1992). Lesbians evolving health care: Cancer and AIDS. *Feminist Review, 41*, 68–76.

Wolfe, M. (1997). AIDS and politics: Transformations of our movement [Speech given at the National Gay and Lesbian Task Force Town Meeting for the Gay Community, 1989]. In M. Blasius & S. Phelan (Eds.), *We are everywhere: A historical sourcebook of gay and lesbian politics* (pp. 638–641). New York: Routledge.

Wolverton, T. (1992). Reunification: changing relationships between gay men and lesbians coping with AIDS. In B. Berzon (Ed.), *Positively gay: New approaches to gay and lesbian life* (pp. 226–231). Berkeley, CA: Celestial Arts Publishing.

Yingling, T. (1991). AIDS in AMERICA: Postmodern governance, identity, and experience. In D. Fuss (Ed.), *Inside/out: Lesbian theories, gay theories* (pp. 291–310). New York: Routledge.

AIDS and Social Relations of Power: Urban African-American Women's Discourse on the Contexts of Risk and Prevention

Margaret R. Weeks
Maryland Grier
Kim Radda
Institute for Community Research, Hartford, Connecticut

Dawn McKinley
Urban League of Greater Hartford

Policymakers, researchers, and community activists have paid increasing attention in recent years to the accelerating illness and death associated with HIV and AIDS among women in the United States. Figures released by the Centers for Disease Control and Prevention (CDC; 1997) showed a significant drop in 1996 in overall deaths associated with AIDS among all racial and ethnic groups and in all regions of the country, but an *increase* among women and those infected through heterosexual transmission. Additionally, of all populations these two exhibit the most rapid increase in new HIV infections (CDC, 1996). Over a decade of prevention efforts have done little to curb this expansion of AIDS among the poorest women in the United States and the world (Farmer, Connors, & Simmons, 1996). Key to understanding this arena of the epidemic's progression and how to interrupt it is recognition of and attention to conditions specific to women that create their risk of exposure to HIV.

Women's experiences with HIV and AIDS, as with all other epidemics, are shaped by an array of complex social, economic, and political factors. These include relations of gender, race, nationality, class, and poverty, each of which are defined by social relations of power. Conditions in the social contexts of women's experience are reflected in their discourse on HIV-related risks and protection from exposure or infection. This chapter explores the role of power in the social relations of women of color, particularly African-American women struggling with poverty and addiction, by presenting their discussion of their own sources of and impediments to power within heterosexual relationships and in their lives in general.

THE INTERSECTION OF GENDER, RACE, AND CLASS

Integral to understanding women's risk of HIV infection is recognition of the complexity of social factors influencing their conditions of risk, their options for taking precautions, and the avenues available to them to reduce the likelihood of their becoming exposed to the virus.

In responding to this recognition, numerous researchers over the past decade have analyzed HIV risk from the perspective of gender relations, and have brought to the fore gender inequality as it affects women's risk and protection (e.g., Amaro, 1995; Carovano, 1991; Kane, 1990; Kline, Kline, & Oken, 1992; Sobo, 1995; Weeks, Grier, Romero-Daza, Puglisi-Vasquez, & Singer, 1998; Weeks, Singer, Grier, & Schensul, 1996; Worth, 1989). Others have focused on issues of race and ethnic culture as these shape and constrain intimate relationships according to prescribed mores and culturally defined sexual roles, and create a context of social oppression resulting from segregation, subordination, and discrimination on the basis of color or language (Amaro, 1988; Flaskerud & Nyamathi, 1990; Fullilove, Fullilove, Haynes, & Gross, 1990; Kline et al., 1992; Marín, 1992; Singer, et al., 1990; Weeks, Schensul, Williams, Singer, & Grier, 1995). Still others have focused on poverty and other class issues as these affect women's HIV risk by limiting their access to health care, reducing their options to reject the support of male partners who refuse HIV/AIDS preventive measures, and oftentimes, creating pressure to use prostitution as a source of income (Farmer et al., 1996; Shayne & Kaplan, 1991; Singer, 1994; Sobo, 1995; Waterston, 1993; Weeks et al., 1998).

These efforts to focus analyses on the factors contributing to and contextualizing women's HIV risk, particularly through heterosexual transmission, indicate the need to develop an integrated approach to understand the full spectrum of mitigating conditions creating and circumscribing HIV risk and women's power to affect transmission, and for furthering the development of effective AIDS prevention approaches for women. Farmer and colleagues (1996) critiqued the predominant behavioral models as inadequate for understanding the epidemic, arguing, "The majority of infected women reside in the world's poorest countries and communities because poverty and gender inequality act to increase women's HIV risks. This dynamic has not been the focus of scientific or public debate" (p. 89). Holland, Ramazanoglu, Scott, Sharpe, and Thomson (1990) additionally pointed out that, "Interpretation [of AIDS epidemiological statistics] is hampered by a general lack of knowledge of the social complexity of sexual behaviour, and by the fact that the quantitative study of human sexual relationships is as yet little developed" (p. 337). They argued that, "the very variable ways in which young women negotiate their sexual practices can be seen as responses to contradictory social pressures" (p. 338). Thus, it becomes necessary to develop more complex conceptual models that take into account these multifarious and contradictory forces and that guide intervention efforts focused on empowerment of women (cf. Mane, Gupta, & Weiss, 1994; Nastasi, Schensul, & Sivayoganathan, 1997).

Connell's (1987) model of the social structure of gender relations provides a framework and method for building such an integrated understanding. He outlined the social relations of gender from the perspective of social structure and historical dynamic, differentiating three key separate but interwoven structural domains of gender relations. These include: (a) the *structure of labor,* which is constituted in definitions of labor such as assignments of tasks as "men's" or "women's," the separation of paid and unpaid labor, segregation, gender-based discrimination, and so forth, (b) the *structure of power,* or authority, control, and coercion in such contexts as the "hierarchies of state and business, institutional and interpersonal violence; sexual regulation and surveillance, domestic authority and its contestation," and (c) the *structure of cathexis,* or the emotional links people create between each other and "the patterning of object-choice, desire and desirability, . . . the production of heterosexuality and homosexuality; . . . antagonisms of gender . . . , trust and distrust, jealousy . . . , and the emotional relationships involved in rearing children" (pp. 96–97). He also defined the "gender order" as the historically constructed pattern of power relations between men and women and definitions of femininity and masculinity, that is, the total elements of the gender structures of labor, power, and cathexis. However, within this structural framework of integrated domains of gender relations are internal contradictions, and thus the possibility for "history," that is, change resulting from conflict and resolution within these structural constraints. Change in social relations depends on specifically targeted action within the social order; the degree of change is moderated by the power of existing structures at any point in time to limit social action and to establish barriers to change. Within this theoretical framework, gender is not a separate categorical component of the social order, but rather gives specific historical content to the elements within and relationships between the three structural domains, as well as the sources of internal contradiction that make possible or limit changes in the social order.

Connell's (1987) analysis of gender offers a means to understanding the process of change in gender relations, and thus the potential for reorganizing these relations in empowering ways for women and others subordinated by these structures (e.g., gay men). This is best illustrated in his discussion of the structure of power within the institution of the family:

> The contestation of domestic patriarchy is so widespread in some settings that it makes sense to talk of a working-class feminism, rooted in these struggles as much as in paid employment. Marital power struggles are often won by wives. . . . [I]t is important to acknowledge that there are genuine reversals of power here. It is not a question of women being conceded an apparent power which can then be revoked, but of *the hard relational outcomes of domestic conflicts and negotiations over years or even decades* [emphasis added]. It is also important to acknowledge that these local victories do not overthrow patriarchy. (pp. 110–111)

Thus, the outcome of practice targeted toward changing structural relations of women's subordination within a social institution such as the family can be a reordering of those power relations. This mechanism is critical for change in any social relations, including those directly defining contexts limiting women's options to reduce their risk of exposure to HIV.

Also important in this theoretical framework is the interplay of the three structures (labor, power, and cathexis) within the gender order. This interplay is most evident within the institution of the family, but exists in all institutions, including the workplace, the state, the streets. For example, Connell (1987) pointed out that power in the family is not just "influence in decision-making" (p. 123), but must include recognition of other kinds of power, such as force (evident in domestic violence) and "fierce emotional pressures that can be brought to bear on family members without any open command or display of power" (p. 123). These include pressures to stay in a relationship (despite the presence of violence and abuse), the power of a mother over a child, and the marital sexual relationship in which the husband "hold[s] the initiative in defining sexual practice" (Connell, 1987, p. 123; cf. Rubin, 1976). Connell summarized, "The gender regime of a particular family represents a continuing synthesis of relations governed by the three structures" (p. 125). This synthesis is critically important in the interplay of family members within and against these structures in daily actions and decision making regarding intimacy, sexuality, communication, and sustaining family members economically and emotionally. Further, this synthesis is fundamental to understanding the context of women's risks and barriers to HIV prevention and other protections and acts of power.

Key in the synthesis of and change in the structures of gender relations is the historical construction of categories or groupings that form the basis of political action within and between institutions and within and between the three different structures (e.g., groupings such as "men" and "women," "homosexual" and "heterosexual"). Thus, women at risk of HIV infection, as individuals or organized groups, taking targeted action toward understanding and changing definitions within social structures that place them in a disadvantaged position of power can create the potential for changing those unequal relationships, redefining their historically specific content and modifying the context of HIV risk (Connell, 1987). An example in this context regarding relations of cathexis is women's purposeful action (as individuals or with the support of other women) to redefine femininity to include women's control of sexual practice with male partners.

Connell's (1987) model of the social structure of gender lends itself to further application, for example, by constructing a parallel model of the social structure of racial or ethnic relations, or of class. The social construction of race and ethnicity (including nationality) and the social hierarchy of one race/ethnicity over others are constituted in structures of labor, power/authority, and cathexis, and present in all institutions. The first two structural domains (labor and authority) have received significant analytical attention, focusing for example on the institutionalization of racism in the division of labor, the exclusion of certain racial and ethnic groups from political power, and the social propensity for the use of state power to control some racial and ethnic groups (e.g., evident in the disproportionate imprisonment of African-American men). These illustrate the process of race relations within these social institutions and the dynamic of practice defined by the social structure of race to change or maintain such inequalities. The structure of cathexis within the social organization of race/ethnicity, however, has received significantly less attention. Yet it is clearly evident in the strong emotions tied to the establishment of racially and nationally homogeneous marriages and sexual relationships and the strong taboos and stigmas attached to interracial intimacy. It is also demonstrated by institutions and political action built upon powerful feelings of hatred toward "other" nationalities or racial groups, evident, for example, in ethnic cleansing and other forms of genocide.

Likewise, the social structure of class relations, constituted most clearly in the structures of labor (with the organization and conceptualization of owners, financiers, workers, the unemployed, and the "underclass," as well as their associated differential resources), and the structure of power (especially to maintain or gain control of those resources) create and define wealth and poverty within the social order and a hierarchy of power within and among different classes. Further, the structural organization of emotions around class relations creates concepts not only of the specification of desirable partners, but also broader definitions of "deserving" and "undeserving" classes, as well as blame and hatred of the poor. In that gender, class, and race/ethnicity each define and constitute the structures of labor, power, and cathexis, they also are inextricably integrated and interactive with each other in the historical process of the social order and social change.

Though Connell (1987) developed this model to organize the structural relations of gender, he made the point that gender as used here is a "linking concept," a "process rather than a thing," and that as such, it holds no a priori ascendancy over other interests (e.g., nationality, class, race) in the targeting of political action. Rather, "The way of defining interest that is ascendant at a given time and place is an empirical question" (p. 138; cf. Farmer et al., 1996, p. xvi). Thus, for women of color in the United States, the question of race/nationality versus gender, class, or sexuality in ranking for salience or priority action becomes an issue for assessment in the process of identifying relevant practice targeted to changing the social relations of inequality around a particular issue, such as HIV/AIDS risk and prevention. This is critical to understanding, for example, African-American women's power in sexual negotiations, their interpretation of the key factors affecting decision making around sexual relations, and their analysis of the sources of their oppression. It is often the inequalities of race and class that take primacy in their discourse on the sources of their disempowerment, despite their concurrent recognition that, as women, they are also disempowered in gender relations, particularly within intimate relationships.

Researchers of women and AIDS have made significant strides toward developing integrated models of the social relations affected by gender, race, ethnicity, and poverty that define the environment in which women must protect themselves from HIV and AIDS.

Paralleling Connell's (1987) concept of the complexity of sexual relations within the gendered structure of cathexis, Holland and colleagues (1990) pointed out that sex cannot be defined only as "a pleasurable physical activity," but "it is redolent with symbolic meanings. These meanings are inseparable from gendered power relations and are active in shaping sexual interaction" (p. 339). They also stated, "The control which young women can exercise over the risks or safety of their sexual practices is constrained by the confusion of their notions of sexuality with their expectations of romance, love and caring. . . . It is difficult for young women to insist on safe sexual practices, when they do not expect to assert their own needs in sexual encounters" (p. 340). Thus, if definitions of desirability as a female heterosexual partner include ascribing power to the man in sexual decision making or conceding power to him to gain or maintain intimacy, whether on the basis of social hierarchies and structures of gender or ethnicity, then the process of empowering women within intimate sexual relations to control some aspects of practice within those relationships requires redefining those structural relations through personal and political action targeted to that end.

Whereas much of the research on limitations to women's power in negotiating sexual practice focuses on this differential role designation in which the male partner controls sex in heterosexual relationships (e.g., Worth, 1989), Holland and colleagues (1990) carried the discussion beyond "a focus on fragmented individual responsibility for personal behaviour change, to seeing safer sex as located in the context of social relationships" (p. 341; see also Amaro, 1995). For example, regarding pressures men exert on women in sexual practice (from persuasion to coercion), they pointed out, "While women have some power to identify and resist these pressures, they do not necessarily want to resist, when love, romance and the fear of losing a boyfriend are critical issues" (p. 342). They further stated:

> Contradictions arise in sexual encounters because women are pulled in different directions by conflicting social pressures. Passion, romance, trust and what you should be prepared to do if you really love a man are inconsistent with mistrust of strangers, social subordination to men, fear of unprotected sex, the use of physical force and concern for reputation. Feminine identity and expectations of sexual passivity pull against the need to be assertive in order to enjoy sex and to ensure personal safety. (p. 343)

Yet, although women may have practical reasons to participate in unequal heterosexual relationships, action directed toward changing or affecting the structure of cathexis itself in their intimate relations with male partners is possible that "attempt[s] to rework patterns of attachment in an egalitarian direction" (Connell, 1987, p. 115). It is this type of practice that may prove critical to constructing effective mechanisms for women to create conditions within heterosexual relationships to reduce their potential exposure to HIV.

In the remainder of this chapter, we utilize this framework in the analysis of women's discussion of their power, its limitations within heterosexual relationships and in the broader context of their lives, and their use of their self-identified power to bring about change. We then discuss implications of these for understanding the contexts of HIV risk and for developing possible approaches to AIDS prevention for women.

WOMEN'S ARTICULATION
OF THE SOCIAL RELATIONS OF POWER

Our research on the social context of HIV/AIDS risk and prevention over the past 8 years has been a collaborative process of working with community organizations to identify, reach, assess the needs and concerns of, and provide education, services, and support to men and women at high risk or already infected through drug use and/or sexual relations. In the course of this collaboration, we had the opportunity to participate together in and observe a support group program for African-American women entitled Sistahs Helpin' Sistahs. This program focuses on substance abuse recovery and empowerment of these women for HIV/AIDS prevention, by building self-esteem through community effort and long-term social and group member support. In a recent session, the group focused its discussion on power and social relationships, particularly intimate relations. The following sections outline the perspectives the women presented in this session as they articulated the complex and conflicting factors that constitute their experiences with addiction, HIV risk, poverty, and intimate relationships. The discourse of these women reflects the complex structures of gender, race/ethnicity, and poverty and the interconnections of these structures as formulated in Connell's (1987) model. They also have important implications both for HIV risk and for political practice targeted toward changing the structures of labor, power, and cathexis that bind these women's practice.

Twelve women from the support group participated in exploring the contexts and sources of power and disempowerment as they have experienced and interpreted them. These women were all African-American, in their mid-30s to mid-40s, and currently in recovery from addiction, having participated in the program for several months to over a year. In the course of this session and in subsequent interviews with a few of the participants, these women described the various social contexts within which they establish and work to maintain intimate relationships, raise and support children, provide financially for themselves and their households, and seek avenues to ensure that their own personal needs are met.

The economic and political context of Hartford, Connecticut, where these women have spent most or all of their lives, is similar to many northeastern urban centers that have been devastated by the loss of industry and the downsizing of businesses, as well as the increasing reduction of social insurance and public assistance for the unemployed and underemployed. Further, Hartford's internal racial and ethnic segregation and White flight to surrounding suburbs have increased the percentage of African Americans and Latinos in the city's poorest neighborhoods who are struggling to find any type of employment. In this context, many impoverished African-American and Latina women have become caught in drug or alcohol addiction, often as an escape from the ravages of poverty, sexual abuse, domestic violence, or the informal economy. They find it an overwhelming task to break away from that addiction and remain in recovery, or conversely, to maintain *both* their families and their addictions, and possibly a partner who also is addicted. Often, given the conventional propensity to blame the poor for their poverty and addicts for their weakness, these women feel a deep sense of shame, self-denigration, self-blame, and worthlessness. In this context, HIV/AIDS is just another in a long list of injustices, becoming a distant threat in relation to the immediate crises of hunger, lack of shelter, physical or sexual abuse, and the pain and demands of addiction.

Perhaps because these social contextual factors are primarily outside their immediate influence, and despite their recognition that job shortages are primary in reducing their economic viability, the women in the support group tended to look for the sources of and solutions to their problems internally. This is not surprising, given the current societal propensity to individualize social problems and to blame women for their own problems and isolate them in their attempts to change their situation. In their struggles to deal with their families, relationships, livelihood, health needs, and addiction, these women focused on personal inner strength and spirituality to become or remain sober, to accept the virtual certainty of their continued financial difficulties, and to seek, establish or reestablish, and maintain intimate relationships with partners, children, other family members, and friends.

During the support group session in which we participated, three recurrent themes appeared in the group members' discussion of power, each of which focuses primarily on internal personal factors related to their ability to make and act on decisions governing their lives and well-being. The first theme is their definitions of themselves as women, and the gendered terms in which they described their roles, options, vulnerabilities, desires, sexuality, and sources of power. The second reflects the process of seeking balance between establishing grounds on which they demand power, particularly in their personal relationships, and compromising to maintain an intimate relationship. The third theme is their discussion of love and *its* power to affect their behavior and choices, including their decisions to concede power in order to keep the love of a partner. We explore each of these themes and discuss its significance and implications for understanding the barriers to and sources of change in social relations of power for African-American women at risk of HIV infection.

Identity, Control, and Internal Sources of Power

Harsh conditions of poverty, addiction, racism, state regimentation (e.g., imprisonment, removal of children, reductions in public support), and personal experiences of abuse and abandonment have devastated many of these women, while at the same time have helped them forge an inner strength and self-empowerment. The building process often occurred through seeking recovery from drug addiction, leaving an untenable relationship, or both, in cases in which they used drugs with their partners. Several of the women in this group felt the key to their success or failure as individuals, in relationships, specifically with children and partners, and in seeking to avoid drug use and to protect against HIV/AIDS was their internal strength, their spiritual beliefs, and their ability to take control of various aspects of their lives. Their definitions of themselves clearly incorporated gendered concepts, for example, regarding the importance of having children. In fact, some suggested that to the degree they were successful at caring for children, that success compensated for other self-identified weaknesses, including their inability to establish or maintain the cultural "ideal" family structure (i.e., two parents plus children) or to control their drug addiction. One woman, in an interview subsequent to the group session, saw confirmation of this perspective in her father's reaction to her drug use: "It took me a long time [before I was ready to quit drugs], but [my father] never badgered me. He never threatened me . . . because I always took care of my children. I always fed [them], always got them ready for school, kept the house clean, kept our clothes washed, and they always had food to eat and stuff. So my father didn't worry too much because I didn't take my habit out on the kids." Fulfilling her mother role defined for her a measure of self-worth in relation to gender-defined structures of labor and authority. Her father implicitly accepted her assessment by not asserting his own power over her (e.g., by taking her children away), and by allowing her to sort out her problems with addiction, given her compliance with her role as mother. Further, this success in motherhood contextualized her actions regarding her drug use. It allowed her to avoid entering treatment until she was ready, but provided a sense of potential for eventual success to quit drugs, and to remain clean when she did stop, given her prior success in this first key arena in which she demonstrated her inner "power."

Gender relations of labor, authority, and cathexis that define the masculine and the feminine in a particular relationship of dominance or hierarchy create understandings of women's and men's inner strength and options for action on the basis of power. One woman defined power for women by contrasting concepts of masculinity and femininity as they relate to it. She said, "As far as power, we don't have to display a bunch of masculinity to show that [we] have power. Lot of people, when they're feminine, they act like they don't have power, that they need help in it and to me that means they're hiding it. Most women that are feminine and have power, they don't show it to the fullest because they are afraid that a man would take it the wrong way. Some men would take it like they're dominating that person." Added another woman: "Most people will call you a bitch because you want to be like the men and want what the men have. If you go about getting what you want, you're considered a bitch." These women recognize that within the social relations of gender is a clear association of men with power and women with powerlessness who concede power to men. They also acknowledge an assortment of negative associations regarding women who seek power or control over their lives, including the concept that these women will not be attractive partners for men who are concerned with having their legitimized power threatened. Thus, these women may fear that asserting power could lead to the loss of love of a male partner. Furthermore, they realize that their struggles with addiction and with seeking and maintaining intimate relations begin by addressing these associations in order to build and use their internal power in political action on their own behalf.

Another woman during the session described her sense of self and her discovery of power as she saw it in relation to general and targeted degradations. She said:

> How I found out that I didn't have power was that I was letting everybody control me, [control] my feelings. When I felt like, "I'm not going to let you do this to me," or "I'm not ugly, I am pretty"; but you telling me I'm ugly all the time, this is what I'm thinking. So I have to grow out of that conditioned mind that you done put me in and learn how to condition my own mind. And I have to keep sticking to my own worth, so that's how we have to learn to [have power].

Given the eroticization of beauty in women, and the importance of it for self-esteem, it is not surprising that she links messages about her beauty, or ugliness, to her internal power. The sense of self-worth or value as an individual is defined in meanings constituted in the structure of cathexis and linked to power (internal and external) to act in relation to those structures. Her decision to reject those concepts of beauty, or redefine them, provided her a means to act against the structures that contributed to her sense of powerlessness and consequently to act in relation to other conditions, including seeking drug treatment, job training, and employment.

Yet another woman in the group discussed the *process* of finding inner strength and internal sources of power:

> You still have to learn [that you have power] on your own. That is what I had to learn. My self-esteem was very, very low. I mean real low, to the lowest that they can come. And within the 18 months [of recovery]—I'm 36 years old; I just learned to have power, to have control, to not let nothing and no one to come in the way of where I stands on my own ground. Relationships, I got power in. When I go to my [support] groups, I got power in . . . helping somebody else that's helping me. You have to learn that empowerment. Empowerment don't just come, it's a process.

This statement expresses her acknowledgment that political practice to change social structures comes not only through her own struggles for self-worth, though such struggles for women often occur in isolation, but also from common action and the support of other women engaged in the same struggle. It also illustrates the significance of group action possible through programs like this one that bring women addicts together around a specific cause (such as substance abuse relapse prevention or AIDS prevention). Moreover, it points to her recognition that such action is a process, with ongoing successes and failures and requiring long-term effort to bring about change.

The difficulty of political and personal action to change drug use or HIV risky practices in intimate relationships is evident in these women's discussion of personal and social barriers to success in this regard. One African-American woman in her late 30s described her most recent relapse to drug use after a period of being clean for several years, and its impact on her sense of her own power and its limitations. She said:

I went through a lot, an awful lot. And I started seeing patterns within my life that was causing this. But it took me to step out there one more time with the drugs to have it hit home. . . . I thought everything was under control. . . . Everything, my brother was so sick, there was a possibility of him dying. I had a relative that I was taking care of and here, what about me? Everybody's leaning on me. I didn't stop and think that I had somebody to give it to and let him [her male partner] carry that. I'm going through this, "Yeah, OK, I'm all right." But I wasn't all right. And it broke me. It broke me. This superwoman stuff; we're so take care, take care. Who's going to take care of us?

Her statement painfully illustrates the conflict between gender roles defining women as caretakers of the family (and all others except themselves) and her own emotional need for support. Her drug-using partner in particular was unable to offer her the kind of support she needed at that time. Her inability to resolve this conflict resulted ultimately in the devastating loss of control over her addiction and her relapse to drug use. Significant also in this experience is her association of her relapse with an increasing awareness of the social structural and gender conditions reducing her power and causing her to break down her defenses and will to continue to fight her addiction.

This woman and several other session participants frequently raised the issue of spirituality and its significance for their efforts at building self-empowerment. They generally distinguished it from religion and church attendance, defining it in terms of their belief in God and feelings of the spirit within themselves. They emphasized the importance of spirituality for gaining a sense of purpose and direction, acquiring strength to establish themselves in a position of power within personal relationships, and addressing daily struggles with poverty and addiction. Although their discourse on this source of inner strength was generally very personalized, their common understanding of its significance in their lives created a common ground and a source of unity among the women in the group.

During the session, many of the women in this group also discussed their personal conflicts and experiences in dealing with structural relations of oppression in comparison to the experiences of their mothers. These women both expressed understanding of their mothers' difficulties and strengths, and saw them as models either to emulate or repudiate. One woman summarized the voices of several in the session with the following words: "You know what, I think my mother suffered in her own ways. My mother is dealing with a lot of things. . . . And she made a lot of mistakes, and she paid for them in her own ways. It's just ways that I don't know about. Because see my mother could be thinking about all them things that I done been through, she could be blaming herself or could be going through the stuff that I done been through, and she's just not opening up and saying it." These women saw their own power or weakness as a reflection of their mothers' and their own sources of strength or barriers to action as stemming from the same conditions their mothers faced, even in cases in which they felt strongly resentful about conflicts between them or unmet expectations for love and support. They recognized similar social relations affecting both them and their mothers, though with variation on the specific struggles and responses to those difficulties relative to their power to bring about change.

Several women in the session discussed women's reproductive capabilities as a unique source of their power within gendered social relations. In defining this power, three of the group members had the following dialogue:

P1: Males are always forgetting one important thing. They try to dominate a woman, they
     try to overpower a woman, but they keep forgetting one thing—they came from a woman.
P2: They have to realize that. They can't get here by themselves.
P1: They would not even be here if it wasn't for us. So we've had the power all along, huh?
     So how do we forget that power?
P3: Society. Just in the way they stigmatize color, like Blacks. It's like that.
P2: Oppression in general, societal pressure, you know.
P1: And because we've fallen in love so we have to continue . . . Yes, we do. We fall in love
     and we have the tendency to forget who we are and we focus everything about us on that
     man.

In this conversation, these women articulate several key interconnected elements of the
three structural domains. First, they recognize that social factors in the structures and relations
of gender transform a potential and unique power of women, that is, their capacity for
reproduction, into a source of their potential disempowerment. Despite its necessity for the
continuation of humankind, including men, women's reproductive capacity is not associated
with power, but rather is ignored or forgotten. Second, they identify the stigmatization and
degradation of women and African Americans as effectively similar, thus associating gender
and race as structural conditions defining relations of hierarchy and inequality within which
they are doubly subordinated. Third, they acknowledge love, and specifically the process of
falling in love with a man, as a potential agent in their loss of power. We discuss this further,
but first look at the ways these women articulated the process of negotiating power with male
partners in the context of intimate heterosexual relations.

Balancing Power in Intimate Relationships

A second primary theme in the discussion of power among women in the support group
session was the various ways they sought to balance their own power with that of their male
partners. Within the constraints of social structural relations shaped by gender, race, and
class, men and women seek to establish intimacy and love while maintaining some level of
power and control over their lives and resources. These women, and others in our AIDS
prevention research studies, spoke of this balancing act in maintaining heterosexual relationships in the context of numerous financial and emotional strains, complicated by addiction,
poverty, racism, and sexism. As is the case with their self-defined and self-identified internal
sources of power, the structure of cathexis in gender relations as it is currently constituted
limits the means these women have to gain even modest control within their intimate heterosexual relationships. Structural relations of labor and authority compound the difficulty for
these women, given their limited resources, the demands of addiction or recovery, the neces-
sities of childrearing, social relations of gender authority that subordinate them to their male
partners, and social relations of race and nationality that subordinate them and their male
partners (should those partners also be of color) to the dominant racial or ethnic group.
    Women in the support group described the difficulty of keeping this balance between
being sexually desirable, maintaining intimacy with a man, facing and dealing with addiction
in combination with family responsibilities, and finding "worthiness" in themselves and their
lives. One woman described the difficulty of and need for compromise in order to maintain
intimacy, and the implications and limitations of such compromise for her power in that
relationship:

It seems like it's harder in relationships with men . . . because you've always got to find a
compromise. So when does the compromise become giving up your power to theirs, especially

when they're doing the same thing? Well you know society got a lot to do with that too because when me and my husband got married, I was, guess you could say, taught to listen to him and do what he say, to give him my check and da da da da. You know what I'm saying? So I lost a lot of power in that relationship, but slowly but surely I gained it back. I started standing up for me. I'll compromise to the bitter end you know with anybody, but when I say what goes, that's what goes. With me, I can take a lot, but when I put my foot down, then that's it.

With these words, she acknowledged the constraints placed on her by gender relations in which the definition of "desirability" of the woman partner in a heterosexual union is conditioned by her listening to the man and by her lesser position of authority in relation to her male partner. This woman also recognized her socialization into accepting these concepts and her structural location in the hierarchy, maintained for the sake of the relationship. Yet, her determination to act against those structures has made possible her ability to change the context of negotiation within her intimate relationship with her male partner, to strengthen the base of her authority within that relationship, and to redefine herself as a partner on more equal grounds in their ongoing interaction. These are key elements in the process of building a basis for successful "negotiation" regarding sexual practice and protection against HIV and other threats, both inside and outside of the relationship.

The experiences with addiction of the women participating in this program and their numerous attempts at recovery, combined with their efforts to deal with protection against HIV or AIDS or a variety of physical and emotional abuses and poverty, have caused them to recognize the importance of and need for tipping the balance of compromise toward addressing their own needs. This recognition generally evolved in the context of reaching the bottom with addiction, illness, or an abusive relationship. One woman in the group poignantly described this as follows:

Right now I'm at a certain point in my life now I'm like, don't mess with me, just don't. . . . I feel like I been through a lot, you know. I'm sick of bein' sick of. Sick of this nonsense and I want to change my life. I want to break that part of my life, that pattern with the pain, pain, pain. Doing the same thing over and over. Turn around and I'm being destructive to myself. I want to break that. It's so easy to have to go there, swallow a few pills, and that's this all over. But it's not all over. And I don't want that. You know I have a lot to live for. I got three beautiful children. . . . And no man and no drugs is worth me killing and taking my life. No man and no drugs are worth me bringing my self-esteem down so low when it can't be picked up again.

Another woman expressed a similar feeling: "Look, I been dictated to all my life from my childhood for 35 years old. Ain't nobody dictating my life no more. When I do that, every day at sometime, something comes my way to show me that I got power. Because I ain't giving it up. Because I like the way I'm living today [clean of drugs]. Ain't nobody telling me what to do, and how to live, and who to see, and what to say."

Many of these woman have come to this sense of determination to be in control of their lives and intimate relationships through harsh experiences as addicts or through experiencing relationships with addicted men, who also were struggling for control. Their struggles have been compounded by numerous experiences of losing in the negotiations or conflicts with their male partners over resources and power within the relationship. Further, both they and their partners struggle together on a daily basis in the context of poverty, racism, and other "structural violence" (Farmer et al., 1996), which compounds the difficulties and deprivations they face and raises the stakes in these struggles. These conditions also create a context within which love, romance, and sexuality are constrained and consequently affect relations of power between partners.

Love and Power in Intimate Relationships

The significance of the gender structure of cathexis in heterosexual relationships for contextualizing HIV risk and prevention is clearest in discussions of love as it affects women's sense of power and powerlessness, and their decisions to concede power to their male partners (Amaro, 1995; Holland et al., 1990; Sobo, 1995). Regardless of the complexities of balancing personal and family needs with the needs of an intimate male partner, several women in the session and in subsequent interviews described in emotional detail the importance of having the love of a man in their lives, and their consequent willingness to take numerous risks and make serious concessions for that love. One woman expressed the significance of her feelings of love for a man who had been her partner for over 20 years, the man who had taught her to inject when she was 18 and for whom she had prostituted to support both her own and his drug use for most of that period. She left him because his continuing drug use jeopardized her recovery, which she was determined to maintain. She said:

> Now in my case, . . . I was blind. . . . I really was in love with him. . . . I want to love again and I want to find that person again. But I'm going to be scared, I'm going to have caution signs up. . . . To me it's an honor whenever you do find that love even if it's just for a year or so. It's something special, it's something that you would never want to forget. I'm glad that I did find somebody in my life that finally loved me for who I am since I couldn't never get it from my family members. . . . I don't have that love from them that I had from this man. And I had to let him go [because he was still using drugs]. I had to find the power within me even though the pain got great enough. But I stood on my two feet. . . . So power is hard. To stand your own ground when you find that empowerment in yourself.

Particularly significant in this statement is that she referred to breaking her love ties with her partner as finding power within herself, and acknowledged the symbolic importance of leaving what she felt was a loving relationship for her own benefit (i.e., her drug abuse recovery). And yet, she described the intensity of her desire for that love relationship, or one like it, to allay her loneliness, when she said, "My greatest pain is I live by myself; . . . no man lives with me. That's the most loneliest thing in the world. To stick that key in that door. . . . I swear it's so hard for me not to have a relationship." Her statement gives painful testimony to the potential cost of establishing and maintaining control over a significant aspect of her life, in this case, her drug use and associated health and well-being.

Another woman tied the significance of a desire for love to risks women take in intimate sexual relationships, including risks directly related to HIV transmission:

> You was talking about the condoms and all that. You know, [my partner and I] used the condoms [once] and the next [time we] did not. It was like because I was *flattered* that he trusted me. Isn't that kind of backwards? He trusted that [I] didn't have nothing, that he was safe. I was flattered! I didn't even think about [whether I trusted him]. It didn't go that far. All I was, was flattered that he trusted me. My self-esteem was so low; again [I was] forgetting about myself—[it was] all about the man still.

Gendered social relations define intimacy in terms of trust, and create this conundrum for AIDS prevention that defies "educational" and "behavior change" strategies. In her statement, this session participant acknowledged the potential HIV risk from not using a condom, and suggested that now, at this point in her life, she might not accept her partner's trust of her as sufficient (or even flattering) to lead her to engage in this risk. Yet, she recognized that her need for love, her limited power in that relationship, and her self-conception in the context of multiple degradations of her past and current situation more directly and effectively determined her interaction with and feelings for that partner, including her decision to engage in "unprotected" sex with him at the second encounter.

RELATIONS OF POWER AND IMPLICATIONS FOR AIDS PREVENTION FOR WOMEN

The tremendous challenge remains of developing successful HIV/AIDS prevention approaches for women that appropriately take into account and target the social conditions that create and shape their "risk," including within heterosexual relationships. Fundamental to developing such approaches is to identify the source of this risk. Much of the context of HIV transmission is characterized by social structures and relations built around hierarchies and oppression on the basis of gender, class, racial, and ethnic distinctions. Although clearly the virus is the agent of the disease, these various social structures and relationships of disempowerment create pathways of least resistance or greatest opportunity for the virus to traverse, resulting in the predominance of the disease among those least empowered and facing the greatest barriers to making "behavioral" changes for the sake of HIV prevention (cf. Farmer et al., 1996).

In general, the women in Sistahs Helpin' Sistahs did not identify the sources of their disempowerment (or the sources of their power) in terms of the global or local economy, or the class structure. They are, nevertheless, affected by these conditions, and by other structures of inequality. Flight of industry and manufacturing from developed to developing countries, combined with the ubiquitous downsizing and restructuring of business and industry to increase the margin of profit, ensure that these women (disadvantaged by racism, sexism, and insufficient or inadequate education and training) will be increasingly less able to attain employment that pays a living wage during their working years. Government policy changes to reduce public spending, specifically on public assistance and support for single mothers and unemployed or displaced workers, increase the likelihood that these women will be unable through any means (barring the informal or illegal economies) to provide sufficient support for themselves and their families. Prejudices and systematic discrimination on the basis of race, nationality, language, gender, and sexuality also coalesce to reduce their options to avoid poverty and its debilitating effects on their health, stability, welfare, and happiness. Thus, the causes of these women's disempowerment and resulting multiple risks are the structures of labor, power, and cathexis as currently constituted by relations of gender, race, and class. These structures and their historical shape create an environment opportune for the rapid spread of HIV through drug use and heterosexual transmission within the communities in which these women live. The solution to the spread of HIV/AIDS, then, is to change those structures, relations, and historical context.

It is unlikely, however, that the next decade of the AIDS epidemic will see a reversal in the creation of poverty resulting from continued downsizing, U.S. exportation of jobs to take advantage of low third-world wages, and a class structure and economic dynamic that increasingly polarize the wealthy from the working classes and the poor. It is also unlikely that global and national relations defined by separating and hierarchically ordering people on the basis of socially constituted definitions of race, ethnicity, and nationality, which are themselves intricately tied to the economic forces of class hierarchy and poverty, will improve for people of color. Nor will gender inequality and gendered hierarchies on the basis of sex and sexuality be eliminated in the near future, certainly not soon enough to interrupt the deadly trajectory of the epidemic among women in the United States and elsewhere. Unfortunately, for many, any effort is too late, and the press of time calls for immediate responses to stem the tide of new infections.

Yet, ignoring or minimizing the significance of social structural relations because of the daunting nature of bringing about such broad-based change to eliminate social inequalities and structural violence misses the fundamental dynamic that is at the root of HIV risk (Farmer et al., 1996). So what, then, should AIDS prevention for women look like? Is it necessary, if not sufficient, to identify individual behaviors and personal and "cultural" factors that affect decision making, and to respond with more education and more "culturally sensitive" behavioral modification programs? To what degree is the focus on individual cognition and behavior the source of and solution to the problem? Furthermore, what are providers' and women's options for addressing the root causes and contexts of HIV risk? Can providers, fettered by compartmentalized and fragmented programming and funding sources, broaden the scope of their efforts to address the social structural context of this risk? Can women, facing isolation and disempowerment, find "mechanisms" or processes to protect themselves and take political action around the common cause of reducing the spread of AIDS? And, if they seek to empower themselves to protect against social structures and relationships that make them vulnerable to HIV infection, can they still find love and intimacy in relationships with male partners?

The women in Sistahs Helpin' Sistahs have come to identify the barriers to and sources of their power, and likewise the sources of their HIV risk, generally through hitting bottom and seeking to rebuild their lives, beginning internally. Their discussion of power in this support group session focused on their personal experiences with poverty, addiction, and disempowerment in intimate relationships, including abusive relationships in their families of origin or with their heterosexual partners. Their response to these problems has been to look for *self*-empowerment, putting one's foot down, building inner strength to face recovery, to demand equality in a relationship, or to live alone. AIDS prevention education and counseling have provided them with the knowledge and "skills" to avoid HIV transmission behaviors, and this holistic program has begun to politicize them to recognize the broader social forces that constrain them in their efforts to redirect their lives around drug abuse recovery. But they identify the process of building inner strength as the key to being able to apply HIV risk reduction behavioral imperatives or to take steps, alone or as a group, to improve their options to achieve economic and social stability. They also recognize the tenuousness of their inner power to protect themselves as they face ongoing struggles with drug relapse, poverty, inequality in heterosexual relationships, and the need for love, intimacy, and balance in their intimate relations.

Gaining and maintaining power under these circumstances, however, requires more than individual inner strength. It requires solidified efforts, often with the support and comradeship of other women who have faced similar experiences. The coming together of the women in this program has had a major impact on their ability to work jointly and separately to identify their inner power, to use it, and to encourage each other to do the same. It has been particularly important for breaking the isolation these women face in dealing with their problems, and for recognizing that their problems are not theirs alone. Understanding the relationships among social structures defined by gender, class, race, and ethnicity, through identification and discussion in group programs like Sistahs Helpin' Sistahs, can further help these women to target political practice for change of the broader conditions of HIV risk and transmission, as well as to provide them with internal resources on which they can draw to fight for their own interests in personal interactions.

On the basis of this framework, and through the experiences of women participating in this program, we can identify six key components of AIDS prevention for women necessary to address the social context of risk beyond affecting individual behavior change. First, given the prevailing and powerful influence of gendered relations of inequality and their disempowerment of women, it is necessary to identify and build on sources of women's inner power so they can begin to contextualize their own issues and barriers to AIDS prevention and thereby begin the process of change (on the personal, group, community, and broader levels) to increase their control over their lives and risks. Prevention programs also need to build upon the process of balancing power in intimate relationships to redefine the gendered structures of labor, power, and cathexis in order to tip the scales in the "negotiating" process in support of women to control more of their sexual activities, resources, and other key components of those relationships.

Second, it is essential to disassociate "blame" from women for the social conditions that shape their disempowerment and HIV risk. Removing this blame takes away one more insult to their self-esteem, sense of self-worth, and inner power, and allows them greater possibility to take a modicum of control of their lives and intimate relationships. It further locates risk not in their individual decisions nor in assumptions about personal weaknesses, but in the many contradictory forces that remove from them the option to make or enforce a decision to act to protect themselves, or that leave available only "choices" that constitute one or another form of "risk" for them to weigh and balance.

Third, it is necessary to recognize individual HIV risk as located within social structures and historically constructed social relationships, that is, as *part* of these larger forces that generally are outside the individual's immediate control. This recognition removes the onus of the AIDS epidemic from the individual. It also allows identification of social structures and relationships as targets for political change that addresses the conditions affecting the continuing and increasing spread of the disease.

Fourth, critical to advancing AIDS prevention for women and others disproportionately affected by the epidemic is organized action through common "agency" as members of self-identified groups in a social and political context. It is more effective to build mechanisms of power, control, and prevention through identification of the common cause of a group, that is, to "unionize" in targeted political practice around a common set of structural relationships and inequalities, than it is to approach the problem as though those at risk were isolated individuals. As structural relations of gender, race, or class create categories of groups defined by their relationships to those structures (i.e., as women, gays, African Americans, the poor), use of these categorical constructs to galvanize individuals in common political action to change social relations of inequality within which they are defined provides a mechanism to effect change that reverses or equalizes that power.

Fifth, programs designed to address HIV/AIDS as a single issue invariably suffer from a lack of resources to address the broader context of the epidemic and the wider social forces affecting its progression. Multifaceted programs that simultaneously address conditions of labor and employment, education and training, general health care and access, housing, food, and drug treatment are generally perceived by funders and service organizations as overly labor intensive and expensive. Yet, such comprehensive designs, combined with long-term efforts and supports, may in the long run prove more effective (and therefore also more cost-effective) for reversing the epidemic's relentless expansion among those facing multiple and complex crises.

Sixth, there are few substitutes for love and intimacy. Many heterosexual women do not want to lose the love of a man. HIV/AIDS prevention providers must acknowledge the importance and power of this type of relationship, including for women's self-definition of internal power and worthiness. Prevention programs can build on love for protection against HIV in an informed way, for example, based on dual respect and recognition of the need for mutual protection and allowing for power of each person in the relationship.

Even small battles and victories that are targeted to the gendered social structures and to structural relations defined by race and class can reverse the order of power and hierarchy that places women at heightened risk for HIV. Ongoing political action targeted at those relations can bring about change in individual relationships and social contexts within institutions that foster relations of inequality.

In addition to organizing and supporting women to identify the broader causes of their risk and the sources of their power, researchers and AIDS prevention and service providers must become advocates of change in the social structures that perpetuate inequity on the basis of gender, race, ethnicity/nationality, and class. They must seek to reverse conditions and social relations that generate poverty and consequent injuries, perpetrated through repressive policies against the poor, against women facing combined joblessness and responsibility for children, against addicts, and against people of color. Needed is a broader political agenda for AIDS prevention to develop policies that prevent the conditions that create the opportunity for the continued spread of HIV disproportionately among those most affected by these inequities in order to curb the expansion of this deadly epidemic.

The empowerment these women identified is individualized, stemming from their lifelong isolation in dealing with problems said to be caused by them. Yet, their voices are better heard together, and their causes better served in common action, supported by advocates that include AIDS prevention researchers, service providers, and AIDS service organizations. Without a focus on policy changes that ensure adequate access to jobs, health care, housing, education or job training, and food, AIDS prevention education and counseling programs ultimately will be rendered ineffective.

ACKNOWLEDGMENTS

The program Sistahs Helpin' Sistahs is supported by the Connecticut Department of Public Health through the Urban League of Greater Hartford. The authors are greatly indebted to the coordinators of that program (including coauthor Dawn McKinley, and Gloria Austin) for their tireless work, and for creating the opportunity to participate with the women of this program for discussing these important issues. Our greatest debt, however, is to the women who shared with us their lives, fears, loves, and hopes for the future, without which we could not have gained their critically important perspectives.

REFERENCES

Amaro, H. (1988). Considerations for prevention of HIV infection among Hispanic women. *Psychology of Women Quarterly, 12,* 429–443.

Amaro, H. (1995) Love, sex, and power: Considering women's realities in HIV prevention. *American Psychologist, 50,* 437–447.

Carovano, K. (1991). More than mothers and whores: Redefining the AIDS prevention needs of women. *International Journal of Health Services, 21,* 131–142.

Centers for Disease Control and Prevention. (1996). *HIV/AIDS surveillance report, 8*(1).

Centers for Disease Control and Prevention. (1997). Update: Trends in AIDS incidence, deaths, and prevalence— United States, 1996. *Morbidity and Mortality Weekly Report, 46,* 165–173.

Connell, R. W. (1987). *Gender and power: Society, the person, and sexual politics.* Stanford, CA: Stanford University Press.

Farmer, P., Connors, M., & Simmons, J. (Eds.). (1996). *Women, poverty and AIDS: Sex, drugs, and structural violence.* Monroe, ME: Common Courage Press.

Flaskerud, J., & Nyamathi, A. (1990). Effects of an AIDS education program on the knowledge, attitudes, and practices of low income Black and Latina women. *Journal of Community Health, 15,* 343–355.

Fullilove, M. T., Fullilove, R. E., Haynes, K., & Gross, S. (1990). Black women and AIDS prevention: A view towards understanding the gender rules. *Journal of Sex Research, 27,* 47–64.

Holland, J., Ramazanoglu, C., Scott, S., Sharpe S., & Thomson, R. (1990). Sex, gender, and power: Young women's sexuality in the shadow of AIDS. *Sociology of Health and Illness, 12,* 336–350.

Kane, S. (1990). AIDS, addiction, and condom use: Sources of sexual risk for heterosexual women. *Journal of Sex Research, 27,* 427–444.

Kline, A., Kline, E., & Oken, E. (1992). Minority women and sexual choice in the age of AIDS. *Social Science and Medicine, 34,* 447–457.

Mane, P., Gupta, G. R., & Weiss, E. (1994). Effective communication between partners: AIDS and risk reduction for women. *AIDS, 8*(Suppl. 1), 5325–5331.

Marín, B. (1992). Hispanic culture: Implications for AIDS prevention. In J. Boswell, R. Hexter, & J. Reinisch (Eds.), *Sexuality and disease: Metaphors, perceptions and behavior in the AIDS era* (pp. 27–36). New York: Oxford University Press.

Nastasi, B., Schensul, J. J, & Sivayoganathan, C. (1997, March). *A community-based HIV/AIDS prevention program for Sri Lankan youth.* Paper presented at the annual meeting of the Society for Applied Anthropology, Seattle.

Rubin, L. (1976). *Worlds of pain.* New York: Basic Books.

Shayne, V. T., & Kaplan, B. J. (1991). Double victims: Poor women and AIDS. *Women and Health, 17,* 21–37.

Singer, M. (1994). AIDS and the health crisis of the U.S. urban poor: The perspective of critical medical anthropology. *Social Science and Medicine, 39,* 931–948.

Singer, M., Flores, C., Davison, L., Burke, G., Castillo, Z., Scanlon, K., & Rivera, M. (1990). SIDA: The economic, social and cultural context of AIDS among Latinos. *Medical Anthropology Quarterly, 4,* 72–114.

Sobo, E. J. (1995). *Choosing unsafe sex: AIDS-risk denial among disadvantaged women.* Philadelphia: University of Pennsylvania Press.

Waterston, A. (1993). *Street addicts in the political economy.* Philadelphia: Temple University Press.

Weeks, M. R., Grier, M., Romero-Daza, N., Puglisi-Vasquez, M. J., & Singer, M. (1998). Streets, drugs, and the economy of sex in the age of AIDS. *Women and Health, 27,* 205–229.

Weeks, M. R., Schensul, J. J., Williams, S. S., Singer, M., & Grier, M. (1995). AIDS prevention for African American and Latina women: Building cultural and gender–appropriate intervention. *AIDS Prevention and Education, 7,* 251–264.

Weeks, M. R., Singer, M., Grier, M., & Schensul, J. J. (1996). Gender relations, sexuality, and AIDS risk among African American and Puerto Rican women. In C. Sargent & C. B. Brettell (Eds.), *Gender and health: An international perspective* (pp. 338–370). Englewood Cliffs, NJ: Prentice-Hall.

Worth, D. (1989). Sexual decision-making and AIDS: Why condom promotion among vulnerable women is likely to fail. *Studies in Family Planning, 20,* 297–307.

15

In Their Own Words: Communication and the Politics of HIV Education for Transgenders and Transsexuals in Los Angeles

Gust A. Yep
San Francisco State University

Myrna Pietri
California State University, Los Angeles

> The crisis surrounding the HIV epidemic exposed America's racism and homophobia in new ways, laying bare the ugly truth that the structure of benevolence—social programs, especially health care—simply were not meant for everyone.
>
> —Patton (1996, p. 7)

> There is nothing in this whole AIDS mess that is not political!
>
> —Kramer (1989, p. 110)

Since early medical reports in 1981, the HIV/AIDS epidemic has become a crisis of intense international concern (Feldman & Johnson, 1986; Osborn, 1989). This epidemic has affected virtually everyone including sexual minority communities (e.g., Carballo-Dieguez, 1995; Choi, Salazar, Lew, & Coates, 1995; Morin, Charles, & Malyon, 1984; Myrick, 1995; Peterson, 1995; Silvestri, 1993; Yep, Miller, & Parker-Cobb, 1994), diverse cultural groups (e.g., Aoki, Ngin, Mo, & Ja, 1989; Bowen & Michal-Johnson, 1995; Carballo-Dieguez, 1995; Gock, 1994; Marín & Marín, 1990; Mays, 1989; Peterson, 1995; Witte, 1992a; Yep, 1992, 1993b), women and men (e.g., Amaro, 1993; Squire, 1993), children, adolescents, and adults (e.g., Curran, 1988; Edgar, Freimuth, & Hammond, 1988; Landau-Stanton & Clements, 1993; Reardon, 1989; Shayne & Kaplan, 1988; Witte, 1992b), hemophiliacs (e.g., Landau-Stanton & Clements, 1993; Scheerhorn, 1995), injecting drug users and their partners (e.g., Landau-Stanton & Clements, 1993; Singer, Jia, Schensul, Weeks, & Page, 1992), and heterosexuals (e.g., Altman, 1986; Catania et al., 1994; Curran, 1988). Of these groups, sexual minorities, including the gender transposed, have been disproportionately affected by HIV. As Herek (1995) noted, "Since the early 1980s, life as a gay, lesbian, or bisexual person has always been lived against a backdrop of AIDS and HIV" (p. x).

Gender transposition "implies that the gender identification/gender role and/or the sexual orientation of a given individual is the opposite of, or discordant with, what we would expect to find in the average man or woman in our society" (Silvestri, 1993, p. 18). It includes, but is not restricted to, transgenders and transsexuals. Broadly defined, transgenders are individuals whose gender self-presentation differs from their biological sex, for example, full- or part-time cross-dressers, whereas transsexuals are individuals who experience consistent gender dysphoria accompanied by a wish for surgical reassignment of their biological sex, for example, individuals before and after sex reassignment surgery (Silvestri, 1993).

HIV infection is a very serious problem among transgenders and transsexuals. Silvestri (1993) maintained that there are at least two additional factors that place this group at "higher risk than most" (p. 83) when compared to other sexual minorities: (a) for the male-to-female (MTF) transgender, sexual activity and hesitancy to negotiate for safer sex are viewed as feminine, thus, a form of gender validation, and (b) needle sharing for hormones. As Silvestri observed, "When someone shows up in the bar with a vial of hormones and a syringe, everyone wants a shot. It matters little how many people may have been stuck with the needle before" (p. 87). As stated earlier, HIV infection already has disproportionately affected sexual minority communities; these additional behavioral factors can further accelerate the spread of HIV among transgenders and transsexuals. Focusing on "their own words," the purpose of this chapter is to examine the social and cultural context associated with HIV infection in this group.

THE POLITICS OF HIV EDUCATION

Government responses to the HIV epidemic have been slow. This was particularly true during the early years of the epidemic. The source of initial silence and negligence at the federal level was reported by Grover (1987): "Gary Bauer, [former] president Reagan's assistant, told *Face the Nation* that the reason Reagan had not even uttered the words AIDS publicly before a press conference held late in 1985 was that the Administration did not until then perceive AIDS as a problem: 'It hadn't spread into the general population yet' " (p. 23). The "general population" is presumed to be heterosexual, middle-class, family-oriented, non-pleasure-seeking (unlike drug users and homosexuals), and nonaddicted, and, as Grover noted, "is the repository of everything you wish to claim for yourself and deny to others" (p. 24), in other words, its members hold power and its accompanying corollary, control over allocation of resources.

Labeling AIDS both as a "transmissible lethal disease and an epidemic of meanings and signification," Treichler (1987, p. 32) noted that AIDS discourse is loaded with dichotomies like homosexual and the general population ("high-risk group" vs. "the general public"), normal and abnormal (heterosexual, vaginal intercourse presuming that women are the "natural receptacles with the rugged vagina" for the male sperm vs. homosexual, anal intercourse presuming that the rectum is fragile and vulnerable to the "killer sperm" of other men), guilty and innocent victims ("actively contracting HIV" like through needle sharing vs. "passively contracting HIV" in the mother's womb). Simply stated, AIDS discourse constructs the self (the general population) and "the other" (social deviants like homosexuals, prostitutes, and injecting drug users), thus creating and maintaining a safe distance between people living with HIV/AIDS and "everybody else."

It is not surprising, then, that early HIV educational efforts focused on "high-risk groups" as opposed to "risk behaviors." The high-risk group approach assumes that being a particular kind of person—homosexual, hemophiliac, heroin addict, Haitian—makes the individual vulnerable to HIV infection. Fueled by homophobia, AIDS-reporting procedures established by the Centers for Disease Control and Prevention (CDC) were also problematic: If a man diagnosed with AIDS was both a homosexual and a drug user, he was automatically counted in the homosexual/bisexual men category, therefore, "the 'gay' nature of AIDS was in part an artifact of the way in which data was [sic] collected and reported" (Treichler, 1987, p. 44).

The risk behavior or risk-based approach, on the other hand, focuses on the behaviors associated with HIV transmission. Currently endorsed by public health officials, this approach has not been supported by government funding (Patton, 1996). Right-wing groups, popularizing the unsupported argument that discussion of low-risk ways to engage in stigmatized sexual practices leads to increasing deviant and undesirable behaviors, successfully passed the Helms Amendment, which made it legal to prohibit funding for HIV education programs that "promote" homosexuality and sexual promiscuity. With the exception of CDC Demonstration Projects, many of these risk-based education programs are currently funded by private sources (Patton, 1996).

According to Patton (1996), the current national AIDS pedagogy advocates a risk-based approach within particular subgroups like homosexuals. Although HIV/AIDS education programs and public communication campaigns have generally increased knowledge about HIV transmission and prevention, such knowledge has not always been manifested in terms of adoption of health protective behaviors, for example, condom use (Edgar et al., 1988). The problem of motivating individuals to change their health behavior and to maintain safer sexual habits is based on communication (Edgar et al., 1988; Metts & Fitzpatrick, 1992; Reardon, 1988; Yep, 1993a). However, such communication campaigns and educational programs have generally not addressed the social and cultural meanings of HIV transmission–interrupting behaviors other than those of Euro-American gay men (Marín & Marín, 1990; Michal-Johnson & Bowen, 1992; Patton, 1996; Stanton et al., 1995; Weeks, Schensul, Williams, Singer, & Grier, 1995; Yep, 1992, 1993b, 1995, 1997, in press). Although gay men, transgenders, and transsexuals are stigmatized, harassed, and treated like perverts, gay men are typically marginalized on the basis of their sexuality whereas transgenders and transsexuals suffer oppression from both sexual and gender transgression (Rubin, 1993). In other words, transgenders and transsexuals experience different social and cultural realities.

To further exacerbate this situation, research on the social and cultural context associated with HIV infection among transgenders and transsexuals is almost nonexistent (Yep et al., 1994). To increase our understanding, this chapter explores and describes their social and cultural realities. More specifically, this article identifies the social and cultural context in which transgender and transsexual persons live, explores socioculturally appropriate HIV/AIDS education, prevention, and service delivery programs for this population, and develops a research agenda that reflects the needs of transgender and transsexual persons. To accomplish this, the PRECEDE model, developed by Green, Kreuter, Deeds, and Partridge (1980), is used as an organizing theoretical framework for the development and design of health education and communication programs for the gender-transposed community.

THE PRECEDE FRAMEWORK

PRECEDE is a model for health education intervention. It is an acronym for "predisposing, reinforcing, and enabling causes in educational diagnosis and evaluation" (Green et al., 1980, p. 11). According to this model, health education is a process in which people are motivated to use health information and to do something with it—to keep oneself healthy by engaging in self-protective behaviors, for example, practice of safer sex to prevent HIV infection. To put it differently, health education is a communication process in which consumers of health messages (a) increase their knowledge of the particular health condition (information dissemination function), and (b) adopt specific behaviors to enhance their health by either reducing health risks, increasing healthy behaviors, or both (motivation and social influence function).

The PRECEDE framework is based on the underlying assumption that the process of communicating about health presumes that health actions, habits, and practices are voluntary behaviors. The notion that health behavior is a voluntary behavior, according to the model, implies that (a) the health communicators and health education recipients must agree on the definition of health-related problems (e.g., both health educators and individuals in the transgender/transsexual community must agree that HIV infection is a serious problem in this community), and (b) health communicators must recommend behaviors and health actions that are compatible with the value system of the target person or community (e.g., recommending to a male-to-female transsexual that she needs to assert herself by saying "no" to unsafe sexual practices would not be compatible to her value system given that self-asserting behaviors are not perceived as feminine or gender validating; on the other hand, telling this same person that condoms are a form of birth control can be perceived as both feminine and gender validating). Emphasizing the need for congruence between value systems, Green and associates (1980) further observed, "Health means different things to different people, serves different purposes for different people, and is more or less important to different people" (p. x). In short, the PRECEDE framework suggests that health education and communication must take into account the social and cultural realities of the target individual or community.

The PRECEDE framework has been widely adapted since its development in 1980. More specifically, it has been applied to a variety of health conditions like HIV/AIDS (Alteneder, Price, Telljohann, Didion, & Locher, 1992), asthma (Bailey et al., 1987), blood pressure (Meagher & Mann, 1990), bulimia (Benson & Taub, 1993), cancer (Chie, Cheng, Fu, & Yen, 1993; Cretain, 1989; Dignan et al., 1995; Earp, Altpeter, Mayne, Viadro, & O'Malley, 1995; Michielutte et al., 1989; Taylor, Taplin, Urban, Mahloch, & Majer, 1994), lower extremity amputation (Grise, Gauthier-Gagnon, & Martineau, 1993), mental health (Wilson, 1986), rheumatoid arthritis (Bartholomew, Koenning, Dahlquist, & Barron, 1994), and schistosomiasis (Kloos, 1995), among others. The model has been used in childbirth and parenting education programs (O'Meara, 1993), nutrition (Mansour & Hassan, 1994), patient health education (Jenny, 1993), and wellness programs (Bonaguro, 1981). It has also been applied to a variety of health threats including automobile child restraint programs (Eriksen & Gielen, 1983), drug abuse (Lohrmann & Fors, 1986), medication-related problems (Opdycke, Ascione, Shimp, & Rosen, 1992), sexuality programs (Rubinson & Baillie, 1981), stress (Dunlap & Berne, 1991), suicide prevention (Frankish, 1994), and tobacco use (Polcyn, Price, Jurs, & Roberts, 1991), among others. In addition to its wide applicability, the PRECEDE framework has received empirical support. For example, Mullen, Hersey, and Iverson (1987) compared three health behavior models (PRECEDE, health belief model, and theory of reasoned action) in terms of their predictive capacity to anticipate changes in smoking, exercise, and consumption of sweet and fried foods over an 8-month interval in a sample of 326 adults, and found that the PRECEDE model accounted for more variance in behavior than the other two models. The PRECEDE framework, with its emphasis on understanding the social and cultural realities of the target individual or community, its broad applicability across populations and health conditions, and empirical support, appears to be especially appropriate for identifying and examining factors associated with the HIV problem in the transgender and transsexual community. We begin by providing a brief overview of the framework by identifying its seven steps or phases associated with the health education process.

The Phases of PRECEDE

The PRECEDE framework directs the attention of the health education planner to outcomes rather than input; in other words, health messages and interventions are designed after an outcome is diagnosed. For example, a health educator might want transgender sex workers to practice safer sex with their clients (outcome) and to accomplish that, she or he needs to find out why these sex workers are not engaging in self-protective behaviors before she or he can design interventions and health messages directed to deal with the problem.

In order to develop proper and effective interventions, this framework suggests a seven-step process. Phases 1 and 2 consist of epidemiological and social diagnoses. More specifically, Phase 1 focuses on the "quality of life" of the target community by assessing some of the general problems that individuals in such a community might experience, for example, unemployment, poverty, and high incidence of sex work (prostitution), and Phase 2 identifies particular health problems that appear to be contributing to the social problems observed in the first phase, for example, high incidence of sexually transmitted diseases (STDs). Phase 3 is a behavioral diagnosis: It focuses on the identification of specific health-related behaviors that appear to be associated to the health problems highlighted in Phase 2, for example, the link between unprotected sexual activity and high incidence of STDs. The primary focus of Phases 4 and 5 is on educational diagnosis. In Phase 4, specific predisposing, enabling, and reinforcing factors are identified. Predisposing factors are those individual's attitudes, beliefs, values, and perceptions that facilitate or hinder behavioral change, for example, negative attitude toward condom use. Enabling factors refer to personal (e.g., low self-esteem), social (e.g., social alienation), and institutional (e.g., exclusionary laws) barriers. Reinforcing factors are those attitudes and behaviors of others—like friends, health care personnel, family members—that may encourage or discourage the target individual to change his or her health behavior; for example, sex without a condom is the "community norm." Phase 5 goes beyond the examination of the predisposing, enabling, and reinforcing factors (Phase 4) to deciding which combination of these factors are going to be the central focus of the health intervention, for example, health messages aimed at changing attitudes and beliefs about condoms and making condom use a new community norm. Phase 6 is an administrative diagnosis and it refers to the actual development and implementation of a health intervention program, for example, design and implementation of an innovative outreach program for sex workers in the community. Finally, Phase 7 is the ongoing evaluation of the program and it includes Phases 1 through 6, for example, soliciting feedback from sex workers in the community (the target audience) and using such feedback to improve the existing outreach program.

Using the steps of this framework, we now turn to qualitative data we collected through a series of three focus groups[1] that included transgender and transsexual persons, researchers, and service providers for the transgender and transsexual community. These focus groups were designed to increase our understanding of the social and cultural reality of transgender and transsexual individuals living in Los Angeles, one of the largest HIV/AIDS epicenters in the country.

THE SOCIAL AND CULTURAL CONTEXT OF TRANSGENDERS AND TRANSSEXUALS IN LOS ANGELES

Our qualitative data were collected from three focus groups. The theme of the first focus group was to identify sociocultural factors underlying HIV/AIDS education, prevention, and service delivery for transgenders and transsexuals. The theme of the second focus group was

---

[1]The focus groups were conducted in Los Angeles, California, October 1995. Each focus group had six participants who were identified as "experts on transgender/transsexual issues" in Los Angeles because of their own personal experiences as transgender/transsexual persons and/or their professional experiences as service providers or researchers in this area of scholarship. We would like to express our gratitude, appreciation, and recognition for their commitment and dedication to the gender-transposed community in Los Angeles.

to explore socioculturally appropriate HIV/AIDS education, prevention, and service delivery programs for this population. The theme of the third focus group was to develop a research agenda that reflects the needs of transgender and transsexual persons.

Although our qualitative data are largely exploratory, and therefore, not generalizable to the larger transgender/transsexual community in Los Angeles, they provide us with a greater understanding of the social and cultural contexts in which transgender and transsexual individuals live. Based on our focus group data and using PRECEDE as the organizing framewok, we report our findings in terms of the different steps of the model.

Phase 1: Quality of Life

As indicated earlier, Phase 1 focuses on the quality of life of the target community by assessing some of the general problems that individuals in such a community might experience. Several problems affecting the quality of life of transgender and transsexual persons were identified: (a) high incidence of prostitution, (b) discrimination, (c) homophobia, (d) sexism, (e) lack of political representation, and (f) family estrangement.

According to our focus group participants, a substantial percentage of transgenders and transsexuals are involved in sex work or "survival sex." As is discussed later, this type of activity is often associated with alcoholism and drug use. Our participants also noted that transgender/transsexual sex workers are most often hired by heterosexual men. Many of them prefer to play the passive role ("the insertee") when they engage in anal intercourse. Further, many heterosexual clients, fearing stigmatization, are not forthcoming about their sexual activities with transgender/transsexual sex workers and, therefore, can easily infect their unsuspecting intimate relational partners. In essence, this situation can be a secret and dangerous path for the further spread of HIV among heterosexuals, or as the government would call it, the general population.

Discrimination was perceived to be both internal and external; as a focus group participant described, "You know, there really is a lot of discrimination both internal and external. For example, internally, there is competition between transsexuals, transgenders, transvestites, and other groups. . . . These different groups view each other as a threat, in competition for social services." The need for more networking and cooperation between these subcommunities was noted. In addition, there appears to be a status hierarchy within the gender-transposed community with transsexuals on the high end of the status continuum and drag queens on the low end. Our focus group members reported that, in some instances, a nontranssexual person would self-identify as a transsexual to increase his or her status in the community. In other instances, individuals who renounce their transgender identity may be perceived as a threat to the identity of the group and pressure is exercised on the individual to maintain such identity, thus creating further psychological conflict.

Discrimination from external sources was also reported. Examples of external discrimination include housing, employment, and health insurance. In addition, discrimination exists against non-HIV-infected members of the community; as one participant indicated, "It's really sad to see that social services are more readily available to transgenders and transsexuals who are HIV-positive."

Homophobia was also documented in the community. Homophobic attitudes may be associated with the confusion between gender identity (the individual's perception and awareness of his or her biological sex) and sexual orientation (the individual's affectional tendencies). This confusion is manifested in the inability of the general public and helping professionals to accept a transgender/transsexual who is also lesbian or gay in their transgender identity—for example, a biological male who has a female gender identity and is romantically involved with a biological woman with a female gender identity would be considered lesbian in terms of sexual orientation even though the two biological bodies might be heterosexually relating. "Those in our community who self-identify in this manner are oftentimes referred to as hysterical lesbians or gays," a focus group participant added.

Sexism is faced by members of the community who are male-to-female transgenders/transsexuals. Focus group participants noted that these individuals are harassed more than female-to-male transgenders/transsexuals. Beauty bias, which may be perceived as an extension of sexism, or as one participant put it, "the *Cosmopolitan* syndrome," also plays an important role in the community. For example, service providers tend to discourage sex reassignment surgery if the patient is less than attractive.

Focus group members also indicated that their quality of life would be significantly enhanced if the transsexual/transgender community had greater political representation at all levels of government. At the present time, transgenders and transsexuals are generally not acknowledged as a legitimate group and, therefore, are excluded from existing antidiscriminatory legislation from which other minority communities benefit.

Family estrangement was a major factor for most transgenders/transsexuals. Focus group participants recalled numerous stories of alienation, hurt, and exclusion from their own families; one participant, a male-to-female transsexual, seemed to succinctly capture the sentiment of the group: "My family hasn't talked to me since my decision to live publicly as a woman." An extension of this problem are issues of lost history that is either repressed, changed, or denied due to gender transposition.

Phase 2: Health Problems

The second phase identifies particular health problems that appear to be contributing to the social problems observed in the first phase. Our focus group participants identified three health problems in the transgender and transsexual community: alcoholism and drug use, sexual compulsion, and needle sharing. As stated earlier, stigma, discrimination, and family estrangement are common experiences in the daily lives of transgenders and transsexuals. Along with this persistent social alienation, focus group members reported that alcoholism and high incidence of drug use was observed in the community. This situation appears to be especially true of transgender/transsexual sex workers who use substances to "get high" to cope with the nature of their work which, in turn, supports the substance dependence, thus creating a cycle of addiction and survival sex.

Sex in the transgender and transsexual community appears to be an important vehicle for: physical survival (survival sex), and gender confirmation and affirmation ("validation sex"). Sex for survival and gender validation are not mutually exclusive and they often occur together. As indicated earlier, survival sex provides the male-to-female transgender/transsexual a way to earn an income to support herself and her lifestyle whereas validation sex offers a sense of psychological affirmation that she is desirable as a woman. Some focus group participants noted that validation sex can often be carried out to compulsive extremes; for example, the more sexual activity a male-to-female transgender/transsexual engages in, the more validated she might feel as a woman.

Hormone therapy (i.e., receiving medical attention from a physician, laboratory tests, and prescriptions) is an extremely expensive treatment. Because of this, many transgenders and transsexuals resort to obtaining hormones through the black market or purchasing them in Mexico. Inexpensive and poor-quality hormones and surgery pose a major health threat to members in this community. Additionally, many members share needles while self-administering hormone therapy; as one participant stated, "You know, you are really desperate to get hormones, so you share needles. What's important is getting those hormones!" Needless to say, the potential for the transmission of HIV and other communicable diseases is quite apparent in the practice of needle sharing.

Phase 3: Behaviors Associated With Health Problems

Phase 3 is a behavioral diagnosis: It focuses on the discovery of specific health-related behaviors that appear to be associated to the health problems identified in Phase 2. Focus group participants noted that unprotected sex and needle sharing are two health behaviors that put many transgenders and transsexuals at risk for HIV infection and other communicable diseases. Some of these participants observed that for many transgender/transsexual sex workers: (a) Sex with a condom with clients might be difficult because they may not feel like that they are in a position to negotiate or that negotiation is not gender affirming, that is, not a feminine behavior for a male-to-female transgender/transsexual, and (b) sex with a condom with an intimate relational partner may be an indication of mistrust in the relationship. Finally, needle sharing for hormones, as discussed earlier, is another behavior that can endanger the health of transgender and transsexual individuals.

Phase 4: Predisposing, Enabling, and Reinforcing Factors

Phase 4 focuses on specific predisposing, enabling, and reinforcing factors. Predisposing factors are those individual's attitudes, beliefs, values, and perceptions that facilitate or hinder behavioral change, for example, the belief that negotiating for condom use is not a gender-affirming activity or the belief that unprotected sexual activity with "someone one loves" is an indication of trust. Enabling factors refer to personal, social, and institutional barriers, for example, financial difficulties, social stigmatization, invisibility, lack of institutional legitimacy. Reinforcing factors are those attitudes and behaviors of others that may encourage or discourage the target individual to change his or her health behavior.

Our focus group participants noted that social service agencies for the transgender/transsexual community generally lack sensitivity to the unique needs of the individuals in this community. For example, many transgenders and transsexuals are turned away at shelters because their gender presentations do not coincide with their gender identity or physiological reality. Additional problems include, but are not limited to, conflicts over which restroom to use, confusion over dormitory assignments, and conflicts over which showers to utilize. According to our participants, agency staff oftentimes, through lack of sensitivity training, imposed their own religious and moral principles upon the client in spite of the obvious conflict with the client's identity. Other examples of insensitivity and incompetence include the use of improper pronouns, by both the staff and residents, when addressing a client, for example, using *she* to call a female-to-male (FTM) transgender when the more appropriate address for this individual's gender self-presentation is *he*. Lastly, many caseworkers tend to treat gender identity issues as an addiction rather than a complex social behavior.

DEVELOPING TRANSGENDER/ TRANSSEXUAL-SENSITIVE PROGRAMS

Focus group participants examined ways to create, design, and implement programs that contain messages that are sensitive to the transgender and transsexual community. Four issues were raised, including the need for a Transgender/Transsexual Demonstration Project, sensitivity training for service providers, advocacy, and additional educational programs. Under educational programs, some suggestions for outreach programs for transgenders and transsexuals were presented.

Speaking for the group, a participant emphatically stated, "What we really need is for the CDC to conduct a Transgender/Transsexual Demonstration Project." The participants suggested several steps for this process. First, the demonstration project should conduct a needs assessment of the community. Second, it should develop educational strategies for the community and the public at large (e.g., appropriate curriculum, motivating messages, etc.). Third, these findings can be incorporated into the demonstration project. Fourth, and finally, a project evaluation should be conducted to assess its effectiveness before it is shared and implemented at a national level.

Sensitivity training for health care providers is another essential aspect of the educational process. A male-to-female transsexual recalled, "Sometimes agency workers use the incorrect personal pronoun, for example calling me 'he' instead of 'she' . . . sometimes, if we are preoperative, we are given dormitory, restroom, and bathroom assignments that we are extremely uncomfortable with like being asked to use men's restrooms and showers." Health service providers need to be sensitized to the special needs and issues of the transgender/transsexual community. Additionally, health care and social service programs need to be designed to include transgender/transsexual clients; in particular, health care programs can allocate resources for transgenders/transsexuals—for example, the Weingart Center in Los Angeles currently holds an HIV clinic specifically for transgenders.

Advocacy is another integral part of education. Advocacy in the form of legislation was most important to focus group participants. Among the legislative activities that were noted are the formation of a Los Angeles County HIV/AIDS transgender/transsexual task force, the creation by the L.A. city mayor of a commission on transgender/transsexual affairs, and legislation passed to account for the transgender/transsexual population in governmental data gathering (e.g., census, city-wide needs assessments, etc.). Other advocacy measures could include incorporating transgenders and transsexuals into the groups currently protected under antidiscriminatory legislation.

The City of Los Angeles, Community Development Department, could, for example, open a one-time request for proposals (RFP) process that would fund agencies working with the transgender/transsexual community. In the past the city has opened up the RFP process to youth and gang development programs and agencies with only 1 year's experience. The advantage of this type of RFP is that they do not have to compete with more established agencies (e.g., organizations with many years of experience and perhaps national funding). The RFP process would work in the following manner: (a) Agencies providing services to the transgender/transsexual community would submit RFPs in order to obtain funding for their agencies, (b) the Community Development Department would make funding recommendations, (c) funding would be granted to agencies upon city council and mayoral approval, and (d) once funded, the agencies become part of the city's human service delivery system. Working with government agencies is rather tedious and time consuming. It would be in the best interest of the members of the transgender/transsexual community to develop working relationships with elected officials (e.g., city council members or county supervisors).

The transgender/transsexual community could also gain clout by forming its own political organization, not unlike ACT UP or QUEER NATION in the gay community, which have been successful in getting the attention of politicians at the local, state, and national levels. Another possibility is to form a "Sexual Minority Coalition" not unlike the "Rainbow Coalition" whereby all sexual minorities could advocate for common needs. What is clear is that advocacy via legislation and the political machinery is necessary for the survival of this marginalized community.

In addition, all participants noted that service providers need to offer more educational programs for the community. Examples of such programs might include: jobs skills training, general equivalency diploma classes, job placement programs, and rapport building with local businesses to improve the level of hiring of transgender/transsexual employees.

Some suggestions were made to improve outreach efforts. First, outreach activities need to provide materials that are sensitive to the members of the community; for example, a male-to-female transsexual in our group indicated, "I want to get a care package that has things that I need like lipstick and feminine hygiene products . . . don't insult me by giving me razors and aftershave!" Second, all outreach efforts should use community outreach workers with whom the target population can relate; for example, hire transgenders and transsexuals as community outreach workers. Third, and perhaps most important, outreach workers must somehow differentiate themselves from commercial sex workers so that the target group does not feel threatened. A participant, capturing the sentiment of others, summarized for the group: "The community itself needs to be a part of the entire service delivery process; they need to be seen in the boardroom, as grant writers, administrators, researchers, designing curricula and of course on the 'front lines.' But don't limit their involvement to just outreach work on the streets." Fourth, and finally, educational literature must be culturally and linguistically appropriate for the target individuals.

DEVELOPING A BASIC RESEARCH AGENDA

Focus group participants noted that a research agenda that reflects the needs of the transgender and transsexual community is twofold: social scientific and behavioral research, and biomedical research. In terms of social scientific and behavioral research, several needs were noted: (a) the development of a more accurate taxonomy for differentiating sex, gender, gender role, gender identification, and sexual orientation, (b) the relationship between social alienation, prostitution, and HIV/AIDS, (c) the rituals of needle sharing for hormones, (d) the social organization and hierarchies in the community including rites of passage and rituals, (e) the sexual behavior of transgender/transsexual sex workers and their clients, and (f) the communication behaviors between sex workers and clients.

Biomedical research needs were also examined. They include: (a) examination of brain differences between women, men, female-to-male transgenders/transsexuals, and male-to-female transgenders/transsexuals, among others, (b) exploration of the connection between hormone use, drug use, and HIV infection, (c) examination of the long-term effects of hormone therapy, and (d) exploration of the aging process among transgenders and transsexuals, among others.

SUMMARY, CONCLUSIONS, AND FUTURE DIRECTIONS

The HIV epidemic has devastated sexual minorities, including the gender-transposed community. Although it has been noted that HIV is a serious health crisis among transgenders and transsexuals, there is a paucity of research in this area. This exploratory study was conducted for fill this important research need.

Because the PRECEDE model takes into account the larger social and cultural context in the creation of health intervention programs, we argue that it is a suitable model for the diagnosis, creation, design, implementation, and evaluation of health messages and educational programs for transgenders and transsexuals. To increase our understanding of such a social and cultural context, three focus groups were conducted. In general, we identified several problems that are related to quality of life in the transgender/transsexual community including high incidence of prostitution, internal and external discrimination, homophobia, sexism, lack of political representation, and family estrangement. Along with these problems, we also found some specific health concerns in the community—for example, alcoholism and drug use, sexual compulsion, and needle sharing—which appear to be linked to some risky behaviors associated with HIV transmission, namely, unprotected sex and needle sharing for hormones. In addition, some of the predisposing, enabling, and reinforcing factors were explored.

Although our research focused on the social and cultural context of transgenders and transsexuals in Los Angeles, several other reports noted similar findings with transgenders in the Tenderloin district of the San Francisco Bay Area (Greenberg, 1993), in Kings Cross and Darlinghurst, Sydney, Australia (Perkins, 1996), and in the streets of London (Gibson, 1995). For example, Greenberg also documented internal (e.g., tensions between preop and postop transsexuals) and external (e.g., housing, police harassment) discrimination, lack of political recognition, and high incidence of prostitution. Although transgenders and transsexuals were integral in the Gay Liberation Movement and the Stonewall Riots, many experience exclusion from social and political activities in the gay and lesbian community.

Perkins (1996) reported that the transsexual community in the Kings Cross and Darlinghurst in Sydney, Australia, also display a hierarchical structure as well as tension from within the community regarding how this hierarchy was ordered. Four distinct groups were identified in the community: the showgirls, the strippers, the sex workers, and the girls who pick up men in bars and clubs. Perkins noted that there were actually three hierarchies in that community. First, according to prestige and community recognition, the following ranking was observed: showgirls, strippers, call girls, bar girls, and street girls. Second, according to financial gain, a different ranking was documented: street girls, call girls, strippers, showgirls, and bar girls. Finally, according to success at "passing" as women, another ranking was noted: strippers, call girls, bar girls, street girls, and show girls. As these hierarchies indicate, a sizable group of individuals in the community is involved in prostitution, sex work, and hypersexuality. Many of the clients are heterosexual.

In her work with sex workers in the streets of London, Gibson (1995) found that transgender and transsexual prostitutes have a history of childhood abuse and family estrangement, drug abuse, HIV infection, internal and external discrimination, and lacking political voice. For example, Gibson noted that these sex workers are routinely fined for soliciting and importuning and highway obstruction, thus maintaining the vicious cycle of selling sex, getting fined, and having a record (which severely limits future employment prospects) that keeps many of them in prostitution. Simone, a male-to-female transsexual sex worker, reported that although her work provides her with a living, drugs, and hormones, it is not always gender validating: "The first thing they [the clients] do is to tell you that they are straight and . . . It's just the willy they're after, not the girly things about you . . . Then they want you to screw them" (Gibson, 1995, p. 89). These situations can create further psychological and identity conflict for the transgender sex worker. They also concur with our own findings in Los Angeles.

Our focus group participants also examined ways to develop education programs and health messages that are sensitive to the characteristics of the transgender and transsexual population and provided some suggestions for a research agenda that reflects the needs of this population. Future research calls for the collaboration between communication scholars, psychologists, sociologists, social workers, health educators, medical practitioners, and biomedical researchers, among others, to increase our understanding of the social and cultural context of transgenders and transsexuals living against a backdrop of psychological conflict, fear, social alienation, discrimination, marginalization, and HIV infection.

ACKNOWLEDGMENTS

This project was partially supported by the California Universitywide AIDS Research Program (Grant Agreement C94-CSLA-141) and the City of Los Angeles Community Development Department Technical Assistance Funding, The Office of the AIDS Coordinator, awarded to the first author. An earlier version of this chapter was presented to the "Social and Cultural Construction of HIV/AIDS" Panel for the Eighty-second Annual Meeting of the National Communication Association, San Diego, California, 1996. Finally, we wish to acknowledge and thank Ferd Eggan, AIDS Coordinator, City of Los Angeles, for his support, and Diana Fisher, Josh E. Miller, and Michael A. Leonard for their assistance.

REFERENCES

Alteneder, R. R., Price, J. H., Telljohann, S. K., Didion, J., & Locher, A. (1992). Using the Precede model to determine junior-high-school students' knowledge, attitudes, and beliefs about AIDS. *Journal of School Health, 62*, 464–470.

Altman, D. (1986). *AIDS in the mind of America.* Garden City, NY: Anchor Press/Doubleday.

Amaro, H. (1993). Reproductive choice in the age of AIDS: Policy and counseling issues. In C. Squire (Ed.), *Women and AIDS: Psychological perspectives* (pp. 20–41). London: Sage.

Aoki, B., Ngin, C. P., Mo, B., & Ja, D. Y. (1989). AIDS prevention models in Asian-American communities. In V. M. Mays, G. W. Albee, & S. F. Schneider (Eds.), *Primary prevention of AIDS: Psychological approaches* (pp. 290–308). Newbury Park, CA: Sage.

Bailey, W. C., Richards, J. M., Manzella, B. A., Windsor, R. A., Brooks, C. M., & Soong, S. J. (1987). Promoting self-management in adults with asthma: An overview of the UAB program. *Health Education Quarterly, 14*, 345–355.

Bartholomew, L. K., Koenning, G., Dahlquist, L., & Barron, K. (1994). An educational needs assessment of children with juvenile rheumatoid arthritis. *Arthritis Care and Research, 7*, 136–143.

Benson, R., & Taub, D. E. (1993). Using the PRECEDE model for causal analysis of bulimic tendencies among elite women swimmers. *Journal of Health Education, 24*, 360–369.

Bonaguro, J. A. (1981). PRECEDE for wellness. *Journal of School Health, 51*, 501–506.

Bowen, S. P., & Michal-Johnson, P. (1995). "Telling them for real": A case of culture-specific HIV education for African Americans in the urban underclass. In L. K. Fuller & L. McPherson Shilling (Eds.), *Communicating about communicable diseases* (pp. 97–112). Amherst, MA: HRD Press.

Carballo-Dieguez, A. (1995). The sexual identity and behavior of Puerto Rican men who have sex with men. In G. M. Herek & B. Greene (Eds.), *AIDS, identity, and community: The HIV epidemic and lesbians and gay men* (pp. 105–114). Thousand Oaks, CA: Sage.

Catania, J. A., Coates, T. J., Golden, E., Dolcini, M., Peterson, J., Kegeles, S., Siegel, D., & Fullilove, M. T. (1994). Correlates of condom use among Black, Hispanic, and White heterosexuals in San Francisco: The AMEN longitudinal survey. *AIDS Education and Prevention, 6*, 12–26.

Chie, W. C., Cheng, K. W., Fu, C. H., & Yen, L. L. (1993). A study on women's practice of breast self-examination in Taiwan. *Preventive Medicine, 22*, 316–324.

Choi, K., Salazar, N., Lew, S., & Coates, T. J. (1995). AIDS risk, dual identity, and community response among gay Asian and Pacific Islander men in San Francisco. In G. M. Herek & B. Greene (Eds.), *AIDS, identity, and community: The HIV epidemic and lesbians and gay men* (pp. 115–134). Thousand Oaks, CA: Sage.

Cretain, G. K. (1989). Motivational factors in breast self-examination: Implications for nurses. *Cancer Nursing, 12*, 250–256.

Curran, J. W. (1988). AIDS in the United States. In R. F. Schinazi & A. J. Nahmias (Eds.), *AIDS in children, adolescents and heterosexual adults: An interdisciplinary approach to prevention* (pp. 10–12). New York: Elsevier.

Dignan, M., Sharp, P., Blinson, K., Michielutte, R., Konen, J., Bell, R., & Lane, C. (1995). Development of a cervical cancer education program for Native American women in North Carolina. *Journal of Cancer Education, 9*, 235–242.

Dunlap, P., & Berne, L. A. (1991). Addressing competitive stress in junior tennis players. *Journal of Physical Education, Recreation and Dance, 62*, 59–63.

Earp, J. A., Altpeter, M., Mayne, L., Viadro, C. I., & O'Malley, M. S. (1995). The North Carolina Breast Cancer Screening Program: Foundations and design of a model for reaching older, minority, rural women. *Breast Cancer Research and Treatment, 35*, 7–22.

Edgar, T., Freimuth, V. S., & Hammond, S. L. (1988). Communicating the AIDS risk to college students: The problem of motivating change. *Health Education Research, 3*, 59–65.

Eriksen, M. P., & Gielen, A. C. (1983). The application of health education principles to automobile child restraint programs. *Health Education Quarterly, 10*, 30–55.

Feldman, D. A., & Johnson, T. M. (1986). Introduction. In D. A. Feldman & T. M. Johnson (Eds.), *The social dimensions of AIDS: Method and theory* (pp. 1–12). New York: Praeger.

Frankish, C. J. (1994). Crisis centers and their role in treatment: Suicide prevention versus health promotion. In A. A. Leenaars, J. T. Maltsberger, & R. A. Neimeyer (Eds.), *Treatment of suicidal people* (pp. 33–43). Washington, DC: Taylor & Francis.

Gibson, B. (1995). *Male order: Life stories from boys who sell sex*. London: Cassell.

Gock, T. (1994). Acquired immunodeficiency syndrome. In N. W. S. Zane, D. T. Takeuchi, & K. N. J. Young (Eds.), *Confronting critical health issues of Asian and Pacific Islander Americans* (pp. 247–265). Newbury Park, CA: Sage.

Green, L. W., Kreuter, M. W., Deeds, S. G., & Partridge, K. B. (1980). *Health education planning: A diagnostic approach*. Palo Alto, CA: Mayfield.

Greenberg, S. (1993, July 13). The next wave. *The Advocate*, pp. 51–53.

Grise, M. C., Gauthier-Gagnon, C., & Martineau, G. G. (1993). Prosthetic profile of people with lower extremity amputation: Conception and design of a follow-up questionnaire. *Archives of Physical Medicine and Rehabilitation, 74*, 862–870.

Grover, J. Z. (1987). AIDS: Keywords. In D. Crimp (Ed.), *AIDS: Cultural analysis, cultural activism* (pp. 17–30). Cambridge, MA: MIT Press.

Herek, G. M. (1995). Preface. In G. M. Herek & B. Greene (Eds.), *AIDS, identity, and community: The HIV epidemic and lesbians and gay men* (pp. ix–xii). Thousand Oaks, CA: Sage.

Jenny, J. (1993). A future perspective on patient/health education in Canada. *Journal of Advanced Nursing, 18*, 1408–1414.

Kloos, H. (1995). Human behavior, health education and schistosomiasis control: A review. *Social Science and Medicine, 40*, 1497–1511.

Kramer, L. (1989). *Reports from the holocaust: The making of an AIDS activist*. New York: St. Martin's Press.

Landau-Stanton, J., & Clements, C. D. (1993). *AIDS, health, and mental health: A primary sourcebook*. New York: Brunner/Mazel.

Lohrmann, D. K., & Fors, S. W. (1986). Can school-based educational programs really be expected to solve the adolescent drug abuse problem? *Journal of Drug Education, 16*, 327–339.

Mansour, A. A., & Hassan, S. A. (1994). Factors that influence women's nutrition knowledge in Saudi Arabia. *Health Care for Women International, 15*, 213–223.

Marín, B. V., & Marín, G. (Eds.). (1990). Hispanics and AIDS [Special issue]. *Hispanic Journal of Behavioral Sciences, 12*(2).

Mays, V. M. (1989). AIDS prevention in Black populations: Methods of a safer kind. In V. M. Mays, G. W. Albee, & S. F. Schneider (Eds.), *Primary prevention of AIDS: Psychological approaches* (pp. 264–279). Newbury Park, CA: Sage.

Meagher, D., & Mann, K. V. (1990). The effect of an educational program on knowledge and attitudes about blood pressure by junior high school students: A pilot project. *Canadian Journal of Cardiovascular Nursing, 1*, 15–22.

Metts, S., & Fitzpatrick, M. A. (1992). Thinking about safer sex: The risky business of "knowing your partner" advice. In T. Edgar, M. A. Fitzpatrick, & V. S. Freimuth (Eds.), *AIDS: A communication perspective* (pp. 1–19). Hillsdale, NJ: Lawrence Erlbaum Associates.

Michal-Johnson, P., & Bowen, S. P. (1992). The place of culture in HIV education. In T. Edgar, M. A. Fitzpatrick, & V. S. Freimuth (Eds.), *AIDS: A communication perspective* (pp. 147–172). Hillsdale, NJ: Lawrence Erlbaum Associates.

Michielutte, R., Dignan, M. B., Wells, H. B., Young, L. D., Jackson, D. S., & Sharp, P. C. (1989). Development of a community cancer education program: The Forsyth County, NC cervical cancer prevention project. *Public Health Reports, 104*, 542–551.

Morin, S. F., Charles, K. A., & Malyon, A. K. (1984). The psychological impact of AIDS on gay men. *American Psychologist, 39*, 1288–1293.

Mullen, P. D., Hersey, J. C., & Iverson, D. C. (1987). Health behavior models compared. *Social Science and Medicine, 24*, 973–981.

Myrick, R. (1995). Communicating about empowerment in an environment of silence: Public and community-based HIV and AIDS education for gay men in Oklahoma. In L. K. Fuller & L. McPherson Shilling (Eds.), *Communicating about communicable diseases* (pp. 113–123). Amherst, MA: HRD Press.

O'Meara, C. (1993). An evaluation of consumer perspectives of childbirth and parenting education. *Midwifery, 9,* 210–219.

Opdycke, R. A., Ascione, F. J., Shimp, L. A., & Rosen, R. I. (1992). A systematic approach to educating elderly patients about their medications. *Patient Education and Counseling, 19,* 43–60.

Osborn, J. E. (1989). A risk assessment of the AIDS epidemic. In V. M. Mays, G. W. Albee, & S. F. Schneider (Eds.), *Primary prevention of AIDS: Psychological approaches* (pp. 23–38). Newbury Park, CA: Sage.

Patton, C. (1996). *Fatal advice: How safe-sex education went wrong.* Durham, NC: Duke University Press.

Perkins, R. (1996). The "drag queen scene": Transsexuals in Kings Cross. In R. Ekins & D. King (Eds.), *Blending genders: Social aspects of cross-dressing and sex-changing* (pp. 53–62). London: Routledge.

Peterson, J. L. (1995). AIDS-related risks and same-sex behaviors among African American men. In G. M. Herek & B. Greene (Eds.), *AIDS, identity, and community: The HIV epidemic and lesbians and gay men* (pp. 85–104). Thousand Oaks, CA: Sage.

Polcyn, M. M., Price, J. H., Jurs, S. G., & Roberts, S. M. (1991). Utility of the Precede model in differentiating users and nonusers of smokeless tobacco. *Journal of School Health, 61,* 166–171.

Reardon, K. K. (1988). The potential role of persuasion in health promotion and disease prevention: Review and commentary. In J. Anderson (Ed.), *Communication yearbook XI* (pp. 277–297). Newbury Park, CA: Sage.

Reardon, K. K. (1989). The potential role of persuasion in adolescent AIDS prevention. In R. Rice & C. Atkin (Eds.), *Public communication campaigns* (pp. 273–289). Newbury Park, CA: Sage.

Rubin, G. S. (1993). Thinking sex: Notes for a radical theory of the politics of sexuality. In H. Abelove, M. A. Barale, & D. M. Halperin (Eds.), *The lesbian and gay studies reader* (pp. 3–44). New York: Routledge.

Rubinson, L., & Baillie, L. (1981). Planning school based sexuality programs utilizing the PRECEDE model. *Journal of School Health, 51,* 282–287.

Scheerhorn, D. (1995). Hemophiliacs talk about HIV/AIDS. In L. K. Fuller & L. McPherson Shilling (Eds.), *Communicating about communicable diseases* (pp. 125–138). Amherst, MA: HRD Press.

Shayne, V. T., & Kaplan, B. J. (1988). AIDS education for adolescents. *Youth & Society, 20,* 180–208.

Silvestri, A. (1993). *Handbook on the gender transposed: A guide for social service providers.* Los Angeles: Author.

Singer, M., Jia, Z., Schensul, J. J., Weeks, M. R., & Page, J. B. (1992). AIDS and the IV drug user: The local context in prevention efforts. *Medical Anthropology, 14,* 285–306.

Squire, C. (1993). Introduction. In C. Squire (Ed.), *Women and AIDS: Psychological perspectives* (pp. 1–15). London: Sage.

Stanton, B., Black, M., Feigelman, S., Ricardo, I., Galbraith, J., Li, X., Kaljee, L., Keane, V., & Nesbitt, R. (1995). Development of a culturally, theoretically and developmentally based survey instrument for assessing risk behaviors among African-American early adolescents living in urban low-income neighborhoods. *AIDS Education and Prevention, 7,* 160–177.

Taylor, V. M., Taplin, S. H., Urban, N., Mahloch, J., & Majer, K. A. (1994). Medical community involvement in a breast cancer screening promotional project. *Public Health Reports, 109,* 491–499.

Treichler, P. A. (1987). AIDS, homophobia, and biomedical discourse: An epidemic of signification. In D. Crimp (Ed.), *AIDS: Cultural analysis, cultural activism* (pp. 31–70). Cambridge, MA: MIT Press.

Weeks, M. R., Schensul, J. J., Williams, S. S., Singer, M., & Grier, M. (1995). AIDS prevention for African-American and Latina women: Building culturally and gender-appropriate intervention. *AIDS Education and Prevention, 7,* 251–263.

Wilson, R. W. (1986). The PRECEDE model for mental health education. *Journal of Human Behavior and Learning, 3,* 34–41.

Witte, K. (1992a). Preventing AIDS through persuasive communications: A framework for constructing effective, culturally-specific health messages. *International and Intercultural Communication Annual, 16,* 67–86.

Witte, K. (1992b). The role of threat and efficacy in AIDS prevention. *International Quarterly of Community Health Education, 12,* 225–249.

Yep, G. A. (1992). Communicating the HIV/AIDS risk to Hispanic populations: A review and integration. *Hispanic Journal of Behavioral Sciences, 14,* 403–420.

Yep, G. A. (1993a). Health beliefs and HIV prevention: Do they predict monogamy and condom use? *Journal of Social Behavior and Personality, 8,* 507–520.

Yep, G. A. (1993b). HIV/AIDS in Asian and Pacific Islander communities in the United States: A review, analysis, and integration. *International Quarterly of Community Health Education, 13,* 293–315.

Yep, G. A. (1995). Healthy desires, unhealthy practices: Interpersonal influence strategies for the prevention of HIV/AIDS among Hispanics. In L. K. Fuller & L. McPherson Shilling (Eds.), *Communicating about communicable diseases* (pp. 139–154). Amherst, MA: HRD Press.

Yep, G. A. (1997). Overcoming barriers in HIV/AIDS education for Asian Americans: Toward more effective cultural communication. In D. C. Umeh (Ed.), *Confronting the AIDS epidemic: Cross-cultural perspectives in HIV/AIDS education* (pp. 219–230). Lawrenceville, NJ: Africa World Press.

Yep, G. A. (in press). "See no evil, hear no evil, speak no evil": Educating Asian Americans about HIV/AIDS through culture-specific health communication campaigns. In L. K. Fuller (Ed.), *Media-mediated AIDS*. Cresskill, NJ: Hampton Press.

Yep, G. A., Miller, J. E., & Parker-Cobb, S. (1994, November). *The transgender and transsexual communities: The last frontier of HIV transmission.* Paper presented at the 80th annual meeting of the National Communication Association, New Orleans.

The Power of Romance: Changing the Focus of AIDS Education Messages

Yvonne Kellar-Guenther
Western Illinois University

The following is a poem I wrote to summarize the findings of a review of HIV literature, input from 48 respondents who participated in in-depth interviews, and input from over 700 respondents who have participated in two quantitative studies. This poem was written to help provide insight into why young adults, who have extensive knowledge of HIV and its impact, do not engage in safer-sex behaviors, specifically sexual history discussions. I entitled this poem, "The Ultimate Sacrifice."

I look at you across the room
And I am overcome by desire.
You are beautiful.

I watch you talk with others
And I want you to talk with me.
I watch you share with others
And I want you to share with me.
I watch you smile at others
And I want you to smile at me.
And then it happens.
Our gazes meet
And our eyes speak of our desire.
You slowly make your way over to me
And I wait.
I will always wait.
You reach me and we decide to go somewhere private.
I follow.
I will always follow.
We sit down
And suddenly you are talking to me,
sharing with me,
smiling at me.

And I am in heaven.
My dreams have come true.

We talk, we share, we laugh
For what seems like hours.
My attraction grows stronger.
I want to share more.

You invite me back to your place and I follow.
I will always follow.
You go to get our coats while I wait.
I will always wait.
I look up and I see myself in the mirror.
Who are you? I ask myself.
No reply.
I continue to look.
The longer I look, the uglier I become.
I am alone, waiting.
Waiting to follow.
I remember times past when I waited and followed
Only to be left.
Still I wait. Still I follow.
Was it worth it?
Will it be worth it?

In the background I hear a voice
"Know your partner," it screams.
I am silent.
You return.

On the drive home I look at you.
I want to ask you questions but I am afraid.
Of what you might say.
Of what you might do.
I am silent.
Finally, I turn away into the night.

What would you think if you knew
I wondered
About the secrets that I keep.
Would you still be interested in talking with me,
sharing with me,
smiling with me?
Or would you turn away?
I wait.
I will always wait.

You walk into your home.
I follow.
I will always follow.
You turn to look at me and I am overwhelmed by desire.
You move to embrace me
And I catch my reflection in the mirror.
I am beautiful again
I am in your arms.

You draw back and I look into your eyes.
What secrets do you keep? I wonder.
But I am afraid to ask.
Inside a voice whispers, "Know your partner."
I look at you and I feel fear.
But I am silent.

You smile at me and I smile back.
Do you know the sacrifices I am willing to make?
Do you understand the price I am willing to pay?
To talk with you.
To share with you.
To smile at you.

The voice whispers again
"Know your partner"
But you reach for me
And it is pushed away
By desire.

In my research I have found that young adults have a strong desire to be in a romantic relationship. AIDS education messages, however, do not appear to account for this desire. Currently, most AIDS education messages focus on disseminating knowledge about HIV/AIDS transmission and safer-sex prevention behaviors (Markova & Power, 1992). To motivate individuals to enact safer-sex behaviors (e.g., condom use, abstinence, sexual history discussions), these educational messages stress the fact AIDS is a deadly disease (Freimuth, Hammond, Edgar, & Monahan, 1990). Although these messages may be very effective for some groups, they are not effective for young adults, the largest at-risk group for contracting HIV (Mahoney, Thombs, & Ford, 1995). In this chapter I argue that educators working to motivate young adults need to change the focus of their message from the danger of AIDS as a health risk to the danger of AIDS as a relational risk. To show this, I review the literature, including my own work, that demonstrates that young adults (a) are not changing their behavior despite their knowledge of HIV/AIDS, (b) do not fear dying, and (c) are interested in being in a romantic/sexual relationship. I also review my research findings, which suggest that this desire can serve to be an effective catalyst for encouraging young adults to engage in safer sex. The chapter ends with some suggestions for ways educators can alter their AIDS education messages to utilize young adults' desires to be in a romantic relationship and some suggestions for future research.

YOUNG ADULTS' AIDS PREVENTION BEHAVIORS

Past research shows that although college students are educated about the acquisition and prevention of HIV/AIDS, infection rates for this group continue to rise (Baldwin & Baldwin, 1988; DiClemente, Forrest, & Mickler, 1990; Stiff, McCormack, Zook, Stein, & Henry, 1990). Approximately 67% of all AIDS cases have occurred in adults 20–39 years of age (Mahoney et al., 1995). HIV is, in fact, the leading cause of death for young adults in the United States (Selik, Chu, & Buehler, 1993). Because the latency period between the acquisition of HIV and the diagnosis of AIDS ranges from 1 month to 10 years, these statistics suggest that

HIV/AIDS is most likely acquired during adolescence or early adulthood (Keller, 1993; Mahoney et al., 1995).

Young adults may become increasingly infected with HIV due to their reluctance to adopt safer-sex practices. For example, whereas gay men as a whole have been the most successful in adopting safer-sex behaviors (Becker & Joseph, 1988), gay men in college continue to engage in risky sexual practices (D'Augelli, 1992). Young heterosexuals also continue to engage in dangerous sexual behaviors. Sixty-three percent of Kusseling, Shapiro, Greenberg, and Wenger's (1996) heterosexual respondents ($n = 652$) reported not having safer sex with their last sexual partner. This statistic becomes more alarming when one learns that 45% of Kashima, Gallois, and McCamish's (1992) heterosexual respondents who stated they did take precautions against HIV/AIDS listed exclusivity as their primary prevention strategy. In addition, DiClemente et al. (1990) found that only 8% of those who reported using condoms used them regularly during sexual intercourse. It is, in fact, this combination of serial monogamy (one partner for several months) and unprotected sex with that partner that places young adults at risk for contracting HIV (Hammer, Fisher, Fitzgerald, & Fisher, 1996; Rosenthal, Moore, & Brumen, 1990). Taken as a whole, these findings show that current AIDS education appears to have little relation to prevention behaviors for young adults (Baldwin & Baldwin, 1988; Caron, David, Wynn, & Roberts, 1992; Edgar, Freimuth, & Hammond, 1988).

Fear Appeals and Fear of Dying

Currently, most AIDS education messages attempt to use fear appeals; specifically, they claim that individuals may die from contracting HIV/AIDS. For example, one AIDS education brochure states, "Even though it's hard to bring up the subject of safer sex, DO IT! Your life depends on practicing only safer sex" (Education Training Research Associates [ETR], 1987). Messages such as this one can be seen in numerous AIDS education brochures and books. Even messages that attempt to show that healthy-looking people can be infected with HIV typically include a life-threatening fear appeal (e.g., America Responds to AIDS campaigns). Research that analyzed the relationship between age and fear appeals, however, reveals that these messages are more effective for older audiences than younger ones (Boster & Mongeau, 1984).

Young adults may reject the fear appeals because they are unable to personalize the risk that is being stated. This lack of personalization is evident in past research that looks at fear of contracting HIV/AIDS. Several studies have revealed that young adults believe AIDS is someone else's problem (Caron et al., 1992; Goertzel & Bluebond-Langer, 1991; Kowaleski, Zeller, & Willis, 1991; Manning, Barenberg, Gallese, & Rice, 1989; Mickler, 1993). For example, a 21-year-old heterosexual male respondent in one of my studies ($n = 48$) stated, "If all these people are supposed to have AIDS, how come I don't know anyone who does?" (Kellar-Guenther, 1994). This was a statement I actually heard several times while collecting data. The message that HIV/AIDS is rampant is not personalized by several of my respondents because it does not fit within their experiences.

This lack of personalization can be explained by Freud's (1918) theory of the fear of death. Freud stated that individuals cannot fear death because they have not yet experienced death. Instead, he argued, individuals have fears regarding death that are centered around past experiences such as the fear of separation or the fear of ceasing to exist. I did, in fact, find that none of my 15 heterosexual respondents in another study feared dying at all (Kellar-Guenther, 1995). Rather, my respondents stated that they feared that their romantic partners would reject them. For these respondents, death seemed unrealistic. Freud would argue that this is because they had not experienced death yet and, as a result, could not fear the unknown. My respondents had, however, been rejected and knew that being rejected was a painful experience.

In addition to not fearing death, young adults have been found to have a low fear of disease (Shayne & Kaplan, 1988; Weinstein, 1984, 1989). This lack of fear is called the optimistic bias. Although people in general tend to underestimate their vulnerability to illness, adolescents who engage in risky behaviors are even more likely to believe they are not susceptible to illness (Shayne & Kaplan, 1988). In past research, young respondents who have placed themselves in high-risk groups for various illnesses still underestimate their susceptibility to that particular illness (Weinstein, 1984, 1989). This optimistic bias seems to be used by respondents in several AIDS prevention studies and serves to highlight the gap between knowledge and behavior.

There have been, in fact, several studies whose findings accentuate the division between young adults' knowledge and condom use. For example, Baldwin and Baldwin (1988) found that although 28% of their 513 respondents had taken a campus sex education course, only 1% of their sample thought there was a strong chance they would contract HIV/AIDS. This is startling considering 66% of their sample reported never using a condom in the last 3 months. DuBuono, Zinner, Daamen, and McCormack (1990) reported that although a majority of their respondents were concerned about contracting HIV, they were unlikely to use a condom regularly.

Similar findings can be seen in the research on sexual history discussions. Although young heterosexuals professed they know they and their partners should discuss their sexual pasts (Edgar, Hammond, & Freimuth, 1989; Metts & Fitzpatrick, 1992), Bowen and Michal-Johnson (1989) reported that 40% of their respondents had, at some time, opted to not talk about AIDS with their romantic/sex partners even though they wished to talk. Similarly, 39% of Cline, Johnson, and Freeman's (1992) 588 respondents reported having never spoken with their sexual partners about AIDS and, of this group, 4.6% reported having wanted to talk. These findings show that although young adults have the knowledge to know how to protect themselves, they refuse to use that knowledge to competently enact safer-sex behaviors.

According to Spitzberg and Cupach (1984), competent behavior is the result of having the motivation to enact the behavior, the knowledge of how to act, and the skills to act adeptly. Past research assures us that young adults are aware of the AIDS risk (Keller, 1993; Stiff et al., 1990) and what precautions they can take (Maticka-Tyndale, 1991; Metts & Fitzpatrick, 1992). Young adults, then, may not be skillfully enacting safer-sex behaviors because they lack the motivation to do so (Kellar-Guenther & Christopher, 1997b; Maticka-Tyndale, 1991). Instead, they seem motivated and able to separate the knowledge they possess from their actual behaviors.

What is dangerous about this division of knowledge and behavior is that young adults may have created biased rationales to alleviate the dissonance this division creates. Maticka-Tyndale (1991) and Hammer and colleagues (1996), for example, found that their interviewees were able to "explain" the contradictions between their knowledge and actual practices in ways which seemingly absolved them of personal risk. These included: (a) an assumption that they were not subject to the "general rules" (e.g., "except for me"), (b) a disbelief of the "knowledge" (e.g., "they say that but they really just don't want us to . . ."), (c) an unwillingness to address the contradictions between their knowledge of transmission and their sexual activities (e.g., "I just don't want to think about that"), (d) the belief that the situation did not allow them to use their knowledge (e.g., they were under the influence of drugs or no condom was available), and (e) the belief that it is too late to take action anyway (e.g., "By that time, if she has it [HIV], you have it, too"). The reliance on these biases can best be explained by motivated reasoning.

Motivated Reasoning

Research on motivated reasoning states that "people are more likely to arrive at the conclusions they want to arrive at" (Kunda, 1990, p. 495). In other words, individuals' rationales for their behavior are motivated by directional goals or desired endpoints. These rationales are used to distort information so that the individual sees a consistency between their behavior and their knowledge. Although very few AIDS researchers have utilized this theory to predict and explain young adults' safer-sex behaviors, I have found this theory to be extremely useful. With motivated reasoning and the Health Belief Model (HBM), a theory used to explain preventive behavior for asymptomatic diseases (Janz & Becker, 1984), my coauthor and I were able to explain 46% of the variance in young heterosexuals' ($n = 317$) decision to engage in a sexual history discussion (Kellar-Guenther & Christopher, 1997b). This is double the amount of variance found by models that use the Theory of Reasoned Action (Ajzen & Fishbein, 1980; Fishbein & Middlestadt, 1989) and the HBM (e.g., Basen-Engquist, 1992).

Also, in another study the same coauthor and I are currently working on (Kellar-Guenther & Christopher, 1997a), motivated reasoning and the HBM enable us to explain 34% of the variance in 399 young heterosexuals' decision to use a condom. Needless to say, I believe motivated reasoning holds the key to changing young adults' behavior.

Here is an example of how motivated reasoning works. If an individual, Pat, desires a romantic relationship, that romantic relationship becomes Pat's directional goal. According to the research on motivated reasoning, Pat will enact behaviors necessary to have a romantic relationship and avoid behaviors that block this goal. If Pat perceives that a sexual history discussion or a condom request is a threat to the goal of initiating or maintaining a relationship, he will avoid those behaviors. Pat must, however, form a logical, rational argument justifying the decision to not engage in the preventive behavior. This argument must be logical enough to persuade a dispassionate observer but may be formed using biased heuristics, which allows Pat to move toward this directional goal (Kunda, 1990). By looking at past research, it is evident that young adults use a plethora of biased heuristics to justify their decision not to request a condom or engage in a sexual history discussion.

Biased Heuristics

When looking at past research on condom use and sexual history discussions, it became clear to me that there are three groups of biased heuristics that young adults appear to use. These include heuristics regarding personal factors, situational factors, and relational factors.

A majority of the biased heuristics identified by Maticka-Tyndale (1991) and Hammer et al. (1996) are personal factors. Overall, respondents in both of these studies were able to incorporate the belief that somehow they were not at risk for contracting HIV. Their arguments centered around the fact that, for some reason, they were not subject to the same rules (e.g., "except for me") as strangers (Maticka-Tyndale, 1991). This may be because they believe that HIV infection is a matter of luck (Kelly et al., 1990) and they are lucky enough not to contract it.

This line of reasoning is similar to the optimistic bias. As stated earlier, the optimistic bias is the belief that one is not susceptible to illness in general (Shayne & Kaplan, 1988). One reason young heterosexuals state they do not fear HIV/AIDS specifically is that they do not personally know anyone who has HIV or AIDS (Kellar-Guenther, 1994). This is similar to Freud's argument as to why individuals do not fear death. Hammer et al.'s (1996) respondents take this one step further and state that they have already exposed themselves to HIV and have not become infected. These young adults appear to be using their past behavior as an indicator that they are "immune" to HIV. Although one may believe that the argument that a group is immune to HIV would not be rational enough to persuade a dispassionate observer, history has shown that it actually is. During the early 1980s, the medical community thought that women could not contract HIV, that they were only carriers (Corea, 1992). For approximately 10 years, a large group of physicians believed women were immune, regardless of the fact that some of their female clients had HIV symptoms. Young adults now appear to believe that they are unable to contract HIV.

Another heuristic bias young adults appear to be using is the idea that one chooses healthy-looking partners and thus avoids having sexual intercourse with someone who is at risk (Maticka-Tyndale, 1991; Metts & Fitzpatrick, 1992). This bias is a blending of personal and situational factors. Young adults believe they control their situation by choosing the right sexual partner. Statements such as, "I won't have sex with someone unless I trust them and know their background" and "I know I'm not HIV positive because every girl I've been with I've known for a little while" (Hammer et al., 1996, p. 385) are seen throughout the literature. In fact, Maticka-Tyndale (1992) noted that selecting a sexual partner from a close circle of friends or friends of a friend was mentioned as the most popular form of protection against HIV for young heterosexuals.

By choosing someone they know or that another knows, young adults are able to apply another biased heuristic—implicit personality theory. Through implicit personality theories young adults are able to ascribe low risk to those the individuals whom they know, like, or love (Offir, Fisher, Williams, & Fisher, 1993; Williams et al., 1992).

Young adults in past research have also mentioned other situational factors that make it all right to forego using condoms. Although a majority of Hammer et al.'s (1996) participants believed that condom use was a responsible way to protect themselves and their partners from HIV, they claimed that there were situations in which it was difficult to use a condom. One situation was when an individual was under the influence of drugs or alcohol (Hammer et al., 1996; Kusseling et al., 1996) and therefore could not think clearly enough to remember to use a condom. Leigh and Miller (1995), however, found that combining sex with alcohol and drugs does not necessarily make an individual more likely to engage in riskier sexual intercourse. Alcohol and drug use, then, may be a ready-made excuse as to why an individual may not practice safer sex but not an actual deterrent.

Another situation that young adults believed inhibited condom use was the times when condoms were simply unavailable (Hammer et al., 1996; Kusseling et al., 1996). The individuals had used all their condoms or did not bring one to the interaction. One participant summed it up by stating "If you run out [before a sexual encounter], what are you going to do?" In fact, 15% of Kusseling et al.'s respondents said they engaged in unsafe sex because they "could not stop themselves." Clearly, for these young adults abstaining from sexual intercourse is not an option.

Finally, young adults appear to argue that they do not need to worry about HIV because they are involved in a romantic relationship (Hammer et al., 1996; Maticka-Tyndale, 1992). Research has, in fact, found that HIV preventive behavior is negatively correlated to the level of intimacy in a relationship (Moore & Barling, 1991; Valdiserri et al., 1988) and feelings of liking and romantic involvement (Edgar, Freimuth, Hammond, McDonald, & Fink, 1992). This is because the security of being in a committed relationship makes young adults feel as though they are no longer vulnerable to the threat of AIDS.

There are several examples in the literature that show that young adults do indeed believe that being in a relationship makes them immune to contracting HIV. For example, Hoff, Coates, Barrett, Collette, and Ekstrand (1996) reported that over 50% of the gay men in a relationship were nonmonogamous ($n = 1,034$). Regardless, a majority of HIV seronegative gay men in relationships were more likely to have anal intercourse than were single men (Hoff et al., 1996). In addition, individuals who are romantically involved with men who are HIV-positive also appear to believe that being in relationship will protect them from contracting HIV. For example, HIV-negative women who were in a romantic relationship with HIV-infected hemophiliac men still engaged in high levels of unprotected sex (Dublin, Rosenberg, & Goedeter, 1992). Sack (1992) also cited several cases of women she treats who know that their romantic partner is HIV-positive and continue to have unprotected sexual intercourse with them. These young adults appear to believe that "love will conquer all."

These biased heuristics are important because they are seen as barriers to safer-sex behavior by young adults. When testing the HBM, perceived barriers were found to be the most powerful, negative predictor of perceived severity of the disease (Janz & Becker, 1984). Furthermore, perceived severity of HIV/AIDS and barriers to sexual history discussions and condom use were found to predict whether young adults engaged in these safer-sex practices (Basen-Engquist, 1992; Yep, 1993). Understanding the perceived barriers to safer-sex behavior is, I believe, the key AIDS educators need to motivate young adults to protect themselves against HIV/AIDS.

Desired Endpoints

All of these biased rationales used by young adults in past research point to the fact that, for this group, there may be some desired endpoint so alluring that rational, fact-based arguments become distorted and fail to keep young adults from enacting safer-sex behavior. I believe that desired endpoint is the wish to be in a romantic relationship or sexual relationship. Research in other health areas has demonstrated the importance of relational variables for individuals in general. For example, Federoff (1991) cited a case where a man died from a heart attack because he stopped taking his medicine due to an unpleasant side effect, the inability to have sex, leading to the conclusion, "It is always a mistake to assume that sexual functioning is a trivial concern" (Federoff, 1991, p. 141). The same may be true of HIV/AIDS. The possibility of exposure to a virus whose effects will not be evident for several years may not compete with the instant motivation a romantic relationship and/or the opportunity for sexual intercourse offers (Kaplan & Shayne, 1993; Leishman, 1987).

Many AIDS educators have ignored the importance of romantic relationships for individuals. For example, in her book on AIDS education targeted toward women, Sack (1992) asked, "is this relationship worth dying for?" (p. 10). As Sack discovered in her interviews, too often the answer to that question is, "Yes." What I have found, along with others studying safer-sex behaviors for young adults, is that maintaining intimacy is a higher priority for young relational partners than AIDS prevention (Bowen & Michal-Johnson, 1989; Fullilove, Fullilove, Haynes, & Gross, 1990; Hammer et al., 1996; Kellar-Guenther, 1994; Kellar-Guenther & Christopher, 1997b; Williams et al., 1992). This is because a romantic partner provides an individual's sexuality needs, intimacy needs, companionship needs, and tenderness needs (Buhrmester & Furhman, 1986; Christopher & Roosa, 1991; Sullivan, 1953).

Sexual intercourse, like relational commitment, can also serve many functions (Sprecher & McKinney, 1993) and, as a result, be a desired endpoint for young adults. Coitus can be an act of self-disclosure (Reiss, 1989), a means of showing closeness, affection, or love toward one's partner (Christopher & Cate, 1984; Waring, Tillman, Frelick, Russell, & Weisz, 1980), a behavior that highlights the interdependent nature of the relationship (Omoto, Berscheid, & Snyder, 1987), an act of relational maintenance (Bell, Daly, & Gonzalez, 1987; Dainton, 1991; Dindia, 1988), or a resource to be exchanged within a relationship (Cate, Lloyd, Henton, & Larson, 1982). These needs and functions met by relational commitment and sexual intimacy are so important to young adults that the perception of HIV risk is decreased or eliminated through the use of biased heuristics (Cline et al., 1992; Hammer et al., 1996; Kellar-Guenther, 1994).

The goals of young adults differ from the desired end goals of AIDS educators. Educators want young adults to discuss their sexual histories so that the couple will choose to use a condom or abstain from sexual intercourse. Young adults, however, believe that by asking relational partners to wear a condom or discuss their sexual past they are communicating a lack of trust, threatening the stability of the relationship, and endangering the opportunity for sexual intercourse (Cline et al., 1992; Hammer et al., 1996; Kellar-Guenther, 1994; Kellar-Guenther & Christopher, 1997b). Furthermore, a condom request may make the sexual encounter seemed planned and logical whereas unprotected sex may make the encounter seem spontaneous and erotic (Adelman, 1991). For young adults then, safer sex may appear to be the barrier to relational commitment and/or sexual intercourse. There is research, however, to support that these goals (wanting to have safer sex and wanting to have a romantic/sexual relationship) are not mutually exclusive.

How to Meet Everyone's Goals

Past research reveals that relational commitment and sexual intimacy can serve to inhibit and promote safer-sex behaviors. According to AIDS research, safer-sex behaviors are avoided because actions that cause the HIV risk (e.g., drug use, any sexual activity with a partner outside the relationship) threaten the partnership (Sprecher, 1989). Young adult respondents in several studies have, in fact, stated that they choose not to engage in safer-sex behaviors because they were worried about offending or losing the relational partner (Harlow, Morokoff, & Quina, 1991; Kellar-Guenther, 1994; Williams et al., 1992). Moreover, my coauthor and I have found that fear of losing the relationship actually inhibits young heterosexuals' perceptions that they could even begin the sexual history discussion (Kellar-Guenther & Christopher, 1997b) let alone request a condom (Kellar-Guenther & Christopher, 1997a).

I have, however, also found that relational variables result in the enactment of safer-sex behaviors. For example, in one study my coauthor and I found that relational commitment and perceived future interaction with the relational partner actually motivated sexual history discussions (Kellar-Guenther & Christopher, 1997b). This was especially true for the women in our study. The only paths that resulted in a sexual history discussion for women originated from relational commitment. Although relational commitment directly led to sexual history discussions, it also promoted the discussion through other relational variables such as sexual intimacy and perceived future interaction.

Relational commitment was also found to be a positive predictor of individuals' perceptions that they had the ability to request a condom (Kellar-Guenther & Christopher, 1997a). This is important because ability to request a condom and fear of contracting HIV/AIDS were the only significant predictors of condom use in our study. These findings strongly punctuate the importance of the dyadic relationship for young heterosexuals at the time the decision is made to engage in sexual history discussions, and, as a result, have important implications for AIDS education. Educators need to take a relational-centered focus to AIDS education messages.

Redefining AIDS Education

Looking at past research, educators can begin to understand why past AIDS education messages have not been effective. Young adults do not fear dying (Boster & Mongeau, 1984); they fear being alone (Kellar-Guenther, 1995). More important, it appears as though young adults view romantic relationships as being dialectically opposed to safer-sex behaviors. They appear to deal with this tension by using what Baxter (1990) referred to as selection; they are choosing to focus on only one side of the dialectic tension (desire for a romantic relationship) and ignoring the other (desire to engage in safer sex).

Educators must help young adults reframe this dialectic so that they understand that they can meet both endpoints at once. Specifically, young adults need to learn that they can use safer-sex behaviors to develop their relationship. This will be a difficult task. Baxter (1990) found that whereas reframing dialectical tension was the most satisfactory way to handle the tension, it was also the most difficult. This is where AIDS researchers need to begin to invest their energies. Researchers need to begin creating and testing strategies that show young adults that safer-sex behaviors can be a relational-building tool. Listed in the next section are some starting points. These include ways to reframe AIDS education messages and some new strategies AIDS educators can teach young adults.

Alternative Frames for AIDS Education Messages

Currently, AIDS education focuses on ways to persuade your partner to take precautions so that you can protect yourself (e.g., pamphlets put out by ETR and "America Responds to AIDS"). This is problematic because the focus on individual health concerns and compliance-gaining techniques imply that your partner will resist your request. When teaching young adults condom request compliance-gaining strategies, educators should stress that research has shown that any request made by the partner to engage in safer sex will most likely receive a positive response. Although the individual may be the one to enact the safer-sex behavior, most young adults will use a condom if their partner asks (Hammer et al., 1996). In fact, Sacco and Rickman (1996) found that sexual partner's preference for condom use accounted for a large amount of variance in gay and bisexual men's decision to use a condom, even after controlling for all personal variables. Furthermore, 14% of Kusseling et al.'s (1996) heterosexual respondents said they did not use a condom when their partner did not want one. These findings show that young adults see the decision to use a condom as a way to show sensitivity to their partner (or empathy). Educators must stress this; a request for a condom is a way to show sensitivity for the partner, a way to take the pressure of the decision out of the partner's hands.

Although it may not seem too important to inform young adults that most are willing to use a condom if a request is made, it may be an important way to change how the condom request situation is viewed. Research on drug educational programs found that their programs had what is called a "boomerang effect." Young adolescents who went to these programs and heard that other students were using drugs began to use drugs rather to than avoid them. Researchers later realized that during these programs young adolescents were getting the perception that drug use was more rampant than it really is, and, as a result, felt they were the only students not using drugs (Donaldson, Graham, Piccinin, & Hansen, 1995). These students decided to "jump on the drug bandwagon" so they would not be the only one not using drugs. The same may be happening for young adults and condom requests. If they continually hear how difficult it is to request a condom from their partner, they may believe requesting a condom is a futile effort because it will lead to conflict and put the relationship in jeopardy. However, if they believe that most people will use a condom if asked, they may be more likely not only to ask, but also to use a condom because "everyone else is." Educators, therefore, may want to reframe compliance-gaining techniques as standard requests.

Educators must also stress how condom requests and sexual history discussions in general are relationship building. This can be done by showing the functions of romantic relationships that these behaviors meet. For example, ensuring that one's partner is protected is a means of attending to tenderness and intimacy needs. Also, engaging in an act that makes one vulnerable (e.g., condom request) is a way of showing trust for the other (Altman & Taylor, 1973). Educators should take time to discuss what relational message is being sent when one requests a safer-sex strategy. Future researchers may also want to devise new strategies that meet relational development goals.

Strategies That Promote Relational Commitment and Safer Sex

There has been some research that has uncovered relationally oriented safer-sex strategies. Interestingly, these strategies have not been framed as being both relationally and safer-sex oriented. Educators will need to be sure they present these strategies so that young adults realize that these messages allow them to meet the needs of their partners and themselves. First, educators can encourage young adults to send "other-oriented" safer-sex requests. For example, Reel and Thompson (1994) found that the statement "Condoms protect both of us" was rated as very effective by their respondents who used condoms during sexual intercourse. These respondents also rated "we" messages as being very effective. These included statements such as "We should talk about condoms to prevent pregnancy," "We both aren't sure if we have AIDS, so I think we should use a condom," and "I think we should use a condom." Both types of messages, other-oriented and we messages, help demonstrate concern for the partner emphasize the relational commitment. Also, according to Knapp and Vangelisti (1991), the use of the term we is a means of showing your partner and those outside the relationship that you have a commitment with your partner. Young adults should be reminded that by focusing on their partners and themselves, they are sending a message this relationship has a future.

AIDS educators may also want to focus on nonverbal condom requests. Research has shown that young adults prefer to initiate sexual intercourse nonverbally (Sprecher & McKinney, 1993). Young adults reported that they preferred to use holding hands (McCormick, 1979), sitting closer (McCormick, 1979; Perper & Weiss, 1987), and touch (Jesser, 1978; Perper & Weiss, 1987) as ways to bring about coitus. Nonverbal strategies have also been found to be effective for persuading one's partner to wear a condom. Young heterosexual college men in DeBro, Campbell, and Peplau's (1994) study reported that getting the woman so aroused that she would forget that he was wearing the condom was the most effective strategy for partner compliance. Fifteen of their 39 men stated they had used this strategy. This strategy should be used with caution, however. These authors found that this strategy was also used when the individual did not want the partner to use a condom (e.g., get partner so aroused that she would not ask). Moreover, individuals often choose to initiate sexual intercourse nonverbally because they are not yet emotionally intimate or able to communicate about sexual intercourse with each other (Breakwell, Fife-Schaw, & Clayden, 1991; Ingham, Woodcock, & Stenner, 1991; Sorensen, 1973). This leads to another possible strategy AIDS educators may recommend, promoting other forms of sexual intimacy initially.

At this time, most AIDS education focuses on condom use, abstinence, or sexual history discussions. Very few AIDS education messages promote other forms of intimacy such as oral sex or mutual masturbation. Educators may want to talk about other forms of sexual intimacy that do not include sexual intercourse as a way for couples to satisfy their need to be sexually involved while at the same time abstaining from vaginal and anal sexual intercourse. In our study on sexual history discussions (Kellar-Guenther & Christopher, 1997b), my coauthor and I found that sexual intimacy was, in fact, a positive predictor of sexual history discussions that took place before the couple had vaginal intercourse. Sexual intimacy in that study included behaviors such as kissing, fondling, oral sex, and vaginal sex. This can be an important strategy because condom use was found to be more frequent for couples who wait to have sex (Ingham et al., 1991). By engaging in other forms of sexual intimacy earlier in the relationship, the couple is more likely to be ready to discuss sexual intercourse with each other, and as a result, feel they can discuss safer-sex behaviors also (Breakwell et al., 1991; Ingham et al., 1991).

As I mentioned earlier, there is not much work on AIDS strategies that account for young adults' desires to be in a relationship. If we want young adults to take precautions, however, we will need to focus on creating and testing some.

SUMMARY

Educators and researchers cannot continue to focus only on individuals' health in their AIDS education campaigns. These campaigns fail to meet the desire young adults have to be in a relationship and, as a result, they are often dismissed through the use of bias heuristics. Although it may sound logical to say that "this relationship is not worth dying for," young adults are often unwilling to believe that the immediate benefits a relationship offers (e.g., intimacy, companionship) can be more costly than the chance they will contract HIV (Kaplan & Shayne, 1993; Leishman, 1987). As a result, AIDS educators need to begin to acknowledge young adults' desires to be in a romantic relationship. Researchers and educators must come up with strategies that enable young adults to develop their romantic relationship while protecting themselves. This may mean reframing the current safer-sex behaviors (e.g., condom use, abstinence) or creating new ones.

The goal of this chapter is to persuade educators and researchers that AIDS education must account for young adults' desire to be in a romantic relationship to be effective. I have also provided the initial steps toward changing the focus of AIDS education messages. If I have been successful, the foundation has been set to design a program that will meet the needs of young adults and AIDS educators. AIDS researchers must now help to build that program. As Reardon (1989) noted, AIDS is the greatest communication challenge since World War II. Understanding the power of romantic relationships in young adults' decisions to enact safer-sex behavior is one step toward meeting that challenge.

REFERENCES

Adelman, M. B. (1991). Play and incongruity: Framing safe-sex talk. *Health Communication, 3,* 139–155.
Ajzen, I., & Fishbein, M. (1980). *Understanding attitudes and predicting social behavior.* Englewood Cliffs, NJ: Prentice-Hall.
Altman, I., & Taylor, D. A. (1973*). Social penetration: The development of interpersonal relationships.* New York: Holt, Rinehart & Winston.
Baldwin, J. D., & Baldwin, J. I. (1988). Factors affecting AIDS-related sexual risk-taking behavior among college students. *Journal of Sex Research, 25,* 181–196.
Basen-Engquist, K. (1992). Evaluation of a theory-based HIV prevention intervention for college students. *AIDS Education and Prevention, 6,* 412–424.
Baxter, L. (1990). Dialectical contradictions in relationship development. *Journal of Social and Personal Relationships, 7,* 69–88.
Becker, M. H., & Joseph, J. G. (1988). AIDS and behavioral change to reduce risk: A review. *American Journal of Public Health, 78,* 394–410.
Bell, R. A., Daly, J. A., & Gonzalez, C. (1987). Affinity-maintenance in marriage and its relationship to women's marital satisfaction. *Journal of Marriage and the Family, 14,* 47–67.

Boster, F. J., & Mongeau, P. A. (1984). Fear-arousing persuasive messages. In R. N. Bostrom (Ed.), *Communication yearbook 4* (pp. 165–176). New Brunswick, NJ: Transaction Books.

Bowen, S. P., & Michal-Johnson, P. (1989). The crisis of communication relationships: Confronting the threat of AIDS. *AIDS and Public Policy, 4,* 10–19.

Breakwell, G. M., Fife-Schaw, C., & Clayden, K. (1991). Risk-taking, control over partner choice and intended use of condoms by virgins. *Journal of Community and Applied Social Psychology, 1,* 173–187.

Buhrmester, D., & Furhman, W. (1986). The changing functions of friends in childhood: A neo-Sullivanian perspective. In V. J. Derlega & B. A. Winstead (Eds.), *Friendship and social interaction* (pp. 41–62). New York: Springer-Verlag.

Caron, S. L., David, C. M., Wynn, R. L., & Roberts, L. W. (1992). "America Responds to AIDS," but did college students? Differences between March, 1987, and September, 1988. *AIDS Education and Prevention, 4,* 18–28.

Cate, R. M., Lloyd, S. A., Henton, J. M., & Larson, J. H. (1982). Fairness and reward level as predictors of relationship satisfaction. *Social Psychology Quarterly, 45,* 177–181.

Christopher, F. S., & Cate, R. M. (1984). Factors involved in premarital sexual decision-making. *Journal of Sex Research, 20,* 363–376.

Christopher, F. S., & Roosa, M. W. (1991). Factors affecting sexual decisions in the premarital relationships of adolescents and young adults. In K. McKinney & S. Sprecher (Eds.), *Sexuality in close relationships* (pp. 111–133). Hillsdale, NJ: Lawrence Erlbaum Associates.

Cline, R. J., Johnson, S. J., & Freeman, K. E. (1992). Talk among sexual partners about AIDS: Interpersonal communication for risk reduction or risk enhancement? *Health Communication, 4,* 39–56.

Corea, G. (1992). *The invisible epidemic: The story of women and AIDS.* New York: HarperPerennial.

Dainton, M. (1991, May). *Relational maintenance revisited: The addition of physical affection measures to a maintenance typology.* Paper presented at the meeting of the International Communication Association, Chicago.

D'Augelli, A. R. (1992). Sexual behavior patterns of gay university men: Implications for preventing HIV infection. *Journal of American College Health, 41,* 25–29.

DeBro, S. C., Campbell, S. M., & Peplau, L. A. (1994). Influencing a partner to use a condom: A college student perspective. *Psychology of Women Quarterly, 18,* 165–182.

DiClemente, R. J., Forrest, K., & Mickler, S. E. (1990). College students' knowledge and attitudes about HIV and changes in HIV-preventive behaviors. *AIDS Education and Prevention, 2,* 201–212.

Dindia, K. (1988, June). *The marital maintenance survey: Toward the development of a measure of marital maintenance strategies.* Paper presented at the International Conference on Personal Relationships, Vancouver, BC.

Donaldson, S. I., Graham, J. W., Piccinin, A. M., & Hansen, W. B. (1995). Resistance-skills training and onset of alcohol use: Evidence for beneficial and potentially harmful effects in public schools and in private Catholic schools. *Health Psychology, 14,* 291–300.

Dublin, S., Rosenberg, P. S., & Goedeter, J. J. (1992). Patterns and predictors of high-risk sexual behavior in female partners of HIV-infected men with hemophilia. *AIDS, 6,* 475–482.

DuBuono, B. A., Zinner, S. H., Daamen, M., & McCormack, W. M. (1990). Sexual behavior of college women in 1975, 1986, and 1989. *New England Journal of Medicine, 322,* 821–825.

Edgar, T., Freimuth, V. S., & Hammond, S. L. (1988). Communicating the AIDS risk to college students: The problem of motivating change. *Health Education Research, 3,* 59–65.

Edgar, T., Freimuth, V. S., Hammond, S. L., McDonald, D. A., & Fink, E. L. (1992). Strategic sexual communication: Condom use resistance and response. *Health Communication, 4,* 83–104.

Edgar, T., Hammond, S. L., & Freimuth, V. S. (1989). The role of the mass media and interpersonal communication in promoting AIDS-related behavioral change. *AIDS and Public Policy Journal, 4,* 3–9.

Education Training Research Associates. (1987). *Talking with your partner about safer sex* (2nd ed.) [Brochure]. Santa Cruz, CA: Author.

Federoff, J. P. (1991). Interview techniques to assess sexual disorders. *Journal of Contemporary Human Services, 72,* 140–146.

Fishbein, M., & Middlestadt, S. (1989). Using the theory of reasoned action as a framework for understanding and changing AIDS-related behaviors. In V. Mays, G. Albee, & S. Schenider (Eds.), *Primary prevention of AIDS: Psychological approaches* (pp. 93–110). Newbury Park, CA: Sage.

Freimuth, V. S., Hammond, S. L., Edgar, T., & Monahan, J. L. (1990). Reaching those at risk: A content-analytic study of AIDS PSAs. *Communication Research, 17,* 775–791.

Freud, S. (1918). *Reflections on war and death.* New York: Moffat Yard.

Fullilove, M. T., Fullilove, R. E., Haynes, K., & Gross, S. (1990). Black women and AIDS prevention: A view towards understanding the gender rules. *Journal of Sex Research, 27,* 47–64.

Goertzel, T. G., & Bluebond-Langer, M. (1991). What is the impact of a campus AIDS education course? *Journal of American College Health, 40,* 87–92.

Hammer, J. C., Fisher, J. D., Fitzgerald, P., & Fisher, W. A. (1996). When two heads aren't better than one: AIDS risk behavior in college-age couples. *Journal of Applied Social Psychology, 26,* 375–397.

Harlow, L. L., Morokoff, P. J., & Quina, K. (1991, August). *Predictors of AIDS-related risk-taking in college women.* Paper presented at the annual meeting of the American Psychological Association, San Francisco.

Hoff, C. C., Coates, T. J., Barrett, D. C., Collette, L., & Ekstrand, M. (1996). Differences between gay men in primary relationships and single men: Implications for prevention. *AIDS Education and Prevention, 8,* 546–559.

Ingham, R., Woodcock, A., & Stenner, K. (1991). Getting to know you . . . Young people's knowledge of their partner at first intercourse. *Journal of Community and Applied Social Psychology, 1,* 117–132.

Janz, N. K., & Becker, M. (1984). The health belief model: A decade later. *Health Education Quarterly, 11,* 1–47.

Jesser, C. J. (1978). Male responses to direct verbal sexual initiatives of females. *Journal of Sex Research, 14,* 118–128.

Kaplan, B. J., & Shayne, V. T. (1993). Unsafe sex: Decision-making biases and heuristics. *AIDS Education and Prevention, 5,* 294–301.

Kashima, Y., Gallois, C., & McCamish, M. (1992). Predicting the use of condoms: Past behavior, norms, and the sexual partner. In T. Edgar, M. A. Fitzpatrick, & V. S. Freimuth (Eds.), *AIDS: A communication perspective* (pp. 21–46). Hillsdale, NJ: Lawrence Erlbaum Associates.

Kellar-Guenther, Y. (1994, May). *A phenomenological inquiry into sexual history discussions.* Paper presented at the meeting of the International Network on Personal Relationships, Iowa City.

Kellar-Guenther, Y. (1995, February). *Too scared to speak: Consequences of losing the relationship vs. contracting AIDS.* Paper presented at the annual Western States Communication Association Convention, Portland, OR.

Kellar-Guenther, Y., & Christopher, F. S. (1997a). *How effective are sexual history discussions?* Manuscript in preparation.

Kellar-Guenther, Y., & Christopher, F. S. (1997b). *Why young heterosexuals don't "Respond to AIDS": Determinants of sexual history discussions.* Manuscript submitted for publication.

Keller, M. L. (1993). Why don't young adults protect themselves against sexual transmission of HIV? Possible answers to a complex question. *AIDS Education and Prevention, 5,* 220–233.

Kelly, J. A., St. Lawrence, J. S., Brasfield, T., Lemke, A., Amidei, T., Roffman, R. E., Vood, H. V., Smith, J. E., Kilgor, H., K., & McNeill, C., (1990). Psychological factors that predict AIDS high-risk versus AIDS precautionary behavior. *Journal of Counseling and Clinical Psychology, 58,* 117–120.

Knapp, M. L., & Vangelisti, A. L. (1991). *Interpersonal communication and human relationships* (2nd ed.). Boston: Allyn & Bacon.

Kowaleski, L., Zeller, R., & Willis, C. (1991). An evaluation of AIDS education: A quasi-experimental exploration. *Journal of Allied Health, 20,* 191–202.

Kunda, Z. (1990). The case for motivated reasoning. *Psychological Bulletin, 108,* 480–498.

Kusseling, F. S., Shapiro, M. F., Greenberg, J. M., & Wenger, N. S. (1996). Understanding why heterosexual adults do not practice safer sex: A comparison of two samples. *AIDS Education and Prevention, 8,* 247–257.

Leigh, B. C., & Miller, P. (1995). The relationship of substance use with sex to the use of condoms among young adults in two urban areas of Scotland. *AIDS Education and Prevention, 7,* 278–284.

Leishman, K. (1987, February). Heterosexuals and AIDS. *The Atlantic Monthly, 259,* 39–49+.

Mahoney, C. A., Thombs, D. L., & Ford, O. J. (1995). Health belief and self-efficacy models: Their utility in explaining college student condom use. *AIDS Education and Prevention, 7,* 32–49+.

Manning, D. T., Barenberg, N., Gallese, L., & Rice, J. C. (1989). College students' knowledge and health beliefs about AIDS: Implications for education and prevention. *Journal of American College Health, 37,* 254–259.

Markova, I., & Power, K. (1992). Audience response to health messages about AIDS. In T. Edgar, M. A. Fitzpatrick, & V. S. Freimuth (Eds.), *AIDS: A communication perspective* (pp. 111–130). Hillsdale, NJ: Lawrence Erlbaum Associates.

Maticka-Tyndale, E. (1991). Sexual scripts and AIDS prevention: Variations in adherence to safer-sex guidelines by heterosexual adolescents. *Journal of Sex Research, 28,* 45–66.

McCormick, N. B. (1979). Come-ons and put-offs: Unmarried students' strategies for having and avoiding sexual intercourse. *Psychology of Women Quarterly, 4,* 194–211.

Metts, S., & Fitzpatrick, M. A. (1992). Thinking about safer sex: The risky business of "know your partner" advice. In T. Edgar, M. A. Fitzpatrick, & V. S. Freimuth (Eds.), *AIDS: A communication perspective* (pp. 1–19). Hillsdale, NJ: Lawrence Erlbaum Associates.

Mickler, S. E. (1993). Perceptions of vulnerability: Impact on AIDS prevention behavior among college adolescents. *AIDS Education and Prevention, 5,* 43–53.

Moore, S. M., & Barling, N. R. (1991). Developmental status and AIDS attitudes in adolescence. *Journal of Genetic Psychology, 152,* 5–16.

Offir, J. T., Fisher, J. D., Williams, S. S., & Fisher, W. A. (1993). Reasons for inconsistent AIDS-preventive behavior among gay men. *Journal of Sex Research, 30,* 53–60.

Omoto, A. M., Berscheid, E., & Snyder, M. (1987, August). *Behavioral and psychological correlates of sexual intercourse in romantic relationships.* Paper presented at the annual meeting of the American Psychological Association, New York.

Perper, T., & Weiss, D. L. (1987). Proceptive and rejective strategies of U.S. and Canadian college women. *Journal of Sex Research, 23,* 455–480.

Reardon, K. K. (1989). Meeting the communication/persuasion challenge of AIDS in workplaces, neighborhoods, and schools: A comment on *AIDS and Public Policy* (Vol. 4, No. 1). *Health Communication, 2,* 267–270.

Reel, B. W., & Thompson, T. L. (1994). A test of the effectiveness of strategies for talking about AIDS and condom use. *Journal of Applied Communication Research, 22,* 127–140.

Reiss, I. (1989). Society and sexuality: A sociological explanation. In K. McKinney & S. Sprecher (Eds.), *Human sexuality: The societal and interpersonal context* (pp. 3–29). Norwood, NJ: Ablex.

Rosenthal, D., Moore, K. S., & Brumen, I. (1990). Ethnic group differences in adolescents' responses to AIDS. *Australian Journal of Social Issues, 3,* 220–239.

Sacco, W. P., & Rickman, R. L. (1996). AIDS-relevant condom use by gay and bi-sexual men: The role of person variables and the interpersonal situation. *AIDS Education and Prevention, 8,* 430–443.

Sack, F. (1992). *Romance to die for: The startling truth about women, sex, and AIDS.* Deerfield Beach, FL: Health Communications, Inc.

Selik, R. M., Chu, S. Y., & Buehler, J. W. (1993). HIV infection as leading cause of death among young adults in U.S. cities and states. *Journal of the American Medical Association, 269,* 2991–2994.

Shayne, V. T., & Kaplan, B. J. (1988). AIDS education for adolescents. *Youth & Society, 20,* 180–208.

Sorensen, R. C. (1973). *Adolescent sexuality in contemporary America.* New York: World Publishing.

Spitzberg, B., H., & Cupach, W. R. (1984). *Interpersonal communication competence.* Newbury Park, CA: Sage.

Sprecher, S. (1989). Expected impact of sex-related events on dating relationships. *Journal of Psychology and Human Sexuality, 2,* 77–92.

Sprecher, S., & McKinney, K. (1993). *Sexuality.* Newbury Park, CA: Sage.

Stiff, J., McCormack, M., Zook, E., Stein, T., & Henry, R. (1990). Learning about AIDS and HIV transmission in college-age students. *Communication Research, 17,* 743–758.

Sullivan, H. S. (1953). *The interpersonal theory of psychiatry.* New York: Norton.

Valdiserri, R. O., Lyter, D. W., Leviton, L. C., Callahan, C. M., Kingsley, L. A., & Rinaldo, C. R. (1988). Variables influencing condom use in a cohort of gay and bisexual men. *American Journal of Public Health, 78,* 801–805.

Waring, E. M., Tillman, M. P., Frelick, L., Russell, L., & Weisz, G. (1980). Concepts of intimacy in the general population. *Journal of Nervous and Mental Disease, 168,* 471–474.

Weinstein, N. D. (1984). Why it won't happen to me: Perceptions of risk factors and susceptibility. *Health Psychology, 3,* 431–457.

Weinstein, N. D. (1989). Optimistic biases about personal risks. *Science, 246,* 1232–1233.

Williams, S. S., Kimble, D. L., Covell, N. H., Weiss, L. H., Newton, K. J., Fisher, J. D., & Fisher, W. A. (1992). College students use implicit personality theory instead of safer sex. *Journal of Applied Social Psychology, 22,* 921–933.

Yep, G. (1993). HIV prevention among Asian-American college students: Does the health belief model work? *Journal of American College Health, 41,* 199–205.

17

Stigma, Secrecy, and Isolation: The Impact of HIV/AIDS on Women in an Australian Study

Lydia Bennett
Michele Travers
University of Sydney

In examining the impact of HIV/AIDS on women, it is necessary to address the current literature regarding people living with HIV and AIDS and to explore what may be unique or different about the experiences of women. We interviewed women living with HIV/AIDS in order to understand their experiences and perspectives. The current chapter focuses on data related to stigma, secrecy, and isolation, and this reflects an important aspect of the study's findings that relate to aversive experiences. However, women interviewed also reported positive experiences and outcomes, such as finding new meaning to life, becoming more open-minded, finding out who their real friends were, and receiving positive and supportive care from health care providers (see Fig. 17.1).

Comparatively little about women with HIV/AIDS has been published, with research treatments and services being based on male-derived data and needs (Rosser, 1991; Stevens, 1996). An examination of the literature on HIV and AIDS by Sherr (1996) states that the dramatic male focus needs exploration, understanding, and redressing. A search conducted by Sherr using Medline found that of the total of 72,491 HIV/AIDS manuscripts identified during 1985–1995, the number of articles on women and HIV/AIDS was only 4.1% during 1985–1990 and increased to only 7.5% during 1991–1995. This lack of representation in the research base and its consequence of "invisible women" compounds the stigma, secrecy, and isolation for women living with HIV/AIDS.

Sherr (1996) identified a number of eras in relation to women and the AIDS epidemic and called the first of these the era of oversight, which was evidenced by women often being overlooked. The focus of the first era concerned questions of procreation and pregnancy rather than women in their own right, whereas the second era was an awakening period where women were acknowledged and addressed. The dawn of the third era is now apparent and Sherr warned that single theoretical approaches such as those that are biological or medical may provide little understanding of important aspects such as the emotional, coping, adjustment, and long-term impact of HIV on women. Approaches during this current era must provide theoretical elasticity that can accommodate gender issues (Sherr, 1996).

Many of the experiences of women are influenced by general attitudes in society regarding women with HIV/AIDS. Attitudes toward these women are often judgmental and involve a

Patriarchal Social Structure

Scientific   Medical
Androcentrism   Disenfranchisement   Dominance

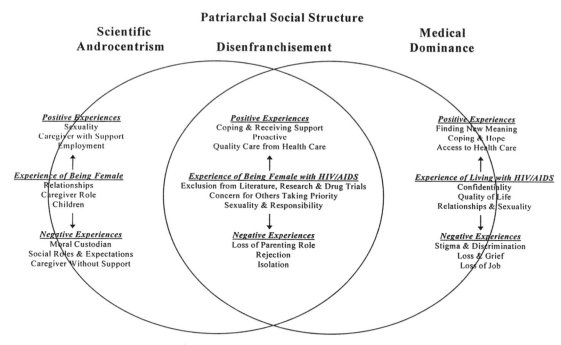

FIG. 17.1.   The experience of being female with HIV/AIDS.

great deal of speculation and assumption about the behaviors that led to infection. The stigma related to women's diagnoses leads to fear of disclosure, and research does indicate that women delay seeking diagnosis and treatment or avoid speaking about their diagnosis (Ward, 1993; Ybarra, 1991).

Furthermore stigma, secrecy, and isolation are complicated by social expectations of what constitutes appropriate female behaviors, morals, and beliefs. For example, differences continue to exist in the judgments made by society about male and female sexual behavior. Practices that are tolerated (or even encouraged) for men are judged more harshly when enacted by women. Because they violate the social expectations of women as "good," either monogamous or chaste, female sex workers with HIV/AIDS may be subject to increased stigma and isolation.

A number of the women in the Australian study had not shared their diagnosis with anyone apart from a sexual partner and a health care professional. This leads to women being unable to gain emotional support from friends and relatives who typically these women would have told about their diagnosis if the women had cancer or another less stigmatized illness.

CONFIDENTIALITY

There is a possibility that confidentiality issues are of greater concern to women than to men and this is an area that warrants further investigation. Fears arising from women's caregiving roles appear to be important in confidentiality issues. For example, a single mother may fear that disclosure of her HIV status could lead to removal of her child from her care. Many women are left to cope on their own because they choose to fiercely shield their family from the revelation of their condition. One woman discussed suicide as a better option than having the family find out the truth. At the time she expressed this intention, she preferred to sacrifice her remaining life, than to have the children live with the stigma and fear associated with having a HIV-infected mother.

Some women perceive that any association with certain HIV/AIDS related groups or services may pose a threat to their anonymity. The decision not to disclose information about their diagnosis can be a source of either empowerment or disempowerment, depending on the reason for the choices made. Although it may empower women to have control over who is told and to be able to tell without that experience leading to discrimination, it disempowers women to not be able to tell for fear of the repercussions. This seems to be especially acute where children may be affected by the decision to confide.

Caregivers need to be extra vigilant to maintain the confidentiality of a woman's diagnosis. How this is carried out can influence women's perceptions of trust and control. If the woman feels empowered by the health care provider, then it is anticipated that she will be more likely to return to caregivers for future help required. Brown (1993) stated in relation to women who are mothers: "Because mothers' rights to confidentiality can so easily be undermined by professionals' stereotypes and institutionalized patterns of unequal power relations, there is a need to increase patients' control over information concerning who will learn about their HIV status" (p. 200). Before agreeing to be interviewed for our study, some women requested that we arrive without any red ribbons or clothing that may identify us as having an association with an AIDS-related service or group.

RESPONSES OF WOMEN AND THEIR CONCERNS FOR OTHERS

In order to appreciate the complexities surrounding stigma, secrecy and isolation for women with HIV/AIDS, it is necessary to recognize that the behavior of many women is, to varying extents, motivated out of concern for others. One woman in discussing helplessness was not talking of her own response, but her concern that "they [the people she told] have a reaction of helplessness because it's not a problem that they can help me to fix." Women are typically concerned about the effect that diagnosis will have *on others* and how they can help reduce the negative impact of their diagnosis on others.

This concern often extends beyond the personal to incorporate a sense of social responsibility. A number of women interviewed spoke of the role they took in educating medical staff (particularly general practitioners) about the medical needs of women with HIV and expressed their concern that other women would not have to go through "what I went through."

Although it is recognized that this reaction of concern by women is one that is fostered and often expected by society, it alerts us to the need for health care professionals and other care providers and supporters of women with HIV to focus first on the individual women's perspectives and needs. For example, if the woman chooses her children or her potential role as a parent as her first area of concern, then this is different to carers presuming that this will be the focus.

The tendency to stereotype women into narrow roles and behaviors may disempower women by failing to recognize the complexity and wide range of needs that women living with HIV/AIDS experience (Travers & Bennett, 1994, 1996). It is crucial to challenge the social structures that function to disempower women. The application of a feminist perspective to theory, research, health care, policy formation, funding issues, and so on, will help to address the current imbalance. Indeed, the feminist perspective is beginning to have an impact on research and practice. For instance, it is reflected in many women's groups and in the work of individual researchers and practitioners. It is crucial to the well-being of women that the entitlements that accompany power are available to them. Disempowerment is a formidable barrier to meeting the health needs of women living with HIV/AIDS and contributes to experiences of stigma, secrecy, and isolation.

AIMS OF THIS STUDY

The main aim was to explore women's experiences and perceptions in relation to living with HIV and AIDS. The study was inductive and explorative. The questions asked were to some extent influenced by other published reports of women's experiences but were broad and open-ended so that women could explain, lead, or focus on the areas of most relevance to them.

Participants.   We interviewed 14 women living with HIV and AIDS. These women were volunteers from the provinces of New South Wales, Victoria, South Australia, Queensland, and Western Australia. Recruitment was conducted with the aid of public notices and information pamphlets. The mean age of women interviewed was 29.7 with the range of ages being from 22 to 37 years. The length of time for which women had known about their HIV status ranged from 6 months to 11 years with a mean of 5.5 years. Half of the women interviewed were mothers with children and the ages of children ranged from 12 months to 12 years of age.

METHODS AND ANALYSIS

Women were given the option to select the place of interview. Most elected to be interviewed in their homes. All women outside of the Sydney metropolitan area were interviewed by phone and some women living within the Sydney metropolitan area requested a phone interview due to either ill health or issues of secrecy. Interviews lasted approximately an hour. Women were asked a series of open-ended questions related to health care needs, disclosure, support, relationships, and coping. Questions were formulated in consultation with counselors (professional and volunteer) who worked with women living with HIV/AIDS. Women were interviewed after they had filled in a questionnaire (the results of this are mentioned as it relates to these interview data, but a full description of questionnaire data does not form part of this chapter). The questionnaire provided women with an opportunity to think about issues that were relevant to them before the interview.

The concept of grounded theory was used in the design of this study (Charmaz, 1990; Glaser & Strauss, 1967; Strauss, 1987; Strauss & Corbin, 1990). Strauss stated that grounded theory is based on a concept-indicator model. This involves empirical indicators being coded according to underlying concepts. The empirical indicators are actual data, which in this research study are the feelings, experiences, or events observed or described by the women. The concept-indicator model is based on the constant comparison of indicator to indicator. The indicators are examined comparatively by the analyst and then "coded" giving them category names.

The analyst is forced into confronting similarities, differences, and degrees of consistency of meaning among the indicators. An underlying uniformity is thereby generated, which results in a coded category. Following this step, indicators are compared to the emergent concepts, and codes are sharpened to achieve their best fits to data (Strauss, 1987).

It is recognized that in formulating categories a substantial *conceptual leap* is made from the actual words of subjects to the resultant conclusions drawn. Considerable attempts have been made to examine the data objectively and to identify what women perceive to be the main issues and areas of concern. During the procedure constant attempts are being made to understand both the positives, needs, problems, and experiences of being a woman with HIV/AIDS.

Categories observed in the data are presented by providing examples of women's statements and then weaving these into, or comparing them with, existing literature in the relevant fields. Where no existing literature can be found to explain a certain phenomenon, creative analysis is presented to attempt to contribute to theory.

Interviewers had previous training in counseling techniques and were able to adapt their role from one of interviewer to counselor if the participants were distressed by recollections of their experiences. Interviewers ensured that, before they left the interview, session women received contact numbers for support or counseling agencies.

One of the main criticisms of qualitative research is that the researchers are seen to be unable to avoid mixing personal impressions with descriptive accounts or to expunge their own biases from data collection, analysis, and interpretation (Borman, LeCompte, & Preissle Goetz, 1986). Accordingly, to reduce the degree of subjectivity and to measure the degree of the reliability of the interpretative and analytical processes, the two researchers conducted the analytical process separately and did not discuss their interpretations together until after the initial coding had been assessed by a third independent researcher. This forms a reliability check, because Wolcott (1975) stated that in qualitative research the researcher is preeminently the research tool.

If researchers can independently analyze data and then compare results, the level of consistency and reliability can be assessed. Following the transcription of interview recordings in this study, the two researchers (Bennett and Travers) independently read and analyzed the data. Each formulated sets of categories from the data on women and HIV/AIDS and identified links and causal relationships between them. They placed these categories and linking themes onto charts, showing their individual perceptions of directions of interactions and examples of the raw data to support or demonstrate themes and/or conceptual areas. Following this procedure, a third social scientist who was not involved in this study was asked to assess the extent of the common ground and overlap of the two conceptual grids. Each of the two initial researchers was interviewed separately by the third person, who ensured an understanding of the meaning of the two conceptual grids.

The third social scientist assessed the extent to which the conceptual categories and their interactions were consistent between the two researchers. There was a high amount of agreement in terms of the variables identified and described by both researchers and the extent of the overlap was quantitatively assessed to be 94%. A statistical computation of this pattern of categories found that there was no systematic variation in the instances where the two differed. This was confirmed by a calculation in SPSS using Kendall's W, "a nonparametric test of the hypothesis that several related samples are from the same population. W tests for agreement among judge's or rater's rankings of several variables and is useful in testing the inter-rater reliability" (SPSS, 6.0) (Result, $p = 1.00$). This procedure and calculation indicates that there is a way of quantifying the reliability of the qualitative interpretation process. This technique addresses some of the criticisms of the interpretative subjectivity of qualitative inquiry and, although time consuming, may be useful for other researchers to incorporate into their research schedules.

RESULTS AND DISCUSSION

Although the research data identified a number of areas that were of concern to women, only a few have been selected for discussion in this chapter. Figure 17.1 demonstrates the concepts and links identified by the researchers. The topics discussed here include the stigma, secrecy, isolation, guilt, and impact on women's relationships and sexuality associated with living with HIV/AIDS.

The Stigma and Secrecy Associated With HIV/AIDS

Many studies have identified the stigma for women associated with an HIV/AIDS diagnosis (Green, 1995, 1996; Sherr, 1993, 1996). Green (1996) stated that maintenance of secrecy related to HIV status may be very stressful and may heighten the sense of shame. Although many people with HIV/AIDS experience the stigma associated with this diagnosis, the stigma assumes an added dimension for women, who are often viewed as "vessels or vectors of HIV" (Sherr, 1993). The focus on women as vectors of transmission (e.g., sex workers, pregnant women) includes an emphasis on the role women play in transmitting the virus to men and children (Rosser, 1991). By adopting such a focus, the mass media and researchers may contribute to attributions of blame and responsibility and, consequently, stigma and isolation.

Green (1996) wrote that it is unclear whether women with HIV are more or less stigmatized by the condition than men, although it has been reported that it is common for HIV-infected women to experience being perceived as promiscuous and/or in some way socially deviant or irresponsible. Experiences of stigma and shame were commonly described by the women involved in our study:

> They think of AIDS . . . as a bad disease. It's something only bad people get.

> People look down on you, they look on you . . . [as if] you are not normal. They don't treat you the same.

> I found it particularly difficult coming from a White middle-class background to suddenly being part of a stigmatized group.

> If you said "HIV" [whispered] it was like, "Shhh," don't let anybody else hear you. You know, it's like, we're dirty.

There was an awareness of the factors that increased the degree of stigma experienced. For example, the labeling by the media of "innocent victims" implies that other people living with HIV/AIDS bear some degree of blame for their condition. By clarifying their source of infection, a number of women sought to reduce the stigma associated with their diagnosis:

> I always say that I was medically acquired, and that seems to get a better reaction that just saying that I'm infected. . . . It just makes things easier.

> You get the sympathy for it, and I'm not stupid. I wanted to be treated nicely. I don't want to be treated like I've got the plague, and it seems that people react so much better. . . . I have the family to think about.

The stigma associated with HIV/AIDS led to many women taking great caution in deciding who to tell about their diagnosis of HIV infection. Some women did not disclose their diagnosis to anyone outside of their health care management. Their need for secrecy was very strong: "Well, at the moment none of my friends know about it. So, you go to the medical department and you . . . my fiancé, just the two of us. It's very hard for me to approach my family, especially when they know you have this disease." In asking a woman to imagine to whom she would disclose her diagnosis, she stated, "But I don't. I don't want to be treated like dirt."

Many women modified their behavior due to the attitudes and beliefs of others. There was a dismissal of the women's own wishes and needs due to fear of being harshly judged or abandoned: "The reason I decided on a termination wasn't because that's what I wanted, because I actually didn't think about what I wanted, but because I know people in the area . . . and I know their views on women with HIV having children, and I didn't want to lose support."

Experiences of Isolation Due to Stigma, Rejection, and Fear

Many women involved in the study spoke about issues of isolation as a result of their diagnosis, and this isolation and abandonment seems to be more commonly experienced by women than by men (Ankrah, 1996; Hankins, 1996; Lamping & Mercey, 1996; Pizzi, 1992; Sherr, 1996). De Bruyn (1992) reported that many women with AIDS in Uganda are abandoned by their partners, often being left with no means to support themselves. The women in this study reported similar experiences:

> I felt very unclean, unwanted . . .

> Well, it's so . . . , it's been a hard life . . . you lose your friends, then you, you just don't want to be around. . . .

> My partner couldn't cope with it . . .

> I don't want to mix around with people . . . don't want to get close to them, because I just felt so different to them.

In Green's (1996) study of people with HIV/AIDS, women listed more people as comprising their social network than was listed by men, and perceived and received more social support than men. However, they also reported more stress arising from their social relationships (negative support). Green suggested that women may be advantaged compared with men with regard to social interaction and social support. However, Green's 1996 study had 66 participants and of these, only 18.2% were women. Many more studies need to be examined before patterns of comparisons and interactions become clearer.

Although Green (1996) reported that her study found no evidence that women were less likely than men to disclose their condition to people in their social network, this finding may be related to variations in women's roles. Women who live alone or have a paid occupational role may score differently than those who have a larger role in relation to caring for a partner, home, and children. The greater the caring role, the greater may be the perceived need by women to protect the family and to avoid the potentially negative impact of disclosure.

Green (1996) stated that, with regard to disclosure, women do not exhibit greater stigmatization or isolation. Nevertheless, the results of Green's analyses may have been different if the number of women in the sample were higher, if it included a scale to measure the perceived need by many women to protect partners and children from the impact of disclosure, and if the analyses included a covariance measure of women's perceived need to protect others. Some of Green's results do support this possible covariance, with Green reporting that women do *feel* more stigmatized than men and that women's home-based role also makes them more visible and more vulnerable to stigma from local residents. In Green's study three women asked to be rehoused after neighbors "found out" about their HIV status, whereas only one man reported being harassed by neighbors; this result becomes more informative when we are reminded that women formed only 18.2% of the total sample.

Wachtel et al. (1992) reported that the women generally had told only one member of their family (often their mother) and when family members were told, those members with small children were the ones who most often rejected their relative with HIV. This indicates the possibility that the people in the community most likely to stigmatize the person with HIV and to limit interactions with them may be those who have children.

Partners may attribute blame for the situation solely to the woman, even should the male partner decide to be tested and found to be infected (Hankins, 1996). The result may be marital breakdown, with the woman often having few skills with which to become self-supporting, abandoned along with her children by her partner (Ankrah, 1996; Hankins, 1996). Such contexts are likely to increase isolation and the perceived need for secrecy.

The women interviewed in our study described their isolation as both externally generated by the actions of others and sometimes internally, when isolation was freely chosen:

> I took myself away from society, and lived in a commune with my daughter. . . . I don't want to tell until I'm ready to.

> You don't want to mix with the community and people, you don't even want to talk to them, you just want to be on your own.

Focus on Needs of Others and Experiences of Guilt

One strong sociocultural expectation of women is that they will place the needs and concerns of others before their own. This is a fundamental aspect of their socialization into the caregiving role, which is perceived as being essentially female (Colliere, 1986). This expectation complicates the issues of stigma, secrecy, and isolation for women with HIV/AIDS (Bennett, Casey, & Austin, 1996). Hankins (1993) stated that although the care of children may reduce a HIV-seropositive woman's sense of isolation, there is the extra burden of concern about disclosure of diagnosis, obtaining child care, eventual placement of children, and possible rejection by other children. Green (1996) stated that women's role as mother and homemaker may place women with HIV at a disadvantage:

> I have the family to think about. I have the children to think about . . .

> It was about a 2-week period that I had of thinking of oh, I'm going to die, and . . . because I had my daughter and I had my husband, I turned to concentrate—I went back through being a mother, and a wife.

> I just wanted to die. I was so full of guilt, especially for my little daughter. That guilt was more than dying. I felt so guilty, I just wanted to kill myself.

> I hadn't told my parents. . . . I guess it's through being concerned about them . . . I didn't want [them to] suffer through something like this.

It has been documented that women are more likely to attend treatment later in their disease course when compared to men (Hankins, 1992; Porter, Wall, & Evans, 1993; Sherr, 1996; Stein et al., 1991). The mother's self-care is often neglected because of the needs of a child or children (Bennett et al., 1996; Delahunty, 1994; Siegel, Karus, & Raveis, 1997; Stowe, Ross, Wodak, Thomas, & Larson, 1993). Women are also more likely to bring their children for appointments than themselves (Sherr et al., 1993), which Sherr (1996) stated is an example of women's self-sacrifice.

Many women described their recognition that placing the needs of others before their own had personal consequences:

I know, being a parent myself, I need that time, I've got to sit back and I've got to say, "where's time for me" . . . I've got nothing for myself, I've given to everybody else but I've not given to me, and so, there are a lot of women saying that we need help.

I was thinking of going to court to get full-time care . . . but the whole thing is . . . "what's best for the child" and going through all that court drama, possibly getting him back but if I do, he comes back for a short period of time and then goes back to maybe a different foster parent, and stability is what he needs.

Impact on Relationships and Sexuality

Worth (1990) stated that women are less likely to leave their partner if he becomes infected than the other way around. More HIV-negative men divorce their HIV-infected female wives; Sherr (1996) argued that this evidence supports more serious consideration of women's fear of rejection as a reason not to disclose their HIV infection status or their recalcitrance to seek care.

Many women stated that their sex life had altered substantially since their HIV diagnosis. In a study by Kamenga et al. (1991, cited by Sherr, 1996), HIV-negative husbands were more likely to abstain from sex when the woman had HIV than when the woman was not infected. Condom use depended on male willingness where negative men at risk of infection from their wives with HIV were able to sustain condom use. In a study by Brown and Rundell (1990), over half of the women reported abstinence, a marked decrease in libido, or at least 50% reduction in the frequency of sexual intercourse since seroconversion.

When we asked women if being HIV-seropositive affected their sexuality, they typically responded, "I'm asexual, nonsexual if that makes sense." And on asking women about the impact their diagnosis has on sexual experiences, one woman stated, "I don't have any." In discussing sexual relationships with a woman who is married and was infected by her husband, she stated, "Oh, there's no physical relationship anymore."

The rejection women experience may not be limited to those outside of their home environment. The lack of sexual relationships may heighten women's feelings of isolation.

IMPLICATIONS OF FINDINGS

Living with stigma, and in secrecy and isolation has major implications for women living with HIV/AIDS. Quality of life, health status, relationships, and self-perceptions are likely to be compromised in such an environment. Keenan (1997) reported that in both Australia and the United States the number of people with HIV who are not accessing treatments or monitoring their health remains high. Keenan asserted that the reason people are not seeking advice about treatment options is not simply because of lack of knowledge. Although funding, access, and informed decisions are some of the possibilities influencing who accesses what treatments, there are many reasons yet to be identified by researchers.

There is evidence that women with HIV/AIDS may be underrepresented among patients receiving antiviral agents and prophylactic treatments (Moore, Hildalgo, Sugland, & Chaisson, 1991; Stein et al., 1991). Siegel et al. (1997) suggested that women in their study may have delayed obtaining medical follow-up for their infection because they were faced with immediate and more pressing daily survival needs or were responsible for the care for others, such as infected partners or children, prior to caring for themselves. The authors also suggested that another prominent barrier to seeking treatment may be a perceived hopelessness about effective treatments for the disease. It is possible that the secrecy and isolation evident in many of the women interviewed in this study may compound this lack of accessing of available treatments and services. Women have stated fear of disclosure due to attendance at clinics or association with groups or organizations that specialize in care for people living with HIV and AIDS. Siegel and colleagues also argued that distrust and suspicion of the health care system can compound women's lack of accessing treatments. If women remain isolated due to fear and secrecy, they will not receive information or be in a position to access support or new treatment options.

In conclusion, HIV/AIDS is a stigmatizing condition that provokes secrecy and contributes to isolation for people with the virus. For women, these negative experiences are likely to be compounded by the expectations of gender-defined behaviors and by the special needs arising from social roles. Women interviewed for this study described experiences of stigma that influenced their behaviors. They also described a need for secrecy often originating out of concern for the effects of their condition on others but also out of fear of being rejected and isolated. By understanding the complexities surrounding these issues, health workers, policymakers, and service providers can work to minimize the stigma and isolation for women living with HIV/AIDS.

REFERENCES

Ankrah, E. M. (1996). AIDS, socioeconomic decline, and health: A double crisis for the African woman. In L. Sherr, C. Hankins, & L. Bennett (Eds.), *AIDS as a gender issue: Psychosocial perspectives* (pp. 99–118). London: Taylor & Francis.

Bennett, L., Casey, K., & Austin, P. (1996). Issues for women as carers in HIV/AIDS. In L. Sherr, C. Hankins, & L. Bennett (Eds.), *AIDS as a gender issue: Psychosocial perspectives* (pp. 177–190). London: Taylor & Francis.

Borman, K. M., LeCompte, M. D., & Preissle Goetz, J. (1986). Ethnographic and qualitative research design and why it doesn't work. *American Behavioral Scientist, 30*, 42–57.

Brown, G., & Rundell, J. (1990). Prospective study of psychiatric morbidity in HIV-seropositive women without AIDS. *General Hospital Psychiatry, 12*, 30–35.

Charmaz, K. (1990). "Discovering" chronic illness: Using grounded theory. *Social Science & Medicine, 30*, 1161–1172.

Colliere, M. F. (1986). Invisible care and invisible women as health care-providers, *International Journal of Nursing Studies, 23*, 95–112.

De Bruyn, M. (1992). Women and AIDS in developing countries. *Social Science and Medicine, 34*, 249–262.

Delahunty, B. (1994). Families and HIV: Personal perspectives. (Australia) *National AIDS Bulletin, 7*(12), 13.

Glaser, B. G., & Strauss, A. L. (1967). *The discovery of grounded theory: Strategies for qualitative research.* Chicago: Aldine.

Green, G. (1995). Attitudes towards people with HIV: Are they as stigmatising as people with HIV perceive them to be? *Social Science and Medicine, 41*, 557–568.

Green, G. (1996). Stigma and social relationships of people with HIV: Does gender make a difference? In L. Sherr, C. Hankins, & L. Bennett (Eds.), *AIDS as a gender issue: Psychosocial perspectives* (pp. 46–63). London: Taylor & Francis.

Hankins, C. (1992). Public policy and maternal fetal HIV transmission. *Psychology and Health, 6*, 287–296.

Hankins, C. (1993). Women and HIV infection. In L. Sherr (Ed.), *AIDS and the heterosexual population* (pp. 21–31). Reading, England: Harwood.

Hankins, C. (1996). Sexuality issues, reproductive choices, and gynaecological concerns affecting women living with HIV. In L. Sherr, C. Hankins, & L. Bennett (Eds.), *AIDS as a gender issue: Psychosocial perspectives* (pp. 1–15). London: Taylor & Francis.

Kamenga, M., Ryder, R., Jingu, M., Mbuyi, N., Mbu, L., Behets, F., Brown, C., & Heyward, W. (1991). Evidence of marked sexual behaviour change associated with low HIV1 seroconversion in 149 married couples with discordant HIV1 serostatus—Experience at an HIV counseling center in Zaire. *AIDS, 5*, 61–67.

Keenan, T. (1997). New hope, new agendas. (Australia) *National AIDS Bulletin, 11*(1) 20–21.

Lamping, D., & Mercey, D. (1996). Health-related quality of life in women with HIV infection. In L. Sherr, C. Hankins, & L. Bennett (Eds.), *AIDS as a gender issue: Psychosocial perspectives* (pp. 78–98). London: Taylor & Francis.

Moore, R. D., Hildalgo, J., Sugland, B., & Chaisson , R. (1991). Zidovudine and the natural history of the acquired immune deficiency syndrome. *New England Journal of Medicine, 324,* 1412–1416.

Pizzi, M. (1992). Women, HIV infection, and AIDS: Tapestries of life, death, and empowerment. *American Journal of Occupational Therapy, 46,* 1021–1027.

Porter, K., Wall, P., & Evans, B. (1993). Factors associated with lack of awareness of HIV infection before diagnosis of AIDS. *British Medical Journal, 307,* 20–23.

Rosser, S. V. (1991). Perspectives: AIDS and women. *AIDS Education and Prevention, 3,* 230–240.

Sherr, L. (1993). HIV testing in pregnancy. In C. Squire (Ed.), *Women and AIDS: Psychological perspectives* (pp. 42–68). London: Sage.

Sherr, L. (1996). Tomorrow's era: Gender, psychology, and HIV infection. In L. Sherr, C. Hankins, & L. Bennett (Eds.), *AIDS as a gender issue: Psychosocial perspectives* (pp. 16–45). London: Taylor & Francis.

Sherr, L., Petrak, J., Melvin, D., Davey, T., Glover, L., & Hedge, B. (1993). Psychological trauma associated with AIDS and HIV infection in women. *Counselling Psychology Quarterly, 6,* 99–108.

Siegel, K., Karus, D., & Raveis, V. H. (1997). Testing and treatment behaviour of HIV-infected women: White, African-American, Puerto Rican comparisons. *AIDS Care, 9*(3), 297–309.

Stein, M. D., Piette, J., Mor, V., Wachtel, T., Fleishman, J., Mayer, K., & Carpenter, C. J. (1991). Differences in access to Zidovudine (AZT) among symptomatic HIV-infected persons. *Journal of General Internal Medicine, 6,* 35–40.

Stevens, P. E. (1996). Struggles with symptoms: Women's narratives of managing HIV illness. *Journal of Holistic Nursing, 14*(2), 142–161.

Stowe, A., Ross, M. W., Wodak, A., Thomas, G. V., & Larson, S. A. (1993). Significant relationships and social supports of injecting drug users and their implications for HIV/AIDS services. *AIDS Care, 5,* 23–33.

Strauss, A. L. (1987). *Qualitative analysis for social scientists.* New York: Cambridge University Press.

Strauss, A., & Corbin, J. (1990). *Basics of qualitative research: Grounded theory procedures and techniques.* Newbury Park, CA: Sage.

Travers, M., & Bennett, L. (1994). Power issues related to women and HIV/AIDS [Refereed article for special edition]. (Australia) *National AIDS Bulletin, 8*(4), 36–38.

Travers, M., & Bennett, L. (1996). AIDS, women, and power. In L. Sherr, C. Hankins, & L. Bennett (Eds.), *AIDS as a gender issue: Psychosocial perspectives* (pp. 64–77). London: Taylor & Francis.

Wachtel, T., Piette, J., Mor, V., Stein, M., Fleishman, J., & Carpenter, C. (1992). Quality of life in persons with HIV infection: Measurement by the medical outcomes study instrument. *Annals of Internal Medicine, 116,* 129–137.

Ward, M. (1993). A different disease: HIV/AIDS and health care for women in poverty. *Culture, Medicine & Psychiatry, 17,* 413–430.

Wolcott, H. (1975). Criteria for an ethnographic approach to research in schools. *Human Organisations, 34,* 111–127.

Worth, D. (1990). Women at high risk of HIV infection. In D. Ostrow (Ed.), *Behavioral aspects of AIDS* (pp. 101–119). New York: Plenum.

Ybarra, S. (1991). Women and AIDS: Implications for counseling. *Journal of Counseling and Development, 69,* 285–287.

18

Mass Media Effects Through Interpersonal Communication: The Role of *"Twende na Wakati"* on the Adoption of HIV/AIDS Prevention in Tanzania

Peer J. Svenkerud
Burson-Marsteller, Oslo, Norway

Nagesh Rao
University of New Mexico

Everett M. Rogers
University of New Mexico

The purpose of the present chapter is to explore the role of interpersonal communication in facilitating mass media effects. We compare (a) the *direct* effects of exposure to a popular entertainment-education radio program in Tanzania, *"Twende na Wakati" ("TNW")* (Swahili for, "Let's Go with the Times") on the adoption of HIV/AIDS prevention behavior, and (b) with the *indirect* effects of this radio program via interpersonal peer communication.

EFFECTS OF MASS MEDIA AND INTERPERSONAL COMMUNICATION ON BEHAVIOR CHANGE

Mass media and interpersonal communication historically have been viewed as separate sub-disciplines of communication (Reardon & Rogers, 1988; Rogers, 1994). Scholars in each subdiscipline have worked independently, with little collaboration or exchange of theories or methodologies. Some researchers (Gumpert & Cathcart, 1986; Reardon & Rogers, 1988) argued that the division between interpersonal and mass media communication, which is based on the history of communication study and on university politics, is a false dichotomy. The rise of new interactive communication technologies, for instance, which possess characteristics of both interpersonal and mass communication, is changing the way we conceptualize mass-mediated and interpersonal communication effects (Reardon & Rogers, 1988). These changes in the communication environment have led scholars such as Gumpert and Cathcart (1986) to argue that mass media and interpersonal communication can be effectively integrated.

The goal of the present chapter is to point to the potential effective integration of mass media and interpersonal channels of communication to jointly trigger prosocial behavior change. We further explore the effects of a specific type of media messages, *entertainment-education* (E-E), on behavior change. We propose that E-E's unique qualities (a) create a climate that triggers interpersonal peer communication about the topics discussed in an E-E radio program, and further, (b) persuade people to change their behavior.

THE ENTERTAINMENT-EDUCATION APPROACH
TO SOCIAL CHANGE

The idea of combining entertainment and education to foster prosocial change began thousands of years ago in the days of oral storytelling and folk drama. However, the conscious use of this strategy in mass communication is a relatively new phenomenon (Svenkerud, Rahoi, & Singhal, 1995). Entertainment-education is the process of embedding educational content with entertainment messages to increase knowledge about an issue, create favorable attitudes, and change overt behavior concerning the educational issue or topic (Singhal, Rogers, & Brown, 1993). Increasingly, such entertainment formats as television serials, rock music videos, comic books, and game shows have been successfully utilized to convey educational messages to promote prosocial ideas (Brown & Singhal, 1993; Coleman & Meyer, 1990).

Entertainment-education draws on Bandura's (1977) social learning theory, which postulates that people model and role-play their behavior after others. Miguel Sabido (1988), creator of E-E *telenovelas* (soap operas) in Mexico, developed a multidisciplinary theoretical framework including elements from Bandura's social learning theory, Bentley's dramatic theory (Nariman, 1993), and Jung's theories of archetypes (Ross, 1993) to effectively promote educational values in an entertaining format.

Entertainment-education efforts focus on six important elements of popular culture: (a) *pervasiveness,* because entertainment and media are everywhere, (b) *popularity,* because most people enjoy being entertained, (c) *personal focus,* because readers of these texts are moved to share the experiences of the characters, (d) *persuasiveness,* because media messages and characters can sway audience members in a variety of ways, (e) *profitability,* because entertainment programs can attract the necessary commercial support to fund educational messages, and (f) *passion,* because these messages can stir strong audience emotions about prosocial issues (Brown & Singhal, 1993; Kincaid, Rimon, Piotrow, & Coleman, 1992). Entertainment media are an effective way to reach the public with prosocial messages (Cambridge, 1992; Church & Geller, 1989; Coleman & Meyer, 1990; Head, 1995; Kincaid et al., 1992; Lull, 1990; Mody, 1991; Nariman, 1993; Sabido, 1989; Singhal & Udornpim, 1997).

Two unique qualities of E-E programs are important in influencing behavior change through interpersonal communication: (a) The audience is a participant, rather than just a target, and (b) E-E may be especially useful for opening discussion and debate, but less useful for directly generating behavior change (Storey, 1995). Our present research analyzes the direct versus the indirect effects of a Tanzanian E-E radio soap opera, *"Twende na Wakati,"* on the adoption of HIV prevention behavior.

MEDIATED VERSUS INTERPERSONAL COMMUNICATION

Communication channels are the means through which a source(s) conveys a message to a receiver(s) (Rogers, 1976). Communication that occurs in face-to-face interaction between two or more individuals is *interpersonal* communication. *Mass media* channels are those means of transmitting messages that involve radio, television, or print media to reach a wide, often noncontiguous audience (Rogers, 1995).

The dominant paradigm of communication in the 1950s and 1960s argued that mass communication was the key to modernization in traditional societies (Lerner, 1958; Rogers, 1962; Schramm, 1964). These modernization theorists embraced the *hypodermic needle model* (Lasswell, 1927), postulating that mass media can influence people directly and uniformly by injecting them with appropriate messages, designed to trigger desired responses.

The hypodermic needle model was challenged by the *two-step flow model,* which sought to explain the relationship between mass media and interpersonal communication. First formulated by Lazarsfeld, Berelson, and Gaudet (1944), the two-step flow model proposed that mass media did not have such powerful, direct effects. Although the model argued that the mass media play a key role in informing and persuading key individuals (opinion leaders) to change their behavior, these opinion leaders in turn magnified their persuasive powers through interpersonal communication links to other audience members (Rogers, 1994). The two-step flow model emphasized the advantage of interpersonal channels over mass media communication in inducing behavioral change (Rogers, 1995).

Several studies conducted in recent years have linked mass media and interpersonal communication to analyze diverse issues like voter behavior and public health concerns such as HIV/AIDS, family planning, and drug prevention. A majority of these studies conclude that the mass media and interpersonal communication are inextricably linked (Coleman, 1993; Endenberg, Flora, & Nass, 1995; Kincaid, Elias, Coleman, & Segura, 1988; Myers, 1994; Valente, Poppe, & Payne-Merit, 1996; Weaver, Zhu, & Willnat, 1992).

In the present chapter we combine lessons learned from the two-step flow model, a mediated theory of interpersonal communication, and the false dichotomy between interpersonal and mass media communication to argue that *"Twende na Wakati"* (and in general, the E-E strategy) triggers interpersonal communication among audience members (Vaughan & Rogers, 1996), and that when such communication is about HIV/AIDS, there is a greater likelihood that a person will adopt an HIV/AIDS prevention behavior (Rogers et al., 1997).

"TWENDE NA WAKATI"

"Twende na Wakati" (TNW) is an E-E radio soap opera that was systematically designed, based on Miguel Sabido's E-E strategy.[1] Creative talent in Tanzania wrote and produced the radio soap opera to ensure that it was culturally appropriate and that the characters, scenes, and circumstances were designed to be realistic for the Tanzania audience.

"TNW" was broadcast in Tanzania since July 11, 1993, for one half-hour, twice weekly in early prime time, at 6:30 PM, on the medium-wave radio channel of Radio Tanzania. Our research project, a large-scale field experiment, in which Dodomo, a region in central Tanzania (which covers the central part of Tanzania, an area in which 3.7 million people reside), served as a comparison (or control) area. For the first 2 years of the project (1993–1995), *"TNW"* was not broadcast to residents in the Dodomo region. The Tanzania Project is the first national field experiment on the effects of the E-E strategy to have a control area in order to measure the effects of the radio program, independent of contemporaneous changes

---

[1]Miguel Sabido, a writer, producer, and director of *Televisa,* the Mexican national television network, designed seven prosocial soap operas in Mexico between 1975 and 1982. These soap operas were highly unusual in that they were grounded in several human communication theories, including Bandura's social learning theory. All of Sabido's soap operas earned high television ratings, and were commercially viable (Nariman, 1993).

underway in Tanzania.[2] In mid-1993 (just before the broadcast of "TNW" began), and at 1-year intervals thereafter (in 1994, 1995, and 1996), POFLEP researchers[3] gathered personal interview data from a national sample. The sample included both the Dodoma comparison area (where broadcasts of the radio soap opera were blocked), and the treatment area (where broadcasts of the radio soap opera could be heard). Our survey instrument measured the effects of "TNW" on knowledge, attitude, and practice of both HIV/AIDS prevention and family planning (Rogers et al., 1997).

The Storyline of "TNW"

"TNW" depicts the daily life of Tanzanians in their struggle against harsh economic difficulties to improve their quality of life (Swalehe, Rogers, Gilboard, Alford, & Montoya, 1995). The radio soap opera attacks certain traditional values of Tanzanian society, such as male chauvinism and son preference, and espouses such modern values as women's empowerment, smaller families, and sexual responsibility through the depiction of positive, transitional, and negative role models. Approximately 6% of the soap opera content deals with HIV/AIDS prevention (Rogers et al., 1997). Other issues are family planning, spousal communication, and gender equality.

The story of "TNW" takes place in the busy town of Milindimo and its neighboring villages. The main characters in "TNW" are Mkwaju and his wife Tunu. Mkwaju is a negative role model. In the early episodes of the soap opera, Mkwaju is a devoted husband and a hardworking truck driver. However, as the story unfolds, his promiscuous behavior and deceitful ways emerge. Mkwaju impregnates three women and all of them give birth to baby girls, frustrating Mkwaju's desire for sons. Mkwaju's wayward ways lead to a worsening financial condition; he resorts to stealing and is eventually fired from his job due to misconduct, absenteeism, and alcoholism.[4] Mkwaju's irresponsible sexual behavior suggests that he is likely to contract HIV, presumably through heterosexual contact.

Tunu, Mkwaju's wife, works as a secretary at the Maendeleo Trucking Company, where Mkwaju is a truck driver. Tunu is brought up according to traditional norms and customs, and is a negative role model in the beginning of the soap opera. Mkwaju and Tunu adopt neither HIV/AIDS prevention methods nor family-planning methods, and Tunu's repeated pregnancies take a toll on her health. Eventually, Tunu is empowered, adopts HIV/AIDS prevention and family planning, and leaves Mkwaju. Thus, Tunu begins as a negative role model and becomes a positive role model during the course of the radio soap opera.

Another positive role model in the soap opera is Bina, a nurse, who advises the main characters of "TNW" on HIV/AIDS prevention and family planning. Other positive role models include Fundi Mitindo, a tailor, and his wife, Mama Waridi, who depict a couple making joint decisions, and practice HIV/AIDS prevention and family planning. When Mkwaju's negative behavior becomes pronounced, Fundi and Mama Waridi provide material support for Tunu and her children.

---

[2]Some 52% of the adults in our treatment area, or about 4.8 million people, reported that they listened to "TNW" during the first 2 years of its broadcasts. The average listener was exposed to 105 of the 204 radio episodes. Two percent of our respondents in the Dodomo comparison area listened to the radio program, mainly on short-wave radios. This unanticipated experimental contamination is not considered a serious threat to the validity of our study.

[3]Population Family Life Education Programme (POFLEP), a Tanzanian research and educational center headquartered in Arusha, Tanzania, served as an important research collaborator and help executing the research on "TNW."

[4]"TNW" focused on the HIV/AIDS issue because a 1992 POFLEP formative evaluation showed that Tanzanians feared the presence and spread of AIDS in their country. On the basis of blood donor data, the National AIDS Control Programme (1995) estimated that 1.2 million Tanzanians were infected with HIV in 1995, about 8% of the 15 million adults in that country.

METHODOLOGY

Our present chapter is based mainly on a personal interview survey administered by trained researchers from POFLEP (Population Family Life Education Programme), a research center in Arusha, Tanzania, with which we collaborated in the present investigation. Our annual surveys were conducted in 1993 ($n = 2,652$) to provide baseline data before *"TNW"* was broadcast, in 1994 ($n = 2,786$), and in 1995 ($n = 2,801$). Each survey represented a nationwide random sample of Tanzanian households. We show how *"TNW"* influenced its listeners to talk about HIV/AIDS prevention and to adopt an HIV/AIDS prevention method. Our main dependent variable is the adoption of a HIV/AIDS prevention method.

We answer three main research questions:

1. What are the effects of *"TNW"* on the adoption of an HIV/AIDS prevention method?
2. Did listeners of *"TNW"* talk to others about the radio program, and if so, with whom did they talk?
3. What are the effects of *"TNW"* on listeners who did not talk with others about the program (the direct effects of exposure), in comparison to listeners who talked with others about *"TNW"* (mass media effects through interpersonal communication)?

FINDINGS

Almost everybody in Tanzania knew about HIV/AIDS when broadcasts of *"TNW"* began in 1993. Knowledge of the existence of HIV/AIDS rose from 96% in 1993 to 98% in 1995. Some misconceptions about the means of HIV transmission existed. For instance, 17% of our respondents (18% in 1993) thought that they could contract AIDS by using a condom,[5] whereas 27% of our respondents in 1993 believed that they could get HIV from a mosquito bite. Some 58% of our 1995 respondents knew someone who had AIDS, an indication of the widespread prevalence of the epidemic in Tanzania.

To answer Research Question #1, we compared the adoption of HIV/AIDS prevention in our treatment versus control respondents in 1994 and 1995 (Table 18.1). Our results show that in 1994 treatment respondents were more likely to adopt an HIV/AIDS prevention method than are the Dodomo comparison respondents. Some 34% of the treatment respondents indicated that they adopted an HIV/AIDS prevention method due to listening to *"TNW,"* compared to 9% of the comparison respondents. In 1995, 44% of our treatment respondents reported adoption of an HIV/AIDS prevention methods due to listening to *"TNW,"* compared to 1% of the control respondents.

Research Question #2 examined with whom the listeners of *"TNW"* talked. In 1994, 46% of listeners in the treatment area talked to others about *"TNW"* (Table 18.2). This percentage increased to 57% in 1995. Table 18.2 shows that most respondents talked (a) with friends (67% in 1994, and 58% in 1995), and (b) with their spouse (21% in 1994, and 35% in 1995).

To answer Research Question #3, we compared listeners/nontalkers with listeners/talkers in the treatment area to determine what effects listening to *"TNW"* had on (a) listeners who did not talk with others, in comparison to (b) listeners who talked to others about the radio program. Responses from our listeners/nontalkers indicated direct effects of exposure to *"TNW"* on adoption of an HIV prevention method: The radio program influenced listeners

---

[5]A widespread rumor in Tanzania was that the lubricant in foreign-manufactured condoms contained HIV.

TABLE 18.1
Treatment Versus Comparison Respondents and Adoption
of HIV Prevention Due to *"TNW"* in Tanzania, 1994–1995

	Adoption of HIV Prevention Due to "TNW"		
Year	*Treatment Respondents*	*Comparison Respondents*	*Total Respondents*
1994	656 (34%)	73 (9%)	729 (26%)
	(*n* = 1,925)	(*n* = 861)	(*n* = 2,786)
1995	847 (44%)	10 (1%)	857 (31%)
	(*n* = 1,939)	(*n* = 862)	(*n* = 2,801)
			5,587

TABLE 18.2
Listeners Who Talk to Others About *"TNW,"* and With Whom They Talk

Year	*Talkers*	*Nontalkers*
1994 (*n* = 885)	411 (46%)	457 (52%)
- Talk to spouse	87 (21%)	
- Talk to friends	278 (67%)	
- Talk to others	21 (6%)	
- No response	25 (6%)	
1995 (*n* = 753)	426 (57%)	309 (41%)
- Talk to spouse	149 (35%)	
- Talk to friends	247 (58%)	
- Talk to others	26 (6%)	
- No response	4 (1%)	

to talk about *"TNW"* with others, which in turn helped persuade them to adopt an HIV prevention method. *Mass media effects through interpersonal communication were considerably stronger than the direct effects of mass media exposure* (Table 18.3). Some 64% of listeners who did not talk to others about *"TNW"* in 1993–1994 adopted an HIV/AIDS prevention method due to the radio soap opera.[6] The comparable figure was 84% for *"TNW"* listeners who talked with others about the program.[7] By 1995, these numbers increased dramatically. Some 69% of the listeners/nontalkers reported adopting an HIV/AIDS prevention method due to *"TNW."* For the listeners/talkers, 92% adopted HIV/AIDS prevention.

We analyzed the relationship between listeners who talked with others, and listeners who did not talk with others: (a) if the respondent was monogamous and had only one sexual partner during the previous year, and (b) if the respondent had never shared needles/razors. Table 18.4 shows that in 1994, listeners who talked with others were more likely to be monogamous (61% compared to 58%) and more likely not to share needles/razors (92% compared to 88%). However, in 1995, the results are somewhat mixed. Listeners who did not talk to others were more likely to be monogamous (67% compared to 52%) than listeners who did talk with others. Listeners who talked were still more likely not to share needles/razors than listeners who did not talk (91% compared to 86%).

---

[6]Because for instance, the use of condoms most commonly is negotiated with a spouse/partner before adoption, we would expect such interpersonal communication to be part of the adoption process of any birth-control method.

[7]The adoption of HIV/AIDS prevention was not related to whether listeners talked to a friend, spouse, or someone else. Respondents who talked about the educational content of *"TNW"* were more likely to adopt an HIV prevention method than were nontalkers.

TABLE 18.3
Adoption of HIV Prevention by Listeners Who Talked to Others
and Listeners Who Did Not Talk to Others in Tanzania, 1994–1995

Year	Listeners Who Talked With Others	Listeners Who Did Not Talk With Others
1994		
- Adopted HIV prevention	347 (84%)	290 (64%)
- Did not adopt HIV prevention	64 (16%)	167 (36%)
Total	411 (100%)	457 (100%)
1995		
- Adopted HIV prevention	563 (92%)	253 (69%)
- Did not adopt HIV prevention	49 (8%)	114 (31%)
Total	612 (100%)	367 (100%)

TABLE 18.4
Validity Check: Responses From Survey Questions Unrelated to "TNW"

Year	Listeners Who Talked With Others	Listeners Who Did Not Talk With Others
1994		
- Respondents practicing monogamy		
Yes	249 (61%)	263 (58%)
No	162 (39%)	194 (42%)
Total	411 (100%)	457 (100%)
- Respondents who did not share needles/razors		
Yes	376 (92%)	406 (88%)
No	35 (8%)	51 (12%)
Total	411 (100%)	457 (100%)
1995		
- Respondents practicing monogamy		
Yes	317 (52%)	244 (67%)
No	295 (48%)	123 (33%)
Total	612 (100%)	367 (100%)
- Respondents who did not share needles/razors		
Yes	556 (91%)	320 (86%)
No	56 (9%)	47 (14%)
Total	612 (100%)	367 (100%)

We believe that these results provide evidence for our three research questions, but the data should be interpreted with caution. Although our respondents were motivated to adopt an HIV/AIDS prevention method due to listening to "TNW," we have to consider other factors (such as a respondent's self-efficacy, access to resources, etc.) to fully understand the effects of the radio soap opera.

Our male respondents with multiple sex partners were more likely to adopt a family-planning method to prevent HIV (and other sexually transmitted diseases [STDs]) compared to the monogamous men in our study (Table 18.5). In 1993, 10% of our monogamous male respondents reported that they had adopted a family-planning method to prevent STDs, which increased to 12% in 1995. The change from 1993 to 1995 was more dramatic for men with multiple sex partners. In 1993, only 8% of our respondents reported that they had

TABLE 18.5
Prevention of STDs as the Motivation for the Use of
Family Planning by Men in Tanzania from 1993 to 1995

Year	Men With One Partner	Men With More Than One Partner	Total Respondents
1993	10.0%	0.7%	389
1994	11.3%	24.7%	552
1995	11.9%	33.9%	530

adopted a family-planning method to prevent STDs; by 1995, this figure was 34% (Table 18.5).

The total cost of 204 episodes of *"TNW"* broadcast by Radio Tanzania from 1993 to 1995 was $346,333. The radio soap opera influenced 4,192,000 listeners (82% estimated on the basis of self-reports) to adopt an HIV/AIDS prevention. Hence, the cost of *"TNW"* per adopter of HIV/AIDS prevention was only about 8 cents ($346,333/4,192,000 adopters).

CONCLUSIONS

Our results indicate that the indirect effects of mass media via interpersonal communication are more powerful than the direct effects of media on behavior change (HIV/AIDS prevention). This finding is consistent with Rogers' (1995) claim that mass media channels of communication are relatively more important at the knowledge stage in the innovation-decision process of adopting a new idea, whereas interpersonal channels are relatively more important at the persuasion stage in the innovation-decision process. Our present findings are limited to E-E media, which have certain unique qualities that facilitate behavior change through interpersonal peer communication.

We believe *"TNW"* (and E-E in general) was effective in causing behavior change via interpersonal communication for several reasons:

1. Knowledge about HIV/AIDS was already high in Tanzania, and 58% of our respondents knew someone with HIV/AIDS. The relative proximity of the disease to the individual Tanzanian made this issue a salient, relevant topic for discussion. The E-E strategy is consciously designed to address educational issues like HIV/AIDS through a realistic plot/storyline, and using role models that are similar (homophilous) in age, gender, socioeconomic status, and so on, with the target audience. The emotional nature of the drama in *"TNW"* catalyzed interpersonal communication among its listeners due to the realistic, culturally proximate design of the storyline of the radio soap opera. The E-E strategy has a unique ability to bring about strong media effects in overt behavior, perhaps because it is based on a theory of behavior change (Bandura's, 1977, social learning model), and because it elicits audience individuals' identification with role models provided by the media (Rogers et al., 1997). Listeners talked with each other, presumably in order to give meaning to the radio message content, such as by speculating about whether (and how) Mkwaju had contracted AIDS.

2. HIV/AIDS is a sensitive/taboo topic in Tanzania, restricting interpersonal communication about this issue. However, an E-E radio soap opera like *"TNW"* stimulated discussion about this sensitive topic, circumventing traditional, more personal ways of talking about this issue.

Interpersonal peer sources/channels are particularly effective in changing behavior due to their credibility, whereas mass media channels are perceived as less personal, and therefore, less likely to initiate behavior change. Although mass media channels are effective in creating awareness and increasing knowledge about an issue, adoption of a behavior change occurs mainly if the message is communicated by an interpersonal, trustworthy channel (Rogers, 1995). Audience members discussed these sensitive issues in relation to the characters' lives (e.g., Mkwaju's), instead of their own, which was more socially acceptable. The emotional and involving nature of the radio soap opera episodes encouraged interpersonal communication about HIV/AIDS prevention, leading to widespread behavior change on behalf of our respondents. Through such peer communication about HIV/AIDS prevention, listeners were influenced to change their behavior (Rogers et al., 1997). Fundamentally, peer communication moves people to behavior change (Rogers, in press).

3. The E-E soap opera had few competing messages on radio or other mass communication channels in Tanzania. "TNW" became extremely popular. Without such widespread exposure by adult Tanzanians in the treatment area, the radio soap opera could not have had its effects on behavior change.

4. What do our present findings mean for the constructed dichotomy between mass media and interpersonal communication in the field of communication study? Entertainment-education can be effective in promoting interpersonal communication about sensitive topics like family planning[8] and HIV/AIDS, which, in turn, promote behavior change. The widespread popularity of the soap opera format, the ability of the melodrama to depict the tussle between prosocial and antisocial behaviors, and their interactive, repetitive nature, makes this genre especially suited for carrying prosocial messages, triggering interpersonal communication.

Other factors than "TNW" could have influenced adoption of an HIV prevention behavior (such as increased coverage in the media about HIV, perceived risk of contracting HIV, etc.). Regardless, "TNW" has been the only systematic HIV/AIDS prevention program over the 2 years of study in Tanzania. Our study benefited from the analytical power provided by a field experimental design, as well as from multiple-method triangulation of our measurements of media effects. The influence of other, contemporaneous factors were removed by our quasi-experimental design.

Our Tanzania research continues. Since mid-1995, "TNW" has been broadcast in the Dodomo area, previously the comparison area. We are currently measuring the effects of the radio soap opera in the Dodomo area with personal interview surveys and other means. The radio soap opera has had similar effects there, with a 2-year lag, to what it had in the 1993–1995 treatment area. Further, we continue to trace the longer term effects of the radio soap opera in the original treatment area. We expect to investigate how "TNW" had different effects in rural and urban people, and whether it had different effects on men and women.

ACKNOWLEDGMENTS

The authors wish to thank Peter Vaughan, Ramadhan M. A. Swalehe, Suruchi Sood, and Krista Alford for their valuable comments on an earlier version of this chapter. We also thank the UNFPA (United Nations Population Fund), the Rockefeller Foundation, the Wey-

---

[8]Our research found parallel results for the effects of "TNW" on family-planning adoption via interpersonal communication (Rogers et al., 1997).

erhaeuser Family Foundation, and the Lang Foundation for funding our research on *"Twende na Wakati."*

REFERENCES

Bandura, A. (1977). *Social learning theory*. Englewood Cliffs, NJ: Prentice-Hall.

Brown, W. J., & Singhal, A. (1993). Entertainment-education media: An opportunity for enhancing Japan's leadership role in Third World development. *Keio Communication Review, 15*, 81–101.

Cambridge, V. C. (1992). Radio soap operas: The Jamaican experience. *Studies in Latin American Popular Culture, 11*, 93–109.

Church, C., & Geller, J. (1989). Lights, cameras, action! *Population Reports, 38*, 1–31.

Coleman, C. (1993). The influence of mass media and interpersonal communication on societal and personal risk judgment. *Communication Research, 20*, 611–628.

Coleman, P., & Meyer, R. C. (1990). *Proceedings from the entertainment-educate conference: Entertainment for social change*. Baltimore, MD: Johns Hopkins University Center for Communication Programs.

Engelberg, M., Flora, J., & Nass, C. (1995). AIDS knowledge: Effects of channel involvement and interpersonal communication. *Health Communication, 7*, 73–91.

Gumpert, G., & Catchcart, R. (Eds.). (1986). *Inter/media: Interpersonal communication in a media world* (3rd ed.). New York: Oxford University Press.

Head, S. W. (1985). *World broadcasting systems: A comparative analysis*. Belmont, CA: Wadsworth.

Kincaid, D. L., Elias, J. R., Coleman, P. L. & Segura, F. (1988). *Getting the message: The communication for young people project*. Washington, DC: U.S. A.I.D. Evaluation Special Study 56.

Kincaid, D. L., Rimon, J. G., Piotrow, P. T., & Coleman, P. L. (1992). *The enter-educate approach: Using entertainment to change health behavior*. Paper presented at the meeting of the Population Association of America, Denver.

Lasswell, H. D. (1927). *Propaganda technique in the World War*. New York: Knopf.

Lazarsfeld, P., Berelson, B., & Gaudet, H. (1944). *The people's choice: How the voter makes up his mind in a presidential election*. New York: Duell, Sloan, Pearce.

Lerner, D. (1958). *The passing of traditional society*. New York: The Free Press.

Lozano, E. (1989). The force of myth on popular narratives: The case of melodramatic serials. *Communication Theory, 2*, 207–220.

Lull, J. (1990). *China turned on: Television, reform and resistance*. New York: Routledge.

Mody, B. (1991). *Designing messages for development communication*. New Delhi, India: Sage.

Myers, K. (1994). Interpersonal and mass media communication: Political learning in New Hampshire's First-in-the-Nation Presidential Primary. *Sociological Spectrum, 14*, 143–165.

Nariman, H. (1993). *Soap operas for social change*. Westport, CT: Praeger.

National AIDS Control Programme. (1995). *HIV/AIDS/STD Surveillance. Report 10*. Dar es Salaam: Tanzania Ministry of Public Health.

Rogers, E. M. (1962). *Diffusion of innovations* (1st ed.). New York: The Free Press.

Rogers, E. M. (1976). Communication and development: The passing of the dominant paradigm. *Communication Research, 3*, 121–148.

Rogers, E. M. (1994). *A history of communication study: A biographical approach*. New York: The Free Press.

Rogers, E. M. (1995). *Diffusion of innovations* (4th ed.). New York: The Free Press.

Rogers, E. M. (in press). When the mass media have strong effects: Intermedia processes. In J. Trent (Ed.), *Communication: Views from the helm for the twenty-first century*. Boston: Allyn & Bacon.

Rogers, E. M., Vaughan, P. W., Swalehe, R. M. A., Rao, N., Svenkerud, P. J., Sood, S., & Alford, K. L. (1997). *Effects of an entertainment-education radio soap opera on family planning and HIV/AIDS prevention behavior in Tanzania*. Albuquerque: University of New Mexico, Department of Communication and Journalism, and Arusha, Tanzania: Population Family Life Education Programme.

Ross, L. B. (1993). *To speak or be silent: The paradox of disobedience in the lives of women*. Wilmett, IL: Chiron Publications.

Sabido, M. (1989). *Soap operas in Mexico*. Paper presented at the Entertainment for Social Change Conference, Los Angeles.

Schramm, W. (1964). *Mass media and national development: The role of information in the developing countries*. Stanford, CA: Stanford University Press.

Singhal, A., Rogers, E. M., & Brown, W. J. (1993). Harnessing the potential of entertainment-education telenovelas. *Gazette, 51*, 1–8.

Singhal, A., & Svenkerud, P. (1994). Pro-socially shareable entertainment television programmes: A programming alternative in developing countries? *Journal of Development Communication, 5,* 17–30.

Singhal, A., & Udornpim, K. (1997). Cultural shareability, archetypes and television soaps. "Oshindrome" in Thailand. *Gazette, 59,* 171–188.

Storey, D. (1995, May). *Entertainment-education, popular culture, and the sustainability of communication: Lessons from Indonesia and Pakistan.* Paper presented at the meeting of the International Communication Association, Albuquerque.

Svenkerud, P., Rahoi, R., & Singhal, A. (1995). Incorporating ambiguity and archetypes in entertainment-education programming: Lessons learned from "Oshin." *Gazette, 55,* 147–168.

Swalehe, R., Rogers, E., Gilboard, M., Alford, K., & Montoya, R. (1995). *A content analysis of the entertainment-education radio soap opera "Twende Na Wakati" (Let's Go with the Times) in Tanzania.* Albuquerque: University of New Mexico, Department of Communication and Journalism, and Arusha, Tanzania: Population Family Life Education Programme.

Valente, T. W., Poppe, P. R., & Payne-Merritt, A. (1996). Mass-media generated interpersonal communication as sources of information about family planning. *Journal of Health Communication, 1,* 247–265.

Vaughan, P., & Rogers, E. M. (1996). *A communication model for the effects of an entertainment-education soap opera on the stages of family planning adoption.* Unpublished manuscript.

Weaver, D. H., Zhu, J. H., & Willnat, L. (1992). The bridging function of interpersonal communication in agenda-setting. *Journalism Quarterly, 69,* 856–867.

V

THE PUBLIC:
PERSPECTIVES ON
MASS-MEDIATED COMMUNICATION

Life on the Edge of the Precipice: Information Subsidy and the Rise of AIDS as a Public Issue, 1983–1989

Timothy N. Walters
Northeast Louisiana University

Lynne M. Walters
Susanna Hornig Priest
Texas A&M University

Driven by the quest for power, a need for ego gratification, and a desperate competition for dwindling dollars, medical researchers intensely promote their causes and programs. They do so because they assume that publicity assists in creating and maintaining goodwill and translates into secure financial support and public policies positive to the organization (Evans & Priest, 1995; Nelkin, 1987; T. Walters & L. Walters, 1992, 1994a, 1994b). To assess the results of their proactive, sophisticated efforts look no further than the pages of newspapers of record such as the *Chicago Tribune,* the *Los Angeles Times, The New York Times,* and *The Washington Post*. On the front pages and between the covers, numerous "discovery" and "announcement" articles dutifully attest to the success that medical groups have had in gaining access to the media (Altman, 1995). Because of this unfettered media access, modeling the source-reporter relationship, examining how that relationship builds the news, and determining how information is funneled from source to reporter to audience helps in understanding how mediated reality is created and defined (Ohl, Pincus, & Rimmer, 1995; T. Walters & L. Walters, 1996; Weaver & Elliott, 1985).

These articles do not appear magically on their own. They are the result of a complex, symbiotic relationship between journalist and institutional information source such as a public relations practitioner. On one hand, sources derive benefit from publicity through the mass media. They gain access to target audiences and the ability to define reality through manipulating the information stock (Nelkin, 1987; T. Walters & L. Walters, 1992, 1994a, 1994b). They believe that placement brings with it legitimacy and attention to an individual institution, program, product, service, or cause, because of the credence and assumption of impartiality that the public attaches to items in the "news" (T. Walters & L. Walters, 1992, 1994a, 1994b). On the other hand, journalists and media organizations derive benefit, too. They receive a flow of cheap, regular, reliable, and usable information. (See T. Walters & L. Walters, 1992, 1994a, 1994b, for listings of these studies.)

Scholars have created colorful metaphors to describe the relationship between source and reporter. Gans (1979) called it a "tango." Hess (1981) labeled it a "personal affinity" that brought together (or kept apart) journalists and their sources. No matter how the relationship is described, the public relations offices and news media work together. For whatever else is true, data have shown that media organizations have neither the economic sources nor the time to cover the entire story of the day.

The medical news cycle begins with academic papers that are often simultaneously published and announced to reporters at pseudoevents like press conferences. Then, the reporter "reveals" the results of the studies to his readers (T. Walters & L. Walters, 1992). Even as they loudly assert editorial independence from the "highwaymen" who inhabit public relations offices, news media officials rationalize using their public relations output. Reporters posit that "balancing of opposing views" and "source attribution" neutralizes inherent one-sidedness. Although such might be true in a perfect world, lack of balance often occurs because of economic necessity, lack of expertise, or just plain ineptitude (Dunwoody & Ryan, 1983; Schoenfeld, Meier, & Griffin, 1979; L. Walters & T. Walters, 1991). That ineptitude is partly the result of the perspective from which many reporters view science. Wishing for neat solutions, some cling to a textbook view of science as a well-managed, orderly, and predictable field when, in reality, the acquisition of science is messy, filled with dead ends, and cluttered with uncertainties (Moore, 1989a).

Because most reporters look for simple solutions and are unable to follow paradigms, translate statistics, or independently evaluate the merits of conflicting assertions, they have become what has been described as incompetent "enough to cover anything" (Cohn, 1989). For news media unusually dependent on medical science sources, the potential arises for a handful of articulate, star-quality scientists, who gather the most attention, to impact profoundly news content (Cohn, 1989; Goodell, 1975; Kreighbaum, 1967; Moore, 1989a; Turk, 1985; L. Walters & T. Walters, 1991; T. Walters & L. Walters, 1992, 1994a, 1994b). This danger is heightened because "the press tends to print the views and interpretations of individual authorities rather than report the results of actual studies" (Shepherd, 1979, p. 134).

Besides obvious problems with errors and purposeful omissions, using information from a small pool reinforces the narrowness of perspective. Because each source may promote selective perceptions, a reporter's choice of sources becomes critical, determining not just who, but what, will be given "standing" as an authoritative voice. This becomes critical because each source may have a different philosophy, organizational background, and primary goal; each may focus on different aspects of a story (Griffen & Dunwoody, 1995). The tendency of newspapers to pull medical stories from the wire service only exacerbates the problem because medical news becomes interpreted by a small number of reporters.

For these reasons, a balancing of viewpoints may not occur if an articulate claims maker dominates the information scene. If this happens, then the one who reaches the broadest audience first may gain the upper hand in making his or hers the dominant ideology. And, as Noelle-Neumann (1984) pointed out, "What does not get reported does not exist, or . . . its chances of becoming part of ongoing, perceived reality are minimal" (p. 150). It follows that the ability of the media to give standing, that is, to include or exclude information from disparate sources, adds or detracts to the context in which a health issue becomes defined, recognized, and considered as a social problem.

This chapter examines a source-media relationship in a nonelection, nonpolitical context using quantitative methods to study the development of HIV/AIDS as an issue. Using a concept known as "information subsidy," the study focuses on sourcing patterns in the *Chicago Tribune*, the *Los Angeles Times, The New York Times,* and *The Washington Post* from 1983 to 1989 to see (a) if there were a subsidy, (b) the source of that subsidy, and (c) what effect, if any, that subsidy had on short- and long-term issue development.

METHODOLOGY

To demonstrate how the process of information gathering and dissemination worked with respect to the development of HIV/AIDS as an issue, a time-series analysis using monthly counts from *Readers' Guide to Periodical Literature, Indicus Medicus* (a medical index), and those of the *Chicago Tribune,* the *Los Angeles Times, The New York Times,* and *The Washington Post* was performed. Samples were drawn from the four newspapers for the period from 1983 to 1989. These were drawn using a computer program to develop constructed months for each year. Using a computer program, samples were chosen from one constructed month for each year. Data were gathered from each newspaper using the same constructed month. To develop a source-comment matrix from the articles sampled, all sources and their messages were identified by two coders with the paragraph as the unit of analysis. A second coder analyzed 25% of all data sets, and intercoder reliability was .920.

Each source was categorized according to affiliation. The nine broad institutional affiliations were: (a) Federal Elected Officials, including U.S. senators and representatives, (b) Federal Health Authorities, including the secretary of health and human services and officials of the Centers for Disease Control, Atlanta, among others, (c) State and Local Elected Officials, including governors and mayors, (d) State and Local Health authorities, including city and state boards of health, (e) Research Physicians, (f) Others (people with AIDS, physicians, and religious leaders), (g) Private Organizations, including the Red Cross and the National Hemophilia Society, (h) Gay Organizations, and (i) Unattributed.

Two coders also examined each paragraph for issue comments. These fell into 14 broad categories defined by L. Walters and T. Walters (1991). These included: (a) Cause: What caused AIDS, (b) Cure: How AIDS might be cured, (c) Education: Developing a public education program, (d) Funds: Who pays and how much, (e) Discrimination: Legal, medical, and personal, (f) Policy: What public policy is best, (g) Prevention: How AIDS might be prevented, (h) Risk Groups: Who is at risk, (i) Statistics: How many had it or could be projected to get it and how many have died, (j) Testing: Development and proposed use, (k) Transmission: How it is spread, (l) Treatment: Drugs and other methods, (m) Symptoms: How to tell if you have it, and (n) Others: All others. From these data, a source-comment matrix was developed for individual newspapers, for specific years, and for combined newspapers and years.

RESULTS

A time-series analysis used monthly totals of articles in each newspaper as the dependent variable and the monthly total of articles in *Readers' Guide* and *Indicus Medicus.* The data showed a strong relationship between the number of newspaper articles and the number of articles in *Readers' Guide* and *Indicus Medicus* (see Table 19.1). A sourcing check of the newspaper articles confirmed the time-order (direction) of the information flow. More than 90% of the articles were the product of news conferences, findings, bureaucratic meetings, or press releases previewing forthcoming academic papers or presentations. Only about 10% were the result of investigative reporting.

The Quantitative Connection. A total of 8,210 paragraphs appeared in the cumulative sample drawn from all newspapers in period from 1983 to 1989. Of this total, 413 appeared in 1983, 136 in 1984, 826 in 1985, 1,144 in 1986, 3,077 in 1987, 1,641 in 1988, and 964 in

TABLE 19.1
Information Subsidy Linear Time-Series Model, 1983–1989

	Readers' Guide	Indicus Medicus
All Newspapers	.816	.611
The Washington Post	.648	.510
The New York Times	.782	.560
Los Angeles Times	.833	.603
Chicago Tribune	.814	.619

Note. The closer to 1, the stronger the subsidy. Number is R2.

1989. Of the identified groups, Federal Health Authorities were the most used both in 1983 and cumulatively over the entire period. The cumulative top four sources over the time period were, in order Federal Health Officials, State and Local Health Officials, Private Groups, and Research Physicians. At the bottom of those selected for use in these newspapers were, starting with those least used, Research Physicians, Gay Organizations, Federal Elected Officials, and State and Local Elected Officials.

Over the time period, the Private Groups and Research Physicians rose dramatically as sources used. In 1983, Private Groups and Research Physicians were about 9% and 5.7% respectively of sources used whereas cumulatively Private Groups and Research Physicians were about 14% and 13% respectively of the sources used. Federal Health Officials fell from the 1983 figure of about 33% of sources used to a cumulative 15%. Despite these fluctuations in magnitude, a comparative chart based on Spearman's Rho showed that the rank order pattern of source usage was relatively stable from year to year during the entire time period and that 1983 set the pattern for the cumulative period with respect to sources (see Tables 19.1 and 19.2).

Only 1985 and 1988 with Spearman's of .492 and .438 slipped below the .500 mark from the sourcing pattern set in 1983. In 1985, the top four sources were, in order, State and Local Health Officials, State and Local Elected Officials, Private Groups, and Research Physicians. In 1988, the top four sources were, in order, Research Physicians, State and Local Health Officials, Federal Health Officials, and Private Groups.

Differences in sourcing patterns also emerged between the newspapers over the time period (see Table 19.2). Examined as a percentage of total newspaper paragraphs, Federal Elected Officials were more often used in The Washington Post and The New York Times than in the Los Angeles Times and the Chicago Tribune. The Chicago Tribune more often used Federal Health Officials than did the other newspapers, whereas The New York Times

TABLE 19.2
Top Four Cumulative Sources and Their Topics of Interest

	1983	1984	1985	1986	1987	1988
Federal Health Officials	Cure	Cause	Symp. Groups	Trans. Groups	Risk	Risk
State and Local Health Officials	Risk	Statistics Groups	Policy	Policy	Testing	Policy
Private Groups	Treatment	Testing	Discrimination	Policy	Testing	Policy
Research Physicians	Cause	Other	Cause	Cause	Cause	Other

Note. Ranking of cumulative sources and topics of interest determined as percentage of paragraphs from newspaper articles.

261

used Private Groups more often that did the other newspapers. *The New York Times* and *The Washington Post* used Research Physicians less often than the other newspapers whereas *The New York Times* and the *Chicago Tribune* used State and Local Health Officials more often than did *The Washington Post* and the *Los Angeles Times*. These findings seemed consistent not only with respect to perceptions about the newspapers as products of the media and geographical environment in which they operate, they also were consistent with reporting traditions.

Less consistency existed between the topic pattern established in 1983 and the cumulative totals for the period 1983–1989 (see Table 19.3). Whereas the top two topics for discussion in 1983 were Cure and Cause, the top two for the cumulative period were Policy and Education.

Because of the consistent sourcing patterns, the change in topic of discussion was not so much the product of changing sources as it was the result of changing focus of the sources selected. Except for 1984 and 1986, the ranking of the messages used in 1983 had little in common with later years. Conversely, 1987, 1988, and 1989 showed topic stability with respect to the cumulative message stock. Used as the base year, 1987 had a Spearman's of .771 with 1989 and .703 with 1990 and the cumulative Spearman's was .588 for 1985, .669 for 1986, .913 for 1987, .736 for 1988, and .690 for 1989.

The differences in the cumulative totals for categories of topics reflected the changed messages of those sources with the most access to the media over the time period as well as the aberrant source patterns of 1985 and 1988. This became clear after looking at a chart of the cumulative top four sources and the main topic of discussion for 1983 and for the period and an analysis of 1985 and 1988.

Although the rank order of the top four sources remained constant over the time period, the principal topics of those sources, except for Research Physician, did not. The data also suggested that the evolution of AIDS as an public issue had a compacted, and somewhat different, topic cycle when contrasted to earlier epidemics of socially connected diseases. Those who have studied analogous previous problems such as syphilis have found a consistent three-part pattern. Typically, in the first stage, mediated messages take on moral overtones. In the second stage, the media begin educating the public and covering the legal maneuvers aimed at containing the disease. In the third stage, the coverage focuses on the attempts to

TABLE 19.3
Top Four Topics of Interest, 1983–1989

	First	*Second*	*Third*	*Fourth*
1983	Policy	Cure	Cause	Risk Grps.
1984	Cause	Cure	Statistics	Education (t)
				Testing (t)
1985	Discrim.	Trans.	Funds	Treat.
1986	Policy	Cause	Education	Risk Grps.
1987	Education	Risk (t)	————	Stats.
		Testing (t)		
1988	Policy	Risk	Test (t)	————
			Trans. (t)	
1989	Policy	Treat.	Funds	Statistics
Cum.	Policy	Education	Funds	Discrim.

Note. The topics were divided into phasic groups using Spearman's Rho. Abbreviations: Cum. = Cumulative; Trans. = Transmission; Treat. = Treatment. Lowercase t indicates rank order tie between groups. Spearman's Rho between 1983 and 1984 (1983 serving as base year), .543; 1985 and 1986 (1985 serving as base year), .636; and 1987, 1988, and 1989 (1987 serving as base year), .771 and .703.

find medical treatments for the illness, with less emphasis on morality (Fuller & Myers, 1940; Schoenfeld et al., 1979; Strodthoff, Hawkins, & Schoenfeld, 1978; Tuchman, 1973; L. Walters & T. Walters, 1991).

Differences between HIV/AIDS and previous epidemics such as syphilis were many. First, most AIDS topics in all phases were centered around policy. Second, discussion of AIDS in moral overtones did not occur until Phase 2. Even so, this discussion was more connected with preventing discrimination than in enforcing morality. Third, the final phase of AIDS coverage was more concerned with policy than with treatment as had been found by studies of previous social diseases. The cumulative matrix of topics demonstrated the changing dynamics of the debate over the time period (see Table 19.3). While Prevention, Symptoms, and Treatment appeared to remain relatively constant over the time period, Cause, Cure, and Discrimination diminished and Funding, Policy, and Risk Groups increased. Education, Statistics, Testing, and Transmission had cyclical patterns that rose and fell like a sine-pulsing wave through the period.

The source pattern-aberrant years 1985 and 1988 also contributed to the truncated topic development pattern. The selected sources helped push discussion from moral to policy and funding issues. In 1985, the top four topics of the top four sources were: State and Local Health Officials—Policy, Transmission, Treatment, and Education; State and Local Elected Officials—Policy, Discrimination, Funds, and Transmission; Private Groups—Discrimination, Policy, Transmission, and Symptoms; and Research Physicians—Cause, Cure, Policy, and Funds.

In 1988, the top four topics of the top four sources were: Research Physicians—Other, Cause, Risk Groups, and Discrimination; State and Local Health Officials—Policy, Funds, Statistics, and Testing; Federal Health Authorities—Statistics, Treatment, and Risk Groups; and Private Groups—Policy, Treatment, Funds, and Statistics. If the periods were subdivided into phasic groups using Spearman's as the factor by which to relate the years, 1983 and 1984 would be grouped together, as would 1985 and 1986, and 1987, 1988, and 1989. These trends were different than that of earlier epidemics of social diseases. Instead of an initial discussion tinged with moral overtones, the AIDS debate launched into policy-related problems, followed by a concentration on discrimination, policy, and education.

DISCUSSION AND CONCLUSIONS

During the period from 1983 to 1989, an information subsidy flowed from sources to the four newspapers of record. Although the sources of HIV/AIDS information remained relatively stable, the topics did not. As might have been expected, Federal and State and Local Health Officials played a prominent role over the time period. But Private Groups, such as the Red Cross and the National Hemophilia Society, and Research Physicians also played a considerable role. Health Officials mostly discussed standard fare such as Cause, Cure, Policy, and Risk Groups; Private Groups and Research Physicians advocated their respective causes. Research Physicians promoted efforts to look for the cause of the disease, while demanding more money to find that cure.

Private Organizations stated their cases, cleaving along lines of risk assessment. On one hand, the Red Cross and other blood banks defended policies concerning donations and blood bank safety, protecting their vested economic interest. On the other hand, private organizations, such as the National Hemophilia Society, demanded closer looks at safety issues because their members were infected with a fatal disease.

Indicating a changed reporting perspective (and perhaps societal values as well) on the connection between public health policy and morality, the topic patterns relative to AIDS differed from those of historic models (Glazer, 1994). Because of the changed perspective, AIDS was addressed as less of a moral problem and more of a public policy problem.

Despite the shift from morality to policy, the AIDS discussion suffered because a "technological" view of medicine was emphasized over a "humanistic one." The discussion of solutions was framed in the wizardry of new science rather than in the more mundane realm of human responsibility and compassion (Nelkin, 1989). That technological frame of reference could have been produced by several influences, but certainly the prevalence of research physicians given standing as sources was a major contributory agent. This emphasis was not novel to either the time period or the issue. This emphasis is deeply ingrained in the mediated culture, dating at least to medical news coverage of "wonder" cures such as penicillin (Evans & Priest, 1995; Moore, 1989b; L. Walters & T. Walters, 1991).

In the United States, as perhaps in no other country, the driving medical ideology has focused "on cure rather than prevention, and is driven by a view of the body as a machine, hospitals as repair shops, and physicians as master mechanics. It is a view that sees cost as no barrier, and to a certain extent, prefers to ignore the common or mundane in pursuit of technical or engineering challenge" (Gandy, 1982, p. 120).

Glorified on stage, screen, and in fiction, these depictions have become ingrained in the culture. As Thomas Thompson (1976) described them, star quality physicians exist in a world apart. They are "performers in a dazzling theater packed with assistants, nurses, paramedics, and a battery of futuristic equipment which could seemingly lift the room into outer space. These are men who relish drama, who live life on the edge of the precipice" (p. 45). So, in fact and fiction, the mass media have helped create, and reinforce, a magic bullet message. Some believe these messages contribute to a willingness to support both expanded government funding for medical research and a demand for more high-technology medicine (Bennett, 1977; Gandy, 1982; Wildavksy, 1977).

As one theory posits the self-fulfilling cycle, the public wants interesting stories about struggles against disease or hopeful news about a cure just around the corner. The physician-researcher needs publicity and prestige brought by media coverage for power, money, and glamour. Moreover, the medical institution's public relations office and the press work hand-in-glove to meet the "perceived" public need (Altman, 1995; Moore, 1989b; Page, 1970).

Although audience expectations may be contributory, the "gee whiz" news frame has become less of an audience-fashioned problem and more of an editorial flaw (T. Walters & L. Walters, 1996). That is because as less and less knowledge is gained through firsthand experience, the audience has become more and more dependent on mediated reports. Exacerbating the problem is the rise of corporate medicine and reduced personal contact with physicians.

Questions that arise about which medical science from which source become facts become more critical in a high-tech society in which information and control are unevenly distributed (Evans & Priest, 1995). The sources given "standing" as outlets for information contribute mightily to the discussion. Because this is an age in which all parties in the health debate must concentrate on an equitable distribution of scarce resources, editors and reporters must rethink the process of how they gather and distribute the news. In doing so, they must address basic questions about what "adequacy" means with respect to medical reporting (Evans & Priest, 1995; Schwartz & Rimmer, 1995).

Can adequacy be defined in terms of objectivity? Does such objectivity mean accuracy, or balance, or a multiplicity of sources? Does objectivity vary from audience to audience? Or, are such concerns even relevant in examining coverage of medical science? Because of such complex questions, newspapers and other media outlets should seriously weigh the consequences of traditional reporting practices as they seek to serve the public interest. This is all the more critical in an era of diminished resources, managed care, strident public outcries over division of available resources, and intense media competition.

REFERENCES

Altman, L. K. (1995, January 10). Promises of miracles: News releases, Where journals fear to tread. *The New York Times,* pp. C1, C5.

Bennett, I. (1977). Technology as a shaping force. *Daedalus, 106*(1), 125–133.

Cohn, V. (1989). Reporters as gatekeepers. In V. Cohn (Ed.), *Health risks and the press: Perspectives of media coverage on risk assessment* (pp. 35–51). Washington, DC: The Media Institute.

Cole, B. J. (1975). Trends in science and conflict coverage in four metropolitan newspapers. *Journalism Quarterly, 52,* 465–471.

Dunwoody, S., & Ryan, M. (1983). Public information persons as mediators between scientists and journalists. *Journalism Quarterly, 59,* 647–656.

Evans, E., & Priest, S. H. (1995). Science content and social context. *Public Understanding of Science, 4,* 327–340.

Fuller, R., & Myers, R. (1940, February). The natural history of a social problem. *American Sociological Review, 6,* 24–32.

Gandy, O. H. (1982). The information subsidy in health. In O. H. Gandy (Ed.), *Beyond agenda setting: Information subsidies and public policy* (pp. 95–120). Norwood, NJ: Ablex.

Gans, H. J. (1979). *Deciding what's news: A study of* CBS Evening News, NBC Nightly News, Newsweek *and* Time. New York: Pantheon.

Glazer, N. (1994). How social problems are born. *The Public Interest, 155,* 31–44.

Goodell, R. (1975). *The visible scientists.* Boston: Little, Brown.

Griffen, R. J., & Dunwoody, S. (1995). Impacts of information subsidies and community structure on local press coverage of environmental contamination. *Journalism and Mass Communication Quarterly, 72,* 271–84.

Hess, S. (1981). *The Washington reporters: Newswork.* Washington, DC: The Brookings Institution.

Krieghbaum, H. (1967). *Science and the mass media.* New York: New York University Press.

Moore, M. (1989a). Beware the bracken fern. In M. Moore (Ed.), *Health risks and the press: Perspectives of media coverage on risk assessment* (pp. 1–18). Washington, DC: The Media Institute.

Moore, M. (Ed.). (1989b). *Health risks and the press: Perspectives of media coverage on risk assessment.* Washington, DC: The Media Institute.

Nelkin, D. (1987). *Selling science.* New York: Freeman.

Nelkin, D. (1989). Journalism and science: The creative tension. In M. Moore (Ed.), *Health risks and the press: Perspectives of media coverage on risk assessment* (pp. 53–72). Washington, DC: The Media Institute.

Noelle-Neumann, E. (1984). *The spiral of silence.* Chicago: University of Chicago Press.

Ohl, C. M., Pincus, J. O., & Rimmer, T. (1995). Agenda building role of news releases in corporate takeovers. *Public Relations Review, 21,* 89–101.

Page, I. (1970). Science writers, physicians, and the public—A menage a trois. *Annals of Internal Medicine, 73,* 641–647.

Schoenfeld, A. C., Meier, R. F., & Griffin, R. J. (1979, October). Constructing a social problem: The press and the environment. *Social Problems, 27,* 38–60.

Schwartz, J. D., & Rimmer, T. (1995). AIDS and the media. *The Public Interest, 25,* 57–71.

Shepherd, R. G. (1979). Science news of controversy: The case of marijuana. *Journalism Monographs, 62,* 97–109.

Strodthoff, G., Hawkins, R., & Schoenfeld, A. C. (1978, Spring). Media roles in social movement: A model of ideology diffusion. *Journal of Communication, 35,* 134–153.

Thompson, T. (1976). *Blood and money.* Garden City, NY: Doubleday.

Tuchman, G. (1973). Make news by doing work: Routinizing the unexpected. *American Journal of Sociology, 79,* 110–131.

Turk, J. V. (1985). Information subsidies and influence. *Public Relations Review, 11,* 10–25.

Walters, L., & Walters, T. (1991, Summer). The conspiracy of silence: Media coverage of syphilis, 1906–1941. *American Journalism,* pp. 246–266.

Walters, T., & Walters, L. (1992). Environment of confidence: Daily use of press releases. *Public Relations Review, 18,* 31–36.

Walters, T., & Walters, L. (1994a). After the highwayman: Syntax and successful placement of press releases. *Public Relations Review, 20,* 174–186.

Walters, T., & Walters, L. (1994b). The four seasons: Cyclical success rates in the placement of press releases. *Southwestern Mass Communication Journal, 10,* 1–12.

Walters, T., & Walters, L. (1996). Agenda building and the 1992 presidential campaign: Was it a failure to communicate or did the audience set the agenda? *Public Relations Review, 22,* 343–356.

Weaver, D. E., & Elliott, S. N. (1985). Who sets the agenda for the media? A study of local-agenda building. *Journalism Quarterly, 62,* 87–94.

Wildavsky, A. (1977). Doing better and feeling worse: The political pathology of health policy. *Daedalus, 106*(1), 105–124.

AIDS as a Legally Defined Disability: Implications From News Media Coverage

Beth Haller
Towson University

The disability rights perspective has been pushing its way into the American public consciousness. This perspective contrasts with the more traditional medical or social welfare perspective in which disability is seen as a physical problem (Scotch, 1988). But federal mandates of the 1990 Americans with Disabilities Act (ADA) have caused the cultural imagery and cultural experiences of disability to change. In this chapter, I argue that the ADA represents the crest of sea change in how Americans think about disabilities, from pitiable partial people to complete citizens deserving of opportunities to pursue the American dream. Not the least among these changes was the clear language of the ADA that defined AIDS as a legally protected disability. This shift occurred not simply because of the ADA's passage, but also as a result of news coverage that portrayed the differing opinions regarding disabilities and the ADA itself. First, I discuss the idea that the news media have the unique ability to influence citizens' perceptions regarding public issues and, consequently, legislation that tries to alter society. Second, I present the predominant American perspectives regarding people with disabilities. Third, I review findings from a content analysis of news coverage of the ADA from 1988 to 1993. Fourth, and finally, I explain how classifying AIDS with more traditionally understood disabilities in legislation and corresponding news coverage influenced American attitudes regarding AIDS, disabilities, and the people who embody them.

NEWS MEDIA AND DISABILITY LEGISLATION

The argument of this chapter rests upon the notion that much of what society believes about people with disabilities and specifically those people with AIDS comes in large part from media depictions. The news media's impact within society leads to certain "constructions" or "frames" of people with AIDS because they may not fit with societal notions of normality. The news media set a certain agenda for the portrayal of disability issues and people with AIDS. The ability of mass media to make people aware and characterize social issues fits with McCombs' (1992) notion of agenda setting: "Both the selection of topics for the news agenda and the selection of frames for stories about those topics are powerful agenda setting roles and awesome ethical responsibilities" (pp. 820–821; see also McCombs & Shaw, 1972).

The passage of the ADA is analogous to Thomas Kuhn's (1970) concept of a paradigm shift in scientific discovery. The ADA acknowledges the full citizenship rights of people with disabilities, just as the Civil Rights Bill for people of color did in the 1960s. The elite news media discourse surrounding the ADA illustrates that AIDS was a "high-profile" disability; these media helped set a new agenda with their reporting on the ADA as they also reinforced existing depictions of disability. These media frames are significant because, as Higgins (1992) argued, we as a society "make disability" through our language, media, and other public and visible ways (see also Kailes, 1988). Studying those depictions helps us understand the media's role in "constructing" people with AIDS as different and their role in framing many types of people who may not fit with "mainstream" constructions.

As Longmore (1985) explained, the language about disability can categorize people in the "handicapped role" as helpless, dependent, or abnormal. This type of language creates a monolithic presentation of people, only in terms of their disabilities, rather than as multidimensional people. Longmore cited terms like *the handicapped, the disabled, the deaf,* or *the mentally retarded* in this stigmatization process. These nouns created from adjectives frame people with disabilities in terms of their disabilities; the term handicapped evokes particularly negative stereotypes: " 'Handicapped' connotes the miserable image of a person on the street corner holding a 'handy cap,' begging for money" (Kailes, 1988, p. 4).

This chapter examines the results when the traditional media stereotypes of disability meet with the disability rights perspective as embodied primarily in the governmental rhetoric of the ADA. The rights-oriented perspective argues that a disability is a phenomenon created by society, which has yet to modify its architectural, occupational, educational, communication, and attitudinal environments to accommodate people who are physically and mentally different (Bowe, 1978). Under the rights perspective, physical difference is acknowledged, and even celebrated as an ethnicity. This perspective focuses not on the individual with a disability, but on society's structures as the problem—structures that can be changed through political action (Clogston, 1990; Scotch, 1988). For example, in applying the rights perspective to people with AIDS, activists fight against attitudinal barriers that might cause employment discrimination.

The 1990 ADA relied on the disability rights perspective as it legislated full civil rights for all people with disabilities. In one sweeping legislative act, the disability rights focus emerged on the public agenda of the United States. The ADA definition of disability is based solely on functioning and/or stigma, not visible appearance. According to the U.S. Equal Employment Opportunities Commission (EEOC, 1992), "An individual is considered to have a 'disability' if s/he has a physical or mental impairment that substantially limits one or more major life activities, has a record of such impairment, or is regarded as having such an impairment" (p. 1). In this definition, "major life activities" include seeing, hearing, speaking, walking, breathing, learning, self-care, working, and performing manual tasks. Temporary or nonchronic impairments such as broken bones are not disabilities. In addition, the act protects people who have an association or relationship with someone who has a disability. The concept of a "record of impairment" helps protect people who have recovered from impairments, such as cancer or mental illness, from discrimination. The idea of "regarded as having" an impairment protects people who may not have an impairment that limits them physically, such as people with facial disfigurement or who are HIV-infected, but may face employment discrimination because of fear. The language of the law specifically addresses past public perceptions of disability gleaned from media. Traditional media imagery associated disability with wheelchairs, canes, or other visible signs. The new legal definition makes it clear that disability has many "invisible" components with which the public and the media have been less familiar.

In addition, the language of the law redefined the notion of a citizen's civil rights, moving it past halting discriminatory practices based on only gender or ethnicity. The ADA outlined how to revise societal structures to accommodate people with disabilities. To prevent employment discrimination in the workplace, for example, the ADA defines reasonable accommodation as "any modification or adjustment to a job or the work environment that will enable a qualified applicant or employee with a disability to participate in the application process or to perform essential job functions" (EEOC, 1992, p. 5). The law allows flexibility because employer accommodation is not meant to cause an "undue hardship." Accessibility must occur, including removal of barriers, whenever "readily achievable," that is, without much difficulty or cost.

The elite news media were familiar with covering the stories of civil rights since the 1960s, so they readily embraced the language of civil rights and minority group politics throughout their news stories. In addition, this was the rhetoric pushed by disability rights activists in lobbying for the ADA. Watson (1993) said the infusion of disability rights language was the greatest accomplishment of the activists in getting the bill passed. First, they established the bipartisan nature of the act and then established the reason for the ADA, "that its protections were an issue of civil rights rather than a charitable obligation or some other rationale" (Watson, 1993, p. 29). The language and perspective of disability rights were perpetuated from the beginnings of the act through the present. Second, the media portrayed the cost effectiveness rationale used by disability activists. This consumer model posits that society is better off if people with disabilities become taxpayers instead of tax beneficiaries (Haller, 1995a, 1995b, 1995c, in press). The language activists clung to most strongly, therefore, was "civil rights regardless of cost" (Watson 1993, p. 30). Disability activists connected the civil rights perspective to similar fights against discrimination faced by ethnic minorities, women, and gays and lesbians. Media stories, however, did not report that specific connection as strongly.

In the late 1980s, the disability rights movement began gaining this power, and AIDS activism helped with that surge of empowerment. Shapiro (1989) argued that AIDS gave "the disability rights movement some momentum, as people with AIDS have depended for protection upon anti-discrimination for people with disabilities" (p. 44). Even before the ADA passed, courts had ruled that AIDS was a disability. So members of the disability rights movement worked from inside and outside the government to craft the ADA to include all aspects of disability. The movement had learned how significant it was to gain the power to frame its own issues (Scotch, 1988). Although legislation protected disability rights, the news media became the only other stumbling block to societal framing of this issue.

PREDOMINANT AMERICAN PERSPECTIVES ON DISABILITY

Today, we say no to second-class citizenship for people with disabilities, no to segregation, isolation, and exclusion, and no to patronizing attitudes. Today, we say yes to treating people with disabilities with dignity and respect, yes to empowerment, yes to judging people on the basis of their abilities, not on the basis of fear, ignorance, and prejudice. (Harkin, 1990, p. 89)

Senator Tom Harkin's characterization of treatment of people with physical differences in terms of "exclusion," "fear," "ignorance," and "prejudice" illustrates that the ADA is meant to combat attitudinal barriers, as well as the architectural barriers that plague people with mobility impairments. Embedded within the language of the ADA is protection from discrimination for people with HIV/AIDS. This is a crucial rhetorical turn because Americans' perspectives on disability tend to focus on the visible representation of disability such as wheelchairs or canes, and that disabled people prefer "to be with their own kind" (Phillips, 1990, p. 849).

AIDS, however, carries with it additional stigma than just disability associations. News media stories depict people with HIV/AIDS with dual stereotypes through associations with the gay rights movement, the disability rights movement, and a highly stigmatized terminal illness. Media stories, therefore, represent people with AIDS both with disability and minority group status (Bernt & Greenwald, 1993). The legislative, social, and cultural concerns of gays and lesbians were mentioned in less than 40% of the AIDS-related stories coded ($N = 1,105$). In addition, Simpson (1992) has delineated in a qualitative way the changes in the way AIDS and AIDS deaths have been covered in major newspaper stories—from effects on traditional families, to effects on gay relationships and the gay community, and, most recently, to allow a gay person to tell his own story about AIDS. Thus, readers receive a multidimensional view of a gay person with AIDS.

These public perceptions of AIDS and other disabilities led to some of the opposition to the ADA. Political conservatives feared the ADA would give civil rights to "deviants," which included the gay community in their view. The business community primarily feared the cost of architectural changes for people with mobility impairments. In May 1989, Zachary Fasman of the U.S. Chamber of Commerce testified before the Senate Committee on Labor and Human Resources that all references to halting discriminatory practices in employment be stricken from Title I of the act. He said the definition of "reasonable accommodation" that employers must provide for people with disabilities was too broad and unnecessary. Fasman questioned the idea in the act that someone is considered a qualified applicant if he or she can perform the essential function of a job with or without reasonable accommodation: "It is too substantial an intrusion on the legitimate prerogatives of employers to ask Federal agencies, the courts and juries to define which aspects of a particular job are 'essential' and which are not" (p. 301).

The ADA considered the capitalistic concerns of businesses without gutting the intent of the law. Businesses with fewer than 15 employees are exempt from the Act. Furthermore, studies found that only 22% of people with disabilities need accommodations at the work site, and that 50% of all accommodations cost $50 or less (Eastern Paralyzed Veterans Association, 1992).

Conservative senators added a variety of amendments before passage. For example, the Helms Amendment, proposed by North Carolina Senator Jesse Helms, clarified the definition of "handicapped" under the Rehabilitation Act of 1973 relating to illegal acts ("Recent Action," 1989). The odd combination of illegal drug users, gays and lesbians, pyromaniacs, and kleptomaniacs are not covered by the act. Helms had also tried to add another component to the ADA that would have barred people with AIDS from working as food handlers, but the Senate voted not to include that proposal (Eaton, 1990). Clearly the Helms Amendment demonstrates the conservative effort to delineate between "good" and "bad" disabilities (see, e.g., Mandel, 1989).

Nevertheless, the ADA definition of disability confronts the implications of a stigmatized disability such as AIDS, making sure that hidden disabilities and those disabilities that invoke unnatural fear are fully covered. The definition even protects from discrimination people who have an association or relationship with someone who has a disability. For example, the definition would protect from discrimination a parent who is caring for a child with AIDS.

The concept of a "record of impairment" helps protect from discrimination people who have recovered or are in remission, such as people with cancer or mental illness. Most important in terms of HIV or AIDS, it helps protect from discrimination people with the diagnosis but no physical manifestations of the disease. The act is carefully worded to ensure employers do not discriminate against people "regarded as having" an impairment. This is a crucial protection for people with AIDS who many times face attitudinal, rather than architectural, discrimination.

A CONTENT ANALYSIS OF ADA COVERAGE[1]

The sample for this content analysis consisted of all news and feature articles written about the ADA from 1988 through 1993 in *The New York Times, The Wall Street Journal, The Washington Post, Christian Science Monitor, Los Angeles Times, Chicago Tribune, The Boston Globe, The Atlanta Journal-Constitution, Philadelphia Inquirer, Newsweek, Time,* and *U.S. News & World Report* ($N = 524$). These publications were chosen because all are indexed and represent the largest newspapers and news magazines of this country that influence our culture. In other words, they are elite news media (Gans, 1980). They also represent four geographic regions in the country, the Northeast, the Midwest, the South, and the West, and include a major business publication and the largest circulation daily, *The Wall Street Journal.*

Questions on the code sheet used in the analysis strove to gather information in four primary areas: demographic data about the types of people and issues that fill the stories; agenda data about the framing of the ADA as either a business concern, a civil right, or a legal issue; disability data about how people with disabilities and disability groups are presented in the cultural context of these stories; and media data about how the media perform when faced with new representations of a group handed down from Congress. One mechanism in doing content analysis of mass media is comparing news coverage to other sources of information that may be more accurate. The overall study (Haller, 1995a) looked for specifics based on numerous demographic characteristics, but this chapter concentrates on representations of disability type, disability-related sources, disability organizations, and language use about disability in the news stories.

One overall finding about the coverage of the ADA illustrates that the notion of disability rights made a moderate amount of headway into news media representations. In understanding the norms of journalism, it would be assumed that the ADA might be covered as a "big story" because it attempts to change the fabric of U.S. society. In addition to affecting 43 million to 48 million U.S. citizens, it legislates how the country organizes its workplaces, how it provides access to most of the architectural structures in the country, and how it communicates with its citizens. However, only 288 stories in 12 prestigious newspapers and news magazines in more than 5 years focused primarily on the story of the ADA. The rest of the coverage assessed in this chapter was typically an incidental mention of the act in a news story. Network television news went for more than a year several times without mentioning the ADA, and only did a total of 27 stories over a 5-year period (Haller, 1995a). In their coverage, news media looked narrowly at the ADA, failing to note the imminent broad cultural changes of this new law. Consequently, a year after the law passed, only 18% of the American public polled knew about it (Louis Harris, 1991). Even with limited coverage, the news media's civil rights coverage of disability issues may have had some resonance with the public. The Louis Harris poll showed that 95% of the people who knew about the ADA

---

[1]Percentages have been rounded for readability in the text.

believed employers should be prohibited from discriminating based on disability, and 96% agreed that discrimination should be banned in public places. However, the other news media frame that embraced business concerns seemed to be a less salient perspective for the public, because the Louis Harris poll found that 89% of the people who knew about the act said that the cost of the new law will be worth it. Although exact links between media coverage and public opinion cannot be made, this chapter argues that news media coverage of the ADA and subsequently AIDS as a disability fit squarely within the powerful agenda-setting function of mass media.

Findings about the content of the ADA print stories show that almost half of the stories had no person with a disability as a source or example (49%). Most of the people with disabilities in the stories were adults (43%). Children were represented in 3% of the stories and teenagers in 2%. A mixture of adults and young people with disabilities was tabulated in 3% of the stories. In the stories, 23.5% of the people with disabilities were men and 10% were women. Both men and women with disabilities were represented in 15% of the stories.

Table 20.1 illustrates the types of disabilities mentioned in the print stories. By comparing Table 20.2, which provides estimates of the incidence of disability in the United States, and Table 20.1, one can see that media stories are inconsistent with statistics on the prevalence of certain disabilities. The visible and more severe disabilities received the coverage. Wheelchair use appears to be the symbolic disability for the news stories, although its actual incidence in the U.S. population is rather low. As a disability, however AIDS also had important symbolic value within news stories. It was the fourth most-mentioned specific disability. In addition, AIDS was mentioned as a social issue in 10.5% of the stories; gay rights/homosexuality was mentioned 2% of the time. Table 20.3 illustrates that only one issue overtook AIDS in news media stories about the ADA and that was the impact of the legislation on the business community. And Table 20.4 illustrates that AIDS ranked high in mention of specific disability-related issues in the stories as well. This "blended" approach in reporting on AIDS, that is, AIDS not as the focus but as a secondary issue in a news story, seemed to be a trend in news coverage of the illness. The Kaiser Family Foundation's (1996) 10-year study of AIDS coverage found that by 1994, 70% of stories on AIDS did not focus on AIDS but just mentioned AIDS in the course of writing about something else.

The print news stories did thorough jobs of characterizing the civil rights nature of the act. About 53% of the stories called the ADA a civil rights bill, and 62% mentioned that

TABLE 20.1
Disabilities Most Frequently Mentioned in News Stories

	Percentage
None	14.5
General	29
Wheelchair use	48.3
Deaf/hearing impaired	23.5
Blind/partially sighted	22.7
AIDS	14.3
Paralysis/para/quad	9
Cerebral palsy	8
Major mental illness	6.9
Cancer	5.3
Mental retardation	4.8
Polio/postpolio	4.8
HIV-positive	4.4

Note. Several disabilities may be mentioned in one story. *N* = 524.

TABLE 20.2
Estimated Incidence of Disability in the United States

Type of Disability	Incidence	Source of Data[a]
Arthritis	30 million people	U.S. National Center for Health Statistics (1990a, 1990b)
Mental disorder (excludes substance abuse)	23.9 million (over a 1-month period)	National Institute of Mental Health (1993)
Hearing impairment	23 million	U.S. National Center for Health Statistics (1990a, 1996)
Heart conditions	19.3 million	U.S. National Center for Health Statistics (1990a, 1990b)
Cancer (excludes skin cancer)	8 million with history (5 million no longer have evidence) (3 million still have evidence)	American Cancer Society (1994)
Visual impairment	7.5 million	U.S. National Center for Health Statistics (1990a, 1990b)
Mental retardation	6 million	National Organization on Disability (1990)
Diabetes	6.2 million	U.S. National Center for Health Statistics (1990a, 1990b)
Paralysis (full or partial)	1.5 million	President's Committee on the Employment of People with Disabilities (1994)
Amputee	1 million	President's Committee on the Employment of People with Disabilities (1994)
Epilepsy	1 million	President's Committee on the Employment of People with Disabilities (1994)
Cerebral palsy	500,000	United Cerebral Palsy Association (personal communication, August 1, 1994)
AIDS	244,939 (Total cases, includes deaths)	CDC (1992)
Use of Assistive Devices (Over Age 15)		
Use a wheelchair	1.5 million	President's Committee on the Employment of People with Disabilities (1994)
Use a cane/walker/crutches	4 million	President's Committee on the Employment of People with Disabilities (1994)
Use a hearing aid	4 million	U.S. National Center for Health Statistics (1990a, 1990b)
Use an artificial limb	250,000	U.S. National Center for Health Statistics (1990a, 1990b)

[a]See reference section for full citation of source.

TABLE 20.3
Seven Other Social Issues Besides Disability Mentioned in the Stories

	Percentage
None	38.5
Business costs	40.5
AIDS	10.5
Unemployment	7.1
Health insurance costs	4.8
Education	4.6
Racial discrimination	3.6
Gay rights/homosexuality	2.1

Note. $N = 524$.

TABLE 20.4
Top 10 Disability Issues Mentioned in News Stories

	Percentage
None	5.3
Accessible public facilities	51.3
Unemployment/jobs	32.8
Discrimination	26.7
Architectural changes	25.4
Accessible transportation	11.8
AIDS	10.7
Access to recreation	9
Societal acceptance of PWD	6.3
Medical insurance for PWD	6.1
Technology	4.2

Note. Several issues may be mentioned in one story. $N = 524$. PWD = people with disabilities.

people with disabilities face barriers in society. About 35% of the stories related the attitudinal barriers people with disabilities face, whereas 58% discussed the architectural barriers people with disabilities face. Many news stories did not give "voice" to people with disabilities or their organizations, although 48% of the stories used a person or people with disabilities as an example in ADA stories.

Table 20.5 indicates the sourcing of the ADA stories. An individual story may contain a number of sources; it is significant that people with disabilities (30%) or representatives of disability groups (35%) appeared frequently. These findings illustrate that government, busi-

TABLE 20.5
Top 20 Sources Cited in the ADA Print Stories

	Percentage
Representative of disability group	35.3
Government agency spokesperson	31.3
Person with disability (no affiliation)	30.2
Businessperson	25
Representative of business group	20
Attorney for disabled person/disability group	15.3
Americans with Disabilities Act/its provisions	12.4
Elected official—local level	12.2
Attorney—general	11.6
Lawsuit/legal document	10.9
Attorney for business/business group	8.4
Government document/report	8.4
Elected official—federal level	7.8
Consultant	6.5
Attorney for government	6.3
Transportation official	6.1
Academic/university researcher	5.9
Independent research report	5.9
Architect/designer	5.5
Teacher/educator	5.5
Gay rights group[a]	1.5

Note. A number of different sources may have appeared in one story. $N = 524$.
[a]Gay rights group added because of topic. It is not in the top 20 sources.

TABLE 20.6
Specific Disability Groups Mentioned

	Frequency	Percentage
None	276	52.7
General—disability activists	8	1.5
Local group	101	19.3
Disability Rights Education and Defense Fund	30	5.7
President's Committee on People with Disabilities	19	3.6
Disabled in Action	17	3.2
Paralyzed Veterans of America	16	3.1
Independent Living Center	14	2.7
United Cerebral Palsy Association	13	2.5
ADAPT	9	1.7
National Organization on Disability	7	1.3
Easter Seals	6	1.1
ARC (Association for Retarded Citizens)	4	.8
World Institute on Disability	4	.8
Children's Defense Fund	3	.6
National Right to Life Committee	3	.6
National Federation of the Blind	2	.4
Variety Club	2	.4
Muscular Dystrophy Association	0	
AIDS group	13	2.5
Gay group	7	1.3

Note. Individual stories may mention more than one disability group. $N = 524$.

ness, and disability interests all appeared in news stories. However, based on being mentioned in the story, government groups were connected to the ADA story more frequently than disability groups. Some type of government group, such as a city council or the U.S. Department of Justice, was represented in 80.5% of the stories, compared to 47% for disability groups.

Reporters on the ADA print stories did seem to find their local disability organizations for comment, however. Local, rather than national, disability groups appeared most often—19% of the time (Table 20.6). Local government sources played a more important role in the AIDS story, according to the Kaiser Family Foundation (1996) study. This study found that state/local officials were the largest group of government spokespeople in AIDS stories at 11%, whereas AIDS activists were major news makers in only 3% of the stories. Significantly, the sources and disability groups mentioned in the ADA stories rarely focused on AIDS, although AIDS was presented as an important social issue in terms of the act itself. Thus, the story of ADA was the one place where the issue of AIDS and government legislation met.

AIDS Defined as Disability

In the news stories on the ADA, did AIDS receive representation as a disability or did it fall into some "special" place in media coverage? In terms of language use, some stories continued to reinforce a "sick role" or medicalization of disability. Examples include people who had been "stricken" with polio earlier in life. People with AIDS were sometimes referred to as "AIDS sufferers," "suffering from" AIDS, "AIDS patients," or "victims of" AIDS. Another association often made among the disabilities covered was the description, "such as mental illness or AIDS" (Fulwood, 1990, p. A25) or "rehabilitated substance abusers, AIDS sufferers and functioning mental patients" (Harte, 1991, p. C6). In other words, many stories linguistically linked the more culturally stigmatized disabilities and thus disassociated them from more "pitiable" mobility impairments.

Though the media may represent AIDS apart from the traditional disability population, disability activists say it is the mutual fight against discriminatory and stigmatizing practices that actually merges people with AIDS into the disability community. Bower (1994) explained this bond among people with different disabilities: "All of us have rejected the terms 'victim' and 'patient' to describe our relationship to our conditions and instead have chosen terms with dignity, which underline our personhood primarily and our condition second, as in people with HIV or people with disabilities" (p. 8). Nevertheless, news reports began to discern these nuances in their ADA coverage, most likely because these new terms were linked to the civil rights message in the ADA and society in general. Although less acceptable terms such as handicapped continued to be used by the news media, news stories reduced the use of medical terms related to disability (see Table 20.7).

In the ADA stories, journalists used these less stereotyping terms such as *wheelchair user, uses a wheelchair,* or *person with AIDS* fairly often. But there was still a high prevalence of the term handicapped, and journalists seem to use it interchangeably with *disability.* For example, a July 26, 1990, CBS television story on the ADA signing used the terms *people with disabilities, the disabled,* and *the handicapped* all in the same story. The language use shows how deeply imbedded cultural notions about ability and health endure with new legislation-related imagery. The most recent version of the *AP Stylebook,* the "bible" on language use for print journalists, disapproves of the word *handicap* to describe a disability

TABLE 20.7
Percentage of Stories Using Disability Language at Least Once

	Percentage
No disability-related language	11.6
The disabled	45.4
Disabled person	36.3
People with disabilities	29.4
In a wheelchair	17.7
Handicapped person	15.5
The handicapped	12.6
Uses a wheelchair	12.2
Person who has _____ (i.e., cerebral palsy)	8.6
Is _____ (i.e., is hearing impaired)	6.7
Wheelchair user	5.9
Person with AIDS	4.8
Special	4
Deaf person	3.8
Suffers from _____	3.6
The _____ (i.e., The blind)	3.1
Confined (to a bed or wheelchair)	2.5
Wheelchair-bound	1.9
Stricken with _____	1.5
AIDS patients	1
Crippled/cripple	1
With _____ (i.e., person with cancer)	1
Other(s)	9.5

Note. The terms are not mutually exclusive. One story may use a number of the terms. The terms *retarded, victim of, physically challenged, deformed, overcoming the disability,* and *in spite of* (disability) all represented less than 1% of language used. *N* = 524.

(Goldstein, 1993). Therefore, in using the traditional language about disability, journalists illustrate that strongly held, imbedded cultural beliefs about ability and health are at war with new perceptions of disability, framed in a civil rights context.

AIDS is particularly salient to these beliefs because of its tenuous status as a traditional disability in the eyes of the press. The news media seemed to embrace the new civil rights metaphor related to mobility-related disabilities, but seemed less certain about that frame when the disability was disease related. However, in terms of amount of coverage, AIDS was definitely not ignored, but more often overemphasized. Though one of the less prevalent causes of disability or death, AIDS was mentioned at a much higher proportion than its actual incidence (see Table 20.2). Kuhn's (1970) notion is that the right metaphor enters society allowing people to perceive new ideas. In the case of ADA news coverage, the right metaphor—civil rights—entered the national conversation about mobility-related disability and the press embraced it. However, a high-profile, disease-related disability such as AIDS retained more of the medical model of representation. Thus, this news media focus within ADA stories continued to depict some people with AIDS-related disabilities as weak, dependent, "abnormal," and financially burdensome to society.

If AIDS symbolizes the highest in disability stigmas, one must consider from where that stigma arises. Wendell (1989) stated that our fears of an imperfect body are great. She argued that it is more than just fear of physical difference at work here. Humans usually can identify with people very different from themselves, different genders, different ages, different races: "Something more powerful than being different is at work. Suffering caused by the body, and the inability to control the body, are despised, pitied, and above all, feared. This fear, experienced individually, is also deeply imbedded in our culture" (Wendell, 1989, p. 112).

Additionally, human emotional reactions to disability are strong, especially when also coupled with a terminal disease such as AIDS. These reactions were documented in a 1991 survey by Louis Harris and Associates for the National Organization on Disability. One component of these reactions is that disability as a minority group is one that anyone can enter at any time. So fears for self are heightened. Of a random sample of Americans ($n = 1,257$), 47% said they are afraid that they may become disabled. About 51% of Americans said they feel lack of concern for people with serious disabilities, but 92% feel admiration for people with serious disabilities. Interestingly, college graduates are more likely than people who did not finish high school to feel these concerns (63% vs. 50%). According to the Louis Harris survey, Americans also have concerns about working and generally interacting with people with serious disabilities. About 30% expressed concern about working closely with a seriously disabled person. Eighteen percent were concerned about being served by a seriously disabled person in a restaurant. And 17% said they are concerned about a seriously disabled person sitting next to them on the bus. This has implications for journalists covering AIDS and disability issues because about 90% of journalists are college graduates (Medsger, 1996).

In another area, the media framed the slow movement of the societal paradigm shift to a disability rights focus. The U.S. business community, fearing the financial ramifications of the ADA, supplied information to the news media to allow for a new frame for the act to emerge—that the ADA would be costly to business. Although the news media embraced the civil rights frame and forgot some patronizing themes used in many stories about disability issues, they also lent much coverage to business concerns, which is not surprising as mass media are businesses. But more important, these journalists ply their trade in the capitalistic society of the United States. As Gans (1980) has argued, news media embody a belief in the goodness of a free-market economy. In a more critical approach, Dines (1992) has called the media "capitalism's pitchmen" because of the conservative nature of the sources they use. Shoemaker and Reese (1991) posited that the mass media perpetuate our core ideology daily:

"Fundamental is a belief in the value of the capitalistic economic system, private ownership, pursuit of profit by self-interested entrepreneurs, and free markets. This system is intertwined with the Protestant ethic and the value of individual achievement" (p. 184). This ideology was upheld by the business focus found in the ADA stories. Unlike the civil rights theme replacing the pity theme, news media presented no new economic frame for the disability legislation, other than the free-market one already in place.

The reliance on these two primary types of frames may have shut out other kinds of information that was significant to the ADA story or stories about disability issues. One frame that logically might have arisen in 1992–1993 was whether the ADA was effective in combating discrimination. But the media followed their norm of event-driven journalism, and only rarely stepped into its watchdog role to scrutinize the impact and enforcement of the ADA. That scrutiny usually came from a lawsuit-related story on someone suing for access or workplace accommodation under the ADA. The *Los Angeles Times,* for example, wrote a 1993 story headlined: "Suit Filed to Preserve AIDS Benefits" (p. D2). The story explained that the EEOC sued after a New York union cut off medical benefits to a worker. Another *Los Angeles Times* story explained how a Ventura medical clinic that refused to treat a man with HIV was being forced under the ADA to pay $85,000 to settle the federal discrimination lawsuit (Hadly, 1993). But these types of scrutinizing stories resulted from lawsuits filed, not journalistic scrutiny of ADA compliance.

So what was the image of AIDS in the ADA stories? First, it was represented as separate from traditional mobility-related disabilities. As a disability, the media portrayed it as a separate social issue more often. Traditional mobility-related disabilities benefited most from media's new frames, which associated accessibility issues with civil rights. However, civil rights as a positive theme was initially designed by the disability community. The major new theme about disability set forth in the news coverage of the ADA was actually the business model. Within this model, news media stories stereotype people with disabilities as burdening society financially with their perceived dependency and costliness (Haller, 1995a, 1995b, 1995c, in press).

Stories about people with AIDS focused on insurance costs and expensive medical care and medications. In a *Chicago Tribune* story for an employment special section, AIDS was characterized as a disability with a high cost: "The health care issue is likely to ignite broad controversy because the disabilities act specifically includes people with HIV" (Gaines, 1992, p. 18). Making society "accessible" for people with HIV/AIDS does not necessarily mean building wheelchair ramps but providing adequate insurance coverage and dealing with attitudinal barriers. Some businesses might complain, just as they do about people with mobility impairments, that hiring people with AIDS is not really worth the cost and over-burdens businesses.

Thus, the positive civil rights rhetoric of the ADA in the stories battled with the business rhetoric in representing AIDS. The disability rights activists who helped craft the ADA may have been mistaken to back off from the consumer model, which could have provided a double-barreled confrontation to business rhetoric. Within the consumer model, mass media stories contain a theme that making society accessible could be profitable to businesses and society in general (Haller, 1995a, 1995b, 1995c, in press).

These media representations of AIDS and the ADA have implications for how the readership thought about the ADA. McCombs explained in 1992 that an agenda-setting attribute of a news media topic can be the perspective journalists or the public use in considering the topics. So agenda-setting theory can be applied to more than just the trans-mission of the significance of an issue to an audience to the significance of perspectives used to present it in the news. In the coverage of the ADA story, the news media added the representational perspective of AIDS as a government policy issue, which had been missing, according to the Kaiser Family Foundation (1996) study. But the news media played on the force of AIDS as a social issue in linking it to the disability legislation so prominently. AIDS has resonated as a sensational news story since the mid-1980s and that potentially added some "charge" to what could have been a dull congressional legislation story. But, AIDS became a high-profile disability for the news media, one that can connote the highest form of a stigma within the range of disabilities, even though other disabilities may be more prevalent in society.

Thus, we see AIDS functioning within the ADA stories as a significant agenda-setting attribute within the news media coverage. In general, the news media transmitted the ADA story within frames of capitalism and civil rights, both of which have high issue salience for the American news media audience. With their use of some perspectives in their reporting and not others, the news media left their agenda-setting imprint on the cultural "story" of the ADA and its relationship to AIDS.

REFERENCES

American Cancer Society. (1994). *Cancer facts and figures—1994.* Atlanta: Author.

Bernt, J. P., & Greenwald, M. S. (1993, August). *Coverage of gays, lesbians, bisexuals and the HIV/AIDS epidemic: A content analysis of seventeen metropolitan daily newspapers.* Paper presented at the annual meeting of the Association for Education in Journalism and Mass Communication, Kansas City, MO.

Bowe, F. (1978). *Handicapping America.* New York: Harper & Row.

Bower, J. (1994, March/April). HIV & disability. *The Disability Rag & Resource, 15*(2), 8–14.

Clogston, J. S. (1990). *Disability coverage in 16 newspapers.* Louisville, KY: Advocado Press.

Dines, G. (1992, May). Capitalism's pitchmen: The media sells a business agenda. *Dollars and Sense, 176,* 18–20.

Eastern Paralyzed Veterans Association. (1992). *Understanding the Americans with Disabilities Act* [Pamphlet]. Jackson Heights, NY: Author.

Eaton, W. J. (1990, July 12). Senate blocks ban on food handlers with AIDS virus. *Los Angeles Times,* p. A20.

Fasman, Z. (1989, December). Should the Senate approve the Americans with Disabilities Act of 1989? *Congressional Digest,* pp. 299, 301.

Fulwood, S. (1990, May 23). Broad disabled rights bill OK'd. *Los Angeles Times,* pp. A1, A25.

Gaines, S. (1992, January 5). Disabilities act breaks new ground in workplace [Employment Outlook special section]. *Chicago Tribune,* pp. 2, 18–19.

Gans, H. (1980). *Deciding what's news: A study of* CBS Evening News, NBC Nightly News, Newsweek *and* Time. New York: Vintage.

Goldstein, N. (Ed.). (1993). *The Associated Press stylebook and libel manual.* Reading, MA: Addison-Wesley.

Hadly, S. (1993, December 1). Clinic will pay $85,000 in HIV discrimination suit. *Los Angeles Times,* p. A34.

Haller, B. (1995a, January). *Disability rights on the public agenda: News media coverage of the Americans with Disabilities Act.* Unpublished doctoral dissertation, Temple University, Philadelphia.

Haller, B. (1995b, November). *Narrative conflicts: News media coverage of the Americans with Disabilities Act.* Paper presented at the National Communication Association annual meeting, San Antonio, TX.

Haller, B. (1995c, May). *The social construction of disability: News coverage of the Americans with Disabilities Act.* Paper presented at the International Communication Association annual meeting, Albuquerque.

Haller, B. (in press). Crawling toward civil rights: News media coverage of disability activism. In Y. R. Kamalipour & T. Carilli (Eds.), *Cultural diversity and the U.S. media.* Albany: State University of New York Press.

Harkin, T. (1990, July 13). Senate. *Congressional Record, 135,* 89.

Harte, S. (1991, December 9). Impending measure touches most bases. *The Atlanta Journal Constitution,* p. C6.

Higgins, P. C. (1992). *Making disability: Exploring the social transformation of human variation.* Springfield, IL: Thomas.

Kailes, J. I. (1988). *Language is more than a trivial concern* [Handout]. (Available from June Isaacson Kailes, disability policy consultant, Los Angeles, CA)

Kaiser Family Foundation. (1996, July/August). Covering the epidemic: AIDS in the news media, 1985–1996 [Supplemental insert]. *Columbia Journalism Review.*

Kuhn, T. S. (1970). *The structure of scientific revolutions.* Chicago: University of Chicago Press.

Longmore, P. K. (1985). A note on language and social identity of disabled people. *American Behavioral Scientist,* *28,* 419–423.

Louis Harris and Associates, Inc. (1991). *Public attitudes toward people with disabilities* [National poll conducted for National Organization on Disability]. New York: Author.

Mandel, S. (1989, September 29). Disabling America. *National Review,* pp. 23–24.

McCombs, M. (1992). Explorers and surveyors: Expanding strategies for agenda-setting research. *Journalism Quarterly, 69,* 813–824.

McCombs, M., & Shaw, D. (1972). The agenda-setting function of the press. *Public Opinion Quarterly, 36,* 176–187.

McCombs, M., & Shaw, D. (1993). The evolution of agenda-setting research. *Journal of Communication, 43,* 58–67.

Medsger, B. (1996). *Winds of change: Challenges confronting journalism education.* Arlington, VA: The Freedom Forum.

National Institute of Mental Health. (1993, August). *Statistics on prevalence of mental disorders.* Rockville, MD: Information Resources and Inquiries Branch.

National Organization on Disability. (1990). *National Organization on Disability* [Information brochure]. Washington, DC: Author.

Phillips, M. J. (1990). Damaged goods: The oral narratives of the experience of disability in American culture. *Social Science & Medicine, 30,* 849–857.

President's Committee on the Employment of People with Disabilities. (1994, October). *Statistical report: The status of people with disabilities.* Washington, DC: U.S. Department of Labor.

Recent action in the Congress. (1989, December). *Congressional Digest,* p. 293.

Scotch, R. K. (1988). Disability as the basis for a social movement: Advocacy and politics of definition. *Journal of Social Issues, 44,* 159–172.

Shapiro, J. (1989). A brief history of the disability rights movement. In J. Shapiro (Ed.), *Reporting on disability: Approaches and issues* (pp. 41–45). Louisville, KY: Advocado.

Shoemaker, P. J., & Reese, S. D. (1991). *Mediating the message.* New York: Longman.

Simpson, R. (1992, August). *Constructing gay death in the newspaper.* Paper presented at the annual meeting of the Association for Education in Journalism and Mass Communication, Montreal, Quebec.

Suit filed to preserve AIDS benefits. (1993, June 10). *Los Angeles Times,* p. D2.

U.S. Centers for Disease Control and Prevention. (1992). *Surveillance report annual.* Atlanta: Author.

U.S. Equal Employment Opportunity Commission. (1992, September). *The Americans with Disabilities Act: Questions and answers* [EEOC-BK-15]. Washington, DC: Author.

U.S. National Center for Health Statistics. (1990a, September 16). *Advance data from vital and health statistics* (No. 217). Washington, DC: Author.

U.S. National Center for Health Statistics. (1990b). *Vital and health statistics* (Series 10, No. 181). Washington, DC: Author.

Watson, S. D. (1993). A study in legislative strategy. In L. Gostin & H. Beyer (Eds.), *Implementing the Americans with Disabilities Act* (pp. 25–34). Baltimore: Brookes.

Wendell, S. (1989). Toward a feminist theory of disability. *Hypatia, 4,* 104–124.

AIDS, the Status Quo, and the Elite Media: An Analysis of the Guest Lists of "The MacNeil/Lehrer News Hour" and "Nightline"

Kevin B. Wright
University of Oklahoma

Since the onset of the AIDS epidemic, the mass media have profoundly influenced the dissemination of information about the disease through a variety of agenda-setting practices. Agenda setting, in general, refers to how the daily selection and display of news stories by the media influences audience perceptions about perceived importance of new topics and issues, and has been the focus of numerous empirical studies over the last 20 years (Protess & McCombs, 1991). Furthermore, agenda setting implies that the priority given to new stories is related to the way in which the audience "incorporates a similar set of weights in their own personal agenda" (Protess & McCombs, 1991, p. 2).

The decision to select or not to select a story is dependent on a number of factors, including time constraints, whether the story is ongoing or "breaking news," the perceived importance of the story by audience members, and the personal judgments of gatekeepers (individuals responsible for deciding what information should be printed or broadcast) within media organizations. Decisions by media gatekeepers are often influenced by forces within the media organization itself, such as policies concerning the types of stories that are appropriate for the target audiences. Even among stories that are deemed worthy of media coverage, decisions within media organizations must be made in terms of what aspects of the story will be told, how the story should be told, and which individuals should be called upon as experts on the issue at hand.

Agenda Setting and Early AIDS Coverage

James Kinsella's (1989) study of AIDS and the American media documents the agenda-setting practices that occurred in the beginning of the epidemic during the early to mid-1980s. According to Kinsella, early coverage of AIDS stories were avoided because the infected population at that time were primarily gay men. Not wishing to offend mainstream target audiences with a story dealing with individuals who might possibly be perceived as engaging in deviant sexual practices, the gatekeepers within the major media organizations, Kinsella contended, made the conscious decision not to include AIDS stories. Although some members within media organizations were aware of the disease and even attempted to make AIDS a news priority (most notably Randy Shilts), Kinsella argued that biases against gay men among key gatekeepers thwarted early efforts to make AIDS stories known to the public.

As the number of AIDS cases began to escalate, the media finally began to include AIDS stories as part of the agenda. However, as Kinsella (1989) argued, most AIDS stories were largely ignored unless the story dealt with a person who was heterosexual or an "innocent victim" of the disease, such as a child contracting HIV through a blood transfusion. Gay men and injection drug users, in contrast, were often portrayed as bringing the disease upon themselves through their deviant behavior."

In addition, Kinsella (1989) raised other concerns in terms of the future of AIDS coverage. He argued that more recent AIDS stories have distorted discussions of at-risk behaviors for HIV infection due to media efforts to sanitize the topic. Kinsella contended that the conscious desire to keep the word choice in AIDS stories purposely ambiguous, so as to not offend advertising sponsors, has led to a number of misconceptions about ways one can contract HIV. Kinsella also voiced a concern that the majority of AIDS patients will largely continue to be political minorities, although the media traditionally have had a poor track record of focusing on minority concerns.

Dearing and Rogers (1992) focused on how news attention to the issue of AIDS was the product of symbiotic relations over which the mass media had only limited control. According to these authors, news organizations are rarely autonomous in setting the news agenda. Outside interest groups, such as government officials, scientists, and political activists, are often the driving force behind helping a health issue become part of the media agenda. Their study examined the role of the media and the early AIDS epidemic, both nationally and locally in San Francisco, and makes a distinction between two types of influences that affect agenda setting and pose problems for traditional quantitative approaches to agenda-setting research. These influences were labeled "endogenous and exogenous" (p. 174). Endogenous influences on the news agenda are factors that originate from within a mass media organization, such as pressures from an editorial staff, whereas exogenous influences are factors that originate outside of mass media organizations, such as pressure from political groups.

Early AIDS coverage appears to be affected by both factors. According to Dearing and Rogers (1992), a long-time editor of *The New York Times* was known for his intolerance of stories about gay lifestyles. It took reporters, who were willing to disregard the internal reward system within the organization, to finally pressure editors to run the first AIDS stories. Even then, *The New York Times* placed its first AIDS article in May of 1983 on page A20.

Exogenous influences on agenda setting came from the Reagan administration's lack of concern about the AIDS epidemic. Gay congressional aides and representatives who had large gay constituencies played "an important role in investigating if and where, within, the government, money for AIDS was being stalled" (Dearing & Rogers, 1992, p. 187). Finally, Dearing and Rogers contended that although AIDS reporting has improved since the beginning of the epidemic, "endogenous and exogenous influences will continue to have an impact on the agenda setting and framing of the AIDS epidemic by media organizations" (p. 177).

Kahn (1993) examined the role of the media in the difficulties involved in authorizing new drugs for AIDS through the Federal Drug Administration (FDA). Kahn contended that the media failed to provide information about AZT and other antivirulent drugs. Although generally supportive of AIDS coverage in the late 1980s and early 1990s, Kahn criticized the media for following the FDA's lead in terms of disseminating information about AIDS drugs.

Agenda Setting and the Elite Media

Traditionally, the mass media have influenced one another in the agenda-setting process. Rather than each media organization being autonomous in the decision-making process of setting the agenda, media organizations read, watch, and listen to one another prior to selecting the information that will be disseminated to the public (Shaw & McCombs, 1989). Events become salient for a variety of reasons, including public concern in the generation of news stories. Far from being a one-way type of communication, audiences and sources outside the media organization influence the daily pool of events that news stories are eventually selected from. Most news media receive information regarding breaking events from wire services and on slow breaking news days have some autonomy in choosing other types of stories to feature.

A small number of media organizations are considered leaders in the news media business, and they have a strong influence on agenda-setting practices of the majority of other media organizations. These leaders are recognized as such for a number of reasons, including their popularity among audiences, high standards of journalism and reporting, and having respected personalities, reporters, and editors in their organizations. *The New York Times* and *The Washington Post* are recognized as two primary leaders among print journalists (Reese & Danielian, 1989; Shoemaker, Wanta, & Leggett, 1989).

In television news, PBS's "The MacNeil/Lehrer News Hour" and ABC's "Nightline" are recognized as two leaders who set the standard for television journalism. Many other television news organizations attempt to follow the lead of these two programs in terms of style, journalistic standards, and types of stories (Hoynes & Croteau, 1989). Like *The New York Times* and *The Washington Post*, these two programs are also leaders in terms of setting the agenda for television news. I will refer to media leaders such as these throughout this chapter as the *elite media*.

Hoynes and Croteau (1989) argued that television news programs such as "The Mac-Neil/Lehrer News Hour" and "Nightline" ostensibly strive to create discussion, analysis, and debate groups on the program that include a wide spectrum of viewpoints and guests. Both programs market themselves as forums that include a representative spectrum of viewpoints on controversial topics that become newsworthy. Moreover, within and outside the journalism community, these programs have gained the reputation of having more liberal viewpoints in contrast to other television news programs.

However, after Hoynes and Croteau (1989) analyzed 865 "Nightline" program transcripts to determine if the show's "guest list" influenced the framing of political and social issues during the discussion portion of the show, the authors provided the following description of what they found to be framing bias within the discussion itself: "As the result of the exclusion of some political perspectives and the promotion of others, *Nightline* helps to legitimize particular positions. *Nightline* certifies spokespersons and 'experts' by giving certain individuals regular opportunities to interpret events. . . . Voices that are systematically excluded from *Nightline* seem to have no role in legitimate public discussion" (p. 104). In their study, Hoynes and Croteau described framing bias as a form of agenda setting in which some viewpoints surrounding an issue are given exposure, whereas others are excluded.

The results of the study found that the debates were "stacked heavily in favor of government spokespersons, assorted 'experts' and journalists, *Nightline's* guest list reflects a profoundly elitist perspective of both domestic and foreign affairs" (Haynes & Croteau, 1989, p. 103). The authors also added that among social issues, "health (42%) is far and away the leading topic featured. Many of these programs dealt with AIDS" (p. 105). However, out of all the social issues presented, political minorities (women, non-White groups, and grass roots political groups) were featured less than 10% of the time. There were no data on gay men or injection drug users in the discussion of AIDS issues. Most of the guests (80%) were well-educated professionals, current or former government officials, or corporate representatives. This suggests that "Nightline" "does not exclude minority voices from appearing, rather they are disproportionately under represented in the class from which *Nightline* draws most of its guests" (p. 107).

Hoynes and Croteau (1989) also stated that the exclusion of political minorities allows a range of spokespersons that is "wide enough to enable 'debates' to occur, yet limited enough to exclude those who might question fundamental tenets of the status quo" (p. 115). This makes it difficult to see the limitations of such a narrow political debate because by "legitimizing differing views within a narrow political spectrum, the appearance of balance is maintained" (p. 115). These authors (Hoynes & Croteau, 1990) conducted a similar study of "The MacNeil/Lehrer News Hour." In addition to analyzing the perspective of the guests who appeared on the discussion forum of the show, in this study the authors were also concerned whether the absence of corporate sponsors was related to a wider perspective presentation of political viewpoints.

The findings were similar to the first study in that the guests were largely affluent, White elites with similar occupations to what was found in the "Nightline" study. According to the authors, "women and people of color were, for all practical purposes, nonparticipants" (p. 144). As far as the supposition that public television would allow for a greater diversity of viewpoints due to the absence of corporate sponsorship, this factor was found to be insignificant. The conclusion drawn from both studies was that "both *The MacNeil/Lehrer News Hour* and *Nightline* fall far short of being politically or socially inclusive. Their limited political scope generally exclude critics in favor of voices of the powerful" (p. 152).

In summary, these elite media programs have been found to have biases in terms of the views that are allowed to participate in discussion of news issues. This is a type of agenda-setting feature by the elite media in the decisions are made by the media organizations to prioritize certain views while simultaneously excluding others. Moreover, because other news media follow the lead of the elite media, the way in which issues are presented, if they are presented at all, by the elite media sets a precedent for other media organizations to follow.

AIDS AND THE ELITE MEDIA

This chapter investigates the ways in which the elite media frame the presentation of AIDS issues. In doing so, this study also examines the relationship between the presentation of these issues by the elite media and the agenda-setting process. This study partially replicates Hoynes and Croteau's (1989, 1990) analyses of both "The MacNeil/Lehrer News Hour" and "Nightline" guest lists in terms of the participants involved in the discussion of HIV/AIDS issues. The rationale for this study is that the framing of AIDS issues by some news media in the past has been shown to distort the public's understanding of AIDS issues in the past, however, no previous studies have focused entirely on the elite media's treatment of AIDS.

Method of Analysis

This study analyzed transcripts of "The MacNeil/Lehrer News Hour" and "Nightline" for a 2-year period (April 1, 1992, to April 14, 1994). The rationale for this time period was an attempt to cover the news during both the Bush and Clinton administrations to assess differences in the coverage of AIDS debates. The year 1992 was chosen as a sample year because the author assumed that a presidential election year would generate more news stories about HIV/AIDS. Each program generated 69 AIDS-related stories that were followed up by focus group debates/discussion surrounding particular AIDS-related issues. Although AIDS and HIV was mentioned in a variety of news stories, this study limited its analysis to those indepth HIV/AIDS stories that were followed either by a debate/discussion or commentary by guests appearing on both shows. These fora were analyzed in terms of the number of guests who represented various demographic groups as well as political perspectives.

From the review of relevant literature, the following research questions were formulated:

R1: Was there an absence of some political perspectives and support for others regarding AIDS/HIV issues that legitimized particular positions and excluded others?

R2: Was there an overreliance upon spokespersons with a particular viewpoint or perspective?

R3: Were the guests invited to participate in the discussion of AIDS/HIV issues typical of individuals primarily affected by the disease?

R4: Did a presidential campaign year generate more stories about AIDS/HIV issues? If so, did the stories represent a limited political perspective?

An analysis of each guest who appeared in debates/discussion sessions on both programs was conducted to determine his or her perspective on HIV/AIDS. Each transcript was analyzed to determine the types of political perspectives or viewpoints surrounding AIDS and HIV issues that were most prominent during the discussions. In terms of my analysis and labeling of political perspectives and viewpoints, I use the terms *conservative*, *liberal*, and *progressive*. Each of these terms is troublesome in that each is relative to an individual's personal political perspective, and therefore they are somewhat ambiguous to define. Although the definitions of each perspective used in the current analysis are somewhat consistent with popular stereotypes and campaign usage, I use the terms in a more general sense. In regard to those HIV/AIDS policy issues that are discussed by the guests in the program transcripts, in some cases I labeled those views that advocated little or no change in policy or that expressed objections or concerns about an issue based on morality (especially surrounding sexual behaviors or drug use in contracting HIV) as conservative, views that advocated moderate change in policy or that expressed less emphasis on morality as liberal, and views that advocated more extreme changes or largely avoided morality issues surrounding policy as progressive. In other cases, the guests themselves were well known to the public in terms of their political viewpoints or they represented groups that officially advocated a particular viewpoint on an AIDS/HIV issue. Finally, each guest was also assessed in terms of whether they were typical or atypical of those individuals most directly affected by HIV/AIDS.

Results of the "Nightline" Analysis

The results of the analysis of "Nightline" transcripts indicate that out of the 18 HIV/AIDS stories that were followed by discussion, the type of guests who appeared largely represented either government officials or other individuals who were not directly affected by AIDS or HIV (see Table 21.1).

The five government officials were directors or members of government AIDS task forces. Although each official tended to favor behavioral changes and prevention strategies, they tended to focus their concerns on the risks of HIV contraction for the heterosexual, non-injection-drug-using population. Out of the 11 AIDS research doctors, 4 held conservative opinions about the efficacy of new antiviral drugs such as AZT or conservative opinions about research dealing with new hypotheses about the HIV virus. Only one of three AIDS activists actually participated in a debate.

Out of the five individuals with AIDS or who were infected with HIV, two were well-known public figures: tennis star Arthur Ashe and Republican spokesperson Mary Fisher,

TABLE 21.1
Analysis of "Nightline" Guest List

Type of Guest	Frequency
Government official	5
Politician	4
AIDS researcher	11
AIDS activist	5
AIDS patient	5
Family of AIDS patient	3

Note. Total number of AIDS debate/discussion sessions = 42.

who appeared twice. The other two individuals with AIDS were a man who was concerned about how candidate Bill Clinton's health care plan would affect his ability to pay for AIDS treatment, and a mother with AIDS who started the Pediatric AIDS Foundation. Four out of five stories in which people with AIDS or HIV appeared were tied in with campaign coverage. Each of these stories was used to emphasize the political angle of either a candidate or a political party's policy on health care reform.

The three family members of people with AIDS came from three different international AIDS stories about the spread of the disease in Uganda and other parts of Africa. These stories relied mainly on government officials from both the United States and Africa. The family members were shown in brief clips about the rising death toll.

In general, the debates on "Nightline" included discussion from mostly government officials, politicians, and AIDS researchers while largely excluding activists and people who are typically affected by the disease. At a time when HIV infection was rising disproportionately among minorities, Arthur Ashe was the only non-White person who appeared on the program to discuss AIDS in a 2-year time period. His celebrity status also makes him an atypical person with AIDS, because he had the financial means to procure alternative sources of health care. Most minorities with HIV or AIDS lack access to adequate health care.

The appearances of Mary Fisher on "Nightline," after the Republican convention, showed that heterosexual women can get HIV, but it was also useful for the Republican agenda. Although the HIV rate has increased considerably among heterosexual women, Mary Fisher was also an atypical person with HIV to appear on the show due to her level of influence. Her father, Max Fisher, is a wealthy businessman and significant contributor to the Republican Party. Mary Fisher's ability to speak about HIV/AIDS was likely due to the connections her father has with the Republican Party. Although she was expressing her concerns about HIV/AIDS, Mary Fisher also was representing the Republican Party and was useful for their agenda. The majority of women with HIV/AIDS typically are from lower socioeconomic backgrounds, are injection drug users, or sexual partners of injection drug users. Moreover, this was one of only three programs in which a woman appeared to discuss AIDS and HIV issues.

One of the other more extensive episodes occurred on March 17, 1994 (Bettag, 1994), when Elizabeth Glaser, the founder of the Pediatric AIDS Foundation, appeared to discuss this particular organization. This story was one of the more extensive HIV/AIDS stories by "Nightline"; however, there was not an issue at stake. Instead of a debate like the majority of AIDS-related issues on "Nightline," this episode focused on a historical account of the development of the organization.

The government officials and AIDS researchers who appeared were also atypical of most people affected by AIDS due to their education, financial means, and influence. These individuals did, however, represent a fairly wide spectrum of political views despite their elite status. Many of the government officials and politicians such as Washington, DC, Mayor

Sharon Pratt Kelly held liberal views on issues, such as favoring passing out condoms to high school students. During the May 15, 1992, program, which also dealt with this issue, she stated, "Forty percent of them (10th-graders) have had four or more partners. And so we have to do what is necessary, not only urge them to abstain, but also, if they persist, to make condoms available through the advice and counsel and support of health professionals" (Bettag, May 15, 1992).

Liberal views within this parameter were often countered with two or three conservative viewpoints on any given AIDS/HIV issue. Mayor Kelly was heavily debated by conservatives such as Tom Jipping (The Free Congress Foundation), who compared her free condom program with "giving a teenager a $100 bill" (Bettag, May 15, 1992), and William Bennet (former Secretary of Education), who stated, "20 years of kind of easy and woozy sex education in the schools have contributed to this problem and made it worse, and I'm worried that condom distribution will simply supplement what's gone on for 20 years, in effect give permission to more children to engage in sexual activity" (Bettag, May 15, 1992).

In one episode that appeared on August 17, 1992, the statements of two AIDS activists appeared in a video clip from the Republican convention. However, their comments were limited short sound bites" from the video footage. Both activists shouted "every seven minutes, a family member dies of AIDS!" (Bettag, August 17, 1992). Pat Buchanan, who was involved in the actual discussion (in the program's studio forum) about the Republican Party policy, responded to the changes in AIDS policy the activists were advocating by extolling family values: "Abortion on demand, a litmus test for the Supreme Court, homosexual rights, discrimination against religious schools, women in combat units, that's changed, all right, but that's not the kind of change America needs" (Bettag, August 17, 1992).

One of the few viewpoints from a progressive spokesperson to surface in an actual debate was on April 8, 1992, when Ken Konstant of ACT UP commented that Arthur Ashe "is now going to meet up with what a lot of people who are HIV-positive have met up with. He will, unfortunately, be chastised for it. There will be people that will think that he should not maybe be in a restaurant eating where they are" (Bettag, April 8, 1992).

With this comment, Ken Konstant attempted to enlighten viewers about some of the problems that are experienced by the majority of HIV-infected individuals, even though the story itself was dealing with a celebrity with HIV. This was one of only four live comments from a progressive spokesperson in the 2-year sample of "Nightline." The other progressive viewpoints came from two gay activists who appeared on December 20, 1993, to support the portrayal of AIDS patients in the movie *Philadelphia*. This debate was centered around whether Hollywood movie producers should promote movies that deal with social issues like HIV and AIDS, but it was presented mainly as a human interest story, which dealt with few controversial issues about AIDS.

The debates among HIV/AIDS researchers provided most of the information about the disease. Issues such as whether the HIV hypothesis is correct and the efficacy of drugs such as DDI and AZT were informative and interesting from a scientific standpoint, but the debates about these issues did not include reactions from people with AIDS/HIV. This was partly due to the technical nature of the debates, but "Nightline" made no attempts to solicit reactions from those individuals who would be most concerned with the efficacy of AIDS/HIV drugs.

Results of "The MacNeil/Lehrer News Hour" Analysis

The transcripts from "The MacNeil/Lehrer News Hour" contained 59 HIV/AIDS stories and 42 debates surrounding AIDS/HIV-related issues. "MacNeil/Lehrer" provided a slightly better demographic representation of guests than did "Nightline" (see Table 21.2).

TABLE 21.2
Analysis of "MacNeil/Lehrer" Guest List

Type of Guest	Frequency
Government official	21
Politician	12
AIDS researcher	14
AIDS activist	17
AIDS patient	4
Academic	4
Celebrity	3

Note. Total number of AIDS debate/discussion sessions = 42.

Sixteen of the government officials held conservative views on HIV/AIDS issues, whereas the remaining 5 held predominantly liberal views. Eight of the politicians held conservative views and four held liberal views. The 14 HIV/AIDS researchers held mostly liberal views during the few times that dialogue moved away from scientific/technical information. The celebrities and academics held predominantly liberal views. Finally, only five of the guests participating in the debates/discussions were from a racial/ethnic group other than White.

Although more AIDS/HIV activists appeared on "MacNeil/Lehrer" than on "Nightline," the majority of spokespersons were government officials, politicians, and AIDS/HIV researchers. More AIDS activists actually took part in discussions about HIV- and AIDS-related issues than on "Nightline"; however, these views were expressed mostly in video clips of demonstrators, by third-person references by the "MacNeil/Lehrer" hosts, or by guests who actually appeared in the studio itself. In addition, the progressive viewpoints that were included on the show were limited to a few statements, whereas other viewpoints would dominate the air time.

An example of this type of underrepresentation occurred on the January 4, 1994, episode when Secretary of Health and Human Services Donna Shalala appeared to discuss the Clinton administration's approach to HIV prevention. The debate was centered around the decision to launch a radio and television advertising campaign that promoted condom use as the best form of protection against infection with HIV.

Shalala contended that the advertisements used more explicit language than previous ads, however, it became evident throughout the discussion that the ads only hinted that some type of "intimate contact" between partners was involved in the spread of HIV. Although the proposed advertisements were an improvement over earlier attempts, the language regarding what intimate contact consisted of was largely ambiguous. Kinsella (1989) charged that the ambiguous use of language regarding the spread of HIV in journalism has contributed to misconceptions about the disease. For example, in an attempt to sanitize HIV prevention advertisements for a mainstream audience, most creators of these advertisements avoid talking about taboo issues such as anal sex or other practices that the assumed heterosexual audience would find offensive.

The only mention of a more progressive viewpoint regarding this issue occurred as follows when Robert MacNeil asked, "Let me ask you about a couple of criticisms of these ads. One from, you might say from the more liberal side of the spectrum, say well, they aren't explicit enough. You never see a condom in one of these ads" (Crystal, January 4, 1994). Although this viewpoint raised a concern about the efficacy of the proposed advertisements, the viewpoint did not come from a spokesperson more directly affected by the spread of HIV itself, namely someone from the gay community or another person more representative of the HIV-infected population.

Another example of underrepresentation occurred on December 1, 1993, World AIDS Day. The discussion was centered around the present state of the epidemic as well as the Clinton administration's creation of a special task force to develop solutions to many issues surrounding the AIDS crisis. Although "MacNeil/Lehrer" devoted the entire show to AIDS/HIV, the majority of viewpoints were presented by government officials. AIDS activist responses to Clinton's HIV/AIDS policies were limited to isolated crowd scene footage or hecklers in the audience during political speeches.

The only presentation of a view by a nongovernment official was by a heckler (amid booing from the crowd) who protested Bill Clinton in video footage of a speech:

> (Man in audience shouting at President) You're so concerned about AIDS, where is the Manhattan Project on AIDS that you promised during your campaign one year [ago]? Lots of talk, no action, where is it? Thirty recommendations of George Bush's commission on AIDS, you promised to implement it during your campaign. Where are they? One year, Slick Willie, the Republicans were right! We should have never trusted you! You are doing nothing, absolutely nothing. (Crystal, December 1, 1993)

This example is typical of a pattern that occurred on a number of episodes, where guests with less progressive viewpoints were allowed to respond to charges on the show itself, whereas individuals with progressive viewpoints were largely excluded from the actual debate/discussion forum. Similar "MacNeil/Lehrer" episodes (Crystal) that showed only video footage of AIDS/HIV activists occurred on May 11, 1992; July 20, 1992; August 10, 1992; October 11, 1992; October 16, 1992; July 23, 1993; June 25, 1993; June 21, 1993; and April 29, 1993.

As opposed to those individuals with more progressive viewpoints, politicians, government officials, and other guests who were allowed to appear in the discussion/debate forums were given an opportunity to respond to what had been said in video footage by progressive spokespersons. However, progressive individuals did not appear to counterargue these comments. For example, in a debate on October 11, 1992, between George Bush, Bill Clinton, and Ross Perot, then-President George Bush responded to video footage of AIDS/HIV protesters by denouncing their efforts to raise awareness about HIV and AIDS:

> And the other thing that is part of AIDS—it's one of the few diseases where behavior matters. And I once called on somebody, "Well, change your behavior. If the behavior you're using is prone to cause AIDS, change the behavior." The next thing I know, one of these ACT-UP groups is saying Bush ought to change his behavior. You can't talk about it rationally. The extremes are hurting the AIDS cause. To go into a Catholic mass in a beautiful cathedral in New York under the cause of helping AIDS and start throwing condoms around in the mass, I'm sorry, I think it sets back the cause. We cannot move to the extreme. (Crystal, October 11, 1992)

No activists appeared to challenge the president's position.

Not all responses to progressive viewpoints were as negative as the preceding example. Bill Clinton and Ross Perot were more sympathetic to AIDS activists in their responses and while discussing their plans to implement HIV/AIDS policy. In the few episodes where AIDS patients did appear via satellite, their comments were few compared to the lengthy discussion by government officials, politicians, researchers, and so forth. Overall, in the episodes during both the Bush and Clinton administrations, the patterns of presenting HIV/AIDS stories changed very little.

For example, on December 1, 1993, there was a debate/discussion surrounding adequate health care for AIDS/HIV patients in the workplace, which was dominated by such figures as Dr. Jocelyn Elders (Surgeon General), Donna Shalala (Secretary of Health and Human Services), Janet Reno (Attorney General), Hazel O'Leary (Secretary of Energy), and President Clinton. During the entire newscast, only one response (to President Clinton) from an AIDS patient, Larry Singletary, appeared: "I just hope for the best, just hope that you appropriate lots of money, so that, you know, research can be done" (Crystal, December 1, 1993).

As with "Nightline," there were a number of debates/discussions on "MacNeil/Lehrer" between AIDS/HIV researchers. Although this dialogue provided the public with information regarding the status AIDS/HIV research, there was virtually no input from AIDS activists or from infected individuals. For example, a debate over the effectiveness of AZT on September 6, 1993 (Crystal), consisted of guests who were demographically typical of other "MacNeil/Lehrer" debate/discussions, such as Dr. David Kessler (FDA Commissioner), Dr. Kathryn Anastas (Bronx Lebanon Hospital), Dr. Debra Cotton (Harvard School of Public Health), and Dr. David Barry (Burroughs Wellcome Company).

"MacNeil/Lehrer" did provide an interesting segment on June 10, 1993, about the Bonaventure House, a group home for AIDS patients. However, this was the only indepth story in the 2-year analysis that dealt with how the HIV/AIDS epidemic was affecting the gay community. In this story, three AIDS patients expressed their feelings about the disease and the state of the crisis.

CONCLUSION AND IMPLICATIONS FOR FUTURE AIDS AND AGENDA-SETTING RESEARCH

The purpose of this study was to examine the agenda-setting practices of two elite leaders of television news, "Nightline" and "The MacNeil/Lehrer News Hour." The study revealed that both programs have largely excluded guests who are representative of those individuals most effected by the epidemic and progressive viewpoints surrounding HIV/AIDS issues. The majority of the viewpoints were expressed by spokespersons who were predominantly White, male, affluent, well educated, and HIV-seronegative.

As leaders in television journalism, "The MacNeil/Lehrer News Hour" and "Nightline" are often emulated by other television news programs throughout the country in terms of style, content, and journalistic standards. Similar to their print counterparts, *The New York Times* and *The Washington Post,* both programs are influential in setting standards of reporting and coverage of news stories. It has been demonstrated that elite media sources often influence the agenda-setting practices of other media on a variety of issues, including HIV and AIDS.

Although AIDS/HIV stories and debates were popular features on both "Nightline" and "The MacNeil/Lehrer News Hour," the guests who dominated the discussion and the viewpoints expressed were found to be atypical of those individuals who are most directly affected by the epidemic. Although individuals such as politicians, government officials, and HIV/AIDS researchers are instrumental in shaping HIV/AIDS policy, they are not the only individuals who have a stake in the outcomes of such policy. When individuals with AIDS or HIV did appear, they seldom participated in the actual discussion/debate that occurred in both programs' fora. Instead, progressive viewpoints or individuals with the disease were heard primarily in video footage of demonstrations rather than on the shows themselves.

Hoynes and Croteau (1989) argued that this practice on both programs places progressive viewpoints outside of the rational and sophisticated discussion that takes place between guests on the show itself. The current study found that AIDS activists were displayed primarily as engaging in deviant behaviors, such as participating in demonstrations. The practice of limiting

AIDS/HIV demonstrators to video footage portrays the views expressed by these individuals as deviant in opposition to the discussion that occurs between the guests invited to participate on both of the programs.

Compared to Kinsella's (1989) assessment of the media's coverage of the AIDS/HIV epidemic, both "The MacNeil/Lehrer News Hour" and "Nightline" have attempted to include HIV/AIDS issues as part of their news agenda on a regular basis. For example, during the 1992 election year, AIDS/HIV was featured as a prominent social issue. However, despite the number of stories and discussion about AIDS/HIV, the discussion was largely limited the guests allowed to appear on the programs. As a result, the public only heard part of the AIDS/HIV story, the viewpoints of those people who are for the most part only indirectly affected by the epidemic. The underrepresentation of those primarily affected by the disease may provide some insight into why coverage of AIDS/HIV stories changed little during the transition from George Bush's administration to Bill Clinton's.

With the tendency of other television news media to emulate the leadership of the elite media, it follows that these two programs have an influence on how the public perceives the state of the HIV/AIDS epidemic. Therefore, the elite media's influence on the agenda-setting process has a major implication for the epidemic. "The MacNeil/Lehrer News Hour" and "Nightline" tend to focus on the implications of the epidemic on White, middle-class, heterosexual concerns. Ironically, at a time when they were most affected by the disease, the concerns of minorities and gay men were given only limited (if any) attention by both of the programs. The public is exposed to only a limited spectrum of viewpoints regarding HIV and AIDS, and this spectrum portrays only a partial representation of reality.

Future Directions.   Future research on agenda-setting and HIV/AIDS issues should take into account the influence of elite media news sources such as "Nightline" and "The MacNeil/Lehrer News Hour." Rather than focusing entirely on the number of stories about AIDS and HIV generated by programs such as these, researchers should also take into account the people who are telling the story and their viewpoints. The influence of elite media on other news media representation of AIDS/HIV issues needs to be empirically verified. Although the current literature on agenda-setting has noted such an effect with other news stories, the unique ways in which the news media portray the most controversial disease of our time should be a continuing concern for communication scholars interested in AIDS and HIV.

REFERENCES

Bettag, T. (Executive Producer). (1992, March 17). *Nightline*. New York: American Broadcasting Companies, Inc.

Bettag, T. (Executive Producer). (1992, April 8). *Nightline*. New York: American Broadcasting Companies, Inc.

Bettag, T. (Executive Producer). (1992, May 15). *Nightline*. New York: American Broadcasting Companies, Inc.

Bettag, T. (Executive Producer). (1992, August 17). *Nightline*. New York: American Broadcasting Companies, Inc.

Crystal, L. (Executive Producer). (1992, May 11). *The MacNeil/Lehrer news hour*. New York and Washington, DC: Public Broadcasting Service.

Crystal, L. (Executive Producer). (1992, July 20). *The MacNeil/Lehrer news hour*. New York and Washington, DC: Public Broadcasting Service.

Crystal, L. (Executive Producer). (1992, August 10). *The MacNeil/Lehrer news hour*. New York and Washington, DC: Public Broadcasting Service.

Crystal, L. (Executive Producer). (1992, October 11). *The MacNeil/Lehrer news hour*. New York and Washington, DC: Public Broadcasting Service.

Crystal, L. (Executive Producer). (1992, October 16). *The MacNeil/Lehrer news hour*. New York and Washington, DC: Public Broadcasting Service.

Crystal, L. (Executive Producer). (1993, April 29). *The MacNeil/Lehrer news hour*. New York and Washington, DC: Public Broadcasting Service.

Crystal, L. (Executive Producer). (1993, June 10). *The MacNeill Lehrer news hour*. New York and Washington, DC: Public Broadcasting Service.

Crystal, L. (Executive Producer). (1993, June 21). *The MacNeill Lehrer news hour*. New York and Washington, DC: Public Broadcasting Service.

Crystal, L. (Executive Producer). (1993, June 25). *The MacNeill Lehrer news hour*. New York and Washington, DC: Public Broadcasting Service.

Crystal, L. (Executive Producer). (1993, July 23). *The MacNeill Lehrer news hour*. New York and Washington, DC: Public Broadcasting Service.

Crystal, L. (Executive Producer). (1993, September 6). *The MacNeill Lehrer news hour*. New York and Washington, DC: Public Broadcasting Service.

Crystal, L. (Executive Producer). (1993, December 1). *The MacNeill Lehrer news hour*. New York and Washington, DC: Public Broadcasting Service.

Crystal, L. (Executive Producer). (1994, January 4). *The MacNeill Lehrer news hour*. New York and Washington, DC: Public Broadcasting Service.

Dearing, J. W., & Rogers, E. M. (1992). AIDS and the media agenda. In T. Edgar, M. A. Fitzpatrick, & V. S. Freimuth (Eds.), *AIDS: A communication perspective* (pp. 165–189). Hillsdale, NJ: Lawrence Erlbaum Associates.

Hoynes, W., & Croteau, D. (1989). Are you on the Nightline guest list? *Extra: A publication of FAIR (Fairness and Accuracy in Reporting), 2*, 2–15.

Hoynes, W., & Croteau, D. (1990). All the usual suspects: MacNeil/Lehrer and Nightline. *Extra: A publication of FAIR (Fairness and Accuracy in Reporting), 3*, 2–15.

Kahn, A. D. (1993). *AIDS: The winter war*. Philadelphia: Temple University Press.

Kinsella, J. (1989). *Covering the plague: AIDS and the American media*. New Brunswick, NJ: Rutgers University Press.

Protess, D. L., & McCombs, M. E. (1991). *Agenda-setting: Readings on media, public opinion, and policy making*. Hillsdale, NJ: Lawrence Erlbaum Associates.

Reese, S. D., & Danielian, L. H. (1989). Intermedia influence and the drug issue: Converging on cocaine. In P. J. Shoemaker (Ed.), *Communication campaigns about drugs: Government, media, and the public* (pp. 30–37). Hillsdale, NJ: Lawrence Erlbaum Associates.

Shaw, D. L., & McCombs, M. E. (1989). Dealing with illicit drugs: The power, and limits, of mass media agenda-setting. In P. J. Shoemaker (Ed.), *Communication campaigns about drugs: Government, media, and the public* (pp. 113–120). Hillsdale, NJ: Lawrence Erlbaum Associates.

Shoemaker, P. J., Wanta, W., & Leggett, D. (1989). Drug coverage and public opinion, 1972–1986. In P. J. Shoemaker (Ed.), *Communication campaigns about drugs: Government, media, and the public* (pp. 68–77). Hillsdale, NJ: Lawrence Erlbaum Associates.

22

What We Say and How We Say It: The Influence of Psychosocial Characteristics and Message Content of HIV/AIDS Public Service Announcements

Timothy N. Walters
Northeast Louisiana University

Lynne M. Walters
Susanna Hornig Priest
Texas A&M University

Because public health campaigns are as much exercises in communication as in medical treatment, they require many vehicles to transmit issue and image salience to the public and to the media. Mindful of this, the communications mix of a sophisticated heath care campaign employs advertising and public relations techniques as part of an integrated strategy. One element of that mix is the televised public service announcement (PSA). Many believe these announcements have the potential to amplify themes and images, as well as to transfer the "legitimacy" that comes from being part of the programming flow. Advocates also believe that these efforts help stimulate news coverage to further advance themes and images. Moreover, there appears to be a relationship between media attention and public policy issues. High levels of attention merit action and funding support from government officials (Gaby, 1980; Mitchell, 1992; Vermeer, 1982; L. Walters & T. Walters, 1992, 1994).

Indeed, in the United States, the televised PSA has been a component of public health campaigns directed toward disease awareness and prevention. Perceived by audiences as crucial and credible sources of health information, PSAs broadcast in conjunction with campaigns conducted by the National High Blood Pressure Education Program, the National Cholesterol Education Program, and the Great American Smokeout have helped reduce illness over the long term.

Treading where others have passed, those concerned with ameliorating the spread of HIV have attempted to orchestrate information and education plans of their own (Katz, 1993). As time has passed, researchers studying these efforts have looked at the communications problem from several angles. They have examined the effects of issue involvement and have found a relationship between the interest a subject brings to the message and the effectiveness of emotional appeals (Flora & Maibach, 1990). Others have examined the problem from the viewpoint of interpersonal relations (Cline, Freeman, & S. J. Johnson, 1990), language discrimination (Norton, Schwartzbaum, & Wheat, 1990), or the constituent executional components of messages (Siska, Jason, & Murdoch, 1992). Underlying this discussion is the need to determine the relationship between the "how we say it," or executional variables, and what the audience brings to the message. This step is essential. Although many studies have found risk groups to be knowledgeable about HIV and AIDS, many have also found that subjects do not apply that knowledge and reduce their risk behavior (Atkin & Wallack, 1990; Christensen & Ruch, 1978; Ratzan, Payne, & Massett, 1994). What is required is an information base regarding target audiences and the actual and potential effects that mediated information can generate in them.

Complicating programmatic development and use of effective campaigns are the disparate priorities of mass media and public health institutions. The mass media want to make a profit, reflect society, cover short-term events, and deliver salient pieces of material. In contrast, public health groups want to improve public health, change society, conduct long-term campaigns, and create an understanding of complex information (Atkin & Arkin, 1990). Suggestions to ease the tension between the two groups have been to increase the quantity and prominence of pro–health and safety messages within the context of entertainment segments, to insert additional disclaimers and positive role models, and to improve the legitimate educational quality of PSAs (Atkin & Arkin, 1990).

Despite the seeming ease and efficacy of these steps, barriers exist to their implementation. Because, like all other media, television's first priority is attracting audiences to remain in business, prohealth depictions always will be sacrificed to audience enjoyment and attention. Because mainstream television avoids controversy, executives are generally reluctant to editorialize about topics such as AIDS or mental illness (Atkin & Arkin, 1990; Cuneo, 1994; Flinn, 1996).

Despite these problems, effective campaigns can be designed and implemented if they are predicated on an understanding of how the media operate, how campaigns fit into the commercial environment, and how messages interact with an audience. Among the seven conditions Flay, McFall, and Burton (1993) identified as necessary for effective health care campaigns were the development of high-quality messages, sources, and channels grounded in theory, formative research, and needs assessment; the frequent dissemination of the stimuli to target audiences over a sustained period; and the accumulation of systematic knowledge about the conditions of maximum impact. If examined with a critical eye, most health care campaigns don't even get off on the right foot. Typically, they fail to recognize the need to begin with research. Unlike their marketing counterparts, some health care PSA developers concentrate on evaluating the result, rather than on preproduction research such as needs assessment and concept testing (Flay, McFall, & Burton, 1993).

This study was a step in that direction of front-end research. It examines extant messages and engages in concept testing and formative research, while looking for better ways to develop high-quality HIV/AIDS messages that attract attention and improve recall of critical information. After examining for-broadcast AIDS PSAs in relationship to demographic variables, this study posits reasons for the failure to communicate effectively and suggests mitigating strategies based on recognizing differences in responses to health care messages among and between groups.

PREVIOUS STUDIES

When examining the potential role of television in promoting the adoption of prosocial attitudes, researchers have studied factors associated with both advertisement and message recipient (Assael, 1987; MacKenzie, 1986). Of the two, the characteristics of the message recipient are perhaps the least understood because models heretofore have been based on externally guided frameworks.

Knowledge of how a group fits into this structure helps construct appeals and executions that are better recalled and/or recognized. Characteristics of the message recipient may be thought of as what a person "brings to the message." The "things" brought to the message have internal and external components. Internal elements include thoughts (attitudes, needs, and perceptions), emotions (experience, emotional state), and characteristics (demographics, lifestyle, and personality). External elements include culture (values, cross-cultural influences, and subcultural influences), social class (collected around norms and values), face-to-face groups (family, opinion leaders, and reference groups), and situational determinants based on an inventory of relevant situations (consumption, purchase, and communication). Broadly defined as the "position of an individual or family based on criteria such as occupation, education and income," social categories or class can be related to the persuasiveness of an advertisement to a population subgroup (Assael, 1987, p. 351).

Looking beyond categorical clustering, advanced systems, such as BrandTab, ACORN, ClusterPlus, Consumers Innovators Plus, Scan-Track, MRI Mediamarket Re-ports, Prism, CUBE, and SRI's VALS 2 combine demographic information with research on activities, interests, and opinions. Taken together, categorical variables and attitudinal dimensions help form psychographic profiles linking advertising executions to group structures (Demby, 1989; Russell & Land, 1988).

Along these lines, some have suggested new ways of looking at what constitutes culture. One possibility is that gender, along with country of origin, conveys a "framing" useful in studying the communication process (Bush, 1986; K. Johnson & LaTour, 1991; Thompson, Pingree, Hawkins, & Davies, 1991). Indeed, Hornig (1990, 1992) and T. Walters and L. Walters (1994) found that the notion of a "woman's culture" helped explain differences between sexes in responding to science and technology. These studies also demonstrated the utility of analyzing differences in response to news about science and technology as a function of membership in distinctive, though intersecting, cultures (Hornig, 1992).

Advertising practitioners and communication scholars have long sought to define elements of messages that work in unison with characteristics of the message recipient to draw attention and improve memory. In doing so, they have isolated cues, or "executional elements," that can elicit, maintain, or terminate attention (Anderson, Levin, & Lorch, 1977; Petty, Cacioppo, & Schumann, 1983). These executional elements may be thought of as the techniques used to construct the message. More simply, they might be thought of as "how we say" something.

In a complex cataloging, Stewart and Furse (1985) separated these "how we say" elements used to create television commercials into almost a dozen categories. Although many have not been standard fare for study of public health awareness and education programs, emotion and information content have been. Because of this long history, the two are natural starting points for examining differences between groups. Even if the history is long, identifying and operationalizing emotion is complicated. Indeed, merely determining what is meant by emotion is complex because of diverse objectives, methods, stimuli, and typologies used in various studies. Despite inconsistency and complexity, the emotion of fear remains a useful starting point because so many previous health care campaigns have used it as a component. Higbee's (1969) definition of fear as the threat of negative consequences produced by a particular behavior is fitting in a health care context, both because of a rich literature connected with fear and because Higbee's definition (and his eight primary emotions scheme) is simple and well tested.

Along with fear, concrete terms also have been a usual ingredient of health education programs (Fish & Karabenick, 1978; Higbee, 1969; Leventhal & Watts, 1966; Miller & Brody, 1988; Rogers, 1983). Many executions have used them, with descriptive words emphasizing undesirable results of a particular behavior, up to, and including, *death*. The lexicography of such nonabstract words includes both those dealing with mortality and those dealing with anatomically explicit words that some consider obscene or profane (Jay & Danks, 1977; Mabry, 1975; Sandwich & Evans, 1977). Rothwell (1971) stated that because obscenity is unacceptable to many in our culture, strategic public use of anatomically specific language may "provide the most jolting, evocative stimulus" (p. 233). One purpose for using sexually laden language is the desire to impact the message recipient, and, in so doing, either attract attention or establish interpersonal identification (Bostrom, Basehart, & Rossiter, 1973).

Despite the simplistic attraction, two potential restraints may limit the widespread use of sexually explicit language over the air waves. The first restraint is strategic. As long as novelty remains, sexually accurate words may serve as a "planned rhetorical strategy to create identification between agitators and potential allies" (Rothwell, 1971, p. 237). Once the novelty disappears, this tactic may become outmoded, and require increasingly explicit language for a desensitized audience (T. Walters & Barnum, 1991). The second potential restraint is the combination of law and custom. The Federal Communications Commission has long prohibited the airing of obscene material, and station managers have long exercised a quasi-statistical sense of community standards when refusing air time for material they consider objectionable. Taken together, the two combine to create a "chilling effect" on PSA makers.

Unfortunately, this chill and conflict over emotional tone, and the perceived need for ever more explicit HIV/AIDS PSAs, threatens gridlock in education efforts. This impasse is dangerous. With disparate increases in HIV infection rates among different populations, the need to know what messages" appeal to "what population subgroup" and "why" is crucial. Thus, researchers should look at socially and legally viable ways to analyze relationships between audiences and messages to circumvent potential problems and make campaigns more potent. One way to do this is to examine the connection between what an individual brings to a message and health-related attitudes using the time-tested variables of fear and explicit sexual words as independent variables. The focus of this chapter is to help understand how determinants such as age, ethnicity, and occupation affect responses to existing PSAs on HIV and AIDS.

RESEARCH QUESTIONS

The research questions addressed in this chapter are:

RQ1: Is there a relationship between the things that an individual brings to a message and recall of verbal and visual themes of AIDS-related PSAs?

RQ2: Is there a relationship between the things that an individual brings to a message and recall of AIDS-related PSAs based on the use of fear and specific sexual explicit words used in these messages.

METHODOLOGY

Subjects were 31 non-Hispanic White (NHW) and 25 African-American (AA) undergraduate communication students at two southwestern universities. The form was a factorial 2×2, within subjects. The independent variables were information content (high or low explicit sexual words) and fear (high or low). Separately, 57 other undergraduate students participated in a preliminary survey to rate independently fear levels in stimulus materials.

Tested HIV/AIDS PSAs were taken from materials produced and designed for on-air use. They came from several sources: 14 television stations, including those in Los Angeles, Miami, Chicago, and New York, as well as major metropolitan areas in Texas; the Centers for Disease Control and Prevention, Atlanta; Planned Parenthood, Houston, Texas; and The American Red Cross.

A preliminary review of more than 100 English-language HIV/AIDS PSAs eliminated those using celebrities or medical professionals as announcers and those that did not feature fear as the primary emotion. Because of potential confounding variables, the need for randomized materials choice, and the desire to provide for analysis of covariance, a panel of 57 students viewed the materials for use. They rated the surviving 20 PSAs for level of fear using Higbee's (1969) definition of fear as the threat of negative consequences resulting from a particular behavior.

The dependent measures were unaided recall items. For recall, the dependent measures consisted of total number of words recalled about the PSA, verbal themes identified, and visual themes identified. Verbal themes were main PSA ideas that could be transmitted and received only through hearing. Visual themes were main PSA ideas that could be transmitted and received only through sight. Two coders identified both the verbal and visual themes. Intercoder reliability as expressed by Pearson product correlations was .950 for verbal themes and .879 for visual themes.

After making a matrix of fear and explicitness for 20 PSAs, 4 PSAs representing high and low levels of fear and and high and low levels of explicit sexual words were chosen randomly for use. Those chosen for use were (a) *Candle*, High Fear, High Explicit Words, (b) *Gun*, High Fear, Low Explicit Words, (c) *Koop*, Low Fear, High Explicit Words, and (d) *Family*, Low Fear, Low Explicit Words. The four PSAs were embedded in an episode of "Northern Exposure" in normal commercial pods. There were four commercial pods in the episode. One PSA was placed in each pod, along with regularly broadcast commercials. Order of presentation of the PSAs was controlled, as was order of appearance within the pod. The content of these PSAs was:

1. *Candle* (High Fear, High Explicit Words):
Visual: Uses lit candles. Starts with a single white candle that lights four others and ends with hundreds of lit candles in the background.
Verbal: "When you have sex with someone, you're having sex with all their former partners. And all their former partners. And all their former partners. And so on. And if any one of them has the virus that causes AIDS, then hundreds of people could be exposed. Including you."

2. *Family* (Low Fear, Low Explicit Words):
Visual: A businessman sits at his desk in his office with a picture of his family. Next, he is shown at home in his living room with his wife and two children. One is a boy; the other is a girl.
Verbal: "Thursday night. My night out with the boys. A few beers, a little action. Sometimes we'd score. Thursday nights. That was the old me. It took AIDS to make me realize that I was putting myself and my family in danger. I was cheating. It's not worth it. I love my family, and I'm not bringing AIDS home. Find out more about AIDS. Call 1-800-342-AIDS."

3. *Gun* (High Fear, Low Explicit Words):
Visual: Shows six people of different races, ages, and genders playing Russian Roulette one at a time. The gun is loaded with one bullet. Ends with a flash across the screen and the sound of a gun firing. AIDS hotline number is used at the end.

Verbal: "Every single day AIDS kills all kinds of people. Randomly. People like you. Men and women. Gay and straight. Single and married. Old and very young. But with your help we can stop AIDS. Call 1-800-992-CURE to give to the American Foundation for AIDS Research. It's nobody's fault, and everybody's problem."

4. *Koop* (Low Fear, High Explicit Words):

Visual: An older man in a uniform with a full beard sitting at a table, with a microphone in foreground and several women in the background.

Verbal: "A message of critical importance for everybody about AIDS and condoms. U.S. Surgeon General C. Everett Koop. The best protection against the infection right now, barring abstinence, is the use of a condom. A condom should be used during sexual relations from start to finish with anyone who you are not absolutely sure is free of the AIDS virus. Brought to you as a public service by the American Foundation for AIDS Research. AIDS. It's everybody's problem."

Procedure.   By means of a script, experimenters followed the same procedure for all subjects. Before beginning the experiment, subjects watched a practice tape and answered questions to practice the procedure. Then, the episode of "Northern Exposure" with the HIV/AIDS PSAs was shown. After viewing the tape, the subjects then were given forms to complete. First, subjects were asked to recall as many of the AIDS PSAs as they could. They were to begin with the first PSA that popped into their minds. They invented a title for the PSA and wrote down as many recollections about the dialogue, the characters, the advice given, or anything else they could remember about the PSA. They were also asked to rate how each PSA made them feel on a scale of 1 (felt not at all) to 10 (felt very much) for eight primary emotions. Second, subjects answered a recognition test that asked questions about program and PSA content. Third, 86 Likert-like statements were answered. Fourth, and finally, demographic information was collected. Although each chosen PSA included fear as part of the execution, all PSAs exhibited other "felt emotions." The literature suggests (and the experiment confirmed) that fear, the primary emotion, did not dominate any PSA to the exclusion of other tested emotions.

Methodological Considerations.   Because of its economy, generalizability, and ability to test real-world situations, the repeated measures, factorial experiment used here offers advantages to other types of experimental designs. In a factorial design, two randomized factors (or independent variables) may be tested across levels. In this type of experiment, all combinations of multiple independent variables and the ways they affect each other are considered. The effect of a factor is the change in response produced by a change in the level of a factor. This is called a main effect. In some experiments, differences in response between the levels of one factor are not the same at all levels of the other factors. When this occurs, an interaction is present.

The mixed design, a variation of the factorial design, combines a repeated measures variable with a between-groups independent variable, such as gender, age, or race, which are variables that can be selected, but not manipulated. The selected natural variable becomes the random-groups independent variable. For example, if the ease of identifying obscene words is to be compared with neutral words for males and females, the type of word has two levels and is the repeated measure. Gender has two levels and is the randomized independent variable (between group) selected by the experimenter because each subject is only one gender (Snodgrass, Levy-Berger, & Haydon, 1985).

A factorial design has specific advantages with respect to communications. Such a design is helpful at the reconstructive stage, where scientists study the real world. A factorial design offers economy in terms of using subjects and is more generalizable. This is because the pattern of results is not necessarily unique to the specific values of other relevant stimulus variables and because the most important uncontrolled source of error is due to individual differences. A randomized repeated measures design accounts for these differences.

In a single-factor experiment, all variables, except the one being manipulated, are maintained at the same level across the different treatment groups. Such control is necessary to guarantee that the differences are due solely to the operation of the independent variable. Yet, this can create problems. One problem connected to nonfactorial experiments is a lack of generality of the results. That is because the particular pattern of results may be unique to the specific values of other relevant stimulus variables maintained at a constant level through the course of the experiment (Keppel, 1973). The factorial experiment provides one solution to this limitation by allowing the effect of an independent variable to be averaged over several different levels of another relevant variable (Keppel, 1973).

Ideally, all important variables except the ones under systematic study would be held physically constant. But, factors not controlled for may be varied randomly across the treatment conditions. Randomization of these nuisance factors is a major way of obtaining internal validity. In doing so, the influence of uncontrolled variables is spread over the treatment groups equally. These variables do not systematically affect the treatment means, and, so, bias is removed. They do, however, influence the sensitivity of the experiment, because any variability due to nuisance variables becomes deposited in the error term. With a larger error term, the ability to detect the presence of real treatment effects is reduced (Keppel, 1973).

Best results from factorial experiments spring from randomization, sensitivity, and power. Relevant randomization of items can include subject populations, assignment, treatment, orders, and materials, and helps guarantee that the treatment conditions will be matched on all environmental factors and subject abilities. The failure to sample randomly from a known population means that results cannot be extended beyond the experiment itself. Reducing treatment variability or subject variability through repeated measures, blocking, and using analysis of covariance, increases sensitivity by reducing error variance. Finally, increasing sample size and the size of treatment effects, and making the experiment more sensitive to experimental effects increases power. The greater the power, the more likely that even a small difference between the experimental groups will make a difference.

Whereas a general weakness of the experimental method is a loss of ecological validity (in this instance an atypical experience with HIV/AIDS PSAs), strong internal validity is obtained by examining the variables in relationship to each other. Because of this, the method eliminates problems with self-reports depending on matching of subject characteristics (Cameron, 1992; Lachman, Lachman, & Butterfield, 1979). Although holding physically constant all variables under systematic study would have been the ideal, real-world factors, including materials expense and a large number of subjects, prevented this. To compensate, factors that were unable to be controlled were varied randomly across the treatment conditions. Randomization spread the influence of the uncontrolled factors over the treatment; although this removed bias, the uncontrolled factors decreased the sensitivity of the experiment. Lastly, the randomization of these nuisance factors helped eliminate biases (Keppel, 1973).

RESULTS

For purposes of comparison, subjects were divided into groups. They were chosen using the following criterion. Both the Likert-scale opinion question ("Math and science are easy for me") and age, which was asked as an open-ended question, were divided using K-means clustering with number of groups set to two. Undergraduate major was used as an indicator of prospective occupation. The group name and number of subjects were: Age, Young ($n = 22$), Mean 19.1, Old ($n = 33$), Mean 22.1; Ethnic, African American, ($n = 29$); non-Hispanic White ($n = 26$); Gender, Females ($n = 28$), Males ($n = 18$); Family Income, Low, $0–$49,000 ($n = 27$), Up, $50,000+ ($n = 28$); Major, Nonscience ($n = 41$), Science ($n = 14$); and Self-Reported Math Skill, Easy ($n = 26$), Hard ($n = 29$).

As was expected, differences emerged along several lines. Ethnic groups and Major plus Self-Report Math Skill accounted for four significant differences between groups when totaled for Verbal and Visual Themes. When similarly totaled, Age accounted for three, and Gender accounted for two. Six significant differences between groups emerged for recall of Verbal Themes and five for Visual Themes (see Tables 22.1 and 22.2).

Some differences can be accounted for in the relationship between group and the "how we say it" variables, which, in this case, were fear and sexually explicit words. With respect to verbal themes, older students recalled more of *Family* (High Fear, Low Sexually Explicit Words), a PSA featuring a family man who had cheated on his wife than did younger students. Similarly, non-White Hispanic students recalled more about *Family* than did African Americans. Science majors, those whose computation skills may be interpreted as above average, recalled more Verbal themes from *Candle* and *Family* than did students who chose careers that did not emphasize math skills. Differences between genders seemed related to certain PSAs.

TABLE 22.1
Mean Recall of Verbal Themes

Demographic Group, PSA
Candle (High Fear, High Sexually Explicit Words)

	Age		Ethnic		Income		Major		Math		Gender	
	19.2	22.1	AA	NHW	Up	Low	Non	Sci	Easy	Hard	F	M
Mean	1.00	1.18	1.04	1.77	1.11	1.11	.86	1.20*	1.04	1.17	1.22	.89*

Gun (High Fear, Low Sexually Explicit Words)

	Age		Ethnic		Income		Major		Math		Gender	
	19.2	22.1	AA	NHW	Up	Low	Non	Sci	Easy	Hard	F	M
Mean	.68	.91	.77	.86	.85	.77	.57	.90	.81	.83	.97	.50

Koop (Low Fear, High Sexually Explicit Words)

	Age		Ethnic		Income		Major		Math		Gender	
	19.2	22.1	AA	NHW	Up	Low	Non	Sci	Easy	Hard	F	M
Mean	.54	.61	.69	.48	.68	.50	.86	.49	.69	.48	.54	.68

Family (Low Fear, Low Sexually Explicit Words)

	Age		Ethnic		Income		Major		Math		Gender	
	19.2	22.1	AA	NHW	Up	Low	Non	Sci	Easy	Hard	F	M
Mean	1.50	1.94*	1.50	2.00*	1.93	1.61	1.36	1.90*	1.65	1.86	1.84	1.61

Note. Groups: Age, Young ($n = 22$), Mean 19.1, Old ($n = 33$), Mean 22.12; Ethnic, Black ($n = 29$), Non-Hispanic White ($n = 26$); Gender, Females ($n = 28$), Males ($n = 18$); Income, Up, $50,000+ ($n = 27$), Low, $0–$49,000 ($n = 28$); Major, Nonscience ($n = 41$), Science ($n = 14$); and Self-Reported Math Skill, Easy ($n = 26$), Hard ($n = 29$).

Age = Mean age; AA = African American, NHW = Non-Hispanic White; Non = Nonscience major, Sci = Science major; Easy = Math and science are easy for me, Hard = Math and science are hard for me; and F = Female, M = Male.

*$p < .05$ between paired groups.

TABLE 22.2
Mean Recall of Visual Themes

Demographic Group, PSA
Candle (High Fear, High Sexually Explicit Words)

	Age		Ethnic		Income		Major		Math		Gender	
	19.2	22.1	AA	NHW	Up	Low	Non	Sci	Easy	Hard	F	M
Mean	1.23	1.67*	1.15	1.79*	1.41	1.57	1.61	1.14	1.23	1.74*	1.57	1.33

Gun (High Fear, Low Sexually Explicit Words)

	Age		Ethnic		Income		Major		Math		Gender	
	19.2	22.1	AA	NHW	Up	Low	Non	Sci	Easy	Hard	F	M
Mean	1.14	1.70*	1.15	1.76*	.86	1.41	1.54	1.61	1.27	1.66	1.49	1.44

Koop (Low Fear, Low Sexually Explicit Words)

	Age		Ethnic		Income		Major		Math		Gender	
	19.2	22.1	AA	NHW	Up	Low	Non	Sci	Easy	Hard	F	M
Mean	.27	.49	.39	.41	.37	.43	.34	.57	.46	.35	.43	.33

Family (Low Fear, Low Sexually Explicit Words)

	Age		Ethnic		Income		Major		Math		Gender	
	19.2	22.1	AA	NHW	Up	Low	Non	Sci	Easy	Hard	F	M
Mean	.86	1.15	.81	1.24*	1.11	1.10	.86	1.65	.89	1.17	1.14	.83

Note. Groups: Age, Young ($n = 22$), Mean 19.1, Old ($n = 33$), Mean 22.12; Ethnic, Black ($n = 29$), Non-Hispanic White ($n = 26$); Gender, Females ($n = 28$), Males ($n = 18$); Income, Up, \$50,000+ ($n = 27$), Low, \$0–\$50,000, ($n = 28$); Major, Nonscience ($n = 41$), Science ($n = 14$); and Self-Reported Math Skill, Easy ($n = 26$), Hard ($n = 29$).

Age = Mean age; AA = African American, NHW = Non-Hispanic White; Non = Nonscience major, Sci = Science major; Easy = Math and science are easy for me, Hard = Math and science are hard for me; and F = Female, M = Male.

*$p < .05$ between paired groups.

Tables 22.3 and 22.4, which present the results of the factorial 2 × 2, within-subjects experiment demonstrate the differences between groups in a variety of ways. Significant differences existed between and among groups for Verbal Themes and Visual Themes. While the results suggested that Fear and Explicit Sexual Words remain potent as individual variables and, as a combination, they also suggest that age, ethnicity, gender, and occupation, among other variables, have an impact on recall of AIDS-related themes. Thus, the results suggest that an effective health campaign requires a variety of messages tuned to audience segments.

CONCLUSION

The results indicated that a relationship exists between what an individual "brings to a message" and recall of verbal and visual themes and that "how we say it" elements such as fear and graphic sexual words are a significant part of the process of communication. The results also indicate that the capacity of individuals to assess risk is directly related to the efficacy of these "how we say it" elements. Whether this capacity is tied to thought and emotion or to culture, social class, face-to-face groups, and situational determinants is unclear. What is clear is that underlying attitudinal dimensions related to gender, age, income, and

TABLE 22.3
Verbal Themes

Between-Subjects Effects		
	F	p
Age	3.662	.061
Ethnic Group	1.484	.229
Gender	3.079	.085
Income	3.972	.050
Major	1.862	.178
Math Skill	.028	.867
Within-Subjects Effects		
Fear	F	p
Fear	6.743	.012
Fear*Age	.666	.418
Fear*Ethnic Group	.023	.881
Fear*Gender	2.535	.118
Fear*Income	.988	.325
Fear*Major	1.862	.178
Fear*Math Skill	.057	.812
Explicit Words	F	p
Words	21.502	.000
Words*Age	.272	.604
Words*Ethnic Group	3.112	.084
Words*Gender	1.068	.306
Words*Income	1.367	.248
Words*Major	5.110	.028
Words*Math Skill	0.091	.764
Interactions	F	p
Fear*Words	73.209	.000
Fear*Words*Age	.032	.859
Fear*Words*Ethnic Group	4.577	.037
Fear*Words*Gender	.406	.527
Fear*Words*Income	.654	.422
Fear*Words*Major	6.506	.014
Fear*Words*Math Skill	1.042	.312

Note. $N = 55$. Groups: Age, Young ($n = 22$), Mean 19.1, Old, $n = 33$, Mean 22.12; Ethnic, Black ($n = 29$), Non-Hispanic White ($n = 26$); Gender, Females ($n = 28$), Males ($n = 18$); Income, Up, $50,000+ ($n = 27$), Low, $0–$49,000 ($n = 28$); Major, Nonscience ($n = 41$), Science ($n = 14$); and Self-Reported Math Skill, Easy ($n = 26$), Hard ($n = 29$).

major (here used as a surrogate for occupation) help separate audiences into groups with differing interpretive frames of understanding science and technology.

Both the quantitative and qualitative data supported the conclusion that youthful population segments have differing abilities in assessing personal risk of contracting HIV. In this experiment, two groups emerged. One was numerate. They could estimate odds in computation manner. The other was less numerate. They required that risk be communicated in a noncomputational, visual manner to reach an understanding of the problem. Although this study dealt with only one college-age group, Eckstein (1989), for one, has suggested that some

TABLE 22.4
Visual Themes

Between-Subjects Effects		
	F	p
Age	4.174	.046
Ethnic Group	7.107	.010
Gender	1.241	.271
Income	.133	.717
Major	.317	.576
Math Skill	.794	.377

Within-Subjects Effects		
Fear	F	p
Fear	41.902	.000
Fear*Age	.293	.591
Fear*Ethnic Group	3.665	.061
Fear*Gender	.005	.945
Fear*Income	.060	.807
Fear*Major	4.654	.036
Fear*Math Skill	2.092	.154
Explicit Words	F	p
Words	4.654	.036
Words*Age	4.174	.046
Words*Ethnic Group	.460	.501
Words*Gender	.021	.885
Words*Income	.009	.926
Words*Major	1.237	.271
Words*Math Skill	.308	.581
Interactions	F	p
Fear*Words	6.340	.015
Fear*Words*Age	.249	.620
Fear*Words*Ethnic Group	1.035	.314
Fear*Words*Gender	1.286	.262
Fear*Words*Income	.043	.837
Fear*Words*Major	.933	.339
Fear*Words*Math Skill	.698	.407

Note. $N = 55$. Groups: Age, Young ($n = 22$), Mean 19.1, Old ($n = 33$), Mean 22.12; Ethnic, Black ($n = 29$), Non-Hispanic White ($n = 26$); Gender, Females ($n = 28$), Males ($n = 18$); Income, Up, \$50,000+ ($n = 27$), Low, \$0–\$49,000 ($n = 28$); Major, Nonscience ($n = 41$), Science ($n = 14$); and Self-Reported Math Skill, Easy ($n = 26$), Hard ($n = 29$).

people suffer from innumeracy throughout their lives. If this is so, then visual communication of risk could (and should) be a useful tactic not only for programmatic HIV/AIDS PSA campaigns but for other health care campaigns as well.

Others outside of communication support this notion. Mathematician John Allen Paulos (1991) has pointed out innumeracy as a common problem that knows no social or class boundaries. Innumeracy exhibits itself in, "an inability to estimate common magnitudes" (p. 134). According to Paulos, "Another way it manifests itself is that people can't gauge risks that they take. They're afraid of things they shouldn't be afraid of, and they're oblivious of things they should be afraid of" (p. 134). Furthermore, he stated, people "don't have any feel for probability, for coincidence, for how likely coincidences are. As it turns out, coincidences are quite likely. If two people were sitting next to each other on a plane, and they had never met, chances are better than 99 percent that they'd be linked after two intermediaries" (p. 135). Differences in the ability to estimate odds have been bemoaned by scholars and observers concerned with behaviors ranging from recidivism to street corner drug sales to seat belt usage. Clearly those who design health-related education campaigns must account for this growing problem.

Many communicators remain confused about the best way to produce a successful health care–related prevention and information campaign. The message standardization school assumes that, because of better and faster communication, the population is becoming more homogeneous. The opposite says that advertisers must recognize differences and tailor communication approaches.

Differences shown here help demonstrate the difficulty of generating executions designed for a mass audience. What was clear from the data presented here is that communications professionals must make a decision on standardization based on whether the approach is feasible for the target audience. In doing so, they should look at language, aesthetics, and values in the context of age, gender, ethnicity, income, and mathematical differences. Because executional variables utilizing age, sensuality, decency, or violence may provoke different responses, reaction to, and interpretation of, advertising efforts may vary (Boddewyn, 1991; Boddewyn & Kunz, 1991; "Global Advertisers," 1992; Johnstone, Kaynak, & Sparkman, 1987; Unwin, 1970). Indeed, as Minnick (1968) noted, the quest for several universal types of fear arousing appeals is perhaps fruitless because such a search is "constrained by the learning histories of the particular message recipient involved" (p. 242).

With these differences in mind, what emerges as a practicable solution is that health care educators, like other marketers, should order their concerns and deal equitably and responsibly with priority publics while acknowledging differences. The best bet for a successful campaign is to start with a single strategy that is adapted to the audience by considering political, social, and cultural conditions (T. Walters & L. Walters, 1994).

As this study has shown, adaptation of strategic solutions to AIDS education demands formulating combinations of executional elements orchestrated for targeted audiences. What the audience brings to a message is important and so only a multifaceted, programmatic approach based on this principle will produce communication programs that help change the attitudes and, ultimately, the behaviors fostering the spread of HIV. In looking at ways to gain attention, improve memory, and induce changes in behavior, health care researchers have turned to fear-based campaigns, believing that morality and guilt are not as effective as fear in raising awareness (Eckstein, 1989). Some even believe PSAs with even higher levels of fear can be constructed and used without causing denial response (LaTour & Pitts, 1989).

Despite these beliefs, the results of this study indicated that fear appeals may have limited potential because fear messages are volatile and unstable in their ability to increase recall. One reason suggested by the data was that other emotions were correlated to fear at different levels for different subgroups. These variable combinations may confound the effect of fear, creating a confused emotional state. Another finding suggested that other emotions, such as "disgust," may be effective in HIV prevention messages for targeted groups. Disgust significantly improved recall of HIV/AIDS PSA messages for young women. Of course, gender is only one way to look at subgroups. Because individuals differ in how they process and use information, media professionals should relate characteristics such as income, age, and occupation to underlying health care attitudes (Capon & Davis, 1984; Childers, Houston, & Heckler, 1983).

Consistent with this viewpoint, the science-related attitudinal measures adapted for this study demonstrated that attitudes about science and technology were related to how much of a risk-related message an individual recalls or recognizes. Of particular interest is the fact that the "how we say it" features of these messages were related to attitudes about science and technology. These measures revealed underlying differences in perspective about science and technology related to age, income, occupation, and gender and so could, with further study, be utilized to design better media campaigns.

But does age bring with it wisdom and experience that affect attitudes? Is income tied to health care and behavior patterns? Is choice of occupation a sign of underlying mathematical skills? Is gender related to responsibility for birth control or risk taking?

The attitudinal factors in this study do not address such questions in depth and so serve as a starting point. They should be developed further for use in a health care context, because age, ethnicity, and occupation also may be associated with differing nurture or nature perspectives on science, medicine, and technology, each of which warrants programmatic study.

Much remains to be done. Health care campaign managers should "choose the customer, focus the product, and dominate the marketplace," just like those who concentrate on products. Citizens must take responsibility for the consequences of their actions. For although birth control devices have been tremendously liberating, they have not made the sexual act without consequences. So, concurrent with training in anatomy and physiology, young adults should be taught some type of behavioral framework. Such an approach is rational, not simply moralistic, because, as recent study has suggested, when risk seems diminished, many develop "offsetting behavior," engaging in increased risk activities spurred by a false sense of security.

Given such concerns, a cooperative effort must be developed to remove politics, emotion, and hysteria from public health discussions about topics such as HIV and AIDS. Only then can a multifaceted, programmatic approach be developed to alleviate a growing communication problem that threatens not only to cripple not only the HIV prevention effort but to create a climate in which other health education and prevention programs become increasingly difficult.

REFERENCES

Anderson, D. R., Levin, S. R., & Lorch, E. P. (1977). The effects of TV program pacing on the behavior of preschool children. *AV Communications Review, 25,* 159–166.

Assael, H. (1987). *Consumer behavior and marketing action.* Boston: Kent.

Atkin, C., & Arkin, E. B. (1990). Issues and initiatives in communicating health information to the public. In C. Atkin & L. Wallack (Eds.), *Mass communication and public health: Complexities and conflicts* (pp. 13–40). Newbury Park, CA: Sage.

Atkin, C., & Wallack, L. (1990). *Mass communication and public health: Complexities and conflicts.* Newbury Park, CA: Sage.

Boddewyn, J. J. (1991). Controlling sex and decency in advertising around the world. *Journal of Advertising, 20,* 25–35.

Boddewyn, J. J., & Kunz, H. (1991). Sex and decency issues in advertising: General and international dimensions. *Business Horizons, 34,* 13–20.

Bostrom, R. N., Basehart, J. R., & Rossiter, C. M., Jr. (1973). The effects of three types of profane language in persuasive messages. *Journal of Communication, 23,* 461–475.

Bush, D. (1986). Gender and nonverbal expressiveness in patient recall of health information. *Journal of Applied Communication Research, 13,* 103–117.

Cameron, G. T. (1992). Memory for investor relations messages: An information-processing study of Grunig's situational theory. *Journal of Public Relations Research, 4*, 45–60.

Capon, N., & Davis, R. (1984). Basic cognitive ability measures as predictors of consumer information processing strategies. *Journal of Consumer Research, 11*, 551–563.

Childers, T. L., Houston, M. J., & Heckler, S. E. (1985). Measurement of individual differences in visual versus verbal information processing. *Journal of Consumer Research, 12*, 125–134.

Christensen, L., & Ruch, C. (1978). *Assessment of brochures and radio and television presentations on hurricane awareness.* College Station: Texas A&M University Press.

Cline, R. J., Freeman, K. E., & Johnson, S. J. (1990). Talk among sexual partners about AIDS: Factors differentiating those who talk from those who do not. *Communication Research, 16*, 792–808.

Cuneo, A. Z. (1994, May 2). Anti-AIDS efforts draws criticism. *Advertising Age*, p. 40.

Demby, E. (1989, January 2). Psychographics revisited: The birth of a technique. *Marketing News*, p. 21.

Eckstein, B. (1989). AIDS awareness study. *Health Marketing Quarterly, 6*, 65–104.

Fish, B., & Karabenick, S. (1978). The effect of observation on emotional arousal and affectation. *Journal of Experimental Social Psychology, 14*, 256–265.

Flay, B. R., McFall, S., & Burton, D. (1993). Health behavior changes through television: The roles of defacto and motivated selection processes. *Journal of Health and Social Behavior, 34*, 322–335.

Flinn, J. (1996, January 6). Fear of condom ads. *The New York Times*, p. A19.

Flora, J. A., & Maibach, E. W. (1990). Cognitive responses to AIDS information: The effects of issue involvement and message appeal. *Communication Research, 17*, 759–774.

Gaby, D. M. (1980). Politics and public relations. *Public Relations Journal, 36*, 10–12.

Global advertisers should pay heed to contextual variations. (1992). *Marketing News, 21*(4), 118.

Higbee, K. L. (1969). Fifteen years of fear arousal: Research on threat appeals: 1953–1968. *Psychological Bulletin, 72*, 426–444.

Hornig, S. (1990). Science stories: Risk, power, and perceived emphasis. *Journalism Quarterly, 67*, 767–776.

Hornig, S. (1992). Gender differences in responses to news about science and technology. *Science, Technology, & Human Values, 17*, 532–542.

Jay, T., & Danks, J. H. (1977). Ordering of taboo adjectives. *Bulletin of Psychonomic Society, 9*, 405–408.

Johnson, K., & LaTour, M. (1991). AIDS prevention and college students: Male and female responses to "fear-provoking" messages. *Health Marketing Quarterly, 8*, 139–153.

Johnstone, H., Kaynak, E., & Sparkman, R. M., Jr. (1987). A cross-cultural/cross-national study of the information content of television advertisements. *International Journal of Advertising, 6*, 223–236.

Katz, J. (1993, May 27). AIDS and the media: Shifting out of neutral. *Rolling Stone*, pp. 31–32.

Keppel, G. (1973). *Design and analysis: A researcher's handbook.* Englewood Cliffs, NJ: Prentice-Hall.

Lachman, R., Lachman, J. L., & Butterfield, E. C. (1979). *Cognitive psychology and information processing: An introduction.* Hillsdale, NJ: Lawrence Erlbaum Associates.

LaTour, M., & Pitts, R. E. (1989). Using fear appeals in advertising for AIDS prevention in the college-age population. *Journal of Health Care Marketing, 9*, 5–14.

Leventhal, H., & Watts, J. (1966). Sources of resistance to fear-arousing communications and smoking and lung cancer. *Journal of Personality, 34*, 155–175.

Mabry, E. (1975). Dimensions of profanity. *Psychological Reports, 35*, 387–391.

MacKenzie, S. B. (1986). The role of attention in mediating the effect of advertising on attribute importance. *Journal of Consumer Research, 13*, 174–195.

Miller, S. M., & Brody, D. S. (1988). Styles of coping with threat: Implications for health. *Journal of Personality and Social Psychology, 54*, 142–148.

Minnick, W. C. (1968). *The art of persuasion.* Boston: Houghton Mifflin.

Mitchell, G. (1992, May 30). Media politics—How it began. *The New York Times*, p. A19.

Norton, R. W., Schwartzbaum, J., & Wheat, J. (1990). Physician breach of patient confidentiality among individuals with human immunodeficiency virus (HIV) infection: Patterns of decision. *American Journal of Public Health, 80*, 34.

Paulos, J. A. (1991). Beyond numeracy: The ruminations of media and medicine. *Journal of Communication, 25*, 132–141.

Petty, R. E., Cacioppo, J., & Schumann, D. (1983). Central and peripheral routes to advertising effectiveness: The moderating role of involvement. *Journal of Communication Research, 10*, 135–146.

Ratzan, S. C., Payne, J. G., & Massett, H. A. (1994). Effective message design: The America Responds to AIDS campaign. *American Behavioral Scientist, 38*, 294–309.

Rogers, R. W. (1983). Cognitive and physiological processes in fear appeals and attitude change: A revised theory of protective motivation. In J. Cacioppo & R. Petty (Eds.), *Social psychophysiology* (pp. 153–176). New York: Guilford.

Rothwell, J. D. (1971). Verbal obscenity: Time for second thoughts. *Western Speech, 35,* 231–242.

Russell, J. T., & Land, R. (1988). *Kleppner's advertising procedure* (11th ed.), Englewood Cliffs, NJ: Prentice-Hall.

Sandwich, M., & Evans, J. D. (1977). Taboo word norms. *Perceptual & Motor Skills, 44,* 865–866.

Siska, M., Jason, J., & Murdoch, P. (1992). Recall of AIDS public service announcements and their impact on the ranking of AIDS as a national problem. *American Journal of Public Health, 82,* 1029–1032.

Snodgrass, J. G., Levy-Berger, G., & Haydon, M. (1985). *Human experimental psychology.* New York: Oxford University Press.

Stewart, D. W., & Furse, D. H. (1985). The effects of television advertising execution on recall, comprehension, and persuasion. *Psychology & Marketing, 2,* 135–160.

Thompson, M., Pingree, S., Hawkins, R., & Davies, C. (1991). Long-term norms as shapers of television viewer activity. *Journal of Broadcasting & Electronic Media, 35,* 319–334.

Unwin, S. J. F. (1970). How culture, age and sex affect advertising response. *Journalism Quarterly, 50,* 735–743.

Vermeer, J. P. (1982). *For immediate release.* Westport, CT: Greenwood.

Walters, L., & Walters, T. (1992). Environment of confidence: Daily newspaper use of press releases. *Public Relations Review, 18,* 31–46.

Walters, T., & Barnum, J. (1991, April). *Proper phraseology: Attracting attention to AIDS public service announcements.* Paper presented at the meeting of the Popular Culture Association, San Antonio, TX.

Walters, T., & Walters, L. (1994, May). *Gender, truth and video tape: Responses to AIDS public service announcements.* Paper presented at the meeting of the International Communication Association, Chicago, IL.

VI

THE PROGRAMMATIC:
RELATIONS BETWEEN
PEOPLE AND INSTITUTIONS

AIDS Information and the National Institutes of Health

Paul A. Gaist
Office of AIDS Research, National Institutes of Health

Information, whether on paper or in electronic form, is crucial in the fight against AIDS. If scientists are to uncover the secrets of the AIDS virus and develop ways to defend against and fight it, if health care providers and patients are to work together to apply what is known, if the public is to know how to protect itself against HIV/AIDS, then we must ensure that our mechanisms for disseminating information are efficient and, most of all, effective.
—Dr. Donald Lindberg, Director, National Library of Medicine, and
Dr. Anthony Fauci, Director, National Institute on Allergies and
Infectious Diseases and Former Director, NIH Office of AIDS Research

When a medical discovery (a new drug, device, procedure, or other treatment or information) is made that can benefit significant numbers of people, or a small number of people significantly, there is an ethical obligation to share that information to benefit the public good (Fitzmaurice, 1997). Recent advances in AIDS, including new knowledge and methods to prevent perinatal HIV transmission and new classes and combinations of drugs to treat HIV infection underscore both the importance and need for communicating AIDS research information in usable forms among all those involved, including researchers, health care providers, and the public, especially those who are HIV infected or at risk of becoming so. When I was approached about writing this chapter, I was told there was a need to better understand the publicly funded AIDS research machinery, both in terms of what it is and how to access it. I was invited to use the chapter itself as an information dissemination vehicle specifically geared to give readers an understanding of what the National Institutes of Health (NIH) and the NIH AIDS Research Program are, to highlight the NIH's information dissemination goals and activities, and to provide guidance on how the reader can access AIDS information at the NIH.

THE NIH AND THE NIH AIDS RESEARCH PROGRAM

The NIH is an agency of the U.S. Public Health Service (PHS), itself an agency of the Department of Health and Human Services (DHHS). The mission of the NIH is to discover and develop new knowledge that will lead to better health for everyone. The NIH accomplishes this mission by supporting and conducting both basic and applied biomedical and behavioral research.

The NIH is comprised of 24 institutes and centers (ICs) each having its own mission and responsibilities. The NIH has a key leadership role in the fight against AIDS. Research supported and conducted by the NIH has led to progress in identifying and understanding HIV and unraveling the means through which infection results in AIDS, in elucidating the nature of the immunodeficiency that occurs, in developing therapies for HIV and for opportunistic infections, and in determining the nature of effective behavioral change strategies.

Currently funded at $1.54 billion (est. FY [fiscal year] 1998), the NIH HIV-related research effort (from here on referred to as the NIH AIDS Research Program) is divided into five major scientific categories and two programmatic categories referred to as *areas of emphasis.* These include: natural history and epidemiology, etiology and pathogenesis, therapeutics, vaccines, behavioral and social sciences, training and infrastructure, and information dissemination. The NIH AIDS Research Program is carried out both through the NIH-sponsored programs of grants and contracts at major universities, research institutes, and science-oriented business and through the NIH intramural research programs.

NIH AIDS RESEARCH PROGRAM AREAS OF EMPHASIS

Natural History and Epidemiology.   The NIH conducts studies to examine the transmission of HIV and the progression of HIV-related disease. Such studies examine the effects of viral factors, host factors, and cofactors on the risk of infection and disease progression. Cohorts of HIV-infected individuals and HIV-uninfected individuals at risk of infection are followed in clinical epidemiology studies at domestic and international sites.

Etiology and Pathogenesis.   NIH-sponsored investigations have facilitated the identification of HIV as the causative agent of AIDS and the development of a highly sensitive diagnostic test for HIV infection. Ongoing studies focus on the elucidation of the role of the structural and regulatory genes of HIV, the delineation of the mechanisms of the HIV-induced cytopathicity, and the immunopathogenesis of HIV disease.

Therapeutics.   The NIH supports two major approaches in the area of drug development, screening and rational (targeted) drug programs, for the purpose of developing agents targeted at inhibiting specific steps in the HIV life cycle. In addition, the NIH supports approximately 100 sites nationwide to conduct clinical trials of candidate drugs/agents.

Vaccines.   In working toward successful strategies for stimulating a protective immune response against HIV infection, the NIH supports a broad program encompassing basic, preclinical, and clinical vaccine research on candidate vaccine products. In parallel, the NIH supports research on risk factors and other preventive interventions that will form an essential foundation for vaccine trials.

Behavioral and Social Sciences.   The NIH sponsors behavioral and social science research related to: developing, implementing, and evaluating behavioral and social interventions to reduce HIV transmission; understanding determinants, trends, and processes of HIV-related risk behaviors and the consequences of HIV infection; developing and evaluating behavioral strategies for preventing or ameliorating the negative consequences of HIV infection; and improving the research methodologies employed in behavioral and social science research.

Training and Infrastructure. The NIH supports several intramural and extramural research resource programs. Included in these programs are grants for training AIDS researchers, support of animal facilities for animal model research, and constructing or improving existing facilities and equipment for AIDS-related research.

Information Dissemination. The NIH has responsibility for obtaining and disseminating information to support research, treatment, and prevention related to HIV and AIDS. Progress in these areas depends on the transfer of information to audiences with varying needs for information in a manner that is understandable and useable. The NIH has ongoing programs and new initiatives to support this effort. Consistent with this philosophy, the Office of AIDS Research (OAR) established a new NIH Information Dissemination Coordinating Committee in FY 1996. This committee is charged with providing planning direction and assisting the OAR and the NIH in identifying and facilitating HIV/AIDS-related information dissemination activities, especially those that are considered trans-NIH.

NIH AIDS-RELATED INFORMATION DISSEMINATION

This section is based on the *FY 1999 NIH Plan for HIV-Related Research* (1998), discussions of the NIH Information Dissemination Coordinating Committee, and discussions with others involved in AIDS communications and information dissemination at the NIH, and provides an overview of the NIH's planning approach and a sampling of the NIH's activities in this area. The most current NIH AIDS Plan (FY 1999 at the time of writing this chapter) may be accessed through the OAR Home Page at http://www.nih.gov/od/oar.

Planning Approach

The NIH AIDS Research Program currently approaches its information dissemination area of emphasis from three primary perspectives: communication, research, and coordination.

Communication. Exchange of information about basic, clinical, and behavioral HIV/AIDS research findings is essential to progress in research and ultimately to improved care and treatment for HIV-infected people. The traditional methods of reporting ongoing studies and research results in peer-reviewed journals and at scientific meetings reach only a limited audience. Health educators, health care providers, patients, and other constituents of the NIH need to know the results of clinical and prevention intervention studies, state-of-the-art recommendations, and the most up-to-date standards of health care. As the epidemic has spread to new and hard-to-reach populations, special information outreach efforts need to be made to provide to provide critical information to those populations and their service providers. This information should be timely, include discussion of the potential implications of research findings for patient care, and be in a form that audiences can use. The latest computer and information technologies should be exploited whenever appropriate. The findings resulting from communications research should be incorporated into the strategies to carry out this objective.

Research. In light of the changing HIV/AIDS epidemic, assessments are needed to identify the important information needs of and barriers for relevant target audiences such as health care providers, service providers, people with HIV and their advocates, at-risk populations, basic and applied researchers, and the general public. Although significant communications efforts have been initiated, some communities still may not be (a) receiving needed information, (b) receiving information in a context appropriate for the audience, (c) comprehending the information, or (d) translating the information into action. New approaches are needed to ensure that the communication of information resulting from HIV/AIDS research is optimally effective.

Coordination. The scientific and lay communities look to the NIH as a central source of information on HIV/AIDS. Because multiple NIH ICs disseminate HIV/AIDS information to these communities, coordination of efforts is essential. In order to make more effective use of limited federal dollars, increase efficiency, make better use of new technologies, and ensure credibility with the scientific and lay communities, there must be ongoing collaboration and coordination of communication activities within the NIH and between the NIH and other federal agencies, public health departments, private companies, international groups, other granting agencies, community groups, and universities.

NIH INFORMATION DISSEMINATION ACTIVITIES

The NIH has a broad and expansive approach to information dissemination and exchange that is ongoing and iterative in nature. Any attempt to provide an inclusive account would surely be voluminous and would always be out of date, missing the new products, activities, and approaches that would have occurred between the time of writing the account and its publication. The same is true here. Instead this section serves as an historic account of key examples of NIH's information dissemination and exchange efforts. It is meant to be illustrative rather than inclusive and relies heavily on the concepts and language provided in the annual AIDS Plans of the NIH.

A major effort to enhance understanding of information needs, resources, and services began in June 1993 when the National Library of Medicine (NLM) and the OAR cosponsored a conference that brought together users of NIH information resources, including health care providers, scientists, information specialists, journalists, and members of the HIV/AIDS community. The purpose of the conference was to review the various HIV/AIDS information services, assess current efforts with respect to needs, and identify additional needs. The resulting recommendations were widely circulated and continue to be utilized for planning and informational purposes.

In response to recommendations from the conference, beginning in FY 1994, the NLM has made awards of up to $25,000 each ($35,000 each for consortia) on an annual basis to enable community-based organizations and public and health science libraries to design their own programs for improving AIDS information access to targeted groups within their communities. Such groups include people with HIV/AIDS and the affected community as well as their caregivers and the general public. Supported activities include purchasing equipment and telecommunications services, implementing Internet access, training in the use of sophisticated information tools, and developing language- and culturally specific materials. The NLM has also funded three major testbeds for improving HIV/AIDS information access: one to examine the functioning of a multitype consortium of academic, public, and hospital libraries along with community organizations as a means to get information to the affected community; another that has developed and field-tested a training curriculum on accessing HIV/AIDS information by nonhealth professionals; and a third that provides access through a dedicated center in a public library.

As part of a larger program of training in the use of online databases that the NLM has been conducting with the Historically Black Colleges and Universities (HBCUs), a new AIDS module has been created. The first pilot training course was taught in 1995 with materials specifically tailored for minority health professionals. Training in the use of electronic resources, based on curriculum developed as a result of this pilot course, continues at the HBCUs and through other groups of minority health professionals such as the National Association for Equal Opportunity in Higher Education.

An important challenge to the NIH is to provide accurate and up-to-date HIV/AIDS treatment information to people in underserved communities and communities of color. A 1993 collaborative workshop provided insights about barriers to effective communication and recommended solutions that are being implemented by individuals and organizations at every level. The workshop was organized by the National Institute on Allergy and Infectious Diseases (NIAID) working with the OAR, the Health Resources and Services Administration (HRSA), and the Public Education Technology Transfer Working Group of the NIAID AIDS Clinical Trials Group.

NIAID is also working to increase understanding of clinical research and the differences between clinical trials and patient care, particularly by those in underserved communities. This communications effort is essential to NIAID's long-standing goal of recruiting hard-to-reach populations into clinical trials. A key part of this effort is building trust and strengthening outreach to local and national community organizations.

Toward this end, NIAID has developed a kit of English and Spanish language materials to assist health care providers, particularly in community clinics, in educating their patients about HIV and the diseases associated with AIDS and how to find out about clinical trials. The kit contains fact sheets on opportunistic infections and a "How to Help Yourself" series of eight attractive brochures for low-literacy audiences. These materials are available in bulk from the National AIDS Clearinghouse.

In December 1995, NIAID prepared and widely disseminated an updated NIAID HIV/AIDS Research Agenda. The document describes the breadth and depth of the comprehensive NIAID AIDS research program and future plans in those fields relevant to the NIAID mission. The document serves to inform others about the scope of NIAID's HIV/AIDS program.

After the National Institute on Drug Abuse (NIDA) conducted a series of meetings with representatives of ethnic minorities and other underserved populations, NIDA began to develop drug abuse- and HIV/AIDS-related materials. NIDA's drug abuse and AIDS public education program provided specifically targeted television, radio, and print materials aimed at audiences at high risk for contracting or transmitting HIV infection. The first campaign, "Stop Shooting Up AIDS," targeted injection drug users, their sexual partners, and others close to them. The target audience of the second campaign, entitled "AIDS: Another Way Drugs Can Kill," was the population aged 12 to 18 years. The third campaign, "Get High, Get Stupid, Get AIDS," was launched in August 1992 and targeted young adults aged 18 to 24 years. These campaigns pointed out the link between drug/alcohol abuse, altered judgment, and risky sexual behavior that can contribute to exposure to HIV. The messages were based on a growing body of research that demonstrated the association between drug/alcohol abuse and high-risk behaviors in these groups.

NIDA has developed material for general populations on the relationship between drug abuse and AIDS. For teens and young adults, NIDA produced two prevention campaigns, "How Getting High Can Get You AIDS" and "How Not to Get High, Get Stupid, Get AIDS."

Early in the AIDS epidemic when the risk of transfusion-transmitted HIV was still significant, the National Heart, Lung, and Blood Institute (NHLBI) established the National Blood Resources Education Program (NBREP). This program facilitated the education of health care professionals about the proper use of blood and blood products in an effort to limit the use of potentially infected blood. The NBREP resulted in the publication and dissemination of multiple education pamphlets and articles in peer-reviewed medical journals.

In 1995, the National Institute of Mental Health (NIMH) established a Consortium on Technology Transfer, supported by discretionary funds from the OAR, Office of the Director, NIH. This consortium has developed and is testing different models of transferring HIV prevention technology from research settings to service settings and from service settings to researchers. This consortium will assess the benefits of translating research findings on effective strategies for HIV prevention for community-based providers, funding agencies, health planners, and policymakers. Areas of focus will include: (a) increased use of methods of behavior change whose effectiveness has been empirically demonstrated, (b) increased capacity to identify and provide outreach to hard-to-reach populations, (c) increased use of more sophisticated and rigorous evaluation designs and methods, and (d) increased coordination of individual prevention methods in comprehensive community-wide strategies to change norms. Ultimately, these studies will be summarized and provided to service providers and policymakers as guidelines for HIV prevention dissemination.

In 1996, the NIMH and the Office of Medical Applications of Research (OMAR) sponsored "The Consensus Development Conference on Interventions to Prevent HIV Risk Behaviors." The goal of OMAR consensus conferences is to review an area of NIH-supported research where there may be a gap between research accomplishments and clinical care. After careful review of the research, a statement was developed and circulated widely to policy- and health-related communities to inform them of the panel's consensus recommendations with respect to HIV prevention programs.

Since 1991, the NIH has used a dedicated system of electronic and print notification, collectively known as Clinical Alerts, to rapidly disseminate to health care professionals, the news media, and the general public information that critically affects the care of patients, such as results of HIV-related clinical trials. This mechanism was recommended by participants, including researchers, medical journal editors, and others, in a workshop convened by the NIH to discuss expedited information dissemination. Although affirming that traditional systems of reporting research results should be maintained, the group recognized that, in some exceptional circumstances, information with immediate clinical relevancy should be expeditiously reviewed and widely distributed prior to publication in a peer-reviewed medical journal. Clinical Alerts are available online on the MEDLARS system and provided for dissemination in academic health science centers and more than 3,000 hospitals; they are also transmitted via Internet to all requestors. The National Network of Libraries of Medicine has developed methods to ensure the wide dissemination of the Clinical Alerts.

In February 1994, NIAID and the National Institute on Child Health and Development (NICHD) utilized Clinical Alerts to disseminate rapidly the results of ACTG 076, which showed decreased transmission of HIV from mother to child when the mother and child received treatment with zidovudine (AZT). A summary of the results was prepared by NIAID and made available online through all Clinical Alerts dissemination mechanisms. In addition, NIH staff played an integral role in the NICHD-chaired PHS Task Force that developed the clinical recommendations based on ACTG 076.

Physicians and patients must have access not only to Clinical Alerts and the results of clinical trials but also to clinical care guidelines, standards of care, and results of state-of-the-art meetings that redefine clinical care guidelines. Recommendations from the NIAID-sponsored state-of-the-art meeting on antiretroviral therapy for HIV-infected adults, held in June 1993, were widely distributed to the AIDS community and to health care providers. In addition, guidelines on OI prophylaxis, PCP prophylaxis for children with HIV, and recommendations for the use of AZT to prevent perinatal HIV transmission, which have been developed by the NIH and other agencies of the PHS, have been made available online in their complete versions as well as through an NIH-supported toll-free service.

It is also critical to ensure that prevention information is effectively disseminated to community service providers. After issuing a series of community alerts to the drug abuse-related HIV/AIDS community on emerging issues of concern in 1992–1993, NIDA developed a special issue of *NIDA Notes,* NIDA's newsletter to the drug abuse field, on AIDS research among drug-abusing populations in summer 1995. NIDA produced an educational videotape for policymakers and professionals working in the drug abuse and HIV/AIDS fields and produced three research monographs in 1994–1995 to keep scientists and practitioners aware of recent developments in research methodologies and prevention approaches.

NICHD provided financial and technical assistance to the Agency for Health Care Policy and Research to develop its educational materials for pregnant, HIV-infected women. These materials provide information on using AZT during pregnancy to reduce perinatal transmission of HIV and are intended to assist pregnant, HIV-infected women in deciding whether to use AZT. The materials consist of a poster, brochures, and handouts, as well as audio- and videotapes in several different languages.

Electronic Information Resources

Existing computerized databases, including those on the MEDLARS system (AIDSLINE, AIDSTRIALS, AIDSDRUGS, and DIRLINE), as well as the AIDS Clinical Trials Information Service (ACTIS) and the HIV/AIDS Treatment Information Service (ATIS), are vital to disseminating research results and clinical information. They provide the foundation for the global dissemination of information concerning basic research, clinical trials availability and results, and standards of care as well as other information of interest to HIV-infected individuals and their advocates.

Information available from the MEDLARS databases includes citations (with abstracts when available) to journal articles, books, and audiovisuals as well as abstracts from many major AIDS-related meetings and conferences (AIDSLINE); descriptions of clinical trials related to HIV, AIDS, and AIDS-related opportunistic diseases and the agents that are being studied in those trials (AIDSTRIALS/AIDSDRUGS); and international, national, and state organizations working in the AIDS area (DIRLINE). In response to recommendations by the AIDS advocacy community, the databases are available free of charge to users. The National Library of Medicine (NLM) has expanded the AIDSLINE database with the addition of abstracts from many scientific meetings. The OAR has worked with the NLM to identify meetings, particularly those meetings supported by the NIH, and obtain copies of the abstracts for inclusion in the database. For example, the abstracts from the Conferences on Retroviruses and Opportunistic Infections are available online through this mechanism. In addition, citations, with brief summaries, to substantive articles from over 20 newsletters have been added to the database.

Initiated in 1989, ACTIS is a centralized resource providing information on NIH- and industry-sponsored clinical trials for HIV/AIDS. This is a free service to users and is jointly sponsored by NIAID, the NLM, and the Food and Drug Administration (FDA) in collaboration with the Center for Disease Control and Prevention (CDC). By dialing a toll-free number, 1-800-TRIALS-A, callers can speak to trained health specialists who access a database featuring information on AIDS clinical trials. Spanish-speaking specialists are available. The information can also be accessed directly through the NLM's AIDSTRIALS and AIDSDRUGS databases. This information is also available electronically from the NLM as part of the Health Services and Technology Assessment Text (HSTAT) database, which includes clinical practice guidelines and recommendations on many health concerns.

To complement the ACTIS project, the NIH collaborated with other agencies of the PHS in the development of ATIS, which provides timely, accurate treatment information on HIV and AIDS. Available since November 1, 1994, ATIS is a toll-free (1-800-HIV-0440), bilingual, telephone reference service for people with HIV disease, their families and friends, and health care providers, providing answers to questions about treatment of HIV infection as well as copies of federally approved HIV/AIDS treatment guidelines and information.

The Internet is an expanding and increasingly important medium for information dissemination. The NIH is increasingly utilizing this medium in tandem with its other information dissemination avenues. For example, NIH home pages such as for NIAID (http://www.nih.gov/niaid) and the OAR (http://www.nih.gov/od/oar) are online, providing extensive HIV/AIDS research and programmatic information for the public, patients, health care providers, scientific investigators, and policymakers. ACTIS (http://www.actis.org/) and ATIS (http://www.hivatis.org/) both have World Wide Web sites that will increase their usefulness. The NLM has created a World Wide Web home page specifically for HIV/AIDS-related information (http://sis.nlm.gov/aidswww.htm). This serves as an entry point to many of the HIV/AIDS-related resources available from the NIH as well as those from NLM. It also serves as a guide to selected resources worldwide.

NIDA has established a telephone- and fax-based information system to provide the public with critical information on all aspects of drug abuse and drug abuse-related HIV/AIDS. Information on these information services is available through the NIDA home page (http://www.nida.nih.gov).

Improved Coordination

The NIH has called for leadership at the PHS level for coordination of activities related to defining standard HIV information needs and related responsibilities. A special interagency working group for HIV/AIDS information dissemination has been formed under the DHHS Office of HIV/AIDS Policy. The working group provides a forum for the coordination of HIV/AIDS information and the formation of policy recommendations on related issues.

A *Guide to NIH HIV/AIDS Information Services* (1998), developed by the NLM and OAR, has been updated annually and made available in both printed and electronic format through NLM's AIDS home page (http://sis.nlm.nih.gov). This pamphlet provides a listing of NIH-supported information services that assist care and service providers, patients, and the public in their quest for knowledge about HIV/AIDS. This pamphlet describes these services as well as selected information services sponsored by other agencies of the PHS. The electronic version provides links to all the NIH and PHS sites and resources that are described in the pamphlet.

There is a growing concern that some of the information disseminated to date has not been fully useful to or usable by health care providers, service providers, people with HIV/AIDS and their advocates, at-risk populations, and basic and applied researchers. It is therefore essential to develop a research agenda that will provide data to help understand and improve all aspects of the information dissemination and communication process. Of particular importance is research designed to understand and improve the information exchange process, especially with respect to identifying and overcoming barriers to effective communication. Additionally, research is needed to evaluate the effectiveness of information and behavior change communication campaigns.

The NIH recognizes the critical importance of disseminating and exchanging information internationally, especially research and treatment information, patient management guidelines, prevention intervention, and research results that impact on the care of HIV-infected individuals. The existing computerized databases from the NLM as well as from ATIS and ACTIS are available worldwide. However, a number of special issues remain, including the lack of computer capabilities and access to journals in many countries, language barriers between the United States and other countries (as well as dialect and cultural barriers within countries), and the lack of resources to provide a standard of care comparable to that available in the United States.

Effective and efficient information dissemination and exchange are important tools in the effort to control and end the AIDS epidemic. The NIH has responsibility for disseminating and exchanging information to support research, treatment, and prevention related to HIV and AIDS. Progress in these areas depends on the transfer of information to researchers, health care providers, those who provide HIV-related services, and HIV-infected individuals and their advocates. These audiences have varying needs for information that is critical in the fight against HIV/AIDS.

ACCESSING HIV/AIDS INFORMATION THROUGH THE NATIONAL INSTITUTES OF HEALTH

This section provides a sampling of HIV/AIDS information that is available through the NIH and contact information for obtaining it and for making additional information-related inquiries. This information appears in the *Guide to NIH HIV/AIDS Information Services* (1998).

National Institutes of Health

The NIH accomplishes its mission to uncover new knowledge that will lead to better health for everyone by supporting and conducting both basic and applied biomedical and behavioral research. The NIH maintains a home page (http://www.nih.gov). The NIH supports and conducts HIV/AIDS-related research through its ICs, focusing on the nature of HIV infection, the genetic and biological properties of the virus, immunopathogenesis, the natural history of HIV, consequences of HIV infection in the body, and the behavioral risk factors associated with HIV infection and its various modes of transmission. The NIH also supports research on vaccine development, tests new agents for the treatment of HIV/AIDS, including opportunistic infections and HIV-associated malignancies, and develops behaviorally based HIV prevention interventions.

A focus of NIH's HIV/AIDS activities in the all key scientific areas—across all NIH institutes—is on information dissemination and publications, particularly on providing information about NIH research and clinical trials. Information services are designed to assist professionals, patients, and the public and cover research, clinical trials, treatment, patient education, professional training, prevention, and general information. The *Guide to NIH HIV/AIDS Information Services* (1998), a publication of the NIH, provides a listing of various information activities of the NIH, some of which has been included below:

NIH, Office of AIDS Research (OAR)
Building 31, Room 4C-02, 9000 Rockville Pike, Bethesda, MD 20892
Phone: 301.496.0357   Fax: 301.496.4843
Home Page: http://www.nih.gov/od/oar

The OAR is located within the Office of the Director of NIH and is responsible for the scientific, budgetary, legislative, and policy elements of the NIH AIDS research program. Congress has provided broad authority to the OAR to plan, coordinate, evaluate, and fund all NIH AIDS research. The OAR is responsible for the development of an annual comprehensive plan and budget for all NIH AIDS research. The OAR supports trans-NIH Coordinating Committees to assist in these efforts in the following areas: therapeutics, vaccines, natural history and epidemiology, behavioral and social sciences, etiology and pathogenesis, training and infrastructure, and information dissemination. The OAR promotes collaborative research in both domestic and international settings. Using the expertise of nongovernment scientists and AIDS community representatives, the OAR has conducted the first comprehensive evaluation of the NIH AIDS research program.

NIH, Fogarty International Center (FIC)
Building 31, Room B2-C32
Bethesda, Maryland 20892
Home Page: http://www.nih/gov

AIDS International Training and Research Program (AITRP): FIC sponsors training for foreign scientists from developing countries through a variety of training options. The training is designed to increase scientists' proficiency to undertake biomedical and behavioral research related to AIDS, to use these acquired skills in clinical trials and prevention and related research, and to stimulate cooperation and sharing of research knowledge.

NIH, National Center for Research Resources (NCRR)
One Rockledge Centre, Room 5040, 6705 Rockledge Drive
Bethesda, Maryland 20892-7965
Phone: 301.435.0888
Home Page: http://www.ncrr.nih.gov

Annual AIDS Research Symposia: NCRR supports two forums each year for the scientific exchange of the most recent advances in AIDS research. The Annual Symposium on Non-human Primate Models of AIDS is attended by scientists from the United States and other nations. The Research Centers in Minority Institutions International AIDS Symposium is designed to stimulate collaborative research on AIDS. Proceedings are published following each symposium.
Stories of Scientific Discoveries: The NCRR Office of Science Policy produces several publications that focus on recent biomedical research findings supported by the NCRR and other NIH components. Articles in the *NCRR Reporter*, a quarterly magazine, and in the *NCRR Highlights*, include AIDS research findings. Specific articles from these publications, or the latest issues of the publications, may be obtained by calling NCRR or accessing its home page.
Access to AIDS Animal Models: The NCRR Comparative Medicine Resource directory lists several research facilities where investigators can gain access to chimpanzees and specific pathogen-free macaque and rhesus monkeys for AIDS studies, including vaccine development.

NIH, National Eye Institute (NEI)
Building 31, Room 6A32, 31 Center Drive, MSC 2510
Bethesda, Maryland 20892-2510
Phone: 301.496.5248
Home Page: http://www.nei.nih.gov

The NEI disseminates information on AIDS-related issues such as the ocular complications of AIDS, basic research, and clinical trials completed and underway.

NIH, National Heart, Lung and Blood Institute (NHLBI)
Building 31, Room 4A11, 31 Center Drive, MSC 2490
Bethesda, Maryland 20892-2490
Phone: 301.496.3245
Home Page: http://www.nhlbi.nih.gov/nhlbi/nhlbi.htm

NHLBI issues a yearly report on its AIDS research programs and issues a yearly catalog of the clinical samples in its repository (which can be obtained by individual investigators for their research).

NIH, National Institute on Aging (NIA)
Building 31, Room 5C-27, 31 Center Drive, MSC 2292
Bethesda, Maryland 20892-2292
Phone: 1.800.222.2225
Home Page: http://www.nih.gov/nia/

NIA produces *AIDS and the Older Adult*, one in a series of "Age Pages." It provides general information to the general public on AIDS in the older population and lists resources for additional information.

NIH, National Institute on Alcohol Abuse and Alcoholism (NIAAA)
Wilco Building, Suite 409, 6000 Executive Boulevard
Bethesda, Maryland 20892-7003
Phone: 301.443.3860
Home Page: http://www.niaaa.nih.gov/

The NIAAA's quarterly bulletin *Alcohol Alert* provides information to health professionals about the relationship between alcohol consumption and HIV infection and AIDS. Select issues of NIAAA's peer-reviewed journal *Alcohol Health and Research World* provide information about the relationship between alcohol consumption and HIV (i.e., PB93160604, "Alcohol, Infectious Diseases, and Immunity," and PB94113503, "Prevention of Alcohol-Related Problems"). Issues are available from the National Technical Information Service (NTIS) at 703.487.4650.

NIH, National Institute of Allergy and Infectious Diseases (NIAID)
Office of Communications
Building 31, Room 7A-50, 31 Center Drive, MSC 2520
Bethesda, Maryland 20892
Home Page: http.//www.niaid.nih.gov

NIAID provides support and direction for the national cadre of scientists conducting research to understand, treat, and ultimately prevent the many infectious, immunologic, and allergic diseases that afflict people worldwide. NIAID disseminates AIDS-related materials describing current NIAID research initiatives (such as information about HIV vaccine development, preclinical drug development, basic research, and epidemiologic studies) as well as materials addressing HIV-clinical trials and treatment issues for health care providers to use in counseling people with HIV or AIDS.

NIH Clinical Trials Information Phone Line: NIAID's Division of Intramural Research/Clinical Center operates a free telephone service for individuals seeking information about participating in clinical trials at NIH (1.800.243.7644).

NIAID Updates on Basic and Clinical Research: NIAID distributes factsheets, press releases, and other print materials about NIAID research results and HIV/AIDS clinical trials. NIAID disseminates research results relevant to clinical practice through press releases, *Notes to Physicians*, and *Clinical Alert*.

NIH, National Institute of Child Health and Human Development (NICHD)
Public Information and Communications Branch
Building 31, Room 2A-32, 31 Center Drive, MSC 2425
Bethesda, Maryland 20892-2425
Phone: 301.496.5133
Home Page: http://www.nih.gov/nichd/

NICHD disseminates reports on Institute supported conferences and workshops related to HIV infection and AIDS in women, adolescents, and children. It produces press releases and newsletters summarizing current research advances in HIV/AIDS prevention, diagnosis, and treatment and makes reprints available of research findings published by NICHD staff in leading scientific journals.

NIH, National Institute on Deafness and Other Communication Disorders (NIDCD)
Policy Planning and Health Reports Branch
31 Center Drive, MSC 2320
Bethesda, Maryland 20892-2320
Phone: 301.496.7243
Home Page: http://www.nih.gov/nidcd/

NIDCD supports and conducts research in the areas of hearing, balance, smell, taste, voice, speech, and language. With respect to HIV/AIDS-related information that addresses people who are deaf or hard of hearing, NIDCD prepares an annual bibliography of HIV/AIDS information materials available to health professionals and the general public. This and other information is available through the NIDCD Information Clearinghouse (1.800.241.1044 for voice or 1.800.241.1055 for TTY).

NIH, National Institute of Dental Research (NIDR)
Building 31, Room 5B-55
Bethesda, Maryland 20892-2190
Home Page: http://www.nidr.nih.gov/

NIDR makes available a literature search on the oral health aspects of HIV infection and AIDS through the National Oral Health Information Clearinghouse (NOHIC). This search is from the Oral Health subfile of the Combined Health Information Database (CHID). Designed with a strong patient education focus, CHID brings together health-related materials that fall outside the scope of more technical, research-based collections. The search focuses on availability of educational materials for both the professional and the patient and includes topics such as the oral manifestations of HIV, oral hygiene for the HIV patient, oral health information for caregivers, adverse oral effects of medical management of HIV infection, and periodontal disease in the patient with HIV (http://www.aerie.com/nohicweb).

NIDR in collaboration with the World Health Organization produces *A Guide for Epidemiologic Studies of Oral Manifestations of HIV Infections,* which provides practical information about the design, implementation, and reporting of epidemiological studies. NIDR also produces training manuals that explain steps for preventing HIV transmission in the dental setting.

NIH, National Institute on Drug Abuse (NIDA)
Room 10A-39, 5600 Fishers Lane
Rockville, Maryland 20857
Home Page: http://www.nida.nih.gov/

NIDA conducts information campaigns to make the general public and specific at-risk populations (e.g., injection drug users or IDUs) aware of the relationships between alcohol or drug abuse and HIV and AIDS. Campaigns include scientific publications, television and radio public service announcements, print media (e.g., advertisements, posters, booklets), and video. NIDA publications addressing drug abuse and drug abuse-related HIV/AIDS issues cover topics such as the reemergence of tuberculosis among HIV/AIDS-infected IDUs, limitations of bleach disinfection of drug-use paraphernalia, medical advice for IDUs, and interventions to prevent HIV risk behaviors.

NIH, National Institute of General Medical Sciences (NIGMS)
Room 2AS-19, 45 Center Drive, MSC 6200
Bethesda, Maryland 20892-6200
Phone: 301.594.0828
Home Page: http://www.nih.gov/nigms/

NIGMS sponsors meetings and disseminates abstracts relating to targeted drug design against AIDS.

NIH, National Institute of Mental Health (NIMH)
Information Resources and Inquiries Branch
Room 7C-02, 5600 Fishers Lane
Rockville, Maryland 20857
Phone: 301.443.4513
Home Page: http://www.nimh.nih.gov

NIMH makes available information on a wide array of HIV/AIDS-related issues. Examples include the NIH Consensus Development Statement on Interventions to Prevent HIV Risk Behaviors (http://odp.od.nih.gov/consensus/statements/cdc/104/104_stmt.html), HIV and AIDS among the severely mentally ill, the role of families in preventing and adapting to HIV/AIDS, and HIV in the brain. NIMH makes available a number of AIDS-related documents and information on its AIDS research grant announcements through the NIMH Mental Health Fax4U system (301.443.5158).

NIMH has published *How to Write a Successful Research Grant Application: A Guide for Social and Behavioral Scientists.* This book provides technical assistance for researchers applying for biobehavioral or psychosocial research funding on all aspects of research, from grantsmanship and completing the applications to understanding the review process. This document (ISBN 0-306-44965-X) is available from Plenum Press (212.620.8000).

NIH, National Institute of Neurological Disorders and Stroke (NINDS)
Office of Scientific and Health Reports
Building 31, Room 8A16
Bethesda, Maryland 20824
Phone: 301.496.5751
Home Page: http://www.ninds.nih.gov

NINDS conducts research on disorders of the brain and nervous system, including the neurological consequences of AIDS, and produces the factsheet, *Neurological Manifestations of AIDS*, which provides information on the neurological sequelae of AIDS and lists resources to contact for additional information.

NIH, National Library of Medicine (NLM)
National Institutes of Health
Bethesda, Maryland 20894
Phone: 301.496.6308/800.272.4787
Home Page: http://www.nlm.nih.gov

The NLM supports a number of vital AIDS-related databases and other information resources that are available to users at no cost. More information on the NLM information resources is available by calling 1.800.FINDNLM (346-3656).

AIDSLINE: This database contains more than 150,000 bibliographic references to published literature about HIV/AIDS and related issues, including prevention and treatment. The database includes citations of journal articles, books, audiovisual materials, and newsletter articles. AIDSLINE also contains abstracts from many AIDS-related conferences.

AIDSTRIALS: This database contains information about HIV-related clinical trials, both open (currently enrolling patients) and closed. Information about NIH-sponsored clinical trials is provided by the NIAID; information about privately sponsored efficacy trials is provided by the Food and Drug Administration (FDA).

AIDSDRUGS: This database contains information about the agents being tested in trials included in AIDSTRIALS.

Health Services and Technology Assessment Text (HSTAT): This searchable database provides access to the full text of the Agency for Health Care Policy and Research (AHCPR) guidelines, NIH Consensus Development Conference Reports, and NIH Technology Assessment Conference Reports.

DIRLINE: This database is an online directory of information resources covering all areas of biomedicine. Included are more than 2,500 HIV/AIDS-specific resources such as organizations, self-help groups, and information systems.

HOME PAGE ADDRESSES OF SELECTED U.S. PUBLIC HEALTH
SERVICE AGENCIES AND RESOURCES THAT PROVIDE
HIV/AIDS-RELATED INFORMATION THROUGH THE
INTERNET AND MANY OTHER CHANNELS
(e.g., information phone lines, print materials, fax services)

Agency for Health Care Policy and Research (AHCPR): http://www.ahcpr.gov

Centers for Disease Control and Prevention (CDC): http://www.cdc.gov

Food and Drug Administration (FDA): http://www/fda/gov

Health Resources and Services Administration (HRSA): http://www.hrsa.dhhs.gov/

Substance Abuse and Mental Health Services Administration (SAMHSA): http://www.samhsa.gov/

AIDS Clinical Trials Information Service (ACTIS): http://www.actis.org

HIV/AIDS Treatment Information Service (ATIS): http://www.hivatis.org

ACKNOWLEDGMENT

Support for this chapter was provided by the National Institutes of Health Office of AIDS Research. The opinions expressed here, however, are entirely those of the author.

REFERENCES

Fitzmaurice, M. J. (1997, February). *Health information infrastructure: Research, privacy, and standards.* Paper presented at the West Medical Design and Manufacturing Conference, Anaheim, CA.

FY 1998 NIH Plan for HIV-Related Research. (1997). Rockville, MD: National Institutes of Health, Office of AIDS Research.

FY 1999 NIH Plan for HIV-Related Research. (1998). Rockville, MD: National Institutes of Health, Office of AIDS Research.

Guide to NIH HIV/AIDS Information Services With Selected Public Health Service Activities (NIH Publication No. 96-3731). (1998). Rockville, MD: National Library of Medicine, National Institutes of Health, U.S. Department of Health and Human Services.

Information services for HIV/AIDS: Recommendations to the NIH. (NIH Publication No. 94-3730). (1994, January). NIH Conference Report.

24

Difference and Identification: Reconsidering the Indigenous Outreach Worker Model

William N. Elwood
Behavioral Research Group
University of Texas—Houston School of Public Health

Epidemics and plagues frequently emanate with disadvantaged populations; unfortunately, such people frequently do not participate voluntarily in public health programs for prevention or treatment. These people usually eschew public agencies due to disillusionment or suspicion of the system, or from fear that program officials will discover and report participants' illegal activities. Consequently, public health programs must reach out to access these hidden populations. Illegal drug users constitute one group of people who have created an underground culture in response to systemic distrust and fear of arrest. Although this strategy facilitates their drug use, it also isolates them from information that can protect them from an epidemic run rampant in their community, HIV. In an effort to educate illegal drug users about risk reduction practices, research and education programs typically have relied on "indigenous" persons to conduct *outreach,* the programmatic location and recruitment of individuals who ordinarily would not participate voluntarily in a program or project. This operating model posits that only individuals of the same gender, race/ethnicity, and HIV risk history have the capacity to educate and recruit members of a target population.

Recent research, however, posits that matching participant and interviewer ethnicity is not essential to recruit and maintain research participants. Thompson, Neighbors, Munday, and Jackson (1996) interviewed 960 African-American and White psychiatric patients and found that matching interviewer and patient race/ethnicity did not influence African Americans' likelihood of participating in or refusing an interview. Similarly, Miranda, Azocar, Organista, Muñoz, and Lieberman (1996) found that demonstrating respect to Hispanic families and elders, using formal titles, taking time to listen carefully, and conducting interviews in a warm and personal manner—rather than matching participant and interviewer ethnicity—are key components for successful recruitment and interviewing of Hispanics for psychosocial research.

In this chapter, I argue that outreach is a powerful health education tool not simply because outreach workers resemble some of the people they contact, but because outreach is a strategic communicative combination of styles and information adapted to members of a target population—in this case, illegal drug users. Outreach workers, who are required *not* to use illegal drugs, achieve solidarity with potential drug-using project participants through identification (Burke, 1969). In this process, outreachers acknowledge their difference from chronic drug users and concurrently demonstrate through their particular communication styles that they also are trusted sources for community knowledge, common street wisdom, *and* HIV prevention.

To elucidate the premise that outreach is explained best as identification, I first provide a brief history of outreach and illegal drug users. Second, I posit that the theoretical approach that best explains the outreach process is Kenneth Burke's idea of identification. Third, I illustrate the premise that outreach workers' abilities to present suitable identification strategies facilitates their HIV intervention success. Fourth, I close with theoretical conclusions and observations relevant to current public discussions on outreach and federal HIV expenditures.

OUTREACH: HEALTH COMMUNICATION TO HIDDEN POPULATIONS

President Lyndon Johnson's War on Poverty programs relied on outreach as a key element to introduce low-income citizens to the availability of economic opportunity programs and to negotiate and secure public health services for people "faced with scattered facilities, hampered by barriers of language, and embittered by the impersonal, officious, and institutionalized manner with which [citizens are] frequently met," when they attempt to access the "only sources of aid available" (Reiff & Reissman, 1965, p. 17; see also Hollister, Kramer, & Bellin, 1974; Office of Economic Opportunity [OEO], 1968). Empirical studies verified the effectiveness of outreach workers and their successors to deliver public health messages (Cauffman, Wingert, Friedman, Warburton, & Hanes, 1970; Diehr, Jackson, & Boscha, 1975; Freeborn, Mullooloy, Colombo, & Burnham, 1978). In turn, residents of low-income urban neighborhoods became accustomed to outreach workers as trusted individuals who provided trustworthy information on social services to the populace and advocated neighborhood concerns to program officials.

Outreach to Injection Drug Users

Impressed with the rapidity with which outreach workers mobilized networks of drug injectors to achieve public health objectives, Patrick Hughes and his associates constructed the Chicago Ethnographic Outreach Worker (CEOW) Model. Under this model, outreach workers acted as ethnographic field assistants to deliver public health services to out-of-treatment heroin users while collecting data on their behaviors. CEOW requirements included knowledge of specific neighborhoods, ability to gain access to drug users' social networks, and their willingness to deliver intervention services to these users (Hughes & Crawford, 1972; Hughes, Crawford, & Barker, 1971). This approach gave Chicago researchers access to populations they had been unable to reach by other means (Schick, Dorus, & Hughes, 1978).

Adapting this approach to early HIV education, Newmeyer (1988) calculated that the use of outreach workers to deliver bleach, condoms, and brief prevention messages was a cost-effective alternative to either treatment-based prevention programs or the unchecked spread of the AIDS epidemic. In fact, studies on drug injectors' HIV/AIDS knowledge and cost analyses led Newmeyer (1989) to recommend, "Use CHOWS" for "outreach education among intravenous drug users" (p. 3130; see also Newmeyer, Feldman, Biernacki, & Watters, 1989; Watters et al., 1990). Researchers and educators followed Newmeyer's directive.

Extant research on community-based interventions to prevent HIV infection among drug users has reported correlations between interventions that involve outreach and reductions in HIV risk behaviors (Birkel et al., 1993; Booth & Wiebel 1992; Flynn et al., 1989; Neaigus et al., 1990; Simpson et al., 1994; Watters, 1987a, 1987b; Watters et al., 1990; Williams, Copher, et al., 1991; Williams, Rhodes, et al., 1997; Woodhouse et al., 1992). These federally funded research and service projects limit outreach to a recruitment activity; their evaluators have been surprised at the projects' respective efficacy to change drug users' HIV risk behaviors. Consequently, using outreach workers to deliver HIV intervention services and to collect data in such projects is now widespread (Koester, 1994), but the precise position of outreach and outreach workers remains less defined than in the initial Chicago model.

Outreach and Ethnic/Racial Indigenousness

The idea that the ethnic and racial, and even gender, characteristics of outreach workers must match their respective target populations also is rooted in the initial conceptualizations of outreach. Reiff and Reissman (1965) advocated the use of "indigenous nonprofessionals" to bridge the social distance between people who needed services and people who provided them. The authors described the indigenous professional as a "peer of the client [who] shares a common background, ethnic origin, style, and group of interests" (p. 81). This notion continued in the early years of the HIV/AIDS epidemic when public health officials wanted to get prevention messages to endangered groups as expediently as possible. At that time, no one knew the target population better than active or former drug users. More than a decade later, we know more about HIV/AIDS and about outreach. Nevertheless, the idea that only people of the same race/ethnicity and gender are the best, if not only, qualified people to conduct outreach intervention continues to endure in two ways.

First, having indigenous outreach workers automatically "ensur[es] cultural sensitivity of intervention presentations," facilitates rapport with members of target populations, enhances program legitimacy, and translates "technical information into readily understood concepts" (Wiebel, 1993, p. 14). In contrast, "nonindigenous professional staff" can be outreach workers if they are willing and able to interact effectively with drug users and have "superior communication skills" (Wiebel, 1993, p. 17). These coexisting and conflicting descriptions of outreach qualifications simply may reflect the growing pains of HIV/AIDS intervention.

Second, these same descriptions also lead me to believe that, in practice, conceptions of outreach may prioritize racial/ethnic complements over communication abilities. In descriptions of intervention project personnel, outreach workers are the only people who are delineated as "indigenous," people who belong to the same minority ethnic groups targeted for intervention and who also may be former drug users "with at least 2 years of abstinence" (Wiebel, 1993, p. 16). In the words of other ethnographers, outreach workers "have street smarts and cultural and ethnic backgrounds similar to the communities in which they work" (Broadhead & Fox, 1990, p. 325). Conversely, professional staff members are "nonindigenous," nor are they required to have a history of drug use and recovery—just a "willingness to work with targeted populations in a natural setting, an ability to respond to the needs of the target population in a culturally sensitive fashion . . . [and] an ability to relate to the target population and understand drug-using behavior" (Wiebel, 1993, pp. 16–17).

Regardless of sociodemographic characteristics, outreach workers have three main responsibilities. First, outreachers must be conversant in contemporary drug subculture to win users' trust. Second, they should avoid influencing drug users' HIV knowledge or questionnaire responses so researchers can measure the effects of an experimental intervention; consequently, and third, outreachers should limit their activities to participant recruitment and data collection.

However, outreach workers often cannot recruit without intervention in some capacity, at least to tell potential participants about the project and the issues it addresses. Furthermore, they must conduct a multitude of social service–related tasks to maintain community relations with people who have come to expect such tasks, even as their official capacity has been narrowed to recruitment. Outreach workers transport people to the public hospital, help others negotiate bureaucracy at the food stamp office, and pull strings to get a destitute person admitted to a free treatment program. Through these acts—symbolic and otherwise—outreach workers demonstrate comprehension and concern for drug users' everyday problems. These acts provide the basis for a core communication strategy.

DELINEATING OUTREACH: COMMUNICATION AND IDENTIFICATION

Although the precise position of outreach workers in intervention research remains imprecise, the rationale for using indigenous outreach workers rests in their traditional credibility and ability to recruit members of drug-using circles, qualities conventional public health workers may not share. Regardless of such characteristics, any outreach worker must win the trust of a skeptical population to recruit and educate members of target populations. An enduring Burkean idea among communication scholars best explains the most important component to the outreach process.

Kenneth Burke (1966) maintained that human beings are symbol-using animals who linguistically delineate situations to which they and other human beings respond. According to Burke (1969), communication is "a symbolic means of inducing cooperation in beings that by nature respond to symbols" (p. 43). Because each of us holds singular characteristics, we constantly must proclaim the similarities among us to compensate for our differences and thus gain the cooperation of others (Burke, 1969, 1973). Thus, communication involves the use of symbols to make strategic connections between diverse individuals or groups to delineate similarities and to win trust. Burke (1969) called the communicative strategy people use to proclaim such unity *identification,* to explain the "common sensations, concepts, images, ideas, attitudes that make them *consubstantial,*" in a way "that does not deny their distinctness" (p. 21).

To identify with someone is not simply a proclamation of a shared value system, but also is an assertion that both individuals are steadfast and sincere in those communal values (Burke, 1969). Indeed, Burke referred to communication "as a general *body of identifications*" (p. 26). He stated that identification is the core and "'unconscious' factor" in human communication (Burke, 1967, p. 63). Using Burke's system, we can characterize outreach workers as symbol users who establish consubstantiality to teach HIV prevention activities to drug users and to recruit them for participation in research.

THE ETHNOGRAPHY OF OUTREACH: DESCRIPTION AND DISCUSSION

It is difficult to separate outreach from the individuals who enact it. Rather than discuss outreach by function, such as recruitment, intervention, and follow-up, it seems most appropriate to discuss the process through two investigators and four outreach workers to illuminate the effectiveness of outreach strategies. For 3 months, the investigator individually spent time with outreach workers during their daily routines involved in recruiting and relocating participants for HIV prevention research projects funded in Houston, Texas, by the National Institute on Drug Abuse and the Center for Substance Abuse Treatment. In addition to observing and participating in project recruitment, travel time was used to ask outreach workers about their personal histories, their outreach philosophies, and to clarify personal observations. Investigators took field notes between outreach encounters, wrote additional descriptions upon return to the office, and shared compiled notes with one another. Outreach workers were consulted if investigators' notes conflicted strongly upon comparison.

Phyllis: The Diva of the South Side Is "All That" and More

South Park and Third Ward are two traditionally African-American neighborhoods in south Houston. There, anyone who's anyone knows Ms. Phyllis and her association with the research project. After hours and on weekends, people approach her for information regarding HIV prevention and drug treatment. Sometimes people even throw themselves on her car to get her attention. Phyllis grew up in these south Houston neighborhoods; to us she is the Diva of the South Side. But Phyllis isn't the Diva of the South Side simply because people know her. She also is "all that." In African-American parlance, a diva is a woman who is attractive, sexy, and well dressed. If she is "all that," she projects an attitude conveying she *knows* she embodies all those adjectives and *you* are darn lucky to be in her presence. One need not be a diva to be all that, but it helps.

Phyllis uses the diva persona and neighborhood knowledge to bring Black men into the research project, and relies on her sex appeal to recruit Black lesbians. Observing Phyllis with both audiences, she flirts, she taunts, she teases, she basks in the attention. The diva seemingly promises everything and delivers nothing—except research participants to the center. For example, a group of men outside a labor hall asked if she and her companion were undercover police officers. Ms. Phyllis rolled her shoulders, waved her arms, and responded, "You know, I ought to just tell y'all to get up against the wall and spread 'em. I've always wanted to do that." At this point, one man threw himself against the wall, an act the rest of the men willingly would have done, along with whatever else Phyllis had requested. Time spent with an attractive, sassy woman has significant appeal. If that time can be extended in a research interview for which one gets compensated, so much the better. Phyllis' communicative strategies work because they invoke the oldest tenet in advertising: Sex sells.

In addition, Phyllis seamlessly integrates HIV education into outreach. Although not the example used in graduate school, Phyllis' work seems to be a 1990s example of speech acts (Austin, 1962; Searle, 1969). Simply by being a diva who explains, demonstrates, and distributes condoms, Phyllis legitimates condom use as acceptable, desirable, and sexy. For Phyllis, intervention is uninterrupted show time.

She tolerates no interruptions during her performance. If you interrupt, she will silence you with a pithy remark or scathing glance. During her show, Phyllis reminds people to use condoms when they're doing the wild thing. Her voice is louder than her customary volume, and her demonstrations are exaggerated. Humor is another component. Addressing the common male complaint that typical condoms are too small to accommodate them, Phyllis thrusts her forearm into a condom and tells them, "Darlin', I know Black men are big, but if you're as big or bigger than this, no one wants to have nothin' to do with you anyway!" Phyllis is also famous for her ability to teach male and female prostitutes how to apply a condom on a customer during oral sex without the john realizing it.

Gabe: Your Best Friend in the Barrio

Gabe has conducted outreach in Houston's North Side Hispanic neighborhoods for 7 years. The most senior member of the project, he knows outreach projects, community folklore, and connections. Gabe grew up in the area and has a special rapport with its members. His neighborhoods have gone through ethnic transitions: from Hispanic, to African American, and now toward Hispanic again. One would think this interethnic cycle facilitates interethnic communication; however relations between Houston's African- and Hispanic-American communities remain strained at best. Furthermore, Gabe never has been an illegal drug user. Instead, he consistently demonstrated a special ability to identify with individuals of both ethnic groups.

Gabe seems to be—and prides himself as—everybody's best friend. First, he continuously maintains a persona as a warm, happy-go-lucky guy who wants men, women, Hispanics, and Blacks to feel comfortable with him. He greets people with "Hey, how's it goin'? What's up, partner?" and never tries to be "one-up" at the close of a communicative transaction. His demeanor may be an intuitive effort to overcome the disdain Blacks and Hispanics have had for one another and the traditional Latina fear and deference to men (Alaniz, 1994; Flores-Ortiz, 1994; Pérez-Arce, 1994). Second, Gabe's concern for the neighborhood extends beyond his job-related activities. He is a member of the Knights of Columbus, and is an active volunteer for a nonprofit community center that provides services to adults and at-risk teenagers. These activities also connect Gabe with community business leaders who view him and the project as a valued community service. In other words, Gabe is concerned and committed to his childhood neighborhood; outreach is just another part of this commitment.

One observes Gabe as he gauges people and situations, then matches his friendly strategies to those constraints. Gabe plays counselor-on-the-street to drug users, the homeless, pregnant women, and prostitutes. He voices a special empathy for homeless people and female prostitutes and seems to provide extra services to help those motivated to change their behaviors. Gabe maintains his rapport by accepting and encouraging incremental behavior changes. For example, White sex workers Ruthie and Joyce continue their drug habits and profession; however, they report reducing their HIV risk behaviors. Ruthie's drug use has increased, but she tells us that she bleaches her needles consistently and always uses condoms with her tricks. As a strung-out prostitute, Pam came to Gabe for assistance. Through the research project, she connected with a treatment program and other services. Pam returned to the outreach center to report on her new life of recovery, employment, a stable living environment, and the imminent return of her son from foster care.

Out of Gabe's presence, Ruthie states that neighborhood drug users talk about Gabe in his absence. Apparently, they respect him a great deal because he doesn't break confidences, accepts people as they are, and encourages the incremental changes they make. For their best friend Gabe, it's simply a matter of "taking care of the people you work with." For Gabe, it's also a matter of taking care of your gatekeepers, the opinion leaders among drug users who provide information and access to the drug subculture. Gabe's gatekeepers are reliable, relatively stable drug users. During his travels, Gabe stops by their homes or hangouts intermittently to connect, buy them a cold drink, see how they are, or give them a ride. In turn, when Gabe needs information or people for a special study, his gatekeepers willingly provide him with information, connect him with new groups of people, and vouch for his integrity.

Occasionally, Gabe must gain entry to a neighborhood without assistance. One method he used has become legendary. Five years earlier, Gabe had tried all his usual techniques of recruitment. Finally, Gabe and his outreacher colleague Mike filled an ice chest with cold drinks, put it in the back of his pick-up truck, and ended up being the Pied Piper of the Near North Side. Dope fiends of both genders and all racial/ethnic groups came out of the woodwork and called to their friends to join the party in the back of the truck. When Gabe returned to the outreach center, he had a truck bed full of drug users and hangers-on. This event solidified Gabe's reputation. One still can hear gatekeepers and locals recall this episode.

During the research for this chapter, we witnessed people introduce Gabe to potential participants and remind them of this story that they had recounted to them earlier. Immediately, these unknown drug users become willing to accompany their new best friend Gabe to the research project.

Mike: Sergeant Viernes Has Just the Facts, Señora

Mike is living proof that one's regular communication styles can be appropriate for both the target population and the outreach worker. Mike is a Hispanic-American man from a non-transitional North Side neighborhood. Raised by grandparents who spoke only Spanish, his given name is Juan Miguel. Mike and Gabe are about the same age, yet the approaches they use and the people they recruit couldn't be more different. Mike's nickname for this study is "Sergeant *Viernes* (Friday)" because, in addition to being a sergeant in the National Guard, he is the strong, silent, military type—clean cut and ramrod straight. Unlike Gabe, he exudes machismo and maintains a no-nonsense persona with potential participants: "I'm part of this neighborhood research project. We test people for HIV and there's $20 in it for you." Although this approach is particularly effective with macho Hispanic men, it can be equally ineffective with women in his own age group and many African Americans.

Though the Guard requires him to be away one weekend each month, Mike never seems to be off duty. Just like the military, everything about Mike is standard operating procedures. He does not order drug users to drop, give him 20, and come to the research center; however, he does provide clear expectations: If drug users want to participate, they must meet requirements and follow program guidelines. Having observed Mike and Gabe, respectively, I am convinced that this militaristic approach may give clients who might perceive Gabe's approach as glad-handing the opportunity to make their own decisions about participating. Mike's approach provides potential recruits with a bottom-line rationale to participate.

Nevertheless, Mike's effectiveness is particularly subtle and culturally specific. Mike is equally fluent in Spanish and English. During the observation process, he instantly would assess individuals and decide in which language to address them. This ability often diffuses any fear Latinas have when they first encounter Mike, although Sergeant Viernes still can be disarming. This innate ability and momentary experience is as effective for Mike as winning friends is for Gabe. Mike's grounding in Latino culture serves him in good stead when identifying with Latinas. For example, he was trying to locate a participant who had been released from jail recently for a follow-up interview. An elderly woman holding a baby and the hand of a 5-year-old girl answered the door at the address the participant had given. Mike not only addressed the woman in fluent Spanish, but also assumed a deferential demeanor unfamiliar in American culture. The *abuelita* provided Mike with her grandson's workplace and hours, the best times to reach him at home and work, and a promise to ask her grandson to contact Mike the same day. Indeed, the man he was seeking phoned Mike, who conducted the follow-up interview.

Gabe might not have been able to achieve the same results as easily as Mike. The woman, accustomed to Latino traditions, likely would have been offended by Gabe's relaxed attitude. In my opinion, Mike's approach is not better than Gabe's, and vice versa. Outreach workers are adept at matching communicative style and substance to individuals. Like any individual, an outreacher will be able to identify with some groups more easily than with others. Mike is particularly effective with a less acculturated Hispanic population; Gabe's forte is with drug users who are, perhaps, as American as they are anything else.

Occasionally, Gabe and Mike work together to achieve results, such as the Pied Piper episode. They also work together at *pinching* a group, putting the fear of God into drug users with whom one has been working, but who have not yet participated. In this effective social network intervention, Mike and Gabe work together, in Spanish and English, to bring a few members through the project. The network members who participate pressure the remaining members because, "We're negative and we're not gonna share [drugs or works] with you unless you get tested." The positive experiences with Mike, Gabe, and other project staff members promote a trusting atmosphere that facilitates additional recruitment. Pinching is an outreach technique and a group-specific risk-reduction intervention that Mike and Gabe have down to a science. Together, Mike and Gabe constitute a winning team for recruitment on Houston's Near North Side.

Daphne: Big Mac Is a Master at Identification Strategies

Of all the outreachers observed for this study, Daphne is the master of multiple communicative strategies. She initially appears nonchalant until her communicative strategies seem to take over. No one can assess her circumstances and continuously change her approaches to identify with a potential participant better than Daphne. A local rap artist with two recordings, she dresses appropriately: baggy shirts and pants, cap worn backward, and Doc Martens boots. Daphne can pull up, get out, approach a group of men and say, "Hey. Y'all remember me?" even if she's never seen them before. She tries to establish rapport by naming neighborhood people she knows and asks if they know them. Given her connections, she usually initiates identification in this way. She then moves to describing the research project and the benefits that ensue.

When naming neighborhood people does not establish a common bond, Daphne is quick to try other, multiple approaches. At a welfare hotel, she tried to recruit a mother surrounded by her children: "Do you know the woman who used to live in 218? Her name was Deborah. It wasn't too long ago. No? Is that your baby? That's a beautiful baby! Sure wish I had one just like it. That baby is beautiful! I like your hair! Where do you get your hair done at? I love your hair." Although Daphne's rapid-fire delivery is similar to a carnival barker's attempt to envelop her audience, her approach with this mother was much softer. In the parking lot at the same hotel, Daphne encountered a woman "on a mission," coming off a crack high and looking for more. Daphne approached and spoke with her cautiously and calmly. When she realized that this woman was beyond reason, Daphne let her continue her mission.

On another occasion, Daphne and this investigator encountered a group of three homeless men downtown, one of whom, Bob, had recently been through the research project. She honked her horn and the men waited for us to approach them on foot. Daphne reconnected with Bob; both attempted to convince the other two to commit to coming to the center that day. After all, a safe place where "nobody'd mess witcha," where "there's air conditioning and you can hang out and kick back" would appeal to many homeless people. But Jimmy Cool, a well-built African-American man with an attitude to match, was particularly unco-operative. After much flattery and several appeals, he told her, "I don't need an HIV test. I always wear a condom. I wear *two* condoms!" Without missing a beat, Daphne replied, "Yeah? Show me one right now! I bet a big stud like you has lots of 'em." Despite his friend's recommendation and Daphne's skill, Jimmy Cool would not be moved. Still, Daphne provided condoms and referral cards to Bob and the third man.

Daphne is a short woman with an ample figure who fancies herself to be a cross between a ladies' man and a woman's woman. Her rapper appearance constitutes part of her Big Mac affectation, an African-American term for a womanizer. Despite her self-definition, Daphne is more feminine than she probably ever would admit. Her masculine, Big Mac persona is counterbalanced by her feminine makeup, jewelry, and hairstyles. Daphne's demeanor and habiliments allow men and women to identify with Daphne's respective male or female characteristics. Whereas Phyllis recruits men primarily through the sexual persona of the diva, Daphne can bring them in as one of the boys. Depending on her situational read, Daphne recruits women as one of the girls or as Big Mac. Daphne's approach may be the most appropriate way to access hard-to-reach populations for this research project. Because she is skilled at matching messages to people, Daphne excels at recruiting heterosexual women, lesbians, gay male injection drug users, and gay male sex workers.

OUTREACH WITH ILLEGAL DRUG USERS: DISCUSSION AND IMPLICATIONS

During investigation, a limitation of the study and of outreach emerged. The main field investigator for this study was a Euro-American man. As in any community, people will be suspicious of anyone who is not part of their milieu. Particularly in Houston African-American communities, the combination of White and Black individuals signifies law enforcement. In Daphne's words, "You can't help it. You're just a clean-cut White guy who's gonna look like an FBI agent no matter what you do." Although people in the streets were nervous at first glance, outreach workers were able to dispel some of that tension. Humor and identification with the trusted outreacher facilitated trust between investigators and community members. For example, Daphne and I (Bill) serendipitously developed an effective routine that made people feel more comfortable:

Daphne: "This is my cousin from California."
Bill: "Yeah. I'm the white sheep of the family."

Daphne used humor to publicly establish consubstantiality and to encourage users to perceive me as someone deserving of the trust they bestow on Daphne. Granted, few people would believe that an African-American woman and a man some project participants call "that Spanish guy" to be first cousins. But Daphne's proclamation of kinship with me is a "shorthand" way to describe the situation for drug users: "He may not look like one of us, but he's cool. You trust me. I trust Bill. You can trust him, too" (see Burke, 1984, p. 29). We recognized the suspicion and spoke to it.

The establishment of consubstantiality is the crucial component to outreach. Recruitment, education, and behavior change occurs by dint of the shared identities that outreach workers institute in the field. It is this recognition of self-in-other that generates the credibility drug users attach to the prevention information they receive and the perception that they can act to prevent HIV transmission. Three implications of this study extend previous research (Simpson et al., 1994; Williams, Copher, et al., 1991, Williams, Rhodes, et al., 1997).

First, Burke's idea of identification illuminates the efficacy of outreach. This application of Burke's enduring concept depicts effective outreach as a public health activity conducted by people who know how to locate and speak to target audiences. In the speaking, outreach workers elucidate the commonalties they share with drug users. Consequently, users endow outreachers with a degree of trust that translates, at least, to project participation and, at most, to sobriety and safer sex practices.

Segregation and congregation, Burke's (1973) definition of a situation that underlies any communicative transaction, accounts for the estrangement between drug user and government-funded, non-drug-using project worker. According to Burke, people act to identify with target groups and perceive themselves to be part of any number of collectivities. Because individuals identify with a variety of groups and the values and norms associated with them, outreach workers have multiple opportunities by which to establish consubstantiality and to teach HIV prevention behaviors. A schema delineating values and norms of drug-using subgroups could help outreach workers' identification and intervention efforts. Granted, identification cannot compensate for every division. For example, a Latina woman simply may be unwilling to discuss negotiation strategies for condom use with anyone but another woman. However, Phyllis' efforts with the Hispanic community and Gabe's dealings with Ruthie illustrate that identification can compensate for multiple differences, allowing outreach workers to do their jobs and drug users to engage in safer behaviors.

Second, the "secret of success" to outreach work is not simply ethnic matching, but the consistent iteration of the similarities that outreach workers share with the people they wish to recruit. Although I agree with Siegal's (1997) assessment that outreach is "a distinctly different culture of work," the essence of its process can be delineated safely as a communication process that hinges on identification. Successful outreachers effectively overcome the estrangement—including human or HIV risk category characteristics—that may exist between drug users and themselves, and between drug users and the institutions from which they likely have withdrawn. Once that estrangement is overcome, they can teach effective HIV prevention methods and refute misinformation.

Therefore, a more appropriate job requirement to conduct outreach with illegal drug users simply may be that outreachers must be able to identify with drug users. Being a former drug user or having lived in the neighborhood where one conducts outreach can provide staff members with advantages in their identification strategies, but successful outreach is not dependent on indigenousness. In our project, African-American women are able to recruit Spanish-speaking men and women, and White gay men. Hispanic-American Gabe has a rapport with African Americans and recruits them easily. Phyllis and Daphne are in recovery and thus have a strong advantage in identifying with drug-using research participants. Mike and Gabe have never been users; yet they have little trouble recruiting types of desired participants.

The success these individuals experience disproves the outreach truisms that dictate that one must resemble clients in every way in order to be effective (Hughes & Crawford, 1972; Wiebel, 1988). Instead, this study demonstrates that outreach workers who can get drug users to believe that they are steadfast and sincere in some shared beliefs can win drug users' trust. Part of establishing consubstantiality is overcoming the difference of illegal drug use. Outreach workers are not users; they discuss common people and topics; they do *not* preach drug treatment. They do ask participants to change their HIV risk behaviors within their current situations. Once drug users endow outreachers with a degree of trust, the users can perceive them as reliable sources of HIV prevention information. Within that consubstantial context, drug users participate in research projects. They will recommend participation to their friends and associates. They stop outreachers in the neighborhood and request bleach samples and condoms. They report changes in their risk behaviors. Some even report teaching HIV risk reduction to their friends (Elwood & Ataabadi, 1996, 1997). When they are ready, some ask for referrals to treatment.

Third, ethnicity should remain an important but not preeminent consideration in HIV prevention research. Currently, many public health researchers are arguing for culturally matched intervention curricula and presenters. Singer (1991) asserted that because drug use patterns and HIV risk behaviors differ among ethnic cultures, "designing 'matched' culturally specific interventions for several ethnic communities and evaluat[ing] their effectiveness in AIDS prevention" (p. 278) should be prominent in the second decade of HIV/AIDS research. Concurrently, an increasing number of minutely defined minorities insist that funds be spent on "culturally specific" prevention and treatment programs designed for and delivered by their particular groups, for example, Asian-American transsexual prostitutes (Burkett, 1995; Yep & Pietri, 1995). Although the human immunodeficiency virus does not discriminate, it is true that some groups within U.S. society are more at risk for HIV infection than are others because members of such groups engage in risk behaviors more regularly than do other individuals (Brown & Primm, 1988). According to Sufian and colleagues (1990), "Ethnic/racial differences may affect life chances, worldviews, the probability that one will become a drug user, drug use behaviors, the probability of having sex with drug users, whether a person becomes infected with HIV, and more" (p. 131). This study demonstrates that understanding cultural values and mores is important for intervention; however, this finding should serve as a basis to establish identification with ethnically diverse individuals in order to educate them.

In fact, difference may be as important as consubstantiality in outreach. Phyllis and Daphne contend that they are successful at recruiting White gay male prostitutes because they can use their jargon and are *not* the same gender or race as these men. According to the outreach workers, the members of this target subpopulation perceive that members of their own group would be overly judgmental (cf. Elwood, 1995; Williams & Elwood, 1995). They also would serve as potential competition for "work." Indigenousness certainly provides an outreach worker with an advantage to teach members of one ethnic group. When conducting outreach with members of one's own ethnic group, an outreach worker has one less estrangement to overcome; the task is made even easier when an outreacher is assigned to recruit individuals from the neighborhoods in which she or he was raised. In other words, you don't have to have belong to the identical racial/ethnic group as your target population—but it doesn't hurt. Nevertheless, the outreachers in this study are able to establish consubstantiality, to recruit, and to educate drug users of both genders and from racial/ethnic groups different from their own.

As social scientists, we have the opportunity to make an instrumental difference on the streets. The results from this applied research study can refocus attention from a universal fascination with difference to create public health programs that can relate universal HIV prevention information in ways that are appropriate for individual program participants. Although an oversimplification, the "secrets" of outreach are as plain as those shared to public speaking students: Know yourself, know your information, and know your audience. We cannot continue to subdivide shrinking resources among groups of people who say differences matter when the people who deliver those services demonstrate daily that those differences can be overcome and, occasionally, can make a beneficial difference in HIV prevention.

Extant research indicates that outreach, an obligatory recruitment function in community-based programs, may be more influential than experimental HIV interventions (e.g., Simpson et al., 1994; Williams, Rhodes, et al., 1997). Therefore, a community-based, HIV research protocol with drug users that uses outreach as intervention can accomplish its goals of recruitment and education more effectively and, perhaps, with less staff members. In other words, recent research suggests that office-based health education is not as effective with out-of-treatment drug users as had been hypothesized and that outreach is the educational "missing link" between the public health research community and hidden populations. Rather than concentrate on the effectiveness of culturally specific interventions, future research should take this exploratory study to determine the relationship between the content of outreach intervention and the influence on behavior changes. We need to know if outreach is effective because drug users can count on outreachers to relate information to them without being judgmental, to always have free condoms, to drive them to the social services office, or a combination. Outreach is presumed to be the most efficacious intervention with this population. Outreach also reflects its own history in community-based programs, dynamics of target populations, and outreach workers' personal experiences. The next generation of research should codify intervention components to determine which activities and in what combination have the most influence on reducing HIV risk behaviors among drug users. According to Burke (1969), "A doctrine of consubstantiality, either explicit or implicit, may be necessary to any way of life" (p. 21, emphasis removed). The results of this study prove that a doctrine of explicit consubstantiality is essential to refine our outreach applications and to save lives.

ACKNOWLEDGMENTS

The data collection for this research was supported by a grant from the National Institute on Drug Abuse Community Research Branch; however, the interpretations and conclusions herein are solely those of the author. The author thanks Mike Lopez, Daphne Moore, Gabriel Sabala, Alan Richard, Phyllis Shephard, and Cheryl Dayton Shotts for their participation in this project.

REFERENCES

Alaniz, M. L. (1994). Mexican farmworker women's perspectives on drinking in a migrant community. *International Journal of the Addictions, 29,* 1173–1188.

Austin, J. L. (1962). *How to do things with words.* Oxford, England: Oxford University Press.

Birkel, R. C., Golaszewski, T., Koman, J. J., Singh, B. K., Catan, V., & Souply, K. (1993). Findings from Horizontes Acquired Immune Deficiency Syndrome Education Project: The impact of indigenous outreach workers as change agents for injection drug users. *Health Education Quarterly, 20,* 523–538.

Booth, R., & Wiebel, W. W. (1992). Effectiveness of reducing needle-related risks for HIV through indigenous outreach to injection drug users. *American Journal on Addictions, 1,* 277–287.

Broadhead, R., & Fox, K. (1990). Takin' it to the streets: AIDS outreach as ethnography. *Journal of Contemporary Ethnography, 9,* 322–348.

Brown, L., & Primm, B. (1988). Intravenous drug abuse and AIDS in minorities. *AIDS and Public Policy Journal, 3,* 5–15.

Burke, K. (1966). *Language as symbolic action: Essays on life, literature, and method.* Berkeley: University of California Press.

Burke, K. (1967). Rhetoric—Old and new. In M. Steinmann, Jr. (Ed.), *New rhetorics* (p. 63). New York: Scribner's.

Burke, K. (1969). *A rhetoric of motives.* Berkeley: University of California Press.

Burke, K. (1973). The rhetorical situation. In L. Thayer (Ed.), *Communication: Ethical and moral issues* (pp. 263–275). London: Gordon & Breach.

Burke, K. (1984). *Permanence and change* (3rd. ed.). Berkeley: University of California Press.

Burkett, E. (1995). *The gravest show on earth: America in the age of AIDS.* Boston: Houghton Mifflin.

Cauffman, J. G., Wingert, W. A., Friedman, D. B., Warburton, E. A., & Hanes, B. (1970). Community health aides: How effective are they? *American Journal of Public Health, 60,* 1904–1909.

Coyle, S. L. (1993). *The NIDA standard intervention model for injection drug users not in treatment.* Rockville, MD: National Institute on Drug Abuse.

Diehr, P., Jackson, K. O., & Boscha, M. V. (1975). The impact of outreach services on enrollees of a prepaid health insurance program. *Journal of Health and Social Behavior, 16,* 326–340.

Elwood, W. N. (1995). Lipstick, Needle, and company: A case study of the structure of a bridge group in Houston, Texas. *Connections, 18*(1), 46–57.

Elwood, W. N., & Ataabadi, A. N. (1996). Tuned in and turned off: Injection drug and cocaine users' responses to media intervention messages. *Communication Reports, 9*(1), 1–11.

Elwood, W. N., & Ataabadi, A. N. (1997). Influence of interpersonal and mass-mediated interventions on injection drug and crack users: Diffusion of innovations and HIV risk behaviors. *Substance Use and Misuse* (formerly the *International Journal of the Addictions*), *32*(5), 635–651.

Flores-Ortiz, Y. G. (1994). The role of cultural and gender values in alcohol use patterns among Chicana/Latina high school and university students: Implications for AIDS prevention. *International Journal of the Addictions, 29,* 1149–1172.

Flynn, N., Jain, S., Sweha, A., Bailey, V., Nassar, N., Siegel, B., Levy, N., Enders, S., Acuna, G., Hom, P., Hinton, B., Webb, D., Ding, D., Koblin, B., McCusker, J., Sullivan, J., Noone, S., Lewis, B., Sereti, S., & Birch, F. (1989). Coordinated community programs for HIV prevention among intravenous drug users—California, Massachusetts. *Morbidity and Mortality Weekly Reports, 38,* 369–375.

Freeborn, D. K., Mullooly, J. P., Colombo, T., & Burnham, V. (1978). The effect of outreach workers' services on the medical care utilization of a disadvantaged population. *Journal of Community Health, 3,* 306–320.

Hollister, R. M., Kramer, B. M., & Bellin, S. S. (1974). *Neighborhood health centers.* Lexington, MA: Heath.

Hughes, P. H., & Crawford, G. A. (1972). A contagious disease model for researching and intervening in heroin epidemics. *Archives of General Psychiatry, 27,* 149–155.

Hughes, P. H., Crawford, G. A., & Barker, N. W. (1971). Developing an epidemiologic field team for drug dependence. *Archives of General Psychiatry, 24,* 389–393.

Koester, S. (1994). AIDS prevention and services: Community-based research. In J. P. Van Vugt (Ed.), *Community based research and AIDS prevention* (pp. 35–57). South Harvey, MA: Bergin & Garvey Press.

Miranda, J., Azocar, F., Organista, K. C., Muñoz, R. F., & Lieberman, A. (1996). Recruiting and retaining low-income Latinos in psychotherapy research. *Journal of Consulting and Clinical Psychology, 64,* 868–874.

Neaigus, A., Sufian, M., Friedman, S. R., Goldsmith, D., Stepherson, S. R., Mota, P., Pascal, J., & Des Jarlais, D. C. (1990). Effects of outreach intervention on risk-reduction among intravenous drug users. *AIDS Education and Prevention, 2,* 253–271.

Newmeyer, J. A. (1988). Why bleach? Development of a strategy to combat HIV contagion among San Francisco intravenous drug users. *NIDA Monograph, 80.* Washington, DC: U.S. Government Printing Office.

Newmeyer, J. A. (1989). Outreach education among intravenous drug users: Use CHOWS. *Journal of the American Medical Association, 262,* 3130–3131.

Newmeyer, J. A., Feldman, H. W., Biernacki, P., & Watters, J. K. (1989). Preventing AIDS contagion among intravenous drug users. *Medical Anthropology, 10,* 167–175.

Office of Economic Opportunity. (1968). *Guidelines: The comprehensive neighborhood health services program.* Washington, DC: U.S. Government Printing Office.

Pérez-Arce, P. (1994). Substance abuse patterns among Latinas: Commentary. *International Journal of the Addictions, 29,* 1189–1200.

Reiff, P., & Reissman, F. (1965). *The indigenous non-professional: A strategy for change in community action and mental health programs, Community Mental Health Journal Monograph Series* (Vol. 1). New York: Behavioral Publications.

Schick, J. F., Dorus, W., & Hughes, P. H. (1978). Adolescent drug using groups in Chicago parks. *Drug and Alcohol Dependence, 3,* 199–210.

Searle, J. R. (1969). *Speech acts.* Cambridge, England: Cambridge University Press.

Siegal, H. A. (1997, August 3). *The human face of HIV prevention.* Speech to the Fourth Research Synthesis Symposium on the Prevention of HIV in Drug Abusers, Northern Arizona University, Flagstaff.

Simpson, D. D., Camacho, L. M., Vogtsberger, K. N., Williams, M. L., Stephens, R. C., Jones, A., & Watson, D. D. (1994). Reducing AIDS risk through community outreach interventions for drug injectors. *Psychology of Addictive Behaviors, 8*(2), 86–101.

Singer, M. (1991). Confronting the AIDS epidemic among IV drug users: Does ethnic culture matter? *AIDS Education and Prevention, 3,* 258–283.

Sufian, M., Friedman, S., Neaigus, A., Stepherson, B., Rivera-Beckman, J., & Des Jarlais, D. (1990). Impact of AIDS on Puerto Rican intravenous drug users. *Hispanic Journal of Behavioral Sciences, 12,* 122–134.

Thompson, E. E., Neighbors, H. W., Munday, C., & Jackson, J. S. (1996). Recruitment and retention of African American patients for clinical research: An exploration of response rates in an urban psychiatric hospital. *Journal of Consulting and Clinical Psychology, 64,* 861–867.

Watters, J. K. (1987a, June). *Preventing human immunodeficiency virus contagion among intravenous drug users: The impact of street based education on risk behavior.* Paper presented at the Third International Conference on AIDS, Washington, DC.

Watters, J. K. (1987b). A street-based outreach model of AIDS prevention for intravenous drug users: Preliminary evaluation. *Contemporary Drug Problems, 14,* 411–423.

Watters, J. K., Downing, M., Case, P., Lorvick, J., Cheng, Y.-T., & Fergusson, B. (1990). AIDS prevention for intravenous drug users in the community: Street-based education and risk behavior. *American Journal of Community Psychology, 18,* 587–596.

Wiebel, W. W. (1988). Combining ethnographic and epidemiologic methods in targeted AIDS interventions: The Chicago model. In R. J. Battjes & R. W. Pickens (Eds.), *Needle sharing among intravenous drug abusers: National and international perspectives* (NIDA Research Monograph 80; pp. 137–150). Washington, DC: U.S. Government Printing Office.

Wiebel, W. W. (1993). *The indigenous leader outreach model: Intervention manual.* Rockville, MD: National Institute on Drug Abuse.

Williams, M. L., Copher, J. I., Knight, K., Stevens, S. J., Vogtsberger, K. N., & Watson, D. D. (1991). Community outreach to untreated IV drug users: An evaluation. *Research in Progress, 1,* 41–44.

Williams, M. L., & Elwood, W. N. (1995). An investigation of the risks of transmitting HIV infection in two networks of male prostitutes in Houston, Texas: A report on preliminary findings. In M. G. Everett & K. Rennolls (Eds.), *Sociology and large networks: Proceedings of the International Conference on Social Networks* (Vol. 2, pp. 151–157). Greenwich, England: Greenwich University Press.

Williams, M. L., Rhodes, F., Elwood, W. N., Camacho, L. M., Bowen, A. M., Simpson, D. D., & Trotter, R. T. (1997). *Community-based programs: Assessing the respective effectiveness of outreach and HIV risk reduction sessions.* Manuscript submitted for publication.

Woodhouse, D. E., Potterat, J. J., Muth, J. B., Reynolds, J. U., Douglas, J., & Judson, F. N. (1992). Street outreach for STD/HIV prevention—Colorado Springs, Colorado, 1987–1991. *Morbidity and Mortality Weekly Reports, 41,* 94–101.

Yep, G. A., & Pietri, M. (1995, November 17). *Reaching out to transgender and transsexual communities: Communication strategies for HIV education and service delivery.* Paper presented at the SCA Seminar Series, A Communication Approach to the HIV/AIDS Epidemic: Theory, Research, Practice, and Experience, San Antonio, TX.

Media Manipulations and the AIDS/Breastfeeding Issue

Linda K. Fuller
Worcester State College, Worcester, MA

The effects of bottle feeding versus breast feeding on the transmission of HIV are unknown. Breast feeding has been recognized as a method of HIV transmission since 1985. Statistical analyses indicate that breast feeding may increase the rate of HIV transmission by 14%. The risk of transmission through breast feeding is higher among women who become infected during the breast feeding period and lower among women who were affected at the time of delivery. However, there are no risk estimates available for bottle versus breast feeding. Without this information, mathematical models calculating the risk of HIV transmission cannot be used. These models could provide criteria for determining whether an infant would be better off being breast fed or bottle fed. In areas such as sub-Saharan Africa where the risk of infectious disease and malnutrition due to bottle feeding are great, breast feeding may be appropriate regardless of the risk of HIV transmission.

—Ziegler (1993, p. 1437)

Confused? If, after reading the preceding quotation, you remain unsure about the certainty of a linkage between breastfeeding and HIV/AIDS, then you are only beginning to understand the politics of this issue. This chapter reviews the literature relative to the politics of HIV/AIDS and breastfeeding, the politics of breastfeeding, and even the politics of breasts.

THE POLITICS OF HIV/AIDS AND BREASTFEEDING

As medical details of HIV transmission were initially being revealed, it was believed that only blood, semen, and vaginal secretions could be implicated. Then, Ziegler (1985) reported the spread of HIV some 13 months after birth to an infant from the milk of a mother who had a two-unit transfusion of blood following an emergency cesarean section. Two years later, cases of other mothers who had received contaminated blood at delivery were also cited in the United States (Lepage et al., 1987) and Europe (Senturia, Ades, & Peckham, 1987).

Still, neither the research nor the reportage on linkages between breast milk and HIV transmission is definitive. In 1988 a team of researchers from Zaire, Belgium, and the United

States reported how a wet nurse who died of AIDS had infected one of her charges and how two of eight Australian babies whose mothers received HIV-infected postpartum transfusions became seropositive (Colebunders et al., 1988). That same year, La Leche League International (LLLI) compiled a bibliographic database search of resource materials from medical and science journals on associations between AIDS and breastfeeding; now, nearly a decade and hundreds of reports later, the overall conclusions of that early baseline compilation remain just as dependent on who has funded and/or performed the studies. The range of countries represented by the research is impressive, the following representing simply a fraction: Haiti (Halsey et al., 1990); Romania (Kerina, 1991); East Bhutan (Bohler & Ingstad, 1996); India (Ravinathan, 1996); Ethiopia, South Africa, Uganda, and other African countries (Brown, 1993; Gray, 1996; Hira et al., 1990; Lemma, 1996; McIntyre, 1996; Nduati, John, & Kreiss, 1994; Nicoll, Killewo, & Mgone, 1990).

Several Russian studies suggest that transmission might be bidirectional (Bartlett & Finkbeiner, 1991; Pokrovskii, Eramov, Kuznetsova, Sliusareva, & Lepetikov, 1990; Scott, 1990). Nduati et al. (1994) raised some doubts with their reportage of an infant who was likely infected by pooled breast milk. Yet, as Pryor and Pryor (1991) pointed out about the United States, "Women who are actively ill with AIDS usually do not have the strength to consider breastfeeding, and in this country are often separated from their babies at birth" (p. 98).

"In countries where the risk of death in the first year is 50 percent from diarrhea and other disease (exclusive of AIDS)," Lawrence (1989, p. 168) decided, "breastfeeding is still the feeding of choice because the risk of dying from AIDS when born to an infected mother is only 18 percent." Bertolli (1996) studied 2,267 HIV-infected women who gave birth in Los Angeles and Massachusetts and concluded that all pregnant women should receive prenatal care, including voluntary HIV testing, and that women with HIV must be counseled against breastfeeding.

One of the few mainstream articles on this subject appeared in 1991 in *The Wall Street Journal,* which reported on research conducted in Africa that concluded women with HIV should use formula if it is available ("Study Cites," 1991). The *Journal* has an impressive circulation of over 2 million worldwide; however, the newspaper with the highest circulation in the United States has barely discussed the economics of infant formula. In 1994, when *The New York Times* reported on a Beth Israel Medical Center agreement urging all women considering breastfeeding to undergo HIV testing, it pointed out how AIDS was the number one killer of American women aged 15 to 44 (Mathur-Wagh, Roche, & Taha-Cisse, 1994).

The U.K. NGO AIDS Consortium (n.d.) stated, among other findings, "Breastmilk also contains a substance which may provide some protection against HIV infection by preventing the virus from binding with uninfected cells." Meanwhile, many breastfeeding advocates question whether blood from cracked nipples, rather than breast milk, is the culprit in the first place.

Another related phenomenon of the HIV/AIDS scare has been the closure of a number of milk banks. The Human Milk Banking Association of North America claims that whereas viruses such as cytomegalovirus and HTLV-1 may be transmitted through human milk, proof of HIV-1 transmission is less clear (Arnold, 1993). Still, as precautionary measures, U.S. milk banks routinely serum-screen all donors for HIV-1 and heat-treat milk according to recommendations from the CDC (Centers for Disease Control) and the FDA (Food and Drug Administration).

The CDC, which recognizes the value of breast milk in conferring immunity from mother to infant via antibodies to protect babies from various infections, nevertheless recommends that mothers refrain from breastfeeding if they have contracted HIV; at the same time, the CDC has amended this recommendation in developing countries, where breast milk is known to be crucial to infant survival. Margaret Oxtoby of the CDC has estimated overall rates of transmission from mother to child range from 25% to 50% ("AIDS Virus May," 1989). Breastfed babies have a slower progression anyway to AIDS, and breastfeeding may even delay it, according to Jacqueline Mok (1993); as she noted, there are probably more questions than answers to this dilemma (see also Nicoll et al., 1996).

In 1987 the World Health Organization (WHO) made a statement on "The Consultation on Breast-Feeding/Breast Milk and Human Immunodeficiency Virus": Instances of a correlation, if they exist at all, are small compared with in utero and intrapartum transmission. Summarizing conclusions arrived at by participants from 15 countries, they used terminology such as how the risks "depend on various factors," how "no definite data were found to substantiate a relationship," and that "further epidemiologic and laboratory investigations are needed" (WHO/UNICEF, 1990).

With colleagues at Family Health, Kennedy (1989) was concerned about all the conflicting evidence available on HIV and breastfeeding. Some 3 years later, those determinants were still being called into play (Program Evaluation Division, 1992). Goldfarb (1993) declared the relative role of breastfeeding in the epidemiology of HIV still uncertain in 1993—a position similar to that of the La Leche League's 1995 press release on how the connection remained "unclear." In 1996, Black labeled the HIV/breastfeeding transmission issue as "controversial," Wellstart International as "not known"—especially in light of a number of risks associated with artificial feeding. Throughout the literature discussing the role of HIV and breastfeeding, the theme is on policy—specifically, the need thereof. For example, the 1987 WHO declaration, which stressed the fact that specific guidelines should be developed to facilitate implementation in individual countries, recommended breastfeeding by biological mothers as the feeding method of choice (regardless of HIV status) when safe and effective alternatives are not possible, the promotion and protection of breastfeeding in both developing and developed countries, the pasteurization of pooled human milk for infants of biological mothers who cannot breastfeed, and, that "HIV-infected women and men have broad concerns, including maintaining their own health and well-being, managing their economic affairs, and making future provision for their children, and therefore require counselling and guidance on a number of important issues."

Recognizing how the HIV/AIDS epidemic influences all phases of women's reproductive lives, Preble, Elias, and Winikoff (1994) urged maternal and child health services providers to understand the nature of both technical and service-related issues. Van de Perre (1995) criticized the bulk of scientific data regarding mother-to-child transmission of HIV-1 by breastfeeding because most are based on observational studies, whereas no intervention trials have yet to be reported. Although it does not deal much with breastfeeding per se, the edited book *HIV, AIDS and Childbearing: Public Policy, Private Lives* (Faden & Kass, 1996) provides valuable insights into legal, medical, social, and ethical issues surrounding these wider issues. "Hanging over the scientific debates is a pall of distrust that is the bitter legacy of the fight over formula in the 1970's," noted Meier (1997, p. 16), "when the product became an emblem of industry's exploitation of the poor."

The Politics of Breastfeeding

This expression is not mine, but reflects the title of a 1988 book by Gabrielle Palmer. Literature on the topic is quite extensive, including a number of books on breastfeeding ranging from how-tos to medical to advocacy-related ones (Anderson, 1995; Black, 1996; Dana & Price, 1985; Eiger & Olds, 1987; Grams, 1988; Huggins, 1986; Kitzinger, 1987; La Leche League International, 1987; Pryor & Pryor, 1991; Woessner, Lauwers, & Vernard, 1987). Surprisingly, and tellingly, little about the overwhelming benefits of breastfeeding is available in the popular press—most noticeably missing in publications like *American Baby, Parents, Childbirth Instructor,* and the like (H. Armstrong, personal communication, March 7, 1997).

Although a complete history is neither appropriate nor possible here, breastfeeding has concerned human beings since time immemorial. The Hammurabi Code (circa 1800 BC) contained regulations on wet-nursing (Fildes, 1986; Golden, 1996b) and "spouted feeding cups" have been found in European infants' graves dating from about 2000 BC. Even royal women were required to nurse an eldest son in Spartan times (Lawrence, 1989), and Hippocrates is credited with saying, "One's own milk is beneficial, other's harmful." Early literature focused on hazards implicated by artificial feeding, and mortality charts marked clear differences between the choice of breast over bottle (e.g., Grulee, Sanford, & Herron, 1934). Issues of culture and class always have been attendant to the breastfeeding process (Golden, 1996a; Raphael, 1979).

One of the first persons to address the malnutrition and mortality problems traceable to bottle-feeding was Dr. Cicely D. Williams, who gave a talk titled "Milk and Murder" to the Singapore Rotary Club in 1939. This pediatrician said, "Anyone who, ignorantly or lightly, causes a baby to be fed on unsuitable milk, may be guilty of that child's death." Commenting on infant formula promotion, she declared, "Misguided propaganda on infant feeding should be punished as the most criminal form of sedition, and that these deaths should be regarded as murder." Although her talk caused quite a stir in its day, it never was published in a medical journal until 1979.

Another health activist, Dr. Derrick Jelliffe (1971), coined the term "Commerciogenic Malnutrition" to describe problems associated with bottle-fed Caribbean babies that he worked with in the 1960s. In 1974, influenced by the work of pediatricians David Morley and Ralph Hendrikse in Africa battling marketing practices of the infant feeding substitutes industry, the British charity War on Want published journalist Mike Muller's *The Baby Killer*—later translated into German and even more provocatively retitled *Nestle Kills Babies.* Around this same time came Peter Krieg's documentary film *Bottle Babies* (1975), a dramatic up-close demonstration of starving, malnourished bottle-fed babies in Kenya; in one particularly poignant scene, a mother scoops water from a filthy stream, then adds it to baby formula.

The era of activism was in full swing, perhaps best exemplified by the formation in 1977 of a consumer organization with the express purpose of monitoring formula companies, circulating their findings, and lobbying for change: the Infant Formula Action Coalition (INFACT). It was supplemented by another advocacy group, the Interfaith Center for Corporate Responsibility (ICCR), whose major claim was the 1976 lawsuit it publicized about the Sisters of the Precious Blood against Bristol-Myers for misleading marketing practices relative to its Enfamil, ProSobee, and Gerber formula. Maher (1992) cautioned us not to assume that women's adoption of formula feeding is based on a simple rationale. She argued that that it makes inroads on male cash income, as women get money for milk powder but hardly for their own bodily resources, and that formula feeding can encourage a more equitable division of labor among family members.

A turning point for public awareness was facilitated by congressional hearings in 1978, chaired by Senator Edward Kennedy of the Subcommittee on Health and Scientific Research. Not only did these hearings encourage a boycott of Nestle, they also served as a catalyst for the 1979 WHO/UNICEF Meeting on Infant and Young Child Feeding in Geneva—leading to the first international consumer code, consisting of these provisions about breastmilk substitutes: (a) There will be no advertising of breastmilk substitutes, (b) no free samples of breastmilk substitutes shall be given to mothers, (c) no promotion of products will be done through health care facilities, (d) no company mothercraft nurses are to advise mothers, (e) no gifts or personal samples will be given to health workers, (f) no words or pictures idealizing artificial feeding, including pictures of infants, should be on product labels, (g) only scientific and factual information should be provided to health workers, (h) all information on artificial feeding, including the labels, should explain the benefits of breastfeeding and the costs and hazards associated with artificial feeding, (i) unsuitable products, such as sweetened condensed milk, should not be promoted for babies, and (j) all products should be of a high quality and take into account the climatic and storage conditions of the country where they are used (WHO/UNICEF, 1981).

Not until 1994, however, did the United States give full support to the code, when President Clinton made a dramatic policy shift at the World Health Assembly in Geneva. "For the first time," Baumslag and Michels (1995, p. 169) gloated, "there is a worldwide unanimity that, in the infant health arena, profit should not come before public health." An encouraging sign for breastfeeding came with the launch, in 1991, of the worldwide Baby Friendly Hospital Initiative (BFHI): a global implementation of lactation management that, according to James Lindenberger (personal communication, March 14, 1997), executive director of Best Start, has been enormously successful. Also, in 1992 the World Alliance for Breastfeeding Action (WABA), headquartered in Malaysia, was formed. Finally, following a human rights perspective, UNAIDS' (1996) Interim Statement[1] concluded, "While in most cases transmission occurs during late pregnancy and delivery, preliminary studies indicate that more than one-third of these infected infants are infected through breast-feeding. These studies suggest an average risk for HIV transmission through breast-feeding of one in seven children born to, and breast-fed by, a woman living with HIV." Recognizing the need for more data to identify the precise timing of transmission of breastfeeding and other interventions, UNAIDS suggested the following elements for establishment of a policy on HIV and infant feeding: (a) supporting breastfeeding, (b) improving access to HIV counseling and testing, (c) ensuring informed choice, and (d) preventing commercial pressures for artificial feeding.

Because this chapter concerns itself with the politics of public access to the AIDS/breast-feeding issue, the saga would be lacking without further amplification of the consumer boycott (1977–1984) against Nestle's marketing practices in Third World countries. In 1866, the Swiss company began marketing the first condensed milk in tin boxes; its more involved marketing practices got the company in trouble in this century. As described in McComas, Fookes, and Taucher (1985), Sparks (1985), Chetley (1994), and Sethi (1994), Nestle became a target because critics thought the multinational company undermined women's confidence in their ability to breastfeed.

In the Western world, women's emancipation was at first associated with bottle feeding. With current interest in nutrition, physical appearance (breastfeeding helps a woman regain her figure faster), and health (breastfeeders have fewer urinary tract infections, reduced risk of osteoporosis, and lower rates of breast, cervical, and ovarian cancer), liberation is taking on new meaning. Breastfeeding advocates would argue that true emancipation would remove medical, psycho-sociological, and employer constraints, along with any guilt feelings related to decisions to breastfeed or not.

Since 1955, the Ross Products Division of Abbott Laboratories has collected breastfeeding statistics. Its most recent publication, "Updated Breast-Feeding Trend, 1986–1994," based on a mailed survey recall of how mothers fed their babies for the first 6 months, reports a resurgence for in-hospital breastfeeding from a low of 26.5% in 1970 to 57.4% in 1994. However, these figures not only include supplemental feeding (which has increased 44% in the last 10 years), but also represent "in hospital" only—when a wide majority of women

---

[1] I am grateful to Helen Armstrong for securing this document for me.

concede to giving breast milk initially to their infants for the known value of its colostrum, but then quit after those first few days. Furthermore, the formula company sponsors these surveys to help its program of giving gift-pack bottles.

A critical component of breastfeeding emerges from social support offered by groups such as LLLI. Started in 1956 by two women who wanted to provide information and encouragement to others about breastfeeding, the organization was one of the first self-help groups for women. Today, some breastfeeding-related journals include the following: *Breastfeeding Review, Journal of Human Lactation, Breastfeeding Abstracts, Birth, Genesis,* and the *International Journal of Childbirth Education.* Traditionally, data show that breastfeeders tend to be better educated and from higher socioeconomic classes. Marriage and assimilation also appear to be factors, immigrants to the United States often thinking it is "American" to bottle-feed, according to Ruth A. Lawrence (1989, p. 12), professor of pediatrics and obstetrics/gynecology at the University of Rochester School of Medicine, who, with Gabriele and Gabriele, stated:

> The impoverished mother is choosing to bottle feed not because she is working, as statistics show she is staying home and bottle feeding. When we interviewed mothers about their infant feeding choice in the prenatal clinic at WIC [Women, Infants, and Children program], they knew mother's milk was best. They said it was too hard to breastfeed and there were too many rules. When we listened to the classes on breastfeeding given by the lactation experts, it was obvious. The instructions on preparing the breasts and diet rules were overwhelming. The mothers said if only their physician would tell them it was important, they would do it for as long as the physician said. (Gabriele, Gabriele, & Lawrence, 1986, p. 175)

In 1995, two very relevant, if disparate books appeared: Pam Carter's *Feminism, Breasts and Breastfeeding* and Baumslag and Michels' *Milk, Money, and Madness: The Culture and Politics of Breastfeeding.* Carter, using "poststructuralist feminist analysis," wanted women's voices included in the debate over what is best for them or their children; from interviews with working-class women in the United Kingdom, she found many associated the concept of breastfeeding with poverty, fatigue, discomfort, embarrassment, restriction, and authoritarian hospital practices. Reminding us of the many diseases that breast milk can help prevent, like diarrhea, sudden infant death syndrome (SIDS), and pneumonia, Baumslag and Michels declared: "Breastfed babies are healthier, have fewer hospitalizations, and lower mortality rates than formula-fed infants. They not only have fewer childhood ailments, they also have less chronic illness throughout their lives" (pp. xxiii–xxiv). Breastfeeding, according to Guttman and Zimmerman (1996), can serve as a metaphor for the precarious position many women find themselves in relative to a number of mixed messages about their bodies, personal identity, social roles, sexuality, and health.

Still, formula feeding prevails—sales tripling, in fact, over the past decade such that the industry generates revenues of $22 million every day. A virtual (90%) monopoly within the formula industry is enjoyed by Ross Laboratories (Similac, Isomil) and Mead Johnson & Co. (Enfamil), the formula subsidiary of Bristol Myers. "In the last 15 years," Walker (1996, p. 4) reminded us, "formula producers have raised their prices by more than 200 percent while the cost of milk, formula's primary ingredient, has risen by only about 30 percent." Of those profits, the U.S. government is responsible for 57% of the formula market share by providing 37% of its infants with free formula under WIC.

Considering social taboos on breast exposure in public next to legislation claiming that breastfeeding is not "criminal behavior," to date only 11 states in the United States[2] have

---

[2]Those states include Florida, Illinois, Iowa, Michigan, Nevada, New York, North Carolina, Texas, Utah, Wisconsin, and Virginia.

taken action on the topic. In 1996, a first-time mother, sitting in a Chevy Blazer discreetly breastfeeding her covered infant daughter in a back parking lot behind a shopping complex in Milford, Connecticut, was warned by a local police officer that it was "inappropriate," and ordered to stop (Foley, 1996). In Florida, a woman who apparently accidentally breastfed a baby born to an HIV-infected mother threatened to sue Broward Medical Center for $200,000 ("Mother Breast Feeds," 1996). There even may be accusations that financially dependent women with HIV who choose to breastfeed rather than use (government-donated) formula might be practicing child abuse. Clearly breastfeeding requires additional legal awareness and support. The politics of breastfeeding run deep, not far removed from the economics of who is profiting—literally—from what might seem like women's decisions.

The Politics of Breasts

Central to this discussion is the increasing objectification of the female breast. Traditionally, Baumslag and Michels (1995) reminded us, breasts were considered simply organs of lactation, exposed without inhibition; then, "As cultures have become 'civilized,' breasts have been transformed from functional items to objects of female decoration and sexual organs whose purpose in life is to titillate and stimulate" (p. 6). One can wonder how breasts came to be associated as sex objects for men's pleasure, and how breastfeeding became associated with indecent behavior. One might also wonder how many Americans, both men and women, have ever seen a woman breastfeeding.

Historian Marilyn Yalom (1997) provided a political, artistic, and cultural examination that includes a range such as Stone Age figurines of women with oversized busts, multibreasted Indian women, Renaissance images of the nursing Madonna, desexualized bare-breasted South Pacific women, Amazon warrior women who chopped off one breast to better draw their bows, and, of course, eroticized breasts. She made us review social issues like wet-nursing, encouraged or discouraged breastfeeding eras, bra burning, even the role of humor. Today, breasts might be associated with silicone-gel implants, surgical enhancements or reductions, mammography, mastectomy and other issues surrounding breast cancer, Cinemax's film *Breasts* (1997), and even the "Wonder Bra" (Fuller, in press).

The Feminist Perspective

Simultaneously underlying and enveloping this entire discussion of AIDS and breastfeeding is a feminist perspective regarding the empowerment of women: physically, psychologically, economically, ideologically, and socioculturally. Breastfeeding is a feminist issue, according to Van Esterik (1989), because "it encourages women's self-reliance, confirms a woman's power to control her own body, challenges models of women as consumers and sex objects, requires a new interpretation of women's work, and encourages solidarity among women" (p. 69). Overall embracing a political ideology encouraging equality for women in all cultural aspects, the feminist perspective sees that whereas historically men have controlled critical theories from their perspectives, and therefore their rhetoric and reflections, male interpretations are distinctly different from women's. HIV/AIDS and breastfeeding might, then, be viewed from a variety of feminist frames. Conservative feminists embrace a maternal view favoring nurturance over any outside constraints. Liberal feminists focus on the political, seeing advocacy and the legal system as their venues, whereas radical feminists take the biological stance of women taking control over their reproductive systems. From whence, one might wonder, does the notion come that a woman's breasts "belong" to her husband?

Marxist and socialist feminists emphasize economics, claiming that capitalism's oppression of the laboring class is key in explaining the oppression of women; gender discrimination, they argue, is inseparable from class discrimination. Consider, for example, the Muslim precept obliging a woman to breastfeed her husband's children for 2 years.

A feminist perspective can help explain divergent attitudes toward obscenity and pornography. Just as conservatives think that a certain set of values should govern both our public and private lives, and liberals argue for freedom of expression, so now must society come to terms with what policies might serve both camps. Although breastfeeding challenges notions of the sexual division of labor, bringing with it a new definition of women's work as productive, not just reproductive, its role vis-à-vis the potential for infectious diseases from a feminist perspective can obviously take many forms. Still, at the core is concern for paternalism: Not only do men still dominate the medical profession as doctors, the overwhelming notion is the idea of "protecting" women rather than giving them credit in decision-making processes.

Repercussions

With economic, cultural, religious, psycho-sociological, legal, and quite clearly political issues looming, the correlation between AIDS and breastfeeding remains at something of a standoff. Although early works like Jelliffe and Jelliffe (1978) or Chetley (1986) seemed to define the issue, the stakes seem much higher now. A number of issues remain: Is the public being informed about current research on the HIV/AIDS breastfeeding connections? If so, who is that public? Who is putting out the research? Where is it being published? Who is funding it? And, most pressing of all, what information is *not* being released? Or, *where* is information being withheld? *Reproductive Health Matters* (May 1995, p. 128) listed some repercussions of what it labeled "HIV and breastfeeding: New information/old dilemmas," including the fact that many African governments have not released this information to their citzenry, that national maternal, child health, and international programs have promoted breastfeeding as protection against disease for decades—and that current HIV prevention curricula countermand such teaching and consequently might not be believed. Furthermore, few mothers actually may know their HIV status; thus teaching that HIV-infected mothers should not breastfeed their children may be ineffective.

At the 11th International AIDS Conference, held in Vancouver, British Columbia, Dr. Peter Piot, head of the United Nations AIDS program, pointed out that 90% of HIV-infected people live in the Third World (in Altman, 1996). Think back to how, owing to the rampant homophobia in the United States that prevented societal concern over AIDS at the beginning of its pandemic, the media didn't pick up on the story until it became more grisly, more heart-rending—such as featuring "victims" of contaminated blood. From the many bibliographic resources for this study, it is apparent that hardly any publications other than medical (with the notable exception of *Ms.;* see Benderly, 1977) have dealt with AIDS and breastfeeding. This report would clearly have been lacking if it had to depend on published reports; hence, input from over four dozen organizations (list available from author) has been invaluable.

On the other hand, those few news items that have gone mainstream tend to be alarmist and/or off base. Finger (1992) referred to the emotional speech by an HIV-infected woman at the Democratic Party National Convention about how she became infected from a blood transfusion during childbirth, unknowingly passing it on to her daughter through her breast milk: "Ten days later, on the July 24 national NBC television news, a reporter covering the closing session of the AIDS conference said, 'Vast numbers of those who escape infection at birth are infected through breastmilk . . . For many infants, breastfeeding has become a death sentence' " (p. 12). Nancy Jo Peck of IBFAN/Geneva (International Baby Food Action Network) sent me an article entitled, "What If the Mother Is HIV Positive?" that appeared in the Pakistani *International News* (October 29, 1996), in which she was blatantly quoted out of context—juxtaposed next to an advertisement for Nestle, no less. She also included some articles from the *Tribune de Genève* representing the other extreme ("Allaitement maternel," 1996; "Un chiffre," 1996), about which she commented, "Interesting because breastfeeding is emphasized far out of proportion to reality" (Peck, personal communication, March 14, 1997).

Despite the fact that media treatment of health issues is critical, its general knowledge of AIDS relative to breastfeeding is alarmingly lacking. One particularly salient example, brought to my attention by Helen Armstrong of Tufts University's School of Nutrition, concerned a report at the XI International Conference on AIDS (Gray, 1996) on an interim analysis of mother–infant pairs in Soweto, South Africa. Her conclusions, stating that exclusive formula feeding significantly reduced HIV transmission, was merely work in progress—as yet unpublished and not at all peer reviewed; yet, its abstract was picked up and reported by a number of sources. Armstrong (personal communication, March 3, 1997), pointing out how an estimated 1.4 million children have died of AIDS since the beginning of the epidemic, cautioned, "There is a danger that tables of child mortality in close association with an article on HIV transmission may suggest a connection which will tend to feed disproportionate panic about breastfeeding."

As to the topic of formula, IBFAN, which was expressly formed to monitor industry violations of the WHO/UNICEF Code, repeatedly reports egregious lacks of compliance. American Home Products, whose Wyeth-Ayerst Laboratories produce SMA, S-26, and Nursoy, gives free supplies to at least 25 developing countries and 7 developed ones, and Nestle donates to some 45 developing countries and 10 developed ones (Baumslag & Michels, 1995). Breastfeeding advocates express particular concern over government-sponsored programs donating formula to WIC recipients, claiming they may be responsible for its high retail price—at special detriment to all taxpayers and to middle-class persons who might prefer to use formula.

Formula makers pay their key executives handsomely (e.g., the chief executive of Bristol Myers reportedly earns over $12 million), contribute to and advertise in journals of organizations like the following: the American Academy of Pediatrics (a million-dollar renewable grant, said to already be worth more than $8 million), the American College of Obstetrics and Gynecologists, and the American Medical Association. Contributions are also made to the Association of Women's Health, Obstetric, and Neonatal Nurses, the American Dietetic Association, and the National Association of Neonatal Nurses, along with extended gifts and benefits to medical students and pediatricians. Quite obviously the public relations departments of these powerful companies reign supreme. Nestle, learning its lessons, could be the best example of what Crable and Vibbert (1985) cited under their Catalytic Issue Management Model for organizations wanting to initiate policy, rather than merely reacting to it. The rhetoric of issue management as described by Elwood (1995) is aptly relevant here; where earlier he explicated various illness metaphors used to describe political issues (Elwood, 1994), it might easily be argued that AIDS and its relationship to breastfeeding symbolize much wider issues.

The biggest foray of formula makers, as research shows that 93% of consumers will maintain brand loyalty with the one they use first, relates to free "discharge" packs of bottles, nipples, rattles, pamphlets, coupons, and formula for new mothers being discharged from hospitals. All this leads to major bidding wars for hospitals that will name them as "discharge" donors. Information about these practices simply does not appear in the news. According to

Baumslag and Michels (1995), "The status quo remains. Formula companies continue to produce artificial milks at great profit. Women continue to choose formula over breastfeeding. And the government continues to pick up the tab, both for the formula and the formula related illnesses" (p. 181).

Throughout this discussion, one of the most critical issues relates to what is absent: information from multinational formula-making corporations about the benefits of breast-feeding, research yet to be performed on the effects of breast milk and of formula, data about the role of formula and juvenile diabetes, and the submerged or subverted discourse, or lack of discourse, about lactation—when the real story is what bureaucracies own the messages and control their dissemination. Culled together, these missing data can present quite a challenge to both medical and economic hegemony. For those who veer toward conspiracy theories, a lot of ammunition hangs temptingly here. For those who question the double standard of bottle-feeding for developed countries, breastfeeding for developing ones, one wonders about the role of ethics, never mind guilt. Clearly, the debate between private profit and public health in the AIDS/breastfeeding issue needs a forum such as this one to be better known to a wider audience.

REFERENCES

AIDS virus may be transmitted through breastfeeding. (1989). *AIDS Alert, 4*(9), 25.

Allaitement maternel et risque du sida [Breastfeeding and risk of AIDS]. (1996, August 22). *Tribune de Genève*, p. 3.

Altman, L. K. (1996, July 7). AIDS meeting: Signs of hope, and obstacles. *The New York Times*, p. A1+.

Anderson, G. (1995, January 14). Breastfeeding: A neglected pro-life issue. *America, 172*(1), 19–21.

Arnold, L. D. W. (1993). HIV and breastmilk: What it means for milk banks. *Journal of Human Lactation, 9*, 47–48.

Bartlett, J. G., & Finkbeiner, A. K. (1991). *The guide to living with HIV infection.* Baltimore: Johns Hopkins University Press.

Baumslag, N., & Michels, D. L. (1995). *Milk, money, and madness: The culture and politics of breastfeeding.* Westport, CT: Bergin & Garvey.

Benderly, B. L. (1977, December). Bottle baby disease: Boycott of Nestle products in an attempt to stop promotion of infant formula in underdeveloped countries. *Ms.*, p. 20.

Bertolli, J. M. (1996, July). *Breastfeeding among HIV-infected women, Los Angeles and Massachusetts, 1988–1993.* Poster presented at the XI International Conference on AIDS, Vancouver, BC.

Black, R. F. (1996). Transmission of HIV-1 in the breastfeeding process. *Journal of the American Dietetic Association, 96*(3), 267–274.

Bohler, E., & Ingstad, B. (1996). The struggle of weaning: Factors determining breastfeeding during in East Bhutan. *Social Science & Medicine, 43*, 1805–1816.

Brown, P. (1993, June 19). Balancing the risks of breast and bottle. *New Scientist, 138*(1878), 10–13.

Carter, P. (1995). *Feminism, breasts and breast-feeding.* New York: St. Martin's.

Chetley, A. (1986). *The politics of baby food.* London: Frances Pinter.

Chetley, A. (1994). Infant feeding row. *The Lancet, 343*, 1030–1032.

Colebunders, R. L., Kapita, B., Nekwei, W., Bahwe, Y., Baende, F., & Ryder, R. (1988). Breastfeeding and the transmission of HIV. *The Lancet, 8626*, 1487.

Crable, R. E., & Vibbert, S. L. (1985). Managing issues and influencing public policy. *Public Relations Review, 11*, 3–16.

Dana, N., & Price, A. (1985). *Successful breastfeeding.* New York: Meadowbrook.

Eiger, M., & Olds, S. W. (1987). *The complete book of breastfeeding.* New York: Workman and Bantam.

Elwood, W. N. (1994). *Rhetoric in the war on drugs: The triumphs and tragedies of public relations.* Westport, CT: Praeger.

Elwood, W. N. (1995). Public relations is a rhetorical experience: The integral principle in case study analysis. In W. N. Elwood (Ed.), *Public relations inquiry as rhetorical criticism: Case studies of corporate discourse and social influence* (pp. 3–12). Westport, CT: Praeger.

Faden, R. R., & Kass, N. F. (Eds.). (1996). *HIV, AIDS and childbearing: Public policy, private lives.* New York: Oxford University Press.

Fildes, V. A. (1986). *Breasts, bottles, and babies: A history of infant feeding.* Edinburgh, Scotland: Edinburgh University Press.

Finger, W. R. (1992, October). Should the threat of HIV affect breast-feeding? *Network,* pp. 12–14.

Foley, M. (1996, August 31). Cop calls breast-feeding "inappropriate." *New Haven Register,* p. 1.

Fuller, L. K. (in press). Confucian conflicts in Singaporean advertising: A case study of the "Wonder Bra" campaign. In J. P. Thierstein & Y. R. Kamalipour (Eds.), *Religion, law and freedom: A global perspective.*

Gabriele, A., Gabriele, K. R., & Lawrence, R. A. (1986). Cultural values and biomedical knowledge: Choices in infant feeding. *Social Science and Medicine, 23,* 501.

Golden, J. (1996a). From commodity to gift: Gender, class, and the meaning of breast milk in the twentieth century. *The Historian, 59*(1), 75–88.

Golden, J. (1996b). *A social history of wet nursing in America: From breast to bottle.* New York: Cambridge University Press.

Goldfarb, J. (1993). Breastfeeding, AIDS and other infectious diseases. *Clinical Perinatology, 20,* 225–243.

Grams, M. (1988). *Breastfeeding source book.* Sheridan, WY: Achievement Press.

Gray, G. (1996, July). *The effect of breastfeeding on vertical transmission of HIV-1 in Soweto, South Africa.* Poster presented at the XI International Conference on AIDS, Vancouver, BC.

Grulee, C. G., Sanford, H. N., & Herron, P. H. (1934). Breast and artificial feeding. *Journal of the American Medical Association, 103,* 735.

Guttman, N., & Zimmerman, D. R. (1996, May). *If I could, I would. But it seems impossible. Women who do it have no respect: Breastfeeding as a metaphor for contradictions in women's lives.* Paper presented at the International Communication Association annual conference, Chicago.

Halsey, N. A., Boulos, R., Holt, R., Ruff, A., Brutus, J. R., Kissinger, P., Quinn, T. C., Coberly, J. S., Adrien, M., & Boulos, C. (1990). Transmission of HIV-1 infections from mothers to infants in Haiti: Impact on childhood mortality and malnutrition. The CDS/JHU AIDS Project Team. *Journal of the American Medical Association, 264,* 2088–2092.

Hira, S. K., Mangrola, U. G., Mwale, C., Chmtu, C., Tembo, G., Brady, W. E., & Perine, P. L. (1990). Apparent vertical transmission of human immunodeficiency virus type 1 by breast-feeding in Zambia. *Journal of Pediatrics, 117,* 421–424.

HIV and breastfeeding: New information/old dilemmas. (1995, May). *Reproductive Health Matters, 5,* 127–128.

Holmes, W. (1992) Breastfeeding and HIV. *The Lancet, 340,* 1095.

Huggins, K. (1986). *The nursing mother's companion.* Boston: Harvard Common Press.

Jelliffe, D. B. (1971). Commerciogenic malnutrition? Time for a dialogue. *Food Technology, 25.*

Jelliffe, D. B., & Jelliffe, E. F. P. (1978). *Human milk in the modern world.* Oxford, England: Oxford University Press.

Jendron, J. (1988). About La Leche League International. In M. Grams (Ed.), *Breastfeeding source book* (p. 175). New York: Achievement Press.

Kennedy, K. I. (1989). Breastfeeding and HIV. *The Lancet, 337,* 333.

Kerina, K. (1991, January/February). A generation imperiled. *Ms.,* p. 20.

Kitzinger, S. (1987). *The experience of breastfeeding.* New York: Penguin.

La Leche League International. (1987). *The womanly art of breast-feeding* (4th ed.). Chicago, IL: Author.

La Leche League International. (1995). *Role of mother's milk in HIV transmission unclear* [Press release]. Chicago, IL: Author.

Lawrence, R. A. (1989). *Breastfeeding: A guide for the medical profession* (3rd ed.). St. Louis: C. V. Mosby.

Lawrence, R. A. (in press). *The medical contraindications to breastfeeding: A discussion of the risk benefit ratio breast-feeding in the face of malnutrition, infection, medications, and environmental toxins.* Washington, DC: U.S. Department of Agriculture.

Lemma, A. (1996, July). *The window of hope for safeguarding youth from AIDS (SYFA) in Africa.* Poster presented at the XI International Conference on AIDS, Vancouver, BC.

Lepage, P., van de Perre, P., Carael, M., Nsengunmuremyi, F., Nkurunziza, J., Butzler, J. P., & Sprecher, S. (1987). Postnatal transmission of HIV from mother to child. *The Lancet, 342,* 400.

Maher, V. (Ed.). (1992). *The anthropology of breast-feeding: Natural law of social construct.* Oxford, England: Berg Publishers.

Mathur-Wagh, U., Roche, N., & Taha-Cisse, A. H. (1994, April 22). Breastfeeding can act as transmitter of HIV. *The New York Times,* p. A26.

McComas, M., Fookes, G., & Taucher, G. (1985). *The dilemma of Third World nutrition: Nestle and the role of infant formula.* Nestle S.A.

McIntyre, J. (1996, July). *Maternal and obstetrical factors in mother to child transmission of HIV in Soweto, South Africa.* Poster presented at the XI International Conference on AIDS, Vancouver, BC.

Meier, B. (1997, June 8). In war against AIDS, battle over baby formula reignites. *The New York Times,* p. A1+.

Mok, J. (1993). HIV-1 infection: Breast milk and HIV-1 transmission. *The Lancet, 341,* 930.

Mother breast feeds HIV baby. (1996, July 16). United Press International.

Muller, M. (1974). *The baby killer.* London: War on Want.

Nduati, R. W., John, G. C., & Kreiss, J. (1994). Postnatal transmission of HIV-1 through pooled breast milk. *The Lancet, 344,* 1432.

Nicoll, A., Killewo, J. Z., & Mgone, C. (1990). HIV and infant feeding practices: Epidemiological implications for sub-Saharan African countries, *AIDS, 4,* 661–665.

Nicoll, A., Newell, M. L., Mansergh, G. Haddix. A. C., Steketee, R. W., & Simonds, R. J. (1996). Preventing perinatal transmission of HIV: The effect of breastfeeding. *Journal of the American Medical Association, 276,* 1552–1554.

Palmer, G. (1988). *The politics of breastfeeding.* London: Pandora.

Pokrovskii, V. V., Eramov, I., Kuznetsova, I., Sliusareva, L. A., & Lepetikov, V. V. (1990). HIV transmission from child to mother during breast feeding. *Zh Mikrobiol Epidemiol Immunobiol March, 3,* 59–62.

Preble, E. A., Elias, C. J., & Winikoff, B. (1994). Maternal health in the age of AIDS: Implications for health services in developing countries. *AIDS Care, 6,* 499–516.

Program Evaluation Division, Family Health International. (1992). Should the threat of HIV affect breastfeeding? *Network, 13*(2), 12–14.

Pryor, K., & Pryor, G. (1991). *Nursing your baby.* New York: Pocket Books.

Raphael, D. (Ed.). (1979). *Breastfeeding and food policy in a hungry world.* New York: Academic Press.

Ravinathan, R. (1996, July). *Prevention of mother to child transmission through perinatal care.* Poster presented at the XI International Conference on AIDS, Vancouver, BC.

Scott, J. (1990, June 22). Nursing mothers got AIDS virus from babies (Soviet Union). *Los Angeles Times, 109,* p. A3.

Senturia, Y. D., Ades, A. E., & Peckham, C. S. (1987). Breastfeeding and HIV infection. *The Lancet, 2,* 200.

Sethi, S. P. (1994). *Multinational corporations and the impact of public advocacy on corporate strategy: Nestle and the infant formula controversy.* Dordrecht, Netherlands: Kluwer.

Sparks, J. A. (Ed.). (1985). *The infant formula feeding controversy: An annotated bibliography 1970–1984.* Dubuque, IA: Kendall/Hunt Publishing Company and St. Martin's Press.

Study cites breast milk in transmission of AIDS. (1991, August 29). *The Wall Street Journal,* p. B5.

U.K. NGO AIDS Consortium. (n.d.). *Breastfeeding and the risk of mother to child transmission of HIV.* Fenner Brockway House, 37/39 Great Guildford Street, London.

Un chiffre resume le defi du sida: plus de 400,000 enfants sont contaminés [Challenging total number as a result of AIDS: More than 400,000 children are infected]. (1996, November 30). *Tribune de Genève.*

UNAIDS. (1996, July). *HIV and infant feeding: An interim statement.* New York: Author.

Van de Perre, P. (1995). Postnatal transmission of human immunodeficiency virus type 1: The breastfeeding dilemma. *American Journal of Obstetrics and Gynecology, 173,* 483–87.

Van Esterik, P. (1989). *Beyond the breast-bottle controversy.* New Brunswick, NJ: Rutgers University Press.

Walker, S. (1996, August 22). Feeding babies vs. fueling competition. *Christian Science Monitor,* p. 4.

Wellstart International. (1996). *Breastfeeding and HIV: Making an informed choice* [Press release].

WHO/UNICEF. (1981). *The WHO/UNICEF international code of marketing of breastmilk substitutes.* Adopted Geneva, Switzerland.

WHO/UNICEF. (1990). *Innocenti declaration on the protection, promotion and support of breastfeeding.* Adopted Florence, Italy.

Woessner, C., Lauwers, J., & Vernard, B. (1987). *Breastfeeding today: A mother's companion.* New York: Avery.

World Health Organization. (1987). *Lactancia natural/Leche materna y virus de la immunodeficiencia humana* [Natural mother's milk/Mother's milk and the human immunodeficiency virus]. Geneva, Switzerland: Author.

Yalom, M. (1997). *A history of the breast.* New York: Knopf.

Ziegler, J. B. (1993). Breast feeding and HIV. *The Lancet, 342,* 1437–1439.

Ziegler, J. B., Cooper, D. A., & Johnson, R. O. (1985). Post-natal transmission of AIDS-associated retrovirus from mother to infant. *The Lancet, 1,* 896.

26

A Tough Sell: The Political Logic of Federal Needle-Exchange Policy

Mark C. Donovan
University of Washington, Seattle

Much has been written about the politics of AIDS; authors commonly stress the failure of government institutions and leaders to respond to the epidemic. Less attention has been paid to explaining how and why the politics and policies surrounding the HIV/AIDS pandemic have taken shape. Calls for "action" and finger pointing at leaders who have "done nothing" about HIV/AIDS were once meaningful, but as David Kirp (1994) has argued, the blame game is played out. In this chapter, I document a substantial government failure in the fight against AIDS—the failure to support needle-exchange programs to prevent HIV infection among injection drug users (IDUs), their sexual partners, and children—but with an analysis that unpacks the factors that structure national AIDS politics and policymaking.

The controversy over needle-exchange programs designed to provide drug users with sterile injecting equipment has simmered for almost a decade. Despite shockingly high rates of infection among IDUs and increasing scientific evidence supporting the efficacy of needle exchange, Congress has repeatedly gone out of its way to prohibit the federal funding of needle exchange. Explaining this puzzle requires understanding the complexities of politics in the United States, and appreciating the bind that elected lawmakers find themselves in when they make policies that single out citizens, in this case the highly unpopular population of "drug users." These quotes highlight the rhetorical dimension of politics, the ways that political language and political communication influence policymaking. Although many needle-exchange proponents bemoan the triumph of "politics" over "science," such a formulation ignores an array of factors that makes needle exchange a tough sell.

I begin the chapter by discussing the link between injection drug use and HIV, then discuss the needle-exchange controversy and its influence on federal policymaking. Having set the context for the analysis, I argue that four factors explain the shape of federal needle-exchange politics and policy: the battle over problem definition, the characteristics of drug users as a population, the important but inobvious role of race, and the political dilemmas involved with making policies that prevent problems. I conclude the chapter by pointing out important differences in the political communication context of local and federal AIDS politics and attempt to draw some the broader lessons from the needle-exchange case.

THE CASE FOR NEEDLE EXCHANGE

Injection drug use is intimately and tragically tied to the HIV/AIDS epidemic. Although much attention in the early years of the epidemic focused on the spread of HIV among gay men, it became clear even in the mid-1980s that the sharing of HIV-infected needles among IDUs was a critical route for the spread of HIV. In 1995, the year for which the most recent data are available, injection drug use was associated directly or indirectly with nearly 35% of newly reported cases of AIDS. Among women and children, over half of all female AIDS cases and over 40% of all pediatric AIDS cases were traceable to injection drug use or sex with an IDU (Centers for Disease Control and Prevention [CDC], 1995a, author's calculations).

As a population, IDUs have experienced dramatically high rates of HIV infection. Estimates in New York City, home of the largest IDU HIV epidemic, have consistently placed the rates of HIV seroprevalence among IDUs at over 50% (Des Jarlais et al., 1994). The most recent, comprehensive estimate of HIV infection (not AIDS) indicates that injection drug use is the largest source of new HIV infections in the metropolitan areas that account for 85% of all reported AIDS cases. Annually, injection drug use is estimated to directly account for approximately 19,000 new HIV infections, *nearly twice the number of infections traced to men who have sex with men* (Holmberg, 1996). In addition, injection drug use has been the biggest contributor to HIV infections among women and children with AIDS. Injection drug use or sex with an IDU has accounted for 64% of all female AIDS cases, whereas mothers who inject drugs or have sex with IDUs account for 54% of all reported cases of pediatric AIDS (CDC, 1996, author's calculations).

HIV prevention among IDUs, then, holds the promise to decrease infections among both drug users and their sexual partners and children. Awareness of this problem, though, has not met with a comparable policy response. In 1988, the National Academy of Sciences noted that "the gross inadequacy of federal efforts to reduce HIV transmission among IV drug users, when considered in relation to the scope and implications of such transmissions, is now the most serious deficiency in current efforts to control HIV infection in the United States" (in Bayer & Kirp, 1992, p. 37). Nearly a decade later, this observation is still accurate.

The key to HIV prevention among IDUs, their sexual partners, and children clearly lies in eliminating the use of infected needles. One way this could happen would be for IDUs to stop injecting drugs altogether, but the way to achieve this result is far from clear. Although drug treatment holds promise, it is not without its problems. First is the fact that one important treatment modality for heroin users, methadone therapy, faces many of the same criticisms lobbed at needle-exchange programs. In fact, some observers have argued that the political trajectory of methadone and needle exchange are analogous (Des Jarlais, Paone, Friedman, Peyser, & Newman, 1995). Second, there are lingering doubts about the effectiveness of drug treatment; the most recent national study of drug treatment showed that over 80% of the patients admitted into treatment dropped out in under 6 months (Hubbard et al., 1989; see also Sharp, 1994). Third, and finally, given current funding levels, a treatment-only approach is unlikely to succeed in reducing drug-related HIV infections because of the mismatch between the number of IDUs and the availability of drug treatment.[1]

Alternatively, and at far lower cost, IDUs could be encouraged to use sterile needles when shooting up, at least until they choose or are able to enter a drug treatment program.

[1]Although this chapter is concerned with the link between *injection* drug use and HIV/AIDS, it is important not to overlook the fact that non-injection-drug use, particularly crack cocaine use, has been increasingly associated with HIV infection. This is particularly the case among women who engage in sex-for-drugs exchanges. The lack of available treatment slots for crack addicts is even more severe than that for heroin addicts. See Forbes (1993).

A barrier to this strategy is the unavailability of sterile needles and syringes to IDUs. In 1995, 45 states had drug paraphernalia laws on the books that effectively limited the sale of syringes and needles for nonmedical purposes. Nine states and the District of Columbia had additional laws mandating prescriptions for the sale of syringes (Valleroy et al., 1995). These laws inhibit IDUs from purchasing syringes at local pharmacies and create a disincentive for them to carry clean syringes and needles because these are considered drug paraphernalia. The lack of availability of sterile needles and syringes has been instrumental in creating the need for needle and syringe exchange in the United States.

The appearance of needle-exchange programs in the United States followed the introduction of an exchange program in Amsterdam in 1986, and the proliferation of domestic street outreach programs designed to educate IDUs about HIV. Often, the centerpiece of many of these U.S. outreach programs was the distribution of bleach kits intended to be used by IDUs to disinfect used needles and syringes. The first organized needle-exchange program (NEP) to operate in the United States opened in 1988 in Tacoma, Washington; others soon followed in San Francisco, New York, Seattle, Portland, Oregon, and New Haven, Connecticut (Lurie et al., 1993). These early NEPs (and most later ones) have often been the subject of controversy. Although these programs were typically initiated by activists, local health departments have often taken over operating these programs.

The controversy over NEPs has revolved largely around concerns that they condone and encourage drug use. Concerns about encouraging drug use have been the key reasons stated for congressional opposition to needle exchange. Beginning in 1988, with the passage of the Health Omnibus Programs Extension Act, Congress effectively prohibited the use of federal funds for NEPs:

> None of the funds provided under this Act or an amendment made to this Act shall be used to provide individuals with hypodermic needles or syringes so that such individuals may use illegal drugs, unless the Surgeon General of the Public Health Service determines that a demonstration needle exchange program would be effective in reducing drug abuse and the risk that the public will become infected with the etiologic agent for acquired immune deficiency syndrome. (P.L. 100-607, Section 256b)

This mandate did more than just prohibit NEPs; it also set the public health research agenda by requiring the simultaneous investigation of whether NEPs reduce HIV infections and also reduce drug abuse. This dual requirement has posed a difficult task for researchers, made all the more difficult by Congress's refusal to provide research funding until 1992 (Hantman, 1995).

Despite these hurdles, needle exchange has been the subject of a profusion of scientific studies. In the late 1980s, reports on the efficacy of European NEPs were published in science and public health journals, and were soon followed by evaluations of U.S. needle exchanges (see Paone, Des Jarlais, Gangloff, Milliken, & Friedman, 1995). Needle exchange was endorsed in reports issued by the National Academy of Sciences (Institute of Medicine, 1986; Normand, Vlahov, & Moses, 1995), the National Commission on AIDS (1991), and the General Accounting Office (GAO; 1993). In a study sponsored by the CDC, researchers at the University of California (UC) reviewed all the extant literature, conducted extensive original research, and produced the most comprehensive review of needle exchange to date. The UC study found no basis for the argument that NEPs increase drug use, and concluded by recommending, "The federal government should repeal the ban on the use of federal funds for needle exchange services. Substantial federal funds should be committed both to providing needle exchange services and to expanding research into these programs" (Lurie et al., 1993, p. vi).

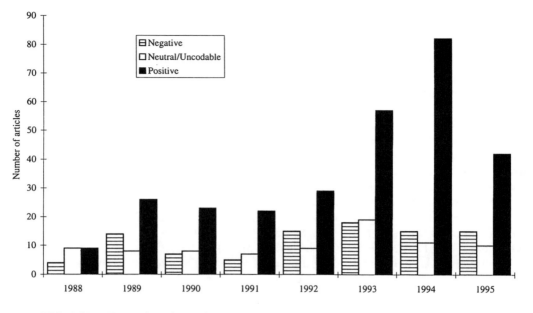

FIG. 26.1.   Tone of needle-exchange headlines in major U.S. newspapers, 1988–1995.

At the federal level, this scientific consensus has so far fallen on deaf ears and the federal funding bans remain. Still, NEPs have become a fixture in many communities due to the efforts of local activists and public health officials. In 1994, at least 55 operated in the United States and reported exchanging over 8 million sterile syringes. In 1995, at least 68 NEPs were in place, operating in 46 cities in 21 states (CDC, 1995b). Public debate over needle exchange has been largely nonexistent, confined to the communities in which NEPs have operated. A 1994 opinion poll, the first national poll on the issue, indicated that 55% of respondents supported NEPs (Lurie, 1995). Although there is no telling how robust such support for NEPs would be if needle exchange became a focus of national debate, the poll results are yet another piece of data that make current federal policy difficult to understand.

Another gauge of needle-exchange sentiment can be found by analyzing press reports about the issue[2] (see Fig. 26.1). From 1988 to 1995, 464 articles with references to needle exchange in the headline appeared in major U.S. newspapers, a median of 50 articles per year. The distribution of this media coverage is relatively easy to understand. From 1988 to 1989, coverage more than doubled from 22 to 48 articles following the first wave of NEP openings. A similar, though more dramatic increase came in 1993 and 1994. Although 53 articles were published in 1992, events culminating in the March 1993 release of the GAO report and the October 1993 release of the UC study dramatically increased needle-exchange coverage in 1993 and 1994. In 1993, 94 articles were published; 103 were printed in 1994. More remarkable is the tone of this coverage. In each year of coverage, more articles reported

---

[2]This section is based on data gathered and coded by the author. The data were gathered from a keyword search of the NEXIS major newspaper and wire service libraries (MAJPAP & WIRE) for occurrences of "needle exchange" in the headline of news articles and editorials from 1988 through 1995. Duplicate articles, resulting mostly from the recycling of articles by news services, were eliminated. Each headline was coded by the author as having a "positive," "negative," or "neutral" tone. Articles were judged to be positive if they reported the opening of NEPs, or favorable comments or studies. Articles were judged to be negative if they reported the problems or obstacles to NEPs, unfavorable comments, or studies in the headline. Articles were judged to be neutral if no tone could be detected in the headline. Where headlines included both positive and negative tones, they were marked as uncodable and collapsed with the neutral articles.

positive news about needle exchange than reported negatively about it. Positive news articles were those with a headline reporting the opening of an NEP, and positive studies or comments about needle exchange. As Fig. 26.1 shows, positive articles have comprised over 50% of all articles in each year since 1989. Since 1993, over 60% of the articles have had a positive tone, rising as high as 75% in 1994.

In the face of overwhelming scientific evidence that needle exchange helps prevent the spread of HIV, the proliferation of NEPs at the local level, suggestive evidence of public support, and consistently positive media, what explains the continued efforts of the U.S. Congress to prohibit funding for NEPs? The remainder of the chapter is devoted to answering this question.

UNDERSTANDING THE POLITICS OF NEEDLE-EXCHANGE POLICY

In recent years, the U.S. Congress has prohibited needle-exchange funding in most major health, HIV/AIDS, and drug laws. Such prohibitions have been part of all but one appropriation bill for the Department of Health and Human Services since 1991. From 1988 to 1995 Congress passed restrictions on needle-exchange funding nine times.[3] The legislature has never voted to support needle exchange. The Congress is not the only branch of government important to the needle-exchange debate. Presidents and agencies within the executive branch, most notably the Office of National Drug Control Policy ("the Drug Czar's Office") have played a significant role in influencing federal needle-exchange policy, but Congress has been at the forefront of the policy process. Furthermore, although Congress has consistently gone on record against needle exchange, what is not obvious is that the needle-exchange restrictions adopted by the body have often been more flexible than other restrictions that were considered and rejected. This fact introduces an interesting twist to the story that I present in the following discussion: Why is it that Congress was opposed to needle exchange—but not as strongly opposed as it could have been? Of the nine restrictive laws passed by Congress, five laws contained these restrictions at the time the bill was introduced to the floor, whereas in four cases NEP funding restrictions were attached by amendment during floor consideration of bills. These battles over restrictive amendments accounted for nearly all the debate about needle exchange in the Congress; each of these disputes originated in the Senate. All told, 11 different amendments were considered relating to needle exchange, and 18 members of Congress rose a total of 55 times to argue over these proposals. The analysis presented in the next two sections is based on these bills and this debate.[4]

---

[3]These restrictions are found in the following public laws: 1988 Health Omnibus Programs Extensions Act, PL 100-607, Section 256; 1988 Anti-Drug Abuse Act, PL 100-690 (Title II, Revisions and Extension of ADAMHA Block Grant), Section 2025; 1990 Labor, Health and Human Services, Education and Related Agencies Appropriations Act, Section 514; 1990 Ryan White CARE Act, PL 101-381, Section 422; 1991 Labor, Health and Human Services, Education and Related Agencies Appropriations Act, PL 101-517, Section 514; 1992 Alcohol, Drug Abuse, and Mental Health Administration (ADAMHA) Reorganization Act, PL 102-321, Section 202; Labor, Health and Human Services, 1993 Education and Related Agencies Appropriations Act, PL 102-394, Section 514; 1994 Labor, Health and Human Services, Education and Related Agencies Appropriations Act, PL 103-112, Section 506; 1995 Labor, Health and Human Services, Education and Related Agencies Appropriations Act, PL 103-333, Section 506.

[4]The relevant debate was compiled by reading issues of the *Congressional Record* associated with consideration of bills containing needle-exchange restrictions. This was cross-checked against a NEXIS keyword search of the *Congressional Record* (RECORD Library) for occurrences of "needle exchange" from 1988 to 1995. I analyzed only debate about actual legislation, ignoring members' Extension of Remarks. The debate was read *in toto* by the author, and passages that directly addressed the question of needle exchange were entered verbatim into a database. The statements in the database were coded according to the protocol available from the author by request.

Though needle exchange is an attractive proposal from the perspective of HIV prevention, it has presented lawmakers with a substantial dilemma. Whereas needle exchange can be justified in that it will prevent the spread of a fatal, infectious disease, it can just as easily be attacked on the grounds that it aids and abets drug use and drug addiction. Members of Congress have overwhelmingly found the second rationale to be the more compelling one. To this point, needle exchange has been an electorally repulsive option for policymakers; those who might favor needle exchange have struggled to justify this stance in ways that do not open them up to sound-bite attacks from political opponents in both the present and future.

I argue that the shape of U.S. needle-exchange policy can be explained by analyzing how problem definitions, the characteristics of IDUs, the racial dimension of the issue, and the dilemma of prevention policies shape lawmaker perceptions of needle-exchange proposals. These perceptions influence how lawmakers judge the political feasibility of such proposals and are subject to manipulation by key lawmakers as they try and secure their preferred legislative outcome. In short, the decision to single out IDUs by prohibiting federal support of needle exchange rather than, for instance, singling them out through the federal support of needle exchange, is the result of problem definitions that privileged the drug problem over the AIDS problem, the fact that IDUs are politically powerless and viewed in highly negative terms, opposition to needle exchange among African-American leaders, and the fact that the prevention of HIV infections provides little benefit to elected lawmakers.

What's the Problem?   Before discussing the debate over problem definition between proponents and opponents, it is important to appreciate that the phrase "congressional needle-exchange proponent" generally has been an oxymoron. During the study period, only three members of Congress went on record as unequivocally supporting needle exchange, whereas nine members rose to denounce it. Because of the political difficulty involved in its support, most votes on the final proposal considered in a debate were landslides in favor of needle-exchange restrictions, with two Senate votes unanimously favoring funding restrictions. But these totals disguise the underlying conflict between those who have been adamantly opposed to needle exchange and those who prefer not to restrict NEPs, but are unwilling to take the political risks associated with clearly supporting needle exchange. These cautious supporters have omitted NEP restrictions from draft legislation, but their tactics have centered primarily on countering highly restrictive amendments with less restrictive ones. Throughout this analysis, references to "needle-exchange supporters" refer to those members of Congress who have opposed attempts to adopt or strengthen restrictions on federal funding of needle exchange.

The cautiousness of these supporters is made clear by contrasting them with needle-exchange opponents. As noted earlier, only three members took positions in favor of NEPs, and each did so only once. Two of these three declarations occurred in 1994 and 1995 after overwhelming scientific evidence supporting NEPs as an HIV prevention strategy. In contrast, the nine members who denounced NEPs repeated their position early and often. All told, over half of all the needle-exchange statements made on the floor of Congress contained a clear statement of personal opposition to NEPs. The relative timidity of needle-exchange proponents carried over into the battle to define the problem being considered by the legislature.

Murray Edelman (1977) observed, "Political and ideological debate consists very largely of efforts to win acceptance of a particular categorization of an issue in the face of competing efforts in behalf of a different one" (p. 25). Differing categorizations of issues carry with them different definitions of the problem at hand, and different problem definitions often imply very different solutions. In this debate, the policy aimed at IDUs was very much a function of the struggle over problem definitions. It is a struggle that opponents of needle exchange clearly won.

Although needle exchange was conceived of and promoted as an HIV prevention strategy, analysis of the rationales offered to support or oppose NEPs in Congress shows that this problem definition was highly unstable. As noted earlier, the public statements that members of Congress make are often designed to justify their preferred policy position and shape the terms of the debate by providing a causal story that links their policy position with a credible rationale. Throughout the 8 years of debate over needle exchange, most statements made on the floor of the House or Senate contained at least one rationale for their stated policy position; some contained none and others contained multiple rationales. In all, 112 rationales were identified and coded in the debate; supporters offered 55 rationales and opponents offered 57. A summary is presented in Fig. 26.2. Briefly stated, over three fourths of the rationales introduced in the needle-exchange debate were not focused on AIDS and AIDS prevention.

The patterns of policy rationales documented in Fig. 26.2 reveal quite a bit about the struggle over problem definition. Refining the analysis yields further clues to the success of the anti-needle-exchange coalition. Unlike would-be supporters, opponents have been consistent and unified in the justification of their opposition to NEPs. Drug-related rationales accounted for 70% ($n = 40$) of all the rationales offered to oppose needle exchange. These rationales argued that unless federal funding for sterile needle and syringe distribution were halted, the government would be "sending the wrong message" about drugs. Needle exchange, it was argued, would increase drug use, signal surrender in the war on drugs, lead to increased drug-related crime, and hamper efforts to bring drug addicts into treatment. The style of these rationales, and the consistency with which they were delivered, is illustrated by an excerpt from a speech by Senator Jesse Helms, which he delivered in a slightly modified form in 1988, 1989, and 1990. Skillfully defining the debate he declared,

> Make no mistake about it. The use of drugs is immoral; it is unlawful; it is killing thousands of Americans. We all know that. . . . Drug users, Mr. President, are not the only ones dying in the drug war. The shopkeeper, the bank teller, the pizza deliverer, the policeman, and thousands of others are dying at the hands of the drug addicts. Drug use is feeding the fires of crime. How many times have you picked up the paper or switched on your radio and read or heard about a violent crime linked to drug use? I think we cannot forget an innocent category of the drug war: the children who are being born right and left addicted to narcotics. . . . I think most people agree that distributing needles will not help these atrocities. (Helms, 1990, p. S6287)

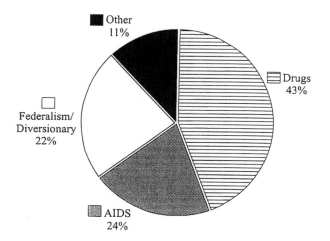

FIG. 26.2. Problem definitions in the congressional needle-exchange debate, 1988–1995. $N = 112$ policy rationales.

Supporting needle exchange was equated with supporting "atrocities," favoring infant drug addiction, and the murder of the Domino's driver. Although this—and all rhetoric—is "just" words, rationales such as these had the powerful effect of changing the terms of the debate. Needle exchange ceased to be about HIV prevention and was instead equated with advocating drugs and death. This rhetoric is representative of NEP opponents. Though many public health professionals and AIDS activists tend to discount such rhetoric, Helms and his allies offered a compelling, easily understood story that put needle-exchange supporters on the defensive. Comments made on the floor of Congress represented needle exchange as a surrender in the war on drugs:

> We are going to taxpayers across the country and say for the first time the Federal Government is not only opting out of the drug abuse business but we are going to go over to parks and give needles, we are going to go across America and give needles to those who abuse drugs. (Shaw, 1992, p. H3383)

> This is a shameful bill. . . . how do you convince a drug addict to come forward and get treatment when the Federal Government itself is handing needles out to them and paying for them? (Holloway, 1992, p. H3387)

> Federal funds should be used to get people off drugs, not to facilitate drug abuse. . . . if we're serious about reducing the spread of AIDS in this country, let's support programs that save lives, not destroy lives. (Ramstad, 1992, p. H3389)

The potency of such arguments can be seen as largely the result of the political inertia of the war on drugs, declared and waged by Presidents Reagan and Bush. During most of the past two decades, being perceived as being "soft on drugs" has been one of the most politically dangerous situations members of Congress can get themselves into; none were willing to take such a risk during the needle-exchange debate. Whether or not the drug war is an efficacious set of policies or merely a symbolic, rhetorical public relations campaign is a separate question (see Elwood, 1994, for a compelling statement of the latter position). It is clear, though, that the political momentum of the drug war was something members of Congress could not—or chose not to—resist. Supporters consistently declared that they too were opposed to any relaxation of the war on drugs, but the unavoidable and uncomfortable reality of NEPs is that they provide people with the equipment necessary to inject drugs.

Unwilling to question U.S. drug policy, supporters of needle exchange opposed funding restrictions with rationales that did not directly support NEPs. The strategy has been to try and change the subject of debate, providing sympathetic legislators with an electorally defensible rationale for not supporting funding restrictions. Typical are the remarks of Senator Ted Kennedy during consideration of the first of four amendments to attach funding restrictions to the AIDS title of the 1988 Health Omnibus Act. He argued, "We are not advocating, as sponsors of this legislation, free distribution of needles. We are saying let's not deny cities where AIDS is burning through some neighborhoods, the power to try new solutions" (Kennedy, 1988, p. S9006). Arguing that NEP funding restrictions unduly regulate the activities of state and local governments has been a favorite, and in some cases successful, rationale of needle-exchange supporters. By invoking federalism, those who are opposed to funding restrictions have argued that congressional restrictions on needle exchange are improper, rather than arguing that needle exchange is desirable or efficacious.

But whereas needle-exchange opponents have been able to "stay on message" with rhetoric about the drug war, its proponents have lacked a clear definition of the problem. The rationale that NEPs will prevent the spread of HIV has been the most common justification offered by supporters, but it has been clearly stated only 15 times, well under half the frequency with which drug-related rationales were offered to oppose needle exchange. In addition to federalism rationales, needle-exchange supporters have also fought funding restrictions with a tactic designed to move the issue out of Congress, calling for more needle-exchange studies, and urging that these decisions should be left up to public health experts, the surgeon general, or the president. These diversionary rationales have proved a somewhat successful strategy given the harsh restrictions on needle exchange that have often been proposed. Twice, for example, amendments were introduced in the Senate that would have halted funding for AIDS or general health and welfare spending to states and localities that used their own money to fund NEPs. In each case, these amendments were defeated through parliamentary maneuvering in which supporters proposed counteramendments with less restrictive language. Given the electoral danger of needle exchange, successful legislative coalitions have had to settle for more lenient restrictions on funding that have left the door for needle exchange open just a crack, most commonly granting the surgeon general the power to waive the restrictions.

As Fig. 26.2 shows, diversionary and federalism rationales together account for nearly a fourth of all policy rationales (22%, $n = 25$). Nearly all these rationales were offered by needle-exchange supporters, accounting for fully 40% ($n = 23$) of all the justifications offered to oppose funding restrictions. These rationales have essentially supported NEP activities without supporting needle exchange per se. This approach clearly seems to be employed by coalition leaders aiming to provide would-be supporters with political cover. With rationales arguing for placing needle-exchange decisions outside the Congress, votes against funding restrictions or in favor of restrictions with a surgeon general or presidential waiver make it difficult for voters to trace the policy effects of needle exchange back to members of Congress. The most obvious effect of NEPs is the one that most lawmakers seem eager to avoid, the distribution of needles and syringes to drug users. The efforts to separate needle-exchange decisions from congressional control thus helps to reduce the electoral liability members attach to the issue, making it difficult for would-be political opponents to "blame" members of Congress for "giving out needles to addicts."

Unpopular, Powerless People.   The trajectory of the needle-exchange debate has been set by the efforts of opponents to define the issue as one of drugs, not AIDS. The reasons for the shape of congressional policymaking becomes even clearer when one considers how IDUs have been linked to the issue and characterized by members of Congress. In general, lawmakers can justify singling out citizens only when they can be credibly linked to the problem at hand. Groups can be viewed as culpable for a problem, the innocent victim of a problem, or as completely decoupled from a problem. The link between a problem and a population is connected to the prevailing public image of group. This image, or social construction, coupled with the political power possessed by a subpopulation, likely influences if and how the group becomes the target of government policy (Schneider & Ingram, 1993).

In the needle-exchange case, the fate of IDUs was determined in large part by the group's relative powerlessness and negative public image. Simply put, IDUs, the targets of federal needle-exchange policy, have no political power. Because drug use is illegal and is a highly stigmatized activity, there are great disincentives for drug users to identify themselves and politically organize. To the extent that this has happened at all, it has been confined to advocates of illegal "soft drugs," the primary one being marijuana.[5] If the interests of IDUs are represented at all, they are represented by organizations of drug treatment professionals

---

[5]Note as well that recent debates over cannabis have often been divorced from general questions of drug use. Advocates of "hemp legalization" have argued that they are in favor of "industrial hemp," not drug use, whereas advocates of medicinal marijuana have also distanced themselves from the considerable population of non-medicinal-marijuana users. Missing from each set of advocates are individuals willing to identify themselves simply as "drug users."

on the one hand, and advocates of drug law reform such as the Drug Policy Foundation, on the other. Both sets of interest groups have significantly different ideas of what is in the best interests of IDUs. AIDS activist groups such as ACT UP and the National AIDS Brigade have taken up the cause of IDUs and have been instrumental in the formation and operation of local NEPs. But none of these groups has developed a serious national political presence advocating for IDUs.

In addition to the political power of group—or lack thereof in the case of IDUs—the prevailing public image of a subpopulation is likely to have an important influence on how lawmakers will treat it in public policies. The more potent and widely accepted the image, the more likely that lawmakers will craft policies and policy rationales that highlight these stereotypes. When, as has been the case with the federal needle-exchange debate, target populations are not visible participants in the policy process, rhetoric about targets is likely to be highly symbolic: "Perhaps the archetypical device for influencing political opinion is the evocation of beliefs about the problems, the intentions, or the moral condition of people whose very existence is problematic, but who become the benchmarks by which real people shape their political beliefs and perceptions. . . . Politicians' statements about unobservable people are often either impossible to verify or quite clearly invalid" (Edelman, 1977, p. 30). The prevailing public image of a population has an important influence on the shape of public policy, working to constrain the choices of electorally minded lawmakers.

The public image, or social construction, of populations does constrain lawmakers, but elected officials also work hard to promote images of groups that are favorable to their goals. They do this by carefully presenting populations in their rhetoric in ways which promote their preferred problem definitions and undermine those of their opponents. As Schneider and Ingram (1993) observed, "Public officials realize that target groups can be identified and described so as to influence the social construction. Hence, a great deal of the political maneuvering in the establishment of policy agendas and in the design of policy pertains to the specification of the target populations and the type of image that can be created for them" (p. 336).

In this debate, IDUs have been clearly linked to the issue in ways that fit with the problem definitions legislators hope to promote. Opponents, having worked to make drugs the issue, see IDUs primarily as the sources of the (seldom defined) drug problem and drug-related crime, and also as sufferers of drug addiction. In contrast, supporters see IDUs primarily as the sufferers of AIDS, and a source of the HIV/AIDS epidemic, in particular the source of infection among women and children. What is striking is the degree to which supporters of needle exchange have failed to characterize IDUs as sufferers of drug addiction, and opponents have failed to characterize them as sufferers of AIDS. Both sets of legislators are making reference to the same, diffuse population of drug users, but each side has taken care to characterize IDUs in a manner that supports their policy position.

No member of Congress, though, made the claim that IDUs, as citizens of the nation, should be entitled to HIV prevention. In all cases, IDUs have been characterized in terms that treat them as nameless, disenfranchised bodies. Whereas debate in the Congress is often filled with stories designed to personalized complex issues, nothing but general characterizations of IDUs were offered during the needle-exchange debate—and they were never flattering. Jesse Helms, for example, defended an amendment prohibiting funding of both NEPs and programs to distribute bleach in order to disinfect used syringes by asking, "How can we expect drug addicts to clean needles when they won't even clean themselves?" (Helms, 1989, p. S15792).

Supporters discussed IDUs in strictly statistical terms. To the extent that they were mentioned at all, it was typically to point out their link to "the spread of AIDS," or more specifically to the infections of their sexual partners and children. Senator Alan Cranston (1989), for example, argued against the Helms needle/bleach amendment by stressing, "The single most important thing we can do to prevent newborn babies from being born with this terrible disease is to reduce the spread of AIDS among IV drug users" (p. S15792). This line of argument is familiar given that care and treatment funding for people with AIDS was largely justified in Congress on the grounds that it would help "innocent victims" of AIDS such as children and hemophiliacs (Donovan, 1993). Yet more general debates about AIDS policy have typically involved the participation of activists representing gays and children with HIV/AIDS who, relative to IDUs, have build considerable political clout. For gay men in particular, negative stereotypes have been partly counteracted by effective political lobbying. In contrast, IDUs have found themselves in the double bind of having a highly negative public image and no significant political mobilization.

Needle Exchange and Race. An understanding of this debate—and all discussions of HIV/AIDS—must include the important role of race and ethnicity. Blacks, Hispanics, Asian/Pacific Islanders, and Native Americans account for just over half of all reported AIDS cases, a shocking enough statistic. Yet among AIDS cases traced directly or indirectly to injection drug use, non-Whites account for nearly 80% of the cases. Furthermore, 85% of pediatric AIDS cases traced to injection drug use have occurred among racial and ethnic minorities (CDC, 1996, author's calculations).

In the needle-exchange case, race considerably complicates the picture as both the biggest need for HIV prevention, and the strongest opposition to needle exchange, can be found among African Americans. The opposition to NEPs among African Americans has been intertwined with, but more complex than the opposition rooted in the war on drugs discourse. The opposition derives from the devastation caused by drug use in urban communities, the important role of opinion leader played by Black churches, and bitter memories of government programs gone awry such as the horrific Tuskegee Syphilis Study (Thomas & Quinn, 1993). For many, needle-exchange programs at best sounds like code for an inexpensive way for government to claim to be dealing with drug use, and at worst like a genocidal plot.

In 1988, 2 years after the first NEP came to the United States, Charles Rangel, Representative from New York City, a key Black leader, and chair of the House Select Committee on Narcotics Abuse and Control, blasted a New York City needle-exchange plan in the *Congressional Record* arguing, "The City Health Commissioner says the idea is to curb the spread of AIDS via intravenous drug use. But rather than seek logical approaches that utilize more and better treatment and rehabilitation our chief health expert is pursuing the kamikaze approach, which is to give addicts needles to help themselves do a better job of killing themselves" (p. H31158). Rangel's opposition to needle exchange has remained steadfast over the years, even as scientific evidence of its efficacy has mounted. This does not make him unique, as most congressional opponents of NEPs have been unmoved by positive study results, but Rangel's opposition is particularly notable given his status as a Black political leader. He has argued that needle-exchange funding would divert resources from treatment programs, and thus has viewed needle exchange as a pernicious attempt to avoid providing adequate treatment to drug users, many of whom are Black.

Thomas and Quinn (1993) have noted the unique importance of churches as gatekeepers to the Black community, and this fact proves to be another barrier to the acceptance of needle exchange. With nearly 70% of African-American adults belonging to churches, they are key sites of social and political organization. Black church leaders have been important, vocal opponents of needle exchange, often using "moral and genocidal arguments" (Thomas & Quinn, 1993, pp. 116–117). These arguments remain quite powerful. The memory of the

Tuskegee Study conducted by the U.S. Public Health Service from 1932 to 1972 has conditioned many African Americans to look at public health interventions with great suspicion (Thomas & Quinn, 1991). In the study, thousands of Black men in Alabama diagnosed with syphilis were monitored by public health researchers, but not provided with treatment or education about the disease and how to prevent its transmission. It is easy to see how such a memory could be evoked when confronted with proposals to distribute needles to drug users. As Thomas and Quinn (1993) noted, "The image of black injection-drug users reaching out for treatment only to receive clean needles from public health authorities provides additional wind for the genocide mill" (p. 111).

Although the racial dimension in the politics of needle exchange may seem clear, what is most striking is the way in which race has dropped out of its congressional discussion. Despite the fact that the HIV epidemic among IDUs is overwhelmingly an epidemic of poor, non-White, urban residents, this fact seldom made an appearance when members of Congress debated needle exchange. This may be a result of the generalized discomfort in the American political system about matters of race, or could also reflect a decision on the part of supporters to avoid associating the discussion of HIV/AIDS and needle exchange with a population that invokes more fear than compassion among wider (and whiter) electorate.

Since the beginning of the epidemic, one of the more obvious rhetorical strategies used by AIDS activists has been to generalize the threat of AIDS. This approach is understandable given the initial tendencies of health officials and the mass media to focus attention on groups at risk for HIV or perceived as "AIDS carriers," and has been instrumental in moving much of the national AIDS discourse toward a discussion of "risk behaviors." But this strategy has also obscured important features of the epidemic, in this case, the degree to which inner-city neighborhoods are bearing a disproportionate share of the epidemic's burden. Though it is true that risky behaviors are primarily responsible for HIV infection, there is also no denying that the risk of HIV infection is spread unevenly through the population. Although "AIDS does not discriminate" may make good public relations copy, it avoids the fact that people with AIDS have faces, and these faces are increasingly non-White.

The Prevention Dilemma.   One difficult thing for needle-exchange proponents to understand is the reluctance of political leaders to support a proposal that seems to have so much promise to save lives. How could political leaders be against such a thing? If they are truly concerned about solving problems, how could they oppose needle exchange? One way to answer this question is to argue that lawmakers simply are not concerned about solving real problems. Though this could easily be the subject of much debate, I suggest two alternate reasons that needle exchange has seemed less attractive to elected leaders than it has to public health researchers and activists. First, lawmakers have been conflicted over which problem needle exchange addresses. To the extent that fighting drug use was perceived as more important than fighting AIDS, needle exchange looks considerably less attractive. The second reason is less obvious: Prevention programs create a dilemma for lawmakers.

Let us assume that elected lawmakers are genuinely interested in solving problems.[6] If this is the case, they must still keep their eye on the next election if they are to have the chance to enact and defend their legislative agenda. Lawmakers, then, are drawn to problems that either they are genuinely interested in, or they expect might be an issue at election time.

---

[6]This assumption might strike casual observers of politics as naive, but it is well documented in the political science literature on Congress (see, e.g., Arnold, 1990; Fenno, 1973, 1978; Kingdon, 1989). Lawmakers are generally regarded as having multiple motivations for their actions, an important one being the wish to adopt their vision of "good policy." The rub is that although a given member may be intensely interested in a given policy area, she must convince other, less interested members that there are electoral benefits—or at least minimal risks—associated with her preferred policy position.

They thus try to solve, or appear to solve, problems they think will benefit their reelections. Although this may be a harsh statement, its roots are fundamentally democratic. *Put differently, elected leaders are responsive to things they think the electorate cares about, or will care about come election time.*

Proposals aimed at preventing problems create a dilemma for lawmakers for two reasons. To begin with, proposals aimed at preventing problems typically involve behavior-changing interventions. In the case of preventing children from smoking or using illegal drugs, the intervention is typically education. Because problems are prevented through a causal chain of (a) intervention, (b) behavior change, (c) problem prevention, it is not certain that the goal—problem prevention—will be achieved. Thus it is important that the early-order effects of a policy, in this example the provision of antidrug or antismoking education, be something a lawmaker can take credit for, or at least cannot be attacked for supporting. Consider needle-exchange proposals in this context. If the HIV prevention goals of needle exchange are not achieved or noticed, lawmakers who advocated the policy would be in the difficult spot of having only supported the distribution of needles to drug injectors.

The second dilemma associated with prevention policies compounds this first problem: Successful prevention policies create nonevents. By preventing a problem from occurring at all, lawmakers have nothing for which to take credit. In the case of HIV/AIDS, elected leaders have moved far more aggressively to fund biomedical research to find treatments and the illusive "cure" than they have to fund and implement HIV prevention programs. The political risk associated with "helping find a cure" has been minimal, whereas the potential electoral benefits—regardless of whether a cure is found—are many. In contrast, HIV prevention whether it be needle exchange, condom distribution to teens, or explicit educational materials aimed at gay men have constituted contentious debates about HIV/AIDS policy in the United States. Each of these proposals was and is arguably an effective prevention strategy. If successful, the outcome of prevention efforts would be fewer incidence of HIV infections. These noninfections likely would not make the news or be the basis of a reelection speech, whereas interventions—needles, condoms, explicit materials—would remain visible and controversial.

Prevention programs become even more unattractive to lawmakers when they are aimed at unpopular people, particularly people without resources to create electoral pressure. With gays and drug users there remains public sentiment that they are responsible for their HIV infections; thus prevention programs come under fire for "encouraging" activities that many think should be stopped. Members of Congress want to claim credit for positive developments in society and politics. Although successful prevention programs may produce such developments, these outcomes may be masked by the controversy surrounding the behavior-changing intervention. Lawmakers may rush to bemoan the tragedy of HIV-infected infants, and they may understand that this is primarily a result of HIV-infected, drug-injecting parents, but it is far more politically palatable to authorize funds to care for these sick infants than it is to authorize fewer funds to distribute clean needles to their unpopular, politically powerless parents.

DISCUSSION

This chapter has explained the political logic that has shaped federal needle-exchange policy in the United States. One theme that I have developed is that whereas congressional opponents of needle exchange have succeeded in securing bans on federal NEP funding, other lawmakers have worked to dilute these restrictions and thwart more severe proposals. From the perspective of needle-exchange activists, the glass is certainly not half full, but neither is it empty. The frustration that many proponents of needle exchange have about federal policy is that the current policy just seems so illogical: Needle exchange would save lives; how can lawmakers not support this? But as I have argued, there is a wide gulf between proposals that are effective and those that are feasible. This does not necessarily mean that needle exchange will always be political infeasible, but so far this has proved to be the case.

Someone who has closely followed the evolution of needle exchange in the United States is likely struck by the difference between the responses of local governments and that of the federal government. City, county, and, occasionally, state governments have been far more willing to embrace needle exchange than our representatives in Congress. This suggests that it is not simply needle exchange that is infeasible, but needle exchange in the context of the national political system. At the local level, needle exchange has typically been brought about by political insurgents (Kirp & Bayer, 1993). Local governments typically have supported NEPs only after committed activists have put themselves on the line to initiate such programs. Whereas local political institutions have often been responsive to such grassroots activity, federal lawmakers operate in a much more complex environment.

This added complexity is illustrated in part by the many issues that members of Congress must juggle and, in the needle-exchange case, by the primacy of the federal war on drugs. Perhaps the most striking differences, though, are differences in the communications context of national politics. For well over a decade observers have noted the appearance and pre-eminence of "sound-bite politics," political campaigns driven by pithy phrases and potent symbols. Although the reduction of complex political decisions to stark portrayals of right and wrong, good and evil is not new, what is new is the saturated media environment in which such politics takes place. The result is that elected lawmakers appear increasingly reluctant to support policies that hold the potential to become the basis of a future opponent's negative attack ad. Would-be supporters of needle exchange must be mindful of attacks that declare: "Congressman Jones voted to use your tax dollars to give drug addicts free needles. Does this sound like America's priorities? Send a message against drugs. Vote Smith for Congress." Deflecting such an attack is harder than avoiding it all together, even if the avoidance worsens a problem everyone agrees must be solved.

Congress is not alone in being flummoxed by the needle-exchange issue. At this writing, the politics of needle exchange in the executive branch continues to be marked by notable contradictions. The latest "czar" appointed to lead the war on drugs—a bona fide general—has reaffirmed the Clinton administration's opposition to needle exchange (Gallman, 1996). Yet, the National Institutes of Health (NIH) has for the first time published a consensus statement calling for a lifting of the federal funding ban and the implementation of federally funded NEPs (NIH, 1997). The administration's response to the consensus statement has been to call for "study" of the issue; whether this is encouraging or discouraging depends very much on what one expects from our complex, democratic political system.

If the needle-exchange debate reveals larger lessons about the politics of AIDS and our political system more generally, it is that political decision making adheres to a logic quite different from that of a simple, single-issue, problem-solving logic. It also reminds us that people who are unpopular and lack political power—drug users, the poor, residents of the inner city—are unlikely to be taken care of by government. In this case, the lack of care stokes the fires of a horrible tragedy, and to date only a handful interest groups with a national profile have championed the plight of IDUs, their sexual partners, and children. But as I have stressed throughout this chapter, there is little about policymaking that is black or white. Congressional supporters of needle exchange, timid though they may be, have resisted more severe restrictions on needle exchange and have opened up opportunities for federally funded needle-exchange studies. Although such incremental steps may seem useless to some in the face of the injection drug–fueled HIV epidemic, successful change will occur only at the margins of federal policymaking, unless some event or heretofore undiscovered political tactic serves to significantly shift the current political context.

REFERENCES

Arnold, D. (1990). *The logic of congressional action.* New Haven, CT: Yale University Press.
Bayer, R., & Kirp, D. L. (1992). The United States: At the center of the storm. In D. L. Kirp & R. Bayer (Eds.), *AIDS in the industrialized democracies: Passions, politics, and policies* (pp. 7–48). New Brunswick, NJ: Rutgers University Press.
Centers for Disease Control and Prevention. (1995a). *HIV/AIDS Surveillance Report, 7*(2).
Centers for Disease Control and Prevention. (1995b, September 22). *Morbidity and Mortality Weekly Report, 44*(37), 684–68, 691.
Centers for Disease Control and Prevention. (1996). *HIV/AIDS Surveillance Report, 8*(1).
Cranston, A. (1989, November 16). *Congressional Record,* p. S15792.
Des Jarlais, D. C., Friedman, S. R., Sotheran, J. L., Wenston, J., Marmor, M., Yancovitz, S. R., Frank, B., Beatrice, S., & Mildvan, D. (1994). Continuity and change within an HIV epidemic: Injecting drug users in New York City, 1984 through 1992. *JAMA, 271,* 121–127.
Des Jarlais, D. C., Paone, D., Friedman, S. R., Peyser, N., & Newman, R. G.. (1995). Regulating controversial programs for unpopular people: Methadone maintenance and syringe exchange programs. *American Journal of Public Health, 85,* 1577–1584.
Donovan, M. C. (1993). The social constructions of people with AIDS: Target populations and United States policy, 1981–90. *Policy Studies Review, 12,* 3–29.
Edelman, M. J. (1977). *Political language: Words that succeed and policies that fail.* New York: Academic Press.
Elwood, W. N. (1994). *Rhetoric and the war on drugs; The triumphs and tragedies of public relations.* Westport, CT: Praeger.
Fenno, R. F., Jr. (1973). *Congressmen in committees.* Boston: Little, Brown.
Fenno, R. F., Jr. (1978). *Home style: House members in their districts.* New York: HarperCollins.
Forbes, A. (1993). Crack cocaine and HIV: How national drug-addiction-treatment deficits fan the pandemic's flames. *AIDS & Public Policy Journal, 8,* 44–52.
Gallman, V. (1996, May 13). U.S. drug chief dislikes needle-exchange tactic. *Seattle Times,* p. A4.
General Accounting Office. (1993). *Needle exchange programs: Research suggests promise as an AIDS prevention strategy.* Washington, DC: Author.
Hantman, J. A. (1995). Research on needle exchange: Redefining the agenda. *Bulletin of the New York Academy of Medicine, 72,* 397–412.
Helms, J. (1989, November 16). *Congressional Record,* p. S15792.
Helms, J. (1990, May 16). *Congressional Record,* p. S6287.
Holloway, C. (1992, May 19). *Congressional Record,* p. H3387.
Holmberg, S. D. (1996). The estimated prevalence and incidence of HIV in 96 large US metropolitan areas. *American Journal of Public Health, 86,* 642–654.
Hubbard, R. L., Marsden, M. E., Rachal, J. V., Harwood, H., Cavanaugh, E., & Ginzburg, H. (1989). *Drug abuse treatment: A national study of effectiveness.* Chapel Hill: University of North Carolina Press.
Institute of Medicine. (1986). *Confronting AIDS: Directions for public health, health care, and research.* Washington, DC: National Academy Press.
Kennedy, T. (1988, April 27). *Congressional Record,* p. S9006.
Kingdon, J. W. (1989). *Congressmen's voting decisions* (3rd ed.). Ann Arbor: University of Michigan Press.
Kirp, D. L. (1994). After the band stopped playing. *Nation, 259,* 14–18.
Kirp, D. L., & Bayer, R. (1993). The politics. In J. Stryker & M. Smith (Eds.), *Dimensions of HIV prevention: Needle exchange* (pp. 77–97). Menlo Park, CA: The Henry J. Kaiser Family Foundation.
Lurie, P. (1995). When science and politics collide: The federal response to needle-exchange programs. *Bulletin of the New York Academy of Medicine, 72,* 380–396.
Lurie, P., Reingold, A., Bowser, B., Chen, D., Foley, J., Guydish, J., Kahn, J. G., Lane, S., & Sorensen, J. (1993). *The public health impacts of needle exchange programs in the United States and abroad.* San Francisco: University of California Press.
National Commission on AIDS. (1991). *America living with AIDS.* Washington, DC: Author.

National Institutes of Health. (1997, February 14). Interventions to prevent HIV risk behaviors: Consensus development statement [Draft]. Retrieved March 30, 1997 from the World Wide Web: http://odp.od.nih.gov/consensus/

Normand, J., Vlahov, D., & Moses, L. (1995). *Preventing HIV transmission: The role of sterile needles and bleach.* Washington, DC: National Academy Press.

Paone, D., Des Jarlais, D. C., Gangloff, R., Milliken, J., & Friedman, S. R. (1995). Syringe exchange: HIV prevention, key findings, and future directions. *International Journal of the Addictions, 30,* 1647–1683.

Ramstad, J. (1992, May 19). *Congressional Record,* p. H3389.

Rangel, C. (1988, October 14). *Congressional Record,* p. H31158.

Schneider, A., & Ingram, H. (1993). Social construction of target populations: Implications for politics and policy. *American Political Science Review, 87,* 334–347.

Sharp, E. B. (1994). *The dilemma of drug policy in the United States.* New York: HarperCollins.

Shaw, E. C. (1992, May 19). *Congressional Record,* p. H3383.

Thomas, S. B., & Quinn, S. C. (1991). The Tuskegee syphilis study, 1932 to 1972: Implications for HIV education and AIDS risk reduction programs in the Black community. *American Journal of Public Health, 81,* 642–654.

Thomas, S. B., & Quinn, S. C. (1993). Understanding the attitudes of Black Americans. In J. Stryker & M. Smith (Eds.), *Dimensions of HIV prevention: Needle exchange* (pp. 99–128). Menlo Park, CA: The Henry J. Kaiser Family Foundation.

Valleroy, L. A., Weinstein, B., Jones, T. S., Groseclose, S. L., Rolfs, R. T., & Kassler, W. J. (1995). Impact of increased legal access to needles and syringes on community pharmacies' needle and syringe sales—Connecticut, 1992–1993. *Journal of Acquired Immune Deficiency Syndromes and Human Retrovirology, 10,* 73–81.

Ethical Choices Regarding Noncompliance: Prescribing Protease Inhibitors for HIV-Infected Female Adolescents

Kathryn Greene
Barbara Cassidy
East Carolina University

Since the advent of the HIV/AIDS epidemic, much effort has been taken to develop persuasive campaigns to promote, for example, safer-sex behavior through increased condom use. Specific messages were developed to persuade HIV-infected persons to: Use condoms, inform sexual partners about their infection, use clean needles, or do not share needles. One missing component has been an analysis of which persuasive strategies are most effective with HIV-infected persons. Given new changes in treatment of HIV and AIDS, understanding how to get HIV-infected persons to comply with health recommendations becomes even more crucial.

At the XI International Conference on AIDS (Vancouver, 1996), scientists met to discuss new treatment strategies and medical regimens for HIV-infected persons. For the first time there was some optimism about combating HIV/AIDS. This unprecedented optimism has come from the new antiretroviral therapies, drug combinations commonly called "cocktails." These cocktail therapies do, however, have associated difficulties. The treatment is expensive and not widespread at present. Side effects for some patients are barely tolerable (e.g., nausea, diarrhea). The antiretroviral therapies require individuals to adhere to strict treatment protocols; noncompliance can lead to the development of drug-resistant strains of HIV.

The advances in HIV/AIDS treatment, however, do not come without controversy. Many affected groups have not been included in new drug protocol studies, just as women were excluded from earlier drug trials (Bartlett, McGovern, Merkatz, Marte, & Mastroianni, 1997). Compliance with treatments (and HIV risk reduction behaviors) will continue to be crucial to combat the transmission of HIV. What will be needed, besides interventions to change behaviors, is a series of campaigns/strategies to maintain and reinforce healthy behaviors. This chapter examines two such behaviors, adolescents' adherence to medication regimens for themselves and for an HIV-exposed infant.

The Centers for Disease Control and Prevention (CDC) reported 3,041 adolescents ages 13–19 have been diagnosed with HIV infection and 2,574 adolescents ages 13–19 have been diagnosed with AIDS through June 1996. In people aged 20–24, 20,228 cases of HIV and 19,997 cases of AIDS were reported. Given that a median incubation period from HIV infection to the development of AIDS in adults is nearly 10 years, many of these individuals likely were infected as teens. HIV/AIDS is the sixth leading cause of death for adolescents and young adults, ages 15–24. AIDS and other HIV-related illnesses have been the fourth leading cause of death among U.S. women aged 25–44 since 1992. AIDS, however, was the leading cause of death for African-American women in 1993, and the AIDS-related death rate for African-American women is nine times as high as for White women (CDC, 1996).

Adolescents with HIV/AIDS are a particularly important group because they are both unrecognized and difficult to reach. Little information is available at present about such adolescents, even less about how to gain compliance with treatment regimens for adolescents, and almost nothing about how to gain compliance with new treatments for HIV/AIDS. The period of adolescence has long been recognized as a likely period of infection. To this point, however, many persons infected as teens were not aware of their infection, and did not receive treatment as adolescents. Today there is a group of adolescents who are being treated for HIV infection. The identification of these adolescents is likely a result of increased HIV testing along with public health recommendations for the testing of pregnant women.

This study includes examination of a subpopulation of adolescents, African-American adolescent women infected with HIV. Teens with HIV/AIDS are likely to be poor and African American (Wortley, Chu, & Berkelman, 1997). Teen women are an especially interesting case because many are or have been pregnant, making it possible to study and compare compliance with treatment regimens for self versus other (care for baby) in relation to HIV/AIDS. The case has been made that socioeconomic status has affected adolescents' visibility as a risk group (King, 1996; Mastroianni, Faden, & Federman, 1994). In this chapter, we explore recommendations for compliance gaining for a particular group of adolescents after presenting case histories of HIV-infected adolescent mothers. First, we review compliance gaining in health care settings and research on compliance gaining.

COMPLIANCE GAINING IN HEALTH SETTINGS

Although communication is a crucial part of health care interactions, Wyatt's (1991) review found that less than 1% of medical literature focused on physician–patient relationships. There is a growing concern about what constitutes the best health compliance-gaining strategies and what verbal and nonverbal strategies physicians use to gain compliance (M. H. Burgoon & J. K. Burgoon, 1990). In the medical context, compliance is viewed as adherence to medical advice or treatment regimens (Stone, 1979), an outcome rather than a process (Charney, 1972). Alternatively, Friedman and DiMatteo (1979) argued for the term *cooperation* rather than *compliance gaining* to focus on the transactional nature of the physician–patient interaction. Physicians often blame patients for noncompliance (see Thompson, 1994), but this will not assist in developing effective strategies to deal with patient noncompliance.

Few other interpersonal contexts are characterized by the urgency of the health care interaction. The medical situation sets up a unique context for compliance gaining. Health care interactions are generally voluntary, patient focused, with varied effects of noncompliance (M. H. Burgoon & J. K. Burgoon, 1990). Although this set of circumstances should create a situation where expected and actual compliance is high (M. H. Burgoon & J. K. Burgoon, 1990), this is not the case. Noncompliance may be the most significant problem in medicine (Eraker, Kirscht, & Becker, 1984). Estimated noncompliance rates generally range from 40% to 60%, studied with behaviors such as appointment keeping and adherence to drug regimens. These surprisingly high levels of noncompliance create health hazards, waste resources, and create frustration (see Thompson, 1994). Stone (1979) phrased this problem more vividly: "Why would someone who has gone to the trouble and expense of seeking out a physician, of undergoing arduous or uncomfortable tests and other diagnostic procedures, and of purchasing drugs and devices on the advice of the physician, then fail to follow the recommendations?" (p. 34). Unfortunately, this lack of compliance is not abnormal, and may be even higher for HIV/AIDS, as patients to this time believed there was no known treatment.

With HIV/AIDS, it is difficult to assess what might serve as effective compliance-gaining strategies from the perspective of the physician or health care worker. Most research has focused on verbal (rather than nonverbal) compliance-gaining strategies. M. H. Burgoon and J. K. Burgoon (1990) indicated severity of illness and past noncompliance should be best addressed by the most aggressive verbal compliance-gaining strategies (e.g., threat). Doctors, unfortunately, overrely on positive expertise strategies and do not use positive or reinforcing strategies (M. Burgoon et al., 1990). Clearly, HIV/AIDS classifies high on severity of illness, but because it has been previously discussed only as a terminal illness, patients perceive themselves as having "nothing to lose," and thus do not comply with their treatment (Rotello, 1995).

Compliance is often studied as an outcome, a special case of unidirectional communication where the physician holds most of the power and resources (cf. Penchansky, 1986). Unfortunately, little is known about the specific strategies health care workers use to gain patient compliance. M. Burgoon and colleagues (1990) stated, "The physician's right to seek the patient's compliance flows naturally from the physician's role and expert power in the situation" (p. 16). Results show physicians report predominant use of expertise strategies but will be verbally aggressive if necessary. Physicians often use liking (acting friendly), promise (offering a reward, such as next visit free), and pregiving (providing free medication samples).

Compliance-Gaining Research. The most widely accepted definition of compliance-gaining message strategies was presented by Seibold, Cantrill, and Meyers (1985): "anticipated and actual discourse patterns performed in the service of a personal or interpersonal agenda" (p. 556). This emphasis on messages and message planning is clear, although research has recognized the significance of patients' perceptions of compliance-gaining messages. The dominant strategy typology includes 16 strategies developed from exchange and power theories by Marwell and Schmitt (1967a, 1967b), later tested by Miller, Boster, Roloff, and Seibold (1977). Although typologies of compliance gaining have been critiqued (see Miller, 1983; Seibold et al., 1985), the 16-strategy system is still widely used. The major criticisms focus on lack of exhaustiveness and mutual exclusiveness. Table 27.1 reproduces the typology and includes an example of each strategy relevant for the present study, compliance gaining with HIV/AIDS drug treatment regimens.

Table 27.1 provides descriptions of the range of 16 compliance-gaining strategies, many positive/negative versions of the same strategy, and examples of compliance-gaining attempts by health care workers/physicians for drug regimen compliance of an HIV-infected patient. A second example is also included for each strategy, targeting compliance with treatment for an HIV-exposed infant. The actor in these examples is the source of the compliance-gaining attempts (the physician, health care worker, or social worker), and the recipient is the HIV-infected patient/client. The illustrations provide examples of the range of choices available and point out the importance of not overusing promise and positive expertise strategies.

One additional critique of compliance-gaining research has been the absence of studies of series of persuasive attempts or sequential messages; surely compliance attempts are not singular events and are likely related to one another. If one tactic works or fails, this would affect choice of subsequent strategies. In the case studies presented, it is possible to see how some sequential message strategies are enacted. Compliance-gaining attempts are not made in isolation; rather they are progressive (become more harsh, e.g., threat of reporting to social services as a last option). Health care workers could use liking and pregiving to establish

TABLE 27.1
HIV/AIDS Examples of Marwell and Schmitt's 16 Compliance-Gaining Strategies

Category	Description
(1) *Promise*	If you comply with my request, I will reward you in some way.
Ex. Self:	"If you take your AZT appropriately, the doctor will prescribe a protease inhibitor."
Ex. Other:	"If you give your baby AZT, the doctor may prescribe a protease inhibitor for you."
(2) *Threat*	If you do not comply with my request, I will punish you in some way.
Ex. Self:	"If you do not take your AZT, the doctor will not prescribe protease inhibitors for you."
Ex. Other:	"If you do not give the baby her medicine, I will report you to child protective services."
(3) *Expertise (Pos.)*	If you comply with my request, you will be rewarded because of the nature of things.
Ex. Self:	"If you take your medicine, your CD4 count will improve and you will feel better."
Ex. Other:	"If you take the AZT, your baby has a better chance of not being infected with HIV."
(4) *Expertise (Neg.)*	If you do not comply, you will be punished because of the nature of things.
Ex. Self:	"If you do not take the medication, you will develop an opportunistic infection sooner."
Ex. Other:	"If you do not take AZT, your baby might contract HIV."
(5) *Liking*	Actor is friendly and helpful to get target in good frame of mind so she or he will comply.
Ex. Self:	"Social worker makes home visits to build rapport with client."
Ex. Other:	"Social worker makes home visits to build rapport with client and child."
(6) *Pre-Giving*	Actor rewards target before requesting compliance.
Ex. Self:	"Give client free phone card, then ask her to take medication as directed."
Ex. Other:	"Give client free baby products, then ask her to give baby medication as directed."
(7) *Aversion Stimulation*	Actor punishes target, making stopping contingent on compliance.
Ex. Self:	"Social worker calls and visits repeatedly until client takes medication."
Ex. Other:	"Child protective services investigates and monitors medication given to baby."
(8) *Debt*	You owe me compliance because of what I did for you in the past.
Ex. Self:	"I helped you get money for medication, so you should take your medication."
Ex. Other:	"I helped get you food for your baby, so you should give baby the medication."
(9) *Moral Appeal*	Say to target, you are immoral if you do not comply with my request.
Ex. Self:	"Taking your medication is the right thing to do."
Ex. Other:	"It would be immoral not to protect your baby from HIV."
(10) *Self-Feeling (Pos.)*	Say to target, you will feel better about yourself if you comply.
Ex. Self:	"You will feel proud of yourself if you take your medication."
Ex. Other:	"You will feel proud of yourself to know that you are helping protect your baby."
(11) *Self-Feeling (Neg.)*[a]	Say to target, you will feel worse about yourself if you do not comply.
Ex. Self:	"You will feel ashamed if you don't take your medication."
Ex. Other:	"You will feel ashamed if you don't give your baby the medication."
(12) *Altercasting (Pos.)*	Say to target, a person with "good" qualities would comply.
Ex. Self:	"You are a very responsible and mature person if you take your medication."
Ex. Other:	"You are a really responsible mother for giving your baby medication to protect him/her."
(13) *Altercasting (Neg.)*[a]	Say to target, only a person with "bad" qualities would not comply.
Ex. Self:	"Only an immature person would not take the medication."
Ex. Other:	"Only an uncaring person would put a baby at risk by not giving medication."
(14) *Altruism*	Say to target, I need your help very badly, so take your medication for me/parents.
Ex. Self:	"It will really help your parents if you take your medication."
Ex. Other:	"Your parents care about their grandchild, so give the medication to help ease their worries."
(15) *Esteem (Pos.)*	Say to target, people you value will think better of you if you comply.
Ex. Self:	"Your family will be proud of you if you take your medication."
Ex. Other:	"Your family will be proud of you if you give your baby the medication."
(16) *Esteem (Neg.)*	Say to target, people you value will think worse of you if you do not comply.
Ex. Self:	"Your family will be disappointed if you don't take your medication."
Ex. Other:	"Your family will be disappointed if you don't give the baby the medication."

[a]These strategies might not be used by social workers or other health care professionals because they could violate the principles of the profession (e.g., "unconditional positive regard").

rapport before asking for the crucial target request, taking their medication as directed. It might also be effective to first gain agreement with smaller requests (Freedman & Fraser, 1966), such as maintaining appointments or filling the prescription, before health care workers target the goal of take every single dose of medication as directed.

COMPLIANCE GAINING IN ADOLESCENCE: THE EFFECTS OF EGOCENTRISM

Compliance gaining of adolescents requires consideration of their special characteristics. Illegal drug use, drunk driving, and sex without contraception and/or with multiple partners occurs frequently among adolescents. Adolescents' own risk-taking behavior is one of the greatest threats to their development. One phenomenon, egocentrism, helps explain why this group is so difficult to reach.

In adolescence, lack of experience may lead to errors in judgment when they make decisions about risk behaviors. An egocentrism perspective emphasizes a specific type of error in judgment that results from a sense of uniqueness or specialness. According to egocentrism, teens focus their attention on their own thoughts, and they assume that others must also be thinking about them. That the assumption is irrational is not apparent to the adolescent. The adolescent is also "blinded" by feelings of invulnerability that accompany feelings of uniqueness. Egocentrism helps explain how adolescents could ignore health messages or compliance-gaining attempts because they feel the messages are not directed toward them, even when, in fact, they are the audience. Egocentrism is, very generally, an overall focus on self, and it refers to a lack of differentiation in subject–object interaction (Piaget, 1929, 1958). Elkind (1967, 1978) argued egocentrism emerges at each of the transitions between stages of cognitive development. For young adolescents, the egocentrism of interest occurs during the transition from concrete to formal operational thought. Elkind (1967) proposed the emergence of two expressions of egocentrism in this transition from concrete to formal operations in adolescence: (a) imaginary audience, where an inability to differentiate the object of thought leads to thinking that others are preoccupied with you because you are preoccupied with yourself, and (b) personal fable, where new ability to think about thoughts leads to a fascination with one's own thoughts, which are surely different from the thoughts of others, and thus a belief in one's uniqueness and invulnerability.

Adolescents have been found to be highest in both imaginary audience and personal fable in the eighth and ninth grades, with a steady decline with age and consolidation of formal operations (Elkind & Bowen, 1979; Enright, Shukla, & Lapsley, 1980). There are also consistent gender differences in egocentrism, with girls scoring higher on imaginary audience measures (e.g., Elkind & Bowen, 1979; Enright et al., 1980; Greene, Rubin, & Hale, 1995; Lapsley, FitzGerald, Rice, & Jackson, 1989) and boys scoring higher on personal fable measures (e.g., Greene et al., 1995; Lapsley et al., 1989). The age effects are significant when examining HIV/AIDS because the height of egocentrism (Grades 8/9) coincides with probable period of infection for many HIV-infected adolescents (most in the present study, particularly). It is possible that egocentrism (especially personal fable) contributed to decisions not to take precautions to avoid HIV infection or pregnancy. In fact, Greene and colleagues reported adolescents higher in personal fable had more negative attitudes toward behavior that could put them at risk for contracting HIV/AIDS. The gender effects are interesting as well. If women are more susceptible to imaginary audience, then it should be easier to persuade them based on what others are doing/thinking (see recommendations section for normative focus).

NEW HIV / AIDS TREATMENTS: PROTEASE INHIBITORS

Standards of treatment for people infected with the AIDS virus are changing rapidly as new studies are reported. Previously, those treated with only one antiretroviral drug, such as AZT, improved initially, but the virus eventually reproduced a version of itself that was resistant to the treatment. This resulted in decreased t-cell counts and increased susceptibility to opportunistic infections. ACTG 175 and the Delta Study showed that combining AZT with another antiretroviral drug such as ddI or ddC prevents the virus from mutating as rapidly (Treatment Review [TR] #20, 1995). In late 1995, the Food and Drug Administration approved the use of 3TC (lamivudine) in conjunction with AZT.

The newest addition to this combination therapy is a group of drugs called protease inhibitors. Protease inhibitors block a part of HIV called protease enzymes, resulting in HIV making copies of itself that cannot infect new cells. Subsequent to the presentation of new studies at the International Conference on AIDS in Vancouver (1996), physicians have been prescribing what has come to be known as cocktails. These triple combination treatments include drugs such as AZT, ddI, d4T and 3TC, along with a protease inhibitor (e.g., Crixivan, Norvir, Ritonavir). Most of the people in one study combining AZT, 3TC, and indinavir (Crixivan) maintained very low or undetectable levels of HIV for nearly a year (TR #22, 1996). Although the initial data are promising, these studies are only entering their second year of tracking, so long-term benefits and risks cannot yet be assessed. Nevertheless, "Researchers are issuing strong warnings that people should try and avoid the development of drug resistance" (TR #22, 1996, p. 2)

None of these trials, however, have included women in sufficient numbers to adequately assess the effects of protease inhibitors on the female body (Bartlett et al., 1997). The recommended dosage, thus, is based on effectiveness in men. As one HIV-infected woman observed, "I don't have the muscle mass that a man does. I think I am taking too high a dose of Crixivan, but no one will listen to me." Inclusion in clinical trials are often based on rigid compliance measures. The necessity for repeated medical visits may hinder a woman's involvement if she is the sole provider of young child(ren). Women are also, at times, excluded because of the possible risk to potential children, but no such concern is expressed in regard to potential genetic damage in men (Bartlett et al., 1997). Moreover, adolescents are not included in clinical trials and often are grouped under the heading "adolescents and adults." Thus, nothing is known about the effects of these cocktail drugs on bodies that are still developing. Anecdotal evidence shows that physicians have begun prescribing protease inhibitors for children, adjusting dosage based on body weight. Adolescents, however, are treated with the same dosage as adults, a questionable practice given the present limited data (King, 1996).

Compliance Problems With New HIV / AIDS Treatments

With these new drugs, compliance with treatment regimens becomes even more crucial. The risk of drug resistance is a major concern with protease inhibitors. If the virus becomes resistant to one of the drugs such as AZT, there are other similar drugs that can be tried. It is believed, however, that if the virus develops resistance to one protease inhibitor, it will be resistant to all. Persons enrolled in early studies of indinavir (Crixivan) were given a lower dose than the one now recommended and subsequently developed resistance to the drug (*Indinavir Fact Sheet*, 1996). All data indicate that it is crucial to take the protease inhibitor as prescribed to keep a constant level in the body, to reduce the possibility of the HIV becoming resistant.

All of the currently prescribed protease inhibitors have side effects, which may contribute to noncompliance. Indinavir (Crixivan) should be taken with lots of water on an empty stomach to avoid dehydration and kidney stones (*Indinavir Fact Sheet*, 1996). With ritonavir (Norvir), side effects included nausea, vomiting, weakness, and diarrhea (*Ritonavir Fact Sheet*, 1996), and should be taken with a full high-protein, high-fat meal (TR #22, 1996)—which many patients report is difficult to consume first thing in the morning. The third protease inhibitor approved is saquinavir (Invirase). This drug produced few side effects; however, studies have shown that very high doses are required for the body to absorb Saquinavir (*Saquinavir Fact Sheet*, 1996). These side effects have a strong association with noncompliance, as patients report many of these problems as reasons why they fail to take medication as directed.

Infectious disease physicians who were interviewed all agreed they face ethical dilemmas when considering prescribing protease inhibitors. One physician (a primary investigator in an AIDS clinical trials unit) responded, "It is definitely an ethical issue. If I prescribe a protease inhibitor and the patient does not take it as prescribed, her virus becomes resistant. If she then transmits that virus, we have an entirely new generation of HIV which is resistant to the one drug that has shown promise of eradicating it." Other health professionals repeated this sentiment. "We don't play. If you are not going to be compliant, you don't get protease inhibitors," stated a physician's assistant in an adult infectious disease clinic. Making this kind of determination requires consistent monitoring of compliance with previous treatments, including the use of patient-completed daily medication calendars, counting the number of pills left in the bottle, and/or telephone calls to pharmacies to determine when prescriptions have been filled and refilled, and how much was dispensed. All of these indicators are considered before deciding to prescribe protease inhibitors.

It is difficult to estimate all the effects of refusal to prescribe the protease inhibitors. The use of threat may increase compliance, but there are other views of effects of choices not to prescribe cocktails to noncompliant patients. For example, physicians may perceive homeless and drug-addicted people as high-risk groups for noncompliance and not prescribe new cocktail treatments for them. Nevertheless, these people are aware of the benefits from the new treatments and may find ways to acquire the medication, including the use of the black market. Those who "acquire their treatment via the black market, would be treating themselves without any supervision, increasing the threat of poor compliance and drug resistance" (Baxter, 1997, p. A35). Although such developments are only speculative at present, it is important to consider consequences of not prescribing these drugs.

Another ethical issue with adolescents' noncompliance is that of possible conception. To date, no studies have been published or released regarding the effects of protease inhibitors and other drugs used to treat HIV/AIDS on the development of a fetus. Some physicians require women of child-bearing age to utilize a reliable contraceptive before they will prescribe protease inhibitors. Is it ethical to intervene in the reproductive choices of female adolescents? Often these requirements do not even consider the adolescent's level of sexual activity or sexual orientation; they simply demand that she use a birth control method, whether she needs or wants it. This intrusion into the reproductive choices of adolescents does not extend to men. Physicians argue that men do not carry a fetus; however, there are no data to indicate that men are not at risk from genetic effects of protease inhibitors.

The new cocktails are expensive, averaging about $1,000 per month. The issue of who will pay for the drugs cannot be overlooked, especially with adolescents. Most adolescents infected with HIV/AIDS are poor (Wortley et al., 1997). If a family is aware of an adolescent's HIV infection, and if it receives public assistance such as Medicaid, the medications will be covered. Many adolescents, however, do not tell their parents. Who then pays? Are they to be denied treatment because they are young and poor? Adolescents cannot apply for Medicaid on their own, as long as they are residing in a parent's home. Other federal or state programs designed to assist HIV-infected people to pay for treatment will not allow a minor to sign consent forms. This creates dilemmas for health care workers who want to prescribe the cocktails but cannot find funding for this long-term prescription treatment.

Adolescents' rights and responsibilities are not federally regulated, and, therefore, may vary from state to state. For example, a North Carolina adolescent may seek birth control or treatment for sexually transmitted diseases without parental consent. In fact, health care providers are prohibited from disclosing this information to parents without the teen's consent. Thus, many adolescents treated for HIV have not disclosed to their parent(s). The only provision for disclosure in most states involves the notification of sexual and/or needle-sharing partners. In these cases, the partner is notified that she or he has had a possible exposure to HIV and is encouraged to be tested, but the name of the HIV-infected individual is not disclosed.

CASE STUDIES OF HIV-INFECTED ADOLESCENT WOMEN

Little data currently exist to examine how health care workers deal with ethical choices regarding (non)compliance in prescribing medication to adolescents. The following case studies are drawn from the pediatric infectious disease clinic in a public tertiary care facility in the Southeast. The following three cases are a representative sample from 35 clients attending the clinic in 1996–1997. The names and personally identifying information have been altered to protect confidentiality.

Janice.   Janice is a 16-year-old African-American adolescent who tested positive for HIV when she was 14. Her mother took Janice to be tested because she knew Janice had been involved with an older man who was rumored to have HIV. Initially, Janice was not put on any therapy. Her virus began progressing rapidly, and she was given a prescription for AZT and ddI within 6 months. She reported that the ddI made her gag and did not take the medication. Many efforts were made to increase compliance. The social worker employed the compliance-gaining strategy of negative expertise: "If you do not take your medication, the virus will weaken your body and you will get sick." A pill crusher was purchased so that she could mix the ddI with applesauce or other food (possible example of promise strategy), but this did not improve compliance. Eventually her physician changed her regimen to AZT and 3TC, which Janice said was much easier to take.

Janice's immune system continued to deteriorate. Phone calls to the pharmacy revealed that Janice did not refill her prescriptions. Several attempts were made to get her mother to accompany her to clinic to discuss the severity of her HIV infection and the compliance problem. When her CD4 count reached 90, her physician became alarmed and lamented the fact that she could not prescribe protease inhibitors because Janice had not been compliant with the previous therapy. In an effort to involve Janice's mother in the process and to utilize an aversive stimulation strategy, the social worker reported medical neglect to the county department of social services. Social services determined that the mother was neglectful in assuring that Janice took her medication, but the strategy was not effective because the agency did not follow through with monitoring or counseling.

The social worker talked at length with Janice about taking her medication. Janice revealed that she felt that her mother did not care. In her words, "The only time we talk about the HIV is when she is throwing it up in my face." She said that she would die anyway and figured that if she did not take her medicine, it would happen sooner and be over with.

As Janice's CD4 count continued to drop, those working with her became even more frustrated. Finally, Janice told her father that she is HIV infected. Her father asked her to please take her medication because he loves her and does not want to lose her. He insisted on going to clinic with her. At this clinic visit, Janice reported that she had started taking the medicine because "my dad asked me to" (compliance-gaining strategy altruism). The physician and the social worker talked at length with Janice, her mother, and her father. Following this meeting, Janice's compliance improved greatly. Janice reports that she has missed only one dose and is working hard to show her physician that she will be faithful at taking her medications, "so I can get that other medicine" [protease inhibitors]. This is an example of the successful implementation of another compliance-gaining strategy (promise), offering the reward (protease inhibitor) for compliance.

Recently, the social worker connected Janice with another HIV-infected teen. The resulting peer support appears to have strengthened Janice's determination to comply with therapy. Three questions remain: How long will she have to adhere to the regimen to convince her physician that she will comply with the dosing schedule for the protease inhibitor? Will she be able to tolerate the side effects, or stop the medication as she did with the ddI? What decisions will be made regarding the possibility of pregnancy? Janice admits she is sexually active, reports using condoms, but not notifying her sexual partner of his risk for HIV infection. Although Janice assures everyone that she uses condoms during sex, she also has asked for several pregnancy tests. Additionally, she has been treated for three different sexually transmitted diseases (STDs) since the discovery of her HIV infection. These facts make it difficult to believe that Janice is complying with safer-sex precautions. Choices to place Janice on protease inhibitors will be complicated by these indicators of possible transmission.

Shaniqua. Shaniqua is a 17-year-old African-American adolescent who was diagnosed with HIV at age 15. No one in her family knows she is infected. Although state law provides for adolescents to be treated for STDs without parental consent, no provision is made for its payment. Through a technicality (living temporarily with her grandmother), Shaniqua was permitted to enroll in a state-funded medical program without parental consent. If she had been living with her parents, she would not have been able to enroll in the program and would have had no source of payment for her clinic visits or medication. Shaniqua is now on Medicaid.

Five months after her diagnosis of HIV infection, Shaniqua was found to be pregnant, indicating noncompliance because she had not notified her partner of her HIV status nor used a condom as required by law. Initially, all clients are informed about the need to (a) use condoms if they are sexually active, and (b) inform potential partners of their risk for HIV infection—using strategies of threat (you can go to jail if you knowingly expose someone to HIV) and two types of positive expertise (use condoms to prevent him from getting HIV, and you from getting an STD, which would be very dangerous given your compromised immune system).

Shaniqua was given a prescription for AZT to reduce the possibility of transmission of the HIV to her child. A moral compliance-gaining appeal was made urging her to take the AZT because it was "the right thing to do" for her unborn child. Because no one in her home knew that she was HIV infected, Shaniqua hid the pills in her room and took them sporadically at best (self-reported and calls to pharmacy). She did not want "anyone asking too many questions." Shaniqua is nearing a point in her disease that medication for herself (not just to protect her baby) will be a consideration. If she was not able to maintain the dosing schedule of a single drug during pregnancy, can she possibly manage compliance with a "cocktail"?

Monisha. Monisha is a 17-year-old African-American adolescent who was diagnosed HIV infected at age 15. Monisha has dropped out of high school, and she has been evaluated by a psychologist and found to be clinically depressed and borderline mentally retarded. Monisha's entire family knows of her HIV infection. She moves between her mother's home, her father's home, and the home of a friend. Her mother is an alcoholic and is not a reliable source of support for compliance.

Monisha's physician prescribed AZT and ddI for her within 2 months of diagnosis. Since being on medication, Monisha has encountered many obstacles. First, her mother lost her public assistance and, therefore, her Medicaid coverage. Monisha moved in with her father; his income was too high to qualify for her Medicaid coverage. Payment assistance came through a pharmaceutical company's indigent drug program and later through the state's HIV drug program. Monisha then moved from her father's home to a friend's home. Not living with either parent, she again qualified for Medicaid. This constant fluctuation in payment sources has drastically affected Monisha's compliance. Although the social worker tries to ensure that she has a source for payment (strategy of pregiving or debt), Monisha often does not notify her until long after she has lost eligibility and run out of medicine.

Strategies employed by the social worker to gain compliance have included negative expertise (If you do not take your medicine as prescribed, you will get sick sooner). Utilizing the rapport that had developed between them, the social worker implemented compliance-gaining strategy liking with some success. The lack of stable social support, a funding source, and Monisha's limited cognitive functioning have contributed to noncompliance with treatment. Additionally, Monisha wants to have a baby. This desire for a child may provide an opportunity to appeal to Monisha to comply with treatment for herself for the good of a child she may carry (altruism). Medically, Monisha is a good candidate now for protease inhibitors, but the indicators of past compliance behaviors for her have been poor. The failure to notify the health care worker until she has missed several days dosage of her medication is alarming, considering the resistance problems with protease inhibitors.

Case Studies of Infected Teen Mothers

Another compliance indicator has come not from the treatment of adolescents themselves, but from their compliance with treatment for their HIV-exposed infants. Following the recommendations of the AIDS Clinic Trials Group (ACTG) Study 076, pregnant women take daily doses of AZT through pregnancy; infants born to HIV-infected mothers require a 6-week course of AZT, followed by a daily dose of Septra to protect the infant from pneumocystis carinii pneumonia (PCP) until the baby's HIV status is determined. The infant's HIV status is determined through two blood tests, both done at birth, and one is repeated at 6 weeks and between 4 and 6 months. If all tests are negative, the child is taken off all preventive medication.

After delivery, mothers/families are educated on the importance of the medication (expertise and liking) and are warned that if noncompliance is suspected, a medical neglect report will be made to the county department of social services child protective services (threat or aversive stimulation). During 1996, the leading cause of reports of medical neglect generated at one pediatric infectious disease clinic was noncompliance with medication. Although this noncompliance with infants' medication was not limited to mothers from the adolescent population, the percentage was higher than for nonadolescent mothers. These adolescents often do not want to consider their own infection; daily doses of medication to their infants are a reminder that the child is HIV exposed. The child looks fine to them, so they can easily deny the need for medication. Some medical providers believe that noncompliance with a child's medication strongly suggests that a mother may not comply with her own therapy. Two cases are described, Reanna and Jeanelle.

Reanna. Reanna is a 17-year-old African-American adolescent with two children, a 2-year-old daughter and a 3-month infant son, Raheem. Reanna was diagnosed with HIV 18 months ago. Reanna and her children live with her mother, sister, and sister's children. Only Reanna's mother knows she is HIV infected and Raheem is HIV exposed. During her pregnancy, Reanna reported that she took the AZT as prescribed, an example of compliance through use of moral appeal ("Taking the AZT is the right thing to do to protect your baby"). Following Raheem's birth, any effort by the social worker to talk with Reanna about her own health care was met with a shrug and a reply of, "I'm fine. I don't think about it." She reported giving Raheem his AZT for 6 weeks and started giving him Septra at 6 weeks.

When Raheem was 2 months old, the social worker called the pharmacy to determine the amount of Septra dispensed and when a refill would be needed. She was told that no such prescription was ever filled. A medical neglect report was made to the county department of social services child protective services unit to exert averse stimulation in the form of investigation and monitoring by a recognized authority. During the investigation, Reanna repeatedly stated that Raheem was not sick and therefore did not need to take any medicine. She had thrown away the prescription. Raheem's physician called the pharmacy to reorder the prescription.

In an effort to assure compliance, the physician ordered a home health nurse to visit the home 3 days a week. The nurse was to measure and mark the amount of Septra left in the bottle and provide education on caring for an HIV-exposed infant (positive expertise). Reanna allowed the nurse to visit only once. The nurse's repeated attempts to visit or call were unsuccessful. Reanna would not answer the door when the nurse knocked. When the nurse called, Reanna would pretend to be her sister and say that she was not home. Reanna told the department of social services social worker that she did not want the nurse visiting because her family and neighbors asked too many questions. The social worker arranged for Reanna and Raheem to meet the home health nurse at the department of social services, but Reanna failed to make this appointment. After several weeks, the department of social services determined that there was insufficient evidence to support medical neglect and closed the case, removing the aversive stimulation. Within a few weeks, Raheem had his third negative test and no longer needed to take Septra.

At present, the medication for her son is not an issue for Reanna. In the course of Reanna's treatment, however, her refusal to comply with her son's prescribed medication strongly indicates she will not adhere to her own treatment regimens (making her a poor choice to start cocktail therapies). Currently, Reanna refuses to keep appointments scheduled for herself, and Reanna's physician will not consider protease inhibitors for Reanna because of past noncompliant behaviors.

Jeanelle. Jeanelle is a 22-year-old African-American woman who discovered she was HIV infected after HIV testing during pregnancy. Jeanelle is not on medication for herself at this time but did take AZT during her last pregnancy. She has three children: two boys, ages 5 and 3, and a 2-month-old girl, Jazmyn. Jeanelle lost custody of her two older children following the court's determination that she was neglectful. She is determined to do whatever it takes to keep Jazmyn. The social worker uses the strategy of promise (if she complies with the treatment regimen for Jazmyn, the social worker will assist Jeanelle in retaining custody of Jazmyn). Additionally, the social worker reinforces Jeanelle's positive feelings about herself by praising her for continuing compliance.

Jazmyn's second test returned positive, indicating that she is HIV infected, and must continue with daily doses of Septra until she is a year old. The social worker stressed the importance of continuing Septra as prescribed to protect Jazmyn from infection (positive expertise). She also will receive a regimen of antiretroviral therapy (i.e., AZT and 3TC). The social worker must maintain the bond with Jeanelle (liking) to provide the support she will need to comply with the treatment. As protease inhibitors become available for children, Jeanelle's compliance with the initial therapies will be considered when deciding to offer them to Jazmyn.

RECOMMENDATIONS FOR COMPLIANCE WITH HIV-INFECTED ADOLESCENTS

There are no easy answers to the dilemmas presented here. On one hand, there is now a group of drugs that, for the first time, give hope to those infected with HIV. The possibility of a future for HIV-infected adolescents is real. These drugs, however, have numerous side effects and require strict adherence to complicated dosing schedules that prevent drug resistance. Physicians and other health care workers will continue to be placed in positions to make judgments or recommendations about who will and who will not comply not only with treatment regimens, but also with public health laws to reduce the risk of transmission. Because it is impossible to monitor patients 24 hours a day, developing compliance-gaining strategies that are effective and meaningful to patients is essential. Based on past research on compliance gaining and adolescent egocentrism, combined with experiences from the case studies presented, recommendations for increasing compliance with HIV-infected female adolescents are presented next.

Recommendations for Self. Based on the case studies, several strategies appear to encourage HIV-infected adolescents to take their medications. Altruism was effective for some adolescents, along with promise (offering the cocktail if she is compliant) and at times liking (creating rapport). What was *not* effective for these adolescents was use of threat or aversive stimulation ("You could go to jail if you expose a partner to HIV"). Thus, traditional fear appeals likely will be ineffective (they often threaten death, not a useful approach for someone who has what to this point has been a terminal disease). Also ineffective was expertise, either positive or negative; this is crucial because physicians often use this strategy (M. Burgoon et al., 1990).

Recommendations for Other. Based on the case studies, several strategies appear to encourage HIV-infected adolescents to give their newborn infants medication. For the "other"-directed strategies, moral appeals and positive self-feeling were effective; these strategies often focused on being a good mother. Positive expertise worked in some but not all cases ("giving your baby AZT can help prevent infection"). What also worked in several cases was threat and aversive stimulation (reporting parental neglect), but this was not consistent and should be considered only as a last resort because of the potential damage to the relationship with the client (loss of rapport).

Social support is also important for compliance gaining. For example, Janice's parental interest and support were critical to gaining compliance with treatment protocols. Because of her father's pleas to "do it for me" and his interest in what is happening with her medically, Janice became more interested in her own treatment. Linking the adolescent with others who are HIV infected, either on an individual basis or through a support group, can also decrease the teen's personal fable and sense of uniqueness (by seeing that others have similar problems and feelings). Janice has voiced more confidence in the expertise, both positive and negative, expressed by members of such a support group because she sees them as similar to herself.

Understanding adolescent egocentrism can be useful in choosing compliance-gaining strategies. Some adolescent risk taking (and associated decision making) is developmental; adolescents will work through some poor decision making themselves in time. Unfortunately, adolescents still are at great risk (and can pose HIV risks to others) until they move beyond these stages. The personal fable component of egocentrism encourages health care workers to avoid threat or aversive stimulation strategies. Using imaginary audience, health care workers could focus on strategies such as altruism, positive esteem, and moral appeal. Indeed, Greene et al. (1995; Greene, Hale, & Rubin, 1997) reported that adolescents' imaginary audience norms were a good predictor of their intentions to avoid higher risk behavior.

Adolescents receive mixed messages about risk behavior, especially sexual behavior. Parents, teachers, and religious organizations tend to promote abstinence (Keeling, 1987), yet other significant figures (e.g., peers or media) may promote risk-taking behavior (Keeling, 1987). Adolescents are particularly influenced by peer opinions (Cohen, Brook, & Kandel, 1991; Gayle et al., 1990), especially regarding sex (Reardon, 1989). For moral issues parent(s) or adults outside the family are reported to be the most influential for adolescents (Niles, 1981; Young & Ferguson, 1979). Thus, to encourage adolescent compliance, it might be possible to change parent attitudes (if they are aware of HIV infection) and get them to support taking medication. Also, peers could support behavior. Respected adults, perhaps a teacher or minister, might also support the behavior. What is crucial is to create social support for the recommended behavior, or compliance.

One finding from this study is that lack of support can contribute to problems with compliance. Many times, this lack of support is associated with unwillingness to disclose their infection. HIV disclosure decisions are extremely difficult. Members of the marital subsystem (lovers, spouses, exspouses, friends) are generally viewed as the most appropriate recipients of disclosure of HIV infection, with the nuclear family rating next highest (Greene & Serovich, 1996; Marks et al., 1992; Serovich & Greene, 1993), and lowest disclosure to extended family and general public. Additionally, the best predictors of willingness to disclose HIV infection are quality of relationship with the recipient and anticipated response to disclosure (Greene & Serovich, 1995). It is understandable, given associated risks, that HIV-infected adolescents would choose not to disclose. Health care workers dealing with these adolescents should be aware of the possible effect of nondisclosure on compliance.

Other approaches have also been shown to increase compliance in some health settings. Inui, Carter, and Pecoraro (1981) recommended asking a question to facilitate discussion about the difficulty of compliance (and assess the directness of responses). They recommended saying to patients, "Most people have trouble remembering to take their medication. Do you have trouble remembering to take yours?" Opening this kind of dialogue could lead to greater compliance; at least it will establish rapport. Behavioral contracts and weekly phone contacts have also increased compliance significantly, but not specifically using an adolescent population (Cummings, Becker, Kirscht, & Levin, 1981). These approaches may have some value, but they also have the potential to increase costs by using additional resources in often already overburdened health settings. Likely, if these plans were implemented, it would be social workers, physicians assistants, or nurses who would perform these behaviors, not the physicians themselves. Because of the psychosocial issues surrounding HIV/AIDS (e.g., poverty and drug abuse), physicians are increasingly dependent on social workers in the management of these complicated cases.

Limitations.   There are three important limitations regarding this study; likely, ethical choices regarding compliance gaining vary by context. First, the clients described here may not be representative of adolescent HIV/AIDS cases in other areas. Specifically, these adolescents are female, African American, many are/have been pregnant; they contracted HIV through heterosexual contact. Thus, it may be inappropriate to generalize to other populations, for example, inner-city adolescent Hispanic men who contracted HIV through homosexual contact. Second, the type of clinic or health care setting is significant here. In the clinic described here, the social worker rather than a nurse or physician made the most persuasive attempts. Other clinics may be set up differently (e.g., structurally, staffing, funding), and compliance-gaining attempts may be different. Third, and finally, is the status of treatment with protease inhibitors. Currently, no one knows how new treatments will affect HIV/AIDS stigma and unwillingness to disclose HIV infection. If the stigma is reduced, compliance gaining might become easier for health care workers.

Future Research.   The introduction of protease inhibitors has changed the treatment of HIV/AIDS dramatically. These changes, however, do not come without associated problems. The case studies presented here, HIV-infected female adolescents, provide but one example of the dilemmas associated with prescribing these new cocktails. If HIV/AIDS treatment remains linked with these cocktail therapies, continued study of access to the medication and compliance with medical regimens will be crucial. The information reported about oft-changing funding sources for medication could have disastrous effects. Careful choices will need to be made to assure equal access to and funding for medication. Health care workers cannot simply exclude adolescents from treatment because they have higher rates of noncompliance or do not have the same funding sources as adults; the matter is clearly complex. Adolescents' absence from trials is additionally disturbing.

   The compliance-gaining strategies recommended here for adolescent women may or may not be similar to effective strategies for other groups. The target, compliance with medical regimens, will remain the same, but what constitutes effective compliance-gaining strategies will differ. As research with protease inhibitors continues, much additional work is required to look at the effects, particularly with compliance.

REFERENCES

Bartlett, J., McGovern, T., Merkatz, R., Marte, C., & Mastroianni, A. C. (1997, October). *Forming equitable research reform: Rationing access to clinical trials and new drugs.* Panel presented at the annual conference of the Duke Journal of Gender Law and Policy, Durham, NC.

Baxter, D. (1997, January 3). Casting off the "unreliable" AIDS patient. *The New York Times,* p. A35.

Burgoon, M. H., & Burgoon, J. K. (1990). Compliance-gaining and health care. In J. P. Dillard (Ed.), *Seeking compliance: The production of interpersonal influence messages* (pp. 161–188). Scottsdale, AZ: Gorsuch Scarisbrick.

Burgoon, M., Parrott, R., Burgoon, J. K., Birk, T., Pfau, M., & Coker, R. (1990). Primary care physicians' selection of verbal compliance-gaining strategies. *Health Communication, 2,* 13–27.

Centers for Disease Control and Prevention. (1996). *HIV/AIDS Surveillance Report: U.S. HIV and AIDS cases reported through June 1996, 8.*

Charney, E. (1972). Patient–doctor communication: Implications for the clinician. *Pediatric Clinics of North America, 19,* 263–279.

Cohen, P., Brook, J. S., & Kandel, D. B. (1991). Predictors and correlates of adolescent drug use. In R. M. Lerner, A. C. Petersen, & J. Brooks-Gunn (Eds.), *Encyclopedia of adolescence* (pp. 268–271). New York: Garland.

Cummings, K. M., Becker, M. H., Kirscht, J. P., & Levin, N. W. (1981). Intervention strategies to improve compliance with medical regimens by ambulatory hemodialysis patients. *Journal of Behavioral Medicine, 4,* 111–127.

Elkind, D. (1967). Egocentrism in adolescence. *Child Development, 38,* 1025–1034.

Elkind, D. (1978). Understanding the young adolescent. *Adolescence, 13,* 127–134.

Elkind, D., & Bowen, R. (1979). Imaginary audience behavior in children and adolescents. *Developmental Psychology, 15,* 38–44.

Enright, R. D., Shukla, D. G., & Lapsley, D. K. (1980). Adolescent egocentrism-sociocentrism and self-consciousness. *Journal of Youth and Adolescence, 9,* 101–115.

Eraker, S. S., Kirscht, J. P, & Becker, M. H. (1984). Understanding and improving patient compliance. *Annals of Internal Medicine, 100,* 258–268.

Freedman, J. L., & Fraser, S. C. (1966). Compliance without pressure: The foot-in-the-door technique. *Journal of Personality and Social Psychology, 4,* 195–202.

Friedman, H. S., & DiMatteo, M. R. (1979). Health care as an interpersonal process. *Journal of Social Issues, 35,* 1–11.

Gayle, H. D., Keeling, R. P., Garcia-Tunon, M., Kilbourne, B. W., Narkunas, J. P., Ingram, F. R., Rogers, M. F., & Curran, J. W. (1990). Prevalence of the human immunodeficiency virus among university students. *New England Journal of Medicine, 323,* 1538–1541.

Greene, K., Hale, J. L., & Rubin, D. L. (1997). A test of the theory of reasoned action in the context of condom use and AIDS. *Communication Reports, 10,* 21–33.

Greene, K., Rubin, D. L., & Hale, J. L. (1995). Egocentrism, message explicitness, and AIDS messages directed toward adolescents: An application of the theory of reasoned action. *Journal of Social Behavior and Personality, 10,* 547–570.

Greene, K., & Serovich, J. M. (1995, November). *Predictors of willingness to disclose HIV infection to nuclear family members.* Paper presented at the annual meeting of the National Speech Communication Association, San Antonio, TX.

Greene, K., & Serovich, J. M. (1996). Appropriateness of disclosure of HIV testing information: The perspective of PLWAs. *Journal of Applied Communication Research, 24,* 50–65.

Indinavir fact sheet. (1996). The AIDS Treatment Data Network. Available: www.aidsnyc.org

Inui, T. S., Carter, W. B., & Pecoraro, R. E. (1981). Screening for noncompliance among patients with hypertension: Is self-report the best available measure? *Medical Care, 19,* 1061–1064.

Keeling, R. P. (1987). Effects of AIDS on young Americans. *Medical Aspects of Human Sexuality, 21,* 22–33.

King, P. A. (1996). Reproductive choices of adolescent females with HIV/AIDS. In R. R. Faden & N. E. Kass (Eds.), *HIV, AIDS, and childbearing* (pp. 345–366). New York: Oxford University Press.

Lapsley, D. K., FitzGerald, D. P., Rice, K. G., & Jackson, S. (1989). Separation-individuation and the "new look" at the imaginary audience and personal fable: A test of an integrative model. *Journal of Adolescent Research, 4,* 483–505.

Marks, G., Bundek, N. I., Richardson, J. L., Ruiz, M. S., Maldonado, N., & Mason, H. R. (1992). Self-disclosure of HIV infection: Preliminary results from a sample of Hispanic men. *Health Psychology, 11,* 300–306.

Marwell, G., & Schmitt, D. R. (1967a). Compliance-gaining behavior: A synthesis and model. *Sociological Quarterly, 8,* 317–328.

Marwell, G., & Schmitt, D. R. (1967b). Dimensions of compliance-gaining behavior: An empirical analysis. *Sociometry, 30,* 350–364.

Mastroianni, A. C., Faden, R., & Federman, D. (1994). *Women and health research.* Washington, DC: National Academy Press.

Miller, G. R. (1983). On various ways of skinning symbolic cats: Recent research on persuasive message strategies. *Journal of Language and Social Psychology, 2,* 123–140.

Miller, G. R., Boster, F., Roloff, M., & Seibold, D. (1977). Compliance-gaining message strategies: A typology and some findings concerning effects of situational differences. *Communication Monographs, 44,* 37–51.

Niles, F. S. (1981). The youth culture controversy: An evaluation. *Journal of Early Adolescence, 1,* 265–271.

Penchansky, R. (1986). Patient–provider concordance: A review and conceptualization. *Medical Care Review, 43,* 293–350.

Piaget, J. (1929). *The child's conception of the world.* New York: Harcourt Brace.

Piaget, J. (1958). *The growth of logical thinking from childhood to adolescence.* New York: Basic Books.

Reardon, K. K. (1989). The potential role of persuasion in adolescent AIDS prevention. In R. E. Rice & C. K. Atkins (Eds.), *Public communication campaigns* (pp. 273–289). Newbury Park, CA: Sage.

Ritonavir fact sheet. (1996). The AIDS Treatment Data Network. Available: www.aidsnyc.org

Rotello, J. (1995, June 13). To protect and serve [Editorial]. *The Advocate,* p. 80.

Saquinavir fact sheet. (1996). The AIDS Treatment Data Network. Available: www.aidsnyc.org

Seibold, D. R., Cantrill, J. G., & Meyers, R. A. (1985). Communication and interpersonal influence. In M. L. Knapp & G. R. Miller (Eds.), *Handbook of interpersonal communication* (pp. 551–611). Beverly Hills, CA: Sage.

Serovich, J. M., & Greene, K. (1993). Perceptions of family boundaries: The case of disclosure of HIV testing information. *Family Relations, 42,* 193–197.

Stone, G. C. (1979). Patient compliance and the role of the expert. *Journal of Social Issues, 35,* 34–59.

Thompson, T. L. (1994). Interpersonal communication and health care. In M. L. Knapp & G. R. Miller (Eds.), *Handbook of interpersonal communication* (pp. 696–717). Beverly Hills, CA: Sage.

Treatment Review #20. (1995). The AIDS Treatment Data Network. Available: www.aidsnyc.org or AIDS-TreatD@aol.com

Treatment Review #22. (1996). The AIDS Treatment Data Network. Available: www.aidsnyc.org or AIDS-TreatD@aol.com

Wortley, P. M., Chu, S. Y., & Berkelman, R. L. (1997). Epidemiology of HIV/AIDS in women and the impact of the expanded 1993 CDC surveillance definition of AIDS. In D. Cotton & D. H. Watts (Eds.) *The medical management of AIDS in women* (pp. 3–14). New York: Wiley.

Wyatt, N. (1991). Physician–patient relationships: What do doctors say? *Health Communication, 3,* 157–174.

Young, J. W., & Ferguson, L. R. (1979). Developmental changes through adolescence in the spontaneous nomination of reference groups as a function of decision content. *Journal of Youth and Adolescence, 8,* 239–252.

Communicating Danger:
The Politics of AIDS in
the Mekong Region

Thomas M. Steinfatt
University of Miami School of Communication

Jim Mielke
UNICEF, Phnom Penh

During 1995, 2.7 million new adult HIV infections occurred throughout the world, with over a third of these new infections occurring in South and Southeast Asia. Indeed, the industrialized world accounts for only 2% of the global total of new infections (World Health Organization [WHO], 1996). Although the spread of HIV in the Mekong countries began later than in the United States and Africa, there are almost 4 million adults in the region infected with HIV (Rosenberg, 1995; see also S. Berkely, 1993; Buchanan & Cernada, 1998; International Union for the Scientific Study of Population, 1994; Tanne, 1991). Yet the number of HIV-infected individuals in the region alone is now more than twice the total number of infected people in the entire industrialized world. But of the U.S.$2 billion spent on AIDS each year, only 10% is spent in the entire developing world. The epidemic is still at an early stage in the Mekong region as a whole, though more advanced in Thailand, with high rates also reported in Burma and Cambodia. In the Mekong region, 2.5 million new infections occur each year (UNICEF, 1995). Underdiagnosis, underreporting, and delayed reporting characterize the region. Nearly 90% of those infected are between 15 and 49 years of age. The predominant route of transmission throughout the region is heterosexual intercourse, with injection drug use second.

Beyond the illness and death caused by AIDS is an additional toll in human misery and secondary problems. Prejudice and discrimination haunt persons with AIDS (PWAs). HIV-infected mothers often deny the protective value of breast milk to their children, switching to less nutritious baby formula dispensed in unsterilized bottles, because one third of infants with HIV are infected through breastfeeding, according to United Nations statistics (Meier, 1997; see also chap. 25 of this volume). Perhaps the greatest burden among the uninfected in the Mekong region is borne by older people in frail health themselves and with scarce resources, called upon to provide care for infected family members who had been the family's principal economic providers, without adequate resources and facing destitute poverty.

Lewis, Bamber, and Waugh (1997) suggested that current conditions with respect to STD (sexually transmitted disease) transmission in the Mekong region can be illuminated through their historical context. Much of this context concerns colonial and postcolonial administrations, which used Western medical models that excluded access to care by the poor and by those outside of urban areas. Western/Middle-Eastern religions such as Christianity and Islam, which were associated with these administrations, crusaded for sexual moralities aligned with their own cultural positions, adding to the problem. Single-god religions normally treat STDs as just punishment from that god, rather than offering educational and medical services to those in need. Ironically, the Leninist anti-Christian doctrines, which replaced the Christian Western influence in much of the Mekong region in the decades following World War II, retained the sexual morality positions of Christianity, with intolerance of commercial sex and prejudice toward persons infected with STDs.

VIETNAM

Officially the Socialist Republic of Vietnam, with a population of about 74 million people, and land area of about 128,000 square miles, Vietnam has one-party democratic communist rule. Since 1986 the economic system has been capitalist/socialist, with the government now encouraging the establishment of private schools and hospitals for the rich, given limited funds available for improving public services for the poor.

There are no official class differences recognized in Vietnam, yet there is a disadvantaged group of people without money or proper legal papers. Such persons are highly restricted in their ability to get welfare, to be admitted to many educational institutions, and to receive government medical care. Thus, most official statistics reflect the situation of persons who are at least upper lower class in status. Both inflation and the presence of the new rich have made the economic status of those who are destitute and undocumented more obvious, and crime and dissatisfaction are rising. HIV/AIDS in Vietnam must be understood within the sociopolitical context just discussed, and with the understanding of the problem of the lowered representation of the paperless in official statistics. Interpretation of official statistics is further complicated by occasional changes in collection method, making cross-year comparisons difficult. For example, injection drug users (IDUs) were listed as 1.21% of the known HIV cases in Vietnam in 1992 and 86.5% in 1993 (Ho Chi Minh City AIDS Committee, 1996). Data collection is hampered further by a chronic lack of funds, with the total budget for blood testing in HCM (Ho Chi Minh) City in 1991 at U.S.$10,000. Articles on relevant issues such as commercial sex are often written without complete citation information, and numbers and statistics are often presented without a discussion of method and without attribution. The policy of information control in Vietnam includes control of scientific data, which does not bode well for information on AIDS.

HIV/AIDS in Vietnam. Historically, the rate of STDs in Vietnam was high under the colonial administrations of France and the United States. In 1931, 92% of commercial sex workers (CSWs) in Vietnam tested positive for at least one STD, whereas the rate was 10% in France (Joyeux, 1933). Few statistics are available on STD infection rates in South Vietnamese CSWs during the American occupation, but it may be suggested by the rate of infection among American servicemen in Vietnam, which varied between 19% and 35% during the 1963 to 1971 period (Greenberg, 1972). In keeping with Leninist thought, STDs and commercial sex were seen as products of the capitalist system and brought shame upon the infected individual; commercial sex is a crime against society. Guenel (1997) referred to the increase in STDs in Vietnam since 1975 as "an established phenomenon" (p. 148).

HIV-1 was first detected in Vietnam 1990, with an official HIV rate in late July 1997 of 0.0084%, given the 6,229 HIV-infected persons, some 2,000 of whom are in HCM City (VNA news agency, 1997). This compares to 3,295 in 1995, 2,214 in 1994, 927 in 1993, and 83 in

1992, officially listed by the government AIDS Committee. Half of the listed 1995 cases were in HCM City, with 9.65% in Khanh Hoa, the province with the second greatest number of infections. Hanoi reported 16 total infections, Hue 33, and Da Nang 124. Of the 1995 total, over 90% were reported in persons aged from 20 to 49, with age unknown for an additional 4.4%. IDUs were 77.03% of the 1995 total, 5.43% were listed as CSWs (HCM City AIDS Committee, 1996). Guenel (1997) estimated 500,000 HIV infections in Vietnam as of December 1996, and a 13.2% infection rate in CSWs. UNICEF estimates the unofficial figure as 84,195, and the Health Ministry estimates 263,229 HIV infections by the year 2000 (UNICEF, 1997).

Methods used to classify multiple-category persons, such as an IDU CSW with tuberculosis (TB), are not clear, and persons falling into multiple categories may not be classified in more than one. The stigmas associated with categories such as IDU, homosexual, and CSW make such classifications less likely and increase their underrepresentation. Within one population subgroup, 32% of IDUs in treatment centers had HIV-seropositive test results in 1995. Among CSWs tested, HIV rates rose from 9% to 38% between 1992 and 1995. Whatever the current level, there is evidence that the epidemic is growing rapidly.

Few surveys of AIDS knowledge among the general public are available. Many Vietnamese believe that HIV cannot be contracted from a friend or spouse, but only from CSWs, foreigners, and homosexuals, according to a 1993 CARE International networking survey of urban areas (Efroymson, 1997). Consequently, they believe that avoiding sex with such persons provides protection from AIDS. Condom requests and condom use are seen as indicating lack of trust. Poirot et al. (1996) gave an AIDS knowledge questionnaire to 570 professional staff members of a Hanoi hospital, principally physicians, nurses, and medical students, 78% of whom considered themselves well informed on AIDS. The most commonly listed source for their information on AIDS was the media, at 80%. Half had discussed the subject with friends, and 57% with fellow workers. Only 17% knew a place where they could get more information. Over 90% knew the principal transmission modes, but drinking water, bathing, kissing, and wearing others' clothes were listed or suspected by 25%, with 40% agreeing to insect bites as a mode. If HIV were to infect a fellow worker, 25% would not want to work with the person, 35% would not invite the person home, and 55% would fear becoming infected.

From the beginnings of the official AIDS campaign in 1990 and up to 1993, CSWs and IDUs were jailed routinely. But Ho Chi Minh City officials in April 1997 approved the creation of a special village in Thu Duc Precinct for about 1,000 HIV-infected persons who are homeless or a financial burden to their families. This means that many of the official HIV cases in HCM City would be concentrated in a single camp, and suggests that a policy of isolation of HIV-infected individuals may be developing. The city's Binh Trieu Detoxification Center became a hospital exclusively for AIDS patients in May 1997 (VNA news agency, 1997).

The opening of Vietnam to capitalism in 1986 has led to possibilities for earlier sexual relations and experimentation with more partners, as young people are more likely to have jobs that remove them from the family home for long periods of time, and give them greater disposable income and a desire to imitate Western habits. Prevention activities targeted for young people include the Youth Union and the Women's Union, which fulfill social functions somewhat similar to that of religious social groups in the West. The leadership of these institutions insist on chastity before marriage and faithfulness within marriage, while recognizing the need for protection from pregnancy, STDs, and AIDS. Government messages concentrate on prevention, warning of the dangers of prostitution, drug use, and multiple sex partners. Earlier government messages made extensive use of fear appeals through the depiction of skulls, skeletons, photographs of AIDS-related skin diseases, and frequent mentions of death. More recent campaigns emphasize love, faithfulness, monogamy, and condom use.

The basic messages in AIDS education materials are to avoid commercial sex, drug use, and multiple sex partners while being faithful to one's spouse, using condoms, and offering support to PWAs. Faithfulness is promoted as the principal method of remaining AIDS free, usually without regard to the dangers of continuous unprotected sex with a potentially infected spouse. As in most of the Western world, the concept that people enjoy sex and drugs because they find them pleasurable does not enter into message content or much AIDS planning. Most messages concentrate on behavioral recommendations in the absence of the reasons for the recommendations with the result that young people invent their own answers and develop belief systems that put them at risk (Efroymson, 1996).

Among the more promising HIV prevention programs is the application of social marketing techniques to condoms. Nguyen, Nhan, and Le (1996) reported on a condom social marketing campaign that distributed more than 30 million condoms in Vietnam from August 1993 to December 1995. The brand names used, "Trust" and "OK," have since become generic terms for condoms in Vietnam, creating a more receptive attitude by the general public to promote condoms openly. The total unit cost of a condom dropped from U.S.$0.13/condom in 1993 to approximately U.S.$0.05/condom in 1995.

The government-run HCM City AIDS Committee occupies several buildings in a large compound on Nguyen Thi Minh Khai Street, including an exhibit hall with visual HIV/AIDS displays. Families may come in for free AIDS education sessions, and the staff is professional and well trained with WHO connections. The program also helps to provide AIDS education activities at government-sponsored clubs such as the Women's Culture House. The few women who have leisure time use the sports facilities and small library, and take classes in traditional women's interest areas such as cooking, sewing, and dancing. AIDS classes are also provided for the Youth Culture House, a former propaganda organization that is now a social club. Youth meetings are held once a week with many students and other young people in attendance to enjoy an evening with other young people. Participants drink Coke and orange juice while watching videotapes showing education programs on AIDS on a big-screen TV. Taped popular music is played from a cassette. Anyone with questions about AIDS is taken to another room within the club where personal information can be imparted in a more private atmosphere. Such programs are available in urban areas. But in rural areas, or for people without the means to attend such functions or exhibits, few governmental alternatives exist.

Nongovernmental Organizations and AIDS in Vietnam.   Despite an overall lack of coordination and cooperation between them, several nongovernmental organizations (NGOs) and international agencies have active HIV/AIDS prevention programs in urban areas. Save the Children/UK maintains offices in HCM City and Hanoi. Its main office is foreign run and is an excellent source of help for the disadvantaged, and of information for social science researchers. The HIV/AIDS program of Save the Children/UK is across town from the main office and entirely run by Vietnamese who are former drug users and sex workers in HCM City. UNICEF is continuing its work with AIDS prevention activities, and the Australian Red Cross has collaborated with the Vietnam National Red Cross HIV/AIDS Prevention Program since 1995, in youth peer education and counseling. Care International in Vietnam has consulted with the national AIDS control program since 1992, with particular attention to gender issues, producing a book with HIV-infected characters who discuss their fears, hopes, and experiences. CARE is also producing 30 episodes of a TV soap opera with an HIV/AIDS theme. Nguyen Friendship, a gay community NGO, has an HIV/AIDS prevention focus.

AIDS education activities in Vietnam are carried out in a climate of increasing poverty and punitive legal crackdowns on sex workers who have little power to resist. Its furtive nature often leads to hurried sex on the street against a wall or tree, which results in little availability or time for condom negotiation or use. Another result of the suppression policy is an increase in the migration stream of young Vietnamese women into Cambodia, to work in the brothels of Phnom Penh and Battambang, where such work is accepted. Vietnamese law supports the equality of women, but among both men and women, men are more culturally valued and are regarded as the rightful decision makers, particularly in the defense of traditional values. Changing attitudes and behaviors to reflect this law is one way to protect women from HIV/AIDS.

CAMBODIA

Officially the State of Cambodia, with a population of 10.7 million people and the smallest land area of the five countries at 69,898 square miles, Cambodian government contrasts with all of its neighbors. Although economically depressed, it is a beginning capitalist multiparty democracy. The country was ruled by twin prime ministers, until a coup in July 1997. No population count was conducted in Cambodia after the 1962 census until March of 1996. Conducted by the Cambodian Ministry of Planning supported by the United Nations Population Fund, the 1996 Demographic Survey of Cambodia studied more than 20,000 rural and urban households, using statistical methods to estimate population parameters. It estimated the 1996 population at 10.7 million, with a median age of 18, giving Cambodia one of the youngest populations in the world. Cambodia's population is young, rural, agrarian, and poor, largely without basic household amenities.

Migration into Cambodia from Thailand is almost nonexistent. Migration from Vietnam, and from China via Vietnam, is substantial. Hong Kong-led smuggling of mainland Chinese into the United States, South America, Europe, and Africa, uses several routes, one of which passes through Vietnam into Phnom Penh. Attractive younger women are occasionally siphoned off from the group in Phnom Penh because using them as labor in the destination countries is too risky. Cambodia has few funds, police enforcement in much of the country is minimal, and human trafficking is only one of many problems. Police estimate 10,000 illegal ethnic Chinese immigrants in Cambodia. Migration of indentured young female Vietnamese labor into Cambodian brothels is also substantial.

HIV/AIDS in Cambodia. HIV-1, as measured by blood donors level in Phnom Penh, was first detected in 1991, and increased from under 0.1% in 1991 to about 10% in 1995. Over 90% of blood donors are men and some are professional donors, both groups with higher infection rates than the general population. More donations occur in urban areas, which are also likely to have higher infection rates. But subpopulations of sex workers, police, military, STD patients, and pregnant women tested under the national sentinel surveillance program have shown similar dramatic rises up to 1995. HIV-1 infection rates among policemen decreased from 8% in 1994 to 5.5% in 1996, in the military from 8% to 6% over the same period, and also dropped slightly among pregnant women to 1.7%. Just over 8% of de-miners, a risky, relatively high paying laboring job, were found infected. Testing by the International Organization for Migration (IOM) of Cambodian emigrants in Phnom Penh found 1.2% positive from January to June of 1995. About 90% of those infected are between 20 and 39 years old (National AIDS Program, 1996).

The National AIDS Program estimates between 70,000 and 120,000 Cambodians are infected with HIV based on testing projections. The Australian Red Cross estimates between 90,000 and 120,000 HIV-infected people as of April 1997, with about 25,000 new infections occurring per year. Over 80% of new infections occur in people between ages 13 and 39, and more than 90% of the infections are through heterosexual sex. United Nations estimates project 30,000 AIDS deaths in Cambodia over the next 5 years, and Cambodia may have the highest percentage of HIV carriers in the Mekong region (UNICEF, 1997). Although very few full-blown AIDS cases have developed, Chin (1996) estimated 15,000 to 40,000 deaths by the turn of the millennium, assuming zero further transmissions versus continuation of transmission at the current rate, with about 12,000 AIDS deaths per year.

Among CSWs in three provinces surveyed by the Cambodian Center for the Protection of Children's Rights, the rate increased from 9% in 1992 to 38% in 1995 and to 41% in 1996, and in provinces bordering Thailand such as Siem Reap, where trade is brisk, to 60%. The coastal cities of Sihanoukville and Koh Kong also have higher rates among CSWs, as does Battambang, Cambodia's second largest city, which has male CSWs catering to men and mixed brothels of men and women, neither normally found in Phnom Penh. Rates in the remote Northeast, near Vietnam and southern Laos, are low.

The first recorded case of infection was in 1991 in a blood donor in Phnom Penh. The first diagnosed case of AIDS was recorded in 1993, with 240 reported cases by September 1996. Actual figures are likely to be 10 to 20 times higher (Chin, 1996) due to lack of testing and reporting. HIV-1 transmission occurs predominantly heterosexually, and mainly among persons with multiple sex partners, so unprotected commercial sex is a prime transmission route. Reuse of needles in health care and in tattooing are other suspected transmission routes, along with vertical transmission. Injecting drug use in Cambodia occurs rarely.

Two rumored initial routes of HIV into Cambodia are the former Cambodian border camps in Thailand for refugees from the Khmer Rouge horrors, and the UNTAC troops, the United Nations transitional force of peacekeepers in place in the 1980s and early 1990s. Guenel (1997) believed UNTAC troops "contributed widely to the dissemination of the virus" (p. 145). Yet both of these routes seem unlikely. UNTAC troops could be easily observed on R & R in the commercial sex center of Pattaya, Thailand, in the early 1990s, where "Danger—Mines" signs in Khmer that they brought with them still decorate some bars. But UNTAC troops did not acquire AIDS at significant rates according to WHO in Phnom Penh, and are thus unlikely as a major initial source. And in the refugee camps, the national blood program of The International Committee of the Red Cross (ICRC) reports only eight HIV-seropositive cases over 6 years, with 100,000 blood donations tested.

Cambodia is almost completely dependent on Western aid in combating AIDS. Whereas the WHO formula for managing AIDS in developing nations calls for expenditures of U.S.$1/person/year, Cambodia is currently spending $500,000/year, or U.S.$0.05/person/year. The projected strain on health resources is massive. The 1,500 to 3,500 land mine casualties per year extend Cambodia's rudimentary health care system to its limits, and there is no place to treat 12,000 additional AIDS patients per year. Additionally 3,000 to 4,000 maternal orphans would be created each year by AIDS if the projections are correct, further straining almost nonexistent social programs.

Limited social research is available with respect to transmission factors in Cambodian AIDS. Khmer culture is very conservative; women are to be chaste before marriage and faithful to their husbands. Sex outside marriage by Khmer men is discouraged, but grudgingly accepted. A common romantic model operates such that young people see themselves as in love, and thus in bed, whereas older people attempt to enforce cultural norms that mirror more ideal conceptions of social reality. Commercial sex is seen as an import from Thailand. Khmer norms suggest that no self-respecting Khmer woman would ever engage in it regardless of economic circumstances. A 2-year study begun in 1993 suggests that Khmer behavior does not follow these norms. Conducted largely by Cambodian high school and university students trained by the government as researchers (Cambodian AIDS Social Research Project, 1996), the survey of youth behavior found that one in three young women are sexually active, whereas just under 90% of young men are sexually active with girlfriends and with CSWs. Homosexual activity was reported by 10% of the men. Condom use was low, with nearly half of sexually active young men reporting never using them.

A 1997 survey of 1,300 people in both urban and rural areas found over 75% of the urban respondents and over 50% of rural respondents were aware of HIV and AIDS and were able to name condoms as a means to prevent infection. Knowledge of STDs other than AIDS was minimal, which has AIDS implications because presence of an STD increases the probabilities for contracting AIDS by 5 to 10 times. Among urban respondents, 16% reported having at least one STD in the past year, as did 12% of rural respondents. Women were twice as likely to report an STD as were men. Over 40% of male respondents between ages 25 and 30 reported visiting CSWs, about half of whom reported using condoms "sometimes" to never. Fewer than 6% of male respondents used condoms with their wives (Australian Red Cross, 1997).

The rural poverty characteristic of Cambodia means it is difficult to reach the majority of the population with education campaigns. Education is beginning on television, radio, and with posters, but the majority of the population does not believe in AIDS. TB is a common cause of death in Cambodia, and only 8% of tuberculosis patients test positive for HIV. TB is also a common cause of death in AIDS patients, so TB is seen as the problem, not AIDS. As with Laos, it is difficult to convince many people that HIV/AIDS is an important concern, when poverty, fires, rats, observable disease, land mines, the remaining Khmer Rouge, crime, and potential political upheaval are common concerns. The dispersed rural population, the legacy of the Khmer Rouge, and the extensive commercial sex industry pose serious problems for the control of AIDS. As in all Mekong countries except Thailand, no "Mechai" has developed in Cambodia to carry the torch to mobilize top-level political leadership, and to address HIV/AIDS on multiple fronts.

Rather than promote condom use as an HIV preventative, the Cambodia Condom Social Marketing project was launched in 1994 to market condoms directly. It developed a condom brand called NUMBER ONE to be sold at a subsidized price of U.S.$0.02. Packaging was designed for local consumers. Thuermer, Warshauer, Mackie, and Deidrick (1996) reported on its results. A comprehensive marketing campaign was launched that included television, radio, puppet shows, contests, workplace programs, school-based education, and sales training. Condom sales have been more than three times higher than initial targets, at a level of 1.3 condoms per capita per year. M. Berkely (1996) reported that sales for the first 5 months after the sales-training intervention rose 158% to an average of 662,714 sold per month.

In the summer of 1997, the government was preoccupied with Pol Pot's uncertain status, the assassination of Sol Sin, the butcher of Phnom Penh, and Hun Sen's coup; AIDS was far from the top of the priority list. Only 2% of the overall inputs to the HIV/AIDS response has come from the government. There is currently no plan of action at national or provincial levels for multisectoral coordination. Programs not directly under the Ministry of Health do not receive the financial and technical support needed to succeed. Because the Khmer Rouge executed most of the educated citizenry, information from outside authorities is not valued.

THAILAND

Thailand is a newly industrialized country (NIC), far better off economically than its neighboring Mekong nations. Its population is 60 million, with 29% under age 15 and 5% over age 65, a population growth rate of 1.24%, and net migration of zero. Infant mortality is 35.7/1,000 live births, compared with 7.88 for the United States. Despite its NIC status, agriculture consumes 62% of the workforce, and accounts for 11% of the gross domestic product. The government in Thailand is in sharp contrast to that of its neighbors, with a dozen or more political parties normally contesting elections and forming a coalition government in a constitutional monarchy. Capitalism and friendship with America are long established traditions, and freedom of speech is generally accepted, though there are several specific exceptions in *lèse majesté,* and military ownership of the electronic media, which normally withholds information when requested by the government. The print media are free. Thai officials tend to be strong on NIH ("not invented here") sentiments, and tend to avoid imported package solutions.

HIV/AIDS in Thailand.   Unlike many other Asian nations, the epidemic in Thailand is among the best documented in the world. The first AIDS case was reported in 1984, and an estimated 750,000 to 800,000 people are currently living with HIV in Thailand, a prevalence rate of 1.25%. Public Health Ministry statistics for October 1996 list 49,091 AIDS cases and 20,584 symptomatic HIV cases with 80% of infections listed as caused by sexual transmission, 6.73% by injection drug use, 0.09% by blood transfusions, 5.39% by parental transmission, and 7.77% by unidentified causes. Within specific groups, median HIV prevalence rates in mid-1994 for drug injectors were 34.27%, direct CSWs 27.02%, indirect CSWs 7.69%, male CSWs 12.50%, patients with other STDs 8.50%, and donated blood at 0.63% in June 1995. In March 1996, the Communicable Diseases Control Department reported 3% of pregnant women in Thailand are HIV infected.

One in every three children born to HIV-infected mothers are infected themselves (Bhatiasevi, 1996b). HIV prevalence of male conscripts by region was 11.7% in the upper North, 2.7% in the lower North, 3.9% in central Thailand, 3.7% in the Bangkok metropolitan area, 2.2% in Isan, and 2.3% in the South (Torugsa et al., 1996). Over 600,000 cases of full-blown AIDS are expected by the turn of the century in Thailand, and over 10,500 Thais have died of AIDS, 2,330 of them in 1996. Identified transmissions sources were 65.9% heterosexual male, 9.3% heterosexual female, 1.1% homosexual/bisexual male, 7.4% IDU, 7.1% vertical, 0.2% blood, and 9.0% unknown (Ministry of Public Health, 1996). Most AIDS patients are of working age, with 64.55% between 25 and 39 years old. Laborers accounted for 46.12% of AIDS patients whereas 21.74% were farmers. Children under 4 accounted for 4.28% of the cases. Chiang Mai and Chiang Rai in the North led Thailand with 6,867 and 5,098 AIDS patients, respectively. Bangkok reported 4,670 AIDS patients.

Thailand's first AIDS case was reported in 1984 in a Thai man returning from abroad, and indigenous transmission cases were not recorded until 1987. In Thailand, extensive transmission of the virus occurred over the 5-year period from 1988 to 1993. The first wave of the epidemic occurred among IDUs, and its occurrence and rapid spread can be pinpointed through three seroconversion surveys of IDU populations by the Ministry of Public Health. In late 1987, 1% of IDUs tested were HIV-seropositive. A few months later, in early 1988, the figure had risen to 16%, and then to 43% among the 1,800 IDUs tested in September of 1988 (Wenniger et al., 1991). From the IDUs, the epidemic spread in its second wave to Thailand's CSWs, mainly women selling sex directly in brothels. Although HIV-1 infection had already been detected in Thailand in male CSWs, it first appeared among Thai female CSWs in 1989, among their heterosexual customers in 1990, and in noncommercial female partners of these customers in 1991. The infection rate among the direct workers across Thailand rose from 3.5% in 1989 to 33% by late 1994. The spread was most rapid in the North, where a group of female direct workers in Chiang Rai was tested four times by the Ministry of Public Health between August 1987 and June 1990, as HIV infection rates in the group increased successively from 0% to 54% (Wenniger et al., 1991). The third wave occurred over the same time period in male customers of these workers, increasing from 0% to 8.6%, and the fourth wave among wives and regular partners of these customers, going from 0% in 1989 to 2.3% in 1995 (Lamptey & Taranatola, 1996) and to 3.0% in 1996. The female–male ratio of people with HIV rose from 1/17 in 1986 to 1/1 by 1996, though Public Health Ministry estimates in 1996 put the ratio at 1/4, and it is expected to be 3/2 by the year 2001 (Anasuchatkul, 1996; Lamptey & Taranatola, 1996). A fifth wave of vertical transmission is now underway.

A decrease in infection rates in Thailand, together with one in Uganda, are the first recorded in the developing world. Infection rates among military recruits and blood donors have both fallen, from 3.96% to 2.5% among recruits between June 1993 and June 1995, and from 0.90% at the end of 1994 to 0.63% in June 1995 among blood donors (Lamptey & Taranatola, 1996). The number of newly infected cases has been declining since 1991 and is expected to remain at about 90,000 per year until 2001 under current policies, but could be reduced to 25,000 new infections per year if strong additional steps are taken (National Economic and Social Development Board, 1996). Substantial increases in condom use with sex workers may partially account for these reductions (Steinfatt, 1998). The Thai Red Cross Society reports a drop from 22% to 10% of men reporting sex with a sex worker from 1992 to 1994. But the rate has continued to rise among pregnant women, from 0% in December 1990 to 3.0% in March 1996, according to Ministry of Public Health statistics. Infection levels in Isan, which has the lowest HIV prevalence, were as high in 1994 as they were in the North in 1991. And even with decreased infection rates, by 2001, 75% of deaths caused by AIDS will be among those aged 20 to 39, the prime wage-earning group (Brown, Sittitrai, Vanichseni, & Thisyakorn, 1994). Over 80,000 Thai children under 10 are expected to die from AIDS by 2001. The budget devoted to AIDS/HIV for 1996 was approximately U.S.$70 million. The effects of the economic crisis of July 1997 on AIDS budgets is uncertain. The overall economic cost of AIDS to Thailand is estimated at about U.S.$8 billion per year, rising to over U.S.$9 billion per year by 2000.

Government Interventions in Commercial Sex in Thailand. Bamber, Hewison, and Underwood (1997) listed three phases of government response to the epidemic: denial in the early years, followed by active monitoring and public education beginning in the early 1990s, and the beginnings of commitment of major resources to monitoring, education, counseling, and community support programs in the mid- to late 1990s. Although blaming CSWs for the spread of STDs, the Venereal Disease Act of 1908 emphasized the medical treatment of the customers of CSWs, essentially ignoring treatment or help for the workers themselves (Mettarikanon, 1983). This model was repeated in the initial responses to AIDS in Thailand. Initial government pamphlets on AIDS suggested foreign partners as a higher risk, listed persons close to infected persons as a source of risk, and kissing as a source of infection (Ministry of Public Health, 1985). Although these statements gave way in later literature to more accepted research findings, in 1989 the administration of Chulalongkorn University, the most prestigious in Thailand, attempted to screen only its foreign staff for HIV. Public health officials called for the arrest of infected CSWs when 40% of a group of direct workers in Chiang Mai tested positive in July. Tourism industry groups denounced the "hysteria" over AIDS in August. As late as 1990 the prime minister made public statements that AIDS was not a problem in Thailand (Bamber, Hewison, & Underwood, 1997). In December of that year, this author spoke at the International Congress on AIDS in Developing Nations, where Ministry of Public Health officials and a former prime minister argued to limit the freedom of CSWs, homosexuals, and IDUs (Bamber et al., 1997; Steinfatt, 1998).

Given high heterosexual transmission rates and an extensive commercial sex industry, in 1989 the government launched a 100% condom use campaign in sex establishments, which took effect over the following 2 years. It ran concurrently with a public education campaign conducted in large part through the media. Over 60 million condoms were distributed annually to 6,029 sex establishments recognized by the Ministry of Public Health's Department of Communicable Disease Control, with an ultimate goal of distributing 120 million annually, to also cover acts of casual sex. Since 1989, condom use in brothels increased from about 6% to as high as 90% in some areas, according the Department of Communicable Disease Control. Steinfatt (1998) found condom use increased from 12% of CSW liaisons in 1988 to 84% by 1997 among indirect workers in Bangkok and Pattaya. Among customers of indirect workers, 15% said they always used condoms in 1988, whereas 70% reported always using by 1996, with lower rates among expatriates (Steinfatt, 1998). Cases of STDs dropped from 0.769% or about 200,000 in 1987 to just 0.164% or about 40,000 cases in July of 1993 (Hannenberg, 1993).

A "model brothel" program and a "Superstar" campaign were also introduced to promote condom use in brothels in Chiang Mai. The model brothel component encouraged all brothel owners to insist on mandatory use of condoms by their workers and to encourage condom use by customers. The program promoted cooperation between sex workers, brothel owners, and customers, on the one hand, and public health officials on the other. Free condoms were supplied as a part of the program involving nearly 500 women from 43 brothels. Superstar refers to the most requested workers, a management designation conferring status and credibility among workers within a brothel. The superstars were trained to conduct repeated small-group training sessions for other workers over a 12-month period, explaining and modeling the use of condoms (Visrutaratna, Lindan, Sirhorachai, & Mandel, 1995).

As a test of the program, volunteers offered to buy off the condom by paying three times the standard fee for sex. Prior to the intervention 42% ($n = 24$) of women surveyed refused sex without a condom. Immediately following the program 92% ($n = 78$) refused, whereas 1 year later 78% ($n = 85$) continued to refuse without additional interventions. Wawer, Podhisita, Kanungsukkasem, Pramualratana, and McNamara (1996) studied 678 CSWs in low-price brothels and tea houses found that the customer's appearance and/or a trusting relationship with the customer were the most common reasons given for not using condoms. They suggested that AIDS education should take attitudes with respect to risk of transmission in the absence of AIDS symptoms into account, and also advocate sanctions for brothel owners who do not enforce condom use. Not all government efforts were equally successful. In early 1995, the Office of the Permanent Secretary of the Prime Minister's Office banned distribution of an anti-AIDS booklet it had produced after complaints arose over sexually provocative illustrations. It contained cartoon drawings of a doctor persuading his female client to strip so he could demonstrate safe sex. The government currently has the 1997–2001 National AIDS Prevention and Control Plan in effect.

Commercial Yes, Noncommercial No, and the Relational Bond Effect. CSWs in Thailand formed the second wave of AIDS, infected by the first wave among IDUs. Partially due to government efforts promoting condoms for commercial sex, AIDS is now more likely to be acquired through a spouse or lover because condom use is low to nonexistent in such relationships. But the effects of earlier messages blaming CSWs for the spread of AIDS make it difficult to convince people that their primary relationship is now the most dangerous. As late as 1995, the Thai Minister of Health blamed migratory foreign sex workers who are unaware of condoms for the continued spread of the disease, a statement the *Bangkok Post* labeled "a hypocritical display of polispeak" ("AIDS Is Not a Problem," 1995).

In support of this notion, Havanon, Bennett, and Knodel (1993) found that most men throughout the social strata engaged in a combination of commercial and noncommercial sexual relationships, normally using condoms when they engaged in sex with prostitutes, but with lowest condom use found among men who were the most frequent patrons. In noncommercial nonmarital relationships, the men tended to screen partners for risk using their own personal criteria, rather than use condoms. The noncommercial partners of these men were largely unaware of their links to a larger network of sexual contacts and the associated risks of HIV infection. Celentano et al. (1996) also found high condom use with CSWs but low or inconsistent use with noncommercial partners. Similar findings were reported by Sittitrai and Brown (1994) and Steinfatt (1998).

In studying condom use among CSWs, Morris, Pramualratana, Podhisita, and Wawer (1995) found that the nature of the relational bond between the commercial partners, rather than the individual characteristics, knowledge, or attitudes of the workers or customers, was the single strongest predictor of consistent condom use for all groups studied. Consistent use drops significantly with regular commercial sex partners as compared with single visit commercial partners. Brothel workers reported that 20% of their commercial partners were regular customers, and 20% of customers also report a regular commercial partner. Thus, these regular relationships provide the highest risk of HIV infection, whereas casual one-time relationships provide the lowest risk due to an increased tendency to use a condom with a one-time partner. The strength of the associative bond between the partners must be considered in messages promoting condom use.

Thus, although condoms are effective in preventing HIV infection, and though condom use has increased dramatically in brothels, the use of condoms in both primary relationships such as marriage, and in secondary noncommercial sexual relationships, such as in *mia noi* (minor wife) and *feen* (girlfriend/boyfriend) relationships, remains low. Casual sex is very common among the large and growing population of young migrant workers from rural areas (Asavaroengchai, 1994). Casual sex among teenagers is not traditional and some believe it is a relatively recent phenomenon, along with an increased tolerance for public knowledge of affairs among adults. This increased tolerance may coincide with the lessened use of brothels due to a fear of AIDS. Many Thai factories operate 24 hours a day and may employ 5,000 female teenagers and young adults on three shifts. Sexual relationships between these young women and their male coworkers, some serious but most casual, are quite common. Most women workers in these factories have a boyfriend, and male workers may have a girlfriend on each shift (Cash & Anasuchatkul, 1995). Ford and Kittisuksathit (1994) studied the sexual awareness and lifestyles of single male and female Thai factory workers aged 15 to 24. Pattalung et al. (1995) found lower sexual activity among female office workers than among female factory workers, and low condom use in both groups.

Premarital sexual activity occurs in a context of relaxation, awareness of social and economic freedom, friendship, and ability to be up to date. According to Cash and Anasuchatkul (1995), a man with a good income or money, who can provide a meal and a good time, is important to female factory workers. The authors found that accepting the man's infidelity both as lover and as husband is seen as a cost of attracting and keeping the man, and that these women perceive condom use requests in a context of their perceived social costs as opposed to their health consequences. Among these were the possible loss of the relationship, loss of trust, loss of belief in their own or their partner's goodness or virtue, loss of social acceptance by peers, and loss of face in making a condom request.

This means that whereas the 100% condom campaign has provided a degree of empowerment to brothel workers who want to use a condom, this is not the case in casual, and especially not in primary and secondary, relationships. Wives and girlfriends lack the power to insist on safe sex from their partners to protect themselves. A man's response to a condom request will normally be, "I am certainly faithful to you. Do you mean that you are not being faithful to me?" The wife or lover has no good response, for she cannot accuse the man of infidelity, nor would she be willing to admit to any degree of infidelity on her own part whether or not it has occurred. In addition, most traditional Thai women feel that condom use should be the man's decision. But a young woman is likely to think that something is wrong with the man, perhaps AIDS or another disease, if he chooses to wear a condom while having sex, and he knows this. Thus men who wish to use a condom also face social pressures against their use.

Discrimination and AIDS in Thailand.   The police can be a major problem for sex workers, including those involved in peer education programs. Raids on brothels, and indiscriminate arrests of adult workers while "rescuing" workers under age 18, are not uncommon. CSWs believe that raids should be conducted only when management abuses or confines workers, and that management, not workers, should then be arrested (Steinfatt, 1998). Police raids move the sex industry underground, where the major abuses such as child workers, indenture, and cheating the workers out of their earnings occur, where health services are unavailable, and where workers cannot file complaints. A particular source of concern to CSWs is the discriminatory treatment they receive with respect to the labor laws. Unlike office work where management will be arrested if there is a problem with the police, workers in legal venues where sex is sold indirectly are the persons arrested; they are not recognized as employees under labor laws, and have no governmental protection.

Although the rights of PWAs are protected by Thai law, these laws are not generally enforced, and most PWAs are reluctant to reveal themselves for fear of further discrimination. Since 1992, government policy has mandated that tests for HIV be performed only with informed consent, yet many public hospitals continue to conduct blood tests on pregnant women and on general patients without informed consent. If HIV is detected, the patient is often refused the services requested. Expectant mothers are often pressured to abort, although abortion is illegal, or are sterilized after delivery. It is common for medical staff responsible for HIV patients to inform each other of the patient's HIV status, thus treating AIDS patients differently from others, as opposed to using universal precautions. The Public Health Ministry encourages couples to have blood tests before marriage, with a strong possibility that an individual testing positive will be rejected by the other partner and by that person's family. This has encouraged the increased sale of counterfeit health certificates (Bhatiasevi, 1996c; Sixth National Conference, 1996).

A policy of dismissal of HIV-infected workers is standard with many Thai employers, who test their employees' blood for AIDS without their consent and dismiss those found HIV-seropositive. Additionally, many companies avoid hiring people with HIV, men wishing to join the monkhood are asked to present a certificate proving HIV-negative status, and such a certificate is required in order to borrow money from the Bank of Agriculture and Agricultural Cooperatives. The National AIDS Prevention and Control Plan under the Eighth National Economic and Social Development Board states that people seeking insurance should not be forced to test for HIV, but they are often refused insurance without such a test. Health officials in rural areas are somewhat removed from control by Bangkok-based officials, and are more likely than urban officials to do what they think is right rather than to follow national policy (Bhatiasevi, 1996c; Sixth National Conference, 1996).

Discrimination Against Support Groups in Thailand.   More support groups for PWAs exist in Thailand than any other country in the region, due primarily to the extent and duration of the Thai epidemic. The groups provide support, attempt to raise the visibility of PWAs, and campaign for the application of human rights to PWAs. Most are located in the North, and secondarily in Bangkok, where the epidemic is most severe. Contrary to Western norms, Thais do not consider it impolite to stare at people with disabilities or deformities. Thus, although some groups have urged PWAs to come out and demonstrate their numbers, particularly on Valentine's Day, which is widely celebrated in Thailand as a day of romantic and brotherly love, crowds gathering to hear a speaker quickly disperse when they realize the group is concerned with support for PWAs. Many Thai politicians invited to attend such events fear possible stigma of identification and do not attend.

Some support groups have faced great prejudice and hostility. When the location of one Bangkok relief center for PWAs, run by the St. Camillus Foundation of Thailand in Soi Rewadee 24, Nonthaburi, became known in the summer of 1995, community opposition was immediate and fierce. Owners of a private kindergarten said the center had scared away customers, and residents expressed fears about the center's water and garbage (" 'Unhappy' Residents," 1995). Shots were fired into the center, which also experienced verbal abuse, intimidation, and bomb attacks. After 9 months of operation the center closed its doors to PWAs, and only a small telephone-counseling service remained. Few citizens were involved in the actual attacks. But even after the center was reduced to telephone counseling, and that fact was clearly explained to the community, a large group of people joined a demonstration against the center in front of the Provincial Hall. It was of sufficient size to impress the Interior Deputy Permanent Secretary, the Governor of Nonthaburi, the Director-General of the Communicable Disease Control Department, and the Public Health Deputy Permanent Secretary, to request that the center move by a specified date. It did. The *Bangkok Post* editorialized against this sequence of events as displaying "profound ignorance and meanness," with the official request for the center to move giving "an official stamp of approval for a campaign of malice and ignorance." It further stated that the officials involved "performed a great service on behalf of the abysmally ignorant" ("Triumph of Ignorance," 1996). Although there are many halfway homes and support centers in Bangkok in areas as such as Silom and Sukhumvit, based on the experience in Soi Rewadee, their location and existence remains secret.

Testing of the Blood Supply in Thailand.   All blood donated in Thailand through the Public Health Ministry undergoes an enzyme-linked immonosorbent assay (ELISA) test, yet an estimated 0.28% of donated blood distributed to hospitals in Thailand is contaminated with HIV. Because about 900,000 units of blood are used in Thailand every year, about 2,520 of the units distributed by the Public Health Ministry each year are contaminated with HIV. By law, a person infected by ELISA-tested blood that did not show HIV contamination is considered infected by accident and the supplier is not liable. The Thai Red Cross Society uses the more reliable and expensive antigen test on blood it distributes. These decisions are financial, and thus political. Persons recently infected with HIV are often more contagious than those with longer term infections, and the antigen test is more accurate in the 4–6 months after a person is exposed to the virus. The risk of infection is weighed against the added cost of the antigen test by the Public Health Ministry, and against the increased work load it would provide to laboratory technicians who are in short supply. The Ministry argued that an increased work load could lead to less accuracy and dependability of results, thus defeating the purpose of the testing, and failing to reduce the number of infections due to contaminated blood ("HIV Lottery," 1996).

14 GENERAL FACTORS IN THE RESPONSE TO AIDS

Beyond the unique factors within each country, 14 general factors serve to summarize much of the response to AIDS across the five countries of Southeast Asia by the degree of their presence or absence:

1. The lack of top-level political leadership in the struggle against AIDS, with the exception of Thailand: If top-level politicians take up an issue, then the issue moves. Otherwise, it does not. The Prime Minister of Uganda never makes a speech without mentioning HIV/AIDS. This does not happen in any Mekong country.

2. The sheer number and extent of competing priorities in underdeveloped and newly industrialized countries: These priorities often include poverty, hunger, political stability, freedom versus despotism, and the residue of prior conflicts as disparate as political enmities and land mines. In situations where so many visible problems are more immediate than the threat of AIDS, it is a luxury to promote the long-term thinking necessary to stem the epidemic.

3. The low salaries typical throughout the ranks and within all areas of the governmental agencies and NGOs that work with AIDS: The lack of sufficient compensation leads to workers who do not care, and/or who can be bribed into actions inducing rather than reducing the spread of AIDS. Governments and NGO leaderships need to set priorities and to use nonmonetary incentives to produce quality work and quality workers. Some of these incentives might include the three Ps: prestige, power, and promotion, in place of scarce funds.

4. The extent to which general information control within a country has constrained the credibility of authorities, thus reducing the likelihood of adoption of desired behavioral change advocated by those authorities.

5. The lack of an overall plan of attack against HIV and AIDS: This is a general lack of coordination between the government, donors, NGOs, local communities, and local community organizations. Although there are normally some structures within each country that provide a degree of coordination between some units, an overall plan and overall coordination is normally lacking, leading to the inefficient use of the already limited resources.

6. The restriction of financial and technical support beyond Ministry of Health programs: When financial and technical support exists, it will seldom be extended to non–Ministry of Health programs. To support non–Ministry of Health programs would mean the diversion of resources away from Ministry of Health control. Officials in charge of such decisions will seldom act to reduce their own power, prestige, and resources.

7. The degree of understanding within AIDS education programs that among those who use condoms, frequency of intercourse with the same partner has a strong inverse relationship to condom use: Condom use is often low in youths' initial encounters where the request for use implies a lack of trust and suspicions of infidelity. But even among individuals who adopt it, condom use is perceived as less necessary and is used far less in marriage, lover, and long-term relations with a specific CSW or regular customer, than in initial and temporary relationships. This proposition is related to Factor 8.

8. The degree to which the sex industry is portrayed as the principal cause of the epidemic: Spurred on by conservative forces who self-label their personal views on human sexual behavior as a "morality" ordained either by a superhuman power or by the will of the proletariat, the sex industry and CSWs are an easy target for the media, politicians, and back-fence gossip. To many minds, the role of CSWs in the initial spread of any STD serves as justification for this attack. An extensive attack on CSWs is easier than an attack on HIV risk behaviors in general. But sex industries and their workers react to the personal examples of AIDS visible within their membership. Workers, energized by their personal risk awareness often adopt risk-reducing recommendations more rapidly and readily than do persons outside of the industry. This produces a sex industry that, having adopted high levels of condom use in the mid-to-later stages of the epidemic, is less risky than normal heterosexual behavior within a marriage, because the infection has now spread among the general population, and married partners do not normally use condoms.

Balance is needed between portraying commercial sex as risky behavior, and an all-out assault on commercial sex as the scourge of humanity. A dilemma is created wherein a degree of public pressure on the sex industry may increase initial prevention efforts. But the media frenzy created by the unleashing of moral zealots will produce and reinforce a very stable public belief that risk lies mainly within commercial sex, and not in primary sexual relationships. When these primary relationships become the preeminent source of infection in the later, more expanded stages of the epidemic, early efforts to portray CSWs as the principal evil make it exceptionally difficult to convince people that it is their "ordinary" sexual behavior that places them most at risk.

9. The degree to which people at risk perceive dangerous activities as negative: Not all population subgroups avoid unprotected sex with infected persons simply because it is dangerous. Some youthful subgroups engage in it directly because it is dangerous.

10. The degree to which condom use and sex education are considered inappropriate topics for public discussion: In parts of the region, particularly outside of Thailand and in most rural areas, safer sex and condom use are not polite or appropriate topics for discussion or advertising. Most people feel that such issues should not be discussed in public, and it is difficult to promote condom use without communication concerning it.

11. The degree of economic, social, and sexual inequality between men and women: Laws concerning marriage and the family usually emphasize principles of monogamy and equality between husband and wife. Yet women are denied equal opportunities for education, economic independence, and a voice in decision making within families, economically, and politically. Women's legal status as relative equals differs from their actual status as subordinate to men. The existence of a market-oriented economy, or transition to it as in Vietnam and Laos, impacts on women more than men. Men hold the societally respectable jobs in government, business, and labor. The woman bears the brunt of providing extra income to the family, and this may often include a form of commercial sex as the simplest and most lucrative means of dealing with a market economy, but without societal help for protection from disease.

12. The existence of a charismatic figure to act as a symbol for the cause: This person must be a vigorous individual with the credentials to be accepted, or at least not lightly dismissed, by the ruling powers. Thailand's Chairman of the Population and Community Development Association, Mechai Viravaidya, was so effective that the Thai people called condoms "Mechais" in the early 1990s.

13. The existence of a government-respected social scientist who can understand, conduct, and explain to the politicians the importance, implications, and needed applications of a broad range of social science research. In a health epidemic where vaccines are unavailable, behavioral change is the only preventative. Thailand was fortunate to have Werasit Sittitrai in this role, as Deputy Director of the Thai Red Cross Society for the Program on AIDS.

14. The degree to which people see AIDS as a personal possibility that could affect them or their loved ones. AIDS symptoms take a long time to appear. People are aware of the existence and danger of AIDS without believing it will happen to them or to those close to them. Resistance to persuasion with respect to changing risk behaviors appears to be a function of the extent of visibility of PWAs who originated within a target individual's village or local area, or who have some other similar demographic characteristics to the target individual. In general, people need to have a personal experience with AIDS, through knowing, seeing, or meeting someone with AIDS, especially someone seen as similar to themselves, in order to effect a change in their own personal risk behaviors. By the time such an exemplar is available, any resulting behavioral change often occurs too late for the individual involved.

ACKNOWLEDGMENTS

Thanks are due to Dr. Le Hoang Son, Director of the HCM City AIDS Committee, to the Institute for Social Sciences in HCM City, to Mark Beukema, Program Manager of Save the Children/UK in HCM City, and to Leah Thayer, Nguyen Thi Thien Hai, Bui Khac Than (Omar), Eli Cawley, William Boyd, and Nguyen Trang, in Vietnam. The resources of Tim France at the South East Asia HIV/AIDS Project/UNAIDS in Bangkok were of major assistance.

REFERENCES

AIDS is not a problem to be passed off as someone else's fault. (1995, February 26). *Bangkok Post,* p. 10.

Anasuchatkul, B. (1996). *Educational interventions for AIDS prevention among single migratory female factory workers in Thailand* [On-line]. Available from SEA-AIDS in pvsex3.txt via E-mail from: ftpmail@@inet.co.th

Asavaroengchai, S. (1994, September 14). Spelling out the threat. *Bangkok Post,* Outlook, p. 1.

Australian Red Cross. (1997, February 28). *Survey of AIDS awareness and related sexual behavior.* Phnom Penh: Australian Red Cross. Also available in summary form from SEA-AIDS dated March 2 as "Risky sexual behavior in Cambodia unchanged by AIDS awareness" via E-mail from: ftpmail@inet.co.th

Bamber, S., Hewison, K., & Underwood, P. (1997). Dangerous liaisons: A history of sexually transmitted diseases in Thailand. In M. Lewis, S. Bamber, & M. Waugh (Eds.), *Sex, disease, and society: A comparative history of sexually transmitted diseases and HIV/AIDS in Asia and the Pacific* (pp. 37–65). Westport, CT: Greenwood.

Berkely, M. (1996, July). *Sales training in a Cambodian CSM program: A way to increase condom use?* Paper presented at the XI International Conference on AIDS, Vancouver, BC, Canada.

Berkely, S. (1993). AIDS in the developing world: An epidemiologic overview. *Clinical Infectious Disease, 17*(Suppl. 2), S329–S336.

Bhatiasevi, A. (1996a, December 14). Burma doing little in fight against AIDS. *Bangkok Post,* p. 2.

Bhatiasevi, A. (1996b, December 12). Gender gap mars fight against AIDS. *Bangkok Post,* p. 5.

Bhatiasevi, A. (1996c, August 28). Law on rights of people with HIV "not properly enforced": Abuses more common here than elsewhere. *Bangkok Post,* p. 3.

Brown, T., Sittitrai, W., Vanichseni, S., & Thisyakorn, U. (1994). The recent epidemiology of HIV and AIDS in Thailand. *AIDS, 8* (Suppl.2), S131–S141.

Buchanan, D., & Cernada, G. (Eds.). (1998). *Progress in preventing AIDS? Dogma, dissent, and innovation: Global perspectives.* Amityville, NY: Baywood.

Cambodian AIDS Social Research Project. (1996). *Two year report.* Phnom Penh: AIDS Social Research Project, Cambodian Ministry of Health.

Cash, K., & Anasuchatkul, B. (1995). *Educational interventions for AIDS prevention among Northern Thai single migratory female factory workers.* Washington, DC: International Center for Research on Women.

Celentano, D. D., Beyrer C., Natpratan C., Eiumtrakul, S., Nelson, K. E., Go, V., & Khamboonruang, C. (1996, July). *Sexual mixing and condom use among high risk HIV seronegative men in Northern Thailand.* Paper presented at the XI International Conference on AIDS, Vancouver, BC, Canada.

Chin, J. (1996). *AIDS report to the Ministry of Health.* Phnom Penh: Cambodian Ministry of Health.

Efroymson, D. (1997). Lack of HIV/AIDS information in Vietnam: A changing Vietnam lacks HIV/AIDS information. *SIECUS Reports: Australia Vietnam science-technology link* (February/March). Also available from SEA-AIDS in news38.txt via e-mail from: ftpmail@inet.co.th

Ford, N. J., & Kittisuksathit, S. (1994). Destinations unknown: The gender construction and changing nature of the sexual expressions of Thai youth. *AIDS Care, 6,* 517–531.

Greenberg, J. H. (1972). Venereal disease in the Armed Forces. *Medical Clinics of North America, 56,* 1087–1100.

Guenel, A. (1997). Sexually transmitted diseases in Vietnam and Cambodia since the French colonial period. In M. Lewis, S. Bamber, & M. Waugh (Eds.), *Sex, disease, and society: A comparative history of sexually transmitted diseases and HIV/AIDS in Asia and the Pacific* (pp. 139–153). Westport, CT: Greenwood.

Hannenberg, R. S. (1993). *The decline of STDs in Thailand: Implications for the AIDS epidemic.* Bangkok: Ministry of Public Health.

Havanon, N., Bennett, A., & Knodel, J. (1993). Sexual networking in provincial Thailand. *Studies in Family Planning, 24,* 1–17.

HIV lottery prompts debate on price of providing safe blood. (1996, April 21). *Bangkok Post,* p. 3.

Ho Chi Minh City AIDS Committee. (1996). [Accumulative HIV positive by age group, provinces, and groups]. Unpublished raw data. Ho Chi Minh City: Author.

International Union for the Scientific Study of Population. (1994). *AIDS impact and prevention in the developing world: Demographic and social science perspectives.* Canberra, Australia: Health Transition Centre, National Centre for Epidemiology and Population Health, Australian National University. [Selected papers from the International Union for the Scientific Study of Population seminar, Annecy, France, December 5–9, 1993. *Health Transition Review* (Supplement to Vol. 4)].

Joyeux, B. (1933). Le peril venerien en Indochine [The perils of venereal disease in Indochina]. *Annales de l'Universite de Hanoi, 1,* 263–275.

Lamptey, P., & Taranatola, D. (1996, July). *The status and trends of the global HIV/AIDS pandemic.* Paper presented at the XI International Conference on AIDS, Satellite Symposium, Vancouver, BC, Canada.

Lewis, M., Bamber, S., & Waugh, M. (Eds.). (1997). *Sex, disease, and society: A comparative history of sexually transmitted diseases and HIV/AIDS in Asia and the Pacific.* Westport, CT: Greenwood.

Meier, B. (1997, June 8). Breast-feeding in developing countries: In war against AIDS, battle over baby formula ignites. *The New York Times,* p. A1.

Mettarikanon, D. (1983). *Sopheni kap nayobai rathaban Thai 2411–2503* [Commercial sex in Thai government policy from 1868 to 1960]. Unpublished master's thesis, Chulalongkorn University, Bangkok.

Ministry of Public Health. (1985). *The AIDS disease.* Bangkok: Author.

Ministry of Public Health. (1996). *Sentinel surveillance by province.* Bangkok: Communicable Diseases Control Department, Ministry of Public Health.

Morris, M., Pramualratana, A., Podhisita, C., & Wawer, M. J. (1995). The relational determinants of condom use with commercial sex partners in Thailand. *AIDS, 9,* 507–515.

National AIDS Program. (1996). *AIDS in Cambodia.* Phnom Penh: Author.

National Economic and Social Development Board. (1996). *The costs of AIDS.* Bangkok: Author.

Nguyen, M. T., Nhan, L., & Le, T. (1996, July). *Condom social marketing in Viet Nam.* Paper presented at the XI International Conference on AIDS, Vancouver, BC, Canada.

Pattalung, R., Mills, S., Wienrawee, P., Benjarattanaporn, P., Sundhagul, D., & Kalumpabutr, N. (1995). *Differences in sexual behavior and condom use among lower income single women employed in factories and offices in Bangkok, Thailand: Results from the Bangkok Behavioral Surveillance Surveys.* Office of Population Technical Assistance (OPTA), AIDSCAP/FHI, Bangkok, Thailand.

Poirot, J. L., Phan, T. L., De Crepy, A., Mary, K. M., Thi Nguyet, N., Thi Bien, T., & Vermeulin, C. (1996, July). *Knowledge and perception of the HIV infection among the staff of a North Vietnam hospital.* Paper presented at the meeting of the XI International Conference on AIDS, Vancouver, BC, Canada.

Rosenberg, P. (1995). Scope of the AIDS epidemic in the United States. *Science, 270,* 1372–1375.

Sittitrai, W., & Brown, T. (1994). Risk factors for HIV infection in Thailand. *AIDS, 8* (Suppl.2), S143–S153.

Sixth National Conference. (1996, August). *Proceedings: The Sixth National Conference on AIDS in Thailand.* Khon Kaen: Ministry of Public Health.

Steinfatt, T. M. (1998). *Working in the bar: Commercial sex, AIDS, and health communication in Thailand.* Manuscript submitted for publication.

Tanne, J. H. (1991). AIDS spreads eastward. *British Medical Journal, 302* (6792), 1557.

Thuermer, K., Warshauer, W., Mackie, B., & Deidrick, J. (1996, July). *Cambodians respond to "NUMBER ONE" condom social marketing campaign.* Paper presented at the XI International Conference on AIDS, Vancouver, BC, Canada.

Torugsa, K., Jenkins R. A., Jamroenratana, V., Krinchai K., Kujareevanich, S., Kongkaew, M., Markowitz, L. E., Mason, C. J., Nitayaphan, S., & Michael, R. A. (1996, July). *HIV risk behavior in young Thai men outside Northern Thailand.* Paper presented at the XI International Conference on AIDS, Vancouver, BC, Canada.

Triumph of ignorance over compassion. (1996, April 18). *Bangkok Post,* p. 10.

"Unhappy" residents behind AIDS center shooting, say police. (1995, August 30). *Bangkok Post,* p. 3.

UNICEF. (1995). *The state of the world's children.* Oxford, England: Oxford University Press.

UNICEF. (1997, December/January). Country level programming: Country reports from the Mekong region. *Mekong Region HIV/AIDS Project Newsletter, 1*(2). *AIDSWatch, News from WHO South-East Asia Region on STDs and AIDS, 1*(1).

Visrutaratna, S., Lindan, C. P., Sirhorachai, A., & Mandel, J. S. (1995). "Superstar" and "model brothel": Developing and evaluating a condom promotion program for sex establishments in Chiang Mai, Thailand. *AIDS, 9*(1 Suppl.), S69–S75.

VNA news agency. (1997, April 27, 1414 gmt). *Ho Chi Minh City sets up village for HIV/AIDS patients* [Radio broadcast in English]. Hanoi: Author.

Wawer, M. J., Podhisita, C., Kanungsukkasem, U., Pramualratana, A., & McNamara, R. (1996). Origins and working conditions of female sex workers in urban Thailand: Consequences of social context for HIV transmission. *Social Science & Medicine, 42*(3), 453–462.

Wenniger, B. G., Limpakarnjanarat, K., Ungchusak, K., Thanprasertsuk, S., Choopanya, K., Vanichseni, S., Uneklabh, T., Thongcharoen, P., & Wasi, C. (1991). The epidemiology of HIV infection and AIDS in Thailand. *AIDS, 5*(Supplement 2).

World Health Organization. (1996). *The world health report: 1996.* Geneva, Switzerland: Author.

VII

THE SYNTHESIS:
CONCLUSIONS AND PROJECTIONS

Diffusion of Innovations and HIV/AIDS Prevention Research

Everett M. Rogers
Corinne L. Shefner-Rogers
University of New Mexico

The purpose of this chapter is to show how the communication theory known as the diffusion of innovations has been applied in research and in programs on the AIDS epidemic, mainly in the United States. The diffusion of innovations is a theoretical perspective concerned with how *innovations,* defined as ideas perceived as new by individuals, spread via certain communication channels over time among the members of a social system (Rogers, 1995). A basic notion of the diffusion model is that once a certain number of individuals (perhaps 10% to 15% of the members of a system) have adopted an innovation, it will continue to spread in a self-sustaining process. The diffusion perspective provides a useful orientation to many public health campaigns, and so, when the AIDS epidemic began in the early 1980s, this theoretical framework was utilized in a number of HIV/AIDS prevention program.

BACKGROUND

The first author of the present chapter originally became involved in research on the AIDS epidemic as the result of an accident of location. In the early 1980s, Rogers was teaching at Stanford University, and thus lived in the San Francisco Bay area. This city was one of three metropolitan centers in the United States in which the epidemic was concentrated (Los Angeles and New York were the others). Unlike the rest of the United States, the mass media in San Francisco gave major news coverage to the issue of AIDS, in part because the virus was spreading via men having sex with men and gay people constituted about 40% of San Francisco's male population (Rogers et al., 1995). Gays in San Francisco were politically active, and the AIDS epidemic became a controversial and newsworthy issue when the city's department of public health tried to close gay bathhouses in the early 1980s. Although the national mass media did not pay attention to the AIDS epidemic for several more years, in San Francisco the AIDS issue received heavy news coverage because it was defined by the media as a political issue (Dearing & Rogers, 1992, 1996).

The Agenda-Setting Process for AIDS

In 1985, author Rogers moved to the University of Southern California, and began scholarly research on the agenda-setting process with a colleague, James W. Dearing. *Agenda-setting* is the process in which an issue climbs to wide attention on the media agenda, then on the public agenda, and finally on the policy agenda. Rogers and Dearing (1988) first critically reviewed the several hundred publications then available about agenda-setting, and concluded that past studies were too aggregate in nature. The typical agenda-setting study investigated the four or five main issues that were on the nation's public agenda at a certain time, and traced how these same issues were influenced by the media agenda (indicated by the amount of media news coverage). Rogers and Dearing argued instead for single-issue studies of agenda setting, in which the agenda-setting process for one issue would be investigated over time.

It is dangerous for relative outsiders to a research specialty to criticize the dominant paradigm guiding that specialty, unless they also conduct research on the alternative paradigm in order to demonstrate its greater usefulness. So Rogers and Dearing began looking for a single issue to study through time. The issue of HIV/AIDS seemed especially intriguing to investigate because it was so slow in climbing the national agenda. Although the first AIDS cases in the United States had been diagnosed in 1981, this issue did not attract much media attention until mid-1985, 4 years later. By that time, more than 10,000 individuals had been diagnosed with AIDS, and about half that number had died. Why were the media so slow in discovering the important issue of AIDS?

Dearing and Rogers received a research grant from the California University Consortium on AIDS Research, to investigate the agenda-setting process of the issue of AIDS in the 1980s. A synthesis of their main findings on the unusually lengthy agenda-setting process for the issue of AIDS in the United States appears in the following section.

The agenda-setting process is related to the diffusion process in that both seek to explain how social change occurs in a society. Most diffusion studies are focused at the individual level, in that individual respondents are asked when they adopted a new idea and which communication sources/channels influenced them to do so (Rogers, 1995). In the typical agenda-setting study, individuals are asked in surveys to identify "the most important problem facing the country today" (in order to measure the public agenda), and these data are analyzed in relationship to the relative position of an issue on the media agenda (measured by a content analysis of the media that indicates the amount of news coverage accorded the issue). The policy agenda is measured by new laws, appropriations, and other policy decisions. Thus agenda-setting research is conducted at the macrolevel of society in order to determine how an issue comes to national attention, whereas diffusion studies are mainly concerned with the microlevel process of how individuals adopt new ideas (of course, in the aggregate such diffusion studies also tell us about societal change).

The Diffusion of AIDS

The HIV/AIDS epidemic is itself a certain type of diffusion process as the virus spreads from person to person among the members of a system. In fact, several mathematical models for the diffusion of innovations come from epidemiological models (Rogers, 1995). In this case, the adoption of a new idea is equivalent to becoming infected with an epidemic. In order to understand the means of transmission of the AIDS virus, an epidemiological investigation by the CDC (Centers for Disease Control and Prevention) in the early 1980s identified 40 men who were among the first in the United States to be diagnosed with AIDS. These individuals, mainly located in San Francisco, Los Angeles, and New York, were connected in a dense network of interpersonal sexual relationships.

One individual, labeled "Patient Zero" by the CDC epidemiologists, played a very key role in the initial spread of the virus. Patient Zero, whose name was Gaetan Dugas, was an airline flight attendant who traveled widely.[1] He was very attractive and led a promiscuous sex life, even after he knew that he was seropositive.[2] He named 72 different male partners during the 2 years just before the AIDS epidemic was identified. Eight were among the other 39 AIDS patients identified in the CDC study. And Patient Zero connected the Los Angeles cluster of AIDS patients with the New York cluster.

The CDC investigators were overwhelmed with the forest of network links connecting the 40 men. It was difficult to make sense out of this information overload. So they turned to Dr. Alden S. Klovdahl, a noted scholar of social networks at Australian National University, who reanalyzed the CDC data with a computer program that he had adapted from molecular chemistry. The vertical dimension in the three-dimensional print-out represented the year in which each of the 40 men had been diagnosed with AIDS. Such a diffusion analysis showed that the role of Patient Zero was even more crucial in the initial spread of the epidemic in America. Although he was not the first of the 40 men to contract AIDS (he was the sixth), once Patient Zero got AIDS, many others soon followed. His 8 direct sexual contacts in turn linked him to 8 other men with AIDS, who in turn linked him to 10 others. In three steps, Patient Zero infected 26 (63%) of the 39 other individuals with AIDS.

This example suggests the power of the diffusion process (and of the spread of an epidemic). Once the diffusion process gets well underway, it is extremely difficult to stop, as it spreads increasingly rapidly in a self-sustaining process. For this reason, the accepted strategy for controlling an epidemic is to identify the cause as soon as possible, and then to immediately throw all the available means of control at the epidemic. Unfortunately, the U.S. government did not follow this obvious strategy in controlling the AIDS epidemic in the early 1980s.

Diffusion Strategies for AIDS Prevention Programs

Diffusion theory also held promise for suggesting strategies for HIV/AIDS prevention by health programs (Dearing, Meyer, & Rogers, 1994). Evidence of this point comes from the STOP AIDS campaign in San Francisco in the 1980s, which was based, in part, on diffusion theory. STOP AIDS recruited at-risk men on the streets and in other public places to participate in small-group meetings that were held in homes and apartments. A speaker who was seropositive and may have been diagnosed with AIDS led the group discussion about the means of transmission of the epidemic, and how to prevent contracting HIV/AIDS through the adoption of safe sex. The STOP AIDS campaign contributed to decreasing the rate of infection of gay men from 20% in 1983 to only 3% in 1989.

Dearing and Rogers applied to the U.S. Agency for Health Care Research and Policy (AHCPR) for an investigation of how HIV/AIDS programs in San Francisco were utilizing (a) the diffusion model, and (b) social marketing strategies, to reach unique populations of at-risk individuals. This project, carried out in 1993–1995, in turn led to a companion study

---

[1]In England, two of the first British patients with AIDS were gay airline stewards. And in India and East Africa, truck drivers and commercial sex workers at truck stops played a major role in spreading AIDS during the first years of its diffusion.

[2]A detailed account of Patient Zero's role in the early diffusion of the AIDS epidemic in the United States was provided by Shilts (1987), Klovdahl (1985), and Rogers (1995).

in Bangkok that was conducted in 1995 by Dr. Peer Svenkerud and Dr. Arvind Singhal of Ohio University (Svenkerud & Singhal, in press). The results of these investigations, focusing on culturally appropriate strategies (based on diffusion theory) for HIV/AIDS prevention, are summarized in a later section of this chapter.

AGENDA-SETTING FOR THE ISSUE OF HIV/AIDS

Rogers and Dearing conducted a longitudinal study of the agenda-setting process for the issue of AIDS in the 1980s. One of the main questions guiding their research was why the AIDS issue was so slow (4 years) in getting on the media agenda. In comparison, the issue of Legionnaire's Disease (a mysterious illness that killed more then 100 older men attending a convention in a Philadelphia hotel) jumped immediately to the top of the U.S. media agenda. Rogers and Dearing measured the media agenda by the number of new stories about AIDS in *The New York Times, The Washington Post,* the *Los Angeles Times,* and the network evening news programs of ABC, NBC, and CBS. From June 1981 through December 1989 (a period of 91 months), these six national media carried 6,694 news stories about AIDS. Although the six media generally agreed in the amount of news coverage of AIDS over the 91 months, there were differences in when the AIDS coverage began.

Climbing the Media Agenda

How does an issue get on the media agenda? *The New York Times* and the White House have the ability to put most issues on the national agenda. If an issue appears on the front page of *The New York Times,* or if the president gives a talk about an issue, the mass media begin to give major news coverage to the issue (Dearing & Rogers, 1996). *The New York Times* published its first Page 1 story about AIDS on March 25, 1983, 12 months later than the *Los Angeles Times* and 10 months later than *The Washington Post,* and 21 months after the first AIDS cases were reported by the CDC. One reason for the delays in the media agenda-setting process was that the management of *The New York Times* did not consider AIDS to be newsworthy in the early years of the epidemic. When a new managing editor was appointed by the *Times* in late 1985, the newspaper's coverage of AIDS expanded dramatically (Rogers, Dearing, & Chang, 1991). Thereafter, *The New York Times* led, rather than lagged, the AIDS news coverage by other national media.

The U.S. president during the 1980s saw AIDS as a budget threat and chose to ignore it. President Reagan did not give a talk about AIDS until May 1987, 72 months into the epidemic, a point at which 35,121 individuals had AIDS. So two reasons for the 4-year delay in the AIDS agenda-setting process were the U.S. president and *The New York Times.*

For some issues, trigger events like personal tragedies set off the agenda-setting process. The number of news stories about AIDS escalated from 14 per month prior to July 1985 (49 months into the epidemic), to 143 per month for the next 42 months of study. Conventional wisdom credits this 10-fold increase in news coverage to the July 1985 announcement that film actor Rock Hudson had AIDS. Rogers et al. (1991) showed that another event, the barring of a young boy, Ryan White, from attending school in Kokomo, Indiana, was even more important than the Rock Hudson tragedy in propelling AIDS up the media agenda. White was the topic of 117 news stories in the six media of study, whereas Hudson was the topic of 74. But the White and Hudson events together accounted for only 3% of the 6,694 news stories of study. More important was the humanization and personification of the AIDS issue by White and Hudson, who served as trigger events to change the meaning of AIDS for newspeople. They responded by giving much more media attention to the issue of AIDS. Here we see how an issue is socially constructed by media gatekeepers over time, and how such perceptions are changed by trigger events.

Other important AIDS-related news events that had occurred previously did *not* push the issue up the media agenda in the United States. Scientific breakthroughs, such as that AIDS was found in the blood supply (in December 1982), that heterosexual contact was a means of AIDS transmission (in January 1983), and identification of the human immunodeficiency virus (HIV, in March 1984), did not put the AIDS issue on the national agenda. Nor did the rapidly increasing number of people who were diagnosed with AIDS or who had died from the epidemic. These real-world indicators did not influence the agenda-setting process, nor have they been found to do so for other issues whose agenda-setting process has been studied (Dearing & Rogers, 1996). *Real-world indicators* are variables that measure objectively the degree of severity of a social problem. Agenda-setting consists of a human process of giving meaning to issues. Tragedies, especially as interpreted by the White House and *The New York Times,* play a much more important role in agenda-setting than do real-world indicators.[3]

The Agenda-Setting Process for AIDS

Does the media agenda influence the public agenda, measured by public opinion polls, as the Rogers and Dearing (1988) model of the agenda-setting process implies? The public agenda for the issue of AIDS was measured by Rogers et al. (1991) by aggregating the responses to 110 polls in which questions about AIDS were asked of 150,000 respondents from 1983 to 1989. However, clear evidence of the effects of the media agenda on the public agenda was not found by Rogers et al., in part because of less-than-perfect measurement of the public agenda (many polls did not asked the "most important problem" question). Nevertheless, early media coverage of the AIDS issue, although relatively sparse, created a sharp increase in public awareness of AIDS (in 1983 and 1984), and corrected the widespread public mis-understandings about methods of HIV transmission (such as that the virus could be spread by contact with toilet seats).

The policy agenda for an issue is usually measured by such policy decisions as the passage of a new law, creation of a new agency, or by increased appropriations. Rogers et al. (1991) operationalized the policy agenda for AIDS by the total federal appropriations for AIDS research, education, and testing. This figure went up from a few million dollars in 1983, to $40 million in 1984, to $70 million in 1985, to $120 million in 1986, to $240 million in 1987, and to $470 million in 1988 (Rogers et al., 1991). So the agenda-setting process for the issue of AIDS resulted in important policy impacts.

Why AIDS Stayed on the Agenda

As we have explained, 4 years were required before the issue of AIDS climbed the media agenda in the United States. But once the issue was on the media agenda, it remained there for the remainder of the 1980s. Why? Most issues follow a rise and fall over a period of a few years. For example, the war on drugs issue shot up the media agenda from 1987 to 1989. The public agenda followed, with a lag. In 1987 only 3% of the U.S. public said (in polls) that drugs were

---

[3]Evidence for this point is also provided by the issue of the war on drugs in the United States, which rose and fell on the media agenda (and the public agenda) in the late 1980s. But during this entire time-series, the real-world indicator of the number of deaths due to drugs was falling. The death of basketball player Len Bias in 1986 was the trigger event that boosted the drug issue on the media agenda (Dearing & Rogers, 1996).

the most important problem facing America. Two years later, this was an incredible 54%. But a year later only 9% said that drugs were the most important problem facing the nation (Dearing & Rogers, 1996). Thus is the rise and fall of an issue on the national agenda.

But AIDS stayed on the agenda during the last half of the 1980s. Why?

Media coverage of the AIDS issue allowed consumers of news stories to experience the consequences of the disease from a variety of perspectives. A subset of 13 categories of news stories about AIDS emerged in the media coverage of this issue, including biomedical accounts of HIV transmission, human interest stories that personalized the disease by describing people with AIDS as victims, accounts of discrimination against people with AIDS, and accounts of children with AIDS (Rogers et al., 1991). Prior to July 1985, a very high percentage of news stories were about the biomedical research findings on AIDS. News stories that personalized the issue of AIDS, using news events such as the Rock Hudson and Ryan White cases, comprised the next phase of media coverage (from 1985 to 1987). Between 1987 and 1988, news stories about AIDS-related government policies dominated the media agenda. In this manner, each of the 13 sub-issues had its day on the media agenda, in a rise-and-fall pattern. As one sub-issue fell, another sub-issue replaced it, serving to keep the overall issue of AIDS high on the media agenda during the last half of the 1980s. New information about AIDS (a) was regularly available over an extended period of time, and (b) was constantly being interpreted in new ways. The continuous shift in focus of the overall issue of AIDS by emphasizing the 13 different sub-issues helped to maintain the topic of AIDS on the media agenda. The enormity of the AIDS issue masked the typical rise-and-fall pattern of issues on the media agenda (Rogers et al., 1991). Obviously, if a cheap and easy cure for AIDS had been discovered over the first 15 years of the epidemic, this issue would probably have dropped down the agenda.

In summary, what was learned about the agenda-setting process for the issue of AIDS in the 1980s? This issue was very slow to climb the media agenda, requiring 4 years from the time of the first reported AIDS cases until this issue received heavy news coverage by U.S. media. Neither the White House nor *The New York Times* played their customary role in putting an issue on the media agenda in the case of the AIDS epidemic. Nor did the real-world indicator of the number of individuals who were HIV-seropositive or who were diagnosed with AIDS propel the issue of AIDS up the media agenda. Not until mid-1985 did two trigger events, the disclosure that actor Rock Hudson had AIDS and the barring of Ryan White from his school in Indiana, change the meaning of the AIDS issue for U.S. media gatekeepers. After 1985, the AIDS issue remained on the media agenda as each of 13 AIDS sub-issues rose and fell in their amount of news coverage. The media agenda seems to have been followed (a) by an increase in the percentage of the U.S. public who regarded AIDS as the most important problem facing the nation (this is the public agenda), and (b) by sharply increased federal appropriations for HIV/AIDS research, education, and testing.

Overall, the Rogers et al. (1991) investigation of the agenda-setting process for AIDS demonstrated the usefulness of single-issue, longitudinal studies of the agenda-setting process, in comparison with the multiple-issue, cross-sectional studies that had previously dominated agenda-setting research (Dearing & Rogers, 1996).

CULTURALLY APPROPRIATE HIV / AIDS
PREVENTION STRATEGIES

As mentioned previously, Dearing and Rogers, in collaboration with several colleagues, conducted an investigation of the way in which diffusion strategies were utilized by HIV/AIDS prevention programs in San Francisco. This project was funded by the AHCPR, a federal government agency concerned with how research-based knowledge is disseminated and utilized by health practitioners. Originally, this research proposal sought only to study diffusion strategies, but the proposal's reviewers suggested that the utilization of social marketing strategies should also be investigated. *Social marketing* is the use of behavior change strategies taken from commercial marketing for use in the nonprofit marketing of products and services like public health.

The AIDS Epidemic in San Francisco

Dearing and Rogers chose to conduct the AHCPR-funded study in San Francisco (a) because of this city's extensive experience with the AIDS epidemic, and (b) because HIV prevention programs had effectively reduced the rate of new HIV infections. Also, Dearing and Rogers had had prior research experience in analyzing the agenda-setting process for the issue of AIDS in San Francisco, which did *not* lag for 4 years, as it had for the rest of the United States (Dearing & Rogers, 1992).

San Francisco is the world's most experienced city in its funding and organized response to HIV infection. San Francisco had the highest number of HIV-infected persons per capita of any major city in the United States (including 48% of the city's gay and bisexual male population), as well as the highest rate of AIDS-related deaths per population (1.7% in 1995). The San Francisco Department of Public Health estimated that this city of 775,000 had 20,273 deaths due to AIDS in 1997. A photograph distributed by the Associated Press in 1994 shows the 122 members of the San Francisco Gay Men's Chorus on stage with 115 dressed in black and facing away from the camera. They represent the members of the chorus who had died from AIDS since 1981. Only seven members of the chorus are dressed in white and face the camera. They represent the members of the Gay Men's Chorus who were still alive in 1994.

HIV Prevention Programs in San Francisco

When the Dearing et al. (1996) investigation began in 1993, San Francisco had 463 organizations providing AIDS-related services of various kinds, with half focusing mainly on HIV prevention. Some 49 of these organizations provided the 100 HIV prevention programs of study by Dearing et al. The degree to which each of these 100 programs was targeted at unique populations was measured by awarding 1 point for each special characteristic of the intended audience for the program. For instance, one HIV prevention program was targeted to African-American, male, runaway, teenage, low-income, low-education prostitutes. This program had a targeting score of 7 (for the seven HIV risk factors characterizing the intended audience).

Why were the HIV prevention programs in San Francisco so highly targeted? The city is a culturally diverse metropolis, with a very high population of Asians, and also with large populations of African Americans and Hispanics. Many of the HIV prevention programs were operated by community-based organizations, which often served a particular ethnic group. For example, a Filipino community-based organization operated an HIV prevention program targeted to young gay Filipino males. The main audience characteristics on which the San Francisco HIV prevention programs were targeted were age, ethnicity, sexual orientation, gender, drug usage, language, socioeconomic status, homelessness, and prostitution (Dearing et al., 1996). One main reason there were so many HIV prevention programs in San Francisco, which has a total population of only 775,000 people, is because of the extreme ethnic/racial diversity of this city. Many of the HIV prevention programs were targeted at a relatively small audience. An extreme case was one program targeted at an intended audience of only about 150 "Deadheads" (followers of the Grateful Dead musical group) who lived in the Haight-Ashbury district.

The most frequently used means through which HIV prevention programs communicated with their target audiences included street outreach, small-group communication, classroom training, and such mass media as radio programs and posters. HIV prevention programs in San Francisco utilized interpersonal communication channels (such as face-to-face outreach) much more than they used mass media communication. Why? Media channels were more difficult to target at a specific audience segment than were interpersonal communication channels.

The typical HIV prevention program was staffed by a relatively small number of individuals. Usually the staff members shared the uniqueness variables with their intended audience. For example, if the target audience consisted of Thai massage girls, the program staff were former Thai massage girls who had received a brief training in HIV/AIDS prevention and in strategies for outreach workers. Many programs utilized volunteers, who were trained and supervised by paid staff. Burnout after a few years of work was common. Often the program staff members were HIV-seropositive, and some had been diagnosed with AIDS. These qualities, including their *homophily*[4] with clients, gave the program staff a high degree of *credibility,* defined as the degree to which a source is perceived as expert and trustworthy.

The importance of homophily in outreach activities was stressed in an interview with a program staff member in an HIV prevention program targeted to gay Native Americans: "I think this is pretty basic for us, the philosophy of Natives helping Natives, and we got 100 percent Native staff, 100 percent Native Board, most of our volunteers are Native, and it's really about hearing the information coming from another Native gay man" (quoted in Dearing et al., 1996).

A crucial quality of the relatively more effective HIV prevention programs in San Francisco was that they communicated their prevention messages in a culturally sensitive manner. Having a culturally homophilous program staff, and communicating in the language of the intended audience members was crucial to success. Dearing et al. (1996) found that HIV prevention programs reported using more social marketing strategies (especially strategies such as designing the social product, audience segmentation, and evaluation) than diffusion strategies (particularly using appropriate communication channels, designing programs with certain perceived attributes, and homophily). Most program staff were para-professionals who did not think in terms of identifying their strategies with a particular model (such as diffusion or social marketing). But Dearing and his fellow researchers were able to categorize most of the strategies reported by their HIV prevention programs of study in terms of these two models.

One important quality of the HIV prevention programs in San Francisco was that their program staff were nonjudgmental in discussing HIV and related matters with their clients. Program staff were careful not to imply to their target audience that injection drug use, commercial sex work, or promiscuity were undesirable. Sometimes this nonjudgmental stance came down to very fine nuances. For example, prevention program staff used the term "drug *user*" rather than "drug *abuser*" when talking to individuals at risk for HIV infection, who in many cases were drug users.

Dearing and colleagues (1996) concluded that the cultural appropriateness of HIV prevention programs in San Francisco was a key factor in their effectiveness. Although program staff members usually had not heard of the diffusion of innovations model or of social marketing, the change strategies they used often fit with these models, especially social marketing.

---

[4]Homophily is the degree to which two or more individuals are similar (Rogers, 1995).

CONCLUSIONS

How has diffusion theory helped us understand the AIDS epidemic, and slow its spread through HIV prevention programs?

The AIDS epidemic itself is a diffusion process. AIDS is communicated through interpersonal channels over time among networks of individuals within a social system. The San Francisco AIDS study (Dearing et al., 1994) showed that HIV prevention programs (a) that utilized interpersonal communication channels to deliver culturally appropriate messages about safe sex, and (b) whose outreach workers were homophilous with the intended audience(s), were more effective in encouraging at-risk individuals to adopt HIV harm-reduction behaviors. A similar study in Bangkok, Thailand (Svenkerud & Singhal, in press), found that more effective HIV prevention programs utilized information dissemination strategies based on homophily. For example, an outreach worker who lived in the same slum area as her target audience of slum housewives was highly effective in outreach prevention activities.

The agenda-setting process for the issue of AIDS led, after a 4-year lag, to increased federal funding for prevention programs. Continuous news stories about the disease and the epidemic helped to demystify AIDS for the U.S. public, and gradually to convince them, and policymakers, that the AIDS issue was of high priority.

How has the AIDS epidemic influenced other prevention programs/campaigns? The success of the STOP AIDS campaign in the mid-1980s in San Francisco, which utilized a small-group, community-oriented approach, promoted the use of peer-networking approaches in other prevention outreach activities. For example, many other U.S. cities and other nations based their HIV prevention activities, at least intuitively, on the "San Francisco model." Further, the diffusion approaches to HIV prevention in San Francisco have spread to other types of prevention programs. For example, the Johns Hopkins University/Population Communication Services *Jiggasha* program in Bangladesh adopted the small-group, community-based approach, led by local leaders who are homophilous with their audience members, to encourage networks of individuals to use family-planning methods.

ACKNOWLEDGMENTS

The authors wish to thank Dr. James W. Dearing, Department of Communication, Michigan State University, for his contributions to the research reported in the present chapter.

REFERENCES

Dearing, J. W., Meyer, G., & Rogers, E. M. (1994). Diffusion theory and HIV risk behavior. In R. J. DiClemente & J. L. Peterson (Eds.), *Preventing AIDS: Theories and methods of behavioral interventions* (pp. 79–93). New York: Plenum.

Dearing, J. W., & Rogers, E. M. (1992). AIDS and the media agenda. In T. Edgar, M. A. Fitzpatrick, & V. Freimuth (Eds.), *AIDS: A communication perspective* (pp. 173–194). Hillsdale, NJ: Lawrence Erlbaum Associates.

Dearing, J. W., & Rogers, E. M. (1996). *Agenda-setting*. Newbury Park, CA: Sage.

Dearing, J. W., Rogers, E. M., Meyer, G., Casey, M. K., Rao, N., Campo, S., & Henderson, G. M. (1996). Social marketing and diffusion-based strategies for communicating health with unique populations: HIV prevention in San Francisco. *Journal of Health Communication, 1*, 343–363.

Klovdahl, A. S. (1985). Social networks and the spread of infectious diseases: The AIDS example. *Social Science and Medicine, 21*, 1203–1216.

Rogers, E. M. (1995). *Diffusion of innovations* (4th ed.). New York: The Free Press.

Rogers, E. M., & Dearing, J. W. (1988). Agenda-setting research: Where has it been? Where is it going? In J. A. Anderson (Ed.), *Communication yearbook 11* (pp. 555–594). Newbury Park, CA: Sage.

Rogers, E. M., Dearing, J. W., &. Chang, S. (1991). AIDS in the 1980s: The agenda-setting process for a public issue. *Journalism Monographs, 126.*

Rogers, E. M., Dearing, J. W., Rao, N., Campo, M. L., Meyer, G., Betts, G. J. F., & Casey, M. K. (1995). Communication and community in a city under siege: The AIDS epidemic in San Francisco. *Communication Research, 22*(6), 664–678.

Shilts, R. (1987). *And the band played on: Politics, people, and the AIDS epidemic.* New York: St. Martin's Press.

Svenkerud, P. J., & Singhal, A. (in press). Enhancing the effectiveness of HIV/AIDS prevention programs targeted to unique population groups in Thailand: Lessons learned from applying concepts of diffusion of innovation and social marketing. *Journal of Health Communication.*

Victories to Win: Communicating HIV/AIDS Prevention and Tolerance

William N. Elwood
Behavioral Research Group
University of Texas—Houston School of Public Health

The chapters you have read address a multitude of issues involved with communication, politics, HIV, and AIDS. Although a final chapter cannot synthesize all topics raised by the contributors, it can comment on themes that emerge throughout the book. Toward that end, I discuss three such themes and explain how we might further our future research and practice.

DISCOURSE, THOUGHT, AND BEHAVIOR

The first theme is that our beliefs and actions regarding HIV and AIDS are premised on the human discourse we create and attend. This discourse, and other actions based on it, also are infused with ideas that exist because they were communicated during previous epidemics. Consequently, we may proclaim HIV to be the enemy, but we fight many individual human beings in its name. As Diane Harney explained, lesbians and gay men fight each other because few gay men have recognized or reciprocated the care lesbians have provided their gay brethren, and because homosexual men and women have less in common than a heterosexual society expects. Steinfatt found that Vietnamese officials planned to place citizens with HIV and AIDS in specially constructed, quarantined areas; whether this policy is enacted as therapeutic communities or as concentration camps remains to be seen. Given the strapped Vietnamese economy and the Marxist philosophy that frames sexually transmitted diseases as crimes against the state, one may expect interred individuals to be treated as prisoners in the war against AIDS. In this worldwide war waged in a commercialized age, nonprofit organizations benefit from the sales of merchandise emblazoned with red ribbons and other HIV-related symbols. Even participants at the XI International Conference on AIDS purchased T-shirts, commemorative Canadian postal stamps, and Starbucks travel coffee mugs, among other memorabilia. Sobnosky and Hauser explained that the commercialization of AIDS memorabilia may help organizations fund research and services; in the process, however, they indirectly may foster intolerance among individuals who believe they practice liberality by wearing a pin featuring the U.S. Postal Service's AIDS commemorative stamp, or by drinking from an AmFAR coffee cup on December first. Nevertheless, they may demur to shake hands with an HIV-infected person, or even may endorse legislative discourse intolerant of people with HIV and AIDS (see Slagle, chap. 8 of this volume).

In the first chapter, I introduced the idea that all illness is infused with a moral aspect. In our culture, to be sick is to endure a moral judgment; to recover is to be redeemed from sin, to suffer and die is to be damned. Thus, the presence of any incurable epidemic will inspire public discourse about disease and morality. When that epidemic is transmitted through sexual intercourse and injection drug paraphernalia, the epidemic and the infected individuals endure an immense burden of sin in addition to their symptoms. As an encyclical prepared for Pope Pius XI and only recently released states, "Zeal against the sin readily becomes zeal against the sinner; but zeal against the sinner soon throws off its mask and shows itself for what it really is, an assault, under the pretense of protecting society from a single social group, upon the very basis of society, an evocation of limited hatred, a license for every form of violence, rapacity, and disorder, and an engine against religion itself" (in Passelecq & Suchecky, 1997, p. 25). The emergence of HIV/AIDS has taught us that we still have many battles to wage with ourselves before we become victorious practitioners of tolerance.

ACHIEVING POWER THROUGH MULTIPLE MESSAGES

The second theme is that disseminating general information through the mass media and more specific prevention information through interpersonal interventions has proven to be an effective means of educating extensive numbers of people in record time—regardless of the methodology chosen for a particular project. In fact, some individuals who have attended public service announcements and interpersonal interventions become amateur educators themselves—teaching friends and family members about HIV and AIDS (Cameron, Witte, & Nzyuko, chap. 12 of this volume; Svenkerud, Rao, & Rogers, chap. 18 of this volume; Elwood & Ataabadi, 1996, 1997; Rogers, 1995). Clearly, diffusion of innovations (Rogers, 1995) is a tremendously influential approach toward fighting a public health pandemic (see Rogers & Shefner-Rogers, chap. 29 of this volume; Svenkerud, Rao, & Rogers, chap. 18 of this volume).

The Irony of Power.   Despite this success, there can be tremendous irony in achieving power—pervasive terminological influence (Elwood, chap. 1 of this volume)—over public health issues. Michel Foucault argued that power is not easily recognizable. It constructs, regulates, and perpetuates itself through individuals, because people attend and internalize the language that delineates hegemonic modes of conduct. As Foucault (1980) stated, "It is in discourse that power and knowledge are joined together" (p. 100). Once internalized, individuals regulate their own behavior and the behavior of others in relation to those dictates (Foucault, 1989, 1990; see also Deleuze, 1988; Elwood, 1992; Foucault, 1961, 1963, 1977, 1978, 1980; Jameson in Stephanson, 1988).

In other words, we use news stories, story lines, public service announcements, and other programmatic efforts to "stimulate the public agenda" (Crable & Vibbert, 1985, p. 15) so that individuals will believe that the ways we delineate ideas regarding HIV/AIDS warrant extensive public attention. Once these ideas become part of the social agenda, they become the commonly accepted ways to discuss HIV and AIDS (for a discussion of this general process, see Crable & Vibbert, 1985). These hegemonic ideas have the prime opportunity to frame individuals' thoughts regarding whether they perceive themselves to be at risk for infection or transmission, how they should regard people with (or without) HIV/AIDS, and how to behave accordingly. Unfortunately, the irony is that once one seemingly achieves power, when people use the terms one advocates in disease prevention messages, there is no guarantee that these same people will apply those terms correctly, or even perform the prophylactic measures associated with such terms.

For example, some researchers posit that extant theory-driven interventions have had little effect on changing people's sexual risk behaviors because program participants can cite prevention methods correctly but also report not practicing those methods (e.g., Gold, 1993; Grimley, Prochaska, & Prochaska, 1997; Hahn, 1991; Kippax & Crawford, 1993; Ostrow & McKirnan, 1997). Drug injectors readily adopted safer injection behaviors after attending such interventions; however, they did not change their sexual behaviors as promptly or as frequently (Booth & Watters, 1994; McCoy & Inciardi, 1995; see also Simpson et al., 1993). A new generation of gay men knows how to prevent HIV transmission. Nevertheless, many of them have unprotected sex because they believe either it is an "old man's disease," or that a cure will arrive between the time they are infected and the time when they develop symptoms (Gallagher, 1997, 1998; Heitz, 1997; Meyer & Dean, 1995; O'Hara, 1997; Signorile, 1997). Furthermore, our investigations have taught us that people can disseminate incorrect information that they believe is accurate. Cameron, Witte, and Nzyuko's chapter (chap. 12) found that some Kenyans living along the Trans-Africa Highway believe that some condoms may be treated with the human immunodeficiency virus (HIV) as part of the American Invention to Discourage Sex. Such findings suggest that future interventions might strive toward reducing the dissemination of inaccuracies while increasing safer behaviors.

INEQUITIES IN SEXUAL ENCOUNTERS INFLUENCE RISK BEHAVIORS

The third theme is that sex constitutes an unequal relationship. Many of the chapters in this book enumerate that personal decisions about whether or when to have sex, whether sex will involve HIV prevention activities, more public decisions about HIV prevention curricula and policy, and even talk about these topics, remain male centered (Fuller, chap. 25; Kellar-Guenther, chap. 16; Stevens & Bogart, chap. 9; Weeks, Grier, Radda, & McKinley, chap. 14). Women's assertions frequently are dismissed; occasionally the women themselves are dismissed altogether. When both partners are male, the decisions regarding penetration and condom use customarily rest only with the assertive, or insertive, partner (Elwood & Williams, chap. 10 of this volume). Women and receptive male partners frequently eschew raising prevention issues for fear of losing the partner; oddly enough, our culture dictates that these same subordinate individuals are responsible to initiate conversation. Clearly, people cannot prevent the transmission of HIV if their circumstances constrain them from speaking.

People also cannot constrain the spread of the epidemic unless HIV-infected people accept their powerful responsibility to prevent the spread of the virus (see, e.g., Bayer, 1997; Garcia, 1998; Mayer, 1997). A sexual relationship also is unequal when the partner with HIV does not reveal his or her infection before sex begins. According to Bayer, people were conditioned not to discuss HIV status, as early HIV education made each person responsible for condom use: "As each person was responsible for his or her own health, neither was ultimately responsible for the other" (p. 47). In other words, to behave as if everyone is infected negated an individual's obligation to inform a partner of a positive serostatus. The negative connotations associated with condom use, and the thrill some HIV-infected people obtain from having unprotected sex (Dotinga, 1998; Elwood & Williams, chap. 10 of this volume; Newman, 1998) create multiple opportunities for HIV infections. Alan Mayer, an HIV-infected architect in Brookline, Massachusetts, asserted, "The emphasis on the individual's rights without an equally strong emphasis on the individual's responsibility is wrong and is a direct cause of the spread of the disease. . . . That is all the more reason that AIDS organizations have a responsibility to encourage, to teach, and to train people who are HIV positive to do what is right" (p. 19A).

Such training may result in a time when people infected with HIV will inform their partners, use condoms, and avoid riskier penetrative activities in as commonplace a manner as we now cover our noses and mouths when we sneeze to avoid infecting others with cold or flu germs. Such a health-related norm may not be a panacea to all inequities associated with intercourse, but it nonetheless may reduce the incidence of infection associated with them.

CONSIDERING SITUATION IN HIV PREVENTION RESEARCH

The opening ceremonies of the 1996 XI International Conference on AIDS featured Doreen Millman (1996), a silver-haired Vancouver woman who was living with HIV. As she sat on a stool in the center of the stage, she told her audience about her experiences revealing her HIV infection and receiving treatment. At one point she uttered, "By now, you're wondering how someone like me, a 63-year-old grandmother, got infected. The answer is very simple. It just doesn't matter!" (p. 1). Her remark drew thunderous applause; upon reflection, it also points to a dilemma of contradiction as regards HIV transmission and treatment. How one contracted HIV should not stigmatize an individual when she reveals her infection, seeks treatment, or speaks in a domed sports arena at an international conference. In such a setting, one need not discuss HIV risk behaviors. Nonetheless, to teach people how to avoid infection, it *does* matter. We must talk about sexual and drug use practices and how people can integrate discussing and performing prophylactic measures with those behaviors. Toward that end, I recommend increased attention to individuals' circumstances in which they are at risk for HIV infection, that is, to examine the relationships among human communication, HIV prevention, and the situations in which individuals may become infected.

The word *situation* is a value-laden, if not explosive, issue in communication theory. Yet unlike the rhetorical criticism controversy (Elwood, 1995b) over whether situations are extant exigencies that elicit particular discourse (Bitzer, 1968; Smith & Lybarger, 1996) or discrete incidents constructed by discourse (Elwood, 1995a; Orr, 1978; Vatz, 1973; Vibbert & Bostdorff, 1992), situational theory is premised on the idea that people are affected by the settings in which they act. Simultaneously, the theory also acknowledges that people affect what occurs in settings by continuously contributing to changes in situational and environmental conditions for themselves and others (Magnusson, 1981). Price (1981) argued that researchers should concentrate on the situation "if we are to discover some of the factors that place a person at risk" (p. 106). In contrast, Pervin (1981) stated that although a situation may modify an individual's behavior, it can do so only within the limits of the potential provided by that individual's personality. In other words, situational theory synthesizes both sides of the rhetorical situation argument to posit that people behave in response to the physical environment in which they exist at any given time, the meanings that they attach to a specific physical environment, as well as in response to behavior by others within their proximity (Cantor, 1981; Magnusson, 1981).

Magnusson (1981) acknowledged that human behavior cannot be understood and explained in isolation from the settings in which such behaviors occur. Magnusson argued that to understand the influence of situations on risk behavior, "we need (1) knowledge about the effective person variables and their interrelations; (2) knowledge about the effective situational variables and their interrelations in relevant terms; and (3) a theory linking these two networks of factors together in the framework of dynamic interaction" (p. 10). The most appropriate theoretical framework that explains the interaction of setting and human behavior is communication, in that discourse is not only the means through which theorists argue about communicative situations, but also the means by which human beings influence the people in their environs and inevitably explain what effects they perceived their surroundings had on their behavior. Situational theory accounts for a specific setting, the individuals within it, their actions, and reactions to others. By involving situational theory, future HIV interventions may acquire the task to change people's perceptions regarding communication itself in specific settings and relationships before they can speak the prevention practices we have taught, and will continue to teach, them.

HIV/AIDS has taught us that there is more than one kind of power in the blood; moreover, the epidemic has revealed how reluctant many of us are to discuss the behaviors that facilitate or prevent the transmission of a lethal virus. It also has revealed anew our prejudices and the inequities of resources, access, and control over one's own body. Mark Twain (1995) stated it more succinctly: "History doesn't repeat itself; it rhymes." The research discussed in chapter one explains that human beings seek individuals or groups to blame when faced with an epidemic. Burke (1973) might argue that this process of scapegoating is an essentially human function in response to disease because it allows certain groups to relieve themselves of guilt or blame by placing it on designated others. Nevertheless, we have progressed significantly in our abilities to speak about behaviors that facilitate HIV infection, prevention methods, treatment approaches, and the multiple barriers to such actions.

The story of the conference speaker reminds me of another silver-haired grandmother. This woman, however, exists in a syndicated television situation comedy, in which four older women share a house and each other's lives in Miami. One episode, taped early in the epidemic, focused on the day's adventures of this grandmother, an immigrant Sicilian woman in her 80s and the eldest member of this alternative family. Part of the day's routine included her volunteer shift at a local hospital, where she gave a nectarine to an AIDS patient, a boy, and encouraged him to eat it. He responded that there were no treatments for his condition at that time, and that there would be no cure before his demise. In short, he was going to die and the nectarine she offered would not alter his destiny. The wise and passionate woman responded that he could fight and win and live if he only had hope—because, at that time, all we had *was* hope—and, of course, a nectarine.

At the close of our millennium, we now have more than hope and nectarines to achieve victory over HIV transmission, and the inequities associated with people, HIV infection, AIDS, and its treatment. Perhaps to inspire us to repeat our past mistakes less often, and preceding Mayer's HIV-specific admonition by generations, Twain (1995) also advised, "Always do right. This will gratify some people and astonish the rest." Let us strive for results that amaze, edify, and lead toward healthier human beings.

REFERENCES

Bayer, R. (1997). Responsibility and intimacy in the AIDS epidemic. *The Responsive Community, 7*(4), 45–55.

Bitzer, L. F. (1968). The rhetorical situation. *Philosophy and Rhetoric, 1,* 1–15.

Booth, R. E., & Watters, J. K. (1994). How effective are risk-reduction interventions targeting injecting drug users? *AIDS, 8,* 1515–1524.

Burke, K. (1973). *The philosophy of literary form.* Berkeley: University of California Press.

Cantor, N. (1981). Perceptions of situations: Situation prototypes and person-situation prototypes. In D. Magnusson (Ed.), *Toward a psychology of situations: An interactional perspective* (pp. 229–244). Hillsdale, NJ: Lawrence Erlbaum Associates.

Crable, R. E., & Vibbert, S. L. (1985). Managing issues and influencing public policy. *Public Relations Review, 11,* 3–16.

Deleuze, G. (1988). *Foucault* (S. Hand, Trans.). Minneapolis: University of Minnesota Press.

Dotinga, R. (1998, January 20). San Diego, Freedom means sex for erotic film star. *The Advocate, 750/751,* 49–51.

Elwood, W. N. (1992). *Critical rhetoric and the issue of drug control: A rhetorical commentary on contemporary discourse in the American war on drugs.* Unpublished doctoral dissertation, Purdue University, West Lafayette, IN.

Elwood, W. N. (1995a). Public relations and the ethics of the moment: The anatomy of a local ballot issue campaign. In W. N. Elwood (Ed.), *Public relations inquiry as rhetorical criticism: Case studies of corporate discourse and social influence* (pp. 255–275). Westport, CT: Praeger.

Elwood, W. N. (1995b). Public relations is a rhetorical experience: The integral principle in case study analysis. In W. N. Elwood (Ed.), *Public relations inquiry as rhetorical criticism: Case studies of corporate discourse and social influence* (pp. 3–12). Westport, CT: Praeger.

Elwood, W. N., & Ataabadi, A. N. (1996). Tuned in and turned off: Out-of-treatment injection drug and crack users' response to media intervention campaigns. *Communication Reports, 9,* 49–59.

Elwood, W. N., & Ataabadi, A. N. (1997). Influence of interpersonal and mass-mediated interventions on injection drug and crack users: Diffusion of innovations and HIV risk behaviors. *Substance Use and Misuse, 32,* 635–651.

Foucault, M. (1961). *Madness and civilization: A history of insanity in the age of reason* (R. Howard, Trans.). New York: Vintage.

Foucault, M. (1963). *The birth of the clinic: An archaeology of medical perception* (A. M. Sheridan Smith, Trans.). New York: Pantheon.

Foucault, M. (1977). *Discipline and punish: The birth of the prison* (A. Sheridan, Trans.). New York: Pantheon.

Foucault, M. (1978). *The history of sexuality: Vol. I. An introduction* (R. Hurley, Trans.). New York: Pantheon.

Foucault, M. (1980). *Power/knowledge: Selected interviews and other writings, 1972–1977* (C. Gordon, Ed., C. Gordon, L. Marshall, J. Mepham, & K. Soper, Trans.). New York: Pantheon.

Foucault, M. (1989). *Foucault live: Interviews, 1966–1984* (J. Johnston, Trans., S. Lotringer, Ed.). New York: Semiotext(e).

Foucault, M. (1990). *Michel Foucault: Politics, philosophy, culture* (A. Sheridan, Trans, L. D. Krizman, Ed.). New York: Routledge.

Gallagher, J. (1997, July 8). Slipping up: Unsafe sex is on the rise—and the new AIDS drugs are only one of the culprits. *The Advocate,* pp. 33–34.

Gallagher, J. (1998, January 20). Are gay men listening? From the front lines: David Ho's right-hand man says the battle is far from over. *The Advocate,* pp. 44–49.

Garcia, J. E. (1998, January 20). Austin, AIDS activist: Sex can be a weapon. *The Advocate,* p. 51.

Gold, R. (1993). On the need to mind the gap: On-line versus off-line cognitions underlying sexual risk taking. In D. J. Terry, C. Gallois, & M. McCamish (Eds.), *The theory of reasoned action: Its application to AIDS-preventive behaviour* (pp. 227–252). Oxford, England: Pergamon.

Grimley, D. M., Prochaska, G. E., & Prochaska, J. O. (1997). Condom use adoption and continuation: A transtheoretical approach. *Health Education Research, 12,* 61–75.

Hahn, R. A. (1991). What should behavioral scientists be doing about AIDS? *Social Science and Medicine, 33,* 1–3.

Heitz, D. (1997, July 8). Men behaving badly: The recklessness of the 1970s and early '80s has reappeared on the party circuit, where gay men are indulging in illicit drugs and wild sex with increasing abandon. *The Advocate,* pp. 26–29.

Kippax, S., & Crawford, J. (1993). Flaws in the theory of reasoned action. In D. J. Terry, C. Gallois, & M. McCamish (Eds.), *The theory of reasoned action: Its application to AIDS-preventive behaviour* (pp. 253–269). Oxford, England: Pergamon.

Magnusson, D. (1981). Wanted: A psychology of situations. In D. Magnusson (Ed.), *Toward a psychology of situations: An interactional perspective* (pp. 9–35). Hillsdale, NJ: Lawrence Erlbaum Associates.

Mayer, A. J. (1997, November 24). Change culture of irresponsibility amid HIV positive [Opinion]. *Houston Chronicle,* p. 19A.

McCoy, C. B., & Inciardi, J. A. (1995). *Sex, drugs, and the continuing spread of AIDS.* Los Angeles: Roxbury Publishing Company.

Meyer, I. H., & Dean, L. (1995). Patterns of sexual behavior among young New York City gay men. *AIDS Education and Prevention, 7,* 13–23.

Millman, D. (1996, July 8). Remarks from the opening ceremony of the XI International Conference on AIDS. *The Daily Progress,* pp. 1, 3.

Newman, J. L. (1998, January 20). New York City, Too much sex? According to whom? *The Advocate,* p. 53.

O'Hara, S. (1997, July 8). Safety first? Anytime you get intimately involved with another human being, there is a risk [Opinion]. *The Advocate,* p. 9.

Orr, C. J. (1978). How shall we say: "Reality is socially constructed through communication"? *Central States Speech Journal, 29,* 263–274.

Ostrow, D., & McKirnan, D. (1997). Prevention of substance-related high-risk sexual behavior among gay men: Critical review of the literature and proposed harm reduction approach. *Journal of the Gay and Lesbian Medical Association, 1,* 97–110.

Passelecq, G., & Suchecky, B. (1997). *The hidden encyclical of Pius XI* (S. Rendall, Trans.). Orlando, FL: Harcourt Brace.

Pervin, L. A. (1981). The relation of situations to behavior. In D. Magnusson (Ed.), *Toward a psychology of situations: An interactional perspective* (pp. 343–360). Hillsdale, NJ: Lawrence Erlbaum Associates.

Price, R. H. (1981). Risky situations. In D. Magnusson (Ed.), *Toward a psychology of situations: An interactional perspective* (pp. 103–112). Hillsdale, NJ: Lawrence Erlbaum Associates.

Rogers, E. M. (1995). *Diffusion of innovations* (4th ed.). New York: The Free Press.

Signorile, M. (1997). *Life outside: The Signorile report on gay men: Sex, drugs, muscles, and the passages of life.* New York: HarperCollins.

Simpson, D. D., Camacho, L. M., Vogtsberger, K. N., Williams, M. L., Stephens, R. C., Jones, A., & Watson, D. D. (1993). Reducing AIDS risks through community outreach interventions for drug injectors. *Psychology of Addictive Behaviors, 8,* 86–101.

Smith, C. R., & Lybarger, S. (1996). Bitzer's model reconstructed. *Communication Quarterly, 44,* 197–213.

Stephanson, A. (1988). Regarding postmodernism—A conversation with Fredric Jameson. In A. Ross (Ed.), *Universal abandon? The politics of postmodernism* (pp. 3–30). Minneapolis: University of Minnesota Press.

Twain, M. (1995). Quotations on history. In *Infopedia: The ultimate multimedia reference tool* [CD-ROM; Future Vision Multimedia, Inc.; 0000-0055-08].

Vatz, R. E. (1973). The myth of the rhetorical situation. *Philosophy and Rhetoric, 6,* 154–161.

Vibbert, S. L., & Bostdorff, D. M. (1992). Issue management in the "lawsuit crisis." In C. Conrad (Ed.), *The ethical nexus: Values, communication, and organizational decisions* (pp. 103–120). New York: Ablex.

Author Index

Subject Index

G

Gay and lesbian liberation, 168–169
  group action during early years of HIV/AIDS epidemic,
    169–171
  ways to understand movement at present, 176–178
Gay men, 12
  blamed for contaminated blood supply, 15–19
  highly self-involved in political vision, 175
  role in HIV epidemic, 13
  working with lesbians in response to HIV/AIDS,
    170–174
  younger ones know about HIV yet engage in unsafe
    sex, 417
Gender relations, 182–185
Gender transposition, 199
  includes transgenders and transsexuals, 200
    HIV a serious problem for, 200
Glaser, Elizabeth, 69, 286
  died of AIDS complications, 74
  effective speaker as political outsider, 69
  narrative style heightened audience emotions, 70
  speech to Democratic convention featured children,
    69–70
    response to speech by, 70–71
GRID (gay-related immune deficiency), *see also*
    HIV/AIDS, 9, 12, 170
Grounded theory, 125, 234

H

Health Resources and Services Administration (HRSA),
    325
HIV/AIDS, 5
  adolescent caseload in United States, 369
    gaining their compliance with treatment, 370–378
    likely to be poor and African-American, 370
  in Africa, 149–150
    in Kenya, 149–150
  and breastfeeding, 341–350
  as excuse for discrimination against certain groups, 5,
    9, 12, 26, 72, 158, 416
    to consider self and others as not at-risk for infec-
      tion, 13–14, 136, 140, 145
  diffusion of virus, 402–403
  educational messages about focus on knowledge regard-
    ing transmission and prevention, 217
    generally use fear appeals that are more effective
      for older audiences than younger ones,
      218
    those targeted for youth should portray AIDS as a
      relational risk, 217
  female adolescents infected with, 369–378
  fostered complex relationships among lesbians and gay
    men, 168
  first mentioned in public by President Reagan in 1985,
    29
  framed by speeches during 1992 Democratic and Re-
    publican National conventions, 67–74
  function of products sold for research and treatment
    funds, 33–37
  has become normalized as an issue, 74
    yet perceived by many as the story of individual per-
      sonal lives, 75
  individuals infected with responsible for preventing
    spread of virus, 413–414
  labeled as judgment on homosexuality by New Chris-
    tian Right members, 54, 93
    who seemed to control debate in late 1980s, 57
  means of infection/transmission, 5, 6, 17, 57–58
  in the Mekong region (Southeast Asia), 381–395
    in Cambodia, 385–387
    in Thailand, 387–393
    in Vietnam, 382–385
  news coverage of, 29–32
    analysis suggests change in reporting practices, 264
    centered mostly on policy, 262
    depicted less as a moral problem than previous epi-
      demics, 263
    depicted people with HIV/AIDS with dual stereo-
      types associated with gay rights and dis-
      ability rights movements, and
      stigmatized terminal illness, 270
    different from coverage of previous epidemics such
      as syphilis, 262
    portrayed HIV as catalyst for unity among gay men
      and lesbians, 167
  and protease inhibitors, 374
    with female African-American adolescents,
      369–378
  people with defined as disabled through news stories,
    275–276
  people confuse fighting individuals with fighting virus,
    415
  perceived in U.S. to be disease only of gay men and ille-
    gal drug users, 93
  politics of, 341–343
    brought attention to societal inequities that facilitate
      transmission, 133
    CDC first notes what would become HIV/AIDS in
      1981, 53
    early reporting strategies skewed appropriate
      representation of risk categories, 200
    inequitable and inadequate diagnoses for
      women, 172–173
  comparisons to other plagues, 4, 25
  consider situation in future prevention research,
    414–415
  culturally appropriate prevention strategies for,
    406–409
  problems with usage of terms, 25
    risk behavior and risk group, 41
  significance of red ribbon, 32, 35
  stimulated affected individuals to organize and demand
    resources to fight the epidemic, 133
  test results, 41
    allow intimates to feel at ease with each other, 141
    can be a ritual with new drug injection partners, 141
    misinterpretation, 41
    negative results used to negotiate unprotected sex-
      ual intercourse, 141, 142
    negative results used in needle-sharing situations,
      142
  women more likely to contract through sexual inter-
    course than are men, 108
HIV/AIDS Treatment Information Service (ATIS), 325